T. E. HOPE

LEXICAL BORROWING IN THE ROMANCE LANGUAGES

A Critical Study of
Italianisms in French and
Gallicisms in Italian
from 1100 *to* 1900

VOLUME II

NEW YORK UNIVERSITY PRESS

NEW YORK 1971

Copyright © 1971 New York University

SBN 8147-3360-3

Library of Congress Catalog Card Number: 79-151224

Manufactured in Great Britain

CONTENTS

Volume II

iii

CHAPTER IV

THE EIGHTEENTH CENTURY

Italianisms in French during the Eighteenth Century

adagio. Music: Adagio.

1726 B-Wart.; 1750 Voltaire; 1751 *Encycl.* It. word, *adagio* (<*agio*, 'ease') which is attested late as a musical term—Alberti, *Diz. universale*, 1797–1805; the *Gr. diz. it.* has Leopardi as its first example—but was certainly in use at a much earlier date. *Adagio* in the general sense is a 14th cent. word.

agrume. Hortic.: Citrus fruits.

It. pl. *agrumi* 1739 de Brosses,[1] who explains the import of the word: 'Ils ont abondamment de ceux (les fruits) qu'on appelle en général *agrumi*, nom qui comprend toute l'espèce citriforme' (II, 74); also ' ... un nombre infini d'*agrumi* confits' (II, 319). <It. collective *agrumi* (m. pl.), used in this sense from 14th cent., P. de' Crescenzi.

allegro, allegretto. Music: Allegro, etc.

Allegro 1726, B-Wart.; both 1751 *Encycl.* Italian words, *allegro*, 16th cent. Annibal Caro as a musical term; *allegretto*.

alto. Music: A singing part; also instrument, viola.

1771 B-Wart.; 1791 *Encycl. méth.* Italian word, *alto*.

ambe. Gambling term; combination of numbers in a lottery.

1762 *Arrêt du Conseil sur la loterie*; 1798 Acad. It. *ambo* in this particular sense.

andante. Music: Andante.

1751 *Encycl.* Italian word, *andante*, 14th cent. (subst.) meaning 'traveller on foot'; 17th cent. (adj.) 'running smoothly, without interruption', etc.

aquarelle. Painting: Aquarelle, water-colour.

1791 *Encycl. méth.* <It. *acquarella, acquerella*; also masculine in the 16th and 17th centuries.

aria. Music: Aria.

1752 Lancombe (Dauz.). Acc. to B-Wart., Fr. *air* in this sense (1608) is a semantic loan from Italian. <It. *aria*, 16th cent., Varchi, as a musical term.

ariette. Music: Arietta.

---

1. Charles de Brosses, *Lettres familières sur l'Italie*, Vols. I and II, ed. Yvonne Bézard, Paris, 1931. Apparently only a small proportion of the *Lettres* were actually dispatched to friends from Italy during de Brosses' visit of 1739–40; others were copied, edited and elaborated for publication subsequently, in many cases a number of years later, though all those in Vol. I were complete in 1745 (*vide* Y. Bézard, introd. to edition cited, pp. ix–x). Dates printed in the letter headings are presumably the *président*'s invention, and his claim that all were written in 1739 or 1740 invalid. Nevertheless the precise circumstantial detail of the work and its convincing impression of actuality suggest that much of the author's information was set down at the time of the events. For this and other reasons which become clear as one reads the *Lettres* attentively—including the unity of their very idiosyncratic style—it is fair to assume that the Italianisms and Italianising *tournures* he uses liberally throughout were known to him at the period of his visit and were in fact related to the circumstances of the time, as his narrative so often implies. I therefore follow the etymologists' usual practice of ascribing to the *Lettres* de Brosses' own date of 1739–40.

'Vers 1710', B-Wart.; 1750 Montesquieu; variant *arietta*. <It. *arietta*, 17th cent., Buon. il Giovane.

arpège. Music: Arpeggio.

1751 *Encycl.*; but *harpègement* occurs in 1690, Furetière, so that *arpège* itself may be earlier. <It. *arpeggio*, first attested in a general sense 'act, technique of playing a harp' (A. M. Salvini pre-1729); back-formation < *arpeggiare*, 18th cent.

asple. Text. ind.: Distaff on which silk is placed to be wound.

1751 *Encycl. méth.* Variant *aspe*. <It. *aspo*, 15th cent., of Germanic origin, cognate with OFr. *hasple* 'reel', still in Oudin (*haspe*). B-Al. derive Fr. *asple* from northern Italian dialects: 'il francese *asple* deriva invece dai dialetti it. sett., dove è prestito dall'oland. e fiammingo *haspel*'. Alberti 1777 defines *aspo* in detail but translates it by the old French term *dévidoir*. I assume that *asple* entered French at the time when a more modern technique was introduced.

avocette. Ornith.: Avocet, *recurvirostra avosetta*.

1760 Brisson (Dauz.); mid-18th cent., Buffon; variant *avoceta, avoseta* (i.e. an Italian form) in 1771 Trévoux. <It. *avocetta, avosetta* of Venetian origin, acc. to B-Al. Alberti, 1788, knows the French word, but not its Italian equivalent; he translates *avocette* by *moriglione*, which is a different bird (*Fulix fuscus*). Though Alberti is well versed in certain technical languages (e.g. concerning ships) his knowledge of natural history is scanty, as other examples of mistaken terminology show.

babilan. Mild euphemism for 'impotent person'.

See F. Letessier, *F.M.*, XX, 1952, pp. 115–16. Noted by Letessier in de Brosses (1740), Casanova, Lalande, *Voyage en Italie* (1769); popularised by Stendhal in his novel *Armance*, 1827, the hero of which suffers from this disability. Also *babilanisme*, 19th cent. From the Italian personal name *Babilano*, apparently a husband who figured in a notorious eighteenth century lawsuit and whose marriage was annulled on grounds of impotence.

bambochade. Painting: Bambocciade.

A humorous genre of painting, esp. rustic tavern scenes. Beginning 18th cent., Dauz.; 1747 B-Wart.; 1762 Acad. <It. *bambocciata*, 17th cent., formed upon the nickname of the artist who popularised this type of subject, Pieter van Laer or Lauwer, 1592–1645, referred to as *Bamboccio* because of his short stature. From 1625 to 1639 van Laer led the Dutch school of painting in Rome. See *bamboche*, 17th cent. It. > Fr. loans.

barcarolle. Music: Barcarole.

Voltaire, Letter of 18th Dec. 1767 (Robert); 1798 Acad. <It. *barcarola*,[1] of Venetian origin (B-Al.; *D.G.*).

belladone. Bot., medic.: Belladonna, *Atropa belladonna*.

1733 Lémery; *belladona* earlier, 1698, Lémery (Dauz.); also 1762 Acad. The position of *belle-dame* (also 1762, acc. to B-Wart.) requires to be clarified. This name, referring to the plant, appears much earlier; cf. Cotgrave: 'Belle-dame, Great Nightshade; or a kind of Dwale, or sleeping Nightshade'; it may be taken as a calque of the Latin form, and doubtless existed in French from early times. It. *belladonna* is attested in 1530, Cibo (B-Al.).

biribi. Game of chance similar to lotto.

1719 Voltaire, *Lettres*, in *Œuvres Compl.*, XXXIII, 54 (Moland) (*Datations 1960* [Arveiller]); 1740 de Brosses, ed. cit., II, 32, 33, 543. <It. *biribisso, -i*, 17th cent., or perhaps from a dialectal form; *biribi* is still used in Siena at the present day (B-Al.).

bouffe. Music, theatre: Comic.

1. The 16th cent. form *barquerolle* referred to by B-Wart. denotes the gondolier himself; see this word in 16th cent. It. > Fr. loans.

Esp. in certain fixed musical and theatrical expressions. *Scène-buffe* 1791 *Encycl. Méth.*; other usages appear in the 19th cent., e.g. *opéra-buffe*, 'comic' as opposed to 'grand' opera, 1835 Acad.; also the phrase *Les Bouffes*, referring to the Italian opera in Paris. <It. *buffo* 'comic, ridiculous' 14th cent., Fr. Giordano.

brasque. Metall.: Luting.

I.e. protective composition lining an oven or crucible. 1751 *Encycl.* < Piedmontese and Milanese *brasca*, tentatively explained by B-Al. (who corroborate the It. > Fr. loan) as a cross between *brasa* (northern form of *brace*) 'coals, charcoal', and *rusca*, 'ash, slag'.

bravo! Exclamation, also subst.

1738 Piron (Dauz.); 1740 de Brosses; 1777 B-Wart., 2nd edition; 1798 Acad. Also *bravissimo!* (not now in use) 1776 *Ann. litt.* (Dauz.) and 1782 Mercier (id., 7th edition).[1] *Bravo!* was originally given a feminine or plural ending as the situation required, a practice continued by *italianisants* in France as late as the Second Empire. <It. *bravo, bravissimo*. See 16th cent. It. > Fr. *brave*.

calmande. Text.: Strong woollen stuff for ladies' shoes; calamanco.

1723 Savary, *Dict. du commerce*. Variant *calamandre*, 18th cent. Very probably < It. *calamandra*, 14th cent., perhaps of Oriental origin. (B-Al. give a reference to a 'calamandra di Cipri').

camée. Fine Arts: Cameo.

1740 de Brosses, *Lettres*, ed. cit., II, 112, 257: 'Ce que l'on admire le plus, c'est le recueil de pierres gravées, entre lesquelles sont ces deux admirables camées'; 'un recueil fort curieux de lampes sépulcrales ... en pierres gravées, camées, etc.' De Brosses still uses the earlier word *camaïeu* (13th cent.) more frequently. <It. *cammeo*, Cellini, etc.

cantaloup. Hortic.: Type of melon, cantaloupe.

Cantalou 1781, *Catalogue du Jardin de Caen* (quoted Dauzat; *vide* F.M., XIV, 300); *cantaloupe* 1791 *Encycl. méth.* (*Cantalupi* appears 1775 in the *Dict. raisonné d'hist. nat.*, s.v. *melon*, acc. to *Datations 1965*, p. 54 [Hutinet-Rittaud]). <It. place name *Cantalupo*[2] (papal villa near Rome) according to almost all sources; B-Wart., however, after admitting a possible It. origin, adds that a locality named Cantaloup exists also on French territory (Hérault).

cantate. Music: Cantata.

1709 B-Wart.; 1718 Acad. <It. *cantata*; *cantada* in 1620, Al. Grandi (B-Al.).

cantatrice. Singer.

1762 Bachaumont, *Mém.*; *vide Datations 1965*, p. 54; 1787 Abbé Richard, *Descr. de l'Italie* (Dauz.). Alb. 1788 translates It. *cantatrice* by *chanteuse*. Used in the first instance to refer to Italian artists. <It. *cantatrice*, 1st half 17th cent., G. B. Doni. Replaced earlier Fr. form *chanteresse*.

caricature. Painting, drawing: caricature.

1740 d'Argenson, *Mémoires*, II, 146, (*Bibl. elzév.*); 1752 *Encycl.*; 1762 *Acad.* <It. *caricatura*. The metaphorical extension 'act of loading, weighting' > 'distortion, exaggeration of certain traits' occurs 17th cent. in Italian and is probably owed to Annibale Carracci.

---

1. De Brosses tells us that he himself used *bravissimo* (but in an Italian linguistic context): 'Je me suis fait beaucoup priser et chérir des principaux musiciens du pays, en criant *bravissimo* à tout propos' (I, 111).

2. Probably a borrowing in French directly from the Italian place-name; *cantalupo* as a common noun is not attested in Italian before the late 19th cent. (Petrocchi, etc.) whereas this variety of fruit appears to have been imported into France much earlier. Cf. Prati: 'Sotto Carlo VIII (secolo XV) fu introdotto nella coltivazione francese, avendolo egli portato dai giardini papali di Cantalupo (Roma)' (*V. Et. It.*, s.v.).

carrare. Archit.: White marble of outstanding quality.

1755 Prévost *Manuel Lexique*, 2nd edition: 'Marbre de Carrare, qui se tire près de Gènes.' (*Datations 1965*, p. 84 [Arveiller]); 1762 Acad.;[1] 1771 B-Wart. <Italian place-name, *Carrara*.

cascatelle. Small cascade.

1740 de Brosses, II, 303. <It. *cascatella*, diminutive of *cascata*. See *cascade*, 17th cent. It. > Fr. loans.

casino. Gaming-house; brothel.

1740 de Brosses, II, 542, 565. Variant *casin*, 1764. <It. *casino*, which originally (16th cent.) was without pejorative connotations. See also 19th cent. Fr. > It. *casinò*.

castrat. Music: *Castrato*, falsetto.

1749 de Brosses, *Lettres*, II, 342, 344. De Brosses also uses *châtré* in this sense on a number of occasions: I, 272; II, 341-2, 434, etc.: 'Ces messieurs les châtrés sont des petits-maîtres fort jolis . . .' (p. 342). <It. *castrato*,[2] 16th cent. in this sense; used initially to refer to Italian singers.

cavagnole. Game of chance similar to biribi.

1745 Voltaire, *Corresp.*; 1746 La Morlière, *Angola*; 1748 Voltaire, *Lettres à d'Argental*, and other examples (for details, see *Datations, 1965*, p. 104). <It. *cavagnola*, the cards being drawn from a receptacle *cavagnolo*, dim. of *cavagno*, 'basket'.

cavatine. Music: Cavatina.

A short air inserted in a larger work not usually repeated. 1767 Rousseau (Dauz.); 1791 *Encycl. méth.* <It. *cavatina*, 18th cent. in this sense.

chébec. Naut.: Type of Mediterranean vessel with both sail and oars.

1771 Trévoux; *chabec Encycl. méth.* (Marine) 1783-87. Vidos also refers to the form *becques* in A. Conflans (1515-22) and quotes Sainéan's opinion[3] that this is the same word with aphaeresis of the initial syllable. <It. *sciabecco*, 1768, Paoli, acc. to B-Al., probably < Arab. *shabbak* 'ship'. Vidos, pp. 313-21.

chipolata. Culin.: Onion stew; chipolata sausage.

1742, *Nouv. traité de la cuisine*, 3, 18 (vide *F.M.*, XIV, 135); 1774 Voltaire (masc.). Both masc. and fem. in 18th cent. Variant *chipoulata* 1751 *Dict. d'Agric.* (Dauz.). <It. *cipollata* 15th cent., B-Al. < *cipolla*.

cicerone. Guide, esp. to ancient monuments.

Ciceroni (pl.) 1739 de Brosses, I, 438, 443; *faire le cicerone*, II, 94. It looks as if these are among the very first occasions when a French speaker used the term. De Brosses is amused by the word's hyperbolical implications: he speaks of 'soi-disant ciceroni' (I, 438). Also 1753 *Encycl.*, etc. Italian word, *cicerone*, with more or less Gallicising pronunciation[4] and corresponding plurals either *ciceroni* or *cicerones*. Originally 'person with the gift of the gab' (< *Cicero*).

---

1. Some authorities reject the reference in Acad., 4th edition, as referring to a place-name. This is not actually the case, in spite of first appearances: '*Carrare*: nom de lieu qu'on donne à du marbre de la côte de Gênes.'

2. *Castrat* as a veterinary term, 'gelding' (1559 R. Le Blanc) is normally taken to be a borrowing from Provençal or Gascon. Though Gascon is frequently a source of terms of horsemanship, Italian is equally important in this respect and may have furnished this term too.

3. L. Sainéan, *La Langue de Rabelais*, I, p. 97.

4. A pronunciation [sisɛrɔnɛ] is also heard in which the vowels are given roughly their Italian value, but the un-French consonant [tʃ] < [k] + palatal vowel is modified according to the French phonemic pattern.

cipolin. Geol., archit.: Type of marble veined like the cross-section of an onion.

Cipollin 1739 de Brosses, *Lettres*, I, 404 (referring to Herculaneum), also *cipolin* II, 98, 225; *cipollani* 1750 Prevost, *Manuel Lexique*; 1757 Cochin et Bellicard, *Observations sur Herculanéum*; 1785 *Encycl. méth.* The variant *cipollini* (i.e. the Italian form) appears in Trévoux, 1771. < It. *cipollino* 16th cent. with northern dialectal pronunciation.[1]

colis. Bale of merchandise, packet, parcel.

1723 Savary. Variant *coli* still in Littré. From the plural of It. *collo* 'neck', used to mean 'burden' already in the early 16th cent. (Ariosto). All authorities agree that the new meaning resulted from a metonymic shift 'neck' > 'burden carried on the neck', though B-Wart. qualify it, with misgivings, I feel, as a 'développement sémantique hardi'. The French word appears to have entered through Marseilles and Lyons (B-Wart., B-Al.).

concetti. Lit. hist.: Conceits, euphuisms.

Pre-1720, P. D. Huet, *Manuscrits* (*F.M.* XIV, 288; *vide Datations 1965*, p. 253); 1739 Desfontaines (Dauz.); 1753 *Encycl.* The variant *concet* appears once in Henri Estienne, (*Nouv. lang. fr. italianisé*) 'ce sont de merveilleux concets, s'il est licite d'user de ce mot' (cited by the *D.G.*). < It. *concetti*, pl. of *concetto*; the French word was felt as a plural form exclusively until a short time ago and governed a plural verb. It. *concetto* with this meaning appears in Tasso and is current during the 17th century.

condottiere. Hist.: Condottiere.

1770 Raynal, *Hist. philos. des deux Indes*, I, 23–4: 'Ces misérables *condottieri*, dont les noms étoient si terribles, et dont les armes l'étoient si peu' (*vide Datations, 1965*, p. 259). A Gallicised ephemeral form *conductier* is found in the fifteenth century (Godefroy).[2] < It. *condottiere*, first used to mean a leader of soldiers in G. Villani, 1st half 14th cent.

conservatoire. Academy of music and similar senses.

1778 Bachaumont, *Mém.* (2 examples) (*vide Datations 1965*, p. 272); Alberti 1788 ('Écoles de musique, dont les plus fameuses sont à Naples'). The *Conservatoire de musique* was founded in 1786, the *Conservatoire des arts et métiers* in 1794. < It. *conservatorio*, 18th cent. in this sense. *Conservatoire* adj., a legal term from the 14th cent. onwards, is a Latinism; the meaning of 'museum, depository' in Fr. and It. during the 18th century is drawn from this.

contorniate. Numism.: Bronze coin ringed by a raised border.

1754 *Encycl.* < It. *contorniato*, used in this technical sense in the 18th cent. B-Al. corroborate the It. > Fr. loan.[3]

contralto. Music: Contralto.

1740 de Brosses: 'un contralto ou haut-contre' (II, 341); 'il y a dans un opéra trois ou quatre voix des dessus, et un contralto' (ibid.); 'quelque fois la voix des châtrés change à la mue, ou baisse en vieillissant, et devient contralto de soprano qu'elle était' (II, 342). Also 1767, Rousseau and 1791, *Encycl. méth.* Italian term, *contralto* (fem.; *contralta*), 16th cent.; replaced indigenous *haut-contre*, 16th cent.

---

1. It is not certain what relation *chipolin* (tech: type of 'grained' and varnished paintwork) bears to this word. Formally a loan from literary Italian as opposed to a dialect is possible, but there may also be an analogy with some other technical word. Semantically a visual metaphor is probable, the grain of paintwork resembling this kind of marble. I have found no convincing evidence that a separate formal or semantic loan took place.

2. Also *conducteur*; cf. Lot, *Art Militaire*, p. 115.

3. I note that *Datations 1965* register an example from the *Journal des Savants*, 30th March 1671. It may well be that *contorniate* is another of the scientific and antiquarian terms which were becoming current already towards the end of the seventeenth century, though the main period one associates them with is the eighteenth century.

crescendo. Music: Crescendo.

1775 Beaumarchais, *Barb. de Séville*; 1791 *Encycl. méth.* Italian musical term, *crescendo*, 17th cent.

da capo. Music: Da capo, repeat.

'Vers 1710', B-Wart.; 1767 Rousseau, *Dict. de musique*. Italian locution, *da capo, daccapo*, 14th cent. Fra Giordano in general usage ('anew, a second time'). De Brosses has it as a nonce-phrase in the general sense, ed. cit., II, p. 8: 'pour reprendre la chose *da capo* . . .'. Or is this a figurative use of the musical term?

descrescendo. Music: Decrescendo.

18th cent. Baini, *Mém. sur Palestrina* (D.G.); 1775 Beaumarchais. Italian term, *decrescendo*, 17th cent.

dilettante. Dilettante. Originally only with reference to music.

1740 de Brosses: 'faites part de ma lettre au petit Potot, qui est un *dilettante*, quasi même un *virtuose*' (II, 370). Italian word, *dilettante* (Filippo Baldinucci, pre-1696) with phonetic adaptation. A plural *dilettanti* is occasionally used. G. Antoine, 'Dilettante. Histoire du mot', *Mélanges Bruneau*, 1954, pp. 161–176.

discrédit. Banking term, initially; loss of credit.

1719 *Arrêt du Conseil d'État*, with reference to the lack of public confidence in the Compagnie des Indes. Very probably < It. *discredito*, 17th cent., Segneri, Magalotti; a formation by prefix from *crédit* is not impossible but unlikely in view of the recent appearance of *discredito* in Italian and the prevalence of banking loan-words from Italy.[1]

dito. Commerce: Ditto.

1723 Savary. It. *ditto*, archaic form of *detto*, p. part of *dire* (13th–16th cent.).

do. Music: Doh (C).

1767 Rousseau, *Dict. de musique*. Italian term, *do*, arbitrarily chosen for reasons of sonority to replace *ut* in the 17th cent. Reputedly coined by G. B. Doni (1594–1697) from the first syllable of his name, though the form *du* appears in the 14th cent. (B-Al.). Other notes of the scale were invented by Guido d'Arezzo in the early eleventh century[2] and are attested in French at various periods: *si* 1690 Furetière, accepted by the Académie in 1835; *ré, mi, fa, sol, la* in the thirteenth century, Gautier de Coincy, but accepted by the Académie only in the eighteenth; *ut* 1648, Voiture (1762, Acad.) but *us* already in Eustache Deschamps, 14th cent.[3] *Fa* is attested elsewhere in the thirteenth century (H.

---

1. *Discréditer*, attested in 1572 (*FEW*, II, 2, 1306b), is doubtless a derivative < *créditer*, though it could be a separate loan, since *discreditare* appears in the 13th cent. *Fiore di Virtù* (Pr.).

2. From the first syllables of each hemistich of the hymn to Saint John by Paulus Diaconus: '*Ut* queant laxis—*Re*sonare fibris—*Mi*ra gestorum—*Fa*muli tuorum—*Sol*ve polluti—*La*bii reatum—*S*ancti *I*ohannes' (the latter giving *si*).

3. The actual reference is:

'Argent monte de l'*us* en *sol*
Ceuls qui bas et povres estoient' (D.G.)

The 't' in *ut* appears to have remained unpronounced in the seventeenth century; cf. the following reference in one of Ménage's *Observations sur la langue françoise* (1672–76), p. 77, where a popular song is quoted in connection with contemporary pronunciation of the past participle of *avoir*:

' . . . que vous avez eü
La, sol, fa, mi, ré, u,
Plus d'amans qu'Angélique'.

d'Andeli, *Bat. des set arts* [*D.G.*]), and others on different occasions before the end of the Middle Ages.[1]

finale. Music: Finale.

1779 B-Wart.; 1826 Mozin, *Dict. franç-allem.*, 2nd edition; 1829 Boiste; 1835 Acad. Phonetic adaptation of Italian term *finale*, 18th cent. as a musical term.

fisolère. Naut.: Portable skiff.

A small boat used in Venice for wildfowling, sufficiently light to be carried by one man. 1702 G. Blondel Aubin, *Dict. de Marine*; 1752 Trévoux. < Venetian *fisolera*, 16th cent., same meaning, formed on *fisolo* (*de mar*), of unknown origin, a small sea-bird found on Venetian lagoons. See Vidos, pp. 397–8.

fonte. Equit.: Leather saddle-purse; later holster for gun.

1752 Trévoux. < It. *fonda*, originally 'sling', but used in the above sense by the 13th cent., Bono Giamboni. The unvoicing of [d] > [t] is usually explained as an analogy with *fonte*, 'cast-iron', though this is scarcely satisfactory from a semantic viewpoint.

format. Printing, etc.: Format.

1723 Savary. < It. *formato*, 18th cent. in this sense; just possibly a derivation from *forme* with learned suffix *-at*. B-Wart. give both alternatives; B-Al. with the majority of authorities support the former, which is the more plausible.

forte, fortissimo. Music: Forte, etc.

1760 Rousseau (Dauz.), also id., 1767, *Dict. de musique*; 1798 Acad. Italian term, *forte*, applied to music in the 16th century. *Fortissimo* 1753 Rousseau, *Lettre sur la musique française.*

franco. Commerce: 'Carriage paid' on merchandise, letters, etc.

1754 B-Wart.; 1771 Trévoux; also *port franc*. Ellipsis of Italian term *porto franco* 17th cent., nowadays more usually *franco* or *franco di porto*.[2]

galvanisme. Physics: Galvanism.

1797 *Annales de chimie et de physique*. Evidence is not sufficient to show whether this word is derived from It. *galvanismo* or, as von Wartburg implies (*FEW*, IV, 48–9), from the personal name Galvani, the Italian physicist who discovered galvanic action in 1780 and died in 1793. *Galvanismo* in Italian is registered by B-Al. as late 18th cent., but by Prati only in 1828, Marco Aurelio Marchi, *Diz. tecnico-etimologico-filologico.*

gavette. Tech., goldsm.: Bar of gold prepared to be made into wire.

1757 *Encycl.* < It. *gavetta*, 16th cent., same sense. B-Al. corroborate the Italian to French loan.

gazetin. Diminutive of *gazette*, usually with slightly depreciative connotations.

1725 *Merc. de France*; 1740 Voltaire, *Lettres*; 1762 Acad. (but removed in 1878). < It. *gazzettino*, 17th cent. in this sense, dimin. of *gazzetta*. See *gazette*, 16th cent. It. > Fr. loans.

gouache. Painting: Gouache.

1752 Trévoux; 1762 Acad. < It. *guazzo*, originally 'stagnant water', 'flooded land' (14th cent.); later, more generally, 'flood, inundation'. The painting term appears in the 16th cent., first as *dipingere a guazzo*.

grandiose. Grandiose.

Grandioso 1740, de Brosses: 'il y a un escalier tout à fait *grandioso*' (II, 52); *grandiose* 1798 *Encycl. méth. Grandiosité* 1787, B-Wart., is probably derived in French, though

---

1. E.g. in the *Farce des deux hommes et de leurs femmes*, P. de Jullev. *Rep. des Farces*, No. 139; *Anc, théâtre fr.*, I, p. 145 (Elzevir edition): 'Somme, il n'y a ne sol ne la/Tant s'effroya en ses riottes/qu'elle excédera de trois nottes.'

2. This term appears to be quite distinct from *porto franco*, 'free port', i.e. a harbour in which no customs dues are levied.

there may be an influence of It. *grandiosità*. *Magnifique, pompeux, illustre, éclatant, splendide, majestueux* are given by Alb. 1788 as French equivalents to the Italian word, while *grandiosità* is glossed as *magnificence, éclat*. <It. *grandioso*, 14th cent. The French borrowing figured initially in contexts relating to the fine arts and later became generalised;[1] compare *pittoresque*, below.

graticule, graticuler. Painting, drawing: Graticule.

Originally term of pictorial arts; framework or 'grid' used to copy a drawing or painting on a different scale. Verb: the action of using this device, or of drawing squares for this purpose. 1701 Furetière (both forms). The variant *craticuler*, 1671 Le p. Chérubin, *Dioptr. Coul.* (reference given by the *D.G.*) is probably a Latinism. <It. *graticola -are*, in these senses; *graticola* 17th cent., but *graticolato* (p. part. and adj.) already in Leonardo da Vinci.

guépard. Zool.: Hunting leopard, cheetah.

Buffon, *Hist. naturelle*, 1794–88. The variant *gapard* appears earlier, in 1706, acc. to B-Wart. A Gallicised form of It. *gatto-pardo*, 16th–17th cent., ult. from Spanish.

influenza. Medic.: Influenza.

1782 Madame d'Epinay. Phonetic adaptation of It. *influenza*, which appears in the medical sense during the 16th century; the first serious epidemic recorded in Italy occurred in 1557. It originally meant 'epidemic' in general: the term entered French usage after the great epidemic of 1743, which spread from Italy. A word much in vogue during the later 19th cent.; now seldom used (= *grippe*).

intaille. Jewellery: Gem cut in intaglio.

De Brosses 1740 uses it in the Italian form in the same context as *camée* (q.v. *supra*) which he is also the first to borrow: ' . . . pierres gravées, camées, *intagli*, etc.' (II, 257, referring to the collection of the antiquary Borioni, 'Lo Speziale'). Partially adapted form *intaille* in 1808, Brard, *Traité des pierres précieuses*; 1828 Mozin, 2nd edition; 1878 Acad. <It. *intaglio*, same sense, 14th cent. (B-Al.).

lazarone. Beggar, one of the rabble.

Used almost invariably when speaking of Naples. 1786 B-Wart.; *lazzaron* 1781, Mercier. De Brosses uses the diminutive *lazarielli* (sic) in precisely the same sense: 'il auroit été mis en pièces, s'il ne se fut enfui, par la canaille *dei lazarielli*' (I, 420; also 422). He later Gallicises it as *lazariels* (pp. 425 and 431). <It. *lazzarone, lazzerone*, the latter form attested in 1612, Neri (B-Al.).

loto. Game of chance, lotto.

1732 Trévoux. <It. *lotto*, 1710 meaning 'lottery', 1739 in this specific sense (B-Al.).

luciole. Entomol.: Glow-worm, *Lampyris italica*.

Lucciole[2] 1704 B-Wart. <It. *lucciola*, 14th cent.

lumachelle. Mineral: Fire-marble.

1740 de Brosses, II, 99; Buffon, *Hist. naturelle*, 1749–88. <It. *lumachella*, dim. of *lumaca*, 'slug'; this type of marble contains fossil snail-shells. The Italian word is given by authorities as a 19th cent. term, but I assume that it was used earlier in technical contexts.

lustrine. Text.: Type of stuff, usually silk, with glossy finish.

---

1. Cf. Acad., 2nd edition, 1835: 'Grandiose . . . T. emprunté de l'italien. Il se dit, surtout dans les Beaux-Arts, de ce qui impose, de ce qui frappe l'imagination par un caractère de grandeur, de noblesse, de majesté. *Composition grandiose. Cette architecture est d'un style grandiose.*'

2. This Italianising graphy continued to be used in the 19th cent.; Dauzat registers *luciole* in Mozin, *Dict. français-allemand*, 1812, but *lucciole* is in fact still the form given in the 1823 edition.

1730 Savary; 1739 Trévoux. <It. *lustrino*, 18th cent. in this sense, but 17th cent. meaning 'spangle used to adorn clothes'. This material is reported to have been first manufactured at Genoa.

mandoline. Music: Mandolin(e).

1740 de Brosses: 'Ils s'entendent aussi à varier le son par la variété de celui des instruments qu'ils emploient, violons, cors, ... violes d'amour, archiluths, *mandolines*, etc.' (II, 358). 1759 Lancombe (Dauz.). <It. *mandolino*, 17th cent., Redi, of Neapolitan origin.

maquette. Fine Arts: Initial sketch or model of painting, sculpture.

1752 Trévoux; the senses 'artist's lay figure' 'model of stage-setting', 'mock-up' (in engineering, etc.) date from the nineteenth century. <It. *macchietta*, 'rapid sketch' (19th cent., acc. to B-Al.) a semantic extension in Italian from the original meaning 'spot, dappling'. Cf. also *macchia*, tech. term in painting, 'handling of colour and shade', documented in Bembo.

maquis. Maquis.

Mackis in a text of 1775 cited by G. Esnault, *F.M.*, XIX, 1951, p. 303: 'On appelle mackis en Corse, ce que nous appellons, en France, taillis ou broussailles'; *taillis ou machies* in 1791. <It. *macchia* or pl. *macchie* (Corsican dialect) presumably an extension from the meaning 'stain' by reason of the appearance presented by patches of scrub on hillsides.[1] *Vide* Wartburg, *FEW*, VI, 17a, 18a.

marasquin. Liqueur, maraschino.

1739 de Brosses. <It. *maraschino*, type of bitter cherry grown especially in Zara, from which this liqueur is made.

mezzo-tinto. Mezzotint.

1762 Acad. Italian word, *mezzo-tinto*, documented at least as early as the 17th cent. First examples of the corresponding loan in English date from 1660 (*OED*).

modénature.[2] Archit.: Proportions and outline of a cornice.

1752 Trévoux. <It. *modanatura*, attested 16th cent., Cellini, < *modano* 'model'.

mouflon. Zool.: Mouflon.

Buffon, *Hist. naturelle* (1749–88); but *muifle*, *muifleron* 1611, Cotgrave ('*muffle*: A kind of Sardinian Sheepe whose wooll is hairie like a goats'); also *mufleron* 1660 Oudin. From an Italian dialect; Corsican *mufru*, *mufrone*, *muvarone*; Sardinian *muvrone*, and forms with metathesis. (Literary It. *muffione* dates from 1803, Alb.). The Italian form *muflone* (used esp. in the fur trade) is a loan < French (q.v., 19th cent. Fr. > It. loans).

octavine. Music: In 18th cent. a very small spinet having only one octave.

1703 Brossard, *Dict. de musique* (*D.G.*): 'Espèce de petite épinette qui pour être transportée plus commodément n'a que la petite octave au petit jeu du clavessin.' 1788 Alb., same sense. <It. *ottavino*, derivative of *ottava*, 'octave'.

oratorio. Music.

'Vers 1700', Dauz.; 1740 de Brosses, *Lettres d'Italie*, II, 152, etc. Plural in -*os* normal from earliest examples. Italian word, *oratorio*, usually explained as a metonymic extension of the term in ecclesiastical architecture, the first works of this nature having been performed at the instigation of San Filippo Neri in the Oratory of San Girolamo della Carità at Rome, and later close to Borromini's Oratorio della Chiesa Nuova.

---

1. The shift of accent *màcchia* > *maquis* presents a certain difficulty, since the term entered French through the spoken rather than the written word. I take it that the stress of the original 18th cent. exoticism was penultimate and that it shifted later when the word became commonly used in French.

2. Close [ę] here is no doubt a reinforcement of mute 'e'; but an analogy with the place name *Mòdena*, Fr. *Modène*, may have contributed.

patine. Fine Arts, etc.: Patina.

1765 Buffon, *Minéraux* (*D.G.*). <It. *patina*, 1681, Baldinucci, acc. to most sources; the *D.G.* derives it tentatively from the verb *patiner*. *Patiner* 'to handle roughly', etc., appears in Cotgrave. Acc. to B-Wart., *patine* was originally a material for polishing calf leather; this is one of the Italian significations.

patraque. Money of little value.

1743 Trévoux; but Oudin has '*patacca*—patac, monnoye de peu de valeur, ou plustost une pièce de 58 sols'. See Prati, *V. Et. It.*, p. 741. Very probably < It. *patacca*, *-o*, 16th cent.

pétéchie. Medical: Petechiae.

Areas of reddish discoloration on the skin accompanying certain diseases. 1741 Col-de-Villars, *Dict. franç.-latin*; 1762 Acad. An earlier example in 1564, Liébault (Dauz.). <It. *petecchia*, more normal in plural, *petecchie*.[1]

piano, pianissimo. Music: Piano (softly), etc.

Piano 1732 Lacomte, *Dict.* (Dauz.) as a musical term; *piano* and *mezzo-piano* as musical terms in de Brosses, 1740 (II, 358), and *piano* in Acad., 1762, as a musical term; but *piano* is used sporadically in other Italian senses, esp. as an adverb ('softly, gently') from the 16th cent.: cf. *pian-pian* in Belleau; *marcher pian*, Cotgrave; *pian piano* 1618, *Fameuse Compagnie de la Lésine*.[2] *Pianissimo* 1775, Beaumarchais.

piano. Musical instrument, piano.

1798 Acad.; but *piano-forte* occurs earlier—1774 Voltaire, and *piano-forté*, 1778 Bedos de Celles, *Art du facteur d'orgues* (*D.G.*); the form *forte-piano* in this sense, also 18th cent., is still permitted by the Académie. The instrument was invented about 1700 by Bartolomeo Cristofori of Padua and was called a *gravecembalo col piano e forte*, whence *piano-forte*.

pittoresque. Picturesque.

Originally 'concerning, pertaining to, an artist or painting'. 1708 Piles (Dauz.); 1721 Coypel (Dauz.) (= 'picturesque', referring both to painting and literature); 1762 Acad. <It. *pittoresco*, 17th cent., Redi.

presto, prestissimo. Music: Presto, etc.

1762 Acad.; *prestissimo* late 18th cent. La Fontaine in 1683 uses *presto* meaning 'swiftly' (Dauz.). Italian terms, *presto*, *prestissimo*.

ristourne. Finance: Refund, rebate.

In maritime law, annulment of a ship's insurance before sailing. *Restorne* 1723, Savary; *ristourne* 1783 B-Wart.; *ristorne*, early 18th cent., Dauz.; *restourne* 1769: also *extorne* in 18th cent. <It. *storno*, in earlier times *distorno* 'annulment', 14th cent.; *storno*, Lorenzo de' Medici.

saltarelle. Country dance: Saltarello.

1752 Lancombe (Dauz.); 1838 B-Wart.; 1842 Mozin, 3rd edition. <It. *saltarello*, 16th

---

1. For the ultimate derivation of the Italian term (< hypothetical *peticula < *petigo*, by analogy with the development *lenticula* < *lentigo*, see G. Alessio's short article in *L.N.*, III (1941) p. 128.

2. *Piano* and *pianissimo* in *Le Barbier de Séville*, 1775, are metaphorical meanings from the musical term rather than direct continuations of the 16th cent. usage. Don Bazile's speech (Act II, sc. 8) contains numerous other musical terms, being indeed a literal orchestration of calumny; it may be acted with gestures similar to those of a conductor. A point of interest is that others of Don Bazile's Italianisms occur also in the *Fameuse Compagnie de la Lésine*; cf. the famous line (in the same scene of *Le Barbier*); 'Oui. Mais vous avez lésiné sur les frais ...' (*vide lésine*, 17th cent. It. > Fr. loans). How far was Beaumarchais familiar with the Italian satire?

cent. (B-Al.), with shift of gender from masc. to fem. It is likely that *tarantelle* exerted analogical pressure upon this word, so similar in form and meaning (q.v., *infra*). Traces of the original gender are few, though they can be found; cf. the entry in the *Complément du Dictionnaire de l'Académie*, 1842: 'saltarelle, n.f. Danse vénitienne ... on dit aussi *saltarello*'.

scaferlati. Type of cut tobacco.

1707 Helvetius. Most authorities give it as of unknown origin; speculation on this score is admirably summed up by Maxime du Camp's remarks in the *Revue des Deux Mondes*, 1st Aug. 1868: 'Selon les uns, c'est la dénomination que les Levantines donnaient à une sorte de tabac qu'on expédiait de Turquie; selon d'autres, c'est le nom d'un ouvrier italien qui, travaillant à la ferme dans la première moitié du XVIIIᵉ siècle, inventa un nouveau procédé pour hacher le tabac (B-Wart. gives this, but provisionally); on prétend encore que scaferlati est la corruption du mot italien scarpelletti, petits ciseaux.' Others prefer a similar derivation from It. *scalpellati*, p. part. of *scalpellare*, 'to shred'. An Italian origin is at all events very probable.

scénario. Theatre, opera: Scenario.

1764 Collé meaning 'canevas, schéma d'une pièce de théâtre'; Lar., 1875, in the sense of 'indications de scene, dispositions de mise en scène', acc. to *FEW*, XI, 294-5. Italian word, *scenario*, 17th cent., Lippi meaning 'didascaglie per gli attori'; 18th cent., 'spazio occupato dalle scene; le scene dipinte' (B-Al.). Only accepted by the Académie in 1934. *F.M.*, XIII, 281.

sigisbée. Cicisbeo, gallant attendant upon a lady.

1740 de Brosses: 'cette odieuse race de sigisbées' (II, 204: also II, 205). 1764 Voltaire, *Dict. philos.* < It. *cicisbeo*, 17th cent., probably an onomatopoeic formation, 'one who whispers', i.e. 'close companion', 'confidant' (B-Wart., B-Al., Prati).

solfatare. Geol.: Solfatara.

1757 Cochin et Bellicard (Dauz.), though the Italian form appears once earlier, 1664, *Voyage d'Italie*; Buffon, *Add. à la Théorie de la terre* (D.G.). < It. *solfatara* (originally place-name, near Naples). *Solphaterie* in Belleforest, 16th cent., is rightly viewed by the *D.G.* as an isolated adaptation of the Italian word.

solfège. Music: Solfeggio, sol-fa.

1790 B-Wart.; 1798 Acad. < It. *solfeggio*, 18th cent., Sacchi (B-Al.), < *solfa*, musical scale.

solo. Music: Solo (instrument, voice).

1703 de Brossard; *les soli* (pl.) 1740 de Brosses (II, 360), who also has *duo* and *trio* (II, 359). Italian word in musical acceptation, *solo*.

soprano. Music: Soprano.

1740 de Brosses (loc. cit. under *contralto*, above); 1768 B-Wart.; 1781 *Mém. pour servir à l'hist. de la révol. de la musique* (D.G.). Both refer to the voice, not the person. Italian word, *soprano*, 1618 Buon. il Giovane as a musical term.

tarentelle. Neapolitan folk-dance, tarantella.

1787 B-Wart.; 1807 Madame de Staël. < It. *tarantella* (1734, A. Casotti) < *tarantola*, either because of the longstanding belief that music cured the tarantula's bite, or because the dance resembled in its movements the effects of the disease known as tarantism or St. Vitus' dance.

tempo. Music: Tempo.

1771 B-Wart.; 1842 Mozin, *Dict. franç.-allem.*, 3rd edition. It. word, *tempo*, Benedetto Varchi (1503-1565) in this sense.

tondin. Archit.: Torus at the foot of a column.

1747 Restaut (Dauz.; = *astragale*). Var. *tondein* 'petite baguette au bas des colonnes', 1828 Mozin, *Dict. franç.-allem.*, 2nd edition. < It. *tondino*, 1570 A. Palladio (= *astragalo*, B-Al.).

trébac. Naut.: Trabacolo.

A type of schooner based on Venice and used in the northern Adriatic. 18th cent., acc. to Vidos, who cites an example in Forfait, *Instit. Mém. scienc.* (pre-1807); *trabac* and *trabacolo* 1858, Bescherelle. The English word *trabacolo* (also borrowed from Italian) dates from 1809 (*OED*). < Venetian *trabàcolo*, attested by Boerio early 19th cent., no doubt current among sailors much earlier. Vidos explains *trébac, trabac* as a back-formation from *trabàcolo* rather than a direct adaptation of an Italian *trabacco*. He rejects Alberti's attestation of *trabacco* (1805) since he considers the *Dizionario universale* to be 'una fonte malsicura' (see Vidos, pp. 590–3).

trille. Music: Trill.

1753 J.-J. Rousseau. Variants *tril, trill.* < It. *trillo*, 17th cent. term, Buon. il Giovane 1618; Giambattista Doni 1640.

trombone, *vide supra*, 16th cent., s.v.

villa. Villa.

1743 B-Wart. Used by Fragonard and other 18th cent. painters; *vide* Migliorini, 'Notules lexicales', *F.M.*, IX, 1941, p. 50. < It. *villa*, 14th cent.

villégiature. Stay, holiday in the country.

Villegiatura (sic) 1739, de Brosses: 'c'est là que les Romains venoient en villegiatura' (I, 453); *villeggiatura*, II, 336. 1755 Abbé Prévost (Dauz.); 1761 *Test. polit. du maréchal de Belle-Isle* (Dauz.). < It. *villeggiatura*, late 17th cent., Redi.

violoncelle. Music: Violoncello, 'cello.

1739 de Brosses (I, 238, 246; II, 91, 576); 1743 Trévoux; 1762 Acad. The Italian word itself is used earlier in French, 1709, B-Wart. < It. *violoncello*, 1680–88, G. B. Borri (B-Al.), diminutive of *violone*, 'double-bass'.

Italian Influences on French Vocabulary during the Eighteenth Century

The eighteenth is a century in which a relatively small number of loan-words passed from Italian into French—a *residuum* period, in the terminology we have proposed.[1]

We can describe political encounters between the two countries at this time more profitably in our next chapter, with reference to the impact of French on Italian. It is enough at this stage to observe that military clashes were largely confined to the earlier and later part of the century and that the free movement of travellers to and from either country was not seriously interrupted at any time before 1789. One event we must record, however; France's purchase of Corsica from Genoa in 1768, and its *de facto* incorporation into the French administrative system from 1770. A word in our list sets the seal on this bargain: *maquis*, originally meaning an area of land allowed to pass out of cultivation through the Corsican peasant's custom of migrating constantly on to new, fallow land.

1. *Vide supra*, p. 273, n. 2.

Though the importation as a whole represents an even, *datum level* of borrowing, one semantic category is conspicuous above the rest, accounting for forty-five of our hundred and six entries. The eighteenth century is the period when Italy's influence on France in the realm of music reached its height, and musical terms reflect this preponderance closely. Italy had not always excelled in this art. During the Middle Ages the epicentre of musical innovation lay in the north; Italian musicians like Italian poets willingly imitated the *troubadours* of Provence or the *trouvères* of Picardy and Champagne. At the close of that period most of the important musical posts in Europe were held by composers who came from Flanders or the Low Countries.

Influence on French music began to be felt and to be confirmed by borrowed vocabulary at the very beginning of the sixteenth century, as part of the great contribution of the Italian Renaissance whose linguistic effects we have already described. *Madrigal*, appropriately, was among the first borrowings to enter usage.[1] Secular, ideal for being performed by amateurs, closely integrated in subject matter with the literary tastes of the time, the sixteenth century Italian madrigal quickly became popular throughout Europe. They were sung at all sorts of social gatherings, but were especially in vogue in France at the Valois court, as in the more important aristocratic seats. The *canzon villanesca* or *villanella*, ostensibly a peasant song but often a parody of the loftier madrigal, appeared around Naples about 1540 and was known in France later in the century (*villanelle* in Montaigne). Dancing as a social pastime, which in the Middle Ages had been associated with folk displays and peasants' wakes, now became popular in the highest orders of society. The most successful poets of the age—Ronsard among them—combined with musicians and impresarios to present masques in which courtiers and even the royal family played parts. Song and dance were intimately related, and the semantic ambiguity of certain loan-words may be traced to the dual function which they performed: in France *ballet* (1578) quickly came to mean a dance rather than the accompanying music of the Italian *balletto*.

Near the end of the century Italy moved to the forefront of European music when the madrigal developed into a new vocal *genre* destined to a brilliant future, the *opera*, which one associates with the man who is best entitled to be called its creator, Claudio Monteverdi (*Orfeo*, 1607). This in its turn reached France, and I have already said a little about its fortunes there. Its sudden rise to favour under Mazarin was short-lived. As time slipped by the current of Italianism gradually fell slack and in the second half of the seventeenth century receded to make way for Lulli and the national French style.

In 1702 a pamphlet entitled *Paralèle des Italiens et des François en ce qui regarde la Musique et les Opéra* by Abbé Raguenet, who had resided for some time in Rome, marked the beginning of a long, bitterly waged but incon-

1. The definitive form is found in 1542, but *madrigale* at the beginning of the century.

clusive controversy about the supremacy of French or Italian music. Up to
the mid-century honours remained with supporters of the national musical
idiom, largely because of the reputation and indisputable excellence of
Rameau, who had shown himself a worthy successor to Lulli and whom many
Frenchmen revered as the man who succeeded in extending the principle of
rationalism to the realm of music. There were even those who compared his
achievement to that of Descartes and Newton; Rameau appeared, and chaos
was no more.[1] During this extended truce or more correctly this period of
desultory skirmishing Italian operas and singers had come to be accepted by all
important musical centres in Europe apart from Paris. Discussion flared into
open hostilities when in August 1752 a troupe of Italian *burletta* singers opened
an eighteen-months' tour in Paris with Pergolesi's *opera buffa La Serva
Padrona*, inserted as an intermezzo between the acts of Lulli's *Acis et Galatée*.
The performance aroused so much admiration that partisans of national
opera took fright; a vigorous exchange of polemic ensued—the notorious
guerre des bouffons—with sixty-three publications on music appearing in Paris
during the space of four years.[2] The brunt of the attack fell on Rameau as the
greatest contemporary exponent of French opera. For a time he remained
aloof, but was at length nettled into replying and committing himself to a
losing battle which saddened the last years before his death in 1764.

The *ordre de bataille* of this campaign, during which 'tout Paris se divisa en
deux parties plus échauffés qui s'il fût agi d'une affaire d'État ou de religion'
is described in animated terms by Rousseau in *Les Confessions*, Book VIII.[3]
Intellectuals, including some contributors to the *Encyclopédie* (Diderot,
d'Alembert) were on the side of the *bouffons*, opposed to 'Les Grands, les
riches et les femmes' who made up the *King's Corner* at the *Opéra*. Grimm
fired the opening salvos for the Italians,[4] but Rousseau soon revealed himself
as their most redoubtable supporter. His *Lettre sur la musique française*, the only
work of real critical value that has come down to us from this confused
affair, drew from Dr. Burney the shrewd observation that 'there was too
much good sense, taste and reason in the letter for it to be read with indifference: it was abused, but never answered'.[5] It also earned for its author the
distinction of being burnt in effigy at the door of the *Opéra*.

Controversy was not stilled by the stalemate of the *guerre des bouffons*, but
burst forth anew during the '70s with the quarrel between supporters of
Gluck and those of the Neapolitan Piccini. The former's very personal

1. Among them de la Borde, in his *Essai sur la Musique*: see Charles Burney, *A General History of Music from the Earliest Ages to the Present Period* (1789), ed. Dover, New York, 1957, Vol. II, p. 969.
2. See Eve Kisch, 'Rameau and Rousseau', *Music and Letters*, XXII, No. 2 (1941), p. 101.
3. *Œuvres complètes, Bibl. de la Pléiade* edition, Vol. I, pp. 384–5.
4. E. Kisch, loc. cit., pp. 99–100.   5. *A General History of Music*, ed. cit., p. 970.

musical contribution had imposed itself on Paris to the extent of being acclaimed as typically French, while Piccini like Pergolesi before him symbolised the music of his native country. 'This admirable composer', reports Dr.
Burney, 'the delight and pride of Naples, as Gluck of Vienna, had no sooner
erected his standard in France than all the friends of Italian Music, of Rousseau's
doctrines, and of the plan if not the language of Metastasio's dramas,
inlisted in his service. A furious war broke out, and all Paris was on the *Qui
vive?* No door was opened to a visitor, without this question being asked
previous to his admission: "Monsieur! estes-vous PICCINISTE OU GLUCKISTE?" '[1]

Contacts in matters of music, as one of the fine arts, are the kind of extralinguistic material one finds most congenial in studying relations between
cultural languages. There is considerable interest for us in the way our words
reflect the vicissitudes of the aesthetic debate in their dating and show by
their content the musical topics upon which attention dwelt. A few terms
enter from the first years of the century, continuing the desultory trend begun
in the later seventeenth (*récitatif, si* [note of the octave] in 1690, *sonate* in 1695);
the largest contribution is made in the middle decades, corresponding to the
disputes of the '50s and '70s. At one time etymologists cited the *Encyclopédie*
as their prime source for this lexical field. Though many words have been
shifted back to the period before 1751, it still remains a productive vein of
information. Rousseau's *Dictionnaire de musique*, 1767, originally part of that
work, contributes two terms (*cavatine, do*) while two more appear in his
Lettre sur la musique (*fortissimo, trille*). Many of the borrowings relate to
singing: *contralto, soprano, alto, solo, cavatine, oratorio, cantatrice, castrat* (the
latter in de Brosses, 1740, but perhaps Parisians were reminded of the word
in 1753 during the visit of the famous *castrato*, Caffarelli).

In the eighteenth century it began to be common practice for a composer
to include indications of expression and tempo in his score. Because of Italian's
ascendancy at the time it was natural that they should come to be written in
that language—a convention accepted internationally which still obtains at
the present day, though national sentiment has impelled certain French composers to use the vernacular in more recent times—Debussy, for one, and
Ravel. Musical expressions in our list appear at dates evenly distributed over
the century—*adagio* and *allegro* 1726, *piano* 1732, *mezzo-piano* 1740, *allegretto*
and *andante* 1751, *forte* 1760, *presto* 1762, *fortissimo* 1763, *crescendo, decrescendo*
and *pianissimo* in the '70s, *prestissimo* late eighteenth century and so on. These
of course are only a sample; greater precision in dating and greater comprehensiveness could only be achieved in a specialised musical survey. All
expressions of phrasing and tempo needed in musical practice are available
in Italian and, as we have observed, are generally drawn from that source.[2]

1. Ibid., p. 973.
2. To give a more faithful impression of the wealth of Italian musical directions current

Let us turn again for a moment to the *Lettre sur la musique française*, which stands at a focal point in our synopsis of lexical and musical trends. What immediately strikes the reader about this brilliant pamphlet is that although Rousseau attacks French opera over all the territory of musical technique appropriate to his subject, contrasting with inexorable logic the role of melody, harmony and tempo in French and Italian compositions, bringing out with recourse to precise musical examples the defects of French *airs, ariettes* and recitative, and developing his criticism right up to the final sweeping condemnation,[1] the point from which his manifesto takes its departure is not musical, but linguistic. The Letter's first dozen pages are a linguistic dissertation. Affirming that 'toute musique nationale tire son principal caractère de la langue qui lui est propre' and that 'c'est principalement la prosodie de la langue qui constitue ce caractère',[2] he begins by sustaining the thesis that 'on peut concevoir des langues plus propres à la musique les unes que les autres: on en peut concevoir qui ne le seroit point du tout'.[3] An unsuitable language would be 'une qui ne seroit composée que de sons mixtes, de syllabes muettes, sourdes ou nasales, peu de voyelles sonores, beaucoup de consonnes et d'articulations' and the like. The reader is left to recognise French in this description. Musical shortcomings following from these defects are then examined. Rousseau does not limit himself to the obvious topic of vocalic or consonantal euphony; he judges French to be inherently unfit as a musical medium on account of its imprecise conventions of length and pitch and its monotone stress, all of which make a harmonious marriage of verbal and musical expression impossible, or at least drive composers to resort to artificial devices—and even because of its vaunted logical word-

internationally I append a list drawn up by V. Adami, *Vocaboli italiani nella lingua francese*, Milan 1935: *allegro non tanto, allegretto grazioso, andante semplice, andantino, andante religioso, animato, un poco animato, agitato, accelerato, armonioso, brillante, ben legato, con disinvoltura, con molta grazia, con forza, dolce, dolcissimo, deciso, energico, grandioso, grazioso, grave, espressivo, lento, leggero, legato, largo, moderato, mosso, più mosso, marcato, marcatissimo, maestoso, pomposo, risoluto, rallentato, rapido, stentato, sostenuto, staccato, tempo di marcia, tuttaforza, vivo.* Cf. also the list of similar terms from English sources cited by Mario Praz, *The Italian Element in English*, p. 60.

1. 'Je crois avoir fait voir . . . que le chant françois n'est qu'un aboiement continuel, insupportable à toute oreille non prévenue; que l'harmonie en est brute, sans expression, et sentant uniquement son remplissage d'écolier; que les airs françois ne sont point des airs; que le récitatif françois n'est point du récitatif. D'où je conclus que les François n'ont point de musique et n'en peuvent avoir, ou que, si jamais ils en ont une, ce sera tant pis pour eux.'

References to Rousseau's writings upon music are drawn from *Les Œuvres de J.-J. Rousseau, nouvelle édition*, Paris, Ledoux et Tenré, 1819. His *Lettre sur la musique française* appears in Vol. XI of this edition, while the *Dictionnaire de Musique* comprises Vols. XII and XIII.

2. Op. cit., pp. 260-1.

3. Op. cit., pp. 257-8.

order.[1] The linguistic aspect of vocal music is so much to the front of his mind that he goes to language for his similes and analogies: French composition is so overloaded with *fredons*, *cadences*, *ports de voix* and other *agréments postiches* that it reminds him of Gothic script;[2] Italian singers attempting to render French scores sound as unconvincing as Arabic read out from French characters.[3]

Italian on the other hand possesses all the advantages that French lacks: 'Si l'on demandoit laquelle de toutes les langues doit avoir une meilleure grammaire, je répondrois que c'est celle du peuple qui raisonne le mieux; et, si l'on demandoit lequel de tous les peuples doit avoir une meilleure musique, je dirois que c'est celui dont la langue y est plus propre. ... Or, s'il y a en Europe une langue propre à la musique, c'est certainement l'italienne.'[4] Thus, circle upon circle, Rousseau builds up an apologia for Italian while defending Italian music: a final contrast takes us beyond the musician's orbit and allows us to glimpse a fleeting vision of Italian as the language of anti-rationalism, intuition and natural harmony.

While he was busy codifying the prosodic limitations of French and seeking to give adequate expression to his findings, Rousseau's sensitivity to language made him aware of inadequacies in current terminology which hindered his efforts to compare the French and Italian tongues in a written treatise, and to some extent acted as a barrier preventing partisans of French opera from appreciating what Italy had to offer. He would dearly like his reader to enjoy with him the manifold beauties of Italian recitative; 'mais pour entrer dans les détails il faudrait pour ainsi dire créer un nouveau dictionnaire, inventer à chaque instant des termes pour offrir aux lecteurs français des idées inconnues parmi eux, et leur tenir des discours qui leur paraîtroient du galimatias'.[5] Nevertheless he does sometimes seek to bridge the gap by consciously adapting an Italian word, e.g. on pp. 310-11: 'Voilà un *trille*, et qui pis est, un repos absolu dès le premier vers...' to which he appends the note 'Je suis contraint de franciser ce mot, pour exprimer le battement de gosier que les Italiens appellent ainsi, parce que, me trouvant à chaque instant dans la nécessité de me servir du mot *cadence* dans une autre acception, il ne m'étoit pas possible d'éviter autrement des équivoques continuelles'.[6] In the case of *tempo*, however, which I regard as one of the key-words to this lexical influence,[7] he fails to take advantage of the other language. A great deal of the musical debate hinges upon the problem of interpreting tempo. Rousseau, who alludes to it on numerous occasions, is

1. 'Les inversions de la langue italienne sont beaucoup plus favorables à la bonne mélodie que l'ordre didactique de la nôtre ... une phrase musicale se développe d'une manière plus agréable et plus intéressante quand le sens du discours, longtemps suspendu, se résout sur le verbe avec la cadence' (op. cit., p. 268).　　　2. Op. cit., p. 259.

3. Op. cit., p. 273. Cf. also p. 260: 'La mesure est à peu près à la mélodie ce que la syntaxe est au discours' (et seq.).　　　　4. p. 266.　　　5. p. 307.

6. He takes over the Italianism *do* (instead of *ut*) for equally pragmatic reasons: *vide* his *Dictionnaire de musique*, s.v., and our word-entry.　　　7. The other is *dilettante*.

often hard pressed to make his meaning clear; yet he makes do with the traditional words *mesure* and *mouvement* and gains semantic precision by using the two in collocation or by adding amplificatory phrases. The loan-word *tempo* was clearly 'in the air' by 1753; Rousseau's continuing use of older equivalents gives us a welcome insight into the conditions which prevail before a borrowing is made.[1]

A few miscellaneous loans show how far the lexical field of Italianisms extended: it took in terms of notation—*arpège, da capo*; music teaching—*conservatoire*; *finale* and *scène-buffe*, referring to the opera's structure; *scénario*, recalling the ancillary aspects of operatic productions, and the acclamations *bravo! bravissimo!* As in the sixteenth and seventeenth centuries there are words denoting dances and their accompanying tunes—*saltarelle, tarantelle*,[2] while the names of several instruments invented or developed in Italy draw out a list already long from previous periods: *mandoline*, associated with southern Italy, *octavine*, a kind of very compact spinet, *violoncelle*, and the instrument destined to be most widely favoured of all—the *pianoforte*.

Another person whose name is seen several times in the eighteenth century list is Charles de Brosses, usually called Président de Brosses, because he was the first president of the *Parlement de Bourgogne*.

De Brosses is a true *dilettante*[3] both of music and of the visual arts. Modern musicologists still cite him for his fresh opinions and remarkable perceptivity, quite apart from the value of his *reportage* on historical grounds. Like the Geneva scholar he feels a deep sympathy with Italian culture, and like him too he is endowed with both the writer's and the scholar's sensitivity to language.[4] But there the resemblance ends, for de Brosses is more a Good Companion than a *Promeneur solitaire* and a natural extrovert into the bargain. Nor is the extended narrative which makes up his *Lettres familières sur l'Italie* quite like that of any contemporary. The little magistrate's journey is not a sentimental one, though the feelings that new sights and acquaintances inspire in him are an important part of his tale. Though he records, weighs

1. Our list's first attestation is 1771. Rousseau naturally knew the Italian word in its native context: cf. his notes on *a tempo* and its equivalent *mesuré* in the *Dictionnaire*; also ibid., s.v. *mouvement*, where *tempo giusto* is mentioned as an expression used in Italian.

2. The social connotation of dancing is more influential than that of vocal or instrumental music (though opera may be considered in some degree a social event). This is why borrowings in the opposite direction, where musical influences are slight, but social ones profound, include a number of dances; *vide allemanda, carmagnola, contraddanza, minuetto* (18th cent. Fr. > It.).

3. The first example of this word registered so far is the one in de Brosses (*vide* word-list).

4. Both Rousseau and de Brosses published serious works on language, the former an *Essai sur l'origine des langues* (1769) and the latter a most substantial *Traité de la formation méchanique des langues, et des principes physiques de l'étymologie*, Paris, 1765. Neither is comparable to the greater philological works of their century—Cesarotti's, for instance —but neither deserves to be wholly lost sight of as they are nowadays.

carefully and comments wisely on all he sees he is not a passive Spectator. Quite the reverse: he launches with relish into each new adventure, savouring everything Italy has to offer; with the confidence of a genuine cosmopolitan he expects to be accepted as an equal by all men, and is accepted. In his own person the Franco-Italian *rapport* which he typifies is intimate because of the traits of character we have just enumerated, his sympathies, and the bent of his genius; but his importance as far as we are concerned lies even more in what he stands for. The author of the *Lettres familières* was a man of many parts—legislator, *philosophe* and contributor to the *Encyclopédie*, philologist, archaeologist and amateur of the arts—but his most successful role was that of the genial tourist. The archetypal tourist, one might say: for not only is his account of the gentleman's voyage the most perfect example of its *genre*, but his attitude towards the foreign language is typical too. He enjoys the sound of Italian just as he enjoys the music of *mon charmant Pergolèse* or, in another medium, *les grâces adoucies de Raphaël*. Italian gaming terms fascinate him—*minchiate, biribi, tre-sette, verzicole,* le fol ou *matto* (i.e. the Joker).[1] He caresses the names of marbles and other stones used by sculptors and builders—*carrare, jaune de Sienne, lapis lazuli, brèche, lumachelle, turquin, cipolin, portor* (opposed to 'ces vilains rances ou autres marbres de Flandre, de couleur terne, terreuse et ferrugineuse' [II, 99]). He complains of unscrupulous *vetturini*, of the post-horse system or *cambiatura*, waxes indignant about *sigisbées* and *babilans* and is scornful of *castrats* (while appreciating fairly their musical talents). Sometimes he ends a chapter with a quotation from Ariosto (II, 68, 186, etc.); ever and anon he enlivens his narrative with snatches of the foreign idiom, partly *bons mots* like Innocent XI's *che si castri meglio,*[2] but mostly the obvious phrases or remarks which a tourist would readily hear: *buona mano, buona mancia, non c'è rimedio, una cosa più stupenda,* with of course the usual exclamations.[3]

De Brosses' *Lettres familières sur l'Italie* were only published in 1799 and therefore did not serve as a written intermediary for the words he borrows (most of which were commonplace by that time) except perhaps among his close friends to whom he showed portions of the manuscript. But we may well surmise that our gifted *raconteur* retained and used a number of these Italianisms in his spoken idiolect, and that the thousands who like him

1. Op. cit., II, 68, 197, 198, etc. He has a taste for puns: cf. his account of the unfortunate *gaffe* made by Legouz ('qui est sujet au quiproquo') in saying *minchie* for *minchiate* at Madame Bentivoglio's (p. 198). There are other gaming terms in our list—*ambe, loto, cavagnole*. Italians seem to have been as fertile inventors of games of chance in the eighteenth as in the seventeenth century (*vide supra*).   2. *Vide* II, 342.

3. 'O *che gusto* de les revoir' (II, 586) '*Cazzo* ! La première pairie du royaume' (II, 287, 542). Cf. also the following: 'Le lendemain matin, ah, messieurs mes amis, *fa fresco, fresco*' (II, 534); '. . . des Corrèges *del primo grido*' (II, 106); 'J'ai de fâcheuses nouvelles à vous apprendre du chemin de Sienne à Rome; il est *cattif*, mais je dis très *cattif* . . .' (II,

went to admire the accumulated treasures of renaissance and baroque Italy, its antiquities or its scenic wonders[1] were in a position to make similar individual contributions to French, some of which by dint of repetition succeeded in entering the language permanently.

Occasionally a term of the plastic and pictorial arts is closely linked with antiquarianism (*patine, camée, graticule*; cf. also the term of numismatics *contorniate*), but most fall within a similar semantic range to those of the previous century, i.e. primarily techniques and *genres: aquarelle, gouache, mezzo-tinto*, the adjective *pittoresque, caricature* and (with a hint of artists' slang) *bambochade. Maquette* 'mock-up' is connected with both painting and sculpture.

There is continuity, too, between commercial terms of the two periods, which again cover an analogous semantic range: commercial practice—*colis, discrédit, dito, format, franco*; insurance—*ristourne*; a selection of products—*calmande, lustrine, scaferlati, gavette*. One or two terms of heavy industry diverge from the previous pattern—*brasque* (luting of a furnace or crucible), *asple*. I see these as indicating in their small way the changing economic structure of Europe as a whole. They are of a piece with the same type of word in the French to Italian list.

Borrowed names of animals, birds and other fauna probably tell us more about Buffon than about Franco-Italian relations (*avocette, guépard, luciole, mouflon*).

Abstracts, the sign of close dependence, are singularly lacking. The only one in our list without specialised affiliations is *grandiose*. Significantly it appears for the first time in de Brosses. Others of the abstract-general-emotive categories are almost all pejorative: *babilan, casino, cicerone, lazarone, lazariel, castrat*,[2] *sigisbée, patraque*. From these too one may draw particular conclusions, which however, we shall keep for a later chapter.[3]

---

386). Sometimes we hear an echo of the other Italophile a century and a half before: 'Mille compliments . . . à nos amés et féaux tutti quanti' (I, 62); deux chevaux . . . moyennant quoi nous ingannions le sortilège qui nous poursuit' (I, 168); 'cette église d'une facilité et d'une vaghezza merveilleuse' (II, 115).

1. Vesuvius was a favourite tourist attraction from early times. De Brosses wrote a monograph on Herculaneum, the first archaeological survey of that city. Pompeii had not been exposed to the light of day when the Président made his voyage; excavations at that site from 1748 onwards greatly increased the number of antiquarian tourists. *Cicerone, solfatare, villa* and to some extent *casino* may be cited as 'touristic' loans. See also observations on *lave*, 17th cent. It. > Fr. list.

2. As regards semantic overtones *castrat* is also partly euphemistic, since it provides an acceptable designation for what in France was widely held to be a distasteful thing. Cf. Rousseau, *Dict. de musique*, s.v.: 'Quoique le mot *castrato* ne puisse offenser les plus déli-cates oreilles il n'en est pas de même de son synonyme français; preuve evidente que ce qui rend les mots indécents et déshonnêtes dépend moins des idées qu'on leur attache, que de l'usage de la bonne compagnie.' De Brosses does indeed tend to use *châtré* in disparag-ing statements: see word-list.   3. *Vide infra*, Part IV, *Pejoratives and Pejoration*.

Remaining words represent the random scatter of borrowings during a period of quiescence, of chance day-to-day contact.[1]

Gallicisms in Italian during the Eighteenth Century

acustico. Scient.: Acoustic.

18th cent., acc. to B-Al. M-D. derive it from Greek, but B-Al. while referring to the ultimate learned origin add that the term appears to have been taken directly < Fr. *acoustique*, 1701 Sauveur, *Mém. de l'Acad. des Sciences*. There is a 17th cent. example of *acustico* in Daniello Bartoli, *Del suono, de' tremori armonici e dell'udito* (1st edition 1679: *vide Gr. diz. it.*) in the phrase *condotto acustico* meaning 'outer ear' (corresponds to *condotto udito esterno* in modern parlance). I interpret this as a Latinism separated in time from the 18th cent. term which became current through French contacts.

addirizzare, addirizzo. To dedicate, entitle.

The above sense appears in A. M. Salvini's annotation of Salvatore Rosa's Satires. Of modern sources, B-Al. consider that in the sense of 'dedicate', 'entitle' or in the reflexive (*addirizzarsi*) 'to inquire of, address oneself to' the It. words are semantic loans from Fr. (*s'*)*adresser, adresse*. Already in the early 19th cent. Parenti (*Catalogo di spropositi*, 1840) reached the same conclusion, condemning the use of the verb in this signification as a recently introduced Gallicism, despite its use in Salvini, who, as he points out, is far from a purist in this respect. F-A. list it as a 'reputato francesimo', but plainly agree with Parenti and Cesari about its foreign origin and extend their censure to the noun *addrizzo*.[2] *Vide M-Stor.*, p. 576.

adepto. Adept, initiate.

Originally a learned borrowing from the mediaeval Latin of the alchemists (cf. Alberti, 1777, who under the form *adetto* still only registers the strict sense of 'Ritrovatore o cercatore della pietra filosofale'), but introduced anew during the later 18th cent. (a) in connection with the secret societies of the time (possible Anglicism?) (b) in a general, figurative sense; cf. Beccaria, *Caffè*, II, p. 9 (*M-Stor.*, p. 570). Rigutini criticises the transferred usage as a definite Gallicism; recent sources also acknowledge a Fr. influence (cf. B-Al.: 'è evidente il tramite francese'). Panz. IX still notes the philosophical or political flavour of the term. <Fr. *adepte*, originally referring to the alchemists (late 17th cent., Bayle); used in the general sense 1771, acc. to Bloch-Wartburg.

aerostato. Aeronautics: Free balloon.

Areostato 1784 (Pr.); Alberti, *Diz. universale*. Neither the Italian nor the French word appears in Alberti 1788. Also adj. *aerostatico* (*areostatico*, same dates). 'Il globo aerostatico' implying 'balloon' in Cesarotti (*Gr. diz. it.*, I, 190a). <Fr. *aérostat* (more usually *aérostate*) and *aérostatique*, 1783, *Hist. de l'Acad. des Sciences*; term originally used by Montgolfier (B-Al., Pr.).

affiorare. Geol.: Of strata: to appear on the surface.

18th cent., M-Stor., p. 576: 19th cent. attestations. Semantic loan < Fr. *affleurer*, 14th cent. (M-D., M-Stor., Pr.). Prati also derives 19th cent. It. *affioramento* 'outcrop of rock' (1861, T.-Bell.) from Fr. *affleurement*, 1593.

---

1. They are: Agriculture: *agrumi, cantaloup*; Architecture: *modénature, tondin*; Botany, medicine: *belladone*; Foods: *chipolata, marasquin*; Historical: *condottiere*; Literary: *concetti*; Medical: *influenza, pétéchie*; Nautical: *chébec, fisolère, trébac* (but no military terms at all); Scientific: *galvanisme; cascatelle*, dimin. of *cascade; gazetin*, a small coin.

2. The native signification 'to set right, correct' dates from G. Villani.

affluente. Geog.: Tributary.

18th cent., acc. to B-Al.   Baretti 1771 has it only as the adj. (pres. part.) = 'flowing, abounding'. Alb. 1777 translates the Fr. word (given as an adj. used as a geographical term) by: 'Luogo dove un fiume mette force, imbocca, si scarica in altro fiume.' The It. > Fr. section still only has *affluente* in the sense of *abbondante*. <Fr. learned geographical term *affluent*, end 17th cent., Furetière (though *affluent* as a pres. part. and adj. meaning 'flowing' appears already in the 16th cent.: 'Terre qui est affluente de laict et de miel', J. Lemaire de Belges; cf. Huguet, I, p. 105). The possibility of a direct Latinism—since the Latin word appears with the above sense in texts of Italy as early as the 10th cent.— must be rejected in view of the term's late appearance in Italian proper.

aggiotaggio, aggiotatore. Fraudulent speculation, speculator.

18th cent. M-*Stor.*, p. 576 (and source cited). 1797 Alb., *Diz. univ.* Used in propaganda and legislation of Revolutionary period against financial abuses. Also in Bernardoni (not good Italian, but 'very expressive'). < Fr. *agiotage*; infl. of Fr. *agioteur* (B-Al., Pr., M-D., M-*Stor.*, etc.), early 18th cent. The Fr. words, together with *agioter* 'to speculate' are derivatives of *agio* (< It. *aggio*; *vide* 17th cent. list).

agremani, agrimani. Type of dress jewellery.

B-Al. register *agrimani* 'guarnizioni a disegno e traforate; diamanti legati in argento' as an 18th cent. loan. It is only in the 19th cent., however, that the term enters general use.[1] Neither Baretti 1771 nor Alb. 1788 register it, the latter translating Fr. *agréments* by *guernimenti, ornamenti, vezzi, guarnizioni*. Also the form *agremani* (19th cent. in general) and the Italianised version *agremà* in F-A., Rig. and Panz. F-A. attack it strongly and with ironical reference to 'le agre mani'. Rigutini, more liberal, considers that *agremà* may ultimately become accepted and compares the similar case of *passamano*, citing as evidence of the word's long denizenship its use in L. Adimari, *Satire*: 'pompose armille, ... orecchini, agrimani (1st edition, 1716: *vide Gr. diz. it.*, I, 267a). The word fell into disuse with the obsolescence of the fashions involved. <Fr. *agréments* (all sources), originally an abstract 'consent, agreement' (15th cent., Chastellain); the signification 'that which is pleasing, agreeable' is normal throughout the 17th cent., while the specific sense of jewellery occurs first in Saint-Simon.

alibi. Legal term, alibi.

1777 Alberti, *Vocab.* A Latin word; but evidence indicates that the legal term entered Italy from France where it existed in this connotation as early as the 14th cent. (1394 Douet d'Arcq, *Pièces relat. à Ch. VI* [D.G.]) (Pr.; B-Al.'s reference to the word's antiquity in French may be taken to indicate a similar view). The fact of a French provenance was known to Alberti, who observes: 'voce latina usata da' *Francesi*[2] in questa frase: *prouver l'Alibi*, che vale Provare la presenza d'una persona in luogo lontano, diverso da quello in cui si pretende qu'ella fosse in certo tempo'. *Alibi* is found as a legal term—usually in a phrase closely resembling the French construction—elsewhere in Europe during the 18th cent.; cf. in English, Arbuthnot, 1727: 'The Prisoner endeavoured ... to prove himself alibi'. Eng. *alibi* as a subst. is first documented in 1774 (*OED*).

allemanda. Country dance and accompanying tune.

---

1. Borrowings in other languages suggest that the Fr. word was disseminated abroad over a long period. Sp. *agremán* is documented only in 1878 (Corominas) whereas in Eng., though the precise sense of 'jewellery' is not found, something very close to the French usage appears already in 1737, Warburton: 'The art of adding *the agreements* to the most agreeable object in the world, which is literary history' (*OED*).

2. In the 3rd edition, 1788. The 1777 edition has 'voce latina usata da' *Forensi* ...' Is the later *Francesi* a misprint? More probably an alteration in the interests of greater precision. The term is at the same time a legal and a French usage.

Although an actual attestation is lacking there is no doubt that the term was used to describe this type of German country dance in Italy as in France, England and elsewhere during the 18th century, though probably not before, if the corresponding English documentation is an acceptable indication of its diffusion elsewhere (1775 Sheridan, *The Rivals*: 'Allemandes (i.e. the Fr. word) and cotillons' [*OED*]). The loan probably took place towards the end of the period; Alberti, 1788, still translates Fr. *allemande* by 'danza tedesca' only. Historical and lexicological sources alike agree that the dance's popularity was at its height in the later 18th cent. French *allemande* appears much earlier in the sense of the tune rather than the dance (16th cent.), as is also the case in English (*Allmands* (sic) as airs for a violin in 1685 [*OED*]).

amatore. Amateur, esp. of sports and pastimes.

The original word *amatore*, *amadore* in OIt. meaning 'lover' (13th cent.) is a Provençalism < OProv. *amador* (which is probably the source of the original OFr. word too; *vide* Bezzola, p. 225 n. 1). A clear semantic influence from French operates from the late 18th cent., first in the broad sense of 'one who cultivates the arts and sciences for pleasure', then during the 19th cent., 'amateur' in the restricted language of sport. The latter may transmit an Eng. influence via French. G. B. Casti, *Il poema satirico*, 1787, speaks of 'un califfo amatore della verdura' who has a garden laid out for his pleasure (*Gr. diz. it.*, s.v.). Bernardoni lists *amatore* as incorrect for *dilettante*; Ugol. and others in the 19th cent. urge readers to reinstate the latter in its original, wider use. Also Fr. form *amateur*, *en amateur* (sport). The French semantic shift has been traced back to J.-J. Rousseau.

ammortizzare, ammortizzazione. Finance: To establish a sinking fund.

Opinions range from that of Prati, who considers both words to be modelled upon Fr. *amortir* (prob. ≠ *amortissement*) to that of B-Al., who explain them as learned legal terms derived from MedLat. Two questions are at issue: (a) the provenance of the form (b) the possibility of a semantic Gallicism only. As regards (a): the presence of Fr. *amortissement* in 1263 and *amortissable* in 1465, the existence of the infix -*iss*- (corresponding to -*izz*-) in the Fr. verb *amortir* together with the Gallicising suffixes -*izzazione*, -*izzare* speak in favour of a Fr. influence, yet the form may equally well be explained by derivation from the MedLat. verb *admortizare* 'to extinguish', attested in 1376. A French influence upon MedLat. itself is, however, not out of the question. As regards (b): there are two distinct meanings to be considered, firstly, 'to place a property in mortmain' (i.e. the sense possessed by the mediaeval Fr. term) and secondly, 'to establish a sinking fund for the repayment of a debt'. The first appears in Paolo Sarpi (1552–1623) (both verb and noun, the latter cited as a term used in France); the second in 1781, *Bandi di Leopoldo* (verb) and Alb., 1797 (noun) (both given by Pr.). The second signification may be assumed to be a Fr. semantic influence,—F-A., Rig. and Panz. have no hesitation in regarding it as such. Little used in the 18th cent., it appears to have become a current bureaucratic and financial term during the 1st half of the 19th cent., when the compound *cassa d'ammortizzazione* is common (Fr. *caisse d'amortissement*) (Pecchio, *Gr. diz. it.*).

andrienne. Fashions: Loose fitting ladies' wrap, with train.

Alberti describes this famous 18th cent. fashion as follows: '*Volg. It.* Sorta di veste femminile, lunga e sciolta. *Andrienne, robe de Chambre*' (1777). The Crusca gives it in G. A. Papini, *Lezioni sopra il Burchiello* (1733); also in Algarotti (1712–64); 1756, G. Gozzi; 1777, Alberti. Venetian form *andriè* in Goldoni and *andrien* in an inventory of 1737. The origin of the word is well known, being the name given to a type of robe similar to that worn by the actress Mlle Dancourt in Michel Baron's *Andrienne* (first night 16th Nov. 1703). *Vide* Migl., *Dal nome proprio*, p. 188.

ardesia. Slate.

G. Targioni Tozzetti (1712–83). Both word and thing seem to have been little known in the 18th century; Baretti 1771 omits the It. word, and describes Eng. *slate* as if the substance were entirely unfamiliar to his readers. Alberti 1777 likewise omits the Italian word, but in the Fr. > It. section has the entry '*Ardoise*. Lavagna, lastra; et quelque part, Ardesia.' <Fr. *ardoise*, 12th cent., Chrétien de Troyes (B-Al., M-D., Pr.); in LowLat. *lapis ardesius*, of uncertain origin, possibly Ligurian (or < *Artesia* Artois)? Cf. the more usual It. term *lavagna* (denoting a closely similar schist) where an analogous generalisation of a place-name occurs.

assegnato. 'Assignat' issued during the French Revolution.

1798 Vincenzo Russo: 'Fondi destinati all'estinzione degli assegnati' (*Gr. diz. it.*); *assignato* 1811, Alberti, *Diz. fr.-it.* Semantic loan < Fr. *assignat* (Panz., Pr., *Gr. diz. it.*), first found as a financial term, 16th cent., but only in common use after promissory notes referred to as *assignats* were printed from 1789 to 1797.

attuale, attualmente. Present, present-day; adv.: at the present time.

Attuale Ferdinando Paoletti, *Opere agrarie*, 2nd edition, 1789 (1st edition, 1778) (Cr.) in this sense, which is fairly rare in the 18th cent. *Attualmente* was used with this meaning at an earlier date; the Crusca V draws examples from P. Segneri, Lorenzo Bellini and A. P. Giulianelli, *Memorie degli intagliatori* (1753). Alberti, 1788, though registering *attuale* only in the sense of 'real', explains the adverb both as 'in atto, in effetto' and 'presentemente, nel tempo presentaneo'. *Attualità*, on the other hand, does not undergo the parallel semantic change until the following century.[1] All three are condemned by 19th cent. purists as a French influence, which is nevertheless confined to the sense alone, since *attuale* 'real, actual' is a word long attested in Italian (Dante; a learned borrowing < *actualis* [Isidore of Seville]). Cf. the theological term *peccato attuale* as opposed to *peccato originale*. The Gallicism is recognised by modern authorities. It would appear that semantic changes in the It. words follow successively those affecting their Fr. equivalents; Fr. *actuellement*, 15th cent. in the original sense, modern sense by 17th cent.; *actuel*, 13th cent. as a philosophical term, modern sense by mid-18th cent. (Buffon); *actualité*, 14th cent. as a philosophical term, modern sense 1830, Balzac.

àuna. Archaic linear measure: ell.

End of cent., Alberti, *Diz. universale* (Prati, under alla[2]); but already in Alb., 1777, Fr. > It. section the following entry occurs: '*Aune*, s.f. Mesure de trois pieds huit pouces, telle qu'elle est à Paris, et le bâton de même longueur dont on se sert à mesurer . . . Sorta di misure nella Francia, che *Auna* si direbbe in Italiano.' <Fr. *aune* (M-L., *REW* 341, *álina*, B-Al., M-D., Pr.); OFr. *alne* c. 1100, *Ch. de Roland*, < Frankish *álina*. The relationship between *auna* and *alla*, the normal word for 'ell' (attested from Dante onwards, *Inf.*, XXXI, 113) becomes clear when one bears in mind what each word signifies: *alla* refers to the English (or Flemish) ell and was borrowed during the Middle Ages either from English (as Meyer-Lübke suggests) or from Flemish; Alberti still defines it as 'nome d'una misura d'Inghilterra ch'è due braccia alla Fiorentina. Sorte de mesure', and obviously sees no connection between this word and *auna*, a French measure (see quotation above) introduced in different circumstances.

baionetta. Milit.: Bayonet.

Fr. Algarotti (1712–64); G. Baretti, *Diz. ital.-ingl.*, 1771; Aless. D'Antonj (1714–86); Alberti, 1777. <Fr. *baïonnette*, 1575 Tahureau (B-Al., M-D., Pr.). The actual meaning and date of entry present problems, as does the ultimate origin. Earliest Fr. examples do not refer to the bayonet as known in the 18th cent. and later but to a type of knife; cf. Cotgrave, 1611: '*Bayonette*: a kind of small flat pocket-dagger, furnished with knives (i.e. like the Gaelic *skean dhu*?); or a great knife to hang at the girdle' (the forerunner of

---

1. I.e. to the sense of 'modernity, up-to-date quality, lively topicality' (*vide* F-A.'s article, 1877). That of 'current affairs, news flash' dates from the 20th cent.

the modern weapon). Oudin translates *bayonette* by *pistolese* (a short dagger). The first Eng. documentation of a bayonet intended to be fixed to a rifle appears in 1704, *London Gazette* (*OED*), and 18th cent. It. examples refer to this particular form of the weapon, which was traditionally introduced by Puységur in Flanders in 1642: cf. Baretti: '*baionetta* . . . a kind of knife used by soldiers at their muskets' top'. Alberti is equally explicit. Most sources derive the word from the place-name Bayonne (cf. des Accords, 1583: *baïonette de Bayonne*); note, however, that Cotgrave still registers *bayonnier*, = *arbalestier*, < OFr. *bayon*, 'quarrel of a crossbow'.

barbetta. Milit. archit.: Barbette.

Defined by Alberti as 'piattaforma senza gabbioni daddove si sparono i cannoni alla scoperta'. First in 1778, D'Antonj, *Architettura militare*; 1788, Alberti (not in 1777 edition); 1844, Grassi, *Diz. militare*. Panzini singles out *cannone messo in barbetta* as an obvious translation of the corresponding Fr. phrase *canon monté en barbette*. The earliest dating is contemporary with the parallel borrowing from Fr. into English, where *barbette* (with Fr. form and accentuation) appears in 1772 (cf. *OED* and Frazer Mackenzie, II, p. 196) D'Antonj's careful definition suggests that the term had but recently entered military usage. <Fr. *barbette*: a semantic loan only, since *barbetta* as a diminutive of *barba* is attested in It. from earliest times. The military metaphor—extension of *barbe*, 'parce que le canon fait le barbe, rase l'épaulement' (Littré)—is found in Fr. by the 13th cent. Nautical *barbetta* = 'bow mooring-hawser of a ship' is on the other hand a figurative use native to Italian.

barlotta. Carpentry: Jack plane.

1797 Alberti, *Diz. universale* (Pr.); but Piedmontese forms already in Maurizio Pipino's *Vocabolario piemontese*, 1783 (cited Pr.). <Fr. *varlope* (*vrelope* late 15th cent., *vuarloppe* 1564, Thierry) (B-Al., Pr.). A northern Italian intermediary is generally assumed; cf. Prati: 'forse per tramite del torinese *varlòpa*, *verlopa* . . . con *-otta* sostituito a *-opa*'. B-Al. give the dialect and archaic form *barlopa* and the adaptation *balotta*. Ultimately < Dutch *voorloper*, lit., 'one who runs before', since the *varlope* is the first plane used to rough out the wood (Eng. *try-plane*)—a task nowadays more usually performed by the general purpose plane or *jack-plane* (Fr. *demi-varlope* or *riflard*, It. *piallone*)—before the actual finish is given by the *smoothing-planes* (Fr. *rabot*, It. *pialla*). The size and nature of the tool suggests that it was used in building or ships' carpentry rather than in finer work such as cabinet-making. All three trades show a strong Fr. influence.

barra. Naut.: Bar of a river.

Alberti, 1788, defined as 'Sfilata di banchi, di sabbione e di scogli che imbarrassano l'ingresso dei fiumi e dei porti'. Not in Alberti 1777, Baretti or earlier sources. <Fr. *barre* in this sense, acc. to Pr. Both B-Al. and Pr. consider as a Gallicism the homonym *barra*, also a naut. term, meaning 'tiller' (in Pascoli acc. to B-Al.; Alberti 1797 acc. to Pr.). Fr. *barre*, which von Wartburg registers as 'neufranzösisch' (*FEW*, I, 2596), is also the source of Sp. *barra*. The original Italian word *barra* ('barrier, entrenchment', first documented in G. Villani, 14th cent.), though of uncertain origin (possibly Celtic) is definitely not a French loan.

barulè. Men's fashions: Hose or knee-breeches with a roll above or below the knee.

Esp. in the phrase *alla barulè*. Pr. notes the form *barolè* (masc. subst.) 1746, in Neapolitan dialect (a kind of cuff where the stockings and breeches meet) and the Gallicising form *baroulè* in Giov. Lami (1697-1770). Petrocchi still has it, though the fashion was out of date by Alberti's time. <Fr. *bas roulés*, acc. to Alb., B-Al., Pr. (17th cent. in Fr.).

basana. Book-binding vellum.

Bazzana, Giambattista Fagiuoli (1660-1742): '(a book) legato in bazzana alla francesca'

(Cr.); rare in the 18th cent. (Alb. translates the Fr. word by *alluda*), entering general usage in the 19th cent. <Fr. *basane*, 13th cent., Estienne Boileau; taken via Spanish and Old Provençal from Arabic *baṭṭana* 'sheepskin, vellum'. (B-Al., Pr.; M-D. give the derivation from Arab. directly).

bastinga, bastingaggio. Naut.: Protection against musketry on a ship's bulwarks.

Lockers or netting fixed to bulwarks of a man-of-war in which could be stowed hammocks, cordage and the like as a protection against small arms shot from opposing vessels. *Bastinga* 1769, B-Al.; 1788, Alb.; *bastingaggio* 18th–19th cent., B-Al. <Fr. *bastingue*, 17th cent., and *bastingage*, 1747 (B-Al.; Panz. has the latter only); ult. < Prov. *bastingo* 'padding'.

battilocchio. Women's fashions: Kind of head-dress, falling down over the forehead.

J. A. Nelli (1673–1767), Gherardini; also *battiloglio*, same source and G. S. Saccenti (rather than Sacchetti, as T-Bell. imply); and both *battiloglia* and *battiloeglie* (adaptation of French pronunciation) during the 18th cent. Version of Fr. *battant l'oeil* (gen. agreement among sources).

berlina. Type of carriage.

Niccolò Forteguerri (1674–1735); Alberti, 1777, who describes the vehicle as 'carrozza a quattro ruote il di cui corpo è piantato su due forti cuoi tirati a forza, che rendon placido il moto'. Still in Petrocchi, 1884. <Fr. *berline*, 1721, Trévoux; but *breline c.* 1700, Saint-Simon (M-L., *REW* 1043, B-Al., Pr.). From the place-name Berlin, where this type of coach was constructed by the Piedmontese Filippo di Chiese for Frederick William of Brandenburg in 1670.

bidè. Bidet.

18th cent., M-*Stor.*, p. 575; end 18th cent., B-Al. Several early 19th cent. examples, e.g. 1829 Boerio, *Diz. dial. venet.* Fr. form often used (Garollo, Panz.). Adapt. of Fr. *bidet* (M-D., B-Al., Pr., etc.), 'pony' in 16th cent.; toilet accessory in 1751, *Relevé des dépenses de Mme. de Pompadour* (*Datations 1960*, p. 90).

bigiotteria. Jewellery.

In Parini with this sense (i.e. of genuine valuables); 1812, Bernardoni. Early 19th cent. and subsequent examples normally mean 'costume jewellery' (theatrical), 'fancy goods'. Rig., Panz. and other sources strongly advocate its rejection in favour of *minuteria*. Also *bisuteri* 1853 (Pr.). <Fr. *bijouterie*, 17th cent. (Purists, Panz., B-Al., Pr.).

bilione. Math.: Billion.

Billione G. Grandi, *Istit. di aritmetica pratica*, 1740 (*Gr. diz. it.*), meaning a million millions; 1777, Alberti, meaning 1000 million, in other words a *milliard*; this graphy still in Petrocchi, 1884. *Bilione* 1855, Fanfani, *Vocab. della lingua italiana*, sense as Grandi. <Fr. *billion*, 1520, E. de la Roche (B-Al., Pr.), a learned coinage < *million* with prefix *bi-*. The Fr. word is synonymous with *milliard*.

blu. Blue.

18th cent., acc. to B-Al. Commonly written *blù*. An adjective of colour used initially in fixed expressions taken from French, esp. connected with textiles and fashions; spread later into wider usage. Cf. Panz. IX, p. 74: 'Ha tolto di seggio ormai le belle parole *azzurro* e *turchino* ' . . *Blù* è entrato nell'uso (d'Annunzio).' First attested in Sicilian, 1751, M. Del Bono, *Diz. sicil.-ital.-latino* (Pr.) and 1785, M. Pasqualino, *Vocab. sicil.* (Pr.). Baretti still translates Eng. *blue* only by *turchino* and *azzurro*. Also *blò*, in Saverien, *Diz. di marina*, 1769, and Alberti, 1788 (starred as a recent addition) as a naval term, 'ship's officer designated by captain to be temporary First Lieutenant' ('Colui che è designato dal capitano d'un Vascello per farvi il servizio d'Ufficial maggiore, quando questi manca' [Alb.]). Meano notes the pronunciation *blè*. All sources give the derivation < Fr. *bleu* (1st example in OFr. *blef*, 12th cent., Ben. de Sainte-Maure), < Frankish **blao*.

The term frequently occurs with the French spelling (1846, Fusinato [Pr.]) though not necessarily pronounced as in French; the pronunciation [blu] is much the most usual 19th cent. onwards. *Un abito blù, il sangue blù* in F-A. 1877 (who print a plaintive letter from *Turchino* on this topic). Both Fr. and adapted forms in Rigutini, 1882. *Bleu électrique* (*blù elettrico*), *bleu gendarme, bleu marine* ('si dice dai mal parlanti *bleu marin*') in Panzini, who adds, 'da noi si pronuncia con un *blù* cosi duro che pare latrato'. *Bluastro* (F-A., 1881) < Fr. *bleuâtre*, and *bleuté* are later 19th cent. terms; the latter was proposed in Parliament as the colour to be adopted by the Italian army (*Atti del Parlamento Ital.*, 1872); General Lamarmora attacked the motion not only on practical but also linguistic grounds, objecting to a colour for which the language had no native term—as opposed to the earlier *azzurro*, which could be considered a national word (F-A., 1877, p. 41).

bordura. Heraldry: Border round the edge of a coat of arms.

1756 Marc'Antonio Ginanni, *L'Arte del blasone* (Pr.). Also in 18th cent. the sense 'illumination on left-hand border of a manuscript' (B-Al.). <Fr. *bordure*, 13th cent., *Garin de Monglane* (B-Al., Pr.). The dress-makers' term (= *orlo, orlatura*) appears later 19th cent.; Panzini suggests in earlier editions of the *Diz. mod.* that *bordura* replaced the more usual *orlo* when intricate decoration of the hem of garments became fashionable —a style introduced from France. Rigutini has both *bordo* and *bordura* as terms used by interior decorators to refer to borders on walls and the like.

borgognone. Naut. (archaic): Iceberg.

Alberti, 1788 (after article on *borgognone, borgognotta,* type of helmet): 'Borgognone chiamono anche i marinai in alcuni luoghi d'Italia i pezzi di ghiaccio staccati che s'incontrano per mare. *Bourguignon.*' Several 19th cent. examples; Panzini still mentions it under *Ice-berg, Diz. mod.* IX, p. 322. <Fr. *bourguignon* (B-Al., Pr.), 1752 (B-Wart.).

brigadiere. Milit.: Brigadier.

Originally 'commanding officer of a brigade', as in French and English; later applied to less important posts. Used late 19th cent. onwards as equivalent to sergeant of police, a further (semantic) loan from French. Baretti, 1771, has *brigatiere* in the normal military sense; also 1778, D'Antonj, *Archit. militare* and 1777, Alberti (*brigadiere*). Prati gives an attestation in 1759 meaning 'subaltern of cavalry'. <Fr. *brigadier*, 1642, Oudin; derivative of *brigade*, ultimately < It. *brigata* (B-Al., Pr.) (see mediaeval It. > Fr. loans).

buccola. Ear-ring, ringlet of hair.

18th cent., M-*Stor.*, p. 575. Bettinelli: 'Si vedono . . . un guardinfante rotondo con un ovale, le buccole della Montespan col chignone della Pompadour' (*Gr. diz. it.*, II, 421c, cited in the sense of 'ear-ring'; but surely this means 'curl of hair'?). <Fr. *boucle* (*d'oreille*), 1676, *FEW*, I, 591a (B-Al., Migl., Gr. diz. it.).

bugrane. Text.: Buckram; used esp. for reinforcing garments.

1788 Alberti. <Fr. *bougran*, 16th cent. (B-Al., Pr.); *boquerant* 12th cent., *Raoul de Cambrai*, < Arabic via OProv. The It. word *bucherame* (14th cent., G. Villani) 'sorta di tela che secondo il Boccaccio si lavora in Cipro e secondo il Villani si fa di bambagia' (Alb.) is probably a direct loan < the Arabic place-name Bukhara; well attested in the Middle Ages, it denoted a type of fine cloth very different from buckram, imported through Venice and Barletta.

buraglia. Text.: Cloth with silken warp and wool or cotton weft.

Savary, *Diz. di comm.*, 1770. <Fr. *burail* (B-Al.), 16th cent., < OFr. *bure* or *burel* with change of suffix.

burò, burrò. Writing-desk or 'bureau'.

Burò, bureau, Il Raguet (1747), Goldoni; *burrò* 1753, G. Gozzi (Pr.); also 1768, *Raccolta di voci romane e marchiane* (publ. C. Merlo, 1932) (Pr.). *Burò* 1850, Rambelli, *Vocab. domestico*; 1860, Ugolini; 1877, F-A. Panzini registers it under the Fr. form (= 'scrittoio, specie di canteranno'). *Burò* meaning 'office', i.e. an apartment where business or adminis-tration is carried on, is also attested in the 18th cent. I note that Vincenzo Monti uses it on several occasions, e.g. in a letter of 14th March 1798: 'Oggi doveva decidersi nel Gran Consiglio l'accettazione, o il rifiuto del Trattato; non mi sono mosso dal Burò . . .' (Bertoldi, *Epistolario di V.M.*, II, p. 72). Other examples appear in Bertoldi, II, pp. 75, 97 ('i capi di burò . . .'; concerning the salaries recently awarded to administrators by the *Gran Consiglio* of the republic), 103, 111, 138 (all 1798). <Fr. *bureau* (Purists, Panz., B-Al., Pr., etc.), *burel* 12th cent., *Saint-Gilles*, meaning a kind of cloth; the sense 'writing-table' is attested in 1552. *Bureau* 'office' is a metonymic extension < *bureau* 'writing-desk'.

cabarè. Table or tray with tea or coffee service.

1768 *Raccolta di voci romane e marchiane* (Pr.); 1770 Savary, *Diz. di commercio*. *Gabarè* 1860 Ugolini; *gabbarè* (as Roman dialect) 1877, F-A. French form *cabaret* in Manfroni (1883) and Panzini. <Fr. *cabaret* (all sources agree), 13th cent. in the sense of 'lowly inn, hostelry'; above meaning end 17th cent., Saint-Simon.

cabotaggio. Inshore navigation; the coastal trade.

Cabottaggio 1777 Alberti; *cabotaggio* 1813 Stratico, *Vocab. di marina*. F-A. 1877 and Rig. 1881 discuss it as a foreign word, with disapproval; Guglielmotti (*Vocab. mar. e milit.*, 1889) considers it an indispensable term. A Spanish origin has frequently been suggested for the It. form (*vide* Rigutini, Panzini, M-D.), ultimately < *cabo*, 'cape'—i.e. to sail from cape to cape, an accurate definition of coastwise navigation. It is for this reason that Rig. suggests the form *capotaggio* as more in keeping with It. pronunciation. Spanish authorities, however, derive Sp. *cabotaje* (first documentation in Jovanellos [†1811]) without hesitation from French (*vide* Corominas). The OFr. Hispanism *cabo*, though rare, is felt by Wartburg and Corominas to be the most likely origin of the French word, the latter rejecting as unconvincing Spitzer's alternative derivation < Fr. *cabot*, 'toad' (an analogy between the leaps of the toad and the short 'hops' of the coastal steamer).[1] Others derive the term from the surname of the famous navigator Sebastien Cabot (important voyages in 1508–9) (Dauz., B-Al.), from a Norman family name (Chabot?) or again from the designation of a type of vessel (see *OED*). The origin of the Fr. verb *caboter* (1690; but cf. *caboteur* in 1542, at a time when the Cabots' voyages were renowned throughout Europe) is equally uncertain. In any event it seems established beyond reasonable doubt that the It. term's immediate origin is Fr. *cabotage*, Furetière 1708 (Wart., *FEW*, II, s.v. *caput*), as B-Al. and Pr. state. *Cabotare* (19th cent.) is probably < Fr. *caboter*. *Piccolo cabotaggio* and *gran cabotaggio* (Panz.) correspond closely to *petit cabotage*, 'coastal trade' and *grand cabotage*, 'trans-oceanic trade' (both 1759 Richelet [*FEW*]). The Fr. word was also adapted into English (*cabotage*) during the early 19th century (*OED*).

caffettiera. Coffee-pot.

Cafettiera (sic) 1729, Veneroni (marked as an editor's addition), 'vaso in cui si fa cuocere il Cafè'. 1754 Del Bono, *Diz. sicil.-ital.-lat.*, Goldoni, P. Verri, etc. Also *caffettiere*, same meaning. *Cafettiera* transl. by 'coffee-pot' in Baretti, 1771. Alberti, 1777. Veneroni 1729 also has *cafettiero* (-e) as a synonym of *cafendiero* and *cafettaio*, meaning 'person who keeps a coffee-house'. <Fr. *cafetière* (B-Al., Pr.), *caffetière* 1690, Furetière, and *cafetier*, 1696.

calancà. Type of cloth painted with floral designs, originally from the Indies.

1771 Savary, *Diz. di commercio*; 1777 Alberti. <Fr. *calencar*, 1762, Acad. (B-Al.), but *calencard* 1730, Savary, *Dictionnaire du commerce*, and *calenca* (Fr.) in Alb.; <Persian *kalamkar*.

---

1. *Zeit. f. r. Phil.*, XLVI, 593 and XLVIII, 98.

calandra. Calender; heavy rollers for finishing cloth and other technical uses.

End 18th cent. Alberti, *Diz. univ.* (Pr.); also *calandrare*, = *manganare*, same source. Usually considered to be a 19th cent. term (registered in connection with a number of other techniques during this period); but the attestation in Alberti proves that it entered It. in the last decades of the previous century with reference to the textile trade. Alberti 1777 and 1788 omit the It. term, translating Fr. *calandre* by 'mangano per lustrar i panni'. <Fr. *calandre* ('roller') (B-Al., M-D., Pr.), *callandre* 1548, < verb *calandrer* (of textiles) 1400; but *calandreur* already 1313, Godef. Prob. < Lat. *cylindrum* < Gk. κύλινδρος.

calosce. Overshoe, galosh.

Galoscia 1777, Alberti: 'Volg. It. Sorta di soprascarpa ad uso di mantener asciutto il piede dal fango ed umido delle strade. *Galoche.*' *Caloscia* 1859, Carena, *Vocab. domestico* (Pr.); *calosce*, F-A. 1877 and Rig. 1881. <Fr. *galoche* (Purists, M-L. (*REW* 1525), B-Al., M-D., Pr.), 1292 *Roole de la taille de Paris*, originally a kind of clog with soft leather uppers and wooden sole, then a similar type of shoe worn over one's ordinary footwear. Prob. of Gaulish origin ultimately. Eng. *galosh* is also a loan from French.

calotta. Skull-cap, as worn by ecclesiastics and also by various tradesmen.

Fr. Algarotti, 1712–64 (T-Bell., s.v. *callotta*); S. Bettinelli (*Gr. diz. it.*). Rare in 18th cent. sources. Alb. 1777 translates the Fr. word by *berrettino*. <Fr. *calotte*, 1394, acc. to T-Bell., M-D., Pr., M-*Stor.* p. 575, though B-Al. favour a learned borrowing in view of the form *calota* (= *berretto*) in MedLat. of the Curia Romana, 1355. The anatomical term *calotta (cranica)* 'brain-pan' (1875, Lessona) is inspired by French medical usage.

calville, calvilla. Variety of red or white apple grown originally in Normandy.

Calvilla 1777 Alberti ('Volg. It.'); attested in 19th cent. technical works on agriculture. The form *calvella* was also used, above all in the 18th cent. (*calvella bianca, calvella rossa*, 1787, Lastri, *Corso di agric. pratica*, [Pr.]); Panzini registers the term under the Fr. form. <Fr. *calville*, 1650, B-Wart.; *caleville* 1680, Richelet (B-Al., Pr.), < place-name Calleville, Dépt. de l'Eure.

carabiniere. Milit.: Carabineer; later member of police force.

Algarotti (1712–64) (Pr.); often refers to mounted troops, cf. Baretti (1771): '*Carabiniere*. A carabineer, a horseman armed with a carbine.' A new term used alongside the original word *carabina*[1] which nevertheless continues to be current during the greater part of the century; only in the 19th cent. does *carabiniere* triumph, largely as a result of the formation of the corps of *carabinieri* (police force) in 1814. <Fr. *carabinier* (B-Al., M-D., Pr.), 1634, B-Wart.

carburo. Calcium carbide.

1797 Alberti, *Diz. universale* (Pr.). Used in tech. contexts throughout the 19th cent. <Fr. *carbure* (B-Al., Pr.) a learned formation coined in France; first attestation 1795, *Encycl. méthodique*.[2]

carcinoma. Medic., scient.: Cancer.

1733 G. Del Papa, *Consulti medici* (Cr.); 1750 Ant. Cocchi (Cr.). Applied before the 19th cent. to various cancerous diseases which were not then recognised to have the same underlying cause; cf. Alberti, 1777: '*Carcinòma*. T. della Chirurgia. Spezie di canchero

---

1. See 17th cent. Fr. > It. loans, note.

2. *Carbonizzare* appears in the 19th cent. (< Fr. *carboniser*, 1803, Boiste) and *carbonizzazione* (< Fr. *carbonisation*, 1789 Lavoisier) slightly earlier, in Alberti, *Diz. univ.* (1797–1805). Though the latter actually antedates 1800 it may in reality be said to enter It. usage together with the verb during the following century *pari passu* with the introduction of industrial techniques from France.

C

che suol offendere la tunica cornea dell'occhio. *Carcinome.*' The term comes to be used in the stricter scientific connotation during the 19th cent. <Fr. *carcinome* (B-Al., Pr.), 1545, Paré; learned borrowing < Gk. καρκίνωμα (used by Hippocrates) < καρκίνος 'crab'.

carmagnola.
A word which assumed various meanings in French during the early years of the Revolution, some of which appear in other European languages, including Italian. These are: (a) a type of garment resembling a bolero or waistcoat fashionable during the first years of the Revolution, until approx. 1795; B-Wart. attest it in 1791; also in the *Supplément* to the *Dict. de l'Académie* 1798. (b) a dance in vogue at the same period, (c) the song *La Carmagnole* (1792) reviling Marie Antoinette ('Madame Veto'), (d) a name applied to the typical revolutionary soldier. The ultimate origin is the It. place-name *Carmagnola* (Piedmont). The garment appears to have been brought to Paris by the *fédérés* of Marseilles who according to some sources adopted it from certain Piedmontese workers from Carmagnola taking part in the initial risings (B-Wart. and Gamillscheg propose this derivation with reservations). Panzini explains the name of the dance and the fashion somewhat differently: 'Carmagnola ... specie di ballo e di vestito repubblicano da Carmagnoli, nome dato ai savoiardi in Parigi, perchè venivano specialmente dalla città piemontese di Carmagnola.' It seems likely that the term *Carmagnole* came to be synonymous with that of 'Revolutionaries from the Midi', whence 'revolutionaries' in general, and that this title was applied to the song and the dance which accompanied it. When were these terms used in Italian? B-Al. give both dress and country dance as 18th cent. words derived from the It. place-name, with the observation that the dress was used by Piedmontese peasants from the 17th cent. onwards—thus rejecting outright the possibility of a Fr. lexical influence. The fashion in question, however, seems to have had more to do with Paris than Savoy. As regards dating it may be justifiably assumed that terms (b) (c) and (d), and possibly also (a) were in common use in Italy before the end of the period, at least when referring to contemporary events in France, and probably in native contexts. Cf. in respect of sense (d) a similar temporary borrowing into Scots, in Robert Burns, *Poem on Life* (1796): 'that cursed carmagnole, auld Satan' (sc. 'revolutionary, trouble-maker' with humorous and ironical implications).

casimiro. Text.: Kerseymere.
A kind of coarsely woven woollen cloth akin to tweed, much used in the 18th cent. (cf. G. Morazzoni, *La Moda a Venezia nel secolo XVIII*, Milan, 1931, p. 54). The term does not seem to be attested in Italian, however, until the very end of the period (*casimir*, 1797 Alberti, *Diz. universale* [Pr.]). *Casimiro, casimirro* in 19th cent. <Fr. *casimir*, 1791, *Journal de Paris*, < Eng. *kerseymere*, a form of *kersey* (perhaps = 'coarse say', a coarse woollen cloth) (cf. Fr. *cariset, carisel*, 15th cent. loan < Eng. *kersey*). Some sources derive the word directly < Eng., but may be influenced by the fact that most Fr. etymologists register the Fr. word as appearing in the late '20s of the following century. Fr. *casimir* undoubtedly precedes the Italian.[1] (cf. *casmir* < Fr. *cachemire*, 19th cent. Fr. > It. loans.)

casserola, cazzeruola. Saucepan.
Casserola 1777, Alberti; *casseruola* and *cazzaruola* 1858, Viani, *Diz. di pret. francesismi*; also in 19th cent. *casserola, cazzeruola.* <Fr. *casserole* 1583, Gay, acc. to B-Al., M-D., Pr. The relationship between forms with -*zz*- and arch. It. *cazza* 'ladle' (14th cent. onwards), 'alchemist's crucible' (cf. Alb., 1777) and *cazzuola*, 'plasterer's, mason's trowel' has been

---

1. See *L.N.*, VII, 1946, p. 7. The history of Fr. *casimir* and It. *casimiro* (together with 19th cent. It. *casmir*) cannot be stated definitively until the contribution of Eng. *kerseymere* and the etymology of *kersey* have been established.

discussed by various etymologists but not precisely defined.[1] In view of the late dating a Fr. loan is undeniable. The earliest attestation clearly reflects the Fr. form, whereas later examples show the influence of existing Italian words.

celibatario. Bachelor, old bachelor.

Pietro Verri (1728–97) (*Gr. diz. it.*); generally condemned by 19th cent. purist dictionaries (= *celibe, scapolo*). <Fr. *célibataire* (Purists, Panz., B-Al., Pr., *Gr. diz. it.*), 1720 B-Wart.

cerniera. Small hinge, clasp.

Used by locksmiths and makers of luxury articles. 1789 Paoletti (Cr.); Alberti 1777 registers it as 'T. de' Magnani e d'altri Artigiani' and describes it as a type of joint or swivel similar to that by which the legs of a pair of compasses are joined together at the upper end. <Fr. *charnière*, 12th cent. (B-Al., M-D., Pr.), prob. < Lat. *cardinaria or *cardonaria.[2]

cervo volante. Kite (child's toy).

1777 Alberti and 19th cent. sources. <Fr. *cerf-volant* (B-Al., Pr. and Panzini: 'È il francese cerf-volant. In italiano, *aquilone*. *Cometa, stella cometa* si dice in Romagna, Lombardia'). The literal (entomological) term (= 'stag-beetle') appears earlier, in Vallisneri, and may also be a loan from French. Against a learned origin it may be urged that the scientific Latin term *lucanus cervus* does not explain the figurative expression *cerf-volant, cervo volante*; on the other hand identity of metaphor does not necessarily imply linguistic borrowing. Some misunderstanding has existed about the dating of the Fr. word. The example from Gay, I, 299b (between 1381 and 1445) refers to a totally different object—a winged stag in heraldry, esp. that supporting the royal coat of arms. See also examples in La Curne, s.v. In Cotgrave it figures as an 'espèce d'escarbot, *lucanus cervus*'. *Cerf-volant* in the sense of 'children's kite' appears even later, in 1669, acc. to the *FEW*, II, 2, p. 614.[3]

chantilly. Culin.: Chantilly cream.

Used initially in Rome. An adapted form *sciantigliè* in Fr. Leonardi dates the borrowing to the late 18th cent. ('durante l'occupazione francese,' acc. to B-Al.). The Fr. form is common in the 19th cent., at which period two further semantic loans were made: (a) name of a famous lace (hexagonal stitching with flower motifs) also called *merlette di Bayeux*, whither the business was transported from Chantilly, (b) style of riding-boot (the racecourse at Chantilly was opened in 1833).

chincaglieria, chincagliere. Small metal ware, fancy goods.

Chincaglieria late 18th cent., 1777, Alberti (as 'voce moderna') though probably in use before in view of the earlier documentation of *chincaglie* 17th cent., and *chincagliere* 'vendor of fancy goods, etc.' early 18th cent., Fagiuoli. Both words are discussed at length by Parenti, F-A. and Rigutini, but all agree that there is no accurate equivalent in Italian with which they might be replaced. <Fr. *quincaillerie* (13th cent., Ét. Boileau) and *quincaillier* (*quinquaillier* 1428, B-Wart.) acc. to Purists, B-Al., M-D., Pr. See *chincaglie*, 17th cent. Fr. > It. loans.

cignone. Women's fashions: Chignon, 'bun'.

---

1. See esp. Rohlfs, *R. Ling. R.*, II, 287 and Prati, *It. Dial.*, XV, 191–2.

2. The nautical term *cerniere* 'ship's fresh water tank' was taken from Fr. *charnier*, a similar tank, originally one in which salt beef was preserved in brine (Lat. *carnarium* 'meat-store'). Brine tanks of this kind were much in use during the 18th century, at which period, however, the native Italian term *dispensa* was normal (Alb., 1788).

3. Godefroy's 15th cent. example in this sense from Chastellain (*Comp.*, IX, 20b) is spurious. The gifts in question are *objets d'art* ('au roy fut presenté un cherf vollant, au duc d'Orliens un blan chisne').

Cignon in *Il Raguet* (1747); *chignone* in Bettinelli (*Gr. diz. it.*); *cignone* in Carlo Gozzi. Also phonetic rendering *cignù* (Petrocchi, etc.) and dialectal *zignòn* (Emilian), *scignò* 'capelli posticci' (Calabr.) (B-Al.). Homonym of *cignone* augment. of *cinghia*, = 'large strap', esp. saddlegirth or braces of a coach. Fr. word *chignon*, 1745 in this sense.

ciniglia. Text.: Chenille, originally a kind of shirred ribbon for decorating dresses. 1777 Alberti (both ribbon and cloth); 1781 *Tariffe delle gabelle toscane.* <Fr. *chenille* (*REW* 1586 [*canicula*] No. 3, B-Al., M-D., Pr.), 1680 Richelet meaning a type of ribbon as above. This is a metaphorical extension from *chenille* 'caterpillar' (13th cent.) on account of the appearance of the ruched ribbon.

civilizzare, civilizzazione. To civilise, civilisation. Trans. verb in Salvini (Cr.); p. part. *civilizzato* Magalotti, *Lett. fam.* (Cr.); Cesarotti. *Civilizzazione* 1770, Paoli (B-Al.); Ant. Lamberti (1757–1832) (*Gr. diz. it.*). <Fr. *civiliser* 1568, *civilisation*, 1756 (coined by Mirabeau in *L'Ami de l'homme*). The semantic development of the Italian words follows closely that of French.

clacche, claque. Kind of overshoe or galosh. *Clacche* in Alberti, 1777: 'Volg. It. Voce moderna ... una spezie di scarpe che si portano su le scarpe ordinarie per ripararle dall'umità a dal fango; disconsi anche *Galoscie. Claque.*' Forms *clacche* and *clach* in Manfroni, 1883, *claque* in Panzini. <Fr. *claque* (Panz., Pr.), onomatopoeic term; 14th cent. meaning 'blow, slap'; 18th cent. in the above signification.

club. Club, esp. political organisation. In a letter of 14th Sept. 1796 Vincenzo Monti lists certain concessions demanded from the Holy See by Napoleon as conditions for an armistice, among them 'Libertà dei club coll' intervento anche delle donne' (Bertoldi, I, p. 450). Another letter dated 19th Dec. 1798 refers to Marco Alessandri's going into hiding in Milan, 'ove si trova Savoldi alla testa di certi Club, di certe congiure, ecc.' (Bertoldi, II, p. 160–1). Ugol. has it as 'parola nuova venuta di Francia' (1860). Ultimately of English origin, but entered Italian via French *club* (B-Al., Purists, M-*Stor.* agree), first attested in 1702, 'mais devenu usuel seulement un peu avant la Révolution' (B-Wart.).

coalizzare, coalizione. To form a political or military coalition, league. *Coalizzarsi* 'to enter into an alliance' in a letter of Vincenzo Monti dated 17th Sept. 1796 (Bertoldi, I, 451). *Coalizzati* (subst.) ibid., referring to the allies who formed the first coalition against France (1793). Both the verb and the substantive *coalizione* appear in a letter of 13th Feb. 1799 (Bertoldi, II, 175). The coalition here is the second coalition against France, viz. that of Britain, Russia, Austria, the Two Sicilies and Turkey formed early in that year. Nineteenth century sources attack the word; F-A. 1877 give as an example the 'lega o colleganza' of 1854 between France, England and Sardinia against Russia. This event may have served to bring the term before the public eye again. Rig. 1886 notes the sense 'trade union'. <Fr. *coalition*, 1544 (Purists, Panz., B-Al.); the political sense is a later 18th cent. semantic loan from English. *Coalizzare, coalizzarsi* < Fr. (*se*) *coaliser*, *Journal de Paris*, 1st Jan. 1791.

coccarda. Cockade. Prati registers the word meaning 'fiocco o rosa di fettuccia portata quale distintivo, e un tempo dai soldati' in Bartolomeo Dotti (1651–1713) and G. Bianchini (1729), but the word is seldom found during the 18th century. Most dictionaries of the period omit an Italian form, translating the French word *cocarde* by *fiocco, nappa, rosa, rosetta*. Baretti glosses the Eng. word *cockade* by 'nastro a mo' di rosa che si porta sul cappello'. The various editions of Veneroni omit Fr. and It. alike; those of Alberti merely explain the Fr. form in terms similar to Baretti's. B-Al. register it in 1817. It would seem that while statements in Rigutini and early editions of Panzini that the word entered Italian during the French Revolution are not literally correct, the implication they make is substantially true, i.e. that the events of the revolutionary period popularised the term. *Coccarda* is frequently attested in writers of the time, and in the immediate post-war years—V. Monti (letter of 14th May 1796), Vincenzo Cuoco (1801), G. Giusti, L. Papi, A. Bresciani. It is discussed as a Gallicism by F-A. and Rigutini; Panzini accepts it as 'voce internazionale, di provenienza francese'. <Fr. *cocarde* (B-Al., M-D., Pr., etc.); *bonnet à la coquarde* 1562, Rabelais; < OFr. *coquart* 'braggart, spry young fellow'.

coc(c)hetta, cochetteria. Coquette, coquetry.

Cochetta Algarotti, Bettinelli; *cocchetta* Cerretti, Fr. Milizia (*Gr. diz. it.* and M-*Stor.* 575). *Cochetteria* (= *civetteria*) in Parenti, Ugol. 1860, F-A. 1877. <Fr. *coquette, coquetterie*, 1651 Scarron.

colare (a fondo). To sink, of a ship.

1777 Alberti, *colare a fondo*: 'T. Mar. Sommergere, mandar a fondo una nave. *Couler à fond.*' Also registered by Alberti in the absolute. 1813–14, Simone Stratico, *Vocab. di marina*; 1860, Viani; F-A., Rigutini. Adaptation of Fr. *couler à fond* (B-Al., M-D., Pr.). Earlier 18th cent. Italian sources only record the indigenous and basic senses of 'to filter a liquid' and 'to cast' (in a mould).

colibrì. Ornith.: Humming-bird.

1745 *Spettacolo della Natura* (Pr.) (translated from Fr.); 1777 Alberti. <Fr. *colibri*; *colibry* 1640 (Pr., Corominas; B-Al. refer also to the Spanish form). It is unlikely that Spanish has played a part in the word's diffusion as far as Italy, either as an immediate or ultimate etymon. The Spanish term is attested about the same time as Italian—*calibre*, 1769 (Corom.)—over a century later than the French. Furthermore, as Corominas points out, the assumption that *colibri* was originally a Carib word does not (even if it be true) necessarily presuppose a Spanish intermediary: 'Las afirmaciones del origen caribe son tardías (1724 vid. Bloch) y están desmentidas por el buen diccionario de Breton (1655). De todos modos el vocablo procede de las Antillas francesas; es desconocido de los historiadores de Indias españoles y aunque hoy se emplea en Santo Domingo, ... en Puerto Rico no es popular (Navarro Tomás, *El Esp. en P.R.*, p. 147) y en otras partes predominan *pájaro mosca, zumbador* (P. Rico) y *picaflor* (Arg., etc.). Las citadas formas calibre y colibre (i.e. the earliest attestations) están aisladas y pueden ser corrupciones' (*Dicc. crit. etim.*, Vol. I, p. 852).

colpo di mano. Surprise attack, coup.

V. Monti, letter of 13th Feb. 1799 (Bertoldi, II, 176): 'Gli officiali francesi che qui abbiamo ... non sanno perdonare a Championnet di non aver ... occupata con un colpo ardito di mano la Sicilia.' Other compounds formed on *colpo* on the analogy of French during the 18th century are *colpo di fulmine* 'love at first sight' (Cesarotti) and *colpo d'occhio* (G. Parini). The latter occasioned much controversy in the 19th century, Viani and Gherardini defending it as a native calque of Latin *ictus oculi*, Arlia and Rigutini denying on semantic grounds that the Latin model was relevant. In general a French influence may be suspected when there is, as Arlia puts it, a 'lungo tratto di cammino metaforico' between the strict sense of *colpo* and that of the resultant compound, as here (*a colpo sicuro* [Fr. *à coup sûr*] is a similar instance). The attestation in Monti clinches the argument; I feel sure that his words echo some remark made by one of his French associates at the time. The Italian compounds are calques of French *coup de main, coup de foudre* and *coup d'œil* respectively.

colza. Bot.: Colza, *Brassica campestris*.

Colzat in G. Targioni-Tozzetti (1712–83); *colza* 19th cent. Not current until the 19th century (Alberti translates the Fr. word by *cavol rapa*). B-Al. give *colzàt* as a Lombard and Venetian form. <Fr. *colza* 1671 (B-Wart.); frequent among early examples are the

alternative forms *colsa* and *colzat* (cf. Savary, 1723); < Dutch or Flemish *koolzaad* (lit. 'cabbage-seed') (*REW* 4731 [*kohlzaad*], B-Al., Pr.).

comitato. Committee.

'Il comitato governativo in questioni di tasse non è che come un tribunale d'appello' (V. Monti, letter of 20th May 1798 [Bertoldi, II, 78], referring to the provisional governing triumvirate of the Cisalpine Republic). Well-attested early 19th cent. onwards. <Fr. *comité* (B-Al., Pr., M-*Stor.*, p. 660), *committé* 1650, du Gard < Eng. *committee*. Semantic criteria indicate a loan through French. As Panzini notes, 'il comitato ha un senso politico e di azione' (*s.v., Diz. mod.*). F-A. are mainly concerned with the expression *comitato segreto*; they add (in the 1881 edition) that the word evokes memories of the *comitato di salute pubblica*. The same is true of French, but not of English except in certain 20th cent. contexts which may themselves reflect Continental usage.

comò. Chest of drawers.

V. Monti, letter of 10th Nov. 1781 (Bertoldi, I, 163): 'Non vi avrei chiesto tutto questo denaro, se non avessi avuto bisogno di farmi abiti, provveder letto, burrò, commò, sedie e mille altre cose.' *Cumò* 1853 D'Ayala; *comò* 1877 F-A., 1886 Rigutini. Current early in dialects, e.g. Venetian, 1829 (Boerio); Prati registers a Piedmontese form *comòda* in 1793. Version of the French word *commode*, used in this sense about 1760.

contabilità. Accounts department.

Used by Pietro Verri (1728–97) in the sense of accounts department or office, i.e. the body of personnel which makes up the department: 'la contabilità sia composta d'un presidente e alcuni ragionati per rivedere i conti di ogni Amministrazione' (*Gr. diz. it.,* III, 626a). The senses 'book-keeping' and 'accountancy' date from the 19th century (G. Boccardo, *Diz. univ. dell'economia politica e del commercio,* Milan, 1881, *Gr. diz. it.*[1] <Fr. *comptabilité,* 1753 in these senses.

contrad(d)anza. Country-dance.

18th cent. B-Al. M-*Stor.* p. 579 (Salvini, Gozzi, etc.). <Fr. *contre-danse,* 1626, < English *country-dance* (M-*Stor.,* M-D., B-Al.).

controsenso. Nonsense, non sequitur.

Late 18th cent. Carlo Gozzi, *Memorie inutili* (*Gr. diz. it.*); 1812 Bernardoni. Also *contrassenso.* <Fr. *contresens* (Rig., B-Al., M-D.), end 16th cent., Sully. Also adverbial phrase *a contresenso,* Cesarotti.

copiglia. Tech.: Wheelwrights' or similar trades: wedge, cotter-pin or split-pin.

1777 Alberti ('T. de' Carradori'); used in 19th century as a current term in almost every branch of engineering ('cotter-pin'). <Fr. *goupille,* 1439, probably < *goupil* 'fox' (Panz., B-Al., Pr.).

corvetta. Naut.: Corvette.

Two different types and rigs of ship are involved here: (a) a long narrow-beamed vessel with mainmast and small foremast, similar to a schooner, able to be propelled by sweeps, (b) a square-sailed ship of war, usually three-masted (occasionally a brig), smaller than a frigate, but used for similar duties. *Corvetta* referring to vessel (a) appears in Alberti 1788 (defined in detail as above). Sense (b) is attested in the 19th century and probably entered use during the Napoleonic Wars. <Fr. *corvette* (Dauz., B-Al., M-D., Pr.), 1476 in a Picard text, probably <MidDutch *korver,* a ship used for pursuit. Corroborative evidence that northern France was the focal point from which the term spread to other languages is provided by the documentation in English, where *corvette* (Fr. form!) appears in 1636 as a vessel captured from the French at Calais, and again in 1711 as a type of ship used as a tender at Calais (*OED*). Both correspond to definition (a) above. The first entry in the *OED* which refers unquestionably to vessel (b) is dated 1798.

---

1. *Contabile* 'book-keeper' on the other hand is a 19th century borrowing (q.v.).

cotteria. Coterie, clique, 'set'.

= *Cricca, consorteria, brigata* (Panz.). In Sav. Bettinelli (*Lettere inglesi*, 1767), who defends it as a term without equivalent in Italian (cited by M-*Stor.*, p. 575 n. 1). Frequent early 19th cent. attestations: *coteria* (Venet.) 1829, *cottaria* (Milan.) 1839. Not initially pejorative in Italian. <Fr. *coterie*, 1376 in the original sense 'group of peasants working a common holding'; modern meaning 1660.

cravatta. Cravat, tie.

Forms with -v-, the typical French pronunciation, appear in the 18th century. First in an inventory of 1705 (cited by L. Frati, *Il '700 a Bologna*, Bologna, 1923, p. 290); *cravata* 1709, Veneroni; *crovatta* G. Gigli (1660–1722); *corvatta* G. S. Saccenti; *cravatta* 1777, Alberti. The word was known in the 17th century under the form *croatta* (registered by B-Al. in Adimari; also in Magalotti). <Fr. *cravate*, 1651, Loret (originally masculine) <Fr. form of the name Croat, the cravat itself having been worn by Croatian auxiliaries fighting with the French in Germany in 1636 (Ménage).

crèolo. Creole.

Originally the name given to a person of pure European descent born in South or Central America (Alberti gives only this sense), later (19th cent. in Italian) used of mulattos and half-breeds of varying degrees. 1777 Alberti; 19th century sources; Panzini. <Fr. *créole, créolle*, 1690, (Panz., B-Al., M-D., Pr., Corominas) < Sp. *criollo* < Portuguese *crioulo* < *criar*, 'to raise, bring up'. Acc. to Corominas Port. *crioulo*, literally 'a chicken raised in the house' in its earliest acceptation was used to refer to Negro slaves born in the household, on the hacienda. It would seem that the sense in Spanish and French (as also in Italian, initially) was restricted to the white population and that the extension to 'mulatto' occurred subsequently. The origin of attestations before the 18th cent. in Fr. and It. is difficult to determine. There is in the late 17th century a period of uncertainty when what seem to be direct loans from Spanish are found both in French and Italian; cf. Fr. *criole* 1680, Furetière (quite apart from the earliest Fr. attestation of all, *crollo*, 1598 in a Hispanising context). B-Al. register *crioglio* ([l] mouillé corresponding to that of Spanish) in the 17th cent. It appears in Magalotti in a patently Spanish setting: '. . . un cavaliere spagnuolo, crioglio di Cile' (*Gr. diz. it.*). These hesitations are finally resolved by a development which has been noted on several occasions elsewhere—the generalisation of Fr. forms in other European languages during the course of the 18th century.

crespone. Text.: A crêpe of fairly heavy stuff, either of wool or silk.

Fagiuoli, *Rime* (Cr.); 1770 Savary, *Diz. di commercio*; 1777 Alberti, who also has the Gallicising form *crepone* (loss of prœ-consonantal [s]) as a separate entry but translated by the same Fr. word, *crépon*. Also *crépon* in Panzini. <Fr. *crépon*, 1660; (B-Al., however, derive it < *crespo* modelled on the Fr. word); < *crêpe*, 12th cent. as an adj., but 16th cent. as name of a textile. See *crêpe, crespo*, 19th cent. Fr. > It. loans.

cretino, cretinismo. Medic.: Cretin, cretinism.

Migliorini (*Stor.*, p. 576) gives both *cretino* and *cretinismo* as 18th cent. Gallicisms. B-Al., while registering *cretinismo* and *cretineria* as 18th cent. terms place *cretino* itself in the 19th; Prati, however, cites an example of the word from Alberti, *Diz. universale*: 'Nel Valese si stima fortunata quella casa che ha un cretino.' *Cretinismo* in 1789, acc. to Prati; both in numerous 19th cent. sources from Melchiorre Gioia onward (1769–1829; *cretino* in a factual description of the inhabitants of the Valais). The attestation of the term used to designate the disease and other derivatives during the 18th cent., strongly suggests that the word *cretino* itself—the actual person in whom the deformity is manifest—was in general usage before the end of this period. <Fr. *crétin*, 1754 *Encycl.*, a Franco-Provençal dialect term of Savoie and the Swiss Valais equivalent to Fr. *chrétien*; the word 'Christian'

used both in the generic sense of 'man, person' and euphemistically for 'imbecile' is found elsewhere in Western Romance.[1] *Cretinismo* < Fr. *crétinisme*, 1786, B-Wart. Cretinism and the effects of inbreeding in remote Alpine valleys began to be studied by French scientists in the mid-18th century. The terms *crétin, crétinisme* have since passed into all European languages (1779 and 1801 resp. in English, for example [*OED*]).

crociera. Naut.: Cruise.

Three senses are involved in Italian, as in French: (a) the act of sweeping or searching a given area of sea for purposes of blockade and the like, (b) the area of sea covered by such a sweep, (c) a luxury or pleasure cruise. Sense (b) is the only one found in the 18th cent.; Prati registers a form *crosciera* with this signification as early as 1715. The It. > Fr. section of Alberti 1777 only has *crociera* in the sense of 'sorta di costellazione formata di quattro stelle situate a modo di croce', i.e. the Southern Cross (cited from Salvini) and entirely omits the nautical significations above. The naval term nevertheless appears in the Fr. > It. section where Fr. *croisière*, defined as in sense (b), is translated by *crociera*. The verb *croiser* meaning 'to patrol or blockade' is translated by 'incrociare uno spazio di mare' while under *crociata* is included the following entry: 'crociata dicono i Naviganti que' luoghi ove i vascelli, benchè vengano da diverse parti, soglion passare. *Croisière*' i.e. roughly the equivalent of 'shipping lanes'. It therefore must be accepted that even before the Napoleonic wars the Fr. word had already begun to be the recognised naval term for this particular manœuvre and had partly replaced the native word *corseggiare*.[2] Meaning (b) also occurs in Stratico, *Vocab. di marina* (1813–14). Meaning (a), which seems to be an early 19th cent. usage (probably of the Napoleonic Wars) is attested in Viani (1858–60) and Guglielmotti (1889). *Crociera* in all nautical significations is a semantic loan < Fr. *croisière*, 1690, Furetière (B-Al., Pr.). *Crociera* 'luxury cruise', a 20th cent. word popular in the mid-'30s, is cited in later editions of Panzini as a Gallicism, though the ultimate origin is probably English.

cupè. Kind of closed carriage with seats for two.

18th cent. Baruffaldi (B-Al.); *cuppè* in G. Fagiuoli (1660–1742). F-A. and Rig. both have *cupè* as a separate compartment in a stage-coach or train. Petrocchi and Panzini still give the main sense as that of a light four-wheeled coach; only earlier editions of Panzini register the railway term. Later editions of Panz. include (under the rubric of the Fr. word *coupé*) the sense 'forma di carrozzeria nelle automobili (a due posti, e di lusso)'. Adaptation of Fr. *coupé* (B-Al., Pr.), 1660 in the sense 'light carriage'; *faire couper son carrosse* meaning 'to take out one of the bench seats of a coach' is in Furetière, 1690 (still in Trévoux, 1771); *carosse coupé* also in Furetière, 1690, meaning 'a coach with only one seat, facing forward through a windscreen in the direction of travel'. The design of the *coupé* roughly resembled half of an ordinary coach. (*Vide FEW*, II, 2, 875).

damigiana. Demijohn.

Large wickerwork-covered flask or carboy for wine or other liquids. 1781, *Tariffa delle gabelle toscane*; 1788 Alberti (a recent addition); Marco Lastri, *Corso d'agricoltura*, 1801–3. <Fr. *dame-jeanne*, acc. to B-Al., M-D., Pr.; Meyer-Lübke (*REW* 2733) draws the It. form directly from a southern French word. Fr. *damejane* is attested in Th. Corneille, 1694, as a naval term; a popular etymology < Prov. *damajano*, which may come from an Arabic *damagan* (< the place-name Damagan in Tabaristan?), but is more plausibly derived from Prov. *demeg*, 'half'; cf. the parallel paronymic attraction in English, where *demijohn* also keeps the idea of 'half'. (*Vide* Migl., *Dal nome proprio*, p. 296).

---

1. See *Arch. Gl. It.*, III, 316; Migl., *Dal nome proprio*, pp. 104 and 326–7.

2. Cf. Baretti, *Diz. it.-ingl.*, 1771, where Eng. *cruise* is translated by (subst.) 'il corso d'un vascello' or 'il corseggiare', (verb) 'corseggiare, andare in corso'.

deboscia, debosciato. Debauchery; dissolute or debauched (adj.), esp. a dissolute person.

Defined by F-A. as 'viver licenzioso, vita sregolata' and by Panzini; 'L'eccesso del bere e del mangiare, e poi sregolatezza dei costumi.' *Deboscia* in G. Fagiuoli (1660–1742). Alberti, 1797. Discussed by 19th cent. purists. Fr. form also found from 18th cent, *Debosciato* (1797, in Alberti, acc. to Pr.) came into frequent use during the 19th cent. F-A. and Rig. condemn it in strong terms; Petrocchi accepts the adj. while omitting *deboscia* itself. Panzini describes both *deboscia* and *debosciato* (the latter given as 'fuori dell'uso' in later editions) as 'barbarismi frequenti su la fine del '800'. B-Al., M-D., Pr., Panz. and 19th cent. sources agree in deriving both terms from Fr. *débauche* (1539, R. Estienne) and *débauché* (*débaucher* 13th cent.). *Débaucher*, which originally meant only 'to sow disaffection among troops' (the original implication of the subst. also; = 'defection, of troops' in the 16th cent.) acquired the moral signification above during the 16th century and passed into Italian with this meaning, though the older sense is still normal in French during the 18th cent.[1]

dentista. Dentist.

1797 Alberti, *Diz. univ.*, (Pr.); 18th cent. acc. to B-Al. An international term, but one which appears to have its origin in France, where *dentiste* is attested in 1735, *Mercure de France*. Little used until 19th cent.; the 18th cent. still normally used native *cavadenti*. Corominas does not refer to a Fr. influence on the Spanish word, but the OED derive Eng. *dentist* unquestionably from French, and the earliest attestation confirms this: 'Dentist figures it now in our newspapers and may do well enough for a French puffer; but we fancy Rutter is content with being called a tooth-drawer' (1759, *Edinburgh Chronicle*). The term *dentifrizio* is older—*dentifritio* in Veneroni (trans. as 'poudre à blanchir les dents'); *dentifricio* Alberti, 1797; *dentifrizio* in 1828, Leone, *Diz. dei termini di medicina*. The It. word is borrowed from Fr. *dentifrice* (16th cent., Paré; learned term <Lat. *dentrifricium* [Pliny]) (B-Al., Pr.). The same may also be true of *dentizione*, 1797, 'cutting of teeth' (Fr. *dentition*, 18th cent.).

dettaglio. Detail.

First in Magalotti with the sense 'detailed relation of facts'. Widely used during the 18th cent. in such authors as G. Lami, A. Verri, M. Cesarotti. Alberti 1797 also has *vendere in dettaglio* (glossed as *vendere al minuto*) 'to sell retail'. The word is frequently criticised throughout the 19th century, by Bernardoni (1812), Ugolini (1850), F-Arlia (1877: esp. the phrases *vendere in dettaglio* and *uffiziale di dettaglio*), Rigutini (1886) and Panzini. <Fr. *détail* (*vendre à détail* as early as 12th cent., *Floire et Blancheflor*). All sources agree on the Gallicism, including B-Al., M-D., Pr.; Alberti, 1797, notes it together with the word *dettagliare*) as a French word 'che l'uso a cominciato a stabilire'.[2] Bernardoni agrees with him and cites with approval Alberti's opinion that 'sì fatti neologismi non si possono nè riprovare nè ammettere, almeno nelle buone scritture, finchè non siano assolutamente rigettati o autenticati da qualche scrittore di grido'. 19th cent. purists note the word's tenacity of life; Panzini, though disapproving, admits that 'è voce che vince nell'uso. . . . Il pubblico si ostina ad usarla'. *Dettaglio* is still far from naturalised; Migliorini gives it as an example of terms 'che hanno continuato a vivere nella lingua corrente, mentre gli uomini di lettere hanno per lo più mantenuto il veto', adding that he himself always avoids it scrupulously.[3]

---

1. The Florentine word *bisboccia* 'revelry, debauch' (19th cent.) is a popular deformation of *deboscia* (B-Al., M-*Stor.*, p. 663).

2. It is noteworthy that Alberti 1788 does not register an Italian *dettaglio* or its compounds and translates the corresponding French term by circumlocutions.

3. *Lingua contemporanea*, pp. 172, 217. See also remarks on purists' reaction to this

dettagliare. To narrate, relate in full detail.

1797 Alberti, *Diz. universale*; Bernardoni, Purists, Panzini. <Fr. *détailler* (19th cent. sources, B-Al., M-D., Pr.), 12th cent., originally meaning 'to cut up,' soon > 'to sell retail'. (See *dettagliante*, 19th cent. Fr. > It. loans.)

dimissione. Resignation (from office, post).

Dare la (sua) dimissione, ricevere la d. on several occasions in Vincenzo Monti (letters of 28th July, 26th Sept., 17th Nov. 1798, etc.); 1812, Bernardoni (as an indispensable technical term). <Fr. *démission* (Purists, B-Al., M-D.), used in this sense by the 18th cent. *Vide dimissionario*, 19th cent. Fr. > It. loans.

disabbigliato, disabigliè. Fashions: In dishabille, in casual dress.

Disabigliè 1703, M-*Stor.*, p. 575 n. 2; *disabbigliata (-o)* in Goldoni and Baretti (ibid.). Well-attested 19th cent. meaning woman's garment ('house-coat' 'dressing-gown'). Also adv. loc. *in disabigliè* (Fr. *en déshabillé*). <Fr. *déshabillé* in the above specialised senses. Panzini also has *déshabillage* ('atto dello spogliarsi').

domino. Mask, esp. at a fancy-dress ball.

Dominò 1729, Fagiuoli (Pr.); Algarotti (1712–64); 1797, Alberti. <Fr. *domino* (Cr., B-Al., M-D., Pr.), 1505 meaning a type of hooded cloak worn by priests for warmth in winter, a jocular appellation taken from the phrase *benedicamus Domino*. Later used to refer to a hood used as a disguise at a masked ball, whence 'mask', early 18th cent. The ecclesiastical sense, attested earlier in Italian (17th cent., acc. to B-Al.) should itself perhaps be considered a loan-word from French rather than a Latinism. See *domino*, 19th cent. loans.

draga. Naut., engin.: Dredger.

In conformity with the original meaning in French the Italian word refers not to a ship but a simple mechanical device, a kind of scoop for removing silt from a river bed; cf. the first example, in Alberti, 1788: 'Draga. Una sorta di pala ribordata da tre lati, con un manico lunghissimo, e serve per estrarre il sabbione . . . dai canali o dai fiumi.' Prati (*V. Et. It.*) registers the fact that according to Corazzini the term *draga* was already in use in 1779. *Dragare* 'to dredge' also appears in Alb., 1788. *Draga* meaning 'dredger' (vessel with continuous chain of buckets, for use as above) is attested in later 19th cent. sources, e.g. Guglielmotti, *Voc. mar. e milit.*, 1889. <Fr. *drague* (B-Al., M-D., Pr.), 16th cent., and *draguer*, 17th cent. The 16th cent. Fr. example denotes a type of net used for trawling; the meaning 'instrument pour retirer du fond de l'eau la vase' appears in Félibien, 1676. Cf. also *drague* 'grapnel' (for recovering lost anchors) in Félibien, 1701 (*draguer* 'to grapple for a slipped anchor', ibid.). *Draguer* 'to dredge' in the above sense is attested in 1634 (see *FEW*, III, 122).

droghetto. Text. (archaic): Drugget, kind of coarse woollen cloth.

1771 Savary, *Diz. di commercio*; 1777 Alberti. <Fr. *droguet*, 1555 (B-Al., Pr.), originally a cheap type of woollen cloth (cf. Engl. *drugget; drogitt, drogatt* in 1580, also a loan from French).

editore. Printer, publisher of books.

In 18th cent.: A. Cocchi (1695–1758) (Pr.); 1777 Alberti. Most authorities, while largely persuaded that the It. form is borrowed from Fr., hesitate to say so without reservations. Parti alone is categorical about it, deriving *editore* < Fr. *éditeur*, 1732, Trévoux. B-Al. register it as a learned term but refer to the Fr. form. The corresponding word in other languages is usually described as a Latinism, though some interrelation is not unlikely: Eng. *editor* greatly antedates the French (if Wartburg's first dating of *éditeur* [*FEW*, III, 205] reflects usage correctly), appearing as it does in 1649 in the above sense. The modern English meaning is an indigenous development of the early 18th century. Spanish *editor* appears late 18th cent. in Esteban de Terreros (Corominas).

word, ibid., 174, 208, and further discussion in A. Schiaffini, *Momenti*, pp. 100–1.

A French influence is generally accepted in the case of the It. verb *editare*, which is found much later (20th cent., acc. to B-Al.; Fr. *éditer* dates from 1784 [*FEW*]); whereas *editoriale* 'editorial' (subst.) is presumed to come via French from English (1856, adj., 1895, subst.).

empirismo. Philos.: Empiricism.

Alberti, 1788 (article added in that edition): 'Carattere, ossia nozione pratica dell' empirico.' The philosophical term is often considered to date from the 19th cent. (1843 Vincenzo Gioberti [see Ugolini], T-Bell.). We may assume, however, that the general term in Alberti was not merely an abstract formed upon *empirico*—which was current as a medical term in the 18th cent.; also used pejor. in connection with quack doctors: first attested in the 17th cent.—but was directly inspired by Fr. philosophical usage. <Fr. *empirisme* (B-Al., Pr.) 1736, probably a version of English *empiricism*. B-Al. also derive the adj. *empirico* from Fr. *empirique*.

equitazione. Art of horsemanship.

1797 Alberti (Pr.). <Fr. *équitation*, 1503 (*FEW*) acc. to Prati; B-Al. note it as a learned word (*equitatio, -onis*, Pliny) but refer to the French term. 19th cent. purists register it as a Gallicism then in vogue, used abusively for the native term *cavallerizza*.

erborista, erborizzare. Herbalist or botanist; to collect simples.

Subst. 18th cent., acc. to B-Al.; verb in G. Targ. Tozzetti (1712–83). < Fr. *herboriste* 1545, *herboriser* 1611 (B-Al., Pr.).

esotico. Exotic.

Esp. referring to plants from foreign countries. 1777 Alberti, who cites Magalotti as an earlier source. 18th cent., acc. to B-Al. *Esoticità* also appears in Magalotti. <Fr. *exotique*, 1548 Rabelais, acc. to Prati; B-Al. give it as a learned term < Lat. *exoticus* (< Greek) but add a reference to the Fr. word. Also *esotismo*, 19th cent., as a general abstract term (B-Al.), 20th cent. as a technical term in painting (Panz., 1908, who suggests *esoticismo* as a more correct alternative). <Fr. *exotisme*, 1849 Bescherelle (*FEW*), a word used by the French Romantics, foremost among them Th. Gautier.

faeton. High elegant carriage with two or four wheels (phaeton).

Faetòn 1797 Alberti, *Diz. universale* (Pr). <Fr. *phaéton*, 1723 (B-Al., Pr.), < name of the Gk. god *Phaeton*, first applied to this type of carriage in France but spreading quickly to other European languages (Eng. 1742, Young, *Night Thoughts*; end 18th cent. in Sp., Esteban de Terreros).

falbalà, falpalà. Folds of veil superimposed upon dresses, esp. at the hem, and worn in the hair.

Much used in 18th cent. The form *farbalà* appears in a Venetian law of 1709.[1] *Falpalà* in Magalotti; also 1733 at Lucca, acc. to B-Al. Prati registers *falbala* in L. Adimari (1644–1708). The Italian word must certainly be dated back to the early 18th century, and may well have been in use at the end of the preceding period. <Fr. *falbala* (Wartburg, B-Al., M-D.), a word of uncertain origin, perhaps from Franco-Provençal (*farbélla* in Lyonnais = 'fringe'); introduced acc. to Ménage by the French courtier de la Langlée in 1692, but now believed to have been in use before this date.[2] The Spanish word *falbala* (mid-18th cent.) is also a loan from French (Corominas, II, 474).

fanfara. Military music for trumpets and drums; brass band.

18th cent. acc. to B-Al. Criticised as a Gallicism by D'Ayala, *Diz. delle voci guaste* . . . (1853). <Fr. *fanfare*, 1546 (B-Al., Pr.), best explained as an onomatopoeic coinage in French, rather than a member of the formal group *fanfaron, fanfaronnade* etc. which are derived from Arab. *farfār* via Spanish. *Vide* Corominas, II, p. 486b.

---

1. *Vide* G. Bistort, *Il Magistrato alle Pompe nella Repubblica di Venezia* (*Miscellanea di Storia Veneta*), Series III, Vol. V, Venice 1912, p. 151.

2. *Vide FEW*, III, pp. 397 and 401; also L. Spitzer, *Arch. Rom.*, VIII, p. 144.

faraone. Card-game, faro.

18th cent. B-Al., M-*Stor.*, p. 576. <Fr. *pharaon*, pre-1725, Dancourt (B-Wart.; the Gallicism appears in Eng. as *farroon*, 1713 [*OED*]).

felicitare, felicitazione, -i. To congratulate, congratulations.

Transitive verb in Salvini, etc.; equivalent to *congratularsi* (*vide* Schiaffini, Momenti, p. 101 and M-*Stor.*, pp. 575-6). *Felicitazione* in Algarotti and elsewhere. Semantic loans from Fr. *féliciter*, 15th cent., *félicitation(s)*, 1623 d'Aubigné. Th. Corneille in 1690 still feels himself obliged to apologise for using it with this signification. The semantic loan soon became more usual than the original sense of 'to make happy'.

feticcio (fetiscio), feticismo. Fetish; worship of fetishes.

Fetiscio 18th cent., *feticismo* end 18th cent. acc. to B-Al. The form *fetiscio* is attested in Giambattista Casti, *Gli animali parlanti*, 1802 ('. . . serpente fetiscio'); this and *feticcio* in T-Bell. *Feticismo* registered by Prati in 1833 (Balbi). <Fr. *fétiche* (Cr. V, B-Al., Pr.), 1732, <Portuguese *feitiço*; *fétichisme* current after publication of de Brosses' *Du culte des dieux fétiches*, 1760.

figurante. Person appearing on the stage.

1777 Alberti. The terseness of Alberti's entry gives rise at first sight to some doubts about its meaning ('add. d'ogni g. . . . Che figura. *Figurant*'), but his corresponding Fr. > It. article confirms that he is referring to a technical term of the theatre—more precisely, of ballet: 'Figurant, ante, . . . Danseur, danseuse qui figure aux Ballets dans les corps d'entrée. *Figurante*; *ballerino*'. Also in Alberti, *Diz. univ.*, Fanfani, Rigutini and numerous 19th cent. sources. <Fr. *figurant* (B-Al., Pr.), 1740.

fiacre, fiacchere. Cab.

18th cent., M-*Stor.* (*fiàccaro*; *vide* p. 575); several early 19th cent. attestations, e.g. 1831, Giac. Leopardi. Discussed in 19th cent. by Ugol., Rig., F-A. ('fiacre, vulgo fiacchere') who point out that there are suitable Italian terms: *pincionella* < Pincio (similar onomastic development to Fr. word) in Rome, *cittadina* in Naples, Milan, etc. Fr. word (and phonetic adapt.) *fiacre*, 1650.

filetto. Culin.: Fillet of steak.

Pr. registers this signification in Alberti, 1797. Though the It. > Fr. section of Alberti 1777 omits the above sense, the Fr. > It. section translates Fr. *filet* 'fillet of steak' by *filetto* or *porso*. A semantic loan (since indigenous meanings of the word date from the 14th century) from Fr. *filet*. (B-Al., Pr.).

filibustiere. Pirate.

Originally used to denote the buccaneers who infested the Caribbean during the 16th and 17th centuries. The history of this word remains controversial both as regards possible French-Italian contacts and its ultimate origin, though interesting new light has been thrown upon it by P. Aebischer's recent article 'Au dossier du fr. *flibustier*, esp. *filibustero*', *R. Ling. R.*, XXXIII (1969), pp. 38-52. Most authorities traditionally derive all Romance forms from English *freebooter*, 1598, which appeared a little earlier as *flibutor* (*flibutors and theeves*, 1587, *OED*), which virtually all sources draw ultimately from a Dutch *vrijbuiter*, with a reference to the MDutch idiom *op vrijbuit gaen*, 'to go on a raiding foray' (*OED*, *D.G.*, B-Wart., Dauz., *FEW* [XVII, 473], Gr. *diz. it.*, Arveiller,[1]

---

1. R. Arveiller, *Contributions à l'étude des termes de voyage en français* (1505-1722), *Doctorat-ès-lettres* thesis, University of Paris, Paris 1963: *vide* Aebischer, p. 40, n. 3.

In English there are three separate words, (a) the original *flibutor* (*freebooter*) (b) *flibustier*, an adaptation from French which came into use in the late 18th century (c) *filibuster*, first applied to certain adventurers whose activity during the '50s of the nineteenth century brought about the present-day political boundaries of Central and South America. I take the latter to be a direct loan from Spanish into AmerEng.

and in particular Corominas, II, 524). Their opinion is supported in the 17th century by Furetière and Ménage, 'parce que les premiers avanturiers dans le Nouveau Monde étoient Anglois' (vide Aebischer, p. 40). Difficulty arises in explaining the presence of pronounced [s] in Romance forms—confirmed by Furetière and Trévoux—from earliest examples: fribustier 1667, Du Tertre, Histoire des Ant-Isles; flibustier 1688 in the Histoire des avanturiers qui se sont signalés dans les Indes, by the ex-pirate Alexandre-Olivier Oexmelin. The back-formation fribuste 'piracy' is attested earlier still, before the mid century.[1] Aebischer rejects the Dutch/English influence entirely, for historical reasons, initially, since Oexmelin's narrative indicates that the pirates' headquarters at Tortuga was mainly dominated by Frenchmen over a long period of time. The true etymon, according to Aebischer, is the phrase finibusterrae, used by Spaniards (among them Cervantes) to signify ne plus ultra, beyond compare, élite, and at the same time by certain authors to signify 'gibbet'. This equivocal, argotic appellation might readily have been applied to the buccaneers either by themselves or the other inhabitants of the Antilles. The new etymology, which has a lot to recommend it, does not however clear up the relative position of French, Spanish and Italian cognates. A majority of authorities considers French to have been the language of dissemination, though Italian sources differ sharply from the rest in laying stress on Spanish. M-D. give a Spanish etymon; B-Al. (s.v. filibustiere) draw it from 'sp. fribustero, flibustero, XVI sec.', although their entry under flibustiere derives the It. verb flibustare 'to engage in piracy' (18th cent.) from Fr. flibuster (1701). The most recent volume of the Gr. diz. it. only makes the issue more confused: 'filibustiere . . . deriv. dallo spagn. filibustero, sec. XVII, attraverso ant. ingl. flibutor . . .' (my italics; see Gr. diz. it., V, 992). In fact the French examples are by far the earliest found in the Romance languages. The first actual attestation of Sp. filibustero appears not in the 16th cent., nor even the 17th, but in the early 19th cent.,[2] as Corominas states, and Aebischer admits. As for Italian, the Gr. diz. it. has no examples before Melchiorre Gioia, who died in 1829 (the edition cited dates from 1848), and other Italian sources have nothing to offer earlier than this. I myself read it fifty years earlier, in Alberti, 1777: 'Filibustiere. T. Marinaresco. Nome che si dà ne' mari dell'America a' Pirati. Filibustier.' The form filibustieri (pl.) is in Stratico, Vocab. di marina, 1813-14. There is nevertheless a clear century between French and other Romance attestations, and this is the main reason why I prefer, with Prati, the French > Italian interpretation. There is also the fact that, although the basis of pirates' slang in the Antilles may have been something which passed for Spanish, French adventurers may well have played a dominant part in developing the buccaneers' terminology. It would also appear from the testimony of Oexmelin himself that the Spanish minority among the pirates had its own terms for buccaneer (matador, montero), and that they remained somewhat aloof from their fellow sea-rovers (vide Aebischer, op. cit., p. 49).

fisciù. Fashions: Woman's scarf, neckerchief.

18th cent., acc. to B-Al.; Magalotti; Fagiuoli. The actual fashion dates from the opening years of the 18th century. < Fr. fichu, 1701 in this sense (B-Al., M-D., Pr.), originally a specialisation of the p. part. fichu = 'mis à la hâte' (Wartburg). The substantive may be earlier in French; but cf. Boyer, The Royal Dictionary, 1699, which

---

1. The [s] is usually explained as an effect of paronymy with farabustear, 1609, 'to steal craftily, scrounge', a term of the germanía (Corominas, loc. cit.), or as a spelling pronunciation (but presumably this term would be transferred by word of mouth?).

2. Corominas observes that 'Cardenas Cano en 1723 y otros autores qui se ocupan de la piratería en el Mar Caribe, sólo se rifieren a los filibusteros con el nombre de piratas o corsarios' (II, p. 524b). The same is true of the other 18th cent. works on piracy.

still only has *fichu* as an adjective meaning 'pitiful, silly' (asterisked as a 'Mean or vulgar Word, or Expression of humour or Burlesk').

flanella. Text.: Flannel.

1758 A. Cocchi, *Consigli medici* (Cr.); 1777 Alberti: 'Sorta di drappo a lana, per lo più a fiori.' *Flanella d'Inghilterra* is mentioned in Alberti, 1788. Also *frenella* (Tuscany), *fanella* (Lucca, Sicily, Calabria, Naples) in 19th cent. <Fr. *flanelle*, 1650 (B-Al., M-D., Pr.) < Eng. *flannel* (earlier *flannan*) < Welsh *gwlanen* 'woollen cloth'.

flauto. Naut.: A type of large transport ship for supplies.

1788 Alberti, meaning (a) ship for transporting stores, (b) hospital ship. It is clear from Alberti's definition that the term is applied to naval units, not to merchant vessels. B-Al. and Pr. derive it from Fr. *flûte* in this sense (16th cent.), a popular etymology for Dutch *fluit* (*vide* Valkhoff, op. cit., p. 139).

framboise. Raspberry.

Magalotti; Alberti, 1777. Italianised into *flambuese* (1738, Pr.), *frambò*(O. Targ. Tozz.), *framboè* (F. Gallizioli, *Elementi botanico-agrari*, 1810–12), *frambosa* (1883 Manfroni). Fr. word, *framboise*, 12th cent. (B-Al., Pr.).

frammassone, franmassone. Freemason.

Forms with *fram-, fran-* have reached Italian through the intermediary of French *franc-maçon* (1740), calque of Eng. *freemason* (1646). The same is true of *frammassoneria* 'freemasonry', 1806, Lanzi (Pr.), 1747 in Fr., but *franche-maçonnerie* 1742. *Franmassone* in L. Pascoli, cited by Bergantini, 1745, acc. to M-*Stor.*, p. 579. Direct adaptations of the English are a little earlier in French and Italian (Fr. *frimaçon*, It. *frimesson* in 1740 (M-*Stor.*). The calque *libero muratore* (or simply *muratore*), inspired either by French or English, is very common in the 18th cent.

fraternizzare, -azione. To fraternise, fraternisation.

Boerio registers the verb as 'voce che cominciossi a sentire dai Demagoghi democratici l'anno 1797 (*Diz. dial. venez.*, 1829). *Fraternizzazione* is attested about that time, e.g. in Rillosi, *La Metamorfosi dell'impostura religiosa diventata politica*, Milan, anno VI repub. (Sept. 1797–98) (cited Hazard, p. 72 [*vide infra*, p. 559, n. 1]).

fricandò. Culin.: Roast leg of veal, etc.

1754, G. Gozzi (Pr.); *fricandò alla francese* in Goldoni, 1760. *Vide* Fanfani, *Uso toscano*. <Fr. *fricandeau*, 1552, Rabelais (B-Al., Pr.).

frisore. Hairdresser.

1798 Alberti (Pr.), who notes it as a 'franzesismo che le donne introducono, e gli scrittori eleganti proscrivono'. Discussed by Ugolini, F-A., Rigutini and Panzini. <Fr. *friseur* (B-Al., Pr.), itself little used in French; attested by Littré but probably current at an earlier date. The verb *friser* (whence It. *frisare*, 19th cent.) appears over three centuries before in 1504.

galetta. Naut.: Ship's biscuit.

Galetta 1777, Alberti, in this sense; also in Stratico, 1813–14. *Galletta* appears during the 19th cent. <Fr. *galette* (B-Al., M-D., Pr.), probably through Genoese *galeta*. The French word, a derivative of *galet*, 'cobble-stone', first appears in the 13th cent. meaning a type of cake or bun; the nautical signification dates from the 17th cent.

gamella. Naut., milit.: Billy-can, dixie (galvanised tin in which rations are served).

1769 Saverien, *Diz. di marina* (nautical term); both naval and military uses in Alberti, 1788: 'catino . . . in cui si pone la minestra, ecc. destinata per cadaun pasto dell'equipaggio sul mare, o per una determinata quantità di soldati ne' reggimenti. *Gamelle*.' <Fr. *gamelle*, 1611, Cotgrave in this sense (B-Al., Pr.). A direct loan from Spanish has been suggested; this is doubtless true in the case of dialectal *camella* 'milking pail' (Campobasso, Abruzzi, Sicily) (*vide Arch. Rom.*, VII, p. 460). Whether directly from Sp. or through the

intermediary of Fr., the form was disseminated from the Iberian peninsula where it appears at an early date as an agricultural term in two distinct senses: (a) 'trough for feeding animals' (1286 in Arabic text of Toledo (*gaméla*), 13th cent., *Libro de los Cavallos*, etc.), (b) 'curved portion at the end of a yoke' (at least from the time of Cervantes). (See Corominas' very detailed article, II, 648–9.)

gendarme. Man-at-arms; policeman.

1777 Alberti (military sense): '*Gendarme* (as an It. word). Volg. It. Voce francese, Soldati a cavallo, distribuiti in compagnie d'ordinanza, senza entrar nel corpo de' reggimenti'. *Gendarme* and *gendarmeria* in Carlo Botta (early 19th cent.). <Fr. *gendarme* (B-Al., M-D., Pr.), first used to refer to 14th cent. cavalry; *gendarmerie* as a collective in 1473, but first used in the modern sense in the later 18th century. Soon replaced in It. by *carabiniere*.

generalizzare. To generalise.

18th cent., acc. to B-Al. (Alberti, 1788, translates Fr. *généraliser* by *generaleggiare*). <Fr. *généraliser* (B-Al.), 16th cent., d'Aubigné. *Generalizzazione*, 19th cent. < Fr. *généralisation*, 1779, Deluc (B-Al.).

gettone. Counter, esp. for gaming or operating automatic machines.

Salvini, *Annot. Fier.*; 1751, Pompeo Neri (both Cr.); 1777 Alberti as 'voce dell'uso moderno', denoting also a counter for use in calculation. The form *gettoni* given by Oudin as a translation of Fr. *jetons* is suspect. <Fr. *jeton*, 14th cent. (B-Al., M-D., Pr.).

ghetta, ghette. Milit.: Gaiters.

Prati registers the word in *Bandi di Leopoldo*, 1780. It is probable that it only entered current usage—together with the article of dress—as a result of the influence of Napoleonic armies. Alberti, 1811, still translates Fr. *guêtre* only by *uosa*. Fairly frequent in early 19th cent.—1812, Bernardoni; pl. *guetri* in 1819 (B-Al.). <Fr. *guêtre(s)*; *guietre*, 15th cent. (B-Al., M-D., Pr.).

ghigliottina, ghigliottinare. Guillotine.

Subst. used figuratively by Monti, letter of 9th April 1797: 'uno scritto . . . che sarà la ghigliottina de' preti' (Bertoldi, II, 9) and in the real sense, id., p. 135 (1798). Also in Alfieri. The verb appears under the form *guillotinare* in 1793, at Bologna (Zaccaria). Venetian *ghilotina* in Boerio, 1829. <Fr. *guillotine*, 1790 (the machine was invented by Guillotin in 1789). B-Al. register *vestire alla ghigliottina* (women's fashions—off-the-shoulder dress with red ribbon round the neck) in 1795.

giacobino. Hist.: Jacobin.

A borrowing of the revolutionary period. Monti uses it from 1794: 'Un uomo . . . segnato a dito come un congiurato, come un Giacobino, e tuttavia buon cattolico e uomo d'onore' (letter of 7th June). He also uses it figuratively: 'si questo è linguaggio da giacobino, spiacemi dunque che la ragione sia giacobina' (20th Aug. 1796). French political sobriquet, *Jacobin*. M-*Stor*. p. 660, B-Al.

giardinaggio. Gardening.

1801–3 Marco Lastri, *Corso di agricoltura pratica* (Cr.; Lastri, 1787, acc. to Pr.). Entered common usage in the 19th cent. <Fr. *jardinage*, 13th cent. (B-Al., M-D., Pr.).

girotta, giruetta, giroetta. Naut.: Wind-indicator, weather-vane.

(= *banderuola*). *Girotta* Alberti, 1788; *giruetta* 1853, D'Ayala; *giruetta* and *giroetta*, 1877 F-A. <Fr. *girouette* (Purists, B-Al., Pr.), 16th cent. (var. *girouet*) ultimately < Old Norse *vedrviti*.

goliè. Necklace.

Alberti, 1798 (Pr.), but used earlier in 18th cent. to mean 'lady's collar or neckerchief of fine material' (Venetian word) acc. to Prati, who refers to G. Gozzi (1756) and Goldoni

(1760). Fr. form still in Panz. IX. Adapt. of Fr. word *collier* (B-Al., Pr.) ≠ It. *gola* 'throat'.

gridellino. Greyish-mauve colour.

Used esp. with reference to fabrics. 1777, Alberti, as a dyers' term: ' . . . colore tra bigio e rosso. *Gris de lin, lilas clair.*' The form *gridelino* appears earlier, in Magalotti. <Fr. *gris de lin* (B-Al., M-D., Pr.).

grosso. Text.: Heavy silken cloth.

T-Bell. define *grosso* as 'stoffa di seta volgarmente detto "*Grò di Napoli*"' and cite examples of *grosso di Napoli, grosso di Tours* from the *Spettacolo della Natura*, 1745. The French word *gros* is used during the 19th cent. (Rambelli, 1850, etc.); F-A. like T-Bell. use an Italianised graphy *grò*. <Fr. *gros* (*gros de Naples* in Oudin) (B-Al., Pr.).

imperiale. Top deck or roof of a stagecoach or omnibus.

Since the reference in Alberti, 1798 (cited Pr.) undoubtedly relates to this particular technical signification, *imperiale* must be classed as a late 18th cent. loan. Earlier editions of Alberti are unaware of the term in Italian, though Alb. 1777 registers the French word as possessing this meaning (among others). *Imperiale* occurs frequently in the 19th cent. <Fr. *impériale*, current in the later 18th cent. but used in an analogous sense by 1648 (*FEW*, IV, 586b) (B-Al., Pr.).

incaricato di affari. Chargé d'affaires, person temporarily in charge.

V. Monti, letter of 15th Aug. 1798: 'Petracchi è stato destituito, e Crespi, minutante del Direttorio, gli succede in qualità d'incaricato di affari' (Bertoldi, II, 102). Early 19th cent., Carlo Botta, etc. Calque of Fr. *chargé d'affaires*, which came to be used by most western European languages as a diplomatic term in the 19th century. (English, 1850 [*OED*].)

ingranare. Engineering: Of gears: to enter into mesh.

Alberti 1788 has *ingranare la tromba* (recent addn.): '*T. Mar.* Toglier via a forza di tromba l'acqua che resta nel fondo d'un bastimento per gettarnela fuori. *Engrener la pompe.*' The Fr. > It. section explains the above sense by a periphrasis, but translates the general meaning of 'to mesh (of cogs), to engage gears' by the two verbs *incastrare* and *ingranare*. *Ingranare* is frequent in technical contexts during the 19th cent.; the substantive *ingranaggio* appears in Tramater. <Fr. *engrener*, 1195 in the sense 'to begin to grind corn' (i.e. by setting the millstones in motion), mid-17th cent. meaning simply 'to put in gear'.[1]

inoculare, inoculazione. Medic.: To inoculate.

The foreign influence, though definite, is a semantic one only; *inoculare* in the sense 'to graft a plant' (archaic) is attested (with *inocchiare*) as early as the 14th century and is a native Latinism. The noun is first to appear in the well-known medical signification in 1761, S. Manetti, *Dell'inoculazione del vaiuolo*. Alberti 1777 has both noun and verb; after defining the usual acceptations of *inoculare* he adds: 'l'uso comincia ad autorizzar questa voce in significato di annestare il vajuolo'; while *inoculazione* is noted as 'voce che comincia ad introdursi'. <Fr. *inoculer, inoculation*, 1723 (B-Al., Pr.), Latinisms originally coined in England (1714, 1722 respectively).

isabella. Name of a colour approximating to 'mustard' or 'coffee-coloured'.

B-Al. register *isabella* as a veterinary term in 1770; Alberti, 1777 and 1788, plainly knows it only in this connection. The phrase *coloretto isabella* appears earlier, in Magalotti.

---

1. Note that, as defined by Alberti, the original usage in Italian closely resembles the older stage of semantic development in French, viz., to set a machine (as a whole) in motion, rather than the more precise technical signification.

<Fr. *isabelle*, early 17th cent. (B-Al., Pr.), from the name of the Infanta Isabella, wife of Albert of Austria, on account of the swarthiness of her complexion.[1]

lama. Lama (Buddhist priest).

1777 Alberti: '*Lama. T. della Storia mod.* Nome de' Sacerdoti presso i Tartari.' Current from late 18th cent. onwards, sometimes with the accentuation *lamà*. <Fr. *lama*, 1629 (B-Al., Pr.), < Tibetan (*b*)*lama*, 'priest'.

lambrí, lambris. Archit.: Wainscoting, panelling.

1768 G. Targioni Tozzetti; Fr. graphy *lambris* in 19th cent. <Fr. *lambris*, 15th cent.; OFr. *lambruis* in 12th cent. (B-Al., Pr.).

lampasso. Text.: Silk damask, esp. for upholstery.

1788 Alberti: 'Sorta di drappo di seta, che ci capita dall' Indie Orientali.' <Fr. *lampas* (B-Al.), *lampasse* 1723 Savary.

lancinante. Medic.: Adj. describing a sudden, stabbing pain.

G. Targ. Tozzetti (1712–83); Gherardini. <Fr. *lancinant*, a learned word first used by Paré, 1546 (B-Al., Pr.).

lasto, lasta. Naut. (archaic): Unit of weight, 'last'; also ship's cargo.

The *last*, a unit of tonnage, was usually equal to two tons. This sense appears (as a 'misura e peso olandese') in Alberti, 1777, under the masculine form; that of 'cargo, burthen of a ship' is added in 1788 as a northern European usage. Both *lasto* and *lasta* (fem.) were in use during the 19th cent. <Fr. *last(e)*, 1702 (*REW* 4922, B-Al., Pr.), < Dutch *last*, 'load'.

letto di giustizia. Royal throne in the *Parlement de Paris*; a sitting of the *Parlement*.

18th cent. Salvini (B-Al.). Calque of Fr. *lit de justice* (sources agree), attested during the Middle Ages: 1318, *FEW*, V, 236; Gace de la Buigne (Tob.-Lomm., s.v. *lit*.)

libertinaggio. Debauchery.

L. Magalotti;[2] Alberti, who gives the word as synonymous with *libertinismo*. <Fr. *libertinage*, 1603 (B-Al., Pr.). The adj. *libertino* has followed closely corresponding semantic developments of Fr. *libertin*, which took on a specific religious connotation after the foundation of the sect who referred to their band as the *libertins* (1525, at Lille), in imitation of the *libertini* mentioned in *Acts*, Ch. VI, v. 9. Once the sect—who might be roughly defined as 'democrats' in their theological attitude—came into serious conflict with established religion the term *libertin* began to assume the meaning of 'irreligious person, freethinker' (still normal in Molière, Pascal). The semantic emphasis shifts during the 17th century from religion to morality; towards the end of the period *libertin* regularly means an immoral, debauched person. It. *libertino* acquires this connotation during the 18th century.

lillà, lilla. Bot.: Lilac; Fashions: Lilac colour.

A late 18th cent. rather than a 19th cent. word, since both the tree (*Syringa vulgaris*) and the colour are mentioned by O. Targioni-Tozzetti. The colour apparently entered first. Both assumptions are supported by the entry in Alberti, 1788 (French to Italian section), where the word *lillà* (with Fr. accentuation) is registered only as the name of the

---

1. See Migl., *Dal nome proprio* . . ., p. 176.

2. The sense in Magalotti (= 'nonchalance, laxness') is idiosyncratic and rather removed from that of the typical 18th cent. loan: 'E per verità parve poi a' miei amici, che questo spirito di libertinaggio regnasse troppo visibilmente in tutte le *Lettere*, essendo riuscite assai slegate, e riconoscendosi per fatte da uno scioperato, che tale era io in quel tempo, più col fine di divertirsi, che di comporre, secondo che ogni *Lettera* aveva per fine sè medesima senza alcuna obbedienza, o correlazione a una precedente idea universale' (Dedicatory essay to the *Lettere familiari*, p. viii of 1762 edition, G. Pasquali, Venice). See also id., ibid., passage cited above, p. 350, in our discussion of 17th cent. Gallicisms.

D

colour: 'Lilas, *T. de Teint. et autres.* Sorte de couleur semblable au gris-de-lin. *Lillà.*
Lilas clair, *Lillà chiaro,* autrefois, *Gridellino.*[1] Lilas pourpré. *Lillà cupo.*' The botanical
term is rendered by *Ghianda unguentaria.* <Fr. *lilas* (Fr. stress retained in *lillà,* which also
appears with the Fr. graphy [Garollo, Panzini]) (Panz., B-Al., M-D.; Pr. in common
with certain Purists registers the colour alone as a definite Gallicism, while conceding a
Fr. influence in final-stressed forms whatever the sense). The dating and historical circumstances persuade me that the word as a whole is of French origin, with the possible
exception of some forms ending in *-ac, -acco* (*vide* Prati); but even these may reflect the
original (archaic) graphy in French—*lilac* 1600, O. de Serres. Ultimately from Persian
via Arabic.

madiere. Naut.: Kelson (of a wooden ship).

Alberti, 1777, has *madieri* (pl.) in the sense of 'Pezzi di legname inchiodati in egual
distanza su la carena d'una galera. *Madriers*', i.e. the *frames* rather than the kelson of the
vessel; but since the basic meaning of the word is 'large baulk of timber' one may assume
that the term was differently applied in different types of construction (cf. the analogous
generic use of 'timbers' in English nautical parlance). Also in Stratico, 1813. <Fr.
madier, madrier (B-Al., Pr.), < OProv. *madier,* < Lat. *materium* 'wood for construction'.

manioca. Botan.: Manioc.

L. A. Muratori (1672–1750); Fr. form *manioc* early 19th cent. In Alberti 1777 (Fr.
section) the Fr. word (graphy *manioque*) is translated by *manioca.* From Fr. *manioc,*
originally *manihot* (1558), from Tupi and Guarani (B-Al., Pr.).[2]

manovra. Naut.: (a) Generic term for cordage, ship's rigging; (b) handling of a ship.

Alberti 1777 has *manovra* in both the above senses. The dialectal form *manuvra*
(handling both of sails and guns) appears earlier, in Patriarchi, *Voc. veneziano e padovano*
(1775), acc. to Prati. *Manovra* meaning 'military exercise' (an acceptation originally
censured by rigorists like Luigi Fincati) appears first in Boerio (1829) and is plainly a
usage introduced during the Napoleonic Wars. Alberti includes this meaning in his
definition of the French *manœuvre* but entirely omits it from that of the Italian word,
while *manœuvre* 'army manœuvre' is translated by 'movimenti d'un esercito'. <Fr.
manœuvre, 13th cent. (B-Al., M-D., Pr.). The verb *manovrare* (naut.: 'to manœuvre a
ship' (Alb.); milit.: 'to carry out army exercises' [1853, D'Ayala]) is taken from Fr.
manœuvrer, originally (12th cent.) *manovrier* (*REW* 5336 [*manuoperare*], B-Al., M-D.,
Pr.). Ugolini also registers it in the metaphorical sense 'to intrigue'.

marabutto. Marabout or guardian of a mosque.

Marabuto in Alberti, 1777, in this signification. *Marabutto* 19th cent. <Fr. *marabout*
(*marabou* 1617, Mocquet) < Arab. *marbut,* same sense—literally, 'bound (to the ascetic
life)'—probably through the intermediary of Portuguese *marabuto* (B-Al.).

marciapiede. Pavement.

1754 G. Targ. Tozzetti, *Viaggi*; 1777 Alberti ('pavement on each side of road or
bridge'; trans. by Fr. *trottoir, banquette*). <Fr. *marchepied,* acc. to F-A., B-Al., M-D., Pr.
The Italian borrowing is taken from a further semantic development of the original
technical extension in French, viz., *marchepied* in the sense of 'canal towpath' (example in
Littré from a Royal Ordinance of 1669). The late 18th cent. nautical signification 'foot-
ropes' (for sailors to stand on, beneath spars) may also be a Gallicism; *marciapiede* for
'step of a carriage', 'railway platform' certainly is.

---

1. q.v., *supra.*

2. The earlier forms with a dental group (*mandioca*), attested first in 1549 and found also
in the 17th century, reached Italy through Portuguese *mandioca,* an alternative form of
Port. *manihoca* documented from the early 16th century.

marcia. Music: March.

Early 18th cent., Algarotti. Alberti, however, still explains the Fr. word in this sense by a periphrasis; 'aria musicale per la marcia de' soldati'. <Fr. *marche*, 18th cent. (B-Al., Pr.).

marna. Geol.: Marl.

F. Paoletti, *Opere agrarie*. Alberti still uses as the Italian rubric the old word *marga* (noted as 'termine de' Naturalisti'), but Fr. *marne* is translated as *marga, marna*. <Fr. *marne*, 1266 (*REW* 5354, B-Al., M-D., Pr.), <Gaulish *margila*.

mascheretto. Naut., hydrog.: 'Bore' on certain rivers.

1769 Saverien, *Diz. di marina*. Alberti, 1788, has *maschereto* (recent addn.) which he defines as the tidal wave on the Dordogne. *Mascheretto* in Stratico. <Fr. *mascaret* (16th cent.) < Gascon *mascaret* (B-Al., Pr.).

melassa. Residue from refined sugar; molasses.

1777 Alberti, as a merchants' term. <Fr. *mélasse* (*meslache*, 1508) < Sp. *melaza* < *mel*, 'honey' (B-Al., M-D., Pr.).

messidoro. Tenth month of the Revolutionary calendar.

23 June 1798, letter of V. Monti (Bertoldi, II, 84). <Fr. *messidor* (B-Al., Pr., etc.), 1793.

metallurgia. Metallurgy.

1749 B-Al.; 1777 Alberti: 'Volg. It. Quella parte della Chimica che attende alla preparazione e depurazione de' sotterranei metalli, e de' minerali per uso di medicina. Métallurgie.' *Metallurgo* and *metallurgico* are also 18th cent. (G. Targ. Tozzetti) while *metallurgista* occurs later (mid-19th cent.). <Fr. *métallurgie*, 17th cent., Oudin, originally 'prospecting for metals' (B-Al., Pr.). The derivatives too are probably Gallicisms.

meticcio. Half-caste.

1777 Alberti (referring to half-caste Indians and noted as 'voce moderna'). Replaced the earlier form *mestizzo* (16th cent., Sassetti), usually regarded as a Hispanism, though the reference in Sassetti (1585) actually refers to Portuguese Eurasians in India. <Fr. *métis* (OFr. *mestiz*, 12th cent.), acc. to B-Al., M-D., Pr.

milord. Wealthy English gentleman.

Attested frequently in the 18th cent., usually with It. flexions—*milorde, milordo* (Parini, Baretti, etc.). A form *milorte* appears once earlier, in Gabriello Chiabrera (†1638), but current use of the term dates from the 18th century. De Brosses refers to the activities of 'milords anglais' in Italy, in 1739. <Fr. *milord*, 17th cent.; *millour* in Old French (B-Al., Pr.). Ultimately from the English form of address 'my lord'. The vocative phrase is shifted grammatically to a substantive in French, creating a false Anglicism; the presence of the same solecism in Italian (as in other European languages) is proof of a French influence.

mineralogia. Mineralogy.

1775 B-Al.; 1777 Alberti, defined as 'scienza e cognizion de' metalli'. Also *mineralogico*, adj., 1777 (B-Al.). Fr. *minéralogie*, 1732 and *minéralogique*, 1751 (B-Al., Pr.).

minuetto. Minuet.

Fr. word *minuet* in Magalotti; *minuetta*, N. Forteguerri (1674–1735); *minuetto*, Algarotti. <Fr. *menuet* (B-Al., M-D., Pr.), an adjective from the 12th cent. onwards, used to refer to a dance in the early 17th cent. The actual minuet popularized in Italy and elsewhere is a late 17th cent. musical form.

miraggio. Meteorol.: Mirage.

18th cent., acc. to B-Al. F-A. (1877) call attention to an observation in G. Torti (1774–1852) (note to the poem *Scetticismo e Religione*) that *miraggio* in this sense was already in use in Italian. Recording the pronunciation *miragio*, T-Bell. recommend that the word (if it must be used at all) should be spelt with the geminated consonant. Among examples of well-known occasions on which mirages have been observed both T-Bell. and F-A. recall that Napoleon's Army of the Nile was greatly hindered in its campaign by meteorological phenomena of this kind. <Fr. *mirage* (T-Bell., F-A., B-Al., M-D., Pr., etc.), 1753, *Hist. de l'Acad. des sciences.*

misantropo, misantropia. Misanthropist, misanthropy.

B-Al. register the abstract noun in 1749; both appear in Alberti, 1777. Frequent attestations early 19th cent. onwards. <Fr. *misanthrope*, 1552 and *misanthropie*, of the same period (B-Al., Pr.).

moerre. Text.: Moire (type of watered silk).

Moerre pre-1764, Algarotti; 1779, *Bandi di Leopoldo*. The form *muerro* appears 1777 in Baldini (B-Al.); Alberti, 1777, translates Fr. *moire* by *moerro*, a graphy which reappears in his definition of Fr. *moiré* (p. part.). Forms with initial [a] (*amoerre* pre-1767, J. A. Nelli; *amuerre* 1749, but *amuer* in a 17th cent. inventory of uncertain date and in one of 1705; *amoerro* 19th cent.) are best explained as a partial agglutination (in Italian) of the French feminine article. The relationship between Fr. *moire*, It. *moerre*, Eng. *mohair* and the older words Fr. *moucaiard*, *moncayar*, It. *mocaiardo*, *mocaiarro*, though complicated, is not difficult to establish. All have as their starting-point Arab. *mukhayyar* (lit. 'chosen, preferred' <*khayyar* 'to choose') which seems to have denoted originally a costly goat-hair cloth from Asia Minor. The word reached Italian certainly by the 16th cent., probably sooner (*mocaiardo* in Cecchi, *mocaiarro* in Sassetti, *Lettere del commercio dei Fiorentini in Levante*, and in a Pistoiese law of 1558); from Italian it entered French in the forms *mouquayat* (1580), *moncayar* (early 17th cent.) (see It. > Fr. 16th cent. loans). Both It. and Fr. terms are still found in the 18th cent. (Veneroni, Baretti, Alberti), the alternative word *camoiardo* being more usual in It. by this time. During the course of the 16th century the Arabic word had reached England—perhaps directly, possibly by several routes—in various guises; it is first attested in Hakluyt (1570): 'cotton wooll, chamlets and mocayres'. The popular etymology *mohair* triumphed in the early 17th cent. *Mohair*, *moncayar* and *mocaiardo* all refer to a type of woollen or hair cloth similar to kersey, often of coarse weave, esp. in France and Italy.[1] The textile *moire* 'watered silk' is first mentioned in Ménage, 1650. A loan from English is unquestionable (cf. *inter alia*, the earlier graphy *mouaire* and direct statements in early documentations that the cloth itself was imitated from an English fabric); it is not clear, however, whether the change of sense took place in France or in England. The latter is more likely. English *mohair* is borrowed a second time in its proper signification, with the English spelling, during the 19th century (*Figaro*, 1868). Fr. *moire* enters Italian late 17th > early 18th cent. (see above) and also returns to England during the Restoration with the French pronunciation and the prestige of French fashions (cf. Pepys, 1660; 'Some green-watered moyre . . .' [*OED*]).[2] The use of the French graphy *moire* in Italian in recent times (Panz., 1905) to mean 'watered silk' may be regarded as a separate influence of *haute couture*.

The shifts may be summed up diagrammatically as follows:

---

1. See definitions in Veneroni and the *OED*. Cotgrave defines *moucayart* and *moncaiart* as two different textiles, the former equated to Eng. *mockado* (a cheap woollen cloth made in Flanders and in Norwich by Flemish weavers) and the latter glossed as 'a silk moccadoe', i.e. a more expensive stuff.

2. It also reaches Spain during the earlier 18th cent.; *vide mué, muer* in the *Dicc. de la lengua castellana*, 1734: 'especie de ormasí de aguas . . . *voz francesa nuevamente introducida.*'

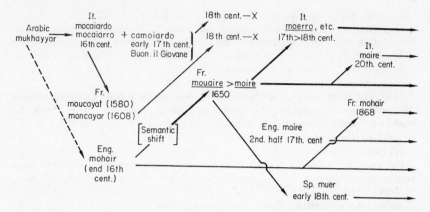

mollettone, molletone. Text.: Heavy woollen stuff with nap on both sides, for winter garments.

1766–77 *Bandi di Leopoldo* (Cr.); 1770 Savary, *Diz. di commercio.* Alberti, 1777, has *mollettone* as a translation of the Fr. word only. <Fr. *molleton*, 1664 (B-Al., Pr.).

monologo. Theatre., etc.: Monologue.

1788 Alberti (under the rubric *monologa* (masc.); but the French word is translated by *monologo* in the Fr. > It. section): 'T. della Letteratura. Scena d'un opera teatrale in cui l'attore parla solo.' <Fr. *monologue* (B-Al.), 15th cent.; originally 'one who speaks incessantly' (pathol. term). The French word was also borrowed by English, with Fr. graphy, in the early 17th cent.; theatrical and literary senses first in Dryden (*OED*).

montura. Milit.: Soldier's uniform, equipment.

L. Magalotti; Alberti, *Diz. universale.* The term is criticised by many 19th cent. authorities—D'Ayala, T-Bell. (who define it as the complete outfit of a soldier's equipment and stigmatise it as a useless neologism), F-A. <Fr. *monture*, 14th cent., Froissart (B-Al., Pr.).

naturalizzare, -arsi. To naturalize, become naturalized (in sense of acquiring nationality).

Naturalizzarsi in Magalotti, who also has *naturalizzato* meaning 'naturalized person' (T-Bell.). *Naturalizzare* in A. M. Salvini, *Annot. Muratori* (Cr.). Alberti, 1777, only registers the p. part. *naturalizzato.* The noun *naturalizzazione* 'act, process of naturalization' appears during the 19th cent. (F-A., Rigutini). <Fr. *naturaliser*, 1553, *naturalisation*, 16th cent. (F-A., Rig., B-Al.).

négligé, negligè. Women's fashions: Négligé.

18th cent. in S. Bettinelli (1718–1808), M-*Stor.*, p. 578. Criticised by purists in 19th cent. A French word, *négligé*, 1694 Acad.; initially a descriptive past participle rather than a substantive. The same term appears in English in 1835, but the obsolete adaptation *negligee* goes back, like Italian, to the previous century (1756, *OED*).

nosologia. Medic.: Nosology (the definition and classification of diseases).

1749 Chambers, acc. to B-Al. Alberti 1777 and 1788 omit the Italian word, but give *nosologia* as a translation of the French term, adding: 'T. de Med. Patholog. Partie de la Pathologie qui traite des maladies en général, abstraction faite des symptômes et des causes.' Early examples usually employ the word in this more general sense (G. Arrivabene, A. Leone) rather than in the strict signification above. <Fr. *nosologie*, 1747 (B-Al., Pr.).

nottambulo. Sleep-walker.

1777 Alberti (who gives as synonyms *sonnambulo* (q.v. *infra*) and *nottivago*); also *nottambolo* in 19th cent. *Nottambulismo* 'sleep-walking' (esp. from a clinical standpoint) appears 1828, in Leone, *Diz. di medicina.* <Fr. *noctambule*, 1701 and *noctambulisme*, 1765 (B-Al., Pr.) <MedLat. *noctambulus.*

òboe. Music: Oboe.

Oboè 1749, B-Al.; *boè* 1748 in Naples, acc. to Prati; *oboè* in Alberti, *Diz. univ.* (though Alb. 1788 omits it, translating Fr. *hautbois* by *chiarina, cennamella*). Forms with the modern accentuation appear early 19th cent. <Fr. *hautbois* (*auxboys* late 16th cent., Et. de Médicis) (B-Al., Pr.).

odalisca. Odalisque, concubine.

18th cent., acc. to B-Al. Archaic form *odalica*, corresponding to the earlier Fr. pronunciation, 1786 (B-Al.). <Fr. *odalisque* (B-Al., Pr.); both forms current in the 17th cent., < Turkish *ôdalyq.*

ottimismo, ottimista. Philos.: Optimism, optimist.

Although the first definite references to *ottimismo* and *ottimista* in lexicographical works appear during the 19th century (Lessona, Petrocchi, etc.) it would clearly be wrong to assign to so late a period terms which in Italy as elsewhere are primarily associated with the theories of Leibnitz. Alberti (1777 and 1788) uses both *ottimismo* and *ottimista* to translate the corresponding French words, but omits them from the It. > Fr. section. <Fr. *optimisme, optimiste* 1737 (used by the Jesuits in their discussion of Leibnitz's philosophical system), diffused throughout Europe after the publication of Voltaire's *Candide, ou l'Optimisme* in 1758 (B-Al., Pr.). *Optimism* appears in English in 1759, *optimist* in 1766 (*OED*).

pacchebotto. Mail steamer.

Paccheboto, Algarotti; *pachebotto* in 1811; *pacchetto* in the same sense, 1814, Stratico. Both *pacchebotto* and *pacchetto* in F-A. Ultimately < Eng. *packet-boat*, but the intermediary role of Fr. *paquebot* (*paquebouc*, 1634) is indisputable (B-Al., Pr.).[1]

palatina. Women's fashions: Kind of scarf made of fur.

1709 Veneroni. Alberti has it in two senses: (a) a fur pelisse worn round the neck in winter (b) a lace stock or neckerchief.[2] The *palatine* was in fashion in France *c.* 1670 and was superseded by that of the *fichu.* <Fr. *palatine*, 1676 (B-Al., Pr.), taken from the title of the duchesse d'Orléans, by whom the fashion was invented.

palissandro. Comm.: Timber of the *Jacaranda brasiliana.*

A hard, dark wood much in demand for marquetry and turnery. 1770 Garcin, acc. to B-Al. <Fr. *palissandre* (B-Al., Pr.), 1723 (*palixandre* in 18th cent.), probably borrowed via Dutch from an indigenous word of Dutch Guiana.

papà. Child's name for father; Papa.

Used in middle-class environment, though not usual in Tuscany, the area of *babbo.* Attested in dialects from the mid-18th cent. onwards: 1754 Del Bono (Sicily); 1775 Patriarchi (Venice and Padua). Not in Alberti. Also the form *pappà.* 19th cent. Tuscan purists react strongly against the Gallicism, though Panz. defends it as a nursery word which appears to have arisen spontaneously in many languages. <Fr. *papa; pappa* 1552, Ch. Estienne (*REW* 6213, B-Al., M-D., Pr.).

---

1. Alb., 1788 (French section), defines Fr. *paquet-bot* (sic) as 'bâtiment qui passe ... d'Angleterre en France et ailleurs' and translates it by *nave da dispaccio*, adding: 'on peut pourtant retenir son nom propre (i.e. the French term in Italian) dans certaines occasions'.

2. Only sense (a) in the 1777 edition.

patriotto, patriota. Patriot.

Though in the sense of 'person who is native to a given country' (Oudin, J. A. Nelli (1673–1767)) the presence of a Gallicism is disputable, most authorities agree that *patriota* 'patriot' represents a French influence. This signification first appears in A. M. Salvini, *Prose Toscane* (1715) and is frequent during the 18th century: *padriotti* (pl.) 1760, Paoli; *patriotto* 1788, Alberti, and several other examples in T-Bell.[1] Bernardoni's *patriotta, patriotto* meaning 'compatriot' (1812), described by Panzini as a popular usage, is doubtless an abbreviation of *compatriotta, -o* which are attested from Boccaccio onwards. Panzini also observes that during the revolutionary and Napoleonic periods, 'patriota valse come giacobino, repubblicano, e anche oggi il senso politico non è disgiunto talora da tale parola'. <Fr. *patriote* (earlier *patriot*) acc. to Purists, Panz., B-Al.; other authorities (Schiaffini,[2] M-Duro, Pr.) though less positive are nevertheless inclined to accept this derivation. Fr. *patriote* appears 1460 and *patriot* 1599 in the sense of 'native of a country' < LateLat. *patriota* < Gk. πατριώτης, 'belonging to the same fatherland'. The semantic shift to 'patriot' occurs towards the end of the 17th cent., seemingly through ellipsis of expressions such as *bon, vrai, fidèle patriot(e)* (Vauban [noun used as epithet], Leibnitz[3]); but a similar development takes place in English during the earlier 17th cent., and historical and political considerations indicate beyond reasonable doubt a decisive influence of English on French in this instance.[4]

pensione. Boarding-house, board and lodging.

Pensione in the above sense is frequently criticised during the 19th cent. as an unnecessary Gallicism. F-A. add to these the meaning of 'boarding school'; Rigutini notes that the term has almost ousted *retta* and *dozzina*; Panz. still considers it a foreign word. All three connotations go back to the 18th century; in the Fr. > It. section of Alberti 1777 *pensione* is given along with *dozzina* as the equivalent of Fr. *pension* in the sense of (a) 'board' (b) 'boarding-house' ('Le lieu où l'on est nourri et logé pour un certain prix') (c) 'boarding school for children'. *Demi-pension* is translated as *mezza-pensione* (explained in precisely the modern sense). Fr. *pension*, originally 'ecclesiastical stipend, (royal) pension' (1255 >) acquired the meaning 'pittance' in the earlier 16th cent. (1535, *FEW*) and both 'payment for lodging' and 'lodging-house' about 1600 (1607 and 1606 resp., *FEW*). The sense 'boarding school' is included in the *Dict. de l'Acad. Fr.*, 1740. Has *pensione* undergone only semantic influence, or is it a formal loan from French? The evidence is evenly balanced; on the one hand, since during the Middle Ages the normal medium for legal transactions referring to pensions and *a fortiori* to ecclesiastical benefices was Latin, one might expect It. *pensione* to be, like Fr. *pension*, a learned borrowing; on the other the comparatively late appearance of It. *pensione* and its derivatives (acc. to T-Bell. 'ecclesiastical benefice' appears in Ariosto, Boiardo; 'emolument' in the 17th cent. (Galileo, etc.); *pensionario*, 16th cent., A. Caro; *pensionare*, 19th cent.) could be taken to imply that they depended upon the corresponding French terms.[5]

persiana. Shutter, Venetian blind.

1. Alb. 1777 still has it only as the equivalent of *paesano*.

2. *Momenti*, p. 103.

3. Though von Wartburg believes that Leibnitz's use of *patriote* in a work written in French is a temporary Germanism unconnected with the definitive English > French semantic loan which took place in the middle of the 18th century (the original MFr. word *patriot* entered German in 1571). See *FEW*, VIII, 24b.

4. The *OED* gives examples of Eng. *patriot* used substantivally with this meaning in 1605, 1644, 1677, 1688 and 1699, and combined with an adjective in 1611, 1641, 1643.

5. *Pensionato* (19th cent.) 'boarding-school' is undoubtedly an adaptation of Fr. *pensionnat* (1798, Acad.).

1777 Alberti: 'Voce moderna derivata dal Francese, che comincia usarsi in Italia, e dicesi d'una spezie di gelosia composta di regoli sottili di legno . . . *Persienne, abat-jour* ou *abajour.*' N. B. Belli's sonnet entitled *Le Perziane* (1835). <Fr. *persienne* (Alb., B-Al., Pr.) 1752, Trévoux, < *persien*, older form of *persan* (14th cent.), since this type of blind was assumed to be of Eastern origin (at a time when Persia represented the 'mystic East' in European eyes; cf. the *Lettres Persanes*).

piano. Plan, e.g. of a building.

18th cent. M-*Stor.*, 577; 1749 Chambers (B-Al.). Alberti appears unaware of it and translates Fr. *plan* by *pianta, idea, disegno, tessitura, ordito, progetto.* Bernardoni rejects it, as do most 19th cent. lexicographers, though Rig. accepts *piano di guerra* (1853 D'Ayala; Fr. *plan de guerre*). Semantic loan < Fr. *plan* (Purists, B-Al., M-D., Pr.), 16th cent. du Bellay (meaning plan of a town).[1]

picchetto. Milit.: Picket, or small detachment of soldiers.

Fr. Algarotti (1712–64); Aless. D'Antonj (1714–86); 1777 Alberti, in sense of 'the guard', i.e. detail of soldiers waiting in readiness to help the sentry on duty should need arise. Still explained by F-A., 1877, and Panzini. <Fr. *piquet* (T-Bell., Purists, Panz., B-Al., M-D., Pr.), 18th cent. in this sense; first used to refer to cavalry (*chevalier de piquet*, 17th cent.), the horses being tethered to *piquets* (= 'posts' in 1380) in readiness for a speedy departure.

picco. Geog., Topon: Peak of a mountain.

1777 Alberti: 'T. Geografico. Nome che si dà ad alcune montagne altissime e dirupate. *Pic.*' <Fr. *pic* in this sense (T-Bell., B-Al., Pr.). The geographical term is only remotely connected with Fr. *pic* 'pick' (pointed instrument used by masons, roadmakers and other trades), a 12th cent. back-formation from the verb *piquer*; the earliest examples of *pic* 'peak' (2nd half 17th cent.) are, as in English, plainly of Spanish origin, being usually attested in the Spanish form, *pico.*[2] The graphy *pic* appears in 1690, Furetière (*FEW*, VIII, 449b). *Pico* 'mountain peak' occurs in Spanish place-names as early as the 11th cent. (cf. Corominas, who mentions examples dated 1085, 1200, 1201, 1244[3]) and appears to have been disseminated from the region of the Pyrenees. The extent to which a Gallicism exists in the It. nautical term *picco* (a) the pointed aftermost top corner of a fore-and-aft sail, (b) that part of the spar which supports the peak of the sail, (c) in such expressions as *andare a picco, colare, mandare a picco*, 'to sink, of a ship'[4] is uncertain. F-A., Rigutini and most 19th century sources class them as French usages.[5] Significations (a) and (b) date from the Napoleonic Wars (Stratico, 1814, Parrilli, Guglielmotti) and are probably of Fr. origin, as the Purists claim. The phrases *andare, mandare, colare a picco*, attested in the 18th cent. (Forteguerri, Alberti) seem at first sight to be Gallicisms, but the presence of *andarsi a picco* as early as 1612, Falconi (B-Al.) brings in the possibility of a

---

1. There is some justification for the theory that Fr. *plan* is itself a semantic loan from It. *pianta*, which is also a 16th cent. word (Vasari). Its appearance in du Bellay hints at a contact in that direction.

2. E.g. Thevenot, *Suite du Voyage de Levant* (written 1665–66), p. 354, who while speaking of the island of Sannas observes '. . . il fait un pico, mais la montagne est plus haute que le pico' (see *F.M.*, XXI (1953), 'Datations nouvelles', p. 294).

3. Back formation from Sp. *picar*; acc. to Corominas a different word from *pico* 'bird's beak', which is an adaptation of Celtic *beccus*.

4. Guglielmotti's explanation of the semantic development is acceptable, viz., 'to sink in the water until the peak alone of the ship (the highest aftermost point) is visible' in other words to be entirely swallowed up by the waves.

5. F-A. include in their condemnation *essere a picco su* . . . 'to tower above, dominate' ('Quelle rocce stanno a picco sulla villetta' (F-A., 1877)), < Fr. *être à pic.*

Spanish loan (< *irse a pico*). I am inclined to consider that both *être à pic* and *aller à pic* are 16th cent. nautical Hispanisms,[1] and that the idioms were borrowed, probably temporarily, from Spanish by Italian sailors also.

pieddritto. Archit.: Upright pillar or pier without moulding, supporting an arch.

Alberti, 1777, has *pilastro, piè-dritto* as equivalents of Fr. *pied-droit. Piedritto* 1829, acc. to B-Al.; *pieddritto* and *pieddiritto* later in 19th cent. <Fr. *pied-droit*, 1694 (B-Al., Pr.).

piroetta. Pirouette.

Originally a term of horsemanship; one of a horse's paces, which involves turning round on the spot. Alberti, 1777: '*Voce Francese usata da' Cavallerizzi*. Moto che fa il cavallo nel voltarsi quant'egli è lungo, senza cangiar sito. *Pirouette.*' The form *piroletta* appears earlier (1749, B-Al.); also *piruletta, pirolè* in various dialects. The modern ballet term dates from the 19th cent. Panzini notes that the Fr. form, *pirouette*, is often heard: '*voce francese usata abusivamente, essendovi piroetta*'. The verb *piroettare* appears late 19th cent. <Fr. *pirouette* (Alb., B-Al., M-D., Pr.), 1510, *Test. de Ruby* (but *pirouet* 15th cent., Gréban) which originally meant 'spinning-top'; used as a term of horsemanship from the 16th cent.

piroga. Dug-out canoe.

1771 Griselini and Fassadoni, *Diz. delle arti e mestieri*, Venice, 1768–75; 1777, Alberti. Masc. *pirogo* slightly earlier, in 1769, Saverien, *Diz. di marina*. <Fr. *pirogue* (B-Al., Pr., M-D., M-Stor.), 1640 < Sp. *piragua*, of Carib. origin. Both French and Spanish have earlier direct Spanish borrowings: *piragua* in Fr. 1555, in It. 1565, Girolamo Benzoni. The same substitution of an original Spanish by a French form is found also in English, where *piragua* is found in 1535, *piroga* 1666 (*OED*).

pomo di terra. Potato.

1749 Bomare (B-Al.), Lastri. Calque of Fr. *pomme de terre*, 1716, Frézier, calque of Dutch *aardappel* (B-Al., Pr., etc.). Used in the north, Sicily and Sardinia.

pot-pourri. Culin.: Pot-pourri; fig. uses predominate later.

18th cent., Salvini (B-Al.), who uses the graphy *popurì*. Frequently registered during the 18th and 19th cent. in various forms—*potpourry*, P. Verri; *potpurrì* F-A., 2nd edition; *pupurrì* Petrocchi—and often criticised, esp. when used figuratively for 'hotch-potch' (= *guazzabuglio*) or 'miscellany' (literary, musical). Fr. word and adapt., *pot-pourri*, 16th cent., Régnier; calque of Sp. *olla podrida*.

purista. Lit., etc.: Purist.

Mid-18th cent. Appears in G. A. Costatini's version of La Bruyère's *Caractères* (1758). 'Vocabolo tolto dal francese per significare, protettori della purità del linguaggio' (Algarotti). M-Stor., p. 573, and sources cited. <Fr. *puriste*, 1625 in this sense. Also *purismo* 1785 *Il Caffè*, Cesarotti, etc.; Fr. *purisme* 1680.

rada. Roadstead (protected anchorage, usually off a port).

18th cent. Magalotti, acc. to T-Bell.; 1788 Alberti (added recently). Veneroni 1729 has it, but marks it as a suspect form. <Fr. *rade* (B-Al., M-D.; Prati suggests either Spanish or French, but the Spanish word is attested over two centuries after the French, in the *Dicc. de la lengua castellana*, 1737), 1483, *Grant Routier* < Old Engl. *rād* (ModEng. *road*).

ragù. Culin.: Ragout.[2]

Ragò 1749, Chambers (B-Al.); *ragù* 1757, G. Gozzi; I. Pindemonte. French form in

---

1. Cf. Fr. *apiquer* 'to be atrip, up and down', of an anchor (i.e. vertically below the vessel). Note also the parallelism between Fr. *apiquer* to 'peak up' a spar (cause it to point upwards) and Sp. *embiquar* (same sense).

2. The 18th cent. sense is the original, etymological one of 'appetiser'. See Panzini's article *ragoût* (*Diz. mod.*) for a description of the *ragoût* at the present day in various regions of Italy.

F-A. 2nd edition, Panzini. Fr. *ragoût* (B-Al., M-D., Pr.), 16th cent. < archaic *ragoûter* 14th cent., Froissart) 'to tickle the appetite'.

ralinga. Naut.: Bolt-ropes (ropes sewn along edge of a sail to strengthen it).

Ralinghe (pl.) 1788, Alberti (recent addn.); *ralinga* 1813, Stratico. <Fr. *ralingue* (Panz., B-Al., Pr.), 12th cent., Wace, adaptation of Dutch *ralijk* (lit. 'spar-rope'). Alberti also has (*fare*) *ralingare* meaning to 'brail up' a sail in order to prevent it from drawing. < Fr. *ralinguer*, 1694, Thomas Corneille.

rango. Rank, degree.

Came into general use from Magalotti's time onwards, acc. to T-Bell. Rigutini gives examples from Giov. Tosi (1748), A. Cocchi, F. Paoletti, *Op. agr.* (1789). Alberti, 1777, describes it as 'voce dell'uso tolta dal francese'. F-A., Panz. give examples of extended uses—*di rango, di alto rango*, 'famous, talented'—as well as the military term 'rank, file'. <Fr. *rang* (all sources agree) 12th cent., of Frankish origin.

rapè. Kind of tobacco or snuff.

'Del rapè della Francia' in F. Paoletti, *Op. agr.* (1789) (T-Bell.). Alberti 1788 has *rape* (sic) '*V. dell' uso*. Sorta di tabacco da naso, che rende odore. *Tabac râpé.*' F-A. have it as a kind of strong tobacco in large shreds. Panzini, who registers it as 'tabacco grosso, da fiuto' notes the It. adaptation *rapato*. <Fr. *tabac râpé* (all sources agree). All dictionaries omit a date of attestation for the Fr. word. The Italian term and those in other languages (e.g. Eng. *rappee, c.* 1740, *Winkle's Snuffs* and 1758, Johnson [*OED*]) are in fact false Gallicisms, in that the substantive does not exist in French; *râpé* in *tabac râpé* (i.e. snuff produced as required by rasping a plug of tobacco with a special file, later tobacco similar to this) is felt as a past participle used adjectivally. Cf. the well-known song by Gabriel-Charles de l'Attaignant (1697–1779); 'J'ai du bon tabac dans ma tabatière/J'en ai du fin et du râpé . . .'.

ratafià. Ratafia (liqueur).

1749 Chambers (B-Al.); 1813 O. Targ. Tozzetti. <Fr. *ratafia* (B-Al., M-D., Pr.), *ratafiat, tafiat* 1675; a Creole term of the West Indies. Alberti translates Fr. *ratafia* by *amarasco* (1788).

realizzare. To realise (one's plans, etc.).

Realisare in Chambers, 1749 (B-Al.) (possibly an Anglicism?). *Realizzare* as a financial term in Algarotti (to realise assets'). 'Se le speranze dateci dal Direttorio Francese si realizzano, il diavolo non sarà sí brutto' (V. Monti, letter of 10th March 1798 [Bertoldi, II, 71]). Bernardoni, 1812, has both the verb and *realizzazione* 'realisation, performance, carrying out of intentions'. <Fr. *réaliser* and *réalisation* (Panz., B-Al., Pr.), 16th cent., Loysel. Alberti translates Fr. *réaliser* by *effettuare*.

rebus. Riddle, conundrum.

1749 Chambers (B-Al.); *rebuss* 1814 in Turin (B-Al.); 19th cent. sources. Latinism coined in France (prob. in Picardy) *rebus*, 1512 (Panz., B-Al., Pr.). Alberti 1788 translates Fr. *rebus* by *equivoco, concettino*.

redingotta. Fashions: Frock coat.

Redingotti (pl.) attested in Lucca, 1748 (Pr.). Goldoni (1763, *Il Ventaglio*) has *rodengotto*; *rodingotto* and *rudingotto* in the 18th cent. Alberti, however, translates the Fr. word by *pastrano* and *palandrano*. <Fr. *redingote*, 1725: 'habillement qui vient des Anglais et qui est ici très commun à présent . . . surtout pour monter à cheval', Barbier, *Chronique de la Régence* (B-Wart.) (B-Al., M-D., Pr.). Fr. term < Eng. *riding-coat*, a garment designed for convenience when riding, an essential feature of the style until recent times being the buttons at the waist which allowed the skirt to be tucked up. The *redingotta* assumed various forms at different periods, and was used particularly in the late 18th cent. and early 19th; in the 20th cent. the word has been applied also to women's fashons (see Panzini's article *redingote*).

regime. Medic., polit.: (a) Diet; (b) Government, regime.

The native word *regimine* in the sense of 'government' (abstract) appears *c.* 1300 in Fra Giordano, but has no direct connection with 18th cent. *regime*, which although ultimately a Latinism from the same source (*regimen*) entered It. through the intermediary of French (T-Bell., F-A., B-Al., M-D., Pr.). T-Bell. (who favour the pronunciation règime as a less offensive Gallicism) register the medical term in A. Cocchi (1695–1758), *Consulti medici*. Alberti is unaware of a single word corresponding to the Fr. *régime* in this sense, but it appears again under the form *reggime* in Leone, 1828. The political signification (pron. *regíme*) dates from the Napoleonic era in view of its first attestation in Bernardoni 1812. In this case the sense, though similar, diverges significantly from that of the mediaeval It. word, denoting a particular system of government (cf. Eng. *regime*, borrowed from French in analogous circumstances [1792]). Fr. *régime* (*regimen* in 13th cent., sense as OIt.) is found in the political acceptation during the 16th cent., and as a medical term in La Rochefoucauld.

reprimenda. Reprimand, rebuke.

18th cent. B-Al.; 1812 Bernardoni; rejected as a Gallicism by T-Bell., F-A., 1877, Rigutini. < Fr. *réprimande* (Panz., B-Al., Pr.), *reprimende* 1549 R. Estienne. Latinising graphy in Italian (*e ~ a*), with resultant phonetic adaptation.

responsabile, responsabilità. Responsible.

T-Bell., who use the spelling *risponsabile*, *risponsabilità*, cite both words in Magalotti, *Lettere*. Alberti, 1777 (who also refers to Magalotti) has the adjective only: '*Risponsabile*. Dal francese Responsable. Ch'è in impegno di render ragione di alcuna cosa.' Bernardoni, 1812, has *responsabile* and *responsabilità* as indispensable technical terms; F-A. register them as legal terms from French, and Panz. adds, '... del primo Ottocento'. Fanfani's assertion that the terms are 'generally condemned' seems an exaggeration, even in the mid-19th century. T-Bell. admit that both words are current among townsfolk. Panz. observes: 'li sancisce pienamente l'uso, e da tempo'. < Fr. *responsable*, *responsabilité*, acc. to Alb., T-Bell., F-A., Panz.; modern authorities are more cautious, but the late 19th cent. opinion is supported by the late dating of the Italian as opposed to the French words. Both French adj. and noun already in the Middle Ages have the sense of 'responsible for one's acts and those of others'—Jehan de Stavelot and a law of 1440 respectively (Godef.). The background is predominantly bureaucratic too.

retroattivo. Legal: Retroactive (of laws).

1788 Alberti, as a legal term. Tramater, 1840, and 19th cent. lexicographical sources generally. Tomm. e Bell. do not register it as a Gallicism, probably because (as Rig. and Panz. point out) it had by then taken firm root in the language. 'Questa parola non è di origine italiana, ma ci venne con le leggi francesi in sul finire del secolo passato' (F-A., 1877). < Fr. *rétroactif*, in an *Ordonnance* of 1534. The abstract *retroattività* is attested a little later, in 1805 (Alb., *Diz. univ.*) and is in all probability borrowed from Fr. *rétroactivité*, though the first example of the French word registered so far slightly postdates the Italian (1812, Mozin). It may well be much older in view of the adjective's dating.

rigodone. Dance: Rigadoon.

An 18th cent. borrowing, acc. to M-*Stor.*, p. 576. < Fr. *rigodon*, *rigaudon*, 1694 Th. Corneille (though presumably current earlier since the corresponding Gallicism in English is registered by the *OED* in 1691). From the name of a certain Rigaud, who invented the dance, according to Rousseau.

risorsa. Resource.

The archaic form *risursa* (usual in 18th cent.) occurs as early as 1753 (B-Al.). *Risorsa* at this period is rare, but appears as a trans. of Fr. *ressource* in Alberti 1777: '*Ressource* ... mezzo, verso. Ceux qui sentent la force de ce mot ont accoutumé de le franciser dans le discours familier, et disent *Risorsa*. Mais c'est une licence un peu forte, eu égard à la délicatesse de la langue Italienne.' *Resorsa* in a 16th cent. text (Marchi) is an ephemeral loan isolated from the 18th cent. transfer: 'Li soldati non hanno più altre resorse, se non andare e bevere alla marina ... e passare in Iscozia' (T-Bell., who give as alternatives to *risorsa* in its different significations *sorgente d'utile, nuova fonte, rinfranco, vantaggio, spediente, partito, ripiego, provento, rendita*). The form *risorsa* is usual from Bernardoni, 1812, onwards. Most lexicographers condemn it—some strongly—while agreeing that usage has accepted it (T-Bell., F-A., Rig.). <Fr. *ressource* (above sources, Panz., B-Al., M-D., Pr.) 12th cent.

rondò. Music: Rondeau, rondo.

The tune accompanying a *rondeau*, or any musical or vocal composition in which the motive is reiterated. Prati registers the plural *rondeaux* in 1812, Minoia, and both Pr. and B-Al. refer to P. Lichtenthal, *Diz. e biografia della musica*, Milan, 1826. Migliorini (*Storia*, p. 576) includes *rondò* among 18th cent. Gallicisms without citing references; but we note that the Italian word has already passed into English (*rondo*) by 1797 (OED), and the shift Fr. > It. > Eng. is not in dispute. <Fr. *rondeau* (*rondel* 14th cent., G. de Machaut), acc. to T-Bell., F-A. (2nd edition, 1881), Panz., B-Al., Pr., M-D., etc.

sanofieno. Botan., agric.: Sainfoin, lucerne.

18th cent. B-Al. Lastri, *Corso di agricoltura pratica*. <Fr. *sainfoin* (B-Al., Pr.), 1600, O. de Serres, but *sainct foin* 1549, R. Estienne.

scialuppa. Naut.: Sloop (one of a ship's boats).

Algarotti (1712–64); 1754 in Sicilian, Del Bono, *Diz. sicil.-it.-lat.*, acc. to Prati; 1777 Alberti. <Fr. *chaloupe* (B-Al., M-D., Pr.), *chaloppe* 1522, probably < Dutch *sloep*.[1]

sciampagna. Champagne.

N. Forteguerri (1674–1735), acc. to Pr.; Gasparo Gozzi (1713–86) (T-Bell.). T-Bell. note the Gallicism, but accept it. Adaptation of Fr. *champagne* (B-Al., M-D., Pr., Panz., etc.), dating from 1732 (B-Wart.) in the sense 'vin de Champagne'. Invented in 1670 (acc. to Panzini) by Don Perignon, cellarer of the abbey of Hautevilliers (Épernay), champagne became well known in France and elsewhere in the early 18th cent.

sciatta. Naut. (*vide infra*).

Two types of vessel are involved here: (a) a light, swift craft, a kind of pinnace, usually a ship's boat, (b) a flat-bottomed barge used to transport merchandise, and esp. as a lighter for unloading ships. In Fr., *chatte* appears in sense (a) mid-18th cent., Savarien; sense (b) is usually given as an early 19th century term (Jal, Boiste, 1838: 'espèce de gabare pour décharger les bateaux'; Chambaud, 1815, Dict. Français-anglais: 'two masted ship, kind of lighter'); but already Alberti, 1777, explains Fr. *chatte* as 'barque qui a les hanches et les épaules rondes, dont les moindres sont de soixante tonneaux'—plainly the second signification. It may be assumed that It. *sciatta* in sense (a) (Saverien, Alb. 1777) is a Fr. loan, despite the fact that the Fr. word appears at the same period, and that Alberti (seemingly unaware of a Fr. cognate) translates It. *sciatta* only by *canot*. Fr. *chatte* 'barge' (sense (b)) has, however, all the appearance of being a popular etymology < It. *chiatta*, 'barge' (< Genoese *ciata*, lit. 'flat bottomed' <Lat. *platta*), which appears in G. Lami, 1770, Baretti (1777), G. Targ. Tozz., but is clearly an older word, possibly dating from the Middle Ages in Genoese. In sum, Fr. *chatte* 'small, swift boat, of uncertain origin' (possibly Dutch? or an indigenous metaphor?) is taken into Italian during the 18th cent.;

---

1. It. *cialupa* in Cirni, 1567 (B-Al.) is a separate loan from Sp. *chalupa* which in turn is probably drawn from French.

on the other hand, It. *chiatta* (a masc. *chiatto*, translated by 'bac, chaland' is also in Alb.) 'large barge or lighter', entering Fr. no doubt directly from Genoese in the later 18th cent., is mistakenly called a *chatte*. A similar paronymic attraction may explain Eng. *cat*, 1699 onward (OED), a barge-like cargo vessel of about 500 tons engaged esp. in the timber trade in north-east England.[1,2]

sofà. Sofa.

Algarotti; Parini; Alberti, 1777, who registers it firstly as an item of furniture used in Turkey, secondly as a 'sorta di letticciuolo ad uso di sedervi sopra' (i.e. used in Italy). <Fr. *sofa* (B-Al., M-D., Pr.). The Fr. *sofa* appears 1560 in the original Turkish sense ('estrade élevée couverte de coussins' B-Wart.) and is found 1657 onward meaning the modern piece of furniture. Ultimately < Arab. *suffa*, a cushion.

sonnambulo. Sleep-walker.

B-Al. give *sonnambulo* in Alb. 1805; but Alberti 1777 translates Fr. *somnambule* by *sonambolo* (sic) and the fact that he registers *sonnambulo* èlsewhere (as a synonym of *nottambulo*) suggests that the term was genuinely in use at that period, not a mere phonetic transposition of the French. Both *sonnambulo* and *sonnambulismo* appear in Leone, 1828. <Fr. *somnambule* 1690, *somnambulisme*, 1730 (B-Al., Pr.).

stallare. Naut.: To stem the tide; to anchor until the tide becomes favourable.

1788 Alberti (not in 1777 edition); 18th cent. Prati. <Fr. *estaler*, *étaler* acc. to B-Al., Pr. OFr. *estaler* 'to halt, rest' in 12th cent.; 'to resist, hold one's own against' in 13th cent.

stato maggiore. Milit.: General staff.

Alessandro d'Antonj (1714–84) (Pr.); 1788 Alberti (in both It. and Fr. sections). Calque of Fr. *état-major* (B-Al., Pr.) 1678, Guillet, prob. < Sp. *estado mayor*.

suicidio, suicidarsi. Suicide, to commit suicide.

Suicidio 1777 Alberti: 'Voce dell'uso. Uccision di se stesso.' Also in Fr. > It. section, as trans. of Fr. *suicide*. The form *suicida* appears in Alberti, *Diz. univ.*, 1805. <Fr. *suicide* 1745 (Panz., B-Al., Pr.), a word coined in Engl. (*suicide*, 1728) ≠ *homicide*. *Suicidare* in Ugolini 1848, *suicidarsi* in 1860 are also Gallicisms (F-A., Panz., B-Al., Pr.). Fanfani notes and condemns the pleonasm of the reflexive, pointing out that the Académie Française is equally critical of the usage. Fr. *se suicider* in 1795 (B-Wart.).

tarantismo. Medic.: St. Vitus' dance.

1749 Chambers (B-Al.); 1828 Leone. <Fr. *tarentisme* (B-Al., Pr.), 1741 Col de Villars < *tarentule* (with back-formation) '*tarantula*'.

teiera. Teapot.

Archaic graphy *theiera* in Magalotti 1711; *teiera* current in 19th cent.; Panzini. <Fr. *théière*, 1723, Savary (Panz., B-Al., Pr.). The form *tettiera* (little used) in Rambelli 1850 was a remodelling upon the alternative French form *thétière* ≠ *cafetière*, used frequently in the 18th cent.

tirabusciò. Corkscrew.

Tirabussón 1752 Goldoni. *Tirabussone* 1788, Alberti (marked as a recent addition); *tirabuscione* in Alb. 1805 (B-Al.); *tirabusòn*, F-A.; *tirabusciò*, Rig.; numerous other

---

1. The English nautical term *cat* mentioned by Chambord (later 19th cent. *cat-boat*, still used to denote a rig of yacht in America) is part of semantic group (a). It enters It. in its turn during the 20th century meaning a kind of pleasure yacht or dinghy.

2. The mediaeval French nautical term *chaz*, *cat*, 12th cent., *gatus* 1175 du Cange is an entirely different vessel. It was so called on account of the grappling-irons with which this boarding craft was provided. *Chat* in ModFr. still means 'grapnel' and other hooked instruments in technology.

graphies. Panz. registers the Fr. form *tire-bouchon* as 'usata per vizio in parecchi dialetti'. Replaced in 19th cent. by *cavatappi*. <Fr. *tire-bouchon*, 1718, Acad. (all sources agree).

toletta. Toilet (*vide infra*).

Veneroni, 1709, translates Fr. *toilette* by *teletta*, described as 'toile qu'on estend sur une table pour y mettre le deshabillé, et les hardes de nuit, comme le peignoir, les peignes, le bonnet, etc.'. *Toelette* 'dressing-table' in Fagiuoli, 1739; *toletta* in Algarotti, Alb. 1777, and elsewhere in the general sense of 'toilet requisites' (for a woman). Prati registers *toeletta* as the name of a Florentine fashion magazine, 1770. Other forms: *tualetta*, *tualette*, *tueletta* in Biscioni and Fagiuoli. The Fr. word is frequent in the 19th century, at which period all forms of the word are strongly opposed by purists; cf. Fanfani (1877): 'I Parrucchieri e i Barbieri ora si sono nobilitati, e le loro Botteghe sono divenute Sale da toeletta, e Saloni—Ah, Figari, Figari!' Fr. word, *toilette*, of which the semantic development passes through four stages: (a) *tellette*, *telette* (1352, B-Wart.) dimin. of *toile*, which becomes specialised for 'embroidered cloth laid on a table' (see Veneroni, *supra*) in the late 16th cent.; (b) by metonymy, the table itself, 'dressing-table', Régnier; (c) the action of dressing, and (d) sum of articles required, later 17th cent.

tormalina. Mineral: Tourmaline (aluminium boron silicate).

Turmalina 1771 B-Al.; *tormalina* 1817, L. Bassi. <Fr. *tourmaline* (M-D., B-Al.), *tourmalin* 1758, prob. < Sinhalese.

tralingaggio. Naut.: Crow's foot, euphroe.

A rope which divides into several other ropes. 1788 Alberti ('cavo a più branche che serve a vari usi'). <Fr. *trélingage* (B-Al.), 18th cent., Bougainville.

tranquillizzare. To calm, pacify.

Used on several occasions by V. Monti meaning 'to set a person's mind at rest' (e.g. about the supposed illness of a relative) (letters of 5th Nov. 1796, 4th Apr. 1798. 'Tranquillizzatevi!' = 'Don't worry!', 12th Sept. 1798, etc.). Also in Parini (B-Al.), Bernardoni (glossed as *tranquillare*). <Fr. *tranquilliser* (B-Al., Pr.), 15th cent., O. de Saint-Gellais. Equivalent of indigenous It. *tranquillare*, 13th cent., *Novellino*.

tuppè, toppè. Toupet, small wig.

Toppè pre-1744 in L. Pascoli (B-Al.), 1760 Goldoni; *tuppè* in G. Gozzi; also *tupè*, *topè* (*vide* M-*Stor.*, p. 579). Referred to a hair style in the eighteenth century; cf. Alberti, 1788: 'Quell' adornamento moderno che si fa de' capelli, tratti dall'insù della fronte all'indietro' (s.v. *toppè*). Adaptation of Fr. *toupet* (B-Al., M-D., Pr., etc.) 'lock of hair' in 12th cent. Prati and Panz. (1931 and subsequently) register the locutions *avere il tuppè*, *avere un bel tuppè* as recent imitations of Fr. *avoir du toupet*, 'to be impudent, cheeky; to "have a nerve" '.

uniforme. Milit., etc.: Uniform.

18th cent. (Lastri) in this sense, acc. to B-Al. 1812 Bernardoni (= '*divisa*, *assisa*'), d'Ayala. Synonym of *montura* (q.v. *supra*). Alberti 1788 has *abito uniforme* (Fr. section) in which the adj. is closer semantically to the French than to the indigenous It. signification, suggesting a transliteration of Fr. *habit uniforme*. <Fr. *uniforme* (19th cent. purists, B-Al., Pr.), 18th cent., but *habit uniforme* end 17th cent., Saint-Simon. Still both subst. and adj. phrase in Alberti. (*Vide uniformizzare*, 19th cent. Fr. > It. loans.)

varecco. Raw soda (originally extracted from sea-weed).

Varec 1771 Bomare (B-Al.); *vareck* 1813 O. Targ. Tozzetti; *varecco* 19th cent. Also *varecchina*, kind of washing-powder. <Fr. *varech*, *varec* (Panz., B-Al., Pr.), 1125 (B-Wart.; cf. also *warec* 1181, du Cange, 'jetsam'); frequently meant 'wreck' in the Middle Ages, though the sense 'seaweed' is found early, esp. in Normandy; ult. < Old Norse or Old English.

French Influences on Italian during the Eighteenth Century

Political relations with France during the eighteenth century fall into three distinct parts. Up to 1748 a series of pan-European conflicts arising out of the rival dynastic claims of Hapsburg and Bourbon led to the intervention of French military and diplomatic power on a number of occasions. Certain key moves of the wars of the League of Augsbourg were played out upon Italian territory (battle of Staffarda, 1690, siege of Turin, 1706), control of which—a coveted prize—was apportioned among the victorious powers by the treaties of Utrecht (1713) and Rastadt (1714). An important shift of sovereignty ensued which in its turn led to a cultural re-orientation whose effects were to become manifest by the mid-century. Northern Italy, Sardinia, Naples and the fortified places of Tuscany fell to the Emperor, and the tutelage of the region as a whole began to pass from Spanish into Austrian hands. A further readjustment of boundaries was sanctioned by the Second Treaty of Vienna, following upon the intervention of the Quadruple Alliance to check renewed Spanish aspirations in Sardinia, Parma and Tuscany prompted by the ambitions of Elisabeth Farnese. The War of the Polish Succession saw French forces committed yet again in northern Italy, this time with the help of Spain as well as Piedmont, for the purpose of limiting Imperial power in that theatre. As for the Wars of the Austrian Succession—though these affected Italy marginally (battle of Piacenza, capture of Genoa by a combined Austrian and English assault) their main centre of activity was outside the territory. The Treaty of Aix-la-Chapelle (Oct. 1748) was the last re-shuffle to affect the Peninsula before the final decade of the century. Austria was now confirmed as master instead of Spain, and under Austrian hegemony Italy was able in her turn to profit by the intellectual tolerance associated with benevolent despotism. This indirect influence—an important one, admittedly—is the only lexically relevant datum which emerges from half a century of jockeying for power between the absolute rulers of Europe.

Developments from 1789 to the end of the century are cast in an entirely different mould. The French invasion of 1794 was more than a feat of revolutionary arms; it was an early instance of ideological warfare in the modern sense. Military, political and cultural aims went hand in hand. Abstract revolutionary ideals were deliberately imposed as well as practical administrative systems, in a spirit close to that of evangelism. The wars of the early eighteenth century had still been largely family affairs among princes; the Revolution applied its tenets to society as a whole, demanding active participation from everyone. Its cult was supported by a highly organised system of literary propaganda[1] and by exploiting all available means of dissemination. In these circumstances official recognition and encouragement of the French language seemed the rational policy to adopt.

But this final decade of the eighteenth century already belongs to another world. Within the eighteenth century proper, as in the seventeenth, the evidence of cultural contacts we are seeking is not to be found in political upheavals. Although the period was at all times one of struggle and change its greatest campaigns were not fought on the battlefield but in men's minds. For this reason the interval of peace and enlightened progress from 1748 to 1789 is of capital importance.

By the middle of the century Venice and Genoa, whose political and commercial domination had in the past often given an impulse to linguistic exchange, as we have seen, were in full decline, but in other places men eagerly pressed on with their search for human betterment. In the monarchies enlightened ministers directed home affairs, Giambattista Bogino in the Kingdom of Sardinia under Carlo Emanuele III, Tannucci in the Two Sicilies (though a more reactionary attitude prevailed later in the century under Victor Amadeo III). The new spirit worked to greatest effect in the states which the Hapsburgs ruled. Under Maria Theresa and Joseph II Milan took the lead. There was scope for bold innovators like Pietro Verri and the Marquis Cesare Beccaria, famous both as reformers in the legal and economic field and as men of letters through their association with the journal *Il Caffè*, modelled on the *Spectator* and launched by Verri in 1764. Similar trends were at work in Tuscany.

But political and social reform was only an end-product of broader principles which have their origin in the international cultural and intellectual climate of the Age of Reason. It is not our place to stray into the cultural historian's preserves by attempting a definition of *Illuminismo*; all we need note is that a vital link existed, even though it was an indirect one, between the spirit of Enlightenment and Franco-Italian linguistic relationships. In Italy as in every other European country the new ideas were propagated through the medium of French. France's part in this respect was the object of intensive research quite a long time ago. The findings are readily accessible.[2]

1. See Paul Hazard, *La Révolution française et les lettres italiennes*, Paris 1910, esp. Chs. II and III (*Les Agents de l'influence française* and *L'Influence française*).

2. See A. Schiaffini, *Aspetti della crisi linguistica italiana del Settecento*, in *Momenti*, pp. 71–115; G. Devoto, *Profilo*, Ch. VII, *Il nuovo bilinguismo*; M-Stor., Ch. X, *Il Settecento*, esp. pp. 497–508, 524–9, 574–9; B. Migliorini, *La questione della lingua*, in *Problemi ed orientamenti critici di lingua e di letteratura italiana* (ed. A. Momigliano), Milan 1948-49, Vol. III, pp. 44–51; id., 'Panorama dell'italiano settecentesco', in *La Ressegna della letteratura italiana*, LXI (1957), pp. 431–5; and G. Maugain's staple survey *Le Français en Italie* in Brunot, *Hist.*, Vol. VIII, Part 1. For French and Italian contacts in general at this time, see H. Bédarida and P. Hazard, *L'Influence française en Italie au dix-huitième siècle*,

Few points of contention remain, though there are understandable differences of emphasis between French and Italian scholars and the universal character of problems raised during this 'crisis of European conscience' often makes it hard to pin-point those factors which are linguistically pertinent. Here again as in the seventeenth century we can help by checking the findings against lexical evidence.

The intermediary role of French has been explained in terms of cultural supremacy, national prestige, intrinsic linguistic merit and pure chance.

The situation is indeed to some extent a fortuitous one, in that French as an authoritative, unified national idiom happened to be available at the right moment in the history of European culture. A suitable medium for international discussion was to hand at the precise time when it was most needed. There is some truth too in the contention—so dear to the eighteenth century —that French was inherently fit to carry out the task which history assigned to it, though the modern linguist cannot read Rivarol's claims for the intrinsic excellence of his mother-tongue without a smile. We no longer feel impelled to speculate whether French is *a priori* more 'logical' than Italian. And yet the question of logic is not entirely irrelevant. French possessed certain characteristics which could be described and accounted for in terms of logic and rationality, and as such it attracted the admiration of a rational age. All through the period claims for the universality of French on the grounds of its immanent rationality were echoed approvingly by Italian intellectuals.[1]

Mere chance and a certain intrinsic aptitude would not in themselves have singled out French to be the interpreter of modern European culture. The decisive factor was that of prestige in various forms. Intellectual prestige, first and foremost. As Schiaffini rightly points out, Classical French was the embodiment of Cartesian thought: it therefore inevitably shared some of the approval which, as we have already seen,[2] Italians felt for this typically French philosophical system: 'Il francese ha avuto potenza di proselitismo idiomatico tra le persone colte di quasi l'intera Europa del secolo XVIII perché strumento e segno del Razionalismo cartesiano e dell'Illuminismo, che è d'origine inglese, ma si era permeato di spirito razionalistico cartesiano, e in Francia aveva assunto una forma genialmente originale e una singolare forza divulgativa ... Dal razionalismo la lingua francese fu l'organo. E fu il riflesso.'[3]

Paris, 1934; C. Pellegrini, *Relazioni*, pp. 63–71 and 91–3 (*bibliog.*); and the first part of A. Graf, *L'Anglomania e l'influsso inglese in Italia nel secolo XVIII*, Turin, 1911, which studies 18th century *gallomania* (and *gallofobia*) as a prelude to *anglomania*.

1. The 'logical order' of French syntax and periodic structure which was felt to reflect an 'ordine naturale delle idee' was contrasted with the 'illogical' patterning of Trecento Italian, which many considered to have been vitiated by Latinism (e.g. Giuseppe Baretti, *Frusta*, Nos. IV and XXV, cited M-*Stor.*, p. 513).

2. *Vide supra*, 17th cent. Fr. > It. evaluation.

3. *Momenti*, pp. 76–7.

E

The *Illuministi* read Locke, Spinoza and Leibnitz; but for them and for Italy as a whole the really great figures were French *philosophes*—Montesquieu, Voltaire, Rousseau, Condillac, d'Alembert—particularly those who contributed to the *Encyclopédie*. Descartes was read in Latin and French before the opening of the century and translated into Italian by 1722. By 1760 a revolution had occurred in Italian thought under the impact of French speculative literature.

In 1700 the reputation of France's novelists and playwrights was already high. Their prestige increased as the century progressed. 'Tout notre théâtre' (Brunot observes) 'passe . . . en italien: les tragédies et comédies de Pierre et Thomas Corneille, Racine, Molière, Crébillon, Destouches, de la Fosse, de la Motte, Pradon, Quinault, Rotrou, Voltaire, pour ne citer que les auteurs les plus connus. De 1708 à 1799 paraissent en Italie quinze éditions en langue italienne de l'*Iphigénie* de Racine . . . la pièce a été traduite par neuf auteurs différents. De 1743 à 1798 on ne compte pas moins de vingt-deux éditions de *Zaïre* en italien; il y a eu dix traducteurs.'[1] One of these literary contacts which has been most assiduously explored is the influence exerted by Molière (whose debt to the *Commedia dell'Arte* we have already acknowledged) upon Italian comic playwrights, above all on his Italian counterpart Carlo Goldoni, who spent thirty years of his life in Paris and whose works include a number written in French itself.[2] French novels and fictional works of a lighter sort were equally prized. 'Chi non sa' asks Algarotti, 'quanti libretti da passar agevolmente il tempo non ispiccino continuamente da quella fonte perenne?'[3] Alfieri bears testimony to the vast number of French novelettes imported in his younger days. According to Graf the vogue of the *roman* set in early, before the end of the seventeenth century, with La Calprenède's *Cassandre*, *Cléopâtre*, *Faramond* and Mlle de Scudéry's *Le Grand Cyrus* in special demand. Fénelon's *Télémaque* was a best-seller; Brunot estimates that the number of editions printed in Italy before 1789 was not less than thirty. Other favoured authors were Fontenelle, Boileau and La Fontaine. Another early literary contact arose through Italian interest in French ecclesiastical writings— sermons, apologies for the Christian religion and hagiography—which came to be widely known largely through the efforts of the Jesuits. Bossuet, Bourdaloue and Massillon were frequently translated.[4]

1. Brunot, *Hist.*, VIII, 1, p. 89. See also the recent extremely detailed article by Renata Carloni Valentini, 'Le Traduzioni italiane di Racine', in *Contributi dell'istituto di filologia moderna, serie francese*, Vol. V (Università cattolica del Sacro Cuore), Milan 1968, pp. 203-448.

2. The reader is referred again to P. Toldo, *L'Œuvre de Molière*, cited earlier and to C. Levi, *Saggio sulla bibliografia italiana di Molière*, in the volume *Studi molieriani*, Palermo, 1922. For a useful bibliography of studies on Molière and Goldoni see Pellegrini, op. cit., p. 90.

3. *Pensieri diversi*, cited Graf, p. 10.   4. Brunot, *Hist.*, VIII, 1, p. 88.

By the middle of the century the impact of French literature of every genre was immense. Even critics whose judgement one respects like Melchiorre Cesarotti and robust Giuseppe Baretti felt at the time that Italian letters were in eclipse, at least temporarily. 'Gli Italiani sono tanto al disotto de' Francesi in fatto di lettere quanto i Marocchini lo sono agl'Italiani.'[1]

It is usual nowadays to attach less importance to French political and military prestige than the francophiles of the eighteenth century did. To our age the reign of Louis Quinze appears at best a pale reflection of that of *le roi soleil*; but we should remember that contemporary observers had not our scale of comparison to go by, did not enjoy a relative prospect in the way we do, and that they would in any event be inclined to make a progressive, optimistic assessment of developments in France, as elsewhere. The later seventeenth century created a stereotype Frenchman whose credentials Europe accepted without question until the Revolution; a person not only possessed of good taste, elegance, wit and learning, but blessed in addition with unparalleled wealth and backed up by political and military power such as the world had not previously known—or could no longer call to mind. Travel between the two countries continued without interruption even in time of war, and obviously played an important part in fostering admiration for things French. The list of those who visited France includes, apart from Goldoni, P. Martello, Scipione Maffei, A. Conti, Alfieri, Algarotti, Lami, Baretti, Alessandro and Pietro Verri, Beccaria, Metastasio, Giuliani, Bettinelli and the two Pindemontes. Among French personalities who helped to interpret their country's outlook by travelling in the Peninsula—whose visits, that is, one associates more readily with disseminating French ideas rather than absorbing Italian culture—special mention must be made of Montesquieu, Madame du Boccage and Condillac. A large, often highly influential French population drawn from all walks of life was established in most of the sizeable Italian cities, particularly Parma, whose court during du Tillot's ministry, as Graf observes, was more French than Italian and worthy to be compared with the Valois court under Catherine de Médicis.[2]

Despite his speculations about the virtues of primitive existence eighteenth century man in practice valued above all else life in an organised society. He was a confirmed city-dweller. A great city was held to be a desirable institution in itself, since among other benefits it stimulated intellectual progress by affording opportunities for human contact. According to Algarotti and his contemporaries it was this lack of a metropolis that most seriously hampered

---

1. Baretti, *Frusta*, XIX. Cf. also Cesarotti: 'La biblioteca delle donne e degli uomini del mondo non è che francese' (*Saggio sulla filosofia delle lingue*, Part II, Sect. XIII, p. 100). I have used the edition by R. Spongano, Florence, 1943.

2. *Anglomania*, p. 9. See also Brunot, *Hist.*, VIII, 1, pp. 100-4. Chs. III–VII deal with the diffusion of French in different regions of Italy (pp. 95–120).

the development of Italian culture. Affirming that 'la vera accademia è un capitale', Algarotti dreams of a centre of civilisation in which 'otto in novecento mila persone si elettrizzino insieme'.[1] No wonder that Paris, the prototype of such a capital, came to be a centre of pilgrimage, the ultimate goal of a Grand Tour made in reverse. Not everyone, of course, went there in search of intellectual enlightenment. Whereas Algarotti held Paris and its society in esteem because they embodied good taste and rational behaviour others found more commonplace features to admire—physical amenities, externals and trappings of the fashionable world.[2] We may consequently expect to find in the lexicon some evidence of a desire to imitate the Gallic way of life in its culturally superficial aspects as well as in those of greater moment.

So much for the question of prestige—the external factor, that is, which exerted its influence upon the Italian *ethos*. It is an unusually strong one: but in this instance the internal impulse, the predisposition towards acceptance is almost equally powerful. Among these circumstances which cleared the way for Gallicism we can detect a certain negative element. Up to a point the intervention of French is encouraged by deficiencies in the native idiom: the need for a simpler, more matter-of-fact prose style in which to discuss the practical sciences, above all political science and economics; the centrifugal effect of dialects, and the existence of a 'netto distacco della lingua poetica così dalla parlata come dalla tecnico-scientifica', all of which factors 'acuiscono l'opposizione fra l'ambiente storico-linguistico italiano, dalle molte facce, e quello francese sostanzialmente unitario'.[3] Far more important, however, is the positive aspect, the mood of active encouragement rather than passive compliance. It was by a deliberate choice that the *Illuministi* exercised their right to take words in handfuls from whatever source they thought useful, and to find new ones if the old ones would not do.[4] Alessandro Verri's mock-legal 'solenne rinunzia alla pretesa purezza della toscana favella'[5] was

1. From a letter written to Voltaire in 1746: cited by Migliorini, 'La questione della lingua', op. cit., p. 46.

2. Graf, pp. 16–19.   3. Devoto, *Profilo*, p. 108.

4. 'Noi vogliamo prendere il buono quand'anche fosse ai confini dell'universo, e se dall'inda, o dall'americana lingua ci si fornisse qualche vocabolo ch'esprimesse un'idea nostra meglio che colla lingua italiana, noi lo adopereremo.'

'Se italianizzando le parole francesi, tedesche, inglesi, turche, greche, arabe, sclavone, noi potremmo rendere meglio le nostre idee, non ci asterremo di farlo per timore o del Casa, o del Crescimbeni, o del Villani, o di tant'altri. . . .'

'Se Petrarca, se Dante, se Boccaccio, se Casa e gli altri testi di lingua hanno avuta la facoltà d'inventar parole nuove e buone, così pretendiamo che tale libertà convenga ancora a noi: conciossiaché abbiamo due braccia, due gambe, un corpo ed una testa fra due spalle com'eglino l'ebbero' (*Il Caffè*, edited by Sergio Romagnuoli (*Collana di periodici italiani e stranieri*, 3), Milan, 1960, pp. 39-40).

5. *Il Caffè*, July 1764, op. cit., p. 39.

made with mixed motives, partly as a boutade against purism and pedantry (which for him were personified in the Accademici della Crusca) and partly an attack by implication in the Voltairean style against prohibitions and interdicts of any kind; but it was also a frank declaration of intention, of action which was to be carried out according to principles consonant with the spirit of the time and accepted without question by the majority of his contemporaries. Towards the end of the century, with the tide of emotion rising all around, Cesarotti still stands upon the authority of cool reason in this matter: 'Se la lingua francese ha dei termini appropriati ad alcune idee necessarie che in Italia mancan di nome, e se questi termini hanno tutti le condizioni [of euphony, phonetic and grammatical conformity[1]] sopra richiesti, per quale strano e ridicolo aborrimento recusarem di accettarli?'[2] A similar reasonable attitude, and despite first appearances a profound liberalism with regard to linguistic problems is revealed even in those passages where Cesarotti seems most strongly to disapprove of Gallicism: 'Io rinforzo le mie proteste, e mi dichiaro di condannar altamente la licenza di coloro chi vanno tutto giorno infrancescando la lingua italiana senza proposito. Quando non ci fossero altre ragioni di condannar questo abuso converrebbe ancora astenersene per non offendere la vanità nazionale, *che nelle cose piccole si fa forse sentir più al vivo che nelle grandi.*'[3]

Nationalistic purism of a kind which becomes so common in the later nineteenth and twentieth centuries was as yet scarcely known. The linguistic patriotism of Rivarol, we note in passing, springs from quite different motives. The formation of Classical French is an incidental accomplishment arising out of cultural unification; it did not prefigure or symbolise a more fundamental unity—social, political—to which its speakers aspired. Hints of a reaction in favour of Italian can be found even during the hey-day of Gallomania, e.g. in Deodati de' Tovazzi's *Dissertation sur l'excellence de la langue italienne* published in Paris in 1761, but only as the century approaches its end does opposition gather impetus, finding expression in the works of Gianfrancesco Galiani Napione (*Dell'uso e dei pregi della lingua italiana*, Turin, 1791), Carlo Gozzi (*Chiacchiera intorno alla lingua litterale italiana*, published posthumously) and a number of lesser-known writers. Most of the linguistic gallophobia prior to 1789 like the outbursts of anti-French feeling in general

1. In the *Saggio*, Part III, Sect. III, p. 76, Cesarotti describes the perfect word as one which is 'conveniente all'idea', i.e. one which 'rappresenta vivamente l'oggetto o colla struttura de' suoi elementi, o con qualche somiglianza o rapporto'; it should also be 'ben derivato, analogo nella formazione, non disacconcio nel suono'.

2. *Saggio*, Part III, Sect. XIII, p. 99. Cesarotti's shrewd, lucid essay, which tells us a great deal about eighteenth century attitudes towards modern linguistic thought, was published first in 1785 with the title *Saggio sopra la lingua italiana*, and again in 1800 as *Saggio sulla filosofia delle lingue*, with minor additions.

3. Ibid., p. 99. The italics are mine.

which occurred from time to time even when French influence was at its peak can be attributed to the back-wash, the natural force of compensation which a pattern of prestige inevitably stirs up. For most of the century, in short, Gallicism had a clear field of action. The liberal element in Illuminism made its path smooth; Rationalism gave it active support on grounds of principle and practical necessity.

The linguistic advantages of French and the force of intellectual, literary, social and political prestige all work in the same direction to make interference at this period potentially the most intensive within the scope of our study. We have to assess our list of 238 borrowings with this cultural and linguistic preponderance in mind.

Three large semantic groupings stand out from the vocabulary as a whole, (a) fashions, including clothing and textiles (32 loans), (b) scientific terms including medical (28), (c) nautical terms (26). The first two have distinct semantic subdivisions, but the cleavage in each case is not so wide that it destroys the group's unitary character. There are special reasons for putting medical terms on a par with those of botany, geography and the like, as we shall see. Names of textiles are usually associated with fashions and enter as a result of the same influences. Almost all denote cloth used in making up garments either as the material of the dress or as an incidental used in the process of tailoring (e.g. *bugrane*, 'buckram').[1] Of textiles registered in the list several are ultimately of exotic origin: *bugrane* from Arabic, *moerre* from Arabic via English, *calancà* from Persian, *casimiro* and *flanella* from English. Those which hail from France are *buraglia, ciniglia, crespone, droghetto, grosso, mollettone*. The colour names *blu, lillà, gridellino* were used mainly to describe cloth. Not all the fashions of clothing are feminine ones (as *cravatta, redingotta, alla barulè* show) though the majority are; these include styles of dress (*alla ghigliottina*), garments (*andrienne, carmagnola, disabigliè, negligè*) and accessories (*buccola* 'ear-ring', *falbalà*—Eng. 'frills and *furbelows*'—*fisciù, goliè, palatina*). *Calosce* and *clacche* denote new styles in footwear. France by now set the tone for European fashions. Parisian creations were promptly copied and the accompanying designations quickly became common currency among tradesmen and their customers in Italy. Many words appear in commercial lists; there are a large number of them which may very well be Gallicisms, though whether they were coined in France, Italy or elsewhere is often hard to prove.[2]

1. The furnishing fabric *lampasso* is an exception.
2. Cf. the following terms selected from Costanza Filippeschi, *La terminologia della moda nei secoli XVII e XVIII* (Thesis, Univ. of Florence, 1950): *Textiles: bat(t)ista*, 1704 L. Bellini, Savary, prob. < Fr. *batiste*; *bettiglia* a fine muslin, inventory of 1707, prob. < Fr. *bétille*; *biancarde*, a linen cloth, Sav., < Fr. *blancards* (?); *bionda*, a kind of white silk lace, 1st doc. in a Venetian law of 1749 prohibiting its use, prob. < Fr.

Other terms which like those of *couture* have a fashionable slant are those relating to hairdressing—*cignone, frisore* itself, *battilocchio, tuppè*—and words denoting social activities in vogue at a certain moment—*domino* 'fancy dress mask', *gettone* in the sense of 'chip or counter for gambling', names of dances, *allemanda, contraddanza, carmagnola, rigodone*.[1] The slightly precious *colpo di fulmine* 'love at first sight' seemed more appropriate to love in a Fragonard-like setting than richer native expressions. Three key-words which sum up this series of borrowings are *cotteria* 'smart set', *toeletta* 'act of dressing, making-up' and the perennial *agremani*, whose indirect, metonymic evocation of meaning seems to reconcile triviality with sophistication and to add more than a hint of snobbery to both.

What the foregoing loans show clearly is that Gallicism of a less serious kind was endemic in a large range of social activities, at least at certain levels of society. In part they represent the 'bibelots et frivolités' which furnished material for light, topical humour in Maffei and Goldoni or which are the object of more serious protests in Napione (cited above) and Parini (e.g. *A Sylvia, sul vestire alla ghigliottina,* 1795). One recalls the disappointment of the fashionable lady in Goldoni's *Le Femmine Puntigliose* on hearing that a certain fine dress-material was made in Italy rather than France, or Vittoria's famous *mariage* ('wedding-dress') which runs like a *leit-motiv* through *Le Smanie della villeggiatura.* The ultimate in this verbal humour is reached of course in Scipione Maffei's *Il Raguet* (1747), where Alfonso and Ermondo's outrageously Frenchified speech provide opportunity for misunderstandings both real and feigned, subtle and obvious—but obvious for the most part. At the beginning of Act II, sc. 3, well-meaning Anselmo makes a little speech of welcome to the stranger Alfonso, and is immediately assailed by a barrage of Gallicisms for his pains:

ALFONSO.   Ed io mi do l'onore,
signor, di rendergli un million di grazie.
È una gran proprietá la sua, di fare
agli stranier tante onestá. Ciò marca
la bontá del suo cuore, io farò in sorte
che mi conosca sempre tutto a lei.

blonde; bisetta 'cheap lace', Sav., prob. < Fr. *bisette; clissone* 'linen for shirts', Sav., < Breton place-name *Clisson* (Breton names are frequent; *Landernò* and *Plougastel* were also apparently applied to names of stuffs); *mignonnette* 'kind of lace', Sav. *Dresses, accessories: amazzone* 'woman's riding-habit', Abate Labbia (1709–75); *paniere* 'frame for skirt', sem. loan < Fr. *panier* (?); *stincherche* (various graphies), Fagiuoli, 'stock made of voile' (the battle of Steinkerke was fought in 1692); *pleureuses* 'broad white cuffs worn on sleeves when in mourning', 1747 in Milan.

1. Also two 'probables', *maronè* (Fr. *marronné*?), a hair-style in Goldoni (1729) and *giga*, Fr. *gigue* a dance ('jig').

ANSELMO.   Ha ragione Despina: questo supera.
               Viaggiando in questo caldo, ella avrá forse
               patito assai.
ALFONSO.   Per veritá ho sofferto
               molto.
ANSELMO.   Ben mi suppongo ch'ella avrá
               sofferto il patimento con franchezza.
               Ella non gradira quest'orto nostro
               di passeggio, ché avrá veduto altro.
ALFONSO.   Io le dimando perdón.
ANSELMO.   Perché mai?
ALFONSO.   Ne sono soddisfattissimo: a l'ingresso
               si gode subito un bel colpo d'occhio.
               Per li giardini io son portato assai.
               Vorrei pariar che molte gran cittá
               non avranno altrettanto; non ci manca
               se non il gazone e il bacin.
ANSELMO.   Ma volendo
               lavarsi, sará subito servita
               dal custode . . .'[1]

The problem is to decide how much of this rigmarole actually reflected
contemporary speech and how much was purely macaronic. G. Maugain
considered the problem in 1934,[2] and recently M. Cigna took it up again
and treated it in admirable detail in an article 'I Gallicismi nel *Raguet* di
Scipione Maffei', *L.N.*, XVIII, 1957, pp. 63–8. The author carefully sifts out
and lists Gallicisms in fifteen similar works of the time—plays by P. Chiari
and Goldoni, translations and adaptations of French—and compares them
with Maffei's text. It is obvious that many of the words Alfonso and Ermondo
use were current already, or became current later in the century.[3] Some
others appeared subsequently in nineteenth century sources, though whether
this means that they were used in Maffei's day is a moot point. Others again
turn up in the *dépouillement* of contemporary works. But there remains quite
a large group to which no parallel can be found elsewhere in Italian; in
numbers it almost exactly equals those which the author considers to be
authentic eighteenth century loans. Miss Cigna by and large finds justification
for Maffei's claim that 'forse neppure uno di questi vocaboli e di queste
maniere di dire è d'invenzione'. Nevertheless a fair proportion of the

1. S. Maffei, *Opere drammatiche e poesie varie*, Laterza, Bari, 1928, pp. 180–1.
2. G. Maugain, 'Le "Raguet" de Scipione Maffei', *Mélanges Hauvette*, Paris, 1934.
3. E.g. *burrò* 'writing-desk' in Act V, sc. 6 (edition cited, p. 222), which Aliso, to
Anselmo's consternation, glosses as 'boia, carnefice' and makes a telling point about the
faulty pronunciation of foreign words. M. Cigna notes down about 40 such words,
many of which are in our 18th cent. list, and some in earlier ones (*travagliare* [med.],
regretto [16th cent.], *dorè, intendente, ramparo, rimarcare* [17th cent.]).

Gallicisms, I feel, must be bogus. Of course the basis of the farce is not fabrication or fantasy but caricature, and caricature without a genuine abuse would be meaningless. A lot of the fun, however, comes from showing the audience its own tendency to Gallicism by exaggerating it outrageously. Many of the expressions peculiar to *Il Raguet* get the best laughs; some of those which appear also in other comedies are very amusing, too, and may on occasion have been poached. To me Maffei's claim that his words were really used seems to be couched rather evasively, and the fact that he does not seriously condemn linguistic misdemeanours of this sort or bring them home to any particular social group (contrast Molière in *Les Précieuses Ridicules* and *Les Femmes Savantes*) suggests that he is keeping his tongue in his cheek. And even if all the words could actually be heard spoken in contemporary society we should still have to decide at what point *use* could be said to have become *usage*. It remains true that despite all these attenuations Gallicism for its own sake had a certain social status in Italy, as for that matter it had in Germany and England too at the same period.[1]

At the present day a large proportion of this section of vocabulary is archaic, if only because the things designated have become obsolete. While the denotata were in use or in being the terms which appear in our list were current and accepted.

There is a common denominator between terms of fashion in the strict sense, or fashionable words in general, and those relating to home life, including culinary terms. The latter are moderate in number but revealing. They include *papà*, widely used in different regions of Italy, *pensione* for 'boarding-house', 'board and lodging', 'boarding school'; *dentista*, now coming into use instead of *cavadenti*; *cervo volante*, a child's toy, and *rebus*, a parlour game as well as a heraldic device. Two architectural borrowings apply to private dwellings: *lambrì*, *persiana*. *Burò*, *bidè*, *cabarè* 'tray, coffee-table', *comò* 'chest of drawers', *toeletta* 'dressing table' and *sofa* are tokens of the reputation of French cabinet-makers under Louis XV and indicate certain ways in which the interior arrangements of the home were disposed in the French fashion. The famous culinary Gallicisms begin to appear in

1. There are a considerable number of other works comparable with Maffei's *Il Raguet* which could be used to assess his Gallicisms more intensively (as indeed Miss Cigna observes). One such is Goldoni's *Il Ventaglio* (1763), which is a treasure house of pseudo-French jargon. The fact that he wrote it in France partially accounts for this. He uses current words like *rodengotto*, *gabinetto*, *salvietta*, *capo d'opera*, *lacchè*; *sufficienza* in the sense of *suffisance* ('self-sufficiency'), *pulito* in the sense of *educato*, *proprio* in the sense of *pulito*, *sortire*, *sortita* for *uscire*, *uscita*, *soggetto* for *persona* (a prospective suitor for the hand of Candida is called 'un soggetto accettabile'). Gambits of conversation like *obbligatissima* = *très obligée* are quite frequent, and so are idioms like *prendere guardia* for *badare*, 'lo trovo perfetto', 'ha del merito', 'amate di sentir delle favole ...?' and many expressions of the same stamp.

strength during this century; they include foods (*filetto, pomo di terra, ratafia*), wines (*sciampagna*), dishes (*chantilly, fricandò, ragù*) and even utensils and table-ware (*caffetiera, casserola, teiera, tirabusciò*).

Taken together the fashionable, social and domestic importation accounts for rather more than a quarter of the total.

The next substantial grouping is associated with intellectual and philo-sophical trends characteristic of the age. Foremost numerically are terms which arise from scientific investigation in several very different fields of knowledge: anthropology: *feticcio, feticismo* (a tribute to the work of the Italophile Charles de Brosses in this field), *meticcio*; geography: *affluente, mascheretto, picco*; geology: *affiorare, ardesia, marna, mineralogia, tormalina*; physics: *acustico*; natural history: *colibrì*; mathematics: *bilione, gettone* meaning 'mathematical counter' (Alb., 1777); meterology: *miraggio* and the nautical term *girotta*, 'weather-vane'. There is also the name of a technology, *metal-lurgia*. Seven botanical terms, *colza, erborista, erborizzare, esotico* (referring to plants), *framboise (frambosa, etc.), lillà* (the plant, not the colour) and *manioca* remind us of the valuable work done by Giovanni Targioni-Tozzetti (1712–83), the celebrated pioneer of botanical studies and the first of a line of eminent naturalists.[1] A typical scientist of the Enlightenment, Targioni-Tozzetti was learned in more than one discipline, happily combining his botanical studies with that of medicine: his doctoral thesis, which was judged to be of outstanding merit, was written in 1734 upon the medicinal use of plants. An empirical approach similar to that of the natural scientists begins to be found in *materia medica* from the middle of the century onwards. The Frenchman Bichat was one of the earlier scientific clinicians, but the movement had its main centre at Leyden, under Boerhaave, who insisted upon strictly objective research freed from the guesswork and rule-of-thumb diagnosis which was all too common in his day. Among those who intro-duced Boerhaave's methods into Italian practice were G. B. Bordieri (1725–85) and M. Sarcone (1732–97). The new empirical approach to medicine succeeded in ridding Europe of some of its worst scourges, foremost among them small-pox (the medical terms *inoculare, inoculazione* reach Italy in 1761). Two other fruitful spheres of research were those of the carency illnesses, particularly cretinism (*cretinismo, cretino*) and the classification of diseases (*nosologia*). Other medical terms borrowed in this period are *carcinoma, lancinante, regime, sonnambulo* (probably *nottambulo*, too) and *tarantismo*. I feel that the part played by French in their diffusion is closely bound up with the shift from Latin to the vernacular which transformed the restricted language

1. Ottaviano Targioni-Tozzetti's works are a major source of botanical terms in the 19th century (q.v.); they also appear in Antonio Targioni-Tozzetti, though less frequently. Of the seven 18th cent. terms three (*colza, erborizzare, lillà*) are first registered in Giovanni, who also has an occasional non-scientific first attestation.

of medicine profoundly in a short space of time during the later eighteenth and early nineteenth century. A corpus of theoretical knowledge was available already in medical Latin; old words were adapted and new words coined simultaneously, with the result that the modern terminology began to be established somewhat earlier than that of the other sciences. As in the case of diplomatic language, where a similar transformation was taking place,[1] French had the obvious advantage of being internationally current.

In this pre-industrial era the doctrines of Illuminism found practical scope chiefly in agricultural and legal reform. A small cluster of agricultural terms appears in the works of Ferdinando Paoletti (*marna, rapè*) and Marco Lastri (*giardinaggio, sanofieno*; early example of *calvilla*). In his *Pensieri sopra l'agricoltura* (1769, 2nd edition, 1789) and *I veri mezzi di rendere felici le società* (1772) Paoletti showed himself receptive to the new theories elaborated by the Physiocrats, yet did not entirely abandon the seventeenth-century mercantilist view of wealth. Lastri was a most interesting personality and a many-sided scholar; apart from his *Corso di agricoltura pratica* in five volumes (1801–3) which concerns us here he tried his hand at translating pieces from Gray and Delille, wrote didactic poetry, tragedy and history and did some research on demography.[2]

The language of eighteenth century economists was examined with very full reference to technical sources by A. M. Finoli in *Lingua Nostra*, IX, 1948, pp. 67–70. For students of lexical interference economic terms are an exasperating group of words. By and large they unquestionably represent a French influence, but it is no easy task to pin down any one word as a clear Gallicism. English also comes into the reckoning and almost all the terms are Latinisms in any case. Most were used very much earlier either in an appreciably different sense, or what is more deceptive, in a sense effectively identical with the scientific usage except that in earlier times it did not represent an item in a recognised body of scientific doctrine. The key-word *industria* (Fr. *industrie*, Eng. *industry*) dates from the Middle Ages in Italian, French and English and originally had several diverse meanings, though that of 'assiduity, diligence' predominated.[3] The modern sense is found in English in 1566

1. Though in a more desultory fashion, at least before 1789. In Italy the situation was complicated by Italian's continuing viability as an intermediary language in the Mediterranean area. At a lower level the *lingua franca* was still widely used, which was largely based on Italian. *Incaricato di affari* is a diplomatic term which qualifies for the present list, though by the narrowest of margins (1798, Monti). It obviously belongs to the revolutionary period.

2. See G. Sarchiani, 'Elogio di Marco Lastri', *Atti della R. Accademia dei Georgofili di Firenze*, VIII, 1817. Lastri died in 1811.

3. In English, for example, it also meant 'a cunning device, a crafty expedient' (*OED*); an early French sense is that of 'cleverness, skill'.

(*OED*) and Italian uses it in much the same way at the same period (Finoli, loc. cit., p. 70). *Political Economy*, used by Adam Smith in the technical signification, is generally derived from French, where A. de Monchrestien has *Économie Politique* as the title of a work published in 1615; but how far was this still a figurative expression for him, i.e. 'political house-keeping'? This is how Hobbes uses it in English when he speaks of 'the oeconomy of a commonwealth' (1651, *Leviathan*, II, xxiii, 124 [*OED*]). *Finanza* and *monetaggio* certainly date from the sixteenth century; both may be from French. Eighteenth century *importare*, -*azione*, *exportare*, -*azione* on the other hand are probably Anglicisms. In *cambiste—cambista* the movement if any is likely to have been from Italian to French.[1] Schiaffini stresses the outstanding contribution made to the study of economics and the spread of its restricted language in Italy by Antonio Genovesi, who occupied the newly created chair of Commercio e Meccanica at Naples from 1754.[2]

Legal terms and political terms prior to 1789 are very thin on the ground. Of the former we may note the use of *alibi* inspired by French, *rettroattivo*, *rettroattività* and *suicidio*, with *letto di giustizia* occasionally used referring directly to crises in France.[3] Among the latter are *naturalizzare*, *naturalizzato* and the all important *patriota*, against which we can set the very probable borrowing *cosmopolita*, its direct antonym.[4] The latter, enshrining a principle which gave rise to repeated controversy, is continuously attested in the political signification from 1715 onward, but the frequency of use rises steeply after 1789. From this date its implications develop *pari passu* with those of Fr. *patriote* which in the early years of the Revolution quickly became a word to conjure with, a catchword of revolutionary tracts both in France and Italy implying 'trustworthy supporter of the Revolution', whence by restriction 'partisan of French intervention in Italy'. Vincenzo Monti frequently commends a colleague or acquaintance by calling him *buon patriotto*, *vero e benmerito patriotto* and the like. In both countries the word fell

1. Other terms mentioned by A. M. Finoli include *monopolio* (*monipolio* is in G. Vill.), *monopolista* (Buon. il Giov.), *concorrenza* 'competition' (which is 15th cent. in the general sense of 'rivalry'), *concorrente*, *azione* 'share in a company' (certainly from Dutch, but possibly via French, see M-*Stor.*, 579–80), *capitalismo*, *capitalista* and *bancarotta* (*vide supra*, mediaeval It. > Fr. loans, *banqueroute* and note).

2. *Momenti*, pp. 105–6.

3. *Processo verbale* belongs to the revolutionary era.

4. *Cosmopolita* appears in F. M. Zanotti, G. Filangieri, Pietro Verri and D'Alberti, with *cosmopolitano* (adj.) in Salvini. Schiaffini considers it a 'francesismo non dubbio' (see *Momenti*, pp. 102–3 and sources cited, esp. Migliorini, *Lingua e Cultura*, Rome, 1948, pp. 277–82); B-Al. suggest that the French word *cosmopolite* (G. Postel, 1560) stood as an intermediary between the Greek etymon and the Italian. It is very much in keeping with the catholicity of eighteenth century French that it should provide the name for these two opposites, the alpha and omega of an individual's political relationship with his fellow men.

into disrepute after the Convention[1] and was used very circumspectly in Napoleonic times. Another key-word of the same period which like *patriotto* —*patriottismo* became invested with an almost liturgical quality was *fraterniz-zare*, together with its abstract *fraternizzazione*.[2] Every bit as revealing in their way are objects of vituperation—the indispensable corollary to revolutionary zeal—the 'counter-revolutionaries' and 'subversive elements' (*elementi sovversivi*), the 'defeatists and rumour-mongers' (*allarmisti*); note, too, the epithet *sedicente*, 'so called', used to create pejorative antonyms to the consecrated words—*sedicenti patriotti, rivoluzionari*, etc. (see nineteenth century word-list, s.v.). Four concrete nouns symbolise the spirit of the times with equal efficacy: *coccarda*, which was attested earlier but acquired a greater frequency of use in these latter years of the century when used to denote the *cocarde tricolore*; *ghigliottina*;[3] and the sobriquets *giacobino* and *carmagnola* meaning 'Revolutionary soldier, *sans-culotte*'. A wide selection of Gallicisms typical of the age may be culled from the almost boundless supply of news-sheets, weeklies, pamphlets, proclamations and tracts which poured from Italian presses in the years between 1796 and 1799. Calling themselves *Osservatore, Tribuno, Giornale, Repubblicano, Democratico, Corriere, Monitore, Imparziale*—all the titles which from French became not only Italian but pan-European, and still are to this day—they modelled themselves upon the style and linguistic form of their French counterparts as well as upon their matter. Often they featured direct translations of French originals.[4] French journals themselves were readily available.[5] A fair proportion of the cant phraseology thrown up by the Revolution, the clichés and other words associated with political episodes of the time tend to be registered by Italian etymologists in the early nineteenth century—in historical, discursive or critical works written by men who had lived through the period and now mulled over its events. Many of these terms could certainly be back-dated to the time to which they refer by sifting through the plethora of contemporary journals. This has already been done with considerable success.[6] Some

1. Cf. the observation, attributed like so many others to Talleyrand, that already under the Directoire 'patriote était devenu une injure'. *Vide* Brunot, *Hist.*, IX, Part 2, pp. 663–5.

2. Mercier's observation upon *fraternisation*, cited by Brunot, Vol. IX, Part 2, p. 668 provides a striking illustration of its affinities with the foregoing term: 'Il n'est aucun qui n'ait dans le cœur la définition du mot *fraternisation*, s'il est *patriote*'.

3. The euphemism *la vedova* for *ghigliottina*, obviously an echo of Fr. *la veuve*, was used also in Italy; *vide* Prati, *Voci di gerganti*, pp. 210–11.

4. In June 1798 for example the *Corriere milanese* advertised itself as a 'traduzione genuina dei principali fogli di Francia'. For details of the remarkable rise of the popular press in these years, with lists of current periodicals and their fortunes see Hazard, op. cit., pp. 44–55.

5. Hazard, p. 53.

6. E.g. in the article referred to during the course of our word-list, P. Zolli, 'Francesismi nel linguaggio politico italiano alla fine del '700', *L.N.*, XXV and XXVI. Among the

of these words must indeed have been heard or written currently in certain environments—*terrore, terrorismo, terrorista* are obvious cases in point; others probably never got beyond the posters on which they were displayed or the pages into which less ardent club members casually dipped. Occasionally we light upon a word which will represent a key concept in the following century, e.g. *funzionario* 'government official', 'member of the administration' (Fr. *fonctionnaire*, like the notion or way of life it enshrines, dates from the outset of the revolutionary period). But it is more stimulating and more informative linguistically to see how political fervour and Gallicising neologism affected an author of standing, a writer with a vested interest in the Italian language; a man like Vincenzo Monti whom we mentioned above, for example, particularly in his day-to-day usage as illustrated by the *Epistolario*.

In his earlier letters, long before he was personally caught up in political events, Monti was not averse to using an occasional French borrowing, e.g. *comò* (q.v.) in an urgent brotherly request for ready cash dated 10th Nov. 1781 and addressed to Francesco Antonio Monti. In this respect he was neither more nor less a purist than the average writer of his day. Always sensitive to atmosphere—perhaps too readily so—he was familiar with the political jargon of the Convention even in his anti-republican period, the period of the *Bassvillana*: he uses *giacobino* (q.v.) in defending himself against a charge of radicalism (June 1794) just as two years later he uses it in justifying his revolutionary propensities. Three more of Monti's first attestations which belong to this word-list date from the period when his sympathies were shifting in favour of the republican cause—*coalizzarsi, club* (referring to Napoleon's demands upon the Holy See, and very likely written by Monti with an actual French text in mind) and *tranquillizzare*. Monti had always been given to affecting an exhortatory mode of expression in his letters (a stylistic Latinism, one assumes, which may be ascribed to his Classical studies during the five years spent in the Seminary at Faenza) and the oratorical *débit* of a Republican comes readily to his pen, all the more so since the revolutionary style had its origins in neo-Classicism. By 1797 he is liable to harangue even his nearest relatives.[1] When later as an official of the Cisalpine

certain or probable Gallicisms which the author collects from propaganda sources dating from 1796 to 1799, are these: *anarchista, civismo, clubista, concussionario, controrivoluzione, -ario, convenzionale* (referring to the Convention), *deportato, detronizzare, direttorio, emigrato, federalismo, indennizzazione, insubordinazione, libertà di stampa, liberticida, montagnardo, proselitismo, refrattario, rivoluzionario, sanculotto, settembrista, terzo stato, constituzionario, realismo* (= *royalisme*), *repubblicanismo, robespierismo, vandeista* (relating to supporters of the rising in the Vendée). Cf. also the list in M-*Stor.*, p. 635.

1. E.g. Bertoldi, II, p. 11, letter to Francesco Monti, 'Vi ringrazio della predica . . .', etc., or II, p. 45 (same addressee): 'Carissimo Fratello—Il mio consiglio è quello di rinunziar a tutto fuorché al titolo prezioso di cittadino' etc.

government he helps to prepare proclamations they have that metallic, *ordre du jour*, remote but coercive quality which comes out so clearly in French.[1] His reports to superiors are full of French bureaucratic jargon: 'Sono già state da noi organizzate constituzionalmente le due amministrazioni centrali del Lamone e del Rubicone ...' (*Al Ministro degli Affari Interni*, 7th Dec. 1797 [Bertoldi II, 50]). The usual metaphors spring to his lips when he prophesies the downfall of the *cabale aristocratiche* and other enemies of the Cisalpine Republic: 'Non ti affliggere tanto ... verrà tempo di fulminarle, e questo tempo non è lontano ...' and 'Si prepara una gran tempesta, ma non sommergerà che i colpevoli', etc. (II, 68); or when he personifies the Cisalpina as a protector of the afflicted: 'No, voi non siete nostri nemici: La Repubblica Cisalpina conquistando la vostra patria ha voluto renderla independente. ... Voi siete divenuti figli della Repubblica, la vostra novella madre sente tutte le vostre perdite, e voi sarete indennizzati' (*Agli Abitanti di S. Leo*, 16th Dec. 1797 [Bertoldi II, 56]).[2] Most of Monti's political borrowings date from this period: *ghigliottina*, 1797; *burò* (political headquarters), *comitato, dimissione, incaricato di affari* 1798; *coalizione, colpo di mano*, 1799. From September 1796 his letters are dated according to Fabre d'Eglantine's Revolutionary calendar, and he continues to use the new names until April 1802: *vendemmiale, brumaio, frimale, nevoso, piovoso, ventoso, germile, fiorile, pratile, messidoro, termidoro, fruttidoro* corresponding to *vendémiaire, brumaire, frimaire, nivôse, pluviôse, ventôse, germinal, floréal, prairial, messidor, thermidor, fructidor*.[3] The honorific *cittadino* is used in addresses from February 1797, but sporadically at first.

What strikes one most forcibly, though, is not how faithfully Monti followed his Gallic mentors but how transient his allegiance to them turned out to be. By the end of 1801 he is able to write to his intimates in the gentle, direct style which had graced many of his letters of earlier days. Moreover like all artists who handle the medium of language he commands several different registers, just as he combines several very opposed personalities. On

1. E.g. Bertoldi, II, p. 48 and 48, *Alla municipalità di Imola* and *Alla m. di Massa Lombarda*.

2. Other phrases taken directly from French: *albero della libertà, comitato di sicurezza pubblica*, etc., *vendita dei beni nazionali, fanatismo religioso* (he calls Rome 'quella santa Babilona' [II, 20]), *capo di burò, commissario organizzatore*, and the formula *salute e fratellanza* (= *salut et fraternité*, on closing a letter). For a survey of relevant usage in French see Brunot, *Hist.*, X, Chs. VII–XI, esp. pp. 62–72, *Figures et Images*.

3. The differences between the French words and their adaptations are interesting. Suffix -*aire* has to be replaced, usually by -*ale*, though *frimaire* itself is found (14th Dec. 1797, etc.) (*vendemmiale, frimale*). *Brumale*, used in 1797 together with the more homely calque *annebbiatore* is finally rejected in favour of the popular suffix -*aio* (*brumaio* consistently by 1799). *Vendemmiatore* and *vendemmiaio* appear occasionally. A desire as in French to invent names which will be novel, distinguished and yet aesthetically satisfying explains most of the changes (including probably *germile, fiorile, pratile* for -*ale*).

assuming the *persona* of a man of destiny, a latter-day Brutus, he took up the linguistic habit which suited it, discarding it in due course when his role altered. Many writers must have done the same. The mass of people, the linguistically unaware, would be even quicker to slough off a jargon which had ceased to be a living force to them.

The impact of Gallicism in this earlier, revolutionary period was great, but for all that not by any means commensurate in the long run with the intense literary and linguistic pressures which propaganda and political journalism exerted upon Italy from 1796 to 1799. We shall find it easier to estimate its enduring effect along with that of Gallicism under the longer-lasting Napoleonic domination, when there is still more copious evidence of lexical transfer.

To return to the lexical contribution made by Illuminism. The semantic category most intimately concerned remains to be examined, i.e. philosophical terms. *Empirismo* and *ottimismo* have a special position here, recalling France's part in interpreting the theories of Locke and Leibnitz to other countries and helping thereby to establish the cardinal principles of European thought throughout Europe. Schiaffini has drawn attention to the connection between Locke's theories on language—that its primary purpose was to communicate thought as quickly and clearly as possible—the precepts followed by the *Encyclopédistes* and the programme of linguistic reform undertaken by contributors to *Il Caffè*.[1] The Hellenisms *filantropo, filantropia* owe their eighteenth century meaning of 'person who aims to further human betterment by practical undertakings', 'the active pursuit of human betterment' to their French equivalents (in Fénelon *et al.*), as do their antonyms *misantropo, misantropia. Civilizzare, civilizzazione* are to be listed under this head.[2]

The third extensive semantic grouping comprises restricted languages of trades, professions and pursuits which are not directly inspired by the intellectual climate of the age. These are the technical vocabularies in their own right, made up of categories which are for the most part represented at all periods: nautical and military terms, terms of trade and commerce, finance, the fine arts and architecture.

1. *Momenti*, pp. 88–90.

2. It is revealing to compare the categories of scientific and philosophical loan-words we have just exemplified with the subject-matter of French works read in Italy at the time. Cf. Brunot's list of books recommended by Genovesi and mentioned in *Il Caffè* during the '60s: Massuet, *Le Philosophe moderne*; Duhamel, *Traité d'agriculture*; Melon, *Essai politique sur le commerce*; La Martinière, *Grand dictionnaire géographique*; De la Porte, *Traité sur la monnaie*; Bidet, *Traité de la culture de la vigne*; Marcandier, *Traité du chanvre*; Montesquieu, *L'Esprit des Lois*; Abbé Coyer, *La Noblesse commerçante*; Alexandre, *Traité général des horloges*; Maupertuis, *Eléments de géographie*; Hénault, *Histoire de France*; Savary, *Dict. du commerce*; De la Caille, *Leçons élémentaires d'astronomie*; Du Bos, *Réflections sur la poésie et la peinture* (*Hist.*, Vol. VIII, Part 1, p. 123).

As we observed earlier, nautical terms are outstanding numerically. There is a purely practical consideration which in part explains this preponderance; a certain statistical exaggeration may have taken place because of the large number of attestations given in the translation of Saverien's *Dictionnaire historique, théorique et pratique de la marine* (Venice, 1769) and in Alberti's dictionaries from 1788 onward.[1] Nevertheless the startling increase compared with the seventeenth century in which very few examples appear[2] requires to be explained more convincingly. What happened historically was this. By the end of the seventeenth century Italian naval construction had entered a slack period. The maritime states, particularly Venice, had suffered grave losses through the shift of trade away from Mediterranean sea-routes yet had failed to win a place in world-wide commerce, partly owing to their disadvantageous geographical situation and partly because of political pressure put upon them by Spain, which still held on to its key position as an oceanic trading nation in the face of increasing Dutch, French and English competition. Venetian and Genoese shipbuilding yards were still occupied in constructing galleys and small craft for the coastal trade. The political and economic reshuffle of the earlier eighteenth century left Italy free to reshape her maritime policy. By 1750 shipyards were launching long-distance trading vessels similar in design and burthen to the East Indiamen of the Dutch and English fleets. Some of the words borrowed came in the first place from Dutch—*lasto (lasta)*, *scialuppa, flauto, ralinga*—and others from English—*rada, pacchebotto* (the latter not immediately accepted into technical usage), but it is significant that the majority are of native French origin. Their most remarkable trait, which emphasises the intensity of French influence in this field, is their wide range of denotata within the limits of the technical vocabulary. We see straight away that many are connected with ocean-going vessels, as one would expect: *marciapiede* 'footrope' and *ralinga* 'bolt-rope', referring to the spars and sails of the larger merchantmen; *lasto* 'ballast'; *tralingaggio* 'euphroe' or system of ropes for large sun-awnings; *scialuppa* small boat or tender carried by ships of greater tonnage. *Corvetta* in the original sense denotes a coastal or river vessel and *sciatta* 'lighter, scow' is also a small craft, but we note that its function is to load or unload the cargoes of ships whose draft is so great that they cannot come close inshore. *Galetta* and *gamella* refer to purser's stores; *madiere* 'kelson' is a term of naval architecture. A further oceanic element appears in terms of navigation and meteorology: *borgognone* 'iceberg', *mascheretto* ' "bore" of a river', applied initially to the

1. Note, however, that while Alberti admits he has enlarged this lexical category considerably in the 3rd edition of the *Nuovo dizionario* (1788) he goes out of his way to justify this added emphasis on grounds of current usage, describing 'la favella marinaresca' as 'ripiena oggidì di francesismi' (op. cit., *Preface*).

2. *Brulotto, diga*; probably *rullare*.

F

Dordogne, *rada* 'roads, roadstead', where deep-sea vessels anchor off, *barra* 'bar' of a river, a navigational hazard especially to deeply laden ships, and *girotta* 'wind-vane'. Evidence of close contact is also provided by words which describe the working of a ship: *stallare* 'to stem the tide', *ingranare* 'to set a ship's pumps in motion' in the earliest contexts, and the key-word *manovra* 'ship-handling'. Only three or four borrowings suggest warlike activities: *blù* (*blò*) as the distinguishing flag of a squadron ('the Blue'), *crociera* meaning 'patrol area' and *bastinga, -aggio*, dunnage or gear used as a temporary protection against small shot. *Colare* (*a fondo*) I take to be an item of official terminology, possibly with a slight euphemistic overtone, for the death of a ship, like that of a man, is fertile ground for linguistic taboo.

Military terms stand for the pre-Napoleonic contact in this sphere. There are not many. Almost all deal with personnel, their accoutrement and organisation, and in this respect they bear some resemblance to the fifteenth century Italian to French borrowings: *brigadiere, carabiniere, gendarme, picchetto*; *ghette, montura, uniforme*; *stato maggiore*. The only weapon—an important one all the same in an army made up mainly of infantry—is *baionetta*, while *barbetta* is an isolated term of fortification. *Gamella* appeared in military contexts (as well as naval) towards the end of the period.

With her settlements in Canada, Louisiana and India, France in the eighteenth century was better placed than any other nation to found a colonial empire. That she did not fully exploit her advantage was due partially to the traditional indifference of Frenchmen in matters of commercial enterprise. We might ascribe to this prevailing attitude the limited number of loans connected with trade and commerce, which—to seek out a statistically appropriate parallel—amount to less than half the corresponding section of seventeenth century Italian to French borrowings, though the eighteenth century total for the whole list is actually larger than the seventeenth.[1] *Cabotaggio* is a revealing word. There was a need for it. Although strictly speaking a nautical term ('coastal navigation') it is most frequently used in all the languages which have borrowed it to describe nationally delimited as opposed to international maritime commerce. The coastal trade was fostered on economic and political grounds, to stimulate production in coastal regions and to provide a reserve of trained seamen in time of war. Cromwell's navigation acts of 1651 directed against the Low Countries are an early example of this practice. The question of protecting inshore sea-borne trade was raised from time to time during the whole of our present period and becomes an increasingly important issue. By 1789 protection was generally practised by most of the maritime nations.

What remains are names of products which French firms usually dealt in: *melassa* 'molasses' and *rapè* from the West Indies, *varecco* from north-

1. Names of textiles omitted in both cases.

western France; *damigiana* is a measure, *bigiotteria* and *chincaglieria* are collectives denoting a range of goods, and (*vendere in*) *dettaglio*, an important term of commercial practice. Other words are marginally associated—we have already noted that certain colour adjectives were commonly applied to textiles and were probably dyer's terms in the first instance (*lillà, gridellino*). And perhaps a commercial context is the best niche for the notorious *filibustieri* who in the eighteenth century as in the seventeenth continued to present a serious problem to traders in the Caribbean.

There are very few indeed of what might be called industrial or engineering terms. *Draga* (*dragare*), which denotes a mechanism used for clearing rivers and dikes with the object of improving agricultural land, is obviously linked to the numerous attempts to impose land reclamation schemes upon property owners by decree during the latter part of the century. *Aerostato* is an excellent instance of a new word borrowed to denote a new invention—man's conquest of the air began in 1783 with the flight of the Montgolfiers' first *aerostat* or heated-air balloon—but the example is an isolated one. *Metallurgia* and *carburo* are the only representatives of heavy industry in the list, and the former has in the eighteenth century an equally valid claim to be placed where we have placed it, among the natural sciences.

Taking together the borrowed vocabulary of commerce, industry and finance[1] one can fairly say that the Franco-Italian influence in this domain had more to do with economics itself than the raw material of economics. France seems to have originated or passed on many ideas about trade and industry in the abstract while contributing rather less than one might have expected to their actual practice. Textiles as usual are well represented, but our previous lists have taught us to anticipate a constant movement of vocabulary in this field and the eighteenth century is not exceptional.

What we do find in this pre-industrial age is a small group of words relating to what we might call the *fine crafts* as opposed to the fine arts. I include under this rubric names of furniture which have already been mentioned (*comò, burò*, etc.), *basana* 'bookbinder's vellum' (incidentally *editore* 'publisher' is also in the list), *bordura* (*heraldry*) and one or two words which suggest the locksmith or cabinet-maker's trade, e.g. *cerniera* 'clasp, hinge' as of a coffer or cabinet.[2] Among these pre-industrial industries, in which few

1. Six items here, *aggiotaggio, aggiotatore, ammortizzare, ammortizzazione, assegnato* and *contabilità. Ammortizzare -azione* and *assegnato* are really bureaucratic since they concern the Exchequer and not private business (establishment of sinking funds; liquidation of confiscated assets during the French invasion), and when viewed in the actual context in which it was borrowed the same is true of *contabilità* as well. Verri is merely proposing a revised system of accounting—a French system, one infers—as a desirable administrative (i.e. governmental) reform.

2. Cf. also the possible Gallicisms *orologiere* 'clock-maker' and *fresa* 'bit, drill' (Fr. *fraise*) which in the 18th century was applied in particular to a small countersink drill for

machine tools were used and the quality of a product depended wholly upon the craftsman's skill, coach-building was probably the most lucrative commercially (*cupè, faeton, imperiale*). It was a universal craft with important centres in Germany, England and Austria besides France and Italy, but in this sphere of activity as so often elsewhere the names of new designs tended to be disseminated through French (*berlina*). An indication that France contributed also to constructional technique is given by *copiglia* 'cotter-pin', etc. (Fr. *goupil*), clearly a wheelwright's term.[1]

Other restricted languages are sparsely represented. Five musical terms *fanfara, marcia, minuetto, òboe, rondò* serve to give perspective to the massive importation of similar loans from Italian to French which we glossed in the previous chapter. Three of horsemanship—the key-word *equitazione*, which corresponds exactly to sixteenth century French *manège* borrowed from Italian, *isabella, piruetta*; two each of the theatre, architecture and literature—*figurante, monologo, piedritto, piano* (though *lambrì* and *persiane* are related), *purismo* and *purista*; and one ecclesiastical term, *calotta*, complete the total. *Adepto* 'initiate', especially into a secret society, is probably one of what Brunot characterises as *relents maçonniques*.

Exoticisms borrowed through French are already numerous though not so abundant as in the next century.[2] There are signs that French was beginning to oust Spanish and Portuguese from their position as intermediaries between Europe and America or India (*meticcio, crèolo* reborrowed from French in preference to the original sixteenth and seventeenth century Hispanicisms). *Meticcio* and *piroga* were used first in descriptions of the North American Indians; two from the Near East, *odali(s)ca* and *marabutto*, evoked the atmosphere of the *Lettres Persanes*. Lastly there is a hint of the part played by France in broadcasting information about English society and institutions (*milordo*).[3]

Proportions within the batch of abstract, general and emotive terms depart unexpectedly from the average. Affective terms are infrequent; a mere handful of words which in some way imply a value-judgement which is unfavourable—*deboscio, debosciato, libertinaggio, controsenso*—and which characteristically refer to behaviour which diverges from the accepted norm,

---

recessing screws in watch and clock mechanisms.

   1. A most informative account of the coachbuilder's trade in France at the time is to be found in the *Encyclopédie*'s article *carosse*, for which Diderot was responsible.

   2. *Àuna, creolo, lama, marabutto, meticcio, milordo, odalisca (odalica), piroga. Minareto* 'minaret' and *pagoda* should perhaps be included.

   3. *Baronetto* (Eng. *baronet*, a rank of the gentry) may also have been borrowed through French, as some claim, though the earliest attestation in Baretti's *Italian-English Dictionary* (1771) seems to imply a direct loan. It remains true that Rivarol's famous protestation: 'N'est-ce pas nous qui avons tiré la littérature anglaise du fond de son île?' could be applied equally to the English language.

whether through incontinence, irreligion or unreason. They contrast in number and substance to the eight or nine comparable terms (out of a very much smaller total) which we encountered in the French borrowings. The pejoration here is more subtle; no abuse, little irony or condescension, scarcely a trace of national ill-feeling. This lack of affectives throws greater emphasis upon other sub-groupings. In their intrinsic value many of the abstract and general terms are outstanding. One or two are the kind of word which is potentially of great service to the language as an informative and analytical system—*dettaglio, risorsa*—while others reduce a complicated pattern of abstract signification to a single term—*amatore, dettagliare, contro-senso* (its semantic opposite, the phrase *buon senso*, is also adapted from French), *esotico, flottare, rango, responsabile, responsabilità, rimarchevole.* Some-times bureaucratic jargon wins a place for itself in general use, e.g. *dimissione, reprimenda (responsabile, -ilità* were probably transferred in this register); occa-sionally a synonym is provided which has a euphemistic slant, e.g. *celibatario,* more dignified than *scapolo,* which was itself originally a substitute-word, viz., a sixteenth century restriction of the meaning 'free'. Borrowings begin to appear in strength with the Gallicising suffix *-izzare* (subst. *-izzaz-ione*), initially associated with a process, an operation of weighty import, later bureaucratic and often used to add apparent substance to an otherwise mundane implication or to act as a blanket term: *civilizzare, civilizzazione, coalizzare, generalizzare, realizzare, tranquillizzare*; cf. also the more specific terms *fraternizzare, -azione, naturalizzare, -azione, erborizzare.* A dozen additional abstract substantives (in the strict grammatical sense) have been accounted for already mainly under science or philosophy. The complete word-list includes no less than seventeen verbs; there are seven adjectives and one adverb, *attualmente.*

In its general articulation our evaluation mirrors the historical *données* with reasonable accuracy. We see evidence for instance of comparatively trivial and transient social contacts beside momentous scientific and philosophical trends. The parallel holds good for certain individual facets, too; the wealth of nautical terms, the contribution of Enlightenment to one or other branch of the social and natural sciences. And yet of all our century lists this one gives rise to the strongest impression of discrepancy between lexical data and the cultural pattern. One recognises that there is an imbalance intuitively, but the actual numbers confirm what one senses to be true. During these hundred years intellectual exchange was intense; mutual interests were as far-reaching as they could possibly be; both countries were deeply absorbed in international cultural movements of which France and the French language were the accredited intermediaries. This is the period when Gallicism in the majority of European countries enters its most productive phase—in places as remote for the eighteenth century as Rumania and the Slavonic-speaking territories, for example. Yet the total of 260 words only marginally exceeds that of loans from Italian to French in the seventeenth century, in which political and intellectual incentives to borrowing scarcely existed and contacts in most other spheres were of secondary importance. Out of all the century lists the present one comes fourth in point of numbers, after the nineteenth century French, the sixteenth century Italian and the mediaeval French influences. The proportion of non-technical to technical loans is moderately high, showing the interference penetrated well below the superficial strata of the lexicon; but if we consider the figures for non-technical words in the absolute the actual number in the eighteenth century is little better than half the average of those in the major centuries just cited. Our historical evaluation cannot hold good until this apparent incompatibility is explained.

There is a risk that we may have over-estimated the language's susceptibility to foreign pressure. We have indicated in global terms that Italian in the Settecento had a certain amount of leeway to make up, that certain areas of vocabulary required to be expanded to meet new demands. Not all the registers of the idiom, however, were equally open to innovation or equally in need of it.

The literary language, by which again I mean the linguistic resources available as a medium for literary art rather than the written language in its broader application—the literary language stood apart from the main stream of Gallicism. Poetic language in particular had its vicissitudes, but France of the eighteenth century, *ce siècle sans poésie*, was in no shape to solve its problems nor were Italian poets inclined to seek stylistic or aesthetic inspiration from that direction. Metastasio's poetic idiom is very different indeed from that, say, of Alfieri, but both are strongly rooted in Italian soil. Parini is responsible for occasional Gallicisms, but how could it be otherwise when the chief butt of his satire, the *mœurs* of high society, were so sensitive to the dictates of France?[1] Resistance to Gallicism or rather indifference to it is an entrenched feature of poetic and tragic diction. The language of comedy on the other hand is less securely based. Directly linked with spoken, conversational usage it necessarily suffers from the latter's heterogeneous nature. Goldoni turns with relief to the language of Molière which has the advantage of being current at the level he requires over the whole range of society which interests him and whose interest in turn he wishes to capture. He is equally comfortable in his native Venetian, though he cannot permanently afford to restrict his potential audience so drastically.

What objective information can our word-list provide about the aesthetic

1. See *bigiotteria, milorde, sofà* in the list. Parini uses several of the words attested earlier in the century. His most pungent Gallicism is perhaps that which supplies the theme of his celebrated ode *A Sylvia, o sul vestire alla ghigliottina* (1795).

status of French in the Settecento—that tenuous but vitally important factor in literary influences?

That Maffei and others make Gallicism an object of fun has little real significance. This is a literary ploy, as we had cause to observe in an earlier chapter. It does not mean either that Frenchmen were scorned or that the French language was considered ridiculous, any more than Anselmo's failure to understand Alfonso's *galimatias* means that French was not understood in Italian society. Sixteenth century French writers use the same gambits with respect to Italian. Estienne's Celtophile fails to understand Philausone in the same way, and Noël du Fail's peasants are flummoxed by the Italianising fecundity of their betters. Nevertheless in either case it is the audience's intimate knowledge of an alien tongue that makes a humorous device of this sort a practical possibility. Both centuries have this familiarity with a foreign literary language in common. And yet there is a difference between the eighteenth century Italian and the sixteenth century French attitude which is crucial, in that despite du Fail's jests and the irony of Estienne, du Bellay and others, Italianism in the sixteenth century had a very real literary status. The poetic overtones of many Italian borrowings which occur in the Pléiade and their near-contemporaries prove conclusively that this was so. To the French Renaissance, stylistic borrowing from Italian was a valued resource, a precious component of the poetic afflatus. The eighteenth century French to Italian contact added no such modulations to the instrument of literature.

Literary Italian's essential self-sufficiency is indicated, too, by the subsidiary role which pro- or anti-French feeling played in the *Questione della lingua*. At this time the struggle to establish a linguistic norm involved proponents of many different points of view. Latin was no longer a serious rival to the *volgare*, though one or two voices were still heard in its favour.[1] The claims of *toscanità* were pressed as strongly as ever. A bitter conflict was rife between advocates of Trecento or Cinquecento purism in one camp and of liberalism or *laisser faire* in the other, according to one's point of view.[2] French comes into the latter confrontation by a side road, since any policy which allowed neologism wider scope automatically favoured borrowing from the obvious source. But Gallicism is still only one of several issues, at least as far as the language of literature is concerned. It is noteworthy that the strongest partisans of *lassismo*, the Milanese Illuminists, are not particularly interested in the literary, aesthetic controversy but are deeply concerned about creating

---

1. E.g. il p. G. Lagomarsini, *Oratio pro lingua latina*, 1737, edition cited M-*Stor.*, p. 522. On the final phases of the conflict between Italian and Latin see M-*Stor.*, pp. 519–24. Vico, we recall, wrote many of his works in Latin.

2. For a synopsis of the main trends of Purism, Tuscanism and the reactions to these movements in the eighteenth century see Migliorini, *La questione della lingua*, loc. cit., pp. 44–8 and M-*Stor.*, pp. 508–16.

a standard language in which to disseminate information and further the intellectual, social and economic ends which we have already discussed. In all its uses save that of uncommitted literary creativity Italian was exposed to the full impact of interference from its sister language. The rather special position which purely literary and particularly poetic usage occupies does not help appreciably to explain away the unbalance between our borrowings and the evidence which history lays before us.

'Chiuso da poco il dialogo col latino' (Devoto observes), 'trattenute le velleità particolariste di centri dialettali, il francesismo ripropone ... nella storia linguistica italiana il problema del bilinguismo, con tutti gli squilibrî, incertezze e polemiche che esso comporta.'[1] At any given moment of history a number of factors intervene to obscure the relationship between one language and another, and also between the individual language and events in the non-linguistic world which for the sake of convenience we have summed up as cultural phenomena. Bilingualism is one of these factors. In eighteenth century Italian its effect is greater than at any other period. The bilingualism which concerns us here is not that which one finds affecting all classes in certain regions, for example Piedmont, but that which applies horizontally— a second language artificially acquired for the most part, current throughout Italy at social levels which embrace those who are in different ways partisans of Illuminism.

The linguistic effects of this situation, above all the way it limited the influx of adapted French forms or modified the overall make-up of the borrowed vocabulary is easy enough to surmise, though far from easy to demonstrate objectively. At any time there are certain aspects of lexical interference which a word-list does not bring out very well; the area of imprecision in this period is greater than usual. There was a broad intermediate zone of Italian words used ephemerally in senses similar to those of French.[2] Sometimes it is difficult to distinguish a genuine semantic loan from a parallel shift of meaning.[3] Others are used in idioms modelled on French.[4]

1. *Profilo*, p. 104.

2. *Paressoso* for *paresseux*, *portreto* for *portrait* (an interesting parallel to the ephemeral English 18th cent. loan *ritrat* < *ritratto*), *degaggiato* for *dégagé*, or the Gallicising uses cited from *Il Ventaglio* above, for instance. This type of borrowing often revives an archaic word which had been taken from French at an earlier date, e.g. *travaglio*, *travagliatore* (= *lavoro*, *operaio*) in Beccaria, originally borrowed during the 13th cent. (*Novellino*, Iac. da Lentino).

3. Semantic loans are notoriously difficult to confirm, but a French influence is very probable in a whole range of words which assumed typically eighteenth-century connotations in Europe as a whole as well as Italy, e.g. *gusto* (*buon gusto*), *genio*, *spirito*, *sentimento*, *sentimentale*, *sensibilità*, *estetica*, *progresso* and so on. Cf. Brunot, *Histoire*, VIII, 1, pp. 132–3; Devoto, *Profilo*, p. 105; Schiaffini, *Momenti*, pp. 108–9; and especially the list of calques cited by Migliorini, *Storia*, pp. 576–7.

4. E.g. *felicitare*, *felicitazione*, *complimento* as in *felicitare alcuno*, *fare i suoi complimenti*, etc. Cf. the list of compound substantives and locutions drawn from French, *Storia*, pp. 578–9.

Words even appear to have been adapted formally to sound more like the French equivalent; no doubt this often happened accidentally in spoken usage.[1]

Beyond this intermediate zone we come to French itself. As far as a literary language is concerned, bilingualism makes for intensive interference only within certain limits. It operates along a certain band. As bilingualism becomes more and more universal, or approaches universality for practical purposes within certain social groups, the tendency to switch wholly into the reserve language rises steeply and adaptation is no longer urgently necessary. At the other side of the intermediate zone, therefore, our loan-word soundings return no echo. The signal is a null.

French was widespread among the middle classes at both formal and informal social gatherings.[2] Our group of 'fashionable and social' terms has to be supplemented by a number—a large number, certainly—of actual French words, or words which passed as French though transformed to a greater or lesser extent by Italian habits of speech. These are precisely the circumstances in which a bilingual speaker is tempted to interpose an occasional foreign term by reason of its greater evocative power, because it says more precisely what he wants to say, or merely because it springs more readily to the lips and obviates in that instance the need to search further for an appropriate expression in his first language. The tendency to be-sprinkle one's speech with foreign words is largely a matter of *parole*, of course, but not wholly so. A quick check through examples of French words and phrases in the extensive personal correspondence which is such a feature of the age[3] suggests that alien elements are not interposed entirely at random and that some kinds of interpolation are more common than others. The reasons why writers resort to these *tournures* are largely argotic in the broad sense—the familiar symbolisation in language of one's affiliations or interests—partly stylistic, with gesticulatory or mimetic *nuances*, but in no small measure semantic, because the foreign element is actually more efficient as regards meaning. At this latter point the extraneous influence touches *langue* as well as *parole*.[4]

1. E.g. *corriggere* for *correggere*, *lutta* for *lotta*, *mantenire* for *mantenere*.

2. By the end of the century Cesarotti reports that the French language is ' . . . communissima a tutta l'Italia: non v'è persona un poco educata a cui non sia familiare e pressochè naturale' (*Saggio*, III, Part XIII). His testimony is seconded by a host of contemporary observers.

3. This is the nearest we can get to actual conversation, which of course correspondence reflects only approximately; though the gap at this period is smaller than one might suppose because conversation in those social groups who used language in the registers which concern us was often highly stylised and self-conscious.

4. We can imagine a progression or *cline* extending from random interpolation of alien elements through conventional stylistic use of certain *tournures* to semantically

The impact of French is strongest in our second major semantic grouping, the vocabulary of Enlightenment. Many words in the list qualify to be included in this section, as we have seen, but they again probably understate the actual influence. Much of the scholarly work of the *Illuministi* was recorded permanently in French, which had the required stock of technical terms and also a convenient phraseology. French itself was widely used in written and spoken contacts between the *philosophes*, who often hailed from very different linguistic regions. This aspect of bilingualism helps to account for gaps in the political, philosophical and legal loan-word categories.[1] In conformity with the liberal and cosmopolitan principles we have mentioned many thinkers frankly preferred and chose to express themselves in French rather than their native tongue. A further explanation of deficiencies in this sector has to do with the abstract, philosophical character of inquiry into natural phenomena during the eighteenth century. It was a long time before genuinely empirical methods triumphed even in what are now the strictly scientific disciplines. Ratiocination and hypothesis, the legacy of cartesianism (and also of scholasticism, to which cartesianism made certain concessions) were still the natural philosopher's principal lines of investigation. Whereas the vocabulary of empirical science—new terms for new discoveries, labels to assist in defining categories—had to be created as research progressed or imported from a language already better furnished in this respect, the language of abstract speculation tended to remain unchanged, making use of native resources which had served thinkers well in previous generations. Exceptions to this rule are names of new philosophical approaches—*empirismo*, *ottimismo* and so on—which come under the heading of 'labelling' or 'classifying' terms and were liable to be diffused internationally along with the system of thought they denoted.[2]

In the third lexical division, 'non-intellectual' technical vocabulary, borrowings are more directly determined by practical needs and reflect more exactly the prevailing professional, commercial or artistic trends. The people who used Gallicising nomenclature belonged to a section of the community who had no preconceptions about linguistic purity, were less likely to be

motivated interpolation and finally borrowing proper once the convention has been received by a sufficiently large body of speakers.

1. Continued use of Latin probably is an additional factor in restricting legal borrowings.

2. A good example of a 'classifying' scientific word is *nosologia*, 'classification of diseases) which we mentioned earlier. Cf. also the modern taxonomy of chemical substances, drawn up by Lavoisier, Guyton de Morveau and collaborators and based largely on the use of learned suffixes (*ite*, *-ate*, *-ide*, *ique*, etc.). The Académie accepted their 'théorie nouvelle' in December 1788 and it was publicised in Italy before the end of the century (translation of Lavoisier's work, *Trattato elementare di chimica*, Venice, 1792).

bilinguals, and would readily adapt and so naturalise foreign words (crafts-men, soldiers, etc.).

To sum up: in this period cultural influences are not fully demonstrable in terms of loan-word categories, though they are unusually strong. The factors which in practice always frustrate an exact evaluation of the lexicon in cul-tural terms are strengthened because of widespread bilingualism especially in philosophical and social circles. Viewed from the standpoint of Italian alone the lexical-cultural discrepancy is more marked than at any other time, but when one takes into account the fact that speaking and writing French had the effect of alleviating the urgent need to use foreign terms in Italian contexts the divergence between linguistic and extra-linguistic phenomena assumes more normal proportions.

Lexical interference during this century enters upon a period of increasing momentum. The needs of technology and science have scarcely begun to be felt. France's political and military prestige has not yet reached its climax. Above all, international contacts are still confined to a select minority. By the time Illuminism has become a spent force new, more far-reaching im-pulses will be at work to raise the fortunes of Gallicism higher still.

CHAPTER V

THE NINETEENTH CENTURY

Italianisms in French during the Nineteenth Century

appoggiature. Music: Appoggiatura.

1829 B-Wart.; It. form *appoggiatura* used in French 1813. Attested in Italian during the 18th century (B-Al.).

aquafortiste. Etcher, aquafortist.

1853 Goncourt. <It. *acquafortista*, borrowed to provide an agent substantive corresponding to *eau-forte* (1832).

aquatinte. Arts: Aquatint.

Aqua-tinta 1819 Boiste; 1820 Laveaux; 1835 Acad. Pronounced [akwatẽta]; further adapted to *aquatinte*, 19th cent. <It. *acquatinta*, early 19th cent.

balancelle. Naut.: Double-ended fishing-boat with single mast and oars.

1823 *Ann. marit. et coloniales* (*vide F.M.*, XXV, p. 308); 1829 V. Hugo, *Les Orientales*; 1831 Willaumez, *Dict. de marine*; 1840 *Rev. des deux mondes*. Vidos (who incidentally omits *balancelle* from his brief synopsis of Fr. > It. loans, pp. 25–9) derives the term ultimately from Neapolitan *paranzella* < *paranza* 'companion, mate'.[1] Two of these fishing craft were required to shoot and recover one net. The word passed into Genoese either unaltered or as *baransella*, with influence of dialectal *baransa*, 'balance', and from thence entered French directly, or, conceivably, via Provençal *balancello* (registered by Mistral as 'espèce d'imbarcation *néapolitaine*' [*Tr. dou Felibrige*]). See Vidos, pp. 226–8.

ballerine. Ballerina, *première danseuse*.

1858 Peschier, Supplt. to *Mozin* (B. Quemada, in *Datations 1960*). Not in Littré or the *D.G.* <It. *ballerina*, 15th cent. (B-Al.).

biscotte. Culin.: Rusk.

1807 *Alman. des gourmands* (*F.M.*, XXIII, 307); 1830 Balzac; 1842 Mozin, *Dict. fr.-allem.* *Biscotin* 'small, hard biscuit' is registered in Richelet, 1680, and by the 1701 edition of Furetière. <It. *biscotto*; *panebiscotto* in Dom. Cavalca, *c.* 1270–1342, *biscotto* itself in G. Villani. *Biscotin* < It. *biscottino*, 16th cent. ('biscottini e biscottoni' in S. Caterina de' Ricci, 1522–90 [*Gr. diz. it.*]). The French word *biscotte* has become feminine through the influence of other feminines terminating in a final consonant (double const. + *e* graphy).

bora. Geog.: Bora.

A violent north wind experienced in the Adriatic. 1830 Stendhal, *Corresp.*, 7, 15 (Le Divan) (*Mélanges Dauzat*, 24). <It. *bora* (Trieste) of Slovene origin.

brio. Liveliness, vivacity, go.

Properly a musical term. 1812 Stendhal (Dauz.); 1829 id., *Promenade dans Rome*; also in the *Chartreuse de Parme*: 'une gaieté pleine de *brio* et d'imprévu' (p. 43 of H. Martineau's critical edition, Paris, 1949) and in Balzac, *La Cousine Bette*, described as 'mot italien intraduisible, que nous commençons à employer' (Brunot, *Hist.*, XII, 382). It. word *brio*, 16th cent., Barozzi (B-Al.); senses as above. *Vide* M. Wandruszka, *Rom. Forsch.*, 67 (1955), p. 20.

---

1. B-Al. register *paranza* meaning the two ships, i.e. two *paranzelle*, in Stratico, 1833.

camoufler. Originally to trick, hoodwink, in thieves' slang.

1829 Forban (Dauz.); 1837 B-Wart. <It. *camuffare*, originally 'to garb, disguise' (Francesco da Buti, 14th cent.; Domenico Cavalca, *c.* 1270–1342), then 'to trick' (first in Luigi Pulci, 1432–84). A borrowing from It. furbesco is beyond doubt; but the relation between this term and Fr. *camouflet* 'snub, affront' (1611, Cotgr.; but *chault mouflet* 15th cent. and *chaumouflet* 17th cent., Oudin, in the original sense of 'smoke blown into the nostrils for medicinal purposes', whence the semantic extension) is far from clear, as also is the position of Fr. argot *camoufle* 'candle' (1821 Ansiaume). Though *chault-mouflet* could be considered an adaptation of an earlier Italian loan from *camuffare*, it is more probably a term of separate origin formed from *chaud* and *muffle*, 'muzzle, snout' (cf. *mouflard* 14th cent., 'heavy-jowled'), or even from *chaume*, 'straw'.[1] The term of thieves' slang is usually traced back to a word *camuffo*, 'panno o bavero che serviva a coprirsi o panno per mascherarsi', acc. to Prati (*V. Et. It.*, s.v. *camuffare*), who supports this form by Venetian *camufo* 'balza, gala', and LowLat. *camuzzo* 'genus panni'. The two terms have a certain affinity of meaning—'to blow smoke into the face, abuse', hence 'to trick, hoodwink'. But all things considered a separate origin is likely. Reciprocal influences both of form and meaning may have occurred at a later date.

carbonaro. Member of the secret society of *Carbonari*.

1820 Stendhal (Dauz.); derivative *carbonarisme*, 1820, id. The secret society was introduced in France by Bazard and Dugied in 1818. <It. *carbonaro* 'charcoal-burner', so called because the movement was first active in the Abruzzi and Calabria, where charcoal was burnt. Carlo Botta says that the sect was formed in this region about 1808 (C. Botta, *Storia d'Italia dal 1789 al 1814* [1834]; *vide* Gr. *diz. it.*).

cardinalice. Eccles.: Adj. corresponding to subst. *cardinal*.

1829 Boiste. <It. *cardinalizio* (adj.), attested 16th cent. (B-Al.). *Grado, abito, cappello cardinalizio* are typical Italian collocations; *charge, fonction, titre cardinalice*, typical French ones.

carlin. Small pug-nosed dog with black muzzle.

1803 B-Wart.; 1814 Béranger (Dauz.); 1835 Acad. Understood to be a jocular extension of Carlin, nickname of Carlo Bertinazzi (1713–83) who played Harlequin in Paris and wore a black mask which the dog's markings resembled. As the name of this breed of dog *carlin* enters Italian (*carlino*) during the course of the 19th century (B-Al., Gr. *diz. it.*, etc.).

carnavalesque. Pertaining to a carnival.

1845 Gautier (Dauz.); 1867 B-Wart. <It. *carnevalesco*, adj. < *carnevale*; *carnovalesco* in Fra Giordano (1260–1311), Crusca. The French borrowing provides an adjective corresponding to *carnaval*, itself drawn from Italian in the 16th century (q.v.).

cartabelle. Eccles.: List of services.

19th cent. Dauz., 7th edition. <It. *cartabello*, originally 'small book, opuscule' (Fra Giordano, 1260–1311).

casquer. Argot: To pay up, fork out.

Initially to 'fall for' a trick. 1837 Vidocq. <It. (regional) *cascare* 'to fall down', attested from Dante onwards. The metaphorical extensions which French usage imitated begin to be found in more recent times, e.g. *cascarci* 'to be taken in by a trick' in Goldoni, *ascare* (absol.) 'to "fall" for someone' (*vide* examples in Gr. *diz. it.*).

---

1. Littré suggests a Picard etymon *cafouma* 'de la préposition *ka, ki*, equivalent à *con-*, et *fumée* . . . d'où le français serait venu par inversion'. There is scarcely need to go so far. A Picard form would well explain initial [k] and the original phrase might be taken as *cau(t)-mouflet* in this dialect.

coda. Music: Coda.

1838 Dauz.; 1842 Mozin, *Dict. fr.-allem.*; 1842 Acad. Italian word, *coda*, transferred to musical signification. Vincenzo Bellini (1801–35) in this sense (*Gr. diz. it.*).

colmate. Agric.: 'Warped' land.

Land reclaimed from rivers or marshes. 1835 B-Wart., but presumably earlier, since the derived verb *colmater* appears in 1820, Lasteyrie (Dauz.). <It. *colmata (di fiume)*, Leonardo da Vinci (*Gr. diz. it.*), < verb *colmare*, 'to fill up', 14th cent. Fr. *colmatage* 1845 is a further native derivative of *colmate*. The practice of reclaiming land on a large scale appears to have developed in Tuscany about 1781 when a legal obligation to carry out such improvements was laid upon landowners by the Grand Duke, later Emperor Leopold II.

confetti. Confetti.

7 Feb. 1852, *L'Illustration*, referring to the Carnival at Rome. The word was popularised by the carnival instituted at Nice in 1873. B-Wart. state that it was used in Paris in 1892. French confetti originally consisted of plaster pellets representing sweets or comfits; the custom of throwing sweets or small coins at baptisms and on other occasions is still widespread in France and Italy. In the 19th century paper confetti (esp. rolls of paper ribbon) were referred to in Nice as 'confetti parisiens' (Dauz.). <It. *confetti*, plural of *confetto*, 'sweet', 14th cent. (possibly a loan from OFr. *confit*).

contrapontiste. Music: Composer who makes use of counterpoint.

1820 Laveaux (Dauz.); 1831 B-Wart.; 1835 Acad. Variant *contrepointiste* ≠ *contrepoint*, Littré. <It. *contrappuntista*, 16th cent.

corso. Parade forming part of the Carnival at Nice.

1869, in the two senses of 'walk, avenue' (in Italy) and 'procession, parade' (B-Wart.). Italian word *corso*, 'wide avenue, parade', attested in Dino Compagni, Bocc., M. Villani, borrowed through the Niçois dialect.[1]

crinoline. Text.: Heavy fabric for skirts, still used for linings, etc.

A material with weft of horsehair and warp of linen. 1829 *Journ. des dames* (Dauz.) in this sense; the corresponding English borrowing with this meaning dates from 1830. <It. *crinolino*, a trade coinage which the *Gr. diz. it.* records in Carena, *Voc. domest.*, 1869, but which was certainly in use much earlier (Carena's dates are 1778–1859). The feminine in French is due to the influence of suffix *-ine* and the analogy of other textile terms (*mousseline, popeline* etc.). See *crinolina*, 19th cent. Fr. > It. loans.

crispin. Type of gauntlet glove; also a cloak in 19th cent.

1825 B-Wart. and Dauz.; 1845 Bescherelle; 1878 Acad. The original sense 'valet in the Italian comedy' dates from Scarron, 1654. *Gants à la Crispin, g. de Crispin* are current in the 18th cent., whence by ellipsis *crispin* 'gauntlet' in the 19th cent. *Crispinade* is registered in 1780. <It. personal name *Crispino*, manservant in the Commedia dell' Arte. Both gloves and cloak were essential items of his costume. Migl., *Dal nome pr.*, p. 181.

dabe. Boss, father (pop.).

Originally a term of thieves' slang, 'king, important person'. 1827 *Monsieur comme il faut* (Dauz.); 1837 Vidocq; also *dabot* id., 'chief of police'. 'Vue la date tardive de son apparition, *dabe* représente une abréviation plutôt qu'une reste de l'accentuation italienne' (Dauzat, *Les Argots*, p. 73). <It. *dabo* (Lat. *dabo*, 'I shall give'), 16th cent. as a gaming term, a sense borrowed sporadically in French also (Larivey, etc.). *Dabo* appears in Oudin 1642 and the derivative *dasbuche*, 'king', in the *Jargon* of 1628, but attestations of *dabe* are interrupted until the 19th century.

---

1. Cf. De Brosses, op. cit., II, 552: 'Nous allâmes le soir faire *il corso*, c'est-à-dire nous promener au petit pas de nos chevaux tout le long de la grande rue.'

désinvolture. Easy, graceful bearing, unconstraint.

Désinvolture in the modern French form 1813, Madame de Staël (Dauz.); 1833 Gautier, *Jeunes-France*: 'Mon ami Théodore, accoudé sur la table avec une désinvolture toute bachique, fumait une pipe courte et noire noblement culottée . . .' (cited by G. Matoré, *Le Vocabulaire et la Société sous Louis-Philippe*, p. 248); Boiste, *Dict. univ.*, 1834, defined as 'jolie tournure, galbe gracieuse de femme' (Matoré, ibid.). The Italian form *disinvoltura* appeared long before in J.-J. Rousseau, 1761, *La Nouvelle Héloïse* and was quite frequently used by the Romantics; Balzac, 1829, *Physiologie du Mariage* (*vide* Matoré, ibid.), Stendhal, 1830, *Le Rouge et le Noir*, Ch. 43: 'La disinvoltura de tous ses mouvements' (referring to the young aristocrat Mathilde de la Mole). <It. *disinvoltura*, 17th cent., ultimately from Sp. *desenvoltura*. V. *désinvolte*, 17th cent. It. > Fr. loans.

dispache. Marine insurance: Assessment.

'Average adjustment' or agreement on payments between an insurance agency and the owners of a vessel. 1826 Mozin, *Dict. fr.-allem.*, 2nd edition. <It. *dispaccio*; used to mean 'lettera di stato o ufficiale o di negozi, di affari' in Sassetti (16th cent.), Galileo, D. Bartoli, etc. (Pr., s.v. *impacciare*).

diva. 'Star' of opera, theatre.

1833 B-Wart. and Dauz.; 1835 Th. Gautier, Pref. to *Mlle. de Maupin* (Matoré, op. cit., p. 248); 1842 Mozin, *Dict. fr.-allem.*, 3rd edition. <It. *diva* lit., 'goddess' (Dante); 19th cent. in this sense. See Panz., 9th edition, p. 202, s.v. *divo*, and *divetta*, Fr. > It. 19th cent. loans.

fantoche. Puppet, marionette.

Dimin. *fantoccini* (i.e. pl. of It. word) 1815 Jouy (Dauz.); 1826 Mozin, *Dict. fr.-allem.*, 2nd edition; admitted by the Académie in 1835. *Fantoche* 1865 Littré; also in Gautier (Dauz.). <It. *fantoccio*, used in this signification by the 17th cent., but *fantoccino* earlier (15th cent., B-Al.).

ferroviaire. Railway (adj.).

c. 1900 B-Wart. <It. *ferroviario*, 1877 F-A., derived from *ferrovia* (probably a calque of Fr. *chemin de fer* rather than Eng. *railway*). *Ferroviaire* entered French via French-speaking Switzerland; *vide* Migliorini, *Saggi sulla lingua del Novecento* (1942), p. 144. The borrowing supplied an adjective corresponding to *chemin de fer*.

fiasco. Theatre, lit.: Fiasco, flop.

Faire fiasco 1820 B-Wart., 1822, Stendhal, 1841, L. Roux. *Fiasco* in Stendhal 1818 meaning 'bottle' (Dauz.). <It. (fare) *fiasco*. The semantic shift from 'bottle' to 'theatrical failure' has not been convincingly explained. French authorities have traditionally interpreted it as an argotic use proper to Venetian glass-blowers—a spoiled vase, no longer fit for anything but a bottle; though Wartburg, one feels, is nearer the truth when he recalls Italian *appiccar il fiasco ad alcuno*, 15th cent., = 'diffamer quelqu'un' (B-Wart., 1960), arising from the custom of hanging a bottle outside a wine-shop, hence 'to claim people's attention' and ultimately, one supposes, 'to make a fool of oneself'. Italian sources for the most part prefer a solution which harks back to some specific context in which the word *fiasco* was used, such as the well-known anecdote of the seventeenth century Harlequin Domenico Biancolelli and his bottle (*vide* Panzini, *Diz. mod.*, 1905 edition onward). *Far fiasco* is attested in F. Pantani, 1766–1837 (Pr.).

fioriture. Music: Grace notes.

1825 Stendhal (Dauz.), Balzac; 1835 Acad. <It. *fioritura*, 18th cent. (B-Al.).

flemme. Laziness (pop.).

Flème 1821 Desgranges. <It. *flemma*, attested 16th cent. in the sense 'calma nel procedere' (B-Al.). The French term is a doublet by borrowing of *flegme* (*flaimme*, 13th

cent.), drawn directly from the Latin Hellenism, which has a distinct though germane signification, 'coolness, imperturbability'.

frangin. Originally argot: Brother.

1829 Le Forban; 1837 Vidocq. Also fem. *frangine* in 1837 (B-Wart.). <It. (Piedmontese) argot *franzin*, a blend of *fradel* and *cüzin*, acc. to B-Wart.; Dauzat on the other hand considers it to have spread from Lyons where it arose as an item of silk workers' slang.

fumerolle. Vulcanology: Fumarole.

1818 B-Wart.; *fumerolles* (fem. pl.) 1826 Mozin, *Dict. fr.-allem.* The corresponding English loan *fumarole* dates from 1811. In the 19th century the graphy *fumarole* was common in French also, but the Académie sanctioned double *l* in 1878. <It. (Neapolitan) *fumarole*, pl. *fumaroli*, corresponding to Tuscan *fumaiolo* and used to refer to the fumaroles of Vesuvius in the first place, as in French. Wartburg registers it correctly as a semantic loan only; other senses are indigenous, e.g. 'spirale de fumée échappant des fours à charbon' (*FEW*, III, 853b and note). The English word *fumarole* is also the doublet of a mediaeval form, viz. MEng. *femerell* ('louvre, chimney in a kitchen') < OFr. *fumeraille*, *fumerole* (*OED*).

gonzesse. Pop.: Mistress, 'bird', 'broad'.

1821 Ansiaume (Dauz.), 1824 *Jargon*. Derivative of *gonze, gonse*, 'bloke, chap, guy' attested in 1684 (*Ragotin*) and the eighteenth century, but only becoming common in popular speech during the early nineteenth. <It. *gonzo*, 16th cent., originally 'dolt, ninny'.

graffite. Graffito.

Graffito 1866 Littré; *graffite* 1878 Acad. Often used in It. plural, *graffiti*, as in other languages. <It. *graffito*, 16th cent., B-Al.

impresario. Director, impresario (theatre, opera).

1824 Stendhal (Dauz.); 1833 Th. Gautier. <It. *impresario*. The sense 'entrepreneur' in general contexts dates from the 16th century; 'director of a theatrical company', etc., appears in the 17th.

irrédentisme, irrédentiste. Irredentism, irredentist.

End 19th cent.; first used (1878 onwards) about Austrian-held territories in which Italian was spoken, later applied to similar political situations in other countries. Corresponding Italian loans in English 1883, 1882. <It. *irredentismo, irredentista* < *irredento* 'unredeemed'.[1]

libretto. Opera: Libretto.

1823 B-Wart.; 1827 Stendhal; 1878 Acad. <It. *libretto* dimin. of *libro* 'book', attested in this sense in Francesco Algarotti, 1712–64. Probably coined in the late 17th century, acc. to M-*Stor.*, p. 559. The indigenous French word *livret* (various technical senses) has been extended of late to include the semantic range of *libretto*.

loge, loggia. Archit.: Loggia.

Esp. relating to ecclesiastical architecture in Italy; also a series of paintings decorating a loggia. *Loge* in this sense 1866, Littré; *loggia* appears later in the 1890 (Dauz.). Semantic loan from It. *loggia* in this signification, which in turn is a formal borrowing from Old

---

1. During a speech in the presence of delegates from Trieste, in 1877, Matteo Renato Imbriani, a writer and politician, referred to Italian territories under Austrian domination as *terre irredente* ('unredeemed lands'). The 'Irredentists' were attacked by the Austrian press and in due course the word *irredentismo* and *irredentista* entered Italian usage. (*Vide* Migliorini, 'The Contribution of the Individual to Language', *Taylorian Lecture*, Oxford, 1952, p. 6).

French (*vide loggia*, medieval Fr. > It. loans). The architectural loan from Italian to French probably took place somewhat earlier than Littré's time; Eng. *loggia* is attested in 1742 (*OED*).

maestro, maestria. Music: A great composer, teacher or conductor; the quality of a *maestro*.

Maestro 1824 B-Wart., 1842 Mozin, 3rd edition. *Maestria* in 1855, Flaubert, *Lettres*. *Maestro* enters German also in the 19th century, English in 1797. Italian words, *maestro*, 16th cent. meaning 'compositore' and 'direttore d'orchestra' (B-Al.), *maestria*, 13th cent. in the sense of 'professional ability' (cf. OFr. *maistrie*).

mafia, maffia. Sicilian secret society, Maffia.

Mafia 1875 Littré. The term entered popular usage in a more general sense—'conspiracy, racket'—as a result of the Stavisky scandal in 1933. Italian word *mafia*, *maffia*, of obscure origin. T-Bell. (1865–79) register *maffia* meaning *miseria*, referring to G.-B. Zannoni, *Scherzi comici* (1st edition, 1819), but giving no other meaning. The word we are concerned with appears first in Sicilian dialect with the sense 'valentia, superiorità, dote di coraggio e di intraprendenza'. One sees how this came to be applied to the private strong-arm men who first figure in Sicilian life during the disturbed periods between 1820 and 1848, and then to the secret society in its typical form from 1860 onwards, when middle-class landed proprietors used it to combat peasant unrest. (*vide Diz. encicl. ital.*, 1957, VII, s.v.). G. Rizzotto's dialect play *I mafiosi della Vicaria* (1863) appears to have helped in vulgarising the word. Prati cites examples in 1868 and 1875 in which the authors still consider it to be a neologism (*Voci de gerganti*, pp. 125–8). F-A., 1877, has an article on it (s.v. *mafia*). The 1875 attestation in French therefore follows hard on the heels of the Italian term in its classical signification, though the latter undoubtedly has priority. See also Spitzer, *Z. f. rom. Phil.*, XLIV, 378–9.

malaria. Medic.: Malaria.

1855 B-Wart.; 1867 Littré. Used first in speaking of marsh fever in Italy, esp. in the region round Rome. It. word *malaria*, lit., 'bad air' (the disease was thought to be caused by harmful exhalations in marshy regions); 1571 Tatti (B-Al.), 19th cent. as a medical term.

manille. Thieves' slang: Convict's manacles, handcuffs.

1849 *Jargon*; 1862 Hugo, *Les Misérables*. The history of Lat. *manicula* in the Romance languages is still obscure, but it is very probable that this particular French word is an Italianism. It. *maniglia*, originally meaning 'bracelet', is attested in the sense 'shackles' during the mid-16th century in Dell'Anguillara. Italian authorities in the main derive Italian forms from Spanish. Fr. *manille* meaning 'ornaments worn by natives', which I find in the 2nd edition of Mozin ('manille ... esp. bracelet de cuivre des Indiens pour bras et jambes', 1828[1]) is probably a direct Spanish or Portuguese loan, and so certainly are *manille* (1696), *menille*, *malille* (1660), technical terms in *jeu d'hombre* and *quadrille* (cf. the Hispanism *manille* = 'second best trump' in English 1674 (*OED*). *Vide* D'Ovidio, *Arch. Glott. It.*, XIII, (1892–94), 395 and Zaccaria, *Elem. Iber.*, pp. 254–7.

mercanti. Bazaar-keeper.

Early 19th cent. Dauz.; 1863 Camus; *mercantiste* 1842, Mozin. <It. *mercante* 'merchant', 14th cent. (B-Al.), either in plural (*mercanti*) or influenced by an Arabic suffix. Originally used in the sabir of North Africa, where the term came to be applied to bazaar-keepers, whence its pejorative connotation.

---

1. No doubt earlier. Eng. *manilla* in this sense dates from 1556 (*OED*).

G

mezzo-soprano. Music: Mezzo-soprano.

1838 B-Wart. (s.v. *soprano*); 1853 *Compl. du grand dict. de Landais* (s.v. *mezzo*). It. term, 19th cent., B-Al.

ocarina. Music: Ocarina.

Late 19th cent. (corresponding loan in Eng. 1877). It. word *ocarina*, coined in 1867 by the inventor of this musical instrument, Giuseppe Donati; < It. *oca* 'goose', either because of the instrument's general shape or because of the mouth-piece resembling a goose's bill.

orlet. Archit.: Type of moulding.

Usually the flat moulding forming part of the cyma or dado, i.e. the projection crowning a cornice. 1842 Mozin, 3rd edition.[1] < It. *orletto*, 19th cent. (B-Al.) acc. to Dauz. and B-Al.; B-Wart. recognise Italian influences generally in the more recent technical senses (s.v. *ourler*). This specific term has obvious semantic and formal links with other words already in French, e.g. *orle*, *ourle*, term of heraldry (narrow band thinner than the bordure of a shield, but also following the shield's outline) and other crafts; and *o(u)rlet* itself ('border', in various uses) attested from 1240 onward.

palafitte. Neolithic lake-dwelling.

Borrowed in 1865 by the French architect Delsor, speaking of the pile-dwellings recently discovered in Switzerland; also 1867, *Rev. des Deux Mondes*. < It. *palafitta*, used in pl. by Pigorini, 1864, to denote the lake-dwellings (B-Al.). *Palafitta* in the original sense of 'bank of stakes forming a rampart or foundations' dates from the 14th cent.

piccolo. Light wine, vin du pays (pop.); Music: Piccolo.

1876 Dauz., B-Wart. It. adj., lit. 'small'; used to mean 'light-bodied wine' in Bernardo Davanzati, 1529–1606. *Piccolo* (musical term) meaning small flute pitched one octave higher than the usual instrument is registered by French sources as an early nineteenth century term (1828 Dauz., B-Wart.); the corresponding word elsewhere dates from the mid-nineteenth (1856 in Eng., *OED*).

pile. Electric storage battery.

Pile galvanique 1812 Mozin, 1st edition; 1866 Littré. < It. *pila* (*pila galvanica*), which originally meant 'pillar, e.g. of a bridge' (G. Vill.), applied by Volta in 1800 (B-Al.) to his electric storage cell, invented in 1799.

pipistrelle. Zool.: Species of small bat, pipistrelle (*Vesperugo pipistrellus*).

1812 Mozin, 1st edition. < It. *pipistrello* (Boccaccio), earlier *vipistrello* (Dante). The shift from masculine to feminine in French is explained by the analogy of forms with pronounced final consonant, that of the suffix -*elle*, and orthography.

polenta. Polenta.

'*Polenta*: bouillie de farine de maïs, en usage en Italie', Mozin, 1st edition, 1812. Italian word, *polenta*, *polenda*, 14th cent.; defined by B-Al. as 'intriso di farina di granturco e di castagne (anticamente d'orzo o di miglio) cotto nel paiolo'. Wartburg considers MFr. *polente* 'oatmeal gruel' (1501, 1552; also in the form *polenta*, 1562) to be a Latinism. It is used mainly in translations of classical texts. The hapax *polenta* 1360 in a text of Avignon is however an ephemeral Italianism (*FEW*, IX, p. 125).

prédelle. Fine Arts: Predella.

Painting or sculpture upon the vertical face of an altar-step. Mid-19th cent., Gautier (Dauz.); 1873 Littré. < It. *predella*, lit., 'bench, step' (14th cent.); 'imbasimento sotto la tavola dell'altare', 1584 Rafaello Borghini (B-Al.).

ptomaïne. Chem., medic.: Ptomaine.

1890 *Larousse*. < It. *ptomaïna*, coined by F. Selmi in 1878 from Gk. πτῶμα, 'corpse'.

---

1. *Orlet*, *orle* are registered earlier, in the 2nd edition of Mozin (1828) with a slightly different signification: 'filet sous l'ove du chapiteau'.

pupazzi. Italian marionettes.

1852 B-Wart.; in vogue late 19th century. It. word, *pupazzi*, plural of *pupazzo*, attested in Forteguerri (1674–1735) in this sense.

putto. Fine Arts: Cupid.

Esp. pl. *putti*, 'frieze of Cupids'. Late 19th cent. (Réau, acc. to Robert, *Dict. analog. de la lang. fr.*). It. word *putto*, 16th cent., P. Giambullari (B-Al.); pl. *putti*, lit., 'little boys'.

quartetto. Music: Quartette.

1838 Acad.; 1846 Bescherelle; 1869 Littré ('terme de musique; mot italien qui signifie petit quatuor'). Plural *quartetti*. The variant *quartette* (pron. [kartɛt]) also appears in Littré ('c'est l'italien quartetto francisé'). *Quartetto* failed to replace the earlier Latinism *quatuor* (1767 Rousseau) and is not in normal use now. Italian word, *quartetto*, 1749 Chambers.

quintette. Music. Quintette.

1838 B-Wart., 1869 Littré; but the Italian form *quintetto* was in use earlier: 1778 B-Wart.; 1835 Acad.[1] Replaced the indigenous Latinism *quinque*, 1772 Voltaire, corresponding to *quatuor*. In 1835 the Académie recognised the Italian word, but as this was rapidly replaced in usage by Gallicised *quintette* the 1878 edition changed its rubric to that form.

rabouin. Argot: the Devil.

1800 *Chauffeurs* (Dauzat); var. *raboin*. <It. (furbesco) *rabuino*, originally onomatopoeic,—'da un *rab*—"folletto", parola indicante in origine un rumore, alla quale si riattacca anche *rabat* (franc. sec. XVI), "folletto"' (Prati, under *rabacchio*). B-Al. and Dauzat agree on the French word's Italian origin. *Vide Les Argots*, p. 72.

ravioli. Culin.: Ravioli.

1834 Boiste; 1842 Mozin, 3rd edition. Gallicised variant *ravioles*, *raviole*. It is hard to say when the term became current. The adaptation *raviole* is actually attested much earlier; cf. B-Wart.: 'attesté en Savoie sous la forme *raviole* depuis le XVI°s., un peu plus tard en Dauphiné et à Lyon'.[2] It. plural word *ravioli*, 14th cent.; but *rabiola* in 1243, considered to be a Cremonese speciality (B-Al.).

risotto. Culin.: Risotto.

End 19th cent., Dauz. *Risotto* is found in English by 1884 (*OED*). Italian word, *risotto*, 1884 Petrocchi.

sabayon. Culin.: Zabaione.

A sweet made of egg yolk, sugar and wine. 1853 *Compl. au grand dict. de Landais*, but *sabaillon* 1827, Acad. <It. *zabaione* (lit. 'mixture'), 15th cent., of northern Italian origin (from Savoy, acc. to Landais). Central Italian *zabaglione* may be a hypercorrection intended to remedy a supposed dialectal pronunciation (yod for *l mouillé*) (Pr.).

---

1. *Quintette* was originally a diminutive form of *quinque*; cf. Littré: 'quintette ... n'aurait dû être adopté que pour qualifier des morceaux de peu d'étendue;' (the Acad. also makes this distinction) 'au lieu de cela, il a complètement remplacé le mot quinque ... et il est aujourd'hui généralement employé pour désigner des morceaux à cinq parties, de quelque importance et de quelque étendue qu'ils puissent être d'ailleurs.'

2. R. Arveiller, 'Notes lexicologiques', *F.M.*, 1947, pp. 297–8 suggests that *ranioles* in *Le Mesnagier de Paris* (c. 1393) should be read as *ravioles*, esp. as this dish is described as belonging to the 'second mes', i.e. entrée, and is obviously of Italian provenance, since *ranioles Lombardes* occurs subsequently in the same text. Arveiller also give examples of the form *rabioles* in the 18th cent.

sangodémi. Interjection.

1835 Th. Gautier, *Grotesques*, 3, 24; also George Sand, *Valentine*. <Venetian expletive *sangodemi*! *Vide* G. Matoré, *Le Vocabulaire . . . sous Louis Philippe*, p. 249.

sépia. Fine Arts: Sepia; a water-colour painted in sepia.

1804 B-Al., 1827 Acad., 1828 Mozin, 2nd edition. *Seppia* in Boiste 1823. <It. *seppia*, attested 14th cent., Z. Bencivenni, in the original sense of 'squid' (the pigment was prepared from the squid's ink-like secretion). Doublet by borrowing of Fr. *seiche*.

spéronare. Naut.: Small sailing boat.

A small lateen-rigged craft with finely pointed stem (hence the name) used in Malta, Sicily and southern Calabria. 1831 Willaumes, *Dict. de marine* ('petit bâtiment maltais'), 1840 acc. to Kemna, *Der Begriff 'Schiff' im Französischen* (Vidos). Variant *speronade* 1874, Sachs-Villatte, *Enzyklopädisches franz.-deutsches und deutsch-franz. Wörterbuch*. <It. *speronara (speroniere)*, < Sicilian *spirunara*. Vidos explains the form *spéronade* as a suffixal derivative rather than a borrowing from an Italian *speronata*, which appears not to have existed. (Vidos, pp. 578–9).

strette. (Music: stretto); *see* 16th cent. loans, s.v., note.

tessiture. Music: Tessitura.

End 19th cent. Dauz., B-Wart. <It. *tessitura*.

tombola. Tombola, raffle.

1835 L. Gozlan (Dauz.); 1853 *Compl. du Grand Dict. de Landais*, in two senses: (a) Game of chance similar to lotto, (b) Kind of lottery or 'raffle' of gifts, 'que les maîtres de certains établissements de plaisir font tirer à la fin de la soirée pour retenir plus longtemps le public'. The sense of 'lottery' is more usual; cf. also Littré, 1867, and the *D.G.* It. word *tombola*, 1805 D'Alb. (B-Al.).

trémolo. Music: Tremolo.

1830 *La Mode* (Dauz.); 1842 Mozin, 3rd edition. It. word *tremolo*, < *tremolare*, 17th cent. G.B. Doni as a musical term (B-Al.).

triduo. Eccles.: Triduum or three-day series of religious observances.

1872 Littré; 1878 Acad. Both of these have the Italian form; later the Latinism *triduum* became usual (1876 *Larousse*). A similar sequence occurs in English where *triduo* dates from 1848 and *triduum* from 1883 (*OED*).

tringa. Ornith.: Tringa or sandpiper.

1812 Mozin, *Dict. franç.-allem.*, 2nd edition; 1835 Acad. It. word *tringa*, first in Oudin.

trombine. Argot, later pop.: Face, 'mug'.

1859 Flaubert (B-Wart.); 1867 Delvau. 1873 Flaubert, *Lettres*. <It. *trombina*, dimin. of *tromba* 'trumpet', or of the same word meaning 'elephant's trunk' (16th cent. Serdonati) (B-Al.).

tromblon. Milit.: Blunderbuss.

1803 Boiste; 1812 Mozin, 1st edition; 1835 Acad. <It. *trombone* 'avec une altération d'origine obscure' (B-Wart.). *Trombone* with this meaning appears in Italian in 1550, Della Valle (B-Al.).

turco. Milit.: Algerian rifleman.

1859 B-Wart.; 1867 Delvau. <It. *turco*, which in the *sabir* of North Africa came to mean 'Algerian' in general (Turkey had possession of Algeria up to 1830) and was therefore used by French sailors to refer to Algerian levies. *Turco* in this specific sense returned to Italian (1946, acc. to B-Al.; but apparently used already by Carducci).

vallisnérie. Bot.: Vallisneria.

Vallisnère 1827 Acad.; *vallisnère, vallisnière* 1828 Mozin, 2nd edition; *valisnère, valisnèrie* and the above graphy (which is preferred) in Littré. From the Italian word *vallisneria*

1831, 'dedicata da P.A. Micheli al naturalista Antonio Vallisneri' (1661–1730) (B-Al.). I assume that B-Al.'s dating does not in fact represent the earliest example.

vasque. Archit.: Basin of a fountain.

1826 Boutard, *Dict. des arts du dessin* (Littré); 1853 *Compl. du Gr. Dict. de Landais*; 1878 Acad. <It. *vasca*, 16th cent. Soderini in this sense (B-Al.).

vendetta. Vendetta, Feud.

1803 C. de Mérimée (B-Al.); 1829 *Rev. des Deux Mondes*; variant *vendette* in Prosper Mérimée, *Colomba*, 1840. Italian word *vendetta* (13th cent. B-Al.) which entered French through the Corsican dialects. Entered general usage as a result of the success of *Colomba*, though Mérimée's Gallicised form has not been accepted.

volt. Electr. engin.: Volt.

Measurement of electrical pressure. 1881, *Congrès d'Electricité*; a word coined by international agreement from the surname of Alessandro Volta (1745–1827). The adjective *volta-électrique* (referring to the phenomenon of galvanism) is registered by the *Compl. du Gr. Dict. de Landais*, 1853. *Volt* appears in Italian in 1895, G. Garollo, and the form *volta* in 1905, Panz., *Diz. mod.*

Italian Influences on French Vocabulary during the Nineteenth Century

The final chapter of our lexico-cultural survey begins in a minor key. In every respect the list of Italianisms entering French after 1800 lives up to the definition I have proposed of a *residuum* period. There is no large dominating category as in the eighteenth century Italian to French list. Abstract terms are very few indeed, *désinvolture* and *vendetta* being the only ones really to have penetrated general usage, with *carnavalesque* standing in as a useful adjective in the precise though limited context to which it belongs. At a modest eighty-one the total number of borrowings is down to the lowest in this direction (i.e. Italian to French) since the fourteenth century, and is closely comparable with the nadir of borrowing in the other direction, the French to Italian contribution of the sixteenth century. Turning forward again to the nineteenth century as a whole, we find that the total in this first list is down to less than one-tenth of that in contemporaneous French to Italian loans. The disparity is striking and significant. At no time during the history of French and Italian does the current of lexical interference run so strongly in one direction.

Very little has been written about Italianisms in French at this time. Official historians of both languages dismiss it with a passing nod and a brief word.[1] Yet even in this quiet backwater there are new things to observe and jot down in our register. Like everything else in language lexical interference

---

1. Brunot limits his comments on Gallicisms in the early part of the century to two sentences, and has little more to add in later volumes (*vide Hist.*, Vol. X, Part 2, p. 889). Migliorini devotes a couple of succinct but helpful pages to them (*Storia*, pp. 666–7 and 743).

is always on the move even when superficially it seems most quiescent. It must necessarily continue that way so long as men speak and remain aware of time and change.

As in the eighteenth century political happenings fall to be considered more appropriately with the larger French to Italian section, but not on this occasion because the effects they exerted were discernible only in the major importation. France was almost as deeply immersed as Italy herself in the events of the Risorgimento, the long-drawn-out struggle for national unity which was successfully concluded in the 1860s and '70s. This mutual involvement can plainly be seen reflected in the minor century list too. *Carbonaro* and *carbonarisme* are a case in point. The secret society of *Carbonari* arose in southern Italy between 1807 and 1812 as an offshoot of freemasonry, though with a definite political bias. In 1815 it acted as a rallying-point for opposition to the Austrian restoration, animating the Neapolitan rebellion of 1820 and that of 1821 in Piedmont. By the end of the second decade *carbonarisme* had spread to France (*vide* word-list) with pro-republican aspirations, and similar *coups* were mounted there (*conspiration des quatre sergents de La Rochelle*, etc.). Later the movement's headquarters migrated to London and, for a time, to Paris. The names *carbonaro* (literally 'charcoal-burner', implying a close-knit group somewhat separate from ordinary society carrying on activities in the wild, remotely) and *carbonarisme* were introduced with the sect itself, and in addition a number of Italianisms describing the fraternity's internal organisation: *bon cousin* (attenuated synonym of *carbonaro*); *vente*, a unit consisting of twenty *carbonari* (It. *vendita*); *baraque* meaning the formal meeting of a *vente* (It. *baracca*) and so on.

Nineteenth century political *démarches* were unusually productive of catch-words and slogans. A *bon mot* uttered by a general or statesman of the day could become a symbol of national unity or an expression of popular execration. Many of these aphorisms shuttled to and fro between Italy and France, and over a limited period had an extremely high frequency of use, e.g. *le concert européen* (1814) echoed by *il concerto europeo; chair à canon* corresponding to *carne da cannone*, attributed to Napoleon; Vittorio Emanuele II and the *grido di dolore*; General Failly's 'les chassepots ont fait merveille' which did so much to embitter Franco-Italian relations;[1] 'O Roma o morte !' (Garibaldi); 'En politique il ne faut pas dire jamais' (Napoleon III). *Faradassé* is a word which won a comfortable place for itself in French during the active years of the *Risorgimento*. An elliptical rendering of what was originally an Italian political motto dating from before 1848—'L'Italia farà da sé'[2] it was inter-

---

1. Referring to a new design of rifle (*Chassepot*) first used with devastating effect by the French garrison protecting the Holy See during the course of their armed intervention against Garibaldi's volunteers, which denied them access to Rome (3rd Nov. 1867).
2. *Vide* M.-*Stor.*, p. 637.

preted in France as a petulant assertion that Italy could achieve unification without French help, and turned back ironically upon the Italians in general (usually as an epithet: les *faradassé*[s]). *Irrédentisme* and *irrédentiste* first appeared in articles referring to Italy's claims on Austrian frontier territory during the 1870s and were later applied to other movements of similar scope, as in other European languages. As for actual Franco-Italian political agreements which are commemorated in vocabulary, we must not forget the Treaty of Turin (24th March 1860) by which France acquired the county of Nice *in perpetuo*. There Italian had been the language of day-to-day business till France took over and a number of words most closely associated with local life and customs were of Italian origin—*confetti, corso* (meaning the carnival procession for which Nice had long been famous). On the other hand in Savoy, which Italy ceded under the provisions of the same treaty, French was already the received official language and the usual medium of educated people.

With three exceptions the nineteenth century importation into French is atomistic, made up of semantically isolated borrowings. Each points the way to some small sector of cultural innovation which is worth our attention for its own sake but cut off from any obvious trend or movement. The three groups which stand apart are not very large, but what there is of interest in this century list centres upon them. Fifteen musical terms, a hang-over from the eighteenth century, make up the first one. The second, seven or eight terms of slang, mainly thieves' slang, is attributable in the long run to what I shall call quite unadornedly the influence of Romanticism. It forms part of a third mode of contact which is more a matter of style and personal literary idiolect than a stable element of *langue* and does not advertise itself very prominently in borrowed words, though there are one or two entries in our list which show us indirectly how it works. These are 'local colour' borrowings: foreign expressions used knowingly as a literary resource because of their exotic connection.

We can draw a helpful distinction straight away between Italianism in themes and their settings, the *mise en scène* of literature, and Italianism in the use of language, in the actual colours and brush-strokes of a literary canvas.

'It was almost inevitable', writes Professor Stephen Ullmann, 'for the young Romantics to give local colour an important place in their aesthetic. It satisfied at once two of their fundamental aspirations: the cult of the picturesque, and the interest in characteristic, distinctive qualities. It was also a tempting outlet for Romantic escapism in the face of a society where they felt neglected and out of place'.[1] More remotely, it served as a token of their desire for absolute freedom both for the person, against the restricting force of social conventions, and for the artist, in the face of academism and literary

1. S. Ullmann, 'Some Romantic Experiments in Local Colour', Ch. 1 of *Style in the French Novel*, Cambridge, 1957.

establishment. And since their chosen medium was language, linguistic exoticism (including lexical borrowing) became for many a practical method of giving body to all these aspects of their aesthetic philosophy.

The captious, provocative element in Romanticism was the one that had the most glaring effects. It is symptomatic that many of those who used barbarisms most wantonly were the militants who frequented, for example, the *Petit Cénacle* and later styled themselves *Les Jeunes-France*; the beatnik fringe who provided shock-troops for the *bataille d'Hernani*: Petrus Borel, Philothée O'Neddy, Aloysius Bertrand, Gérard de Nerval, Augustus Mackeat and their friends. Borel's use of calculatedly grotesque and un-French words reflects the jarring perversity of his themes and through them his *humour noire*, as Le Breton would have called it, together with the anarchical, satanic urge of his personal *daemon*.[1] And yet among the *lycanthrope's* borrowings and those of his fellow *bouzingots* very few Italianisms are to be found. English and German were the languages best calculated to produce the verbal and visual discords necessary *pour épater le bourgeois*; they also offended the wounded nationalism of the Napoleonic generation in a way no Italianism of the nineteenth century could ever do. But the reasons why Italian words are almost absent from these contexts and rare in most Romantic writings are not purely negative, one feels. This is not the whole truth of the matter.

Similar queries hang over the use of Italian as a genuine stylistic resource.

The Romantics ranged very widely indeed in their search for suitable sources of local colour. Once they realised what the precious metal was that they were seeking they quickly unearthed and exploited all the rich lodes of picturesque and evocative material which could be found. They journeyed back in time to mediaeval history and legend, crossed the Rhine for sombre German *Märchen*, explored northward to the lands of the Sagas, southward to Spain, eastward to the mystic regions of the thousand and one nights, and if necessary, by an induced afflatus, plunged into the deep romantic chasms of a fictitious Xanadu. Any *milieu* their public knew just well enough to allow the imagination play and establish the 'distance' needed to make fantasy acceptable was drawn into their productions. Or at a pinch a new background could be invented and endowed with an appropriate lore. The realm of local

1. Petrus Borel is especially given to choosing barbarisms for his titles or chapter headings where their impact is greatest. Cf. his short story *Monsieur de l'Argentière* in *Champavert*, which is headed as follows: 1. *Roccocco* 2. *Was-ist-das?* 3. *Mater dolorosa* 4. *Moise sauvé des eaux* 5. *Very Wel* (sic). *Rococo* was a recently coined term of *avant-garde* slang expressing disgust with anything old-fashioned or established, very closely equivalent in sense and register to the contemporary English epithet *square* (1966) (*vide* Matoré, *Le Vocabulaire et la société*, s.v., p. 239 and references cited). 'Very well' (sc. a direct calque of 'très bien') provides a sardonic twist to end the tale. The remark is made by an affluent Englishman watching the public execution of the heroine, who has been falsely condemned. Borel's actual spelling is *wel* in both text and heading.

colour, in a word, was unbounded—except for one limitation: anything hum-drum, workaday or prosaically familiar was inadmissible. This rule was of iron.

In Romantic literature an Italian *décor* is far from rare (Hugo, *Cesare Borgia*; Lamartine, *Graziella*; Madame de Staël, *Corinne*; Musset, *Lorenzaccio*, etc.); but when one searches one's recollections for examples it is hard to escape the conclusion that their number is not nearly so great as one might expect. It is not immediately clear, for instance, why early nineteenth century writers go to Spain so much more frequently to find settings and plots for their plays, poems and novels. The contrast comes out more forcefully because both Spain and Italy stand in the same geographical relationship with their northern neighbour. That Italy should have sometimes been passed over—or appear to have been—in the course of this universal prospecting is all the more odd since classical antiquity, real dead-bone, graffiti and hewn stone antiquity as revealed by Pompeian diggings and later archaeological reconstruction offer-ed excellent material for imaginative, vivid writing, not least because of the contrast between its plastic reality and the philosophical meta-world of French Classical drama. Rome, like Greece and the other ancient civilisations, was destined to return abruptly to favour under the new poetic dispensation of the *Parnasse*, but meantime traditional classicism was ruled out of court and so was anything that smacked of it. Italianism may have been overshad-owed by this general eclipse.

A further point. Italian local colour in the French Romantics tends to be peripheral in time or place, depicting either aristocratic environments of the Renaissance or physically remote regions like Corsica, which provide a *locale* for the blend of violence, passion, uncompromising virtue and villainy as well as the dour dignity of the human spirit which one associates with Mérimée and his *Mateo Falcone* or *Colomba*.

I think the answer to all these problems lies in the special relationship which obtained between France and Italy in the first half of the nineteenth century, and which for that matter can be traced back much farther, even to the early fifteen hundreds. We have seen something of its workings in the seventeenth century with regard to the plastic arts and in the eighteenth with reference to music. We shall find that a similar spirit animated Italians in their dealings with France. Italy was too close to France in many ways, above all in modern, real, factual and therefore non-Romantic terms. We have to remember too that many Frenchmen lived the most memorable period of their lives in Italy during the Napoleonic conflicts—among them Stendhal, the greatest Italophile of all the nineteenth century writers—and that up to 1850 a large section of the French population must have retained green memories of the days when Italy or certain regions of it were actually part of French territory, accepted into the French homeland, at least as far as France and her allies were concerned.

This as I understand it is why literary Italianism whether in themes, narrative fabric or linguistic medium elicits rather different values from the artist's sensibility than local colour does when derived from other cultural backgrounds. Italianism is not an appropriate device for those who create literature primarily by imposing their personality upon plots and words, and who tend to be the ones who 'make' local colour, *qui font de la couleur locale*, in Hugo's phrase.[1] Nor do I think it accidental that the chief *Italianisants* are to be found among the more sober, formally scrupulous and realistically disposed of the great nineteenth century literary figures (Stendhal, of course; but also Gautier, Musset). Romantic Italianism has little to do with fantasy and the imagination. It usually proceeds from the heart, as a real experience. This is why Stendhal, especially, excels in evoking and developing an Italian environment.[2] Italian, for instance, does not lend itself to 'onomastic' local colour of the Bug-Jargal, Zim-zizimi, Jérimadeth type, and there is very little sign in Stendhal of a disposition to exploit this resource, either in *La Chartreuse de Parme* or elsewhere. Superficial or *decorative*[3] Italianisms are used sparingly; Ullmann only brings to light half a dozen examples. It is extremely rare to find entirely otiose borrowing in the sense of words inserted by a kind of reflex, without linguistic plausibility ('Eh quoi, le *porco* s'est donc défendu?'[4]), or even without adequate psychological or narrative preparation. The descriptive, pictorially evocative power of local colour—its main function—is put to work by means of a variety of techniques. Stendhal is always well documented, even to the extent of glossing his own Italianising

1. 'Non qu'il convienne de *faire*, comme on dit aujourd'hui, de la *couleur locale*, c'est à dire d'ajouter d'après coup quelques touches criardes sur un ensemble du reste parfaitement faux et conventionnel. Ce n'est pas à la surface du drame que doit être la couleur locale, mais au fond, dans le cœur même de l'œuvre' (*Préface de Cromwell*, cited Ullmann, op. cit., p. 40).

2. *Vide* Ullmann, op. cit., pp. 44–52, 'Portrayal of a Foreign Milieu. Italy: Stendhal, *La Chartreuse de Parme*', and works on Stendhal's language cited there. For a summary of publications on Stendhal and Italy in general previous to 1948 see Pellegrini, op. cit., pp. 94–5. Pellegrini also has a useful section on the literary connection between Italy and France as a whole (id., pp. 71–83). I have not laid stress on this plane of contact simply because historians of literature have explored it in meticulous detail already. It is to be taken for granted, however, that the literary dialogue between France and Italy forms an extremely important part of the 'special relationship' mentioned above.

3. For a definition of this term *vide* Ullmann, loc. cit., p. 47. Local colour may of course be classified in many ways; see Matoré *Le Vocabulaire et la Société*, pp. 157–62, where *la couleur locale* is presented as one ingredient only in Gautier's remarkably rich colour vocabulary; also the general section of Hovenkamp, *Mérimée et la couleur locale: contribution à l'étude de la couleur locale*, Nijmegen, 1928.

4. Ullmann, p. 47. These vicarious snatches of foreign vocabulary begin to have point when the word's content is delimited by them in a particular way, where the image is vivid, or the sound expressive; cf. Ullmann's further examples 'la dénonciation de cet infâme *col-torto*'; 'un abominable *seccatore*, ce marquis del Dongo!' (id., p. 47).

usage on a number of occasions; he has an obvious affection for the language as such quite apart from its incidental associations. Many of his contemporaries strip off their garb of local colour at crucial moments in the action and psychological development of their story—leaving their elbows free, so to speak; with Stendhal on the contrary these nodal episodes are precisely the points where his Italianising becomes most significant. A good example is the well-known passage where he uses *disinvoltura* to evoke the uninhibited, easy grace of the young aristocrat Mathilde de la Mole at the moment when Julien Sorel's feeling for her is ripening into the passion which forms the psychological crux of the tragedy.[1] *Brio* is a similar pregnant term. Stendhal appears to have been the first to use it in print.[2] Other Italianisms whose first attestations to date appear in his works are *carbonaro* (1820), *bora*, the notorious tornado experienced in the northern Adriatic in winter (1830), *fiasco* in its proper sense of 'bottle' (1818), *fioriture* (1825), *impresario* (1824).

Théophile Gautier is another of the names one associates with Italian borrowings, though first documentations in his works are quite few (*carnavalesque*, *prédelle* and *sangodémi!* in our list). But he is well in the forefront of those who do italianise and on numerous occasions the earliest example of a borrowing discovered so far only ante-dates him by a short span of time, as we can readily verify by checking our word-list against the date when he first uses *diva* (Preface to *Mademoiselle de Maupin*, 1835, written 1834), *désinvolture* (1833, *Jeunes-France*), *impresario* (1835, *Mlle. de Maupin*), *maestro* (1831, *Jeunes-France*) and *polenta* (1834, *Grotesques*). Others not in our list are *prima donna* and *bravo* 'hired assassin' (both *Jeunes-France* 1833), *cadre* in its Italian sense of 'painting' (of Titian, in this instance) and *cameriere*, both in *Nouvelles*, 1837 and *zingari* 'gipsies' in *Grotesques*, 1834. Gautier was well known and well liked in Italy ('miracolo d'artista' the minor poet Giovanni Marradi called him) and his attitude towards Italianism was like Stendhal's, informed, tasteful and restrained. His journey through Italy in 1850 was one of the greatest artistic experiences of his life.[3] Early in his career he was an assiduous *habitué* of the *Petit Cénacle*—perhaps its leader, at a given moment— and some of the *Jeunes-France's* linguistic habits, mostly bad, had rubbed off on him.[4] But his meridional origin pre-disposed him in favour of Hispanicisms, which were much kinder to French ears than the outlandish usages of his fellows. Quite apart from this, Gautier's attitude to foreign words and

1. *Vide* word-list.

2. *Vide* word-list and Wandruszka's article noted there; also Ullmann, loc. cit., p. 52.

3. Most of the Romantics visited Italy at some period of their lives; several, like Gautier, published an account of their stay there. See H. Bédarida, *Théophile Gautier et l'Italie*, Paris, 1934.

4. For an account of what Gautier's language owed to his early literary connections see Part II, Ch. 1 of Matoré, *Le Vocabulaire et la Société*, 'Gautier et le *Petit Cénacle*'.

therefore to Italianisms even in those days was intrinsically different from that of his companions: I am thinking of course of his sensitivity to the plastic, formal qualities of language and his gift for exploiting them as an essential process of his *transposition d'art*.

Local colour associated with Italian has its positive and its negative aspects, but both have something to teach us about Italianism in its wider connotation.

Some of the words which were originally borrowed for their foreign aura entered French permanently. *Désinvolture* described a trait of human behaviour well, so it took root. Mérimée's arch-exoticism *vendetta* kept its original flavour while handily denoting a perennial facet of man's relations with his fellow-men. In much more recent times *maquis* (*vide* eighteenth century list) succeeded in breaking the shackles of its regional use, but its survival, like that of the third Corsican commonplace *mouflon* (also eighteenth century) was in any case assured by continuing interest in the region it came from—through tourism, in recent times. Another exoticism which has prospered away from home is *mafia* (q.v. in word-list); *mercanti* 'bazaar-keeper' 'street trader' on the other hand has retained the North African or Arabic atmosphere appropriate to its origin.

Another expressive device dear to the Romantics was the use of slangs, vulgarisms, rare and recondite words of all kinds. The terms traceable to thieves' slang in our list[1] are only a tithe of those from non-Italian sources which are to be found in a work like Hugo's *Les Misérables* (mainly indigenous and dialectal with Provençalisms to the fore). Most were culled from the Romantics' staple source of criminal jargon, the memoirs and dictionary of Fr.-Eugène Vidocq (1785–1837), a former convict who became head of the *Sûreté*. If there is some doubt nowadays whether Vidocq's work is accurate or even authentic in parts this does not materially affect the stylistic value of its contents, nor would the mere fact of imprecision have troubled novelists of the time. I do not wish to stress the 'local colour' aspect unduly, however. Interest in the lower levels of society was widespread at all periods of the century and in many Western countries. It provides a common bond for poets, sociologists and political reformers, puts Hugo on a footing with Dickens, Mazzini, George Sand, Engels and a host of others too numerous to mention. Our sample of slang has other Italianisms apart from those connected with the *pègre*; *gonze* 'chap', *gonzesse* 'bird, moll' and *flemme* 'laziness' were part of popular speech. It is well known of course that terms are perpetually migrating from true criminal *argot* to general usage in all languages and are constantly being replaced to maintain the original secrecy of the restricted idiom.

I said earlier that musical terms were a hang-over from the eighteenth

---

1. *Camoufle, camoufler, casquer, dabe, frangin, manille, trombine.*

century. My reason for doing so was that French music was no longer indebted to Italian in the nineteenth century as it was in the earlier period. There were naturally some cross-currents; music-makers have always been a race of travellers, and in recent times increased wealth and growing popular demand made it possible for composers and performing musicians to move even more freely from one centre of patronage to another. In this period the attractions of Paris were pre-eminent.

In practical terms the break with Italy came after the success of Meyerbeer's 'grand opera' in the '30s. Up to then Italians had had a permanent foothold in France. Napoleon maintained the operatic establishment which was considered an essential part of a French royal household by patronising first Cherubini, whom he disliked, then Gasparo Spontini, who suited him well and whom he made a kind of musical dictator. The link with Italy was retained in the '20s with Gioacchino Rossini (1792–1868). It seemed natural that Rossini, the greatest figure in opera of his day, should bring his genius as a gift to France, and equally natural that he should amplify his refined, graceful style in deference to the prevailing French fashion for pomposity and grandiloquence. But in the end his incomparable melodic gift and masterly portrayal of character proved an unequal match for Meyerbeer's musical diplomacy and the *science des planches*, the 'theatrical technology' of Eugène Scribe, who collaborated with Meyerbeer in producing triumph after triumph in the grand manner up to the beginning of the 1860s—works well furnished with striking subjects, sensational episodes, plenty of costume and musical techniques appealing principally to the emotions. In *Guillaume Tell* (1829) Rossini showed that he too could be bombastic, though at the same time musically brilliant, sonorous and controlled. But after this final success, seeing how the land lay, he ceased to write for the stage and left French opera to its own extremely successful devices.

Since opera was the dominant musical *genre* most of our words are linked with it. Large-scale productions demanded the specialised management of *impresarios*. The *poème* which Lulli, Rameau and Gluck had set to music became a *libretto*. A leading singer, perhaps a *mezzo-soprano*, was referred to as a 'goddess', *diva*, or a *ballerine*; a successful composer became a *maestro* and his talent *maestria*. *Appoggiature, strette, fioriture* and *tremolo* call to mind grand opera's embellishments and virtuosity. *Quartetto* could be used of voices as well as small instrumental pieces (cf. also *tessiture*) and *fiasco* in its figurative sense was applied first to operatic failures. A small minority of borrowings are left to denote new instruments and techniques applicable to other *genres—piccolo, ocarina, coda, contrapontiste, quintette* and *brio* used in musical directions.

The loan-words which remain can be dismissed briefly. As before, there are words in the traditional categories of visual art and architecture, but they too are fewer.[1] 'Social' terms are absent, but there is a group of words referring to the home, not all of which are foods: cf. *carlin* 'pug' (breed of dog), *crinoline* in its original sense of a heavy fabric used for dresses, *crispin*, a style of gloves, the game of *tombola* and names of Italian puppets, *fantoche*, *fantoccini* and *pupazzi* which correspond to *marionnette* in the section on French to Italian loans.

The residue of technical words corresponds very closely in the main to contemporary Gallicisms as far as meaning is concerned, but differs radically in point of number, usually giving just a hint, a preview of the massive transfer in these categories which we shall examine shortly. *Colmate, colmater* (concerning land reclamation) are semantically parallel to Fr. > It. *drenaggio*; *malaria* to Fr. > It. *paludismo*; *volt* (Electr. Eng.), from the name of the great Italian physicist Alessandro Volta, goes with *ampère* and *coulomb* named in honour of French scientists (cf. also *pile* [*voltaïque*]). *Graffite* (often *graffiti* in plural or collective) is an interesting archaeological term which links up with this facet of our eighteenth century evaluation, and so is *palafitte* 'neolithic pile-dwellings, lake villages' (< It. *palafitta*). The latter is an unexpected word to find borrowed from Italian since these traces of prehistoric civilisation first came to light in Lake Zurich, about 1823. But Italians were prominent among the early scientists working in this field. A systematic programme of research was carried out during 1853–54, mainly in Switzerland, where unprecedented drought conditions gave access to large areas of lake-beds normally under water. About the same time A. Stoppani made important discoveries of *palafitte* in the neighbourhood of Lake Varese, while in 1860 B. Gastaldi found them on Lake Maggiore and elsewhere.

Three ecclesiastical terms provide an appropriate *omega* to our list—*cardinalice* (adj.; pertaining to a cardinal or the office of cardinal), *cartabelle* 'list of services' and *triduo* (*triduum*). They are a token of the greatest cultural influence our word-lists fail to register; another language, Latin, has tutelage over it. The whole category of which they are part is not very large, but such borrowings as there are relating to Christian ritual and the Church correspond well to historical truth in that they appear consistently throughout the centuries, representing the constant relevance of religion to cultural history, and for the most part they have Italy rather than France as their point of origin.[2]

1. *Aquafortiste* (agent noun corresponding to *eau-forte*), *aquatinte, prédelle* already cited, *putto* (pl. *putti*) and *sépia* (colour, also technique); *loge* (*loggia*), *orlet, vasque*.

2. The remaining items in this list (mainly scientific and technical) are: *dispache* (Insurance); *ferroviaire* (referring to railways); *fumerolle* (Vulcanology); *piccolo* (Agric. in the sense *vin du pays*); *pipistrelle* (Zool.); *ptomaïne* (Medic.); *balancelle* and *spéronare* (Naut.); *tringa* (Ornithol.); *tromblon* (Milit.; but really an archaism ['blunderbuss']); *turco* (Milit.; 'Algerian rifleman', a term of North African *sabir*); *vallisnérie* (Botany). There are a few names of foods and dishes: *biscotte, polenta, ravioli, risotto, sabayon*.

Gallicisms in Italian during the Nineteenth Century

The first edition of Panzini's *Dizionario moderno* (1905) has been included as a source for the following list. It was prepared during the last decade of the nineteenth century from a fichier which in part went back further still, according to Panzini's own statement in the preface to his second edition (1908), where he recounts how the work came to be written and his attempts to find a publisher: 'Da molto tempo, prima ancora che giungessi al mezzo del cammino della vita (he was born in 1863), io mi ero messo a far raccolta di parole nuove. V'è chi fa collezione di francobolli, chi di pipe, chi di cartoline illustrate: io mi divertivo ad inventariare parole; è più ne trovavo di bislacche e di barbariche, più ero soddisfatto, e il commentarle gaiamente constituiva un mio svago nelle ore di ozio.'

By 'Purists' I mean certain specific authors of nineteenth century dictionaries which have an anti-French bias. See below, p. 559f. and Bibliography.

abat-jour. Shade, lampshade, blind.

Abagior 1883, F. Manfroni, *Diz. di voci impure; abajour* F-A. 1877, *abagiur* 1881. B-Al., registering it under *abagiur*, has also Calabrian *abbaggiù*. All sources derive it < Fr. *abat-jour* (1690, Furetière), originally an architectural term, which is still the basic sense given in Alberti 1788 ('fenêtre . . . dont l'embrasement de l'appui est en talus pour recevoir le jour d'en haut'), trans. by It. *abbaino, spiraglio*. The same source gives Fr. *abat-jour* 'shutters' as a recent French technological improvement (= It. *persiane*). This sense and that of 'lampshade' entered It. during the 19th cent. together with the objects denoted.

abbonarsi, abbonamento. To subscribe (to); subscription.

Abbonare and *abbonamento* appear in Alberti only in the sense of 'render buono' (translated by Fr. *abonnir*). The transitive verb in its meanings of 'reclaiming, improving land' (Soderini) and 'approving an account' is a native derivative of *buono* (as also is the reflexive in the sense 'to grow mild', of weather [Soderini]). *Abbonarsi* 'to subscribe to a society, to buy tickets', etc., is a Gallicism (B-Al., M-D., Pr.). It first appears in Bernardoni, 1812. <Fr. *s'abbonner* (early 14th cent.); *abbonamento* < Fr. *abonnement* (13th cent.). 18th cent. sources translate Fr. *s'abonner* by *far patto, appaltarsi, associarsi*.

abbrutire, abbrutimento. To brutalise; brutish dejection or degeneracy.

Both 1812, Bernardoni, *Elenco* (also *-irsi*), as incorrect usage. *Abbrutimento* defended by Viani (1858). <Fr. *abrutir* (1541, Calvin), *abrutissement* (16th cent.) (B-Al., M-D., Pr.).

abrasivo. Tech., esp. engineering: Abrasive (noun and adj.).

'Nel senso "detersivo" . . . è un recente francesismo' (B-Al.). <Fr. *abrasif* in this specialised sense (possibly ultimately from English); otherwise a Latinism. *Abrasivo* (adj.) as a medical term appears as early as the 16th cent. (Fracastoro, 1530, *Syphilidis sive morbi gallici* [Pr.]).

abregè, in abregè. Précis, brief account.

1860 Ugol., *Vocab.; abregé* (sic), 1877 F-A., who strongly condemn the use of these terms for *sunto, compendio*. French forms *abrégé, en abrégé* registered in Panzini and other recent sources. B-Al., Pr., 19th cent. purists. Fr. word *abrégé* (14th cent.) < OFr. *abregier*.

abrupzione. Medic.: Transverse fracture.

19th cent. scientific term. '(*Abrupzione*) è venuta a noi attraverso il franc. *abruption*, prestito dotto' (B-Al.).

absentismo. Excessive drinking of absinthe.

1877 F-A. *Absintismo* in Panzini. <Fr. *absinthisme* (F-A., Panz., B-Al.), an ephemeral word (though one widely current at the time) attested in 1872, popularised as a result of French legislation on the abuse of absinthe during the latter half of the 19th century. The length and vehemence of Fanfani and Arlia's article show that the word was well known in It. in 1877, and probably a little earlier; its use is still deplored in Panz. IV, but more recent editions register it as of purely historical interest.

acagiù. Mahogany, esp. timber.

Acajou (acaiou) is in Vallisneri (1661–1730) and O. Targ. Tozzetti, *Istituzioni botaniche*, 1802, and *acaju* in Alberti, 1777, etc.; but this word is substantially different from the Gallicism in meaning as well as form. These pre-19th cent. examples are physicians' and botanists' terms rather than cabinet makers'. They either refer to the fruit, used in medicine (Vallisneri, Alberti[1]) or to an actual tree, which in fact seems to be a different one from the mahogany tree, viz. *Cassuvium pomiferum*, not *Swietenia mahogoni*; cf. Targ. Tozz., who after describing the fruit adds, 'Il legno è bianco, e serve per farne mobilia' (T-Bell.). Alberti apparently does not think of *acajù* as a furniture-maker's term. But Tozzetti by 1802 is aware that it is used as such, and also that it can mean the same wood as is denoted by Fr. *acajou* or Eng. *mahogany*, since he goes on to say: 'Comunemente si dice Legno d'acajou un legno rosso cupo, il quale non appartiene a questa pianta (i.e *cassuvium pomiferum*); ed altre volte si dà il nome di Acajou al Maogani, quando per esser vecchio è diventato molto colorito.' *Acagiù* is attested in Gherardini, *Suppl.* (1852–57), the Crusca V, F-A. and elsewhere in the 19th cent. 19th cent. sources also have *cagiù*; the Crusca V has it, with one reference to Filippo Sassetti, *Lettere* (16th cent.) which must be regarded as an isolated early example. The older term *acajù* was a direct borrowing from Portuguese (the same thing occurred in the earlier French attestations, e.g. *acaïou* in 1558) replaced by Gallicising forms (influence of Fr. [ʒ]) at the beginning of the 19th cent. These were associated with the new signification, i.e. that of the timber rather than the plant or fruit. <Fr. *acajou* (M-D., Pr.; B-Al. see it as only a possible loan), 1578, Léry, from the Tupi language of Brazil via Portuguese.

accantonare. Milit.: To billet troops in a locality.

1806 (Jan.), *Giornale Italiano*; 1812 Bernardoni, *Elenco* (also reflexive); 1835 Lissone, *Fraseologia*; frequent examples later. Also *accantonamento* 'cantoonment' in Bernardoni, 1853 D'Ayala, etc. <Fr. *cantonner, cantonnement* as a military term (Purists, Panz., B-Al., Pr.) with addition of Italian prefix.

acchito. Opening shot in billiards.

1852–57 Gherard., *Suppl.*; esp. in the metaphor *di primo acchito* already in Gius. Giusti (1809–50), quoted by Gherardini. <Fr. *acquit* (B-Al., M-D., Pr.), < *acquitter*, 'to free oneself'. It. *acchitare* and *acchitarsi* as tech. terms of the game of billiards are also taken from the Fr. forms.

accidentato. Uneven, esp. of ground.

1877 F-A. in this sense. *Accidente* and its derivatives attested in other significations

---

1. Alberti's definition runs as follows: '*Acajù*. T. di Stor. nat. Sorta di frutto Americano'; the author then refers to *anacardo*, glossed elsewhere as a 'sorta di frutto come una piccola castagna ... che nasce da un albero Indiano: *Anacarde, acajou*'. The entry *acajou* in the Fr. > It. section refers to the mahogany tree, but adds: 'Son fruit est une noix en forme de rein dont on fait usage en Médecine. *Acaju*.'

(music, etc.) from Dante onwards are Latinisms. The meaning 'uneven, undulating terrain' is a semantic loan < Fr. *accidenté* (B-Al., Pr., and Panzini, who registers it as 'francesismo manifesto; assai in uso'). The same may be true of the slightly earlier usage = 'struck by misfortune' (early 19th cent., Giusti), which F-A. allow.

acclimatare, acclimatarsi. To acclimatise.

Trans. verb 1812, Bernardoni; reflexive 1877, F-A.; also *acclimatazione* 1875, Lessona, and Panzini, 1905, who also has *acclimatizzare*. Most purists, the Crusca and Viani approve of *acclimare* as the correct form; Petrocchi accepts both this and *acclimatare*. <Fr. (s')*acclimater*, 1782 (Panz., B-Al., M-D., Pr.), neologism coined by Raynal. *Acclimatazione* < Fr. *acclimatation*, 1834. The It. word was used esp. to translate Fr. *Jardin d'Acclimatation*.

accumulatore. Tech., elect. and auto engin.: Accumulator, battery.

19th cent., B-Al. 1892 Garollo, *Picc. encicl. Hoepli* (Pr.) as a scientific (electrical) term, though the sense 'one who collects' is already in the 17th cent. (P. Segneri) and registered by 18th cent. lexicographers. Other late 19th cent. examples, including D'Annunzio. <Fr. *accumulateur* in technical acceptance (B-Al., Pr.); Latinism coined by Planté in 1860 to describe his electrical storage cell.

acròbata. Acrobat.

Crusca, V; 1855 Fanf.: *acrobate* 1875, Lessona. <Fr. learned term *acrobate*, 1797, Gatel acc. to B-A. and Pr., both of which sources also consider *acrobatico* (Giorgini, *Nov. vocab.*: compiled 1870 >) and *acrobatismo* (Lessona, 1875) to be directly influenced by Fr. *acrobatique*, acrobatisme.[1]

aeraggio. Tech.: Ventilation.

1877 F-A. <Fr. *aérage* (Panz., B-Al., Pr.), early 19th cent. A French influence in the case of *aerare, aerato* is less certain. Both verb and adjective appear comparatively late— 18th cent. (B-Al.) as opposed to French *aérer* in an *ordonnance royale* of 1398; neither is much used until the 19th century. Alberti translates the French technical term *aérer* (= 'donner de l'air à un bâtiment, chasser le mauvais air') by a periphrasis, and *aéré* (referring to the siting of a house) by (*casa*) *ariosa*. A Gallicism is very probable in *aerazione* (Fr. *aération* coined at about the same time as *aérage*, i.e. early 19th cent.).

affarato. Busy, occupied.

1860 Ugolini; 1877 F-A.: 'Affarato per affaccendato, per es. "Sono tanto affarato da non poter venire al teatro" è l'affairé francese.' <Fr. *affairé*, same sense, 16th cent.

afferente. Concerning, referring to.

1877 F-A.; condemned as a Gallicism when used instead of *riguardante, concernante*. <Fr. legal term *afférent* (B-Al.), Latinising form of OFr. *aferant* from the archaic verb *aferir* (12th > 16th cent.). Though a bureaucratic word, *afferente* appears to have entered Italian after the Napoleonic period. Bernardoni does not register it.

aggiornare. To adjourn.

Aggiornare meaning 'to dawn, of day' 'to appoint a day' (legal, referring to the day upon which an accused person must appear to answer a charge) is a native term attested

---

1. According to Panzini there is no formal French influence in the learned Hellenism *acròbata*, but only certain of its semantic (metaphorical) extensions, as when 'per traslato, dicesi di chi con salti e sforzi di logica manifesti e ridicoli si studia di coprire e mascherare un proprio difetto od errore'. This sort of usage may be taken from French—especially from political journalese—but the loan is probably more than simply a semantic one in view of dating and context. There are several other examples of traditional music-hall and cabaret terms replaced by French equivalents from the mid-19th cent. onward, e.g. *prestidigitatore, chanteuse*.

H

in 14th cent. texts. A French influence comes in with certain 19th cent. extensions of meaning. Parenti (*Catologo di spropositi*, 1840) distinguishes between 'to appoint a day' and 'to adjourn', condemning the latter, though without mentioning a French semantic loan. Later authorities (F-A., Panz.) summarise the earlier purists' arguments and ascribe the new sense to the influence of Fr. *ajourner*. B-Al. and M-D. agree. *Aggiornare* 'to adjourn' came into use soon after and as a result of the French revolutionary armies' invasion of northern Italy. Fr. *ajourner* 'to dawn' and 'to fix a day' are attested in Ville-hardouin and the Menestrel de Reims; 'to adjourn' is a later extension. An example of *aggiornamento* 'adjournment' appears 1812 in Bernardoni (*ritardo* suggested as an alternative).

agitatore. Political agitator.

F-A., 2nd edition, 1881 register *agitatore* together with *agitare* 'to conduct political agitation' and *agitazione* 'political agitation' as inadmissible usages, without discussing their provenance; Rigutini, however, (1882) insists that all three are Gallicisms. B-Al. concur in the case of *agitatore* (< Fr. *agitateur*, 1687, Dauz., itself perhaps < English *agitator* in this sense); in the verb and abstract noun a French influence is less certain. Rigutini's observation that the terms entered Italian during the First Republic is worthy of note, though I feel that if this were the case earlier 19th century examples would be available.

alaggio. Naut.: Towing, towage.

19th cent. Also *scala d'alaggio* 'slipway'. <Fr. *halage*, 1488, < verb *haler* (12th cent.) 'to haul' < Low German *halen* (M-L. [*REW* 3997], Panz., B-Al., M-D.).

alcolico, alcolismo. Alcoholic; pathological state induced by excess of alcohol.

Earlier forms with double *o* graphy, which Panzini condemns as 'scrittura francese accolta da tempo in italiano'. *Alcoolico* 1863, Crusca V; *alcoolismo* 1874, Lessona. <Fr. *alcoolique*, 1789; *alcoolisme*, 1863, Littré (Panz.; Prati considers the derivation possible, though not certain).[1]

alienista. Specialist in psychopathology.

1883 Manfroni. <Fr. *alieniste* (1863 Littré) (Pr.).

alinea. Printing, etc.: Section, paragraph, esp. of an official document.

Leopardi in a letter adds the word *alinea* in brackets after the word *capoverso* (Gr. *diz. it.*) (pre-1837). *Allinea* 1860, Ugolini; *alinea* 1877, F-A. F-A., Panz., M-D., Pr. accept the derivation < Fr. *alinéa* (17th cent., Guez de Balzac), < the Latin adverbial phrase *a linea*. F-A. and Panzini consider It. *alinea* a superfluous substitute for *capoverso, paragrafo*.

allea. Tree-lined walk or avenue.

19th cent. B-Al., 1877 F-A. Purists and modern sources (Panz., B-Al., Pr.) agree that *allèa* is a Piedmontese word (Turin) of the nineteenth century borrowed from French *allée*. The 17th cent. attestation *aléa* (equated to Fr. *allée*) in Oudin is suspect. Veneroni

---

1. Is there a French influence in the case of *alcolizzare*, as Prati tentatively suggests? The specific sense 'to fortify wine with alcohol' may be a semantic loan, but this is a 19th century usage, whereas the Italian word appears much earlier in a variety of technical significations usually connected with alchemy or chemistry, which correspond to the wide range of senses assumed by *alcole* itself in earlier times. Cf. Veneroni, 1729: '*Alco-lisato*. Fortifié avec du sel armoniac.' French *alcooliser* (1636, E. de Clave) has a similar breadth of meaning; cf. Alberti, 1788, Fr. > It. section: '*Alcooliser: T. de Chimie.* Réduire en poudre impalpable. Réduire une substance en un acide ou esprit inflammable.' In French the sense 'to fortify wine' is not current before the late 18th century. It is of course possible that even in the 'alchemic' significations It. *alcolizzare* is borrowed from French, but not likely.

incorporates it into his work, but the editors of the 1729 edition mark it as doubtful, adding that the correct term is *spasseggiata*. The same edition translates Fr. *allée* (Fr. > It. section) as *viale, andata*.

all'insaputa. Adv.: Without the knowledge of.

1st half 19th cent. M-*Stor.*, p. 662. F-A., 1877, reject *all'insaputa*, though they are prepared to accept *a mia insaputa*, etc., an idiom which is equally typical of French. It. *saputa* is attested in the 16th cent. Calque of Fr. *à l'insu*.

almea. Arabian woman dancer and singer.

1874 Lessona (Pr.); Panzini (the intermediate role of Fr. *almée* is mentioned only in later editions). <Fr. *almée, almé* 1813 (B-Al., Pr.) > Arab. *'ālme*, 'instructed' (>*'alima* 'to know').

altruismo. Altruism, esp. philosophical term.

1874 Lessona. <Fr. *altruismo* (B-Al., Pr.), 1830, coined by Auguste Comte from *autrui* remodelled ≠ Lat. *alter*. Panzini does not criticise the philosophical term, but adds 'per carità, amor del prossimo, sentimento, pietà, non va, è brutto . . . e fuori posto come un vaso di notte in cucina . . .' (!)

alturiere, -o. Naut.: Sea-going, pertaining to the high seas.

Esp. in *navigazione alturiera, piloto alturiero*. 1870 Luigi Fincati, *Diz. di marina* (Pr.). Italian version of Fr. *hauturier, hauturière* (B-Al., Pr.); the adjective appears in French with this signification in 1671, from ModProv. *auturié*.

amarrare. Naut.: to moor a ship.

1813–14 Simone Stratico, *Voc. di mar.*; *amarrare* in Guglielmotti, *Voc. mar. e milit.* (1889). <Fr. *amarrer* (B-Al., M-D., Pr.) 13th cent., *Rôles d'Oléron* < Dutch *maren*, 'to make fast'. The It. substantive *amarra* is probably also a borrowing (< Fr. *amarre*), rather than a back-formation, in view of its appearance together with the verb in Stratico.

ambulanza. Originally milit.: A travelling field-station for troops.

1812 Bernardoni, *Elenco* (an 'expressive word'). <Fr. *ambulance*, 1752 Trévoux (M-D., Pr.). The alternative term in French, *hôpital ambulant* (1762) is also found in Italian: *ospedale ambulante*, 1828, Leone (Pr.).

ampère. Electr. engin.: Ampère.

Name given in 1881 to the unit of electrical force, in honour of the French physicist A. M. Ampère (1775–1836) (Panz., M-D. etc.).

ància. Music: Reed (of woodwind, etc.).

1826 Pietro Lichtenthal, *Diz. e bibl. della musica* (Pr.). <Fr. *anche* (B-Al., Panz., M-D., Pr.), 16th cent., Ronsard. Prob. from a western dialect; ultimately < Germanic *ankja*.

anisetta. Liqueur: Anisette.

Anisetto, anicetto, -a 1829 Boerio, *Diz. dial. venez.*; *anisetta* 20th cent. Panzini registers the French word in early editions, Italianised *anisetta* in later ones. <Fr. *anisette*, (B-Al., M-D., Pr., etc.) 1798, Acad. Alberti, 1788 (Fr. section, under *anis*) still does not mention the liqueur, though he describes a type of *dragée* made from aniseed.

appello. Milit: Roll-call, muster; idiomatic usages.

1812 Bernardoni, *Elenco* (= *chiamata, rassegna*); mid-19th cent., Ugolini, 1877 F-A., 1882 Rigutini. <Fr. *appel* in this sense (Purists, Panz., Pr.). F-A. cite as un-Italian both 'l'appello dei soldati' and the extended usages *rispondere al appello, fare appello a-*; Rigutini adds *appello nominale* (= Fr. *appel nominal*), but concedes that the military terms are accepted. Panzini notes the Gallicism while condoning its use. The juridical term *appello* on the other hand is a 14th cent. derivative of the legal Latinism *appellare* 'to appeal'.

apprendissaggio. Apprenticeship.

1877 F-A., who equate it to It. *noviziato, pratica, tirocinio* and consider it to be largely a dialect term of the northern provinces. Panzini refers to it as a *'brutto adattamento'* of French. <Fr. *apprentissage* (Purists, Panz., B-Al.), 1395.

appretto, apprettare. Text.: Dressing or filling of cloth (to improve finish).

Appretto 1877, F-A; both in Panz. <Fr. *apprêt* (Panz., B-Al., M-D., Pr.), 15th cent., *apprêter*, 10th cent.; but technical senses 16th cent. onwards.

appuntamento. Emolument, salary, soldiers' pay.

1812 Bernardoni, *Elenco* (general sense); Leopardi; D'Ayala, *Diz. delle voci guaste* (milit. term); Crusca V; F-A., Rigutini. F-A. claim that this signification dates back to the Regno d'Italia. Alberti still registers only the indigenous sense (16th century onward; *vide* sources cited by Rigutini) of 'pact, agreement'. <Fr. *appointement*, 14th cent., 'agreement, arrangement'; 'pay, stipend' 17th cent. onward.

appuntato. Milit., police: Title of senior grade in the Carabinieri or similar forces.

1877 F-A.: 'Altra gioia di voce per indicare una specie di Pubblico agente, Ufficiale, e propriamente di quelli addetti alla Pubblica Sicurezza . . . *Brigadiere, Vicebrigadiere, Sargente, Sottosargente, Commesso, Aiuto, Aiutante* e così via via . . .' The *appuntato* had, however, a somewhat different status from any of the available terms Arlia suggests. Generally considered to be a version of Fr. *appointé*, 'soldier who holds a special appointment' (signification current in 18th cent. French) (Purists, M-D., B-Al.). The military term registered by Prati (*V. Et. It.*) as an indigenous derivative from *appuntare* 'to jot down, make a note of' has a very different meaning, viz., 'cadet on probation, not yet received on the strength of the unit concerned'. The presence of two semantically distinct homophones within the same technical vocabulary is an additional indication that the one is of extraneous origin.

ara. Metric measure of area: are.

T-Bell.; F-A. 1877. Arlia strongly criticises 'i dotti Francesi institutori del sistema metrico' and notes that metric weights and measures were introduced by the *Legge sui pesi e le misure* of 16th July 1861 (*vide* F-A., 2nd edition, 1881). Montferrier, *Dizionario di scienze matematiche*, Florence, 1838, is cited as an earlier source together with Parenti, *Esercitazioni Filol.*, No. 8. Fanfani urges that in any event the masculine *aro* should be used to avoid a clash with *ara* 'altar'. <Fr. *are* (masc.) (formed upon Latin *area*), introduced 1795, *Décret du 18 germinal*. The fem. form has persisted in It.; masc. *aro* used in early sources (C. Cattaneo also has *decaro* and *ettaro* [†1869]).

arbitraggio. Finance and banking: Arbitrage.

Crusca V; 1875 Fanfani e Rigutini, 1877 F-A., 1882 Rigutini, etc. Panzini has two principal significations (a) recourse to arbitration in financial matters, esp. banking, (b) a banking operation; purchase of shares to sell when the market is more favourable. The Crusca (who like the Purists are aware of the term's French origin) accept sense (a); Rigutini also permits this use, and F-A. and Panz. are inclined to agree. <Fr. *arbitrage*, 13th cent.; financial terms 19th cent.

armoàr. Display or show-cabinet, glass-fronted cupboard.

Late 19th cent. word. Panzini I (1905) registers the French form as 'non raro fra i mal parlanti'. 'Francesismo della Lombardia, dell'Emilia e altrove', acc. to Prati. Phonetic adaptation of Fr. *armoire*, 16th cent. (earlier *armarie, armaire*).

armònio. Music: Harmonium.

Harmonium 1883, Manfroni (Pr.); *armonium* Della Corte, *Diz. di musica* III, 1930. Panzini gives both these forms, 'alla francese', and makes a plea for the Italian orthography, as above. <Fr. *harmonium* (Panz., B-Al., Pr.) invented by Debain; patent taken out in August 1840.

arrangiamento. Terms agreed between a hotel-keeper and his client.

1881 F-A., 2nd edition; 1882 Rigutini; 1883 Manfroni (Pr.), Panz. <Fr. *arrangement*, acc. to Purists, Panz., Pr.

arrangiare, -arsi. To arrange, settle, adapt.

Mid-19th cent. Ugolini; 1877 F-A. Panzini registers *rangiarsi* and *arrangiarsi*, the latter as 'verbo speciale del gergo di caserna. Per euphemismo, *rubare*'. Earlier Fanfani described it as a 'verbo francioso de' dialetti cisalpini' which had recently found its way into Tuscan usage (*vide* also M-*Stor.*, p. 725). B-Al. think it may equally well have been drawn from southern dialects, 'dove è prestito antico ed endemico'. <Fr. *arranger*, *s'arranger* (Purists, Panz., B-Al., M-D., Pr. etc.), 12th cent.

(pozzo) artesiano. Artesian well.

1859 Giacinto Carena, *Vocab. domestico*. Panzini proposes the alternative 'pozzo modenese', since traces of ancient wells of this kind were discovered near Modena. <Fr. (*puits*) *artésien* (all sources) < *Artois*, where this type of well was common; the geographical name is first registered in this connection by Boiste, 1803.

articolo. In the following senses: (a) article of merchandise (b) article in a written publication (c) 'leading article' in the phrase *articolo di fondo*.

All three have been censured as Gallicisms, though with varying degrees of reprehension. (a) (article of merchandise) 1812 Bernardoni, *Elenco* (= *cosa derrata*), as an incorrect usage. Crusca V. F-A. (1877) condemn it out of hand, particularly in the phrase *articolo di commercio* and Italian versions of Fr. *article de luxe*. Panzini observes 'nel senso di *oggetto, genere, capo* (*di mercanzia*) appartiene al numero di quei gallicismi che sono sanciti dall'uso; tuttavia evitati in decorosa prosa'. (b) (written article) G. Gherardini; but already used by G. Villani (1st half 14th cent.) in the sense of 'chapter, heading in a document' (cf. also *articolo della fede*). Condemned only by the most rigorous purists. (c) (*articolo di fondo*). 1897 Giorgini, *Novo vocabolario*. <Fr. *article de fond*, a loan-rendition of English *leading article* (term first used in early 19th cent. by editor of the *Times* (Prati). (c) is certainly a French loan, introduced through the technical language of journalism; *articolo* in the general sense of 'article in a written work, magazine, newspaper' on the other hand is probably a semantic development native to Italian. Sense (a) may again be taken as a French influence, especially since the signification 'article of merchandise' is attested in French as early as the 16th century (1597 Dauzat).

ascensore. Civ. engin.: Lift.

1890 Prati; Panzini. Earlier editions of Panz. give the French word, observing that although an It. version exists in recent dictionaries the Fr. form is prevalent, esp. in hotel prospectuses, etc. 'Questa parola francese è ormai sostituito da ascensore' replaces these remarks in later editions. <Fr. *ascenseur*, late 19th cent. in this sense.

assenteismo. Absentee possession of property.

1905 Panz. I; but *assentismo* 1892, Garollo, *Picc. enc. Hoepli*. <Fr. *absentéisme* (*absentisme* 1829, *Rev. des Deux Mondes*, *absentéisme* 1834) < Eng. *absenteeism* (B-Al., M-*Stor.*). Both Garollo and Panzini refer specifically to the practice of absenteeism in Ireland under English rule, but 20th cent. examples apply to similar situations in Italy. Italian forms reflect the original and remodelled versions of the French.

assunzionista. Member of religious order of the Assumption.

Later 19th cent.; Panz. I. <Fr. *assomptioniste* (Panz., B-Al., Pr.). The order was founded in Nîmes in 1843.

atavismo. Physiol., bot.: Atavism.

1874-75 Lessona, *Diz. univ.*; A. G. Cagna, 1847-1931 (the latter in *Gr. diz. it.*), also *atàvico* and *atavistico* 1924 G. Darchini, *Voc. ital.-franc.* (Pr.). <Fr. *atavisme*, 1863, B-Wart.; *atàvico* prob. < Fr. *atavique*, 1808, Boiste.

atelier. (a) Shipbuilding yard; (b) Artist's study, workshop.

Sense (a) *ateliere* 1866, Gius. Parrilli, *Diz. di marineria militare* (Pr.). Sense (b) 1883 F. Manfroni; Panzini, who adds 'voce francese . . . talora usata dai mal parlanti'. Fr. word, *atelier*; OFr. *astelier*, 1332, originally 'carpenter's workshop'.

attaccato, attaché. Attaché, esp. to an embassy.

1st half 19th cent. M-*Stor.*, p. 662 (= *addetto*), but *attaccato al burò* registered as in Monti, 1798. *Attaccato* (diplom.) in Ugolini. *Attaché* 19th cent., B-Al. <Fr. *attaché d'ambassade* (=*addetto diplomatico militare*). Corresponding Gallicisms in English and elsewhere.

attivare. To stimulate, expedite.

Vincenzo Cuoco, *Saggi stor. sulla rivol. napol. del 1799* (1st edition 1801): 'Io non veggo altro modo di attivare una rivoluzione che quello d'indurci il popolo' (*Gr. diz. it.*); 1854 Valeriani, *Voc. di voci e frasi erronee* (Pr.); Viani; T-Bell. Not in Alberti or Bernardoni, though the latter objects to *attività* in the phrase *mettere in attività* 'to put into force, circulation' (as of a decree). We may assume that *attivare* was initially a term of revolutionary political jargon which quickly became established in officialese. <Fr. *activer* (Purists, Pr.). A French influence is also likely in certain uses (esp. legal) of *attivazione* (1853, D'Ayala) as well as *attività*.

attruppamento. Noisy or seditious assembly, gathering.

1812 Bernardoni, *Elenco* (= 'adunanza tumultuosa, sedizione'); 1877 F-A. ('tumulto, branco, moltitudine'). <Fr. *attroupement*, 16th cent., de l'Estoile, acc. to F-A. (esp. *Loi contre les attroupements* [= Riot Act]). B-Al. draw *attruppare* from French (attested in Viani).

autoclave. Scient.: Type of pressure container for sterilisation.

1874 Lessona; T-Bell. Panzini adds a separate (nautical) signification 'water-tight bulkhead door'. <Fr. *autoclave* (B-Al., Pr.), 1820, *Descr. des brevets*.

autòcrate. Autocrat (esp. political contexts.)

1828-29 M. A. Marchi, *Diz. tecnico-etimologico-filologico* (Pr.) (also *autocrazia*); *autòcrata* 1851 A. Fusinato (Pr.). Ultimately a learned Hellenism: but both B-Al. and Pr. consider the immediate source to be Fr. *autocrate* (1768 Dauz.). *Autocrazia* may be < Fr. *autocratie* (1798 *Acad.*).

automobile. Automobile, motor.

End 19th cent., both as adjective (1892 Garollo [Pr.]) and substantive; *automobilista* 1899 (Prati); *automobilismo* and *automobilistico* Panz. I (1905). <Fr. *automobile* (B-Al., Pr., M-*Stor.*, p. 734), 'vers 1890' acc. to Dauzat; but *voiture automobile* in 1876. Most of the later compounds with *auto-* are native Italian coinages; a French influence is, however, detectable in *autoscafo* (Panz., 1908) *autobruco* (Panz., 1918) and the calque *autobruco* < *autochenille*, type of half-track vehicle for crossing the Sahara. (cf. Migl., *Saggi*, pp. 11-12).

autoritarismo, autoritario. Authoritarianism, authoritarian.

B-Al. register *autoritarsimo* as a late 19th cent. loan, and the adjective as 20th cent. Neither F-A. nor Rig. have them. *Autoritario* in Panzini both as a substantive ('an authoritarian') and an adjective (esp. *stati autoritari*). <Fr. *autoritaire* (Littré), *autoritarisme* (late 19th cent.) acc. to Panz. and B-Al.

autorizzazione. Authorisation.

1812 Bernardoni, *Elenco*; 1829-40, Tramater. F-A. reject it as an unnecessary Gallicism; Rig. accepts it with misgivings. <Fr. *autorisation* (Purists, Panz., B-Al., Pr.), 1419. The position of *autorizzare* is less clear. M-*Stor.* has it as an 18th cent. semantic loan in the sense of *permettere*. F-A. observe that though a Latinism, it is of French origin, and reprove as a blatant Gallicism the sense of 'permettere, dar facoltà, approvare'. Viani accepts the sense 'give permission' but not that of 'confirm, make valid'. B-Al. consider

it a French loan, but of the seventeenth century; *autorizzare* is in fact used to mean 'authorise' and 'to accept as authentic' in D. Bartoli and Galileo respectively. The original Latinism appears very early in French (*autoriser*, 12th cent.). English *to authorise* (1393 Gower) is considered by the *OED* to be a *formal* loan from French; the sense 'to give permission, authorise' appears already in 1571. Florio (1598) has It. *autorizzare* 'to give power, freewill or authoritie'; so has Minsheu (*authorizare*, 1627). The substantive at least can be attributed to the influence of French, and so also can the rise in frequency of use of the verb during the early 19th century.

avallo. Commerce: Endorsement on a bill.

Girolamo Boccardo, *Diz. della economia e del commercio*, 1857–63. B-Al. agree that it is a 19th cent. loan. Alberti in 1811 still gives only *girata* as equivalent to Fr. *aval* in this sense. The dating in Italian invalidates B-Wart.'s assumption that the French word was drawn from Italian. <Fr. *aval* (M-D., B-Al.), 1675 Savary, *Parfait Négociant* as a commercial term, probably an abbreviation of *à valoir*.

avambraccio. Med.: Fore-arm.

Avanbraccio 1874 Lessona, *Diz. univ.* <Fr. *avant-bras* (late 13th cent.), acc. to Pr. and B-Al.

avamposto. Milit.: Advanced post.

1st half 19th cent., M-*Stor.*, p. 660. <Fr. *avant-poste* (Migl., B-Al.).

avancorpo. Fore-part (of a building, etc.).

1892 Garollo. <Fr. *avant-corps* (M-D., Pr., B-Al.).

avantreno. Fore-carriage, esp. (milit.) of a gun-carriage or limber.

1829 Boerio, *Diz. dial. venez.*; 1863 Gregorio Carbone, *Traité de l'artillerie*. An extraneous term dating from the Napoleonic Wars (not in Veneroni, Baretti, Alberti) which ousted native words already established in the It. military vocabulary from the 17th cent. onwards (*berro, carretto; vide* Prati, *V. Et. It.*, under *berro²*).

azoto. Chem.: Nitrogen.

A 19th cent. word; 1854 Baretti, *Ital.–Eng. Dict.* has it (10th edition), together with *nitrogeno*; Eng. *nitrogen* (Eng. > It. section) is translated by *nitrogeno*, *azoto*. A learned term ('α- privative + ζωή 'life') coined by G. de Morveau in 1787 and transmitted through French *azote* to other European languages (M-D., B-Al.).

babà. Type of sweet-cake.

19th cent., acc. to B-Al. P. Artusi, *La scienza in cucina e l'arte di mangiar bene* (1st edition 1891) (*Gr. diz. it.*). *Baba* in this sense appears 1864 in English, as an accepted Gallicism. Described by Panzini as 'specie di *dolce* . . . fatto di lievito, condito con uva di Corinto, cedrato e liquore'. <Fr. *baba* (Panz., B-Al.) 1767, Diderot, as a Polish word; 1827, *J. des Dames et des Modes*, in a French context (*F.M.*, XV, 136). <Polish *baba*, introduced according to tradition by followers of Stanislas Leczinski.

baccarà. Gambling game: baccarat.

Baccarat 1892–95, Garollo; *baccarà* 1905, Panz. I. <Fr. *baccara¹* 1855, Dauz. (B-Al., Pr.);

---

1. Usually registered as of unknown origin. My own feeling is that it may be connected with the Arabic collective بَقَرَة [baqara(t)] 'cattle'. Cattle are a traditional symbol of wealth (no less to the Arabic-speaking nations than to others), and the real or symbolic transfer of wealth is a feature of most games of chance. That we have here a sophisticated modern card-game played for money stakes is immaterial: titles of games are frequently transferred or handed down. The Fr. word *baccara(t)* appears at a time when French power in North Africa, Egypt and the Levant was in the ascendant and linguistic contacts were frequent, as the number of Arabisms borrowed at this period indicates (*almée, burnous, cheik, zouave*, etc.).

also -*at* in Fr. (as in English) though less usual. B-Al. note that the actual game was of Italian origin and that it reached France under Charles VIII.

baiadera. Indian (woman) dancer.

'Un scritto su Le Bajadere è nel Cosmorama Teatrale (Milano 1838)' (Prati); 1865 Tommaseo-Bellini. <Fr. *bayadère* (B-Al., M-D., Pr.), 1638, *Hist. de la navig. de J. de Linschten aux Indes orient.* (*F.M.*, IX, 46); *balliadère* 1770. <Portuguese *bailadeira* 'dancer'.

ballottaggio. Second scrutiny of votes.

1877 F-A.; 1884 Rigutini (= 'secondo scrutinio'; observes that the *Nuova Crusca* rejects it, though the word is firmly established); Panzini. <Fr. *ballotage*, 1519 (Purists, B-Al., Pr.), a derivative of *ballotte*, end 15th cent., itself a borrowing < Italian (see mediaeval It. > Fr. loans).

banale, banalità. Commonplace, banal; triteness, banality.

1877 F-A., 1884 Rig., 1884 Petrocchi, Panzini. Also *banalità* 1884, Rig., Petrocchi, Panz. <Fr. *banal* (Panz., B-Al., M-D., Pr., etc.), originally (1293) confined to the feudal sense 'pertaining to the domain'; modern signification later 18th cent. *Banalità* < Fr. *banalité* 1602 Charondas (feudal term); modern sense 19th cent.

bancarottiere. A bankrupt person.

1877 F-A; 1884 Rig. (who strongly criticises it); Panzini. B-Al. describe it as a 15th cent. loan-word, but without reference to sources. Generally accepted as a borrowing < Fr. *banqueroutier* (*Ordonnance* of 1536) (Purists, Panz., B-Al., Pr.).[1]

banchisa. Naut., geog.: Pack-ice.

Banchiglia 1870 Luigi Fincati, *Diz. di marina* (Pr.); *banquise* 1892–95, Garollo—the form given in earlier editions of Panzini. <Fr. *banquise* (B-Al., M-D., Pr.), 1798 *Acad.* (not in Alberti, 1788).

basculla. See-saw (or machine device of similar action); weigh-bridge, bascule.

1853 D'Ayala; 1877 F-A. (movable device for weighing or lifting heavy objects); 1892 Garollo ('see-saw'). Panzini has the French form *bascule* (also *barculla*) and mentions that the word is also used to mean the bascule of a guillotine. <Fr. *bascule* (B-Al., M-D., Pr., etc.) 1549 R. Estienne; *bassecule* 1600 Olivier de Serres.

basare. To base, found (upon).

1812 Bernardoni (incorrect usage for *fondare*); Vincenzo Bellini (1801–35) *Epistolario*; Crusca V; 1877 F-A.; 1884 Rig. Panzini states that 'nel senso figurato di fondare, fondarsi detto delle opinioni, dei giudizi ecc. è voce neologica tolta dal francese *baser*'. B-Al., Pr. and M-*Stor.* also derive it from *baser*, a comparatively recent word in French also (1788).

bastrè. Dance, esp. in a cabaret.

'Ballo pubblico senza il freno della decenza: bordello' (Prati). 1863 Fanfani, *Voc. dell'uso toscano* (Prati, who also registers the form *bastrengo*). <Fr. *bastringue* (B-Al., Pr.) 1802.

bauxite. Mineral., metall.: Bauxite.

19th cent. B-Al., Panzini, VII (1935). <Fr. *bauxite* (B-Al., M-D.) 1847 (Dauzat), < place-name *Les Baux* (B. du Rhône) where the mineral was discovered by P. Berthier.

bavarese. Milk and chocolate drink: sweetmeat made with cream, sometimes iced.

1850 Gianfr. Rambelli, *Vocab. domestico* (Pr.); 1863 Fanfani, *Vocab. dell' uso toscano*; *bavaresa* in Panzini, who refers to Cherubini (*Vocab. milanese-italiano*, 1839–43). <Fr. *bavaroise* (B-Al., Pr.) 1743 Trévoux, a drink traditionally popularised by the princes of Bavaria at the Café Procope.

---

1. See *banqueroute*, med. It. > Fr. loans.

bazar. Multiple stores, emporium.

'Nel secondo decennio dell'Ottocento rientra in Italia *bazar* con l'ortografia francese e nel senso moderno europeo di "emporio" ' (E. Visconti, *Conciliatore*, 1819) (M-*Stor.*, p. 664). *Bazzàr* 1860 Ugol. *Vocab.* in the same sense; F-A., 1877. Semantic loan < Fr. *bazar* (Migl., Pr.) which assumed this signification early in the 19th cent. See attestations in *Datations 1960*, pp. 64–5. It. *bazarro* or *bazzarro* 'Eastern market' (1487) and Fr. *bazar* (*bathzar* 1432) are direct Arabisms.

bebè, bébé. Baby.

Bébé leggere sa già: title of a child's reading primer, 1881 (Prati); Panzini I. French word, 1793 Sophie Arnould (*F.M.*, VIII, 111) < English *baby*, occasionally remodelled ≠ English during the 19th cent. (Balzac, 1841). The same tendency appears also in Italian: cf. *bèbi* 1892 Garollo. Panzini (who also criticises the term of fashion *abito da bébé*) observes: 'voce francese che racchiude nella felicità di quelle due sillabe uguali la grazia del bambino insieme a non so quale amabile balordaggine signorile'; and under *baby*: 'vuol dire lo stesso che bébé francese, ma sembra più elegante perchè meno comune'.

beninteso (che). Provided (that).

1858 Ipp. Nievo (*Gr. diz. it.*); 1858 Viani; 1877 F-A.; Panzini. Understood by most authorities to be a calque of the Fr. conjunction *bien entendu (que)* in the sense of *purchè, a condizione che, a patto che* (Purists, Panz., B-Al., Pr.), dating from the early 19th century. The borrowing may have occurred earlier still, say late 18th cent. Alberti (under Fr. *entendu*) translates *bien entendu (que)* (conjunction) by *ben inteso che, purchè,* but under It. *inteso, ben inteso,* only registers the aesthetic term (= 'well proportioned, well designed'[1]). We cannot of course dismiss the possibility that Alberti himself may be guilty of Gallicising in this instance.

berlocca. Milit.: 'Stand easy': drum-roll announcing end of work period.

1853 D'Ayala (Pr.). <Fr. *berloque* 'drum roll', etc., in the above sense, probably onomatopoeic; *brelique* in the 16th cent., *breloque*, 17th cent.

berma. Milit. (fortif.): 'Berm' or ledge forming a continuous path part of the way down a counterscarp.

1853 D'Ayala (Pr.). <Fr. *berme* (B-Al., Pr.), *barme* 1611, Cotgrave, < Dutch *berm* 'slope'.

bersò. Arbour, bower (of trained plants, etc.).

Bersò 1820 Ferrari (Pr.); *berzò*, Parenti, *Catal. di spropositi* (1839–59), F-A., Rigutini; *berceau* and *bersò* in Panz. Italianised form of Fr. word *berceau* (end 15th cent.) in this sense.

berta. Womens' fashions (archaic): small pelerine or shawl with jewels worn over low-cut dresses.

1853 Ferrari (Pr.). Fashionable in '50s, under patronage of the Empress Eugénie; lost favour after the Empress omitted this accessory from her ensemble at a Tuileries ball of 1859, though still occasionally worn during the following decade. <Fr. *berthe* (B-Al., Pr.) 1840, acc. to Esnault < personal name *Berthe* (*aux grands pieds*), mother of Charlemagne, hence presumably a model of propriety. *Datations 1960*, p. 80.

---

1. Eighteenth century lexicographers are familiar with both It. *beninteso* and Fr. *bien entendu* (also their contraries *malinteso, mal entendu*) in the sense of 'bien assorti, bien pratiqué, parfait en son genre' (Alberti, 1788; goes back to Baldinucci). They are most frequently used to criticise the composition of a painting or proportions of a building. Some recognise a French influence here too (*vide* F-A., 1877, s.v. *inteso*). But since the epithet has in practice so close a link with the fine arts it is conceivable that the movement may have taken place in the opposite direction.

besciamella. Culin.: Béchamel.

French form *béchamel* 1892 Garollo and Panzini: the latter refers to an Italian adaptation *balsamella*; *besciamella* in 1904, acc. to Prati. < Fr. *béchamel* (B-Al., M-D., Pr., etc.) 1735 *Cuis. mod.* as *Béchamelle* (*F.M.*, XXIII, 306); modern form 1742 (Arveiller, *Datations 1960*, s.v.) < surname Béchamel, majordomo of Louis XIV.

béton, betoniera. Civ. engin.: Concrete; concrete-mixer.

Later 19th cent., M-*Stor.*, p. 738; Panzini (= *calcestruzzo*). Fr. word, *béton* (OFr. *betun* 12th cent., <*bitumen*: used to mean 'cement' already in Middle Ages). *Betoniera* < Fr. *bétonnière* (Migl., B-Al.); also *betonaggio* < Fr. *bétonnage*.

bibelot. Bric-à-brac, ornament, curio.

1889 D'Annunzio; Panz. Fr. word *bibelot*, 1432 Baudet Hérenc (Dauz.), probably onomatopoeic, as are so many terms denoting small trinkets and objets d'art. Cf. OFr. 12th cent. *beubelet* 'jewel'.

biberon. Baby's feeding bottle.

1883 Manfroni. Also *biberò*. Panzini uses as his rubric the French word (1st edition [1905] onward) but mentions the Italianised form *biberone*, 'voce .. di brutto suono'. French word *biberon* 1301; initial signification 'neck of bottle'.

bidone. Can, tin vessel; originally (naut.) keg for wine.

1853 D'Ayala; but *bidòn* (Milanese) in F. Cherubini, *Vocab. milan.-ital.*, 1839–43. <Fr. *bidon* (B-Al., M-D., Pr., Panz.), 15th cent. in texts of Normandy; prob. of Scandinavian origin.

biella. Engin.: Crank, connecting-rod.

Later 19th cent., M-*Stor.*, p. 738. <Fr. *bielle*, 1751 (Migl., B-Al.).

biffare. To strike out, cross off, cancel.

19th cent. B-Al., Panz. F-A. do not give this meaning, though they object to the legal signification *biffare una porta*, i.e. 'sigillarla in modo che non si possa aprire senza rompere il sigillo'. Sem. loan < Fr. *biffer* (B-Al., Panz.), 1584.

bigiottiere. Jeweller.

1812 Bernardoni; 1877 F-A.; 1882 Rig. Fr. form in Panzini. Rigutini and Panzini draw a distinction between *bigiottiere* 'seller of knick-knacks, trinkets', and *gioielliere*, 'jeweller'. <Fr. *bijoutier*, 1706 in this sense.

bigiù. Jewel, trinket.

V. Monti (†1828) *Epistolario* (*Gr. diz. it.*); 1863 Fanf., *Voc. dell'uso tosc.*; 1877 F-A., 1882 Rig. Also the adaptation *bisù* 'trinket' (= *minuterie*) in Monti ('un piccolo bisù' sent as a gift) and elsewhere. Though occasionally used literally in the sense of 'jewel' (e.g. in Monti), *bigiù* attracts the purists' attention principally on account of its abuse in figurative expressions; cf. Panzini: 'Una piccola casa, una donnina graziosa, tutto ciò insomma che è piccolo, ben lavorato, gentile, può essere onorato dall'epiteto di *bijou* . . .' (*Diz. mod.* IX, p. 71). Adaptation of Fr. word *bijou*, 1460 Lobin, *Hist. de Bretagne*.

bignè. Culin.: Fritter.

Defined by Panzini as 'Nota specie di dolce, fatto di pasta rigonfia e spesso imbottita di crema'. 1846 Tomm. Azzocchi, *Vocab. domest.* II (Pr.); Fr. form *beignet* 1892 Garollo and 1905 Panz. I. <Fr. *beignet* (Panz., B-Al. [who observe: 'l'epicentro del nostro *bignè* è Milano'], Pr.), originally *bignet* (14th cent.).

bisboccia. Revelry.

See note to *deboscia*, 18th cent. loans.

bistro. Low-class café or bar.

1st half 19th cent., M-*Stor.*, p. 661; Panz. (= *bettola*, *osteria*). Fr. word, *bistro*, of uncertain origin; 1884, Moreau, *Souvenirs de la roquette*, 2, 3. (*F.M.* XIX, 203; *Datations*

1960, 105). B-Al. and others also register *bistro* adj. of colour, 'bistre', as a Gallicism (Fr. *bistre*, 16th cent.; also a Gallicism in English and other languages [Eng. 1727, *OED*]).

bivacco. Milit.: Bivouac (temporary camp); also night patrol.

1831 A. Lissoni (Pr.); 1853 D'Ayala. Rigutini considers it a term of the Napoleonic wars, though Grassi, the most reliable military source for this period, omits it. <Fr. *bivouac* (Panz., B-Al., M-D., Pr.) 1650, Ménage < Swiss German *bîwacht* 'night watch'. The earlier Fr. form *bivac* indicates more precisely the pronunciation which prevailed throughout the 18th cent. and early 19th cent. even when the spelling *bivouac* was used (*vide* Alberti's testimony under *bivouac*, *Dict. fr.-it.* 1788). It. *bivacco* is a direct phonetic adaptation of this form.

blaga. Boasting, bragging.

Late 19th cent., M-*Stor.*, and B-Al.; *senza blaga!* (Fr. *sans blague!*) 1897, Carducci (cited by Migl.). An ephemeral Gallicism; Fr. *blague* 'tobacco-pouch' 1722, < Dutch. The sense 'tall story' 'bull' is in military slang by 1809 (B-Wart.). Also 'tobacco-pouch' in Piedmont (B-Al., etc.).

blindaggio. Protection by means of armour.

(Cf. *blindare*, below). 1853 D'Ayala. <Fr. *blindage* (B-Al., Pr.) 1752 Trévoux. The more recent synonym *blindatura* (similar sense; used also for sand-bag protection round monuments of historical interest, 1942 [Migl. *Suppl.*]) is a native derivative of the verb.

blindare. Milit., naut.: To protect with armour-plate.

The verb appears first as a naval term in Simone Stratico, *Voc. di marina*, 1814. Wider technical application in mid-19th cent. Baretti, 1860, *It.-Eng. Dict.* IX, defines it as 'to render bomb or shot-proof'. <Fr. *blinder* (B-Al., M-D., Pr.) 1697 Guillet (also used as naval term). It. *blindato* 'armoured' (adj.) (1892 Garollo) is probably < Fr. *blindé*.[1] See *blinde*, 17th cent. Fr. > It. loans.

blocco. Block.

A number of 19th cent. significations of *blocco* are semantic loans from French. (a) 'Block of stone or similar material': 1860 Ugolini, *Vocab.*; 1877 F-Arlia, who ask with indignation whether even the terminology of art is to be borrowed from France? and quote Michelangelo who in his diary speaks of purchasing 'un *pezzo* di marmo'. Rigutini's remark (1882) that the term was applied particularly to concrete blocks used in the construction of harbours (i.e. the habitual method of building in Mediterranean ports) suggests that the initial contact was not within the realm of art but of civil engineering. Parallel instances support this explanation. (b) 'Block system' on railways (also *cabina*, *posto di blocco*). Ultimately < English, but via Fr. (c) *Blocco* in the commercial idiom (*vendere*) *in blocco* (1860 Ugol.; F-A., Rig., Panz.) < Fr. (*vendre*) *en bloc*. The early 20th cent. signification 'political party, union of political parties' may be registered here. Acc. to Panzini, who objects to the Gallicism, this semantic loan entered Italian in 1907: 'famoso il blocco di Roma, cioè l'unione dei partiti democratici del 1907; il blocco dei liberali e nazionali nelle elezioni del 1921'. All < Fr. *bloc*, 13th cent. B-Al. also register the verb *bloccare* as a Gallicism in the senses (a) 'to "block up" on a railway system' (b) Tech.: Typography: to use a reversed letter temporarily as a substitute for missing type (i.e. the sense of Fr. *bloquer* in this context).

---

1. *Blindato* (like Fr. *blindé*) has been widely used during recent times in compound military neologisms, some of which may be directly inspired by French; e.g. *treno blindato* c. 1900 (Pr.), *autoblindata* (M-D.), *auto-blindo-mitragliatrice* (Panz.) and *carro blindato* (Panz., etc.) reduced to *carro* (compare Fr. *char*) referring to various armoured fighting vehicles (M-D., Migl.-*Suppl.*).

blonda. Type of light coloured lace, 'blonde'.

1850 G. Rambelli, *Vocab. domest.* (Pr.); Panz. <Fr. *blonde*, 1743, Trévoux (B-Al., Pr); a remodelling under Fr. influence of the earlier It. word *bionda*, *biondo* in this sense (*biondi* (pl.) in Gasparo Gozzi).

blusa. As in French, blouse or smock for women or men.

Blouses for women became fashionable in Italy during the 1860s. Attested 1859 G. Carena, *Vocab. domest.* (Pr.); Rig. (1876 and 1882); 1877 F-A., etc. Petrocchi 1884 accepts the adaptations *bluse*, *blusetta*, *blusettina*; *blusina* in Rigutini. <Fr. *blouse* (B-Al., M-D., Pr.), 1788 in an inventory; *vide F.M.*, XXIII, 142 (Alberti 1788 only has Fr. *blouse* in the sense of 'pocket of a billiard table').

bobina. Text.: Bobbin, spool; Auto engin.: Induction coil.

A technical term of the later 19th century. Synonym of *spola*. Fr. form in Garollo; *bobina* in Manfroni, *Diz. di voci impure* II (1901), acc. to Prati. Esp. *bobina di induzione*. <Fr. *bobine* (B-Al., M-D., Pr.) 1544, Martin's trans. of Sannazaro's *Arcadia* (textile term) (Hug.).

bohème, bohémien. Bohemianism, Bohemian.

I.e. dissolute way of life, usually associated with artists. Later 19th cent.; Fr. words (M-*Stor.*, B-Al.). *Bohème* translated by *scapigliatura* (*vide* M-*Stor.*, p. 714). This sense in Fr. end 17th cent.

boicottaggio. Boycott, act of boycotting.

Panzini; 1907 Arlia, *Suppl.* <Fr. *boycottage*, 1889, Cl. Jannet (no abstract in Eng. with *-age* ending). The verb *boicottare* (*boycottare*, in first instance) is often listed as a Gallicism (Fr. *boycotter* 1880, *Parlement* (Dauz.), ult. < English [B-Al., M-D., Pr.]); but M-*Stor.*, p. 712, notes that the first example, in the *Illustrazione ital.* (2 Jan. 1881) was felt to be an Anglicism. The Boycott episode occurred in 1880.

boîte, boatta. Box.

Panzini, 1905, notes that Fr. *boîte* is 'usata dai mal parlanti' to mean '. . . scatola, specie se vi annette l'idea di eleganza e di finezza, come per dolci, profumi ecc.'. *Boatta* for *scatola* is current in Rome to refer to tinned food. Prati, quoting Carena, *Vocab. domest.*, 1859, points out that *boeta* was regularly used in the Grand Duchy of Tuscany during the Napoleonic period to denote an official package of tobacco about a pound in weight sold to retailers by the French authorities. Rigutini, 1876, registers *buetta* in this sense. Cf. also *boîte de nuit* and *boîte à surprise* ('Jack in the Box') (Panzini).

bombè. Rounded, convex, hog-backed, hunchbacked.

Capello fondo bombè in Fusinato, 1846 (Prati), Panzini I, D'Annunzio. Also describing a type of carriage, Boerio 1829 (Pr.). The adaptation *bombato* is well attested in the 19th cent. both as an abstract (e.g. '*bombato*: curved, convex' in Baretti XI, 1860) and in specific technical acceptations: it may well be older than the French pronunciation, of which early attestations are confined to the vocabulary of fashion.[1] Fr. past part. and adj. *bombé* 1690, Furetière.

bombò, bombòn. Sweet, toffee.

Bomboni (pl.) Foscolo, *Epistolario* (letters written from 1794 to 1815) (*Gr. diz. it.*); *bombò* 1860 Ugolini; *bombòn* 1877 F-A., 1882 Rigutini. French form in Panzini, M-D. *et al.* Fr. *bonbon* 1604 G. d'Héroard (physician to the Dauphin).

---

1. We have evidence that at least one technical use of *bombato* existed by the later 18th cent. in Alberti's entry (1788, as a recent addition) '*Bombato*. Aggiunto che si dà ad un legno che è piegato o curvo. *Bombé*' (no corresponding entry in the Fr. > It. section). This is a usage introduced through the restricted vocabulary of naval architecture.

bomboniera. Box for sweets, sweetmeats.

(See *bombon*, above) 1877 F-A.; Panzini. Fr. *bonbonnière* (B-Al., M-D., Pr.), late 18th cent.

bonne. Child's nurse, governess.

1877 F-A., who give as example a typical newspaper advertisement of the time 'si cerca una *bonne* savoiarda', and register in addition the pronunciation [bona]. Panzini also has *bonne* in the sense of *maestra di francese* and *damigella di compagnia*. Fr. word *bonne*, 1708 Saint-Simon in this sense.

bonomia. Geniality, kindliness.

(= *bonarietà*). V. Bellini (1801–35) (*Gr. diz. it.*); 1860 Ugolini; Crusca V; 1877 F-A.; 1891 Rigutini, 2nd edition; Panz. <Fr. *bonhomie* (M-*Stor.*, B-Al., Pr.), 1758, Grimm, *Corresp. (Datations 1960*, p. 129).

bon-ton. Good manners, social elegance.

Bontò, B-Al.: 'lusso, ricercatezza nel vestire'. Cf. *bontonista* 1877 F-A., 'one who dresses in the height of fashion'. Generally used ironically in the last century to mean the class of people to whom this epithet would be applied, i.e. 'smart set, socialites'. Attested in the earlier 19th cent., 1847 Fusinato, acc. to Prati; cf. also Giusti, *Il Ballo*: 'Stretto per l'andito/ Sfila il 'bon-ton';/Si stroppia e brontola/Pardon, pardon' (F-A., *s.v. pardon*). Strongly censured by F-A. and Rig. Fr. phrase, *bon ton*.

borderò. Banking, commerce: Memorandum, schedule.

1860 Ugol.; 1877 F-A. (bureaucratic term); 1882 Rig. (bankers' term). Panzini has Fr. form *bordereau*, and gives the additional sense of 'theatre returns'. Fr. word, *bordereau*, 1539 R. Estienne; but *bourdrel* 1493.

bordò. Bordeaux wine; usually claret, as in English.

Pre-1850, G. Giusti; 1857 Fusinato (Pr.); Panzini. Also term of fashion, = 'wine-coloured' of cloth. Phonetic version of Fr. (*vin de*) *Bordeaux*.

borsa di studio. Bursary.

Borsa alone in this sense 1868, acc. to Prati, who also cites an example from Alfredo Trombetti (1902) which suggests that *borsa di studio* was used in 1880. Panzini. Semantic loan < Fr. *bourse* (B-Al., Pr.), attested in this sense not later than the 18th cent.: but *boursier* (= *élève boursier*) as early as 1430, Fauquembergue.

bottoniera. Button-hole (esp. in lapel).

1883 Manfroni. The older, native Italian sense, 'row of buttons' (16th cent., acc. to B-Al.) is the only one given by Baretti, 11th edition (1860); the French sense is apparently unknown to F-A. and Rigutini. Semantic loan < Fr. *boutonnière* (B-Al., Pr.) 'button-hole', 14th cent. in this signification.

boudoir. Boudoir.

1875 Prati; Panzini. F-A. and Rig. have the phonetic adaptation *budoàr*. Fr. word *boudoir*, 18th cent. Crébillon, *Coin du feu*.

boulevard. Boulevard.

Initially and usually referring to the boulevards of Paris, but applied also to 'ogni via larga, arborata . . . che traversa una città' (Panz.). 1892 Garollo. French word, *boulevard* (< MDutch *bolwerk*) used in this sense 19th cent.; popularised during the Second Empire when Haussmann constructed the Grands Boulevards.

bouquet. (a) Bouquet of flowers; (b) Aroma, esp. of wine.

Sense (a) (= *mazzo, mazzolino*) Phon. adapt. *bucchè* in Basilio Puoti, *Voc. domest. nap. e tosc.*, 1841 (*Gr. diz. it.*); 1883 Manfroni; also *boché, bocchè, buchè*. Sense (b) 1890 F-A., 3rd edition. Also borrowed by Eng. in 1846 (*OED*) and other languages. Both connotations in Panz.; earlier editions give (b) as 'voce con valore quasi technico' (omitted later). MFr. word meaning 'small wood, knoll' (15th cent.); sense (a) in 16th cent.; (b) 19th cent.

bouquiniste. Bookseller of Paris quays.

19th cent., acc. to B-Al. (also adapt. *bocchinista, bochinista*); Panz.; *bochinista* in Arlia, *Suppl.*, 1907. Fr. word, 1752, Trévoux, of Dutch origin.

boxe. Sport: Boxing.

Later 19th cent. M-*Stor.*, pp. 738–9; 1905 Panz. I. (also has *boxare, boxeur*); = *pugilato, pugilatore*, etc. Fr. word, often phonetically adapted, *boxe*, end 17th cent. (M-D., Pr., Panz., B-Al., M-*Stor.*), < Eng. *boxing, (to) box*.

bracconiere. Poacher.

1881 F-A., 2nd edition. <Fr. *braconnier* (F-A., B-A., M-D., Pr.), 12th cent., Wace (= 'master of hounds'; 'poacher' in 17th cent.), derivative of *braconner* 'to hunt with hounds', of German origin. *Bracconaggio* 'poaching' (later editions of Panzini) could be a native suffixal derivative, but is more probably a direct loan from the long-established French abstract *braconnage* (1228 Godef.) (criterion of *-aggio* suffix).

breloque. Locket, pendant.

(= *ciondolo, medaglione*). *Brelocco, breloc* 1877 F-A., Rig.; *breloque* Panz.; *brilocche* Panz., as Roman usage; *brelocche*. A form *berlocco* was given by Alberti, *Diz. univ.*, 1797; late 18th cent. editions of Alberti's *Diz. franc.-ital.* translate Fr. *breloque*, defined as 'bagatelles, ou petites curiosités de peu de valeur' only by *bagattelle, cose da poco*. Fr. word, *breloque* (Purists, B-Al., Pr.) 17th cent., *brelique* 16th cent., of uncertain origin.

bretella, -e. Braces.

1851 Fusinato (Pr.); other mid-19th cent. forms *bretelle, bertella*. <Fr. *bretelles*, 13th cent. (B-Al., M-D., Pr.) < OHG *brittil* 'reins'.

brillantina. Polishing powder, hair cream; silken cloth.

First two senses in 1892, Garollo (Pr.). Both are adaptations of the Fr. trade name *brillantine* which was applied to these commodities mid-19th cent. (1867 *Larousse*). The name of the textile is a rather earlier loan; Dauzat notes the Fr. word in Mozin, 1842.

brioche. Culin.: Brioche.

Panz. I, 1905; also adapt. *brioscia*. French word, 1404, of Norman origin (M-D., B-Al.).

briscola. Game of cards; 'trump'.

Pre-1850 in Giusti (Pr.); 1863 Fanfani, *Uso tosc.* A term of uncertain provenance having related forms in many European languages. The dating strongly supports Prati's assumption that Fr. *brisque* (1771 Trévoux) is the prototype from which the Italian word (like the others) was borrowed; and—if Coromines' explanation is correct—the ultimate origin points to the same source (< the personal name Briscambille (Bruscambille) a 17th cent. actor). Sp. *brisca* (game of cards), also a Gallicism, appears in 1832 (Corominas).

broche, brosche. Brooch.

1877 F-A.; 'La moda d'oggidì chiamalo col nome francese *broche*, o al più, *broscia*' (Carena, s.v.); 1886 Rig.; Panzini, who also notes the phrase *arrosto à la broche*, 'in gergo mondano e degli alberghi di lusso, per spiedo'. = *spillone, fermaglio*. Fr. word, *broche*.

brochure. Brochure.

Esp. *libro in brochure*, 'stitched', of a book, as opposed to bound. Earliest examples in dialects: *a la brossúr* 1829 Boerio (Venet.) (Pr.); *brosciúra, in brosciúra* 1839 Cherubini (Milan.; mod. *brosciür*). *Brosciúr* (subst.) 1877 F-A.; this form together with *brosciú* in Rigut. Panz. observes 'fu tentato l'adattamento *brossura*'. Fr. *brochure* (of a book) 1718 Acad. Also *broschè* 1877 F-A.: Fr. *broché*.

brulè. Spiced and heated, of wine.

Brulé, vin brulé 1839 Cherubini (Pr.); 1860 Ugol.; *brulè* and *ponce brulè* ('punch') in F-A., 1877. Fr. past part. and adj. *brûlé* (usually *vin brûlé*).

buffetteria. Milit.: Belts, webbing of a soldier's uniform.

1853 D'Ayala; also the form *buffetteria*, Panzini. <Fr. *buffleterie(s)* (B-Al., M-D., Pr.) of which the [l] has been effaced owing to loss of semantic transparency during the transfer to Italian. Oudin has the French term ('rare jusqu'au dix-neuvième siècle' [Dauzat]), which is a derivative of *buffle* (itself a borrowing from Italian: see medieval It. > Fr. loans), implying 'objects made of buffalo-hide'.

bullone. Engin.: Bolt, screw.

Bulone 1877 F-A. as an agricultural term; *bullone* 'bolt or screw' 1892 Garollo; Panzini (who registers the alternative spelling *bollone*). <Fr. *boulon* (Panz., B-Al., M-D., Pr.), which is found in the 13th cent., but as a diminutive of *boule*; the modern sense appears during the seventeenth century as a builders' term meaning a bolt for fastening joists, etc., of a building. Cf. also *boulonner* in the same modern technical sense, 1694 Thomas Corneille.

burocrazia, burocratico. Bureaucracy, bureaucratic.

Subst. 1828, Marchi (Pr.), adj. 1839 *Panlessico italiano*. Not registered by Bernardoni. Both are listed by F-A., 1877 (characterised as 'voci greco-galliche'), Rig., 1886, and Panzini. Rigutini notes that the terms were making great headway in usage during the early '80s, adding shrewdly that they would stay because of their pejorative connotation. <Fr. *bureaucratie*, coined by Gournay in the early 18th cent., *bureaucratique*, 1798 Acad. (Purists, B-Al., M-D., Pr.). It. *buròcrate* (Panz., 3rd edition, 1918) < Fr. *bureaucrate*, 1798 (B-Al., M-D., Pr.).

cabestano. Naut.: Capstan. Also gen. engineering.

1853 D'Ayala, *Diz. di voci guaste*. Used esp. to denote a capstan for hauling waggons during the process of making up trains in a railway marshalling yard. <Fr. *cabestan* (B-Al., Pr.), late 14th cent. < Provençal.

cabina. Naut. and gen. usages: Cabin.

1853 D'Ayala (naut.); V. Imbriani (*Gr. diz. it.*); 1892 Garollo ('bathing-hut'); Panzini registers 'telephone-booth'. *Gabina* (Rom.) in Guglielmotti 1889, Panz. <Fr. *cabine* (B-Al., M-D., Pr.) 1688 < English < OFr. (Picard) < OProv.

cabriolet, cabriolè. Light two-wheeled carriage, cab.

Earlier in dialects: 1839 Cherubini (Milanese *cabriolé*; 1845 De Ritis (Neap.), *capriolè* 'Vettura di recente introduzione ed ora dimessa' (cited Pr.). Tuscan in 2nd half 19th cent. Also meaning 'automobile chiusa a due posti', Panzini. Fr. word *cabriolet*, July 1755, < verb *cabrioler* (cf. 16th cent. It. > Fr., s.v. *cabriole*).

cachemire, casmir(e). Text.: Cashmere.

Casmirra in G. Giusti (*Gr. diz. it.*); Fr. form in 1857 Fusinato (Pr.); Panz. IX still uses this rubric. Adaptation *casimir* in T-Bell., *casmir* in Garollo, *casmirra, cascimirra* in Petrocchi, *casmire, casmirre* in Panzini. Fr. word *cachemire*, 1811 B-Wart., < name of the Indian province, Kashmir. The part played by English in transferring the name is uncertain; cashmere itself seems to have come into fashion in France immediately after Napoleon's campaigns in Egypt. The above word is semantically distinct from the earlier loan *casimiro* (q.v. 18th cent. Fr. > It. loans)—also attested 19th cent. as *casimirra*—which denotes an entirely different textile, viz., a kind of coarse tweed, whereas cashmere is a fine wool of the very highest quality. A formal contamination between the two is however clearly discernible in the Italianised words.

cachet, cascè. Capsule, tablet of drugs.

1892 Garollo; Panzini. The latter directs his criticism not so much against any technical sense as certain metaphorical extensions of meaning inspired by French idioms:

'*indole, maniera, modo di fare*, e più specialmente *fascino, seduzione, malia*'. Fr. word *cachet*, 1539, R. Est., 'seal'; figurative usages 19th cent., medical term later 19th cent.[1]

cadeau, cadò. Tip, present, gift.

Cadò, 1839 Cherubini (observes that the word was in great vogue a few years before); 1846 T. Azzocchi, *Vocab. domest.* (Pr.); 1877 F-A., 'gift' (= *regalo*). Fr. word *cadeau*, 17th cent. in sense of 'gift', 15th cent., 'rubric of a manuscript', < Prov. *capdal, cadau*.

café-chantant. Music-hall, variety cabaret.

'Attestato almeno dal 1896 in Italia' (Prati); Panz. I. Adapt. *caffè-cantante* end 19th cent. (B-Al.). 'Locuzione francese: tradotta in *caffè-concerto*, o *varietà* (Panz.). *Caffè-concerto* 1900 acc. to Pr.; Panz. I. Fr. compound noun, used mid-19th cent.

calandra. Entom.: Weevil, *Sitophilus granarius*.

1829 Marchi, *Diz. tecnic.-etim. filologico* (Pr.). Semantic loan < Fr. *calandre* (B-Al., Pr.), 1539, R. Estienne.

calembour. Pun.

1883 Manfroni; *calembourg* in Lessona, *Diz. univ.*, 1875 (Pr.); Panzini. Fr. word *calembour*, 1768 Diderot. Early editions of Panz. register *calemburista* 'punster' as a 'goffa versione del fr. *calembouriste*', though later ones have it only as a native derivative of the borrowed noun.

calicò. Text.: Calico.

Calicot 1875 Lessona; *calicò* 1889 Zambaldi, *Diz. etimol.*; Panz. Fr. word (and It. adaptation) *calicot* 1613, rare until 19th cent. (Acad., 1835), < English.

cambusa. Naut.: Victualling store.

Genoese *cambüsa* mid-19th cent. (B-Al., Pr.). <Fr. *cambuse* (B-Al. M-D., Pr.) 1783 *Encycl. méth.*, < Dutch *kabuys* 'ship's galley' (cf. Amer. Eng. *caboose*). *Cambusiere* 'victualling officer or rating' (Panzini) < Fr. *cambusier* 1835 Acad. (= *dispensa* and *dispensiere*).

camicetta. Womens' fashions: Blouse.

1866 Crusca V, in this sense. 'Voce nostra del linguaggio della moda, che si alterna con la francese *chemisette*' (Panzini). Semantic loan[2] < Fr. *chemisette* (Panz., B-Al., Pr.), 13th cent. as diminutive of *chemise*, mid-19th cent. as a term of women's wear (previously a man's garment). Also It. *camiceria* 'shirt-factory', 'shirt manufacture' (Panz.;[3] '20th cent.', B-Al.). <Fr. *chemiserie* 1845, Bescherelle.

campo di Marte. Milit.: Parade-ground.

1853 D'Ayala; 1884 Petrocchi (= *piazza d'armi*). Fr. phrase *champ de mars*. Also *campo d'onore* 1918 < Fr. *champ d'honneur* 'field of battle' (phrase used by Châteaubriand).

canard. Hoax.

1873 Prati; Rigutini 1886 (tr. by *fiaba, frottola*); Panz. Fr. word *canard*, used figuratively *c.* 1860 onwards. *Canàr* 'duck' in menus in 18th cent. M-*Stor.*, p. 527.

cancàn. Dance: Can-can.

1874 Lessona, *Diz. univ.* (the dance); Panzini, who adds the sense of 'gossiping' and 'din, shindy': 'Più antico significato, *pettegolezzo*. "Successe un *cancan*", un pandemonio, un putiferio' (*Diz. mod.* IX, p. 105). Fr. word *cancan*, 1822 in this sense, probably < 'quanquan de collège' 1554, = oration in Latin; later > 'bruit autour d'une nouvelle' (Dauz.), 1602, Sully, whence 'scandal, gossip'.

canottaggio. Boating, yachting.

1. *Lettera di cachet* plainly corresponds to the Fr. phrase; cf. also the Fr. compounds (cited by Panzini) *cache-nez, cache-pot, cache-sexe*.

2. B-Al. register *camicetta* dim. of *camicia* in 15th cent., and as a synonym of *involucro*, 18th cent. The latter recalls 19th cent. *camicia* 'loose-leaf folder' (1877 F-A.; 1886 Rig.) which purists hold to be a semantic loan.

3. Defined by Panz. as 'negozio ove si vendono camicie ed oggetti a camicie attinenti'.

1898 G. Croppi, *Il canottaggio* (Milano) (Pr.). Not in Rig., 1891. <Fr. *canotage* 1863, Littré (B-Al., M-D., Pr.).

canottiere, -a. (a) Oarsman, yachtsman; (b) kind of sports vest; (c) straw hat ('boater').

(a) 1876 Rigutini; 1877 F-A.; (b) *canottiera* 20th cent. (Prati refers to Meano, *Comm. diz. it. della moda*, 1936). (c) *canottiera* 1918, Panzini III; but probably borrowed by the end of the 19th cent. (B-Al. agree). <Fr. *canotier* (B-Al., M-D., Pr.); sense (a) 17th cent.; (b) and (c) late 19th cent.

cantoniere. Rail: Linesman; also roadmender.

Later 19th cent., M-*Stor.*, p. 737. <Fr. *cantonnier*, 18th cent. meaning 'road-mender'.

capoluogo. Chief, principal town.

Used by Manzoni: 'Le sedi poi di questi *giudici* supremi, i capoluoghi, come ora si direbbe, di loro provincie ... erano appunto le città' (*Gr. diz. it.*). 1897 Giorgini, *Nov. vocab.* Calque of Fr. *chef-lieu*, 1327 (B-Al., Pr.), prob. itself a calque of Flemish *hoofd-oord.* Other compounds of *capo* inspired by French equivalents are *ingegnere-capo*, *segretario-capo*, 1877 F-A. Both are in Rig. (who particularly condemns *in capo* as an imitation of Fr. *en chef*) and Panzini.[1]

cappotta, capotta. Hood of a carriage; bonnet of a car.

19th cent. B-Al. Later 19th cent., M-*Stor.*, p. 713 (Fr. form *capote*). Panzini. <Fr. *capote*, 1688 meaning 'cloak' (B-Al., M-*Stor.*). T-Bell. and Carena have *cappotta* as a term of women's fashions (style of small cap or hat), possibly also < French.

caribú. Zool.: Caribou.

Pre-1803, Giamb. Casti. <Fr. *caribou* (B-Al., Pr., etc.) 1607 (Bloch), from a North American Indian language (prob. Algonquin *kalibú*).

carnet, carnè. Notebook.

Carnetto 1890 F-A., 3rd edition (an ephemeral adaptation); *carnet* 1892 Garollo; Panz. Fr. word *carnet* (*quernet* 1516, Godef.).

carrick, caric. Style of overcoat.

Originally a heavy coat worn by cab-drivers. 1839 Azzocchi, *Vocab. domest.* (Pr.); forms *carrich, chiri, chiric* attested by Cherubini, 1839, in Milanese. <Fr. *carrick* (B-Al., Pr.). <English *carrick*, name of a type of light carriage; the sense 'cab-driver's coat' seems to have arisen by metonymy in French (neither sense of the English word is attested by the *OED.*).

carta velina. Vellum (kind of paper).

Pre-1828, V. Monti. In Venetian 1829, acc. to Boerio, who mentions the Fr. term. Central Italian later 19th cent. <Fr. *papier vélin* (Carena, M-D., Pr.) early 19th cent.: process invented by the Englishman Baskerville (†1775).

carter. Engin.: Chain-case, crankcase or similar.

End 19th cent.; originally applied to the chain-guard of a safety bicycle, invented by the Englishman J. H. Carter in 1891. Panz. wrongly derives it from the common noun *carter = carrettiere.* I cannot find a word *carter* with this sense in English, though it appears early (1891) in French, where it is still the current engineering term for any metal receptacle forming part of a machine (also in Spanish and elsewhere). A false loan, therefore, coined in France, transmitted from French to Italian. (Analogous to the false loan *rover* 'bicycle' in some languages < 'Rover safety cycle'.)

cartomanzia. Divination by playing-cards.

1829-40 Tramater (*Gr. diz. it.*); 1874 Lessona, *Diz. univ.*; Panz. <Fr. *cartomancie* (Panz., B-Al., Pr.) 1832 Raymond, *Dict. général.*

---

1. *Capoluogo* is cited previously by P. Zolli in 1799, *Mercurio Britannico* (*L.N.*, 1964, p. 12), referring to Glasgow.

I

cartonaggio. Articles of cardboard; manufacture of the same.

1877 F-A., meaning 'chocolate-box'; 1886 Rigutini in the second sense above, also 'cardboard binding' (books); Panzini (cardboard industry, bookbinding in boards). <Fr. *cartonnage* (Purists, Panz., B-Al., Pr.), 1785 *Encycl. méth.*

cartucc(i)era. Milit.: Cartridge belt, pouch.

Both *cartucciera* and *cartucciere* are 19th cent. borrowed forms, acc. to B-Al. Prati refers to Pietro Colletta (pre-1831) and Carlo Botta (pre-1837). Already in 1788 Alberti registers *cartocciere* (added in that edition): 'Tasche o sacchette, entro le quali si tengono piccoli cartocci', translated by *gargoussières*; I hesitate to accept this attestation unconditionally (and so to class the word as an 18th cent. loan) because in the same edition both Fr. *cartouchier* and *gargoussière* are translated by words or phrases in which It. *cartocciere* is not mentioned. This is probably a personal military Gallicism of Alberti's, but one that nevertheless only narrowly anticipates the general borrowing, which probably occurred during the revolutionary wars. In French the masc. form is attested long before the fem., viz., *cartouchier* 1752 Trévoux (also in Alberti, and many examples early 19th cent.; Boiste, Bescherelle, etc.) as opposed to fem. *cartouchière* 1863, Littré.

casa di salute. Nursing home.

1884 Petrocchi. Panz. Calque of Fr. *maison de santé* acc. to Panz., Pr. Other compounds of *casa* which echo the corresponding French usage are *casa di commercio* (1828, Pr.), earlier *casa di negozio* (in Alberti, 1777) which Prati compares with Fr. *maison de commerce*, the euphemism *casa di tolleranza* (Panz.) 'licensed brothel' < Fr. *maison de tolérance* and *casa* alone in the sense of 'commercial establishment, firm' esp. with a personal name following.

cascialotto. Zool.: Sperm-whale.

Caccialotto 1875 Lessona *Diz. univ.*; *cascialotto* 1892 Garollo. <Fr. *cachalot* (Pr.) 1730 B-Wart. <Port. *cacholote*.

casinò, casino. Casino, i.e. sumptuous gaming establishment.

19th cent. B-Al.; Panz. All sources derive it in this sense (generally with oxytonic stress, as in French) from the Fr. 19th cent. semantic development of the word *casino* (originally borrowed from It.; *vide* 18th cent. It. > Fr. loans).

cassazione (corte di). Jurid.: Court of Appeal.

A technical term of the Napoleonic period used frequently (C. Botta, V. Cuoco, etc.) and generally accepted by 19th cent. Italian dictionaries. It. *cassare* 'to quash, annul' and *cassazione* are Latinisms of long standing. <Fr. (*cour de*) *cassation* in this context, 1790 (M-*Stor.*, p. 660, Pr., Panz., etc.).

caucciù. Rubber.

Caoutciou O. Targ. Tozzetti (1755–1829); *caoutchouca* 1828 Leone, *Diz. term. medic.* Fr. form later 19th cent.; *caucciù* Panz. <Fr. *caoutchouc* (Panz., B-Al., M.D., Pr.) 1751, *Mém. de l'Acad. des Sciences*, < Carib. *kahuchu*. Indiarubber itself was brought to Europe by La Condamine about 1736.

ceramista. Tech.: Worker, craftsman in ceramics.

1892 Garollo. <Fr. *céramiste* (B-Al., Pr.) 1836 Landais. Prati also considers adj. *ceramico* (1865 T-Bell.) to be a loan-word (< Fr. *céramique*, 1829 B-Wart.).

chalet. Chalet.

1891 Prati; Panzini. The erroneous graphy *châlet* is frequently found. Fr. (Swiss) word *chalet* (Panz., B-Al., Pr.) 1723, Savary, but popularised by *La Nouvelle Héloïse*.

chaperon. Chaperon (usually a middle-aged lady).

1886 Rigutini; Panzini. Both strongly condemn it. Rigutini suggests the alternative terms (*inter alia*) *guida, matrona regolatrice* (!) Fr. word, *chaperon*, 12th cent. in sense of 'hood': the figurative usage (also *grand chaperon*) is current in the 18th cent.

charivari. Din, hubbub, uproar; discordant music.

1851 Fusinato (Pr.). Panz., B-Al. and Pr. agree upon the French origin, though the ultimate provenance is far from certain (see Prati, and bibliography there cited). *Chalivali* appears in Fr. 14th cent.; an early signification is that of 'mock serenade (rattling of cauldrons, pans and the like) at the wedding of those judged to be past marriageable age', hence 'uproar', 'free-for-all'. *Charivari* 'dust-cover for protecting garments, esp. when travelling', in Italian early 19th cent., is a further semantic loan from French.

charlotte. Culin.: Fruit pudding.

Italianised form *sciarlotta* 1843 Cherubini (Pr.); *ciarlotta* Panz. I. Fr. word, *charlotte*, 1804 Kotzebue. Personal name (*Vide* Migl., *Dal nome proprio* . . . , p. 298). A separate 20th cent. loan is the milliners' term (esp. used in It. form *ciarlotta*) denoting a style of woman's hat ('cappello con frappa' [B-Al.]) which was in fashion both in France and Italy about 1910.

châssis. Chassis of a vehicle: frame of a machine.

1905 Panz., 1st edition (first registered as a photographic term). Adapted to *sciassì*. B-Al. note the Piedmontese word *ciasìl* 'window-frame'; cf. Eng. *chassis* 1664, same meaning (later corrupted to *sash*). French word dating from 13th cent. (Panz., B-Al., Pr.).

chauffeur. Chauffeur; driver of a motor vehicle.

Later 19th cent. M-*Stor.*, pp. 713, 737; Panz., 1st edition. 'La voce francese fu variamente adattata nei dialetti, ad es. ven. *sofèr*, *safèr*, rom. e pis. *scioffè*, *sciaffè*, march. *sciafóre*, calab. *sciafèrre*, etc.' (B-Al.). In earlier editions Panz. observes 'il termine ha preso stabile radice fra noi'; later its glaringly foreign form and orthography singled it out for puristic attacks. *Autista* was officially introduced as a substitute (law of Jan. 1932). Fr. *chauffeur* dates from 1680 in the sense 'stoker' (of a forge, furnace), whence stoker and therefore 'driver' of a steam traction engine, locomotive, etc., in the 19th cent.

chef. Chef (de cuisine).

Panzini I, 1905; but certainly in use much earlier. *Chef* is well attested in English by the mid-19th cent. (1842, Barham, 1850, Thackeray, etc. [*OED*.]). Fr. word *chef* (*de cuisine*).

chemise. Style of light overcoat.

Southern dialect, esp. Naples, of varying pronunciation: *scemisse* Abruzzi, Apulia; *sciammisu*, Calabria, etc. (B-Al., Pr.). Registered 1877 by F-A., whose article includes a lengthy discussion between four allegorical figures, Chemise, Pardessus, Sopratutto and Cappa, in which Cappa has the best of the exchanges. Fr. word, *chemise*.

chèque. Finance: Cheque.

1874 Lessona; *scech* 1877 F-A.; 'L'assegno, o Check', 1874, in Fanfani's *Il Borghini* (cited Pr.); graphies *ciècch*, *scècche* end 19th cent., Petrocchi. Fr. word *chèque*, 19th cent., < English; first attested 1835 in 19th cent. English form *check* now replaced in British Isles by the French graphy, though not in North America.

chiffon. Text.: Chiffon.

A later 19th cent. word. Italianised graphies *ciffone* and *cifone* in Lessona 1874 and Manfroni 1883 respectively (Pr.). Used earlier in dialects. The sense 'tutte quelle gale che servono al vestire muliebre', which Panzini quotes from Littré, is the first to appear in Italian. The more recent, accepted meaning 'type of fine cloth' belongs to the 20th cent. Fr. word, *chiffon*, 1611 Cotgrave.

chilòmetro, chilometraggio, chilolitro, chilogrammo, chilo. Kilometre; distance in kilometres, kilolitre, -gram, etc.

19th cent., B-Al. Also *chilolitro* and *chilogrammo*, with shortened version *chilo* (early 19th cent., M-*Stor.*, p. 660). French accentuation *chilò* still used in Leghorn and Sienna

(Migl.). Technical terms taken from learned French equivalents *kilomètre, -gramme, -litre*, coined in 1790 and adopted with the metric system as a whole in 1795 (B-Al., M-D.). *Chilometraggio* (Panz.) is a late 19th cent. loan < Fr. *kilométrage* (Littré) (B-Al., M-D., Panz., etc.). F-A. register it as a bureaucratic term of railways, postal services meaning 'travelling allowance' (2nd edition, 1881); Panz. has it in the above sense.

china. Term of dice: two fives at one throw.

1870 Fanfani, *Voci e maniere del parlar fiorentino*. <Fr. *quine* (B-Al., Pr.) 12th cent., Wace.

choc. Medic.: Shock.

Choc traumatico, choc operatorio 1892 Garollo; Panz. notes that *commozione, colpo, collasso, depressione* are not adequate synonyms. *Squasso* suggested as a substitute (Donaggio, Piccini) (Migl., *Suppl.* to Panz., 9th edition). French word *choc*, 1523; med. term 19th cent.

christofle. Metall.: Alloy of copper, zinc and nickel.

19th cent.; Fr. word, name of French industrialist Ch. Christofle, 1805–63 (B-Al.).

cicca. 'Quid' of chewing-tobacco; cigarette-end, cigar-butt.

1863 Fanfani, *Vocab. dell'uso tosc.*, Panz., as a Tuscan word: but in northern dialects earlier (suggesting a Fr. loan); 1843 Cherubini. The verb *ciccare* 'to chew tobacco' (and later 'to grumble' in naval and milit. usage) appears in Boerio, 1829 (*cicàr*). Cf. also Genoese *ciccà* (Pr.). As to the borrowing, It. authorities hold opposed views; M-D., Pr. and Panz. derive it < Fr. *chique, chiquer*, while B-Al. consider the French words to be Italianisms. The dating supports a Fr. > It. transfer: *chique* 'piece of chewing-tobacco' is attested 1798, Catineau, while the form itself dates from the 17th cent. (*chique* 1642 Oudin 'bowl' (game of bowls) prob. < German; also 1694 Th. Corneille, 'type of mite which burrows in the skin (in English, 'jigger' or chigoe) current from the end of the century onwards (Alberti, etc.).

cicchetto. Nip, dram of liquor.

A slang term in Piedmontese registered in 1814 and 1830 acc. to Prati. Attestations in literary usage late 19th cent. <Fr. *chiquet* (Panz., B-Al., Pr.); also *chiquette*. A later (semantic) loan from Fr. is the military slang term meaning 'dressing down', 'reprimand' (other than an official one) (20th cent., B-Al.; before 1900, Pr.; Panz. II, 1908).

ciclismo, ciclista. Cycling, cyclist.

Ciclismo 1895, Arlia (Pr.); late 19th cent., De Amicis; Panzini. *Ciclista* late 19th cent., Olindo Guerrini; 1907 Arlia, suppl. to F-A., 2nd edition. <Fr. *cyclisme, cycliste* (B-Al., Pr.). Prati also derives *ciclistico* (1899) and *ciclodromo* (1890) from French. All the French terms appear after 1889 when the original word *cycle* was borrowed from English (Dauz.).

ciclone. Meteorol.: Cyclone.

1874 Lessona; Panzini. <Fr. *cyclone* (B-Al., Pr.), 1863 < Eng. *cyclone*, coined 1848 by the meteorologist Piddington.

ciminiera. Factory chimney; ship's funnel.

1853 D'Ayala; Panz. <Fr. *cheminée* (Panz., B-Al., M-D., Pr.) 12th cent., Saint-Gilles, with change of suffix (a form *ciminea* appears in Oudin; *sciminea* still in Lucca [Pieri, *Arch. Glott. It.*, XII, 114]).[1]

---

1. Apparently borrowed on a previous occasion in the Middle Ages; cf. B-Al.: 'ben rappresentato nei dialetti ital. merid. dove il prestito è molto antico: cfr. *chemineria* 1361, a Roma.' Bezzola (*Abbozzo*, p. 201), referring to *REW* 1548, notes its presence in Genoese and Southern dialects, 'dove giunse forse cogli Angiò e con tutti i Francesi ch'essi portarono con loro', adding, however, that 'le voci meridionali possono ... essere anche prestiti spagnuoli' (ibid., note 5).

cislonga. Chaise-longue.

1863 Fanfani, *Vocab. dell'uso toscano*; 1881 F-A., 2nd edition; 1886 Rigutini. *Sislunga* 1883 Manfroni. Panzini registered the Fr. word. <Fr. *chaise-longue* (Panz., B-Al., Pr. etc.).

claque. Theatr.: Claque.

1877 F-A.; Panz. *Claqueur* registered (same sense) by Panz. I, 1905. Fr. word, *claque*, 14th cent. (= 'blow, slap'); 19th cent. in figurative sense above. Fr. *claqueur(s)* attested 1787.

cliché, cliscè. (a) Typog.: Stereotype plate or print; (b) Well-worn phrase, cliché.

Tech. sense 1892 Garollo; figurative use Panz. I 1905. *Sottoclisce* 'caption' (usually beneath a photograph), Migl., *Suppl.* Fr. word (and adaptation) *cliché*, 1813 B-Wart., < German. (*L.N.*, III, 139; V, 70).

clivaggio. Tech.: Cleavage (of precious stones).

Either tendency of a precious stone to split along certain planes of the crystal, or the act of splitting a crude gem prior to cutting. French also has both senses. 1853 D'Ayala; 1874, Lessona. <Fr. *clivage* (B-Al., M-D., Pr.), 1771, Trévoux (but *cliver* 1723, Savary) prob. < Dutch.

clou. Culminating point, chief attraction, highlight.

End 19th cent. B-Al. 1907 F-A., *Suppl.*; but early editions of Panzini note that the term was current before the turn of the century, and cite as an example 'il *clou* dell' Esposizione' (inspired by reports of the 1889 Paris Exhibition? Or the 1900 one?). The French word appears to be attested in this signification only in the later 19th cent. (not in Littré).

cocotte. Caritative term for prostitute.

19th cent. F-A. Panz. cites *cocottes* in G. Pascoli (1855–1912); *cocot* 1901 Manfroni (Prati). Fr. word *cocotte*, 1789 *Cahier . . . des Dames de la Halle.*

codificare, -azione. Legal: To codify.

L. Fornaciari (1798–1858) (Pr.). Not in Bernardoni. Both abstract and verb *codificare* in 1886 Rigutini, 1890 F-A. The latter suggest replacement by *codificicazione* (i.e. derivative of It. *codice* rather than Fr. *code*). <Fr. *codification* 1819, Saint-Simon and *codifier*, 1842, Mozin (Purists, Panz., B-Al., M-D., Pr.).

cognàc (cògnac). Brandy.

Cognacche late 19th cent., Petrocchi; *cognac* later 19th cent., Carducci (*Gr. diz. it.*), Panz. ('*cognacche* è poco nell'uso'). Fr. word *cognac* < place-name Cognac (Charente).

coiffeur. Hairdresser, barber.

19th cent. B-Al.; 1883 Manfroni (Pr.); Panzini, who also registers *coiffure*. Taxed and later prohibited. Fr. word *coiffeur*, 1767, Voltaire; but *coiffeuse* in 17th cent. *Coiffeure c.* 15 o, Jean d'Authon.

colbàc. Milit.: Type of bearskin shako worn by light cavalry.

Colbak 1874 Lessona; *colbacche, colbacco* late 19th cent., De Amicis, Petrocchi.[1] <Fr. *colback* (B-Al., M-D., Pr.), which entered French during the campaigns of Napoleon as First Consul (esp. in Egypt [1798]) as a result of contact with the Mammeluks, who wore this headgear (Turkish *qalpaq*). Panzini notes that the *colbac* was adopted by Italian cavalry under General Ricotti.

collettivismo. Polit.: Collective ownership of natural resources.

19th cent. B-Al.; 1892 Garollo (Pr.); Panz. *Collettivista* Panz., 2nd edition, 1908.

---

1. *Kalbak*, late 17th cent. (Redi) is an ephemeral loan direct from Turkish. Cf. Fr. *kalepac* in La Boullaye (1657) as an exotic (Turkish) word.

Also *collettivizzare, collettivizzazione*, Panz., 1st edition, 1905. <Fr. *collectivisme* (Panz., Pr.), coined at the political congress held in Basle 1869. *Collectiviste* 1876.

colpo di stato. Polit.: Coup d'état.

1853 D'Ayala; Ugol.; De Sanctis (*Gr. diz. it.*); 1886 Rig. Calque of Fr. *coup d'état*. Other 19th cent. compounds formed on *colpo* in accordance with French patterns are *colpo di grazia* (*coup de grâce* 1671), used in metaphorical sense by Monti, letter of 3 June 1807 (Bertoldi, III, 157), *colpo di testa* 'whim, caprice' (*coup de tête*, 1680), criticised by F-A., 1877; probably *colpo de sole* (*di calore*), Carducci (*coup de soleil*, Montaigne). Cf. also *colpo di fuoco, di telefono, di spugna, di pollice, di fortuna, d'ala* (generally in T-Bell., Rig., F-A. and Panz.). See *colpo di mano*, 18th cent. loans.

compressa. Medic.: Surgical compress.

1828 Leone, *Diz. term. med.* (Pr.); Tramater; 1877 F-A.; 1886 Rigutini. In a lecture given to the Circolo Filologico Fiorentino on 5th April 1875 published by Rig. as a preamble to his *Neologismi buoni e cattivi*, the word *compressa* is cited as a typical example of unnecessary Gallicism in scientific vocabularies (= 'piumacciuolo'). <Fr. *compresse* 13th cent., *Roman de la Rose*, but first found in medical sense 1539 R. Estienne.

comunismo, comunista. Communism, Communist.

Both in Giuseppe Giusti, letter of 24th Dec. 1846 written from Pisa referring to an egalitarian movement among peasants based on Pisa and Leghorn (*Epist. di G. Giusti*, ed. Martini, Florence 1932, II, pp. 488–92). Panzini. <Fr. *communisme*, 1843, *communiste*, 1841, B-Wart. (B-Al., Pr.).

comunardo. Hist., polit.: Communard.

19th cent. B-Al.; Carducci (*Gr. diz. it.*). There is no doubt that the word was used in Italian journalism at the time when the Fr. word itself was current, immediately after the Franco-Prussian War. It. version of Fr. *communard*, 1871, name given to supporters of the revolutionary movement (*Commune*) of 18th March 1871.

confezione, confezionare. Ready-made clothes: to manufacture ready-made clothes.

Confezionare 1874 B-Al.; both in F-A. 1877, Rigutini, Petrocchi, Panzini. Fanfani notes that the verb was currently used to mean the manufacture of various products— 'clothes, cannon, bread, even laws'. Later authorities are concerned only with the first of these. The word seems to have entered It. in the mid-19th cent. at which time the ready-made-clothes industry was established. Petrocchi still gives both verb and noun as popular usage. Semantic loan < Fr. *confection* (up to 16th cent. an abstract or pharma-ceutical term only) and *confectionner* 16th cent., Marnix, rare until 19th cent. Above sense mid-19th cent. (Purists, Panz., B-Al., M-D., Pr.).

consolle. Console-table.

'Mensola, . . . mobile elegante sul quale si posano minuterie, vasi, bronzi, ecc.' (Panzini). 1877 F-A. Other late 19th cent. sources. Attested earlier in northern dialects: *tavol a consòl* 1839 Cherubini (Milan.). Also adapt. *consòlida* (Naples, Rome) (Panz.). Adapt. of Fr. word *console* (B-Al., M-D., Pr.), 16th cent.

consumè. Culin.: Consommé: concentrated stock, let down with water as required.

1870 Prati; *consommè* (with *consumè* as popular pronunciation) in Rigut., 1886; 1881, F-A., 2nd edition. The Purists urge a return to the old term *consumato* (the Crusca V cites examples from the *Ricettario fiorentino*; cf. also 'brodo di cappone consumato' in Bandello [*Gr. diz. it.*]). Adaptation of Fr. word *consommé* (B-Al., M-D., Pr.), mid-16th cent. (Paré) in this sense.

constatare. To ascertain, verify.

1812 Bernardoni, *Elenco*; *Constatare* and *costatare* 1877 F-A., 1886 Rigut., who also register the abstract *co(n)statazione*. <Fr. *constater*, 1726, and *constatation* 1586, Scaliger; but little used before 18th cent. (Purists, B-Al., M-D., Pr.).

contabile. Accountant, book-keeper.

1812 Bernardoni: Ugol.: 'Durante l'invasione francese si scambiò la prima volta in *contabile* il vecchio e italiano nostro *"computista"*, che anche dicesi *"ragioniere, calcolatore, abbachista, abbachiere"*.' Attacked strongly, together with *contabilità*, by all the 19th cent. lexicographers. Most agree with Ugol. in suggesting *computista* and *ragioniere* as substitutes, and for the abstract, *computisteria, ufficio dei conti*, or *conti* alone. <Fr. (*agent*) *comptable* (Panz., B-Al., M-D., Pr., etc.). See *contabilità*, 18th cent. loans.

controllo, controllare, controllore. Inspection, to inspect, inspector, etc.

1812 Bernardoni, *Elenco*[1] (all three forms, abstract and verb equated to *registro, -are*; *controllore* to *siniscalco, maggiordomo, registratore*). Verb in Boerio, 1829; all three registered by mid- and later 19th cent. lexicographers. Rigutini mentioned the use of these terms on the railway in Florence, and elsewhere. Panz., 4th edition, 1922, adds *controllo di fabbrica* < Fr. *contrôle d'usine* (participation of workers in management). <Fr. *contrôle* (all sources) 1611, Cotgr., but *contre-role* 14th cent.; *contrôler* 1455; *contrôleur* (*contre-roleur* 1372).

contrarotaia, controrotaia. Rail. engin.: Check-rail.

19th cent. B-Al. Calque of Fr. *contre-rail* (B-Al.).

coperto. The requisites for setting a table.

Esp. in idiomatic uses, e.g. 'pranzo di cinquanta coperti' (for 50 people), as in French. 1877 F-A., Rig., Panz. in this sense. <Fr. *couvert* (B-Al., M-D., Pr.), 13th cent. meaning 'covering' in general. Cf. earlier *coverto* = 'roof, shelter' (Boccaccio, Ariosto) which may also have been borrowed.[2]

coprire. To cover, meet (expenses).

Esp. in idiomatic uses, e.g. *coprire le spese, l'interesse*, etc. 1812 Bernardoni, *Elenco* (*coprire una spesa, coprire un impiego*); T-Bell.; 1886 Rig. (*coprire un ufficio, un posto, impiego, una carica*; also as in 'i guadagni cuoprono le spese'); Panzini. <Fr. *couvrir, se couvrir* in this sense (Panz., B-Al., Pr.). B-Al. also treat as a Gallicism *coprirsi* 'mettersi il cappello' (*se couvrir*).

cormorano. Ornith.: Cormorant.

19th cent. B-Al.; early 19th, M-*Stor.*, p. 661. <Fr. *cormoran*, 1393; *cormarenc* 12th cent. (B-Al., Migl.).

cornalina. Mineral.: Cornelian.

1875 Lessona (Pr.). <Fr. *cornaline* (B-Al., M-D., Pr.), 12th cent. (graphy *corneline*).

corporazione. Guild, corporation.

1812 Bernardoni. 'La letteraria corporazione' in Monti, meaning the body of writers in general, letter of 15th March 1816 (Bertoldi, IV, 279). Monti uses *corporazione* in a rather different acceptation at the very end of the 18th cent. (in a letter of March 1798, Bertoldi, II, 72) when he states that 'tutte le *corporazioni ecclesiastiche* sono soppresse' (i.e.

---

1. Possibly 18th cent.; cf. Alberti 1788, s.v. *contrôle, -eur*: 'Quelque part on dit abusivement controllo . . . et quelque part, controllore.' Machiavelli used the title of *contrarolo* (a person), no doubt from the older French form *contreroleur*, speaking of a 'maestro contrarolo, che è quello che spaccia le poste' (*Gr. diz. it.*). P. Verri used an abstract *controlleria* meaning 'action of inspecting' (id.).

2. Monti describes as 'un pranzo di parata in numero di quaranta coperte' a banquet held by the French in Rome with the intention apparently of dispelling hostility to the invaders and winning supporters for their cause. Monti was present (Letter of 1st March 1797, Bertoldi, II, p. 5).

the religious Orders). Frequent 19th cent. examples. <Fr. *corporation*, 1672, < English (Purists, B-Al., Pr.; M-D. derive it from Latin, adding, 'entrato nell'uso mod. prima in Francia e poi in Italia').

corsè, corsetto. Fashions: Corset, stays.

Both forms in Carena, *Vocab. domest.*, 1846; also in sense of 'bed-jacket'. Ugol. gives as equivalents *giubba, giustacore, corpetto, busto.* <Fr. *corset* in what is widely understood to be a 19th cent. signification, though the English word *corset* in this sense, clearly a Gallicism, appears in 1795 (*OED*).

corvè. Milit.: Turn of duty, fatigue.

Also in everyday speech, = 'thankless task'. Milit. sense 1853 D'Ayala. General usage 1877 F-A.; both explained in Panzini. Also It. form (disus.) *corvata*, 1860 (Pr.), 1877 F-A. Fr. word *corvée*, 12th cent. B-Al. note that *corvè* as a military term was officially replaced in 1940 by *comandata*.

cotiglione, cotillon. Dance: cotillon.

Cotiglion, Petrocchi; Fr. form *cotillon* 1892 Garollo (Pr.); Panzini. Fr. word, *cotillon*, originally (1461) style of petticoat; dance, early 18th cent.

cotoletta. Culin.: Cutlet, chop.

19th cent. B-Al.; 1886 Rigutini; Panzini. Italianised form *costoletta* 1859 Carena (Pr.). <Fr. *côtelette* (Panz., B-Al., Pr.) 14th cent., *Ménagier de Paris.*

coulisse. Tech.: Groove, channel, slide; Theatr.: Wings.

Colisse and *culisse*, 1877 F-A. (= *scanalatura*); 1880 Nicotra, *Il Gallicismo in Italia*, 2nd edition (Pr.) (tech. sense); term of automobile engineering ('gate' of gear-change) in Panzini, who also notes the sense 'sliding door' (*porta a coulisse*), and the figurative usages 'office for "outside brokers" on the *Bourse*' and 'behind the scenes' (= *dietro le quinte*). Fr. word, *coulisse*, 12th cent. *Coulissier* 'outside broker' appears in 1842 (Mozin).

crampo. Medic.: Cramp.

1891 Petrocchi (Pr.). 19th cent., acc. to B-Al. <Fr. *crampe* (B-Al., M-D., Pr.) 13th cent., Jean de Meung, < Frankish.

cremagliera. Engin.: Toothed rack, rack and pinion.

1853 D'Ayala (Pr.); 1886 Rigutini (tr. as 'asta dentata'). Used especially of the toothed rack on certain mountain railways ('rack-railways'), fairly widely used in 19th cent. Arlia (1907, Supplement to F-A., 5th edition) speaks of a *strada ferrata a cremagliera* running from Saltino to Vallombrosa. <Fr. *crémaillère* (B-Al., M-D., Pr.), 13th cent. in sense of 'pot-hanger' i.e. vertical toothed rack upon which cooking vessels are suspended over fire; tech. sense 18th and 19th cent.

crêpe, crespo. Text.: Crêpe.

1839–43 *Gran dizionario del commercio* (*Gr. diz. it.*); 1851 Fusinato; Manfroni; Panz.; Meano, Monelli, Jacono. *Velo crepè*, Ugol. Many examples are of the Italianised form *crespo*, which the *Gr. diz. it.* registers as the name of a textile on a previous occasion, in Bernardino Rota (16th cent.). Indigenous It. *crespo* adj. 'curled', etc., dates from the Middle Ages.

cretonne. Text.: Cretonne.

(Strong cotton fabric.) 1874 Lessona, *Diz. univ.* (Pr.); but *Il Mondo Illustrato* 1870 shows that dresses of cretonne were already in vogue as seaside wear. Early editions of Panzini criticise the erroneous spelling *creton* then in use. Adapted more recently into *cretona, cretonina.*[1] Fr. word (*toile*) *cretonne*, 1723, < Creton, a town in Normandy renowned for textiles in the sixteenth and seventeenth centuries.

---

1. An isolated example of *cretona* (a textile woven in Normandy) appears in the 18th cent., 1770 Savary, *Diz. di commercio.*

crinolina. Women's fashions: Crinoline (hooped skirt).

In this sense the It. word is documented from 1854 onwards. Numerous subsequent examples. <Fr. *crinoline* (B-Al., M-D., Pr.), usually given as first attested 1856, but probably in use a decade before. The original French word *crinoline* meaning a heavy linen cloth (1834) is borrowed from Italian (see 19th cent. It. > Fr. loans).

croccante. Culin.: Kind of crisp almond cake, and similar sweets.

1837 Giovanni Zanobetti, *Nuovo diz. portatile della ling. it.* (Prati) as an adjective 'crunchy' (applied to foods); 1841 Tommaseo. Boerio has *crocante* in Venetian as early as 1829. <Fr. *croquant* (B-Al., Pr.) pres. part. of verb *croquer* 'to crunch' (15th cent.).

crochetta, -e (pl.). Culin.: Croquettes.

1859 Carena, *Voc. domest.*; diminutive, *crocchettine* 1863 Fanfani, *Voc. dell'uso tosc.* Adaptation of Fr. word *croquette(s)* (B-Al., Pr.), 1835 *Acad.*, < verb *croquer* (*vide supra, croccante*).

crocè, croscè. Crochet-hook, crochet-work.

Crochet 1851 Fusinato (Pr.); *cruscè* 1859 (Neapolitan); *croscè* 1877 F-A. (who also register *lavori al crochet*); *crocè* Rigut., Petrocchi (who observes that the Fr. word is in such general use that to use the It. term *uncinetto* would be an affectation. Adaptations of Fr. *crochet* (B-Al., M-D., Pr.), 12th cent. meaning 'hook' in general.

crumiraggio, crumiro. Working during a strike, 'blacklegging'.

Crumiraggio 1905 Panzini (also *crumiro*, 'blackleg'). 'Dai Crumiri, predoni alla frontiera fra la Tunisia e l'Algeria, che diedero pretesto alla Francia per l'occupazione della Tunisia: nome adoperato spregiativamente contro gli operai non solidali negli scioperi' (M-D.). B-Al., M-*Stor.* note the Gallicism in *crumiro*, Pr. in both *crumiro* and *crumiraggio*. <Fr. *kroumir, kroumirage*.

cupone. Coupon.

(= *cedola*). *Coponi* (pl.) 1840 in Naples; *cupone* 1877 F-A., Rigut. 1886, Panz., who also registers *coupon d'hôtel* (kind of travellers' cheque issued by Cook's used internationally with this name). <Fr. *coupon* (B-Al., M-D., Pr.), 12th cent.

dadà. Hobby, favourite idea, 'bee in bonnet'.

1881 F-A., 2nd edition; Panzini. Fanfani's proposed substitute—'fissazione, se serio' misses the mark in that a *dada* is usually not serious. B-Al. note as 20th cent. the meaning 'persona infantilmente ricercata nel vestito'. The word *dada* was disseminated in Italy and elsewhere above all in connection with *Dadaism*, the school of art founded in Paris by Tristan Tsura in 1916. Fr. word *dada*, child's word for 'horse' (1611 Cotgrave), whence 'hobby-horse' and the above senses (late 18th cent.; N.B. influence of Sterne's *Tristram Shandy*). Also *dadaismo* 1927 Panz., 5th edition. <Fr. *dadaïsme* 1916.

dagherrotipo. Photog.: Daguerrotype.

Daguerrotipo 1854 (Pr.); *dagherròtipo* 1892 Garollo (print made by this process); Petrocchi (apparatus for taking the photograph). Also *dagherrotipia*, the process of making a Daguerrotype (upon iodised silver plate): *daguerrotipia* 1875 Lessona (Pr.); *dagherrotipia* 1892 Garollo, etc. Both words and both senses of *dagherrotipo* in T-Bell. <Fr. *daguerrotype* (B-Al., Pr.) 8th Sept. 1839, from the name of the inventor L. J. Daguerre (1769–1851) who discovered the process in that year. *Dagherrotipia* < *daguerrotypie*, 1863.

danzante (festa, veglia-). Various social functions where dancing is held.

Mattinata danzante 1877 F-A; Rig.; *serata d.* 1877 F-A.; *tè danzante* 1895 Garollo; *musica danzante* 1886 Rig. Also *veglia d.* (Panz.), *festa d.* (B-Al.), *trattenimento d.*, *cena d.* (Prati). Expressions formed upon the model of Fr. *thé dansant*, etc. (Purists, Panz., B-Al., Pr.). 'Modo traslato conforme all' indole della lingua francese, difforme al modo italiano di concepire' (Panz.).

dattilografo, -ia. Dactylograph, typewriter, typist.

End 19th cent., Petrocchi. Meaning 'typist', 1908 Panz. 2nd edition (also *dattilografa* [fem.]). <Fr. *dactylographe* (B-Al., Pr.). The machine was originally a French invention (1818) to enable the blind and deaf-mutes to communicate with the outside world (attested Mozin, 1842; registered by B-Al., as 19th cent. in It.). The sense 'typewriter' appears in Fr. 1873 (Dauz.) and 'typist' late 19th cent. 'Seguendo la falsariga francese, il doppio significato si delude usando dàttilo (f.) per macchina dattilografica' (B-Al.). Also *dattilografia* 'typewriting', 1908 Panz., but *dactilografia* 1905 Panz., 1st edition; B-Al. register as 19th cent. <Fr. *dactylographie* (B-Al., Pr.) late 19th cent.

débâcle. Collapse, catastrophe.

Later 19th cent., M-*Stor.*, p. 738; *c.* 1880, B-Al.   Fr. word, *débâcle*, 1690.

debordare. To overflow (esp. of river); to go beyond.

1812 Bernardoni, *Elenco* (in general and figurative senses); 1877 F-A., 1886 Rig. (of a river bursting its banks); Panzini ('venir fuori, sporger fuori dal suo posto o orbita'). <Fr. *déborder* (Purists, Panz., B-Al.), 14th cent. *Debordamento*, in Bernardoni and F-A., is probably a loan < Fr. *débordement* (15th cent.) since it appears at the same time and in the same contexts as the verb.

debuttare. To make one's début on the stage, or elsewhere.

Debutàr in Venet. 1829 (Boerio) as a word used on theatre bills: *debuttare* F-A., Rig. <Fr. *débuter* (Purists, Panz., B-Al., M-D., Pr.), *desbuter* 1539 R. Estienne.

debutto, debuttante. Theatrical début, introduction into society; debutante.

Debú 1829, Boerio, as a word introduced a few year before; *debutto* 1831 Anton. Lissoni *Aiuto allo scrivere purgato* (Prati); Ugol., F-A., Rig. *Debuttante* in the same sources. <Fr. *début* 1642 Oudin, *débutante* 1787 Féraud (Purists, Panz., B-Al., M-D., Pr.).

decalcare. To take a tracing.

'Riportare il "calco" d'un disegno o quadro' (B-Al.). 19th cent., (B-Al.), < Fr. *décalquer*, 1694.

decalcomania. Hobby of collecting 'transfers'.

The formal group of which Fr. *décalcomanie* is a member was transferred originally from Italian to French (see *calquer*, *calque*, It. > Fr. 17th cent. loans). The terms transferred are of the fine arts and refer to the process of taking a tracing, impression or cast of paintings or sculpture. There is evidence of some slight reciprocal influence in respect of these words during the 19th cent., in the use of *decalco*, *decalcare* for *calco*, *calcare* in technical significations. During the 19th cent. Fr. *décalque* (1849, Bloch) and *décalquer* (1694, Th. Corneille) were used in the new, limited sense of coloured pictures which when wetted could be transferred to a scrapbook, i.e. 'transfers'. The hobby of collecting transfers, 'delizia degli scolaretti, e sciupio dei libri' (Panz.) became in the later 19th cent. a veritable *décalcomanie* (1876, Littré). Both the craze and the name were introduced into Italy from France: *decalcomania*, Petrocchi, Panz.; also *calcomania*, Panz., 1st edition. It. *decalco* and *decalcare* in these contexts are also borrowed from French.

declassare. To demote, reduce in status.

19th cent. B-Al. <Fr. *déclasser*, 1813. *Declassato* (adj.) 'one who is not recognised by his natural social group' (Panz., 8th edition, 1942) is a further semantic loan from French.

décolleté. Dressm.: Fashions: Low neckline.

Later 19th cent., M-*Stor.*, p. 737; Panz., 1st edition. 'Corrisponde la nostra scollato . . . ma ormai la voce francese è prevalente' (Panz.; omitted in later editions). Fr. term, *décolleté*, < verb *décolleter*, used in the early 18th cent. to mean 'to remove one's scarf' (*collet*).

dedalo. Labyrinth; figurative uses.

1877 F-A. ('labirinto, imbroglio'). <Fr. *dédale* (M-D., Pr.) 1555 Pasquier.

defilare, defilè (défilé). Milit.: To review troops; march past.

Both verb and subst. in F-A. 1877 and Rigutini. Fr. form *défilé* in Panz. B-Al. add a further military signification: 'sottrarre al tiro nemico diretto' (20th cent.). <Fr. *défiler* (all sources) 1648, and *défilé*, 18th cent. in the above sense.

demarcazione, demarcare. Demarcation.

Demarcazione 1812 Bernardoni, 1829–40 Tramater, 1877 F-A., Rig. *Demarcare* in Bernardoni, F-A. <Fr. *démarcation* 1752 Trévoux, *démarquer* 16th cent. (Purists, B-Al., Pr.), < Sp. *demarcación, demarcar* used to refer to the arbitrary demarcation line established in 1493 by Pope Alexander VI between the Spanish and Portuguese spheres of influence in the Americas. From Arlia's observations the word seems to have become familiar to Italians during the demarcation of Italy and Austria which took place in 1866.

demi-monde, demi-mondaine.

Demi-monde 1892 Garollo, Panz.; *demi-mondaine* 1905 Panz. (19th cent., B-Al.). Fr. word *demi-monde* (and derivative), title of play by Dumas fils, 1855.

demoralizzare, demoralizzazione. To demoralise, demoralisation.

1812 Bernardoni: 1886 Rigutini, who registers it as a recent Gallicism used generally of soldiers, but also of civilians. Panz. approves of the verb. <Fr. *démoraliser* 1798, Acad., *démoralisation* 1800, Boiste (Purists, Panz., B-Al.).

dentiera. Set of false teeth, denture.

19th cent. acc. to B-Al., though Pr. registers the word in Alberti 1797–1805. Also tech. engineering: 'toothed wheel, rack', 1874 Lessona, Petrocchi. <Fr. *dentier* in above sense (B-Al.) with change of gender. Fr. *dentier* appears 16th cent., meaning 'jaw'; the signification 'set of (natural) teeth' (1690, Furetière) is given by Alberti in 1788 as archaic (the only sense mentioned there). When the word was revived to mean 'false denture' is uncertain, though examples may be found in the early 19th cent.

deperire. To decay, depreciate, waste away.

M-D. register the semantic development as a Gallicism; the 19th cent. Purists draw a careful distinction between *deperire* 'to perish utterly' and the above sense (Rigutini, especially). The latter are registered with disapprobation by Bernardoni 1812, Ugolini, F-A. and Rigutini (who cites among his references Zannoni, early 19th cent.), but the bureaucratic term has remained in use. A semantic loan < Fr. *dépérir* (Purists, M-D.; Panzini concurs by implication). Similar criticisms are levelled at the subst. *deperimento* (registered by all the above sources). 'Cattiva traduzione del fr. *dépérissement*' (Ugolini). The Fr. word dates from 1600.

deragliare. Rail. engin.: To be derailed.

1877 F-A.: '*Rail* e voce inglese . . . ma a noi il verbo provenne dal *dérailler* francese.' <Fr. *dérailler* (B-Al., M-D., Pr.), 1842 *Journal des chemins de fer*. Also *deragliamento*, F-A. < Fr. *déraillement* (1842).

dettagliante. Retail merchant.

1891 Rigutini, 2nd edition; Panzini. <Fr. *détaillant* (B-Al., M-D., Pr.), 1649 in this sense.

digiunè. Breakfast.

19th cent. B-Al.; 1877 F-A., who also register the sense 'tavolino dove si suol far colazione, il quale è generalmente di figura rotonda e col marmo. Il proprio suo nome è *desco*.' Panzini has the French form. Adapt. of Fr. *déjeuner*, or rather *petit-déjeuner*, 'breakfast'. (= *colazione*.)

dimissionario. One who has tendered his resignation (from a post, office).

1812 Bernardoni, *Elenco*; Rig. <Fr. *démissionnaire* (Purists, Panz., B-Al.), 18th cent.

dinamismo. Phil.: Physics: Art: Dynamism.

1874 Lessona (Pr.); 1892 Garollo (Pr.). As a theory of movement in art connected with futurism, 1918 Panz., 3rd edition. <Fr. *dynamisme* (philos.) 1835 *Acad.* (B-Al., Pr.).

dinamitardo. Revolutionary saboteur, anarchist.

End 19th cent. Petrocchi; Panz. <Fr. *dynamitard* (late 19th cent.) (Panz., B-Al., Pr.) 'revolutionary who uses dynamite for destructive political activities'. Also the technical word *dinamitare* 'to blow up with dynamite', 1905 Panz., 1st edition. <Fr. *dynamiter*, late 19th cent. Both Prati and B-Al. consider that the original word *dinamite* (explosive, 'dynamite', 1874 Lessona) reached Italian through French.

dirigible. Airship; dirigible.

End 19th cent., acc. to B-Al., M-*Stor.*; 1905 Panz., 1st edition. <Fr. *dirigeable* (init. *ballon dirigeable*) 1851 Giffard (B-Al., Pr.).

divetta. Woman cabaret singer, 'starlet'.

Divette (Fr.) 1905, Panz. I: 'divinità di ordine inferiore al tempo del furoreggiare dei caffè-concerto'. <Fr. *divette* (Panz., Pr.) 1890, dimin. of *diva* (q.v., 19th cent. It. > Fr. loans).

dolomia, dolomite. Mineral.: Dolomite.

Both 19th cent. acc. to B-Al. Panzini. <Fr. *dolomie, dolomite*, 1792 Saussure (B-Al., M-D., Pr.); formed on name of geologist Dolomieu (1750–1801).

domino. Game of dominoes.

Dominò (Fr. accentuation) 1855 Fanfani; 1874 Lessona (Pr.). Petrocchi has *dòmino*. 'Giuoco che prende forma definitiva in Italia nel XVIII sec. e si espande rapidamente in altri paesi' (B-Al.). <Fr. *domino* (B-Al., Cr. V, M-D., Pr.), 1771 Trévoux, probably from the appearance of the domino, which resembles a mask; possibly from *dominus* 'master'. Early editions of Panzini relate the anecdote whereby the game was said to be derived from the words *benedicamus Domino* (the traditional origin also of *domino* 'cloak': see *domino* 18th cent. Fr. > It. loans) spoken by a monk of Montecassino who invented the game to combat boredom.

dormeuse. Lounge chair; type of carriage.

'Carriage': *dormös* 1840 in Milanese (Cherubini). *Dormeuse* in both senses, 1892 Garollo. Also Italianised as *dormosa, durmosa* (Pr.). Fr. word *dormeuse* (B-Al., Pr.), 'chair' 1858; both senses in Littré.

dorsay. Mens' fashions: Style of tail-coat.

19th cent. B-Al. Panzini I, 1905. Fr. word, *dorsay* (B-Al., Pr., Panz.), 1870; < name of the English nobleman Alfred d'Orsay, a beau of Parisian society in the 1st half of the 19th century. The *OED* does not register a corresponding term in English.

drenaggio. Drainage, esp. in land reclamation.

1860 Ugolini; 1886 Rigutini; other late 19th cent. examples. Also as a medical term (evacuation of cysts, etc.) 1892 Garollo. <Fr. *drainage* (Purists, B-Al., M-D., Pr.), 1849, borrowed (together with *drain, drainer*) as agricultural terms < English. Med. term 1859. M-D. consider It. *drenare* a loan < Fr. *drainer*; B-Al. draw it directly from English.

droma. Naut.: A sailing-ship's spare masts and spars.

1879 Luigi Fincati, *Diz. di marina* (Pr.). <Fr. *drome* (B-Al., Pr.) 1755, *Encycl.* < Low German.

dublè (doublé). Rolled gold; imitation gold.

(= *similoro*). *Dublè* 1877 F-A.; Panzini. <Fr. *doublé* (p. part. and adj. < *doubler* in sense 'to line' (of cloth, etc.); cf. 18th cent. *doublage*, panelling or lining of a ship's side), 1755 *Encycl.*; there may be some influence of *doublet* (18th cent.) a double glass disc with coloured paper between cut to imitate emeralds, etc.

écarté. Card-game: écarté.

Current during 19th cent. Panz. I, 1905. Fr. word, *écarté*, 10th March 1810, *Mercure de France*. Attested in Eng. 1824 (*OED*).

eccentrico. (Adj.) Eccentric, bizarre.

1860 Ugolini; 1886 Rigut.; Panz. <Fr. *excentrique* (Rig., Panz., B-Al., Pr.); fig. sense 1736, acc. to B-Wart., <Eng. *eccentric* (Littré). Also *eccentricità* (Ugolini) in similar sense, < Fr. *excentricité*.

eccezionale. Exceptional.

1886 Rigutini; esp. as political, legal term—*poteri eccezionali*, etc. <Fr. *exceptionnel* (Rig., B-Al.), 1739.

éclatant (eclatante). Brilliant, magnificent, striking.

1865–79 Tomm. e Bell.; *eclatante* 1877 F-A.; 1886 Rigut. (strongly attacked by Purists). Panz. registers the Fr. form. Under *eclatante* Migl. *Suppl.* remarks: 'è stato adoperato (speriamo de ischerzo) come addattamento del fr. *éclatant*'. 'Voce ... penetrata nel piemontese e lombardese', acc. to B-Al. Also *éclat* (B-Al.). French words *éclatant* and *éclat*, with similar figurative uses.

écraseur. Medic.: Écraseur (surgical instrument).

(A miniature chain-saw operated by a screw.) 1877 F-A. (suggests *schiacciatore*). Panzini. Fr. word; applied to the instrument by its inventor, Chassaignac (1804–79).

edredone. Ornith.: Eider-duck: also eider-down.

1874 Lessona (Pr.); Panz. <Fr. *édredon* (Panz., B-Al., Pr.) 1700 Liger. <Icelandic, prob. via German.

effetti (pl.). Effects, chattels, stocks.

B-Al. register as 19th cent. Gallicisms the sense (a) *capi di vestiario*, (b) *titoli commerciali*. Rigutini 1886 already expressed a similar opinion about the same two acceptations ((b) translated by *cedola*), which he rejects, while concurring with the *Nuova Crusca* in accepting the sense 'goods and chattels' (examples in Sassetti, Fagiuoli, etc.). Panzini enlarges upon this distinction: 'Effetti per *oggetti minuti, roba, biancheria, capi di vestiario*, è francesismo dell'uso, *effets* = *meubles, vêtements*.... *Effetti* nel senso di *sostanze, averi, beni mobili e immobili* è ritenuta voce ottima e come tale registrata dalla Crusca, ancorchè non molto usata in tal senso.' F-A., 1877, give *effetto* in the second signification ('*roba, oggetto, arnese*') as French also. Fr. word, *effets* (pl.), 'goods, chattels, luggage, movables of various kinds', and (finance) 'stocks, bills, funds' (*effets publics, de commerce*, etc.).[1]

egotismo. Philos.: Egotism.

End 19th cent., Petrocchi (Pr.); Panz. <Fr. *égotisme*, acc. to Pr.; B-Al. register the English origin but add that the word was disseminated as a result of Stendhal's *Souvenir d'égotisme*; first attested in Fr. 1726.

élite. Elite (of society); ruling classes.

1877 F-A., who quote a ministerial dispatch of 10th March 1861: 'Il Parlamento rinchiude nel suo seno l'elite (sic) della nazione.' Fr. word; *eslite* 12th cent.

endemico. Medic.: Endemic (of diseases).

1828 Leone (Pr.). Remodelling under the influence of Fr. *endémique* (1608) of the original It. adj. *endemio* (Vallisneri, Alberti, Leone) < Gk. ενδήμιος, 'indigenous'.

en tout cas. Small umbrella-cum-parasol.

19th cent. B-Al. Panzini (also 'leggero impermeabile'). Fr. phrase *en tout cas* substantified (un *en-tout-cas*) (Littré).

---

1. It now appears that *effetti* was extended semantically and brought into wider use by its being used in proclamations, etc., in the Revolutionary period: *vide* example dated 1797 in P. Zolli, *L.N.*, 1964, p. 13 and note.

entremets. Culin.: Side-dish, sweets.

Earlier 19th cent., M-*Stor.*, p. 660. French word, 12th cent.

equilibrista. Tight-rope walker: acrobat.

1895 Garollo. Also used in figurative sense (as in French), particularly of political figures. *Equilibrismo* likewise. <Fr. *équilibriste* (B-Al., Pr.) 1780.

escursione. Outing, trip.

1860 Ugolini; 1877 F-A.; Panz. F-A. accept only the original (16th cent.) It. sense of 'raid, sortie' (= *scorreria*), even though the wider connotation exists in Latin. Rigutini while noting this fact is prepared to add the French signification to It. usage. He continues: 'Dove è il suggello della gallicità è nel traslato, come *far un escursione nella storia, nella filosofia*, ecc.' Semantic loan < Fr. *excursion* (B-Al., Pr.), 16th cent. Also *escursionista* 'tripper' 1883 Manfroni (Pr.) < Fr. *excursionniste* (B-Al., Pr.) 1852. B-Al. also register 20th cent. *escursionare* (Panz.), *escursionismo* as Gallicisms.

esergo. Numism.: Exergue.

1855 Fanfani. <Fr. learned term *exergue* (B-Al., Pr.), 1636.

esploatare, esploatazione. To exploit, exploitation, esp. of mineral deposits.

Both in 1877 F-A; Rigutini; Panzini. Adaptations of Fr. *exploiter, exploitation* (Purists, B-Al., Pr.) used in this sense mid-18th cent. onwards. Later replaced by *sfruttare*.

esteriorizzare, -azione. Spiritualism: To 'exteriorise' a medium's spirit.

'Il transferirsi della sensibilità di uno individuo fuori di lui durante il sonno ipnotico' (B-Al.). Both 19th cent. acc. to B-Al.; Panzini. <Fr. *extérioriser* (1869), *extériorisation* (Panz., B-Al.), i.e. Gallicising forms of It. *esteriorare, esteriorazione* (Panz., same senses).

estradosso. Archit.: Extrados (of arch vault).

19th cent., acc. to B-Al.; Panz. <Fr. *extrados* (Panz., B-Al.) 1694, Th. Corneille.

étagère. Set of shelves, 'what-not'.

1877 F-A.; Rigutini; Panzini. B-Al. note that this item of furniture came into fashion a little before 1825. Fr. word *étagère*, 1823 Boiste.

etnografia. Ethnography.

1843 (Prati); Crusca V. Used earlier (Marchi, 1829, acc. to Prati) for historical description of races. <Fr. *ethnographie* (B-Al., Pr.), 1823. Also *etnologia* (19th cent.) < Fr. *ethnologie* 1842, Mozin.

fàglia. Geol.: Fault.

1892 Garollo (Pr.); Panz. <Fr. *faille* (Panz., B-Al., Pr.), 1779 Le Camus, originally a mining term of the Walloon dialects.

falaise. Geog.: Cliff at sea's edge.[1]

1883 G. Marinelli (Pr.); other late 19th cent. attestations. Panzini. Also It. versions *falesa, falesia*. Fr. word *falaise* (B-Al., Pr.); *faleise* 12th cent., *Enéas*. (Norman or Picard word referring initially and principally to cliffs of northern France.)

fanoni. Zool.: Whalebone, i.e. cartilaginous filter lining a whale's mouth.

1874 Lessona. <Fr. *fanons* (pl.) (B-Al., Pr.), 12th cent., 'pennant'; above sense not later than 18th cent. B-Al. also derives the ecclesiastical terms (19th cent.; 'maniple'; 'pendant of a mitre') from French.

farmacia. Chemist's shop, drug-store.

1828 Leone (Pr.); 1st half 19th cent. M-*Stor.*, p. 662. Semantic loan < Fr. *pharmacie* 1314, but originally (as in It.) used solely to mean 'pharmacy', i.e. dispensing of medicines (Pr., Migl.).

---

1. 'Si suole indicare anche da noi, una sponda rocciosa che dirupa a perpendicolo nel mare' (Antonio Jacono, *L.N.*, III, p. 43 (q.v.), also *L.N.*, IV, 39 and *It. Dial.*, X, 113).

favoriti (pl.). Fashions: Side-whiskers.

19th cent. B-Al.; Carducci (Pr.); 1877 F-A.; *favorite* in Venetian 1829 (Boerio). <Fr. *favoris* 1829 (Panz., B-Al., Pr.), subst. from the adjective *favori*, which is an Italian loan (*vide* 16th cent. It. > Fr. borrowings).[1]

femminismo. Feminism.

Appears as the title of a work by L. Ficheri publ. in Venice 1897: *Femminismo* (*terzo sesso*): *satira sociale.* Panzini; Arlia, *Suppl.* 1907. The movement came into prominence in the last decade of the 19th century and first of the 20th, and was strong in Italy immediately after the Great War. <Fr. *féminisme* (Panz., B-Al., Pr.) 1872. Also *femminista* < *féministe* (Panz., B-Al.).

fiamma, fiammetta. Veter. Surgery: small spring-loaded scalpel for bleeding horses.

Both in Leone, 1828 (Pr.). <Fr. *flamme, flammette* (Prati), a popular etymology of OFr. *flieme* < Lat. *fletomus* < *phlebotomus* (cf. OIt. *fiotano* [T-Bell.]).

finanziera. Double-breasted frock coat (as used still by station-masters).

19th cent. B-Al.; Panzini I, 1905. <Fr. *financière* (B-Al., Pr.) 18th cent., so called because understood to be worn by bankers, financiers and the like. Also 19th cent. is the culinary term, 'manicaretto di rigaglie di pollo e, se si vuole, con animelle e funghi' (Panz. IX), corresponding to Fr. (*à la*) *financière*.

flacone. Small glass flask, bottle for perfume.

Word of the luxury trades. 19th cent., B-Al.; 1877 F-A., Rigutini. <Fr. *flacon* (B-Al., M-D., Pr.) 14th cent. (*vide fiasco*, 19th cent. It. > Fr.).

flagioletto. Music: Flageolet.

19th cent. B-Al. <Fr. *flageolet*, 14th cent.

flambò. Torch.

End 19th cent. acc. to B-Al. <Fr. *flambeau* (B-Al.) 14th cent., *Ménagier* < OFr. *flambe*, 'flame'.

flan. Culin.: Flan.

1877 F-A. (refer to use of the word earlier in Milanese); Garollo; Panz. Fr. word, *flan* (B-Al., Pr.), *flaon* 12th cent. < Frankish.

fonazione. Scient.: Production of speech sounds.

1874 Lessona. <Fr. *phonation* (B-Al., Pr.) coined < Gk. φωνή by Chaussier (1828).

foncé. Fashions: Dark, applied to colours.

19th cent. acc. to B-Al.; Panzini. Fr. word *foncé*, 1690.

fondant. Toffee, fondant.

19th cent. B-Al.; Panzini. Fr. word *fondant*; subst. in Littré ('bonbons qui contiennent . . . une liqueur ou une pâte sucrée et parfumée'), but not later than 18th cent. as an adj. in similar connotations ('une poire fondante' i.e. which melts in the mouth).

fondiario. (Adj.) Pertaining to funds.

Pre-1832, Carlo Botta (cited by Rigutini); other 19th cent. attestations. A learned word coined as equivalent of the Fr. adj. *foncier* (Rig., Panz., B-Al.); *cens fonsier* 1370, Godef. Most 19th cent. purists consider certain usages of *fondo* to be derived from French, esp. *fondi* in plural, e.g. *fondi pubblici* (= *fonds publics*); the more intransigent (Arlia, for instance) condemn *fondo* itself in the sense of *somma, denaro, assegnamento*.

fonduta. Culin.: Kind of savoury with cream cheese and eggs.

Fondua in Petrocchi (late 19th cent.), which represents the Piedmontese dialect term

---

1. *Favore* in Savary, *Diz. di commercio*, 1770 (= 'thin, light ribbon') may be < Fr. *faveur* 'ribbon', 1564 Thierry.

fondüa; *fonduta* in Manfroni 1901 (Pr.), Panzini. <Fr. *fondue* (Panz., B-Al., Pr.) 1768, Rousseau, taken < Swiss dialects; entered It. via Piedmontese.

forfait (forfè). Commerce: Contract at a fixed price.

Usually *vendere, comprare, trattare a forfait,* = 'on contract'. *Prezzo a forfait,* inclusive price for a job lot of miscellaneous items. 1886 Rigutini; 1895 Garollo; Panzini (also phon. adapt. *forfè*). Italianised form *forfatto* in F-A., 2nd edition 1890 (Pr.). Fr. word *forfait, Ordonnance* of 1647 in this sense.

fotografia. Photograph.

1865–74 T-Bell., where *fotografo, fotografare, fotografico* are also registered. <Fr. *photographie,* 1846 (B-Al., Pr.) < English *photograph* (1839). B-Al. derive all four of the above forms from their French equivalents.

foulard. Fashions: Neckerchief of fine silk or cotton; the name was later applied to the material used.

1846 Fusinato (Pr.), but *folard* 1840 in Cherubini (Milan.). Phon. adapt. *folàr*, Petrocchi. Fr. word *foulard,* 1771 < Prov. *foulat* (past part. of *fould*) (B-Al., Pr.).

foyer. Foyer (of theatre).

1895 Garollo (Prati); Panzini. Fr. word, *foyer*: in 18th cent., by metonymy, 'common-room in theatre' (with fire) where actors rested; above sense 19th cent.

frac. Evening dress (men's).

Frac-paré in 1851, Fusinato; *fracche, fracco* 1883 Manfroni (Pr.); *frac,* Rigutini. The fashion passed from France into Italy a little before the time of Napoleon III and became the accepted evening dress of all western European countries about 1860. Fr. word, *frac* (*fracq* in Beaumarchais 1767), < English *frock (-coat).*

franco-tiratore. Irregular militia, guerrillas.

19th cent. B-Al. Calque of Fr. *franc-tireur,* itself a calque of German *Freischütz* (B-Al., Panz.). The *franc-tireurs* were constituted in eastern France to harass invaders in 1792, and again in 1815 and 1870.

fregata. Ornith.: Frigate-bird.

1874 Lessona (Pr.). 19th cent., B-Al. <Fr. *frégate* (Buffon) (B-Al., Pr.), figurative extension of *frégate,* 'small, swift man-of-war', itself a borrowing from Italian (q.v., 16th cent.).

frenologia. Phrenology.

1829 M. A. Marchi, *Diz. tech.-etim.-filol.* (Pr.). <Fr. *phrénologie,* (B-Al., Pr.), attested 1829 but no doubt existing a little before. The 'science' was invented by Franz Gall (1828), a German doctor resident in Paris from 1807 onwards.

fumasigari. Cigar-holder.

19th cent., acc. to B-Al. <Fr. *fume-cigare,* 19th cent. (B-Al.).

fumista. Stove-setter, stove-repairer.

'Operaio che lavora a stufe, camini, termosifoni' (B-Al.). In Milanese 1840 (Cherubini); Tuscan, end 19th cent. Figurative sense in Italian parallel to those of French ('practical joker, trickster, smart Alec'). <Fr. *fumiste* (Panz., B-Al., M-D., Pr.) 1762; fig. senses 1852, les Goncourt. Also *fumisteria* (late 19th cent.), trade of 'fumiste', whence 'mystification', etc., < Fr. *fumisterie* 1845, Bescherelle.

fumoir. Smoking-room, e.g. in theatre.

Later 19th cent., M-*Stor.,* p. 737; Panz. Fr. word dating from the mid-century (1865, B-Wart.).

funicolare. Funicular railway (esp. cable railway, *téléférique*).

Late 19th cent., Petrocchi, Giorgini (Pr.); Panzini. <Fr. *funiculaire* (Panz., B-Al., Pr.) 1725 Varignon as adj.; subst. mid-19th cent.

funzionarismo. Excessive tendency to seek employment in public offices.

1877 F-A. <Fr. *fonctionnarisme* (1870 Littré; F-A. quote an attack upon the neologism by de Castellane in *La Patrie* during 1871). Panzini has *funzionale*, medical and architectural term < Fr. *fonctionnel*. *Vide funzionario*, 18th cent. Fr. > It. loans.

fuor d'opera. An irrelevancy, unnecessary digression.

19th cent. Gioberti (B-Al.); Rigutini; Panz. Calque of Fr. *hors d'œuvre* (Rig., Panz., B-Al.) in this sense (see *hors d'œuvre*, below).

furgone. Covered waggon, van.

Forgone 1812 Bernardoni, glossed as *carrettone*; *forgone* and (metath.) *frugone* in Ugolini and F-A., 1877; *furgone* in Panz., 1905. Originally a milit. term, 'large covered cart in which to transport food, equipment'. This is the sense in Cherubini 1840 (Milanese, *forgón*) as well as most of the above sources. <Fr. *fourgon* (B-Al., M-D., Pr.), 17th cent., Voiture.

gaffa. Naut.: Grappling-iron; gaff (for landing fish).

Masc. *gaffe* in early attestations. 1814 Stratico; 1853 D'Ayala. The usual sense in It. as in Fr. is that of a long pole with a curved spike at the end, to assist in landing large fish (this signification enters English from Fr. in the middle of the 17th cent.). <Fr. *gaffe* (fem.) (B-Al., Pr.), 1393; above senses (also that of 'boathook'); < Prov. *gaf*.

galoppo, galop. Type of lively dance.

1847 Arnaldo Fusinato; 1865–79 T-Bell. Fr. form *galop* in later attestations; also used as word of command in the quadrille. <Fr. *galop* (Panz., B-Al., Pr.), name given in France to this dance (and accompanying tune) about 1830, when it was introduced. The dance itself is apparently of German or Hungarian origin. (See also *galoppo, galoppare* in the original sense, medieval Fr. > It. loans).

garage. Shed, coach-house, garage.

= *Rimesso, autorimesso*. A 19th cent. term, acc. to B-Al. and M-*Stor.*; 1905 Panz., 1st edition; 1918 Panz., 3rd edition, in the meaning which now predominates, viz. 'garage for motor vehicles'. Fr. word, *garage* (*Ordonn.*, 1802), which originally meant the action of docking a ship, or halting a train in sidings (*c.* 1840); also storage for goods or coaches and garage for motor vehicles (1899 Larousse). The semantic range in It. is narrower than Fr. (as it is in English). B-Al. derive 20th cent. *garagista* ('garage-hand, -proprietor') from Fr. *garagiste*.

gargotta. Low-grade eating-house.

1864 Rigutini (Pr.). Prati refers to a dialectal *gargota* attested in Turin, 1783 (Morizio Pipino, *Vocab. piemontese*). B-Al. consider it a 19th cent. loan. <Fr. *gargote* (B-Al., M-D., Pr.), 1680 < *gargoter* 'to eat gluttonously'.

gattò. Culin.: Cake.

Gatò 1877 F-A. (= *focaccia, dolce*); 1905 Panzini, 1st edition. Widely used earlier in dialects, esp. southern. Venet. *gatò* 1829, Boerio; Sardinian *gattò* 1832 (Prati). Adapt. of Fr. *gâteau* (all sources agree), *gastel*, 12th cent.[1]

gè. Jet.

Petrocchi; Panzini (also registered Fr. *jais* and adapt. *getto*). Fr. word, *jais* (Panz., B-Al., Pr.), 13th cent.

genio. Milit.: Corps of engineers.

Esercito del Genio, Raffaello Lambruschini (1788–1873) (Pr.); *genio* 1853 D'Ayala, F-A. 1877, Rigutini. <Fr. *génie* (B-Al., M-D., Pr., etc.) 1759, shortened version of *ingénieur*.

---

1. F-A. also reject *gatò* as a foundryman's tech. term, = 'mass of solidified metal' (Fr. *gâteau* has this connotation in the 18th cent.), pointing out that when Cellini described the casting of his *Perseo* he used the traditional term *migliaccio* (used also by Alberti to translate Fr. *gâteau* in this sense).

K

Genio meaning 'genius' (abstr.) or 'a man of genius' is an 18th cent. semantic loan (= *potenza d'intelletto, o d'ingegno* [F-A.]). F-A. cite Leopardi to the effect that Italian has no precise equivalent.

gerenza. Management, administration.

Gerenza and *gerente* ('manager, administrator') 1886 Rigutini. <Fr. *gérance* (Rig., B-Al.), 1866 Littré, *gérant* 1787. Prati considers the synonym *gestione* (1812 Bernardoni) to be a loan < Fr. *gestion* (15th cent.).

ghepardo. Zool.: Hunting-leopard or cheetah.

1874 Lessona (Pr.). <Fr. *guépard* (B-Al., Pr.) for earlier *gapard* (1706), term applied by Buffon to the above species which he had defined precisely. The word *gapard* itself is borrowed from It. *gatto-pardo* (cf. Fr. *chat-pard* 1690), used to refer to the *serval (Felis serval)* which in former times was popularly thought to be a cross between a cat and a *leopard* or *pard*.

ghisa. Metall.: Cast-iron.

1877 F-A.; 1886 Rigutini. <Fr. *gueuse* (Purists, B-Al.), or more correctly, from the parallel form *guise* (now obsolete), also 16th cent., in which the German etymon (*Gans, Göse*) may have been influenced by Germ. *giessen*.

giaccheria. The Jacquerie; any popular riot.

Mid-19th cent., T-Bell. <Fr. *jacquerie* (B-Al., Pr.) 14th cent. <Jacques(Bonhomme), traditional name denoting the peasant and used to refer to the peasants' revolt of 1358 in the first instance. *Jacquerie* in the extended signification dates from 1821 (P.-L. Courier). (Cf. Migliorini, *Dal nome proprio*, p. 224).

giacchetta. Fashions: Jacket.

See *giacchetta*, medieval Fr. > It. word-list.

giada. Jade.

1855 Fanfani; *giado* in Lessona and Petrocchi (Pr.). <Fr. *jade* (B-Al., Pr.), *ejade* 1633 < Sp. *ijada*.

giaguaro. Zool.: Jaguar.

1874 Lessona (Pr.); E. Zaccaria, *L'Elemento iberico nella ling. ital.* gives examples of forms *giagaro, sciaguaro* from authorities of the first half of the 19th cent. (earliest *c.* 1821) (*vide* Prati, *V. Et. It.*, p. 491), while *jagar* appears in Giambattista Casti (Pr.). <Fr. *jaguar* (B-Al., Pr.), mid-18th cent., Buffon, < Tupi *yaguara*.

giambone. Culin.: Ham.

19th cent. B-Al.; 1883 Manfroni (Pr.); Panzini (also has *maniche à jambon* (women's fashions) 'leg of mutton sleeves'). A Lombard and Piedmontese word, (*giambón, giambún*, Milanese, Turin). <Fr. *jambon* (Panz., B-Al., Pr.), 13th cent.

giardiniera. Flower-stand; waggonette.

Two main senses borrowed from French during the course of the 19th century: (a) ornamental stand for indoor plants: 'mobile di varie forme spesso a più bracci, adoperato per sostenere vasi di fiori e pianti ornamentali' (*Diz. encicl. ital.*) (1863, Fanfani), (b) Large horse-drawn cart with side-benches, originally used for taking garden produce to market (end of cent., Petrocchi). The culinary term (Fanfani 1863—applied to various dishes composed of mixed vegetables) may also owe something to French, as Panzini claims. The French word is used in similar contexts in English. <Fr. *jardinière*; sense (a) 1777, *FEW*; (b) 1877, *Larousse*.

gibus. Opera-hat.

Cappello alla Gibus 1846 Fusinato (Pr.); Petrocchi; Panz. Fr. word *gibus* (Panz., B-Al., Pr.); hat invented by person of that name in 1834 (cf. Migliorini, *Dal nome proprio*, p. 194).

gilè, gilet. Waistcoat.

1804 D'Alberti, acc. to Prati. Fr. form *gilet* in Fusinato 1846, *Fisiologia del Lion*. F-A., Rig. register it under *gilè*; an adaptation *giletto* dates from the late 19th cent. Synonym of *panciotto*. Fr. word, *gilet* (all sources), 1736 < Sp. *jileco* < Turkish *yelek*.

girondino. Hist.: Girondin: by extension, moderate republican.
Early 19th cent. (B-Al.) in strict sense; end 19th cent. (Petrocchi), meaning 'moderate republican' (*vide* Panzini). <Fr. *girondin(s)* 1793. (B-Al., M-D., Pr.).

giuliana. Culin.: Julienne (soup).
1892 Garollo (Pr.). <Fr. *julienne* (B-Al., Pr.); *potage à la julienne* in 1722.

giurì. Jury.
Early 19th cent. (B-Al.), M-*Stor.*, p. 660. In Piedmont in 1848, acc. to Prati, who registers the signification 'commissione incaricata di giudicare di meriti, ricompense, quistioni' in 1868. Fully italianised form *giurìa* in Panz. I, 1905. 'Giurìa sembra oggi raramente usato come termine giuridico e cavalleresco' (cf. *giurì d'onore*, Panz.) 'mentre predomina nel senso di "giudici" di competizioni sportive e artistiche' (B-Al.). <Fr. *jury* (18th cent.) (B-Al., M-D., Pr.) <Eng. *jury* (ultimately < OFr.).

goletta, goeletta. Naut.: Type of schooner.
1870 Luigi Fincati, *Diz. di marina* (Pr.); *goeletta* in Botta, early 19th cent. (Pr.). <Fr. *goëlette* (B-Al., Pr.), *goualette* 1752, prob. < *goëland* 'seagull' of Breton origin.

grafia. Philol.: Graphy (usually of a manuscript).
19th cent. B-Al.; Petrocchi. <Fr. learned coinage *graphie* (B-Al., Pr.), 1762.

grafologia. Graphology, i.e. study of handwriting as an index of character.
19th cent. B-Al.; 1892 Garollo (Pr.). <Fr. *graphologie* (B-Al., Pr.), coined in 1868 by Jean Hippolyte Michon. B-Al. derive *grafologo* < Fr. *graphologue* 1877.

grammo. Metric system: gramme.
Opening years of 19th cent., M-*Stor.*, p. 635. Also *gramma*. Adapt. of Fr. gramme, 'loi du 3 avril 1793, au sens moderne; en 1790 comme terme d'antiquité' (B-Wart.).

grand guignol. Puppet, Punch and Judy show.
19th cent., B-Al. Also as in French applied to 'rappresentazioni rapide, in cui col terrore e con l'orrore impreveduto si studia di commuovere la sensibilità atrofizzata di noi moderni ... Agg. *granguignolesco*! (o *granghignolesco*)' (Panz., 9th edition, p. 305). Equivalent to Eng. 'blood-and-thunder'. Fr. phrase, < *Guignol*, name of an outstanding masque of the French puppet theatre (Lyons; 18th cent. onwards).

grattoàr. Scraper, eraser.
1877 F-A.; 1886 Rig.; Panzini. Applied usually to a small knife for erasing writing or printing, but also to similar tools in technical contexts. Fr. form in Panz. Adapt. of Fr. *grattoir*; similar significations 1611 (Cotgrave) onwards.

grenadina. Fashions, Text.: grenadine.
'Stoffa leggera di seta granulosa a trafori, simile a un merletto, per abiti femminili' (B-Al.). Panzini. 19th cent., acc. to B-Al., who with Panz. derive it < Fr. *grenadine*, 1828.

grenetina. Chem.: Preparation of pure gelatine.
1874 Lessona (Pr.); Petrocchi. Fr. *grenetine*, < surname of inventor, *Grenet*, of Rouen (B-Al., Pr.).

grès. Ceramics: Stoneware.
'Materiale ceramico a pasta dura compatta, sonora, impermeabile, ottenuto per cottura fino ad incipiente vetrificazione dell'impasto e spesso anche ricoperto da una vetrina impermeabile' (*Diz. encicl. ital.*, s.v.). Also used as a scientific term (petrology: type of stone) in Italian. 1853 D'Ayala (Pr.); B-Al. give it as a 19th cent. term, with phonet. adapt. *grè*. Fr. word *grès*, 12th cent. in original sense of 'sandstone'; 1330, Gay, in the sense 'terre sablonneuse dont on fait de la poterie'; 1837 meaning 'object de poterie de grès' (*FEW*, XVI, pp. 56-7).

gribana. Naut.: Shallow-draught sailing coaster of about 50 tons used off coasts of Picardy and Flanders.

A 19th cent. term, acc. to B-Al. (not in Alberti, where the French word is rendered by a descriptive periphrasis). <Fr. *gribane* (B-Al.), 1612, *gabanne* (possibly not the same vessel?) 1436, Monstrelet.

griglia. Grating, grille.

1812 Bernardoni (*grata, inferriata*). B-Al. register the meaning 'shutters' from 1836; also F-A., 1877 (esp. in pl. *griglie*), Rigutini, Panzini. <Fr. *grille* (Purists, B-Al., M-D., Pr.), *greille* 13th cent.

grippe. Medic.: Influenza.

Grippo, grippa A. Guadagnoli (1798–1858) (B-Al.); 1874 Lessona (Pr.). Fr. word *grippe*, 1763 *Journal de médecine*.

grisette. Grisette; 'good time girl' of modest social position.

'Grisette è una delle voci francesi che vennero di moda fra noi dal tempo della Monarchia di Luglio' (Panzini). *Grisetta* 'donna di facili amori' in Petrocchi. Fr. word, *grisette*, originally type of cheap grey cloth (Scarron), whence the sense 'working-class girl, esp. seamstress' in later 17th cent. Though *grisette* in the well-known French sense is largely a 19th cent. word similar connotations already existed in the 18th cent.; cf. Fr. *grisettier* in Alberti 1788 (= 'amante di donniciuole, di femmine volgari e plebee').

grisou. Coal-mining: Fire-damp.

Orthog. adaptation *grisù* (B-Al.). 1874 Lessona; Garollo (Pr.); Panz. Fr. dialect word (Walloon) *grisou*, 1796. Also *grisutina* (20th cent.), Ital. version of Fr. *grisoutine*, explosive used in mines where fire-damp is prevalent (B-Al.).

guipure. Fashions, text.: Type of lace.

(= *merletto a rilievo: intaglio* suggested as alternative). 1892, Garollo; Panzini; *guipur* 1897, Prati. Fr. word, *guipure*, attested 1393, < OFr. *guiper* 'to cover with silk, do *appliqué* work.'

habitué. Habitual frequenter of cafés, theatres, etc.

1890 F-A., 2nd edition. Fr. past part. and subst. *habitué* with (as in English) complete substantivation and the addition of semantic overtones (mild pejoration and satire) not inherent in French.

hors d'œuvre. Culin.: Hors d'œuvre.

(= *antipasto*). 19th cent., acc. to B-Al. Fr. compound, *hors d'œuvre* (1616), in this specialised sense (initially an architects' and builders' term).

hôtel. Hotel.

19th cent. B-Al. Manfroni (1883) is registered by Prati as the first authority to remark upon the fashion of using the French word on Italian hotel signs—a practice forbidden in 1940, after having been the object of a penal tax since 1925 (substituted by a wider use of native *albergo*). Fr. word, *hôtel*, specialised in the sense of 'demeure somptueuse d'une personne éminente ou riche' (Littré) in the early 17th cent.; the sense 'hotel' belongs to the 19th, though Alberti (1788) already gives one of the senses in Fr. as 'palazzo o gran casa mobiliata ad affitto'.

hurrà! (urra!). Interj.: Hurrah!

1860 Ugolini; 1877 F-A. ('urlo di belva del settentrione') (!); Panzini. Prati notes that the interjection was in use in the Italian navy. Also *urrà*, and French and English forms. <Fr. *hourra* 1835 Acad. (*hurra* 1830, Mérimée) < English.

idealogia. Ideology.

Originally a philosophical term (science of the formation of ideas) coined in 1796 by G. L. Destutt de Tracy which entered Italian in the early 19th cent.; 1822 M. Gioia; 1827 G. Zanobetti. The extended, pejorative signification—involved or spurious system of thought, usually surrounding a political creed (in It. end 19th cent.)—is a semantic loan from later 19th cent. Fr. usage (Littré has *idéologiste*, *idéologue* in the unfavourable sense of 'rêveur philosophique et politique').

illusionista. Conjuror.

19th cent. B-Al.; 1905 Panz., 1st edition. <Fr. *illusioniste* (B-Al., Pr.). Panz. cites Eng. *illusionist* beside the Fr. word. The Eng. term appears at least as early as the French (1864 in this sense, *OED*; French examples in later 19th cent.) but even if the usage were originally English the intermediary language in this instance was French. *Illusionismo* (end 19th cent.) < Fr. *illusionisme*, acc. to B-Al.

imbarcadero. Naut.: Pier.

(= *imbarcatoio*). 19th cent., B-Al. <Fr. *embarcadère* 1723 (Panz., B-Al., Pr.). <Spanish *embarcadero*. A more obvious Gallicism is the use of It. *imbarcadero* for 'platform' on a railway station (F-A., 1877; rendered by *montatoio*), or 'railway station' itself (regional usage, Genoa). The transfer of Fr. *embarcadère* from a term used in connection with inland waterways to railway parlance (by analogy of use, or even in some measure because of the physical proximity of railway and canal installations,[1] had taken place by 1834 (Wexler); the double meaning of 'platform', 'halting place for trains', and therefore 'station' also arises in French.

impressionista, impressionismo. Painting: Impressionist, -ism.

The former in 1895, Garollo (Pr.); the latter end 19th cent. (B-Al.). <Fr. *impressioniste* (Panz., B-Al., M-D., Pr.) 1874; originally used by the critic L. Leroy, speaking in disparaging terms of Monet's *Impression: soleil levant* (first public viewing 1863). *Impressionismo* < Fr. *impressionisme* (late 19th cent.).

impromptu. Impromptu, esp. music.

19th cent. B-Al. Panz. and B-Al. see it as a borrowing from Fr. *impromptu*, Loret, 1651, 'morceau improvisé, fait sur-le-champ (chanson, petite pièce de théâtre, etc.)' (*FEW*, IX, *promptus*, p. 444a). Corresponding loans in English, German, etc.

incoloro. Scient.: Colourless.

1874 Lessona (Pr.). F-A. note that the term is fairly current, though not in everyday use. Also *incolore* (more recent). <Fr. learned *incolore*, 1829 (B-Al., Pr.).

incosciente. Unknowing, unaware.

Incosciente 1883 Manfroni (Pr.); *incosciente*, Panzini: 'nel linguaggio comune si abusa di questo vocabolo *incosciente* per significare privo di discernimento, mezzo matto, sciocco, cattivo, secondo i casi'. <Fr. *inconscient* 1853 (B-Al., Pr.). *Incoscienza* (subst.) 1899 (Pr.), < Fr. *inconscience* 1846; *cosciente* may also be a borrowed word (Fr. *conscient* 1754).

indelicato, indelicatezza. Indelicate, unscrupulous, unscrupulousness.

Both in T-Bell. 'Eufemismo neologico che spesso vale *truffatore*, *ladro*. Una serva *indelicata*.' (Panz.). <Fr. *indélicat* 1786, *indélicatesse* 1808 (B-Al., Pr.), generally used euphemistically.

individualizzare. To individualise, specify.

(= *specificare*, *individuare*). Vincenzo Gioberti (1801–52), acc. to Panz.; Crusca; Rigutini (also *individualizzazione*). <Fr. *individualiser* (Rig., Panz., B-Al.). F-A. and Rigut. also condemn French uses of the noun *individuo* = 'person' ('chi è quell'individuo?' [F-A.]).

inodoro. Scient.: Odourless.

1877 F-A.; 1886 De Nino, *Errori di lingua italiana che sono più in uso* (Pr.). <Fr. scient. Latinism *inodore* (B-Al., Pr.) 1762.

---

1. P. J. Wexler, op. cit., pp. 88–90, 95.

insuccesso. Failure, fiasco, flop.

1877 F-A., 1886 Rig., Panz. Usually applied to theatrical failures and the like. Arlia suggests '(l'opera) *poco o non piacque*, e, familiarmente, *fece fiasco*'. <Fr. *insuccès* (Purists, Panz.), 1796.

interpellare, interpellanza. Polit.: To ask a question in Parliament.

1886 Rigutini; Panzini ('l'atto con cui un deputato domandava ad un ministro risposta o spiegazione su affari direttamente dipendenti dal Governo'). A semantic loan (as opposed to the original legal Latinism (Varchi) and the sense 'to interrupt' also initially in French). <Fr. *interpeller, interpellation* (polit. terms of 1st Republic; legal, etc., 14th cent., Bersuire) (Rig., Panz., B-Al.).

intervista. Journalism, etc.: Interview.

1877 F-A.; 1886 Rigutini. *Intervistare* 'to interview (someone)', Rig. and Panzini. The Purists derive both subst. and verb from French. B-Al. see them as Anglicisms which entered through Fr. *entrevue*; Panzini derives both directly from Eng. *interview* (supposed to have been coined by an American journalist in 1869). In concurring with B-Al.'s interpretation we should add that the French intermediary may be not *entrevue* itself (though *entrevue* possessed the above meaning early in the century) but the more specialised Fr. word *interview* (<Eng.; 1884, but may have been earlier). It. *intervistare* in particular is more easily derived from the Fr. verb *interviewer* (1885) than from Fr. *entrevue*.

intransigente. Uncompromising (esp. in politics).

1886 Prati. Also abstr. *intransigenza* 19th cent., B-Al. <Fr. *intransigeant, intransigeance*, 1875 (B-Al., Pr.) taken from Spanish *intransigente*, a word which became current after having been applied to the Federalist Republicans in Spain, 1873–74.

intravedere. To see dimly, catch a glimpse of, begin to perceive.

Travedere in Leopardi 1817 with the signification of Fr. *entrevoir*, acc. to M-Stor., p. 661 (the sense 'to be mistaken' is traced by Pr. back to the 16th cent.). Later the usual form is *intravedere* (Gioberti, Mazzini: *Vide* Migl., ibid.). Sem. loan < Fr. *entrevoir* (Purists, M-Stor.).

introspezione. Medic.: Internal inspection of the body.

'Esame dell'interno dell'organismo' (B-Al.). 1895 Garollo (Pr.). <Fr. *introspection* (medic.) (B-Al., Pr.), 1842 Mozin. The more recent psychological or psychiatric term originated in English (Binnet, 1909).

invergare. Naut.: To set up a ship's spars and bend on the sails.

19th cent. Not in Alberti. <Fr. *enverguer* (B-Al.), 1690, < *vergue* 'spar', 1369.

jabot. Fashions: Frill of a shirt—stock, jabot (at neck).

19th cent. B-Al.; Panzini. Fr. word *jabot*, 1546 Rabelais.

kermesse (chermesse). Kermess (in the Low Countries); church social, field-day.

c. 1870 B-Al.; *caramesse* in the 16th cent., (Guicciardini) referring to the Low Countries. *Kermessa* in Lessona 1875 (Prati). 'Parola adoperata nei Paesi Bassi e nel settentrione della Francia per indicare la festa annuale della parrocchia ... *Kermesse* poi indicò senz'altro una fiera, e con questo senso venne fra noi, ma la parola straniera, per il solo fatto che è tale, inchiude un senso di nobiltà!' (Panzini IX). Fr. word *kermesse* (B-Al., Pr., etc.) 1391 < Flemish *kerkmisse*.

lamantino. Zool.: Manatee, sea-cow.

1875 Lessona (Pr.). <Fr. *lamantin* (B-Al., Pr.), *lamentin* 1640, remodelling by pop. etym. of Sp. *manatí* (Carib.).

lamè. Fashion: Lamé (cloth with metallic thread).

19th cent. B-Al. Fr. word *lamé*, 1723 Savary < *lame* (see *lama*, 15th cent. Fr. > It. loans).

lampista. Lamp-maker, lamplighter.

1877 F-A.; 1886 Rigutini; Panzini. Also *lampisteria* 'lamp-room' (on stations, etc). <Fr. *lampiste*, 1835, *lampisterie* (Purists, Panz., Pr.).

lasciapassare. Milit., police: Pass, safe-conduct.

1846 Azzocchi, *Vocab. domest.* Version of Fr. *laissez-passer* (B-Al., Pr.), 1675 Savary (esp. concerning dutiable goods).

lavabo. Wash-bowl, wash-stand.

In the sense of 'lavabo' in a sacristy the Italian word (like the French and English) is an ecclesiastical Latinism (1803, Alberti, in It.). The broadening of application to articles of furniture in domestic use takes place in French and is found in Italian at the end of the 19th cent. (B-Al.; Panz. 1905). A semantic loan in this signification < Fr. *lavabo* (Panz., B-Al., Pr.), 1823 Boiste.

lavaggio. Tech., miner.: Washing of ore in mining operations.

1st half 19th cent., M-*Stor.*, p. 662; 1877 F-A. < Fr. *lavage* (Panz., B-Al., M-D., Pr.), 15th cent.

legiferare. Legal: To promulgate laws.

End 19th cent., B-Al. <Fr. *légiférer* (B-Al., Pr.) 1846; *légisférer* 1796.

liana, -e. Bot.: Liana, climbing plant of tropical forests.

1869 A. Pozzi, *La Terra* (Pr., B-Al.); Lessona (Pr.). <Fr. *liane(s)* (B-Al., M-D., Pr.), *liene* (≠ *lien*) 1640; term of the Antilles < Spanish.

libero scambio, libero scambista. Free-trade, free-trader.

Libero scambio 1874, Lessona (Pr.), 1877 F-A.; *libero scambista* Tomm. e Bellini. Calque of Fr. *libre-échange*, 1853, *libre-échangiste* 1846 (T-Bell., F-A., B-Al., Pr.), in turn < English *free-trade* (1823), *free-trader*.

libresco. Bookish: culled from books.

19th cent. B-Al.; Panzini. Adapt. of Fr. *livresque* (Panz., B-Al., Pr.), Montaigne, revived in the 19th cent.

limiere. Bloodhound: fig., sleuth.

1st half 19th cent., M-*Stor.*, p. 663. <Fr. *limier*, 12th cent. (originally 'hound on a leash' [*lien*]).

linciare, linciaggio. To lynch: practice of lynching.

Linciare 1877 (B-Al.); *linciato* 1884: *linciaggio* 1907 Arlia, *Suppl.* Both in Panzini. <Fr. *lyncher* 1867, *lynchage* 1883 (Panz., B-Al., Pr.) < English verb *to lynch* (< name of John Lynch). A French intermediary is confirmed in the case of the substantive (and hence in all probability, in the verb) by the suffix *-age*, *-aggio* which in this instance is without an English parallel.

lingotto. Ingot (usually of gold or silver).

1877 F-A. <Fr. *lingot* (F-A., Panz., B-Al., M-D., Pr.), 1327. <Eng. *ingot* (Chaucer [*OED*]). B-Al. derive *lingottiera* 'ingot-mould', 1890 < Fr. *lingotière* (1611).

lion, lionne. Beau, elegant young man-about-town.

1833 Pecchio, *Osservazioni semi-serie*;[1] 1846 Fusinato, *Fisiologia del Lion*: 'Fu petit-maître chiamato un di,/Poi muscadin, indi dandy,/E finalmente Parigi e Albione/Lo battezzarono per un leone;/Il che significa, con sua licenza,/ch' egli è la bestia per eccellenza' (cited Panz.). Also *lionne* (1851), 'fashionable young woman' (particularly the horsey, adventurous young heroine of the Romantic era). F-A., 1877, have *lione* (m.)

---

1. Cited by Anna L. Messeri, 'Voci inglesi della moda accolte in italiano nel XIX secolo' *L.N.*, XV (1954), 47–50. The exact position of English and French as sources of this borrowing is still uncertain. The 1833 example may be a direct Anglicism. No doubt exists, however, about the Gallicism in *lionne*.

and *lionne* (f.), and *a la liò* 'in the height of fashion'. <Fr. *lion* (1839 *Mérimée*), *lionne* (1830 de Musset). Form and sense are clearly from French, but we note that the Fr. word is an early 19th cent. version—reflecting specifically Parisian society under Louis-Philippe—of the 18th cent. English usage (1715, Lady M. W. Montagu, etc.) which was applied to persons in general who for any reason chanced to be in the public eye, i.e. those who were 'lionised' by society (cf. Mrs. Leo Hunter in *The Pickwick Papers*).

litro. Cubic measure: litre.

19th cent., B-Al. Lessona (Pr.). <Fr. *litre* (B-Al., M-D., Pr.), 1793.

locale. Building, piece of property, room, place.

1812 Bernardoni in these senses, which are well attested throughout the century and reproved as Gallicisms by purists. *Località* (= *luogo, paese*) is condemned for the same reason (1812 Bernardoni, 1877 F-A.; Rig.). <Fr. *local* (B-Al., Pr.) 18th cent. as a substantive in the above senses (the It. adj. *locale* is on the other hand an indigenous term [Dante]). *Località* prob. < Fr. *localité*, 16th cent., but 19th in the senses relevant here.

localizzare. To circumscribe, localise.

1877 F-A.; 1886 Rigutini (the basic meaning registered is 'to localise warfare, civil unrest'). <Fr. *localiser* (B-Al., M-D., Pr.) 1823, Boiste.

locomobile. Steam traction engine.

'Per la trebbiatura' (Rig.). 1874 Lessona, who notes that this type of machine was used in France from 1850 onwards (cited Prati); 1877 F-A.; Panzini. <Fr. *locomobile* (subst.) 1861 in this sense (*FEW*);[1] adj. 1808.

locomotiva. Railway Engin.: Steam locomotive.

1846 Carlo Conti, *Idea generale della Locomotiva* (Pr.); but adjective already in 1839 (B-Al.). The substantivising of the original adjective has a similar history in French and English. A decade or so elapses between the developments in English and French, and between French and Italian. Fr. *locomotive* (subst.) appears in 1834, current by 1837 (Wexler); *machines roulantes ou locomotives* in 1825 (Wexler): Eng. *locomotive* (subst.) in 1829 (memorandum to Liverpool and Manchester Rly Co.), but *locomotive engines or steam horses* in 1815 (*OED*). It. *locomotiva* therefore < Fr. *locomotive* (Rig., B-Al., Pr.) < Engl. *locomotive*.[2]

locomotore (adj.). Scient., medic.: Locomotor, motor (of muscles, etc.).

1828 Leone. *Apparato locomotore* of animals in Lessona 1874 (Pr.). Also *locomozione*, referring to living beings, 1828, Leone. <Fr. *locomoteur* (adj.) 1690, *locomotion* 1772 (B-Al., Pr.).

longarina. Naut., railway, civil engin.: Beam, girder.

Longherina 1866 G. Parilli, *Diz. di marina militare* (Pr.); *lungherina* 1870 L. Fincati, *Diz. di marina*; *longarina* 20th cent. The nautical term usually denotes the 'ground-ways' of a slipway, i.e. the long wooden beams down which a vessel is launched. 1890 as a term of railway engineering, acc. to B-Al. (meaning part of permanent way). Civil engin., 20th cent. <Fr. *longrine* (B-Al., Pr.), *longueraine* 1716, H. Gautier *Traité des ponts* (civ. eng.); 1792 Romme, *Dict. de Marine* (naut.). The railway engin. term, 'longitudinal sleeper along which the permanent way is bolted' appears 1867 (*FEW longus*, V, p. 410a).

lorgnette. Lorgnette.

A pair of eye-glasses, usually fixed to a long handle. 1895 Garollo (Pr.). Also *lorgnon*,

---

1. Wexler, however, has an example as early as 1840, from P. Grouvelle, *Guide du chauffeur*, 2nd edition. The definition clearly refers to the same machine (op. cit., p. 104 n. 50).

2. *Vide* Migl., *Saggi Novecento*, p. 22; *L.N.*, II, 103.

'eye-glass', 19th cent. (B-Al.). Fr. words *lorgnette* (1694: sense now rendered by *face-a-main*), *lorgnon* 1835. Cf. English *lorgnette*, 1820, *lorgnon* 1846 (*OED*).

luna di miele. Honeymoon.

1803 B-Al. Calque of Fr. *lune de miel* (1748, *Zadig*), acc. to B-Al., M-*Stor.*, p. 663, itself a calque of Eng. *honeymoon* (*Migl.*) attested in 1546 (*OED*).

lunette (pl.). Spectacles.

1860 Ugolini; 1881 F-A. (who insist that in Italian *lunetta* is an architectural term only). Fr. word, *lunettes*. Ephemeral equivalent of indigenous It. *occhiali* (13th cent. onwards, Fra Giordano).

màcabro (macabro). Macabre (esp. concerning stories or paintings dealing with the subject of death).

Danza macabra in A. Bazzarini (1829), Tramater (1829–40); *canto anatemico e macabro* in A. Bòito (1865, Prati). General use of the adjective in later 19th cent. The stress vacillates between the Fr. pattern *macabro* (as early as 1824, acc. to B-Al.) and the proparoxytone during the 19th cent. < Fr. *macabre* (B-Al., M-D., Pr.), 1842; *danse macabre, danse macabré* 15th cent.

macedonia. Culin.: Macedoine.

'Mescolanza di frutta tagliata a pezzi, con un po' di liquore' (Panz.). 19th cent., B-Al. <Fr. *macédoine* (Panz., B-Al.) 1771, originally dish of assorted chopped vegetables.

macuba. Brand of snuff renowned for its bouquet.

1879 Prati; dimin. *macubino* (an imitation '*macuba*') Petrocchi. <Fr. *macouba* (B-Al., Pr.), < place-name Macuba (Sp.), a region of Martinique which produced tobaccos of high quality.

madampolàm. Text.: Madampollam.

A strong white cotton cloth imported initially from India into western Europe by English merchants, later manufactured in France. 1827, B-Al. <Fr. *madampolam* 1823 (B-Al., Pr.) < place-name Mādhavapalam via English. Most sources assume that the Fr. word was drawn from English. This is historically plausible, though in point of fact the *OED* dates the first English example from 1832.

maddalena. Culin.: Kind of tea-cake.

19th cent. B-Al. <Fr. *madeleine* (B-Al.), 1846 Bescherelle. The name of the variety of peach (It. *maddalena* 19th cent., B-Al.) is probably also < Fr. *madeleine*, 17th cent., Le Duchat.

magazzino. Large shop, emporium, chain-store.

1877 F-A., who also (with Panzini) register the pronunciation *magazzeno, magasèn* as a phonetic influence of French. A semantic loan, in this specific meaning, from Fr. *magasin* (Purists, B-Al., Pr.), since the semantic shift 'warehouse' > 'retail store' is peculiar to French (19th cent.). The Fr. word is a formal loan < It. *magazzino* (see mediaeval It. > Fr. word-list).

maionese, -a. Culin.: Mayonnaise.

Fr. form *mayonnaise* 1895 Garollo; *maionese*, Panzini. Fr. word (and adaptation) *mayonnaise* 1807, Viard (B-Al., M-D., Pr.).

maître d'hôtel. Steward, majordomo, butler.

1895 Garollo (Pr.). B-Al. register an adaptation *maestro d'(h)ostello* in the 16th cent. (from Botero). Fr. compound, *maître d'hôtel*.

mal del paese. Homesickness, nostalgia.

1828 Leone; *mal du pays*, Panzini. Calque of Fr. compound *mal du pays* (Pr., B-Al., though the latter consider as an alternative etymon German *Heimweh*). The French term dates from 1827, Scribe (*FEW*, VII, 469b).

malinteso. Misunderstanding (subst.).

1st half 19th cent., M-*Stor.*, p. 662. Calque of Fr. *malentendu*, 1558.

malversare, malversazione. To embezzle; peculation.

Both in F-A. 1877; *malversazione* in Bernardoni, 1812, and Rig. 'Voce franciosa fatta italiana, perchè fanno noia le buone voci *Prevaricazione, Sottrazione, Dilapidazione, Peculato*' (F-A., s.v. *malversazione*). <Fr. *malverser, -ation* (Purists, B-Al.), 1527.

mammellone. Geog.: Hillock.

With geminated *m*, 1853 D'Ayala, Panzini; *mamellone* 1877 F-A. <Fr. *mamelon* (B-Al., M-D., Pr.), geog. term in Bernardin de St.-Pierre (*FEW*, VI, 131a). Also borrowed by Eng., *mamelon*, 1830 in this sense (*OED*).

mangusta. Zool.: Mongoose.

Mangosta 1875 Lessona (Pr.); *mangusta* 1895 Garollo (Pr.). <Fr. *mangouste* (B-Al., Pr.; M-D. cite both Fr. and Sp. forms), 1703 Biron, < Spanish *mangosta* (a Marathi word). Alberti translates the Fr. word by *icneumone* or *topo di Faraone*.

manichino. Puppet, artist's lay figure, mannequin.

First two senses in 1870 (Pr., B-Al.); 'tailor's dummy', 'mannequin' in Panzini. Also Fr. form. Substituted in the latter sense by *indossatrice*, 1937. Semantic loan, since *manichino* dimin. of *manico* 'sleeve' is an indigenous 16th cent. word (= 'lace cuff'; also 'muff' for the hands [Alberti]). <Fr. *mannequin* (Rig., B-Al., M-D., Pr.), 15th cent., < Dutch *mannekijn*.

manitu, manitù. Anthrop.: Guardian spirit of North American Indians.

Manitù 1870, B-Al.; *manitu* 1895 Garollo (Pr.). <Fr. *manitou* 1633 (B-Al., Pr.) < Algonquin.

marengo. Numism.: Gold coin of 20 gold lire (napoléon).

Coined by Napoleon at Turin after the battle of Marengo (14th June 1800): dated years 9 and 10 (1800–2). A *napoléon* in French parlance.

margarina. Margarine.

1874 B-Al. <Fr. *margarine* (B-A., Pr.) coined by Chevreul as a chemical term, applied in 1871 to margarine itself (the foodstuff) by Mège-Mouriès when this industry was founded in France. The word quickly entered other European vocabularies (in Eng. 1873 [*OED*]).

marionetta. Marionette, string-puppet.

Fr. form *marionnette* 1808, Pananti (B-Al.); *marionetta* 1812 Bernardoni; T-Bell.; 1877 F-A. (who claim that the word originated in Italy, entered French and returned to NIt. dialects). <Fr. *marionnette* (T-Bell., F-A., B-Al., M-D., Pr., *FEW*), *maryonete* 1517; 'string puppet' 1556, Gay (*FEW*, VI, 336b).

marmitta. Cauldron.

19th cent. B-Al. There is a strong possibility that the borrowing is older. Bernardoni's attestation places it not later than the opening years of the century, and we often find that words Bernardoni criticises were current in the Revolutionary period. Alberti does not register it directly, but translates the Fr. word *marmite* by *marmita, ramino*. There are examples in Oudin and Veneroni, but these are suspect; the 1729 edition of Veneroni 'stars' the entry as an expression of jargon or a barbarism. Prati notes *marmitta* in Luigi Fiacchi, 1754-1825. <Fr. *marmite*, 1313 (Purists, B-Al., M-D., Pr.). The It. loan entered military terminology in the first instance (cf. the semantically related It. > Fr. loan *gamelle*). Also from French is the argotic military term *marmitta* 'large shell' (e.g. for a howitzer). Fr. *marmite* 'bomb fired from a mortar', 1758 (La Chesnaye); used widely during the Great War.

marmittone. Milit. slang: Lazy or gluttonous soldier; 'skiver'.

19th cent. B-Al.[1] *Marmitone* as a translation of Fr. *marmiton* 'scullion' in Oudin is suspect (see *marmitta*, above). Veneroni 1729 asserts that the form *marmitone* is merely the French word transcribed; *'guattero* est le mot italien'. B-Al., Pr. and certain Purists derive the It. military usage < Fr. *marmiton* (1525 in the sense of 'scullion').

marrone. Adj. of colour; Maroon.

End 19th cent. Petrocchi. Fr. form *marron* in Panz., 1st edition, 1905. As an adj. of colour (esp. used of fashions, luxury goods), It. *marrone* is generally regarded as a semantic loan < Fr. *marron* (18th cent.), which in the original sense is an earlier, formal, borrowing from Italian (*vide* 16th cent. It. > Fr. list) (B-Al., Pr.). It. *marrone* in the primitive senses is an indigenous word of doubtful origin (= (a) 'chestnut' (b) augment. of *marra* 'hoe', both 14th cent.).

marron glacé. Culin.: Marron glacé.

19th cent. B-Al.; *marrons glacés* 1895 Garollo (Pr.); also adapt., *marroni glassati*. Fr. compound, *marron(s) glacé(s)*.

massacrare. To massacre.

1812 Bernardoni. <Fr. *massacrer*, 13th cent., rare before 16th cent. (B-Al., Pr., Bezz., M-D., etc.). The French word was initially confined to the butcher's trade, like *massacre* (12th cent.). Hyperbolical uses of both verb and subst. parallel to those of French are common in the 19th cent.

matinée. Morning or afternoon performance or reception.

1895 Garollo (Pr.); Panzini. Adapt. *mattinata* end 19th cent. (*mattinata musicale*, Petrocchi). Also *matinè*, *matinée* (fashions) 'woman's housecoat for use in the mornings': a 19th cent. term (Panz., 1905). Fr. word *matinée*, borrowed in the above meanings.

medium. Spiritualism: Medium.

1875 Lessona (Pr.); Italianised > *medio* 1895, Garollo. Fr. *médium* (1856) (B-Al., Pr.) < English Latinism *medium*. The *OED's* earliest examples in English (1853, 1854) show the word as current and accepted in usage.

menestrello. Lit. hist.: Minstrel.

Musician who provided instrumental accompaniment for the troubadour: the troubadour himself. 1875 Lessona (Pr.); *ministrello* earlier in 19th cent. (T-Bell.). <Fr. *ménestrel* (B-Al., M-D., Pr.) revived for literary purposes and drawn from OFr., where the sense is, however, more frequently conveyed by the variant *menestrier* (13th cent., whence probably OIt. *ministriere* [G. Vill., Boccaccio], though an OProv. etymon is not impossible).

mentoniera. Fashions: Floral trimming of a hat.

'Mazzetto di fiori artifiziali sotto la tesa dei cappelli da donna' (Prati). Carena (1859) and Gherardini, acc. to Pr. <Fr. *mentonnière* (B-Al., Pr.), Voltaire; originally 'lower part of a mask or domino' (14th cent.).

menu. Menu (in restaurant).

(= *lista, carta*). *c.* 1868 B-Al.; 1877 F-A.; form with Fr. stress, *menù*, in F-A., 2nd edition. Fr. word *menu*, 18th cent. in this acceptation.

mercuriale. Commerce: List of market prices.

1860 Ugol. <Fr. *mercuriale* (subst.) (Pr.) in this sense 1800. B-Al. adds the semantic loan *mercuriale* = 'reprimand, scolding', also < Fr. *mercuriale*, which has this meaning

---

1. T-Bell. have *marmittone* as a political term in the sense 'one who is only concerned with what he can get out of a change of government'. I see this as a secondary shift from the original metaphor which gave rise to the military argotic term ('cauldron' > 'glutton' > 'soldier who shirks work, looks after Number One', etc.).

in the 17th century (first applied to sessions of the Parlement which were held on Wednesday, *Mercurii* dies.

meringa. Culin.: Meringue.

Marenga 1850 G. Rambelli, *Vocab. domest.*; *meringa* end 19th cent., B-Al.   <Fr. *meringue* (B-Al., M-D., Pr.), 1739, Menon. Alberti translates Fr. *meringues* (plural, *sic*) as 'sorta di marzapane'.

metallizzare, metallizzazione. To apply a coating or plating of metal to other surfaces.

Both verb and subst. in Lessona, 1875. <Fr. *métalliser, métallisation* (B-Al., Pr.) in the specialised, mid-19th cent. signification above. The French verb (like the English) is well attested from the later 16th cent. onwards, but invariably in the senses (a) 'to make a mineral, etc., become metal' (e.g. by smelting) (b) (more rarely) referring to the formation of metals in the earth's crust (applies more particularly to the abstract *metallisation*). These two senses are still the only ones given by earlier 19th cent. sources (Boiste, Bescherelle, etc.). Littré has in addition the definition 'Garnir d'une couche de métal. Métalliser une glace' (used esp. of lustre-ware and the like). This is the signification borrowed by Italian.

metraggio. Tech., commerce: Length measured in metres.

1890 F-A., 3rd edition; Panzini. Often used in the 20th century as a tech. term of the film industry; *Film a lungo metraggio* = 'long-running film'. <Fr. *métrage*, 19th cent. (Panz., B-Al., M-D., Pr.).

metro. Metre (measure). (i.e. basic measurement of the metric system). Early 19th cent., M-*Stor.*; 1791 Prati. Adapt. of Fr. *mètre*, 1791. Italian compounds of *metro* correspond to French.

midinette. Parisian working-girl, midinette.

1905 Panzini. Fr. portmanteau word (end 19th cent., G. Charpentier) made up of *midi*+*dînette* (B-Al., Pr.).

miliardo. A thousand million, usually referring to money. 1855, Fanfani, *Vocab. della ling. it.* <Fr. *milliard*, 1544 (B-Al., M-D., Pr.), formed upon *million*. Also *miliadario*, 1877 B-Al., Panzini, 'multi-millionaire', <Fr. *milliardaire*, 19th cent. (B-Al.).

militarismo. Militarism.

'Preponderare dei militari su gli altri ceti' (Panz.).   1853 D'Ayala (B-Al.); 1868, Pr. < Fr. *militarisme* 1846 (Panz., B-Al., Pr.).

militarizzare, militarizzazione. To militarise, militarisation.

Verb in D'Ayala 1853, F-A. 1877; subst. 1890, B-Al. <Fr. *militariser*, 1846, *militarisation* 1863 (B-Al., Pr.).

mimare. To mime, in sense of act without words.

1905 Panz., 1st edition. <Fr. *mimer* (Panz., B-Al., Pr.) 1846 Bescherelle.

mistificare. To mystify, pull wool over the eyes.

1890 B-Al.; Rigutini. 'Noi abbiamo moltissime voci: *burlare, canzonare, ingannare, corbellare, ciurmare* ecc. Eppure a mistificare si annette un senso—come dire?—di modernità e di eleganza nell'inganno' (Panz.). <Fr. *mystifier*, 1764 (Purists, Panz., B-Al., M-D.).

mitragliatrice. Machine-gun.

1875 Lessona (Pr.). Adaptation of Fr. *mitrailleuse* (M-D., Pr.), 1869 (machine guns were first used in action by the French in August 1870).

mobilizzare, mobilizzazione. Milit.: to mobilise, mobilisation.

Mobilizzare 1853 D'Ayala; 1877 F-A. <Fr. *mobiliser* 1836 (B-Al., Pr.). *Mobilizzazione* 1876, Pietro Ellero, *Scritti politici* (vide *L.N.*, XXI (1960), p. 121); De Nino, *Errori di lingua ital. che sono più in uso*, Turin, 1886; 1877 F-A. <Fr. *mobilisation* (B-Al., Pr.).

Both Fr. words appeared earlier as banking terms (1808 and 1823 resp.), probably borrowed < English. The It. native word *mobilitare* (18th cent., Marchetti, in the original sense 'to move, set in motion') was influenced semantically either by *mobilizzare* or (as is more likely) by the Fr. military signification of *mobiliser*, and eventually became the established term. Grassi (1835) registers *mobilitare* in this sense, which was extended to the abstract *mobilitazione*. F-A. treat both verbs as Gallicisms, but feel that *mobilitare* is 'meno francese che *mobilizzare*'.

modista. Designer, dealer, shop-keeper, who specialises in women's fashions (esp. millinery).

1808 Pananti. Antonio Guadagnoli mentioned the term in his *Poesie e versi giocosi* (Pisa, 1824), acc. to T-Bell. Gherardini; F-A. Gradually replaced Tuscan *crestaia*. <Fr. *modiste* (Purists, B-Al., M-D., Pr.) 1801 Mercier (Dauz.), though Alberti 1788 registers *modiste* in a sense germane to this, viz., 'qui suit les modes, qui affecte les modes'.

moffetta. Zool.: Skunk.

1869 B-Al.; Lessona. <Fr. *moufette* (B-Al., Pr.), Buffon.

monolito (-e). Monolith.

1829 B-Al.; 1843 V. Gioberti; T-Bell. <Fr. learned coinage *monolithe* (B-Al., Pr.), 1532; rare before 18th cent.

monopolizzare. Commerce: To monopolise.

1812 Bernardoni; 1860 Ugolini; F-A.; Rig. (registers both commercial and figurative uses). <Fr. *monopoliser* 1791 (Purists, B-Al., M-D., Pr.). The abstract *monopolizzazione* (F-A.) may also be a direct loan < Fr.; a borrowing in the case of other derivatives, even those appearing first in the 19th century, is unlikely (It. *monopolio* like Fr. *monopole* is a medieval Latinism).

montagnardo. Mountain-dweller.

(= *montanaro*). 1881 F-A., 2nd edition. <Fr. *montagnard* (B-Al., Pr.), 1512.

montagne russe. Helter-skelter, scenic railway (at a fun-fair).

1875 Lessona; Panzini. <Fr. *montagnes russes* (B-Al., Pr.), Littré. Lessona's explanation that the amusement was invented in Russia is debatable. I suspect that whatever the origin of the pastime itself the creators of the name given to this artificial version of the sport of tobogganing were probably French fairground constructors. The phrase is a suitably exotic one.

montante. Finance, commerce: Sum of money, amount.

1860 Ugolini; T-Bell.; F-A. <Fr. *montant* (B-Al., Pr.), 12th cent.

montatore. Engin.: Mechanic who assembles machinery.

1895, Pr. < Fr. *monteur* (B-Al., Pr.), originally jeweller who mounts precious stones. Also *montaggio* 'assembling of machinery' 1901 Manfroni. Later used with special meaning in the cinematograph industry: assembly of 'shots' to form a complete film; 'special effects'. <Fr. *montage* (both senses) (Panz., B-Al., M-D., Pr.); 1842 Mozin. Migliorini traces the verb *montare* (technol.) back to the 18th cent. (*Stor.*, p. 576).

morena. Geol.: Moraine of a glacier.

1860, Pr. < Fr. *moraine* (B-Al., M-D., Pr.), 1779 Saussure, < Savoyard *morêna*.

morfina. Chem., medic.: Morphine.

1822, Pr. < Fr. *morphine* (B-Al., Pr.), 1817 P. L. Courier.

morga. Mortuary, morgue.

1st half 19th cent. (M-*Stor.*); 1877 F-A.; both *morga* and *morgue* 1883 Manfroni; Rig. 'L'introduzione di questo francesismo incontrò difficoltà, ma *obitorio* si cominciò ad usare solo dal 1937' (B-Al.). The periodical *Unità della Lingua* invited suggestions for an alternative name (I, 1869–70, pp. 371–2), but none caught on (M-*Stor.*, p. 737 n. 1). *Riconoscitorio* was favoured. <Fr. *morgue* (Purists, Panz., B-Al., Pr.), 15th cent. in sense

of 'haughtiness, arrogance'; inspection-room where prisoners were placed so that their features could be memorised, late 17th cent., Veneroni; modern sense 18th cent.

mortissa, mortesa. Carpentry: Mortise (of a joint).

Mortissa early 19th cent., M-*Stor.*; *mortesa* 19th cent., 'termine dei legnajoli di Prato' (Pr.). Prati regists *mortisa* in Oudin and Stratico (early 19th cent.); the former is suspect for reasons we have already mentioned. <Fr. *mortaise* (13th cent., *mortoise*) (Migl., Pr.).

morva. Veter.: Glanders.

(= *cimurro, moccia*). 1812 Bernardoni; Lessona. <Fr. *morve* (B-Al., M-D., Pr.), 1506, < Prov. *morvo*.

muflone. Zool.: Mouflon (of Corsica, Sardinia).

1895 Garollo; *muflone, mufflone*, Panzini. <Fr. *mouflon* 18th cent. (B-Al., Pr.) in view of (a) group [fl] (b) frequent use of this form as a fashion term (furriers'). B-Al. consider It. *muffione* (*mufione* 1803 Alb.) to be an adaptation of the Fr. word rather than an importation from the Corsican dialects (the word's ultimate source; cf. *mouflon* in 18th cent. It. > Fr. loans). The dating supports Battisti's hypothesis. Under various guises the Corsican/Sardinian dialectal forms (see p. 363) appeared in peninsular Italian (as in French) some two centuries before the first attestation of *muffione*; Fr. *mouflon* appears half a century before. It is not unreasonable to suppose that the regular, Tuscan form *muffione* was imposed from without; the presence of other natural history terms borrowed from Buffon indicates a French loan in this respect also.

mughetto. Medic.: Inflammation of the mouth in young babies.

(Also veter.; name of a disease common in lambs.) Medical term 1806, Cesari (B-Al.); veterinary term T-Bell. Semantic loan < Fr. *muguet* in this sense (B-Al., Pr.) (*vide* 16th cent. Fr. > It. *mughetto*).

mugic (mougik). Russian peasant, moujik.

Panz., 1st edition, 1905 (also *mujich, mujick*). <Fr. *moujik* (B-Al., Pr.), *mougik* 1862, Victor Hugo < Russian *muzhik*.

musetta. Horse's nosebag; Milit.: kit-bag.

1853 D'Ayala; 1883 Manfroni. <Fr. *musette* (B-Al., Pr.), 19th cent. in this sense.

mussare. To foam, sparkle, esp. of wines.

1860 Ugolini; 1877 F-A.; Rig. (also *mussare una cosa*, 'to make a thing seem more than it is', French usage [Rig.]). Semantic loan < Fr. *mousser* (Purists, B-Al., M-D., Pr.), 1680 in this sense.

mutismo. Dumbness.

Referring to the incapacity of a dumb person, 1875, Lessona; 1877 F-A. The Purists reserve a special criticism for the meaning 'obdurate silence' typical of Fr. usage. F-A. insist that more specific terms are necessary to distinguish between *mutezza, mutolezza* on the one hand and *silenzio, taciturnità* on the other (see also Panzini's article, s.v.). <Fr. *mutisme* (Purists, B-Al., M-D., Pr.), 1741 in the true sense; restricted meaning 19th cent.

nazionalizzare, nazionalizzazione. To nationalise, nationalisation.

1836 Tramater (verb); subst. 19th cent. (B-Al.). <Fr. *nationaliser* (B-Al.) 1794, *nationalisation* (B-Al.) 1877, Littré.

negriero, -e. Slave-trader, 'blackbirder'.

Meaning either the person or the ship. Naut. term *negriere* 'slave-trading vessel' 1866 Giuseppe Parilli, *Diz. di marina militare* (Pr.); *negriero*, both vessel and sailor involved in slave-trading, 1870 L. Fincati, *Diz. di marina* (Pr.). 'Slave-trader' in general given as a 19th cent. term by B-Al. <Fr. *négrier* (Panz., B-Al., Pr.), 1752.

nevato. Glaciol.: Snow crystals which form glacier: névé.

1807 B-Al.; 1886 G. Giacosa (Pr.). Panz. registers the Fr. form. <Fr. *névé* (Pr.;

B-Al. consider it a possible adaptation of the Fr. word only), 1867 (Littré). Wartburg (*FEW*, VII, 156b, 157a) draws the Fr. as well as the Eng. and It. words from dialectal usage of Savoie and the Dauphiné.

nomadismo. Anthr., geog.: Nomadism.

1877 F-A. <Fr. *nomadisme* (F-A.; B-Al., Pr.), end 18th cent.

nuance. Shade, gradation, nuance.

1883 Manfroni; Panz. Adapt. *nuanza* 1901 Manfroni, 2nd edition. Fr. word *nuance*, 1611 (Cotgr.), in the modern sense.[1]

òasi. Oasis.

1877 F-A. (who note the frequency of metaphorical uses similar to French). 'La voce latina è passata nelle lingue di cultura nel XVII sec. . . . ed è pervenuta all'italiano attraverso il francese' (B-Al.). Pr. concurs. Adapt. of Fr. *oasis*, 1561, but rare until 1766 (Dauz.) <Gk. <Old Egyptian.

oficleïde. Music: Ophicleide (wind instrument with keys).

1834 B-Al.; 1875 Lessona; variant *ofleide* in Petrocchi; *offlè* 1883 in Nicotra, acc. to Pr. 'Fu più usata, fino dall'inizio, la traduzione *serpente a chiave*' (B-Al.). <Fr. *ophicléide* (learned coinage <ὄφις 'snake', χλεῖς 'key') instrument invented in France in 1820 and played at the Opéra in 1822 (B-Al., Pr.).

olona. Naut.: Type of sailcloth.

Alona, Iona, lonetta, Stratico 1813. <Fr. *toile d'Olonne* (B-Al., M-D., Pr.) < place-name Olonne, where sailcloth was made.

oltramontani. Hist.: Partisans of the Pope's absolute authority in France.

1843 (Pr., B-Al.). Also *oltramontanismo* end 19th cent. (1895, Pr.). Semantic loans < Fr. *ultramontain* (B-Al., Pr.), *ultramontanisme* 1739. *Oltramontano* (adj. and noun) in the strict sense of 'beyond the mountains' (G. Villani, etc.) is a native Latinism (parallel to the Fr. word in this sense, also used from the Middle Ages onwards).[2]

omeletta, -e. Culin.: Omelette.

Omelette 1877 F-A. (as a term used principally in the north of Italy); Panzini. Banned in 1940; the Sindacato dei pubblici esercizi recommended *frittata*, but as Panz. pointed out, the Italian word does not exactly correspond to the French. Fr. word (and adaptation *omelette*; *homelaicte* 1552 Rabelais.

omnibus. Transport: Omnibus.

1835 (Turin) acc. to B-Al.; 1839 in A. Bresciani, *Saggio di alcune voci toscane di arti, mestieri e cose domestiche* (Pr.); 1850 G. Rambelli, *Vocab. domest.* <Fr. *(voiture) omnibus* (B-Al., M-D., Pr.) 1825 acc. to *FEW*, VII, s.v. *omnis*, p. 353a. *Omnibus* 'local stopping train' is a later semantic loan from Fr. (1875, Lessona).

ordàlia. Hist.: Ordeal (by fire, water, etc.).

1820 B-Al.; *ordalie* (pl.) 1895 Garollo. Ultimately < OEng. *ordāl* (usual MLat. form, *ordalium*), but with Fr. *ordalie* (*c.* 1775 Duclos) as intermediary (Pr.; B-Al. tentatively concur).

organdis, organdi. Text.: Organdie.

1875 Lessona (*organdi*); Panz., 1st edition. Petrocchi has *organdisse*. <Fr. *organdi* (B-Al., M-D., Pr.), 1723 < mediaeval name of the city of Urganj in Turkestan, a

---

1. It. *sfumatura* 'gradation of colours, shades', which now does duty for Fr. *nuance* appears to have been influenced semantically by the Fr. word in the 18th cent. See M-*Stor.*, p. 577 and source cited.

2. In a letter of 23rd Oct., 1793, V. Monti uses the substantive *oltramontano* from an Italian's point of view, i.e. meaning 'Frenchman' (Bertoldi, I, p. 387).

famous silk market. See C. Battisti, 'Vecchi nomi di stoffe derivati da nomi di luogo', *L.N.*, March 1946, and 17th cent. It. > Fr. *organsin.*

organismo. Scient., biol.: Organism.

1827 as a biological term: 'complesso e struttura degli organi' (i.e. organs of a living creature) (B-Al.); 1828 Marchi, referring to a biological theory (B-Al.); also 1828 as a synonym of 'living creature' (B-Al.). <Fr. *organisme* (B-Al., Pr.), 1729 which served as intermediary for the scientific Latin term *organismus.*[1]

paccottiglia. Commerce, naut.: 'Trade goods'.

(I.e. trinkets, beads and the like used by ship's crew for trading on their own behalf). 1814 Simone Stratico; *pacotiglia* 1877 F-A. (also *roba de pacotiglia*, 'remnants, broken lots' etc., to be sold at clearance sales). <Fr. *pacotille*, 1723 Savary, ultimately < Spanish *pacotilla* (B-Al., Pr.).

pacfong. German silver.

Various forms in 19th cent.: *pacfond* T-Bell.; *panfò* 1877 F-A., Rig.; *pachfong* 1875 Lessona; *pacfòn, pàcfon.* <Fr. *packfong, packfond* 19th cent. < Cantonese word meaning 'white copper'.

paciulì. Patchouli (essential oil used in perfumes).

Various forms in 19th cent.; *pascioli* 1847 Fusinato; *patchouly* 1875 Lessona; *pasciulì* Panz. 1st edition ('Era il profumo del romanticismo'). <Fr. *patchouli* 1846 (19th cent. sources, B-Al., M-D., Pr.) < Hindustani via English.

paltò. Fashions: Overcoat, originally for men; more recently for women also.

1841 Cherubini, in Milanese (also *pantò*); *paltò* 1847 A. Fusinato; *paletò* in F. D. Guerrazzi (1804–73); Fr. word in Manfroni. Other forms: *paltoss* (1839 acc. to Pr.), *paltòn* (Roman, acc. to Panz.), *paltonne.* This fashion—which replaced the *redingotta*—was known in northern Italy, though perhaps not generally accepted, as early as 1838 (*vide* Panzini's article). <Fr. *paletot* (all sources), *palletot* 15th cent., < Middle English.

paludismo. Medic.: Malaria.

End 19th cent., B-Al.; Panzini: *impaludismo* a little earlier, 1875 Lessona. <Fr. *paludisme* (B-Al., Pr.) 1884; the form with prefix, *impaludisme*, is also common in Fr. (1873, *FEW*, VII, 531a).

panorama. Panorama.

In original sense of 'a large painting, usually on the walls of a circular room, lit in such a way as to give an illusion of depth': 1829 Marchi, *Diz. tec.-etim.-filol.* Meaning 'view of countryside from a lofty vantage point': 1853, Fanfani. The panorama was invented by an English artist Robert Barker in 1789 and was first called a *cyclorama*; the appellation *panorama* dated from 1796. Fr. *panorama* (1799) acted as intermediary

---

1. No Fr. influence appears to have operated in the other derivatives of *organum* (ὄργανον), except perhaps a semantic one in respect of *organizzare, organizzazione.* Bernardoni condemns their use in a general signification. V. Monti uses both subst. and verb on several occasions, usually referring to the process of setting up a governing body with its ancillaries in various parts of the Cisalpine Republic ('l'organizzazione dell' Emilia' 16th Nov. 1797). Cf. also the typically Gallicising context of 'si è formata una commissione di otto legislatori per organizzare un piano di finanze, che tutte le sere si occupa di quest'oggetto' (letter of 26th Sept. 1798). Rigutini is prepared to sanction only the primitive sense of 'forming body tissues' in the verb; current Gallicising uses of the abstract are to be rendered by *esercito, scuola, festa, dimostrazione* and other precise terms. *Organo* itself in the sense of 'newspaper' is also rejected. *Disorganizzatore*, used to mean 'saboteur, counter-revolutionary' and corresponding abstract *disorganizzazione* appear in 1797 and may very likely be Gallicisms (*vide* P. Zolli, *L.N.*, 1964, p. 13; 1965, p. 17).

between Eng. and It. (B-Al., Pr.). Panzini and B-Al. register *panoramico* (adj.) as a borrowing < Fr. *panoramique* (1842).

pantaloni (pl.). Trousers.

1829 Boerio (Venetian) ('voce qui introdottasi e naturalizzata dopo la rivoluzione politica' [s.v.]); 1850 Rambelli; T-Bell.; *pantalone* (sing.) 1877 F-A. ('voce gallica'; the authors insist that, though fashions have changed, It. *calzoni* is still the right word); 1886 Rigutini ('voce francese introdotta senza alcun bisogno ... per opera specialmente dei sarti'). <Fr. *pantalon(s)* (all sources agree), originally borrowed from Italian as the name of the mask Pantaleone (Commedia dell'Arte), but soon used to refer to the typical garment worn. By the mid-17th cent. *pantalon* could mean a pair of breeches resembling the lower half of Pantaleone's costume (cf. Migliorini, 'Notules lexicales', *F.M.*, IX (1941), pp. 46–50, and *Dal nome proprio*, pp. 103, 175, 256, 270). Veneroni's article (1709) describes the 17th cent. significations in detail. *Vide pantalon*, 17th cent. It. > Fr. loans.

panzea. Pansy.

In O. Targioni-Tozzetti (d. 1829) acc. to Migliorini, *Suppl.*, who also registers *pansè* in G. Manzini. 'Francesismo usuale, oltre che in Toscana, sulla Riviera di Ponente, a Napoli (*pansè*) in Sicilia (*panzè*) e Sardegna (*pansé*)' (B-Al.). Adj. *pansè* 'violet-coloured' 1870 (B-Al., Pr.), 1877 F-A., etc. <Fr. *pensée* (all sources), 1545 Guéroult.

papeterie. Stationery; compendium of writing materials.

Papetteria (first sense) 1854 G. Valeriani, *Vocab. di voci e frasi erronee* (s.v.); 1877 F-A. (also gives *papeteria*); *papeterie* 'writing compendium' Rigutini, Garollo, Panz. Fr. word (and adapt.) *papeterie*, 1553 Ch. Estienne, originally 'paper-mill', 'paper industry', but more commonly used 19th cent. onwards in the above senses.

papigliotti (pl.). Fashions: Curl-papers.

1846 A. Fusinato; 1877 F-A.; Fr. form in Panz. Dialectal variants somewhat earlier. Adapt. of Fr. *papillotte* (F-A., Panz., B-Al., Pr.) originally 'gold spangle' (to be sewn on a dress) (1420); above sense dates from 18th cent.

pappiè. Paper, document (used jokingly or pejoratively).

1863 Fanfani, *Uso toscano*; *papiè* in Petrocchi; both forms in Panz.: 'francesismo popolare ... per *carta, biglietto, documento, cartavalore*'. 'Volgarismo toscano, umbro e romano' (B-Al.). Italianised form of Fr. *papier* (B-Al., Pr.).

paracadute. Parachute.

1832 Papi, *Nuovo diz. univ. tecnol.* (Pr.); Tramater. Calque of Fr. *parachute* (Panz., B-Al., Pr.) 1786 Bachaumont. The parachute itself was invented in 1784 or 1785 by the balloonist Blanchard. 'La sua conoscenza si diffuse (sc. in Italy) nel 1797 per opera di Garmeni' (B-Al.).

parafare, paraffare. Diplomatic term: to initial a document prior to ratification by government concerned.

Form *paraffare* in 1839 (B-Al.). <Fr. *parapher* (Panz., B-Al., M-D.), 1565 Tahureau. The noun *paraffo* (*paraffa*) 'paraph, flourish after signature or sign manual' appears previously (early 18th cent., Salvini). <Fr. *paraphe* (Panz., B-Al., M-D.), 1390, originally 'paragraph' (cf. *pàrafo* 'paragrafo (di codice)' in Ariosto, which B-Al. derive from Spanish). Specialised as a graphological term in 16th cent.

parafulmine. Lightning-conductor.

1824 C. Botta (Pr.); Prati registers the term as occurring in the title of a book published in 1808; T-Bell. Calque of Fr. *paratonnerre* (Pr.; B-Al. refer to Fr. *parafoudre*). The lightning-conductor was invented by Franklin in 1752.

paralizzare. To paralyse, literally or figuratively.

1812 Bernardoni, who rejects the implications 'prevent, stop, place obstacles in the way of a transaction or undertaking'. Typical officialese of the Revolutionary period, dating back to 1797 in Venetian, if Boerio's affirmation is accepted: '*paralizàr* fu introdotto nel 1797 e poi usato per *impedire, incagliare, troncar le gambe*' (1829). F-A. and Rig. (under *paralisare*) both condemn the exaggerated uses and semantic extensions in terms similar to Bernardoni, the former ascribing them largely to journalism. The medical term proper is generally accepted. <Fr. *paralyser* (Purists, B-Al., M-D., Pr.), mid-16th cent., Paré.

parapioggia. Umbrella.

1859 Carena, *Voc. domest.*; 1877 F-A. A 19th cent. term, now disused or provincial. <Fr. *parapluie* (Purists, B-Al., Pr.) 1622 Tabarin, current in 18th cent. The Fr. word is created on the formal pattern of *parasol*, <It. *parasole* (q.v., 16th cent. loans).

parcella. Legal: Parcel of land.

1839 as an admin. term, acc. to B-Al. <Fr. *parcelle* (Panz., B-Al., M-D., Pr.), 13th cent. The senses 'account, list of expenses', which B-Al. derive from Milanese *parcela* at the end of the 19th cent. are presumably indigenous semantic developments of the borrowed term.

pardessus. Fashions: Overcoat.

Pardessù 1877 F-A., Rig.; Petrocchi and Panz. have the French graphy. Obsolescent during 20th cent. Fr. word *pardessus*, 1846 Bescherelle, subst. formed by ellipsis of prepositional phrase (Littré still has un *par-dessus*).

pardon! Interjection: Excuse me!

(For *scusa! scusi! permesso!*). B-Al. refer to the example in Giusti (relevant passage cited above under *bon-ton*). A usage deplored by the Purists (*vide* F-A., 1877), which without any doubt was current in certain circles well before Giusti's *Ballo*—presumably even in the 18th century among bilingual speakers. Panzini records its obsolescence. A French word.

parlamentarismo. Parliamentary government.

1874 T-Bell.; Panzini. Panz., 3rd edition (1918) refers to affective connotations: 'Il sistema . . . parlamentare; ma con intenzione di alludere ai difetti ed alle inframmettenze non buone di tale sistema politico nella vita della nazione'. <Fr. *parlementarisme* (B-Al., Pr.) coined in 1852 by Napoleon III, acc. to V. Hugo, *Napoléon le Petit*, V, VIII.

parola d'ordine. Milit.: Password; watchword, motto.

1817 Grassi (B-Al.); 1863 Fanfani, *Voc. dell'uso tosc.* Also *motto d'ordine*, F-A., 1877. <Fr. *mot d'ordre* (F-A., B-Al., Pr.). *Parola* alone is used by Montecuccoli in this sense, but I see this as a special application of 'word' in its own right rather than a Gallicism, i.e. rather than an ellipsis of *parola d'ordine*. *Motto* in Tomaso Garzoni (16th cent.) is a similar case.

parquet. Parquet floor-covering.

19th cent. B-Al. Also *parchè, parchetto.* *Tassellato* suggested as equivalent in this sense (Migl., *Suppl.*, under *tassellato*). Also used in It. in metonymic extensions: 'recinto, poi lo spazio nell'aula d'udienza riservato ai magistrati' (i.e. the principal sense in ModFr.); 'alla borsa (il recinto) delle grida' (i.e. stockbrokers' ring or enclosure, as in French) (B-Al.). Adapt. *parchè* in F-A., 1877: 'uffizio, Segreteria del Procuratore del Re'. Fr. word (and adaptations) *parquet*, originally 'small enclosure' (1339). 'Le sens "parquet de salle" (dès le 14ᵉ siècle) vient du développement sémantique "compartiment", "assemblage de compartiments" ' (Dauz.). (This signification is usually rendered by *parquetage* in ModFr.) The extension 'small enclosure' > 'enclosure reserved for judges' > 'bar of Court' > 'bench of magistrates, office', etc., occurs from the 16th century.

parvenu. Self-made man, nouveau riche.

1848 Ugolini; *parvenù* F-A. 1877, Rig. Panzini, after citing several Italian equivalents, observes ' . . . ma in francese non v'è quel grave senso di spregio che si ha in italiano'. Fr. word *parvenu*, 1779 Mme de Genlis (current in later 18th cent.).

passerella. Naut.: Gangway (for embarcation).

1895 Garollo. Also 'footbridge, over-bridge' 1905, Panzini, and in later editions the further nautical meanings of 'bridge of a ship', 'catwalk' (= *candelieri*). <Fr. *passerelle* (Panz., B-Al., M-D., Pr.). 1835 Acad.

pastorizzare, -azione. Scient., agric.: To pasteurise, pasteurisation.

End 19th cent. *Pasteurizzare, -azione* in Panzini, who adds 'per la più facile pronuncia si dice *pastorizzare, pastorizzazione*'. The corresponding Eng. loan *to pasteurise* appears in 1881 (*OED*). <Fr. *pasteuriser, isation* (Panz., M-D.), late 19th cent., formed on the name of Louis Pasteur (1822–95).

patibolare. Patibulary.

Viso patibolario ('a gallows face, gallows look') 1848 Ugolini; *faccia patibolare* Rigutini. <Fr. *patibulaire* (Rig. equates *faccia p.* to mine *patibulaire*) (B-Al., Pr.). In French 1408.

patois, patoà. Patois, local dialect.

19th cent. acc. to B-Al.; *patoà* and *patuà* 1877 F-A. 'Voce di larga diffusione un secolo fa in tutta l'Italia settentrionale, ora limitata alla Liguria, al Piemonte, alla Lombardia e al Trentino' (B-Al.). Fr. word (and adapt.) *patois*, 13th cent.

pattinare, pattinaggio. To skate, skating.

Verb in F-A., 1877; B-Al. gives it as 19th cent., but registers *patinare* already in the later 18th cent. (1789; form also used in 19th cent.; Gargiolli, F-A.). Subst. end 19th cent. (Panz. 1905). <Fr. *patiner* 1732 (B-Al., M-D., Pr., etc.); *patinage* 1868 (B-Al., Pr.). The word *pattino, -i* is understood by all It. sources to be a French loan word, but dating is uncertain. The actual form appears in It. in the later Middle Ages meaning kind of shoe (Luigi Pulci: 'Chi si cava pattini, e chi pianelle' [Cr.]); still used in the 17th cent. Oudin translates *patin d'Hollande* (i.e. 'skate') by *zoccolo*, and Veneroni's *remaniement* of this entry leaves no doubt that by *zoccolo* ice-skate is meant. *Zoccoli di diaccio* are mentioned by Bini, 16th cent. (see Prati's article in the *V. Et. It.*, s.v. *pàttini*).

pècari. Zool.: Peccary.

1831 B-Al.; 1850 Rambelli. <Fr. *pécari* (B-Al., Pr.), 1640 < a Carib. dialect.

pedicure. Chiropodist.

End 19th cent., Petrocchi; Panz. <Fr. *pédicure* (B-Al., M-D., Pr.), 1781, Laforest.

pelusce. Text.: Plush.

Peluscio 1853 D'Ayala; *plusce* 1863 Fanfani (as dial. term, Lucca); Fr. form in Garollo, Panz.; *pelusce* 20th cent. Adapt. of Fr. word *peluche* (Cotgrave), itself a loan < It. *peluzzo* (see 16th cent. It. > Fr. loans).

pepiniera. Seed-plot, breeding-ground, esp. in figurative uses.

1812 Bernardoni; 1839 B-Al. Metaph. use 1853 D'Ayala, 1877 F-A., Rig., Panz. <Fr. *pépinière* (Purists, Panz., B-Al., M-D., Pr.), 1539 R. Est. in literal sense.

percalle. Text.: Percale, percaline, cotton cambric.

Percale 1829 (B-Al.); *percalli* (pl.) 1851 Fusinato. Fr. form *percale* in Panz. ('la voce francese si alterna con l'italiana *percalle* o *percallo* (e *percalletto, percallina*)'). Adapt. of Fr. *percale* (Panz., B-Al., M-D., Pr.), 17th cent. Thévenot < Persian *pärgâl*.

perfettamente. Perfectly.

Used with adj. for emphasis as in 'perfettamente inutile' (T-Bell.) and as interjection, = 'precisely! exactly!' 1829 acc. to B-Al.; Pr. refers to Giusti; Tomm. e Bellini ostracise it in the above usages as a useless barbarism. Also 1877 F-A. ('questa modo di assentire è francese scrivo scrivo'), Rig.; Panz. ('uno dei gallicismi più comuni'). Imitation of idiomatic/syntactical use of Fr. *parfaitement* (19th cent. sources, B-Al., Pr.).

personale (subst.). Personnel.

Registered as a barbarism by T-Bell. in the sense 'personnel of an office' (esp. Government dept.); also *personale insegnante* (the former already in 1839, acc. to B-Al.); 1877 F-A.; 1886 Rigutini ('nuovo gergo dei pubblici uffici'); Panzini ('... è il *personnel* francese. Brutta voce burocratica'). Adapt of Fr. *personnel* in this sense (above sources; B-Al.). Cf. the corresponding loan in English, dating from 1857.

personalità. Personality.

In sense of 'important personage', 'public figure', *personalità* is generally accepted as a semantic loan < Fr., as opposed to the indigenous Latinism (14th cent.; abstract < *persona*). 1839 in this sense (B-Al.); Rigutini also draws from French the meaning 'personal remark', 'affront'.

pessimismo. Pessimism.

1875 Lessona; *pessimista* in T-Bell. <Fr. *pessimisme* (B-Al., Pr.), 1823 Boiste, but understood to have been created by Mallet du Pan (1747–1800). Fr. *pessimiste* 1836.

piantone. Milit.: Orderly; unarmed guard.

Boerio (1829) registers the term as a 'neologismo popolare' used to refer to certain soldiers detailed for police duty at key points in the city of Venice (*vide* Prati). Usual milit. term in 1853, D'Ayala. Semantic loan < Fr. *planton* (Boerio, Panz., B-Al., Pr.); *être de planton* 1790, 'to be on duty'. M-D. give it as an extension of the indigenous word *piantone* 'shoot, young plant, cutting' (14th cent.) 'per l'immobilità di chi sta di guardia'. A similar metaphor is usually cited as the origin of the French military term.

piazzare. To place; to lay out, allocate money, funds.

1812 Bernardoni; 1877 F-A. (esp. financial and military, concerning deployment, stationing of soldiers); Panzini (general sense, financial, sport ['placing' of horse in a race]). <Fr. *placer* (19th cent. sources, B-Al., M-D., Pr.), 1606 Nicot.[1] V. Monti uses *rimpiazzare* meaning 'to replace' (= Fr. *remplacer*) at the end of the 18th century. Contexts usually refer to replacing an official or a committee, especially one judged inefficient or politically compromised; e.g. 'Ginguené è stato già rimpiazzato...' (Letter of 17th Oct. 1798. See also Bertoldi, II, 40, 57, [1797]).

picchetto. Peg, stake for driving into ground.

1860 Ugolini (Pr.); Panzini. <Fr. *piquet* (Panz., B-Al., M-D., Pr.), 1380 (see *picchetto* 18th cent. Fr. > It. loans).

piedatterra. Small dwelling used occasionally; *pied-à-terre.*

1891 Petrocchi; the Italianised form is mentioned by Panzini 1905 under the rubric of the Fr. word. Fr. *pied-à-terre*, 17th cent., Chifflet.

pierrot. Pierrot.

Pierrotto 1891 Petrocchi; Fr. form in Panzini, who explains the term as follows: 'Nome maschile francese di nota maschera; abito e volto candido, anima candida e maltrattata. Comune travestimento di carnavale. Il *Pierrot* fu creato in Francia (secolo XVII) deducendo da *Pedrolino* e da *Pulcinello*, maschere italiane.' Fr. *pierrot* registered in this sense 1834, Boiste (*vide* Migl., *Dal nome proprio*, p. 230).

---

1. Some uses of *piazza* are held to be imitations of French by the Purists, e.g. the sense 'situation, job' (F-A., Rig.), 'seat' (Rig.). Panzini describes as 'locuzioni volgarissime entrante pur troppo anche nell'uso del popolo, specie delle grandi città, dall'uso francese del vocabolo *place*': *letto a due piazze*; *trovare una buona piazza* (job); *fare piazza* 'to make room'.

pilè. Crushed, granulated sugar.

Also *pillato* 1836, B-Al. <Fr. (*sucre*) *pilé*, < *piler* 'to crush with a pestle', *c.* 1165, *FEW*, VIII, 489b. *Pilare* 20th cent. also < Fr., acc. to B-Al., used esp. of polishing rice.

pinguino. Ornith.: Penguin.

1804 Alb., *Diz. Univ.* Alb. 1788 explains the French word but offers no simple It. equivalent: 'Sorta d'uccello acquatile, che si chiamerebbe *Germano magellanico*'. <Fr. *pingouin* (B-Al., Pr., M-*Stor.*); *penguyn* 1600, probably from a Celtic language (Breton *penn guenn* 'white head' is the most likely source).

pioniere. Pioneer.

As a milit. term ('soldier who prepares the way for the army') 1853 D'Ayala; 1877 F-A. (= *guastatore, piccioniere*); 1886 Rigutini (= *zappatore*). Extended senses end 19th cent., Petrocchi. Panzini notes the transferred sense of 'pioneer-coloniser', adding, 'vuol dire più nobile cosa, cioè colui che audacemente avanza, aprendo la via della civiltà, *araldo, antesignano*'. <Fr. *pionnier* (all sources agree) 12th cent., 'foot-soldier', whence modern milit. signification.

piovra. Octopus.

1891 Petrocchi; Panzini. Both also register the metaphorical uses ('persona o istituto che strugge e assorbe' (Panz.), etc.) which are a major portion of the word's connotation. <Fr. *pieuvre* (B-Al., Pr.) 1866 V. Hugo, *Travailleurs de la mer* (from Norman dialect). Cf. Petrocchi: 'La piovra sarebbe il polpo; ma de Vittor Hugo a preso questo significato esecrabile' (s.v. *piovra*).

piqué, picchè. Text.: Piqué.

Venet. dial. *pichè* 1829 Boerio; *picchè* 1876 (B-Al., Pr.); Fr. form in Garollo and Panzini (false Gallicism *piquet* in the latter). The substitutes *piccato* and *picca* proposed in the late 1930s failed to gain acceptance. Fr. word *piqué*, 1823 *Boiste*. Eng. *piqué* in this sense is also a 19th cent. loan (1852, *OED*).

pista. Race-track, track of a sports stadium.

1891 Petrocchi; Panzini ('cycle-track' 1905; later editions have the meaning 'aerodrome runway'). Semantic loan < Fr. *piste* (Panz., B-Al., M-D., Pr.) in these senses; in Fr. 1562 du Pinet. The French word itself is an earlier loan < It. (dialectal) *pista* (see 16th cent. It. > Fr. *piste*). The signification 'race-track' (1860, *FEW*) as opposed to the original sense (and that of Italian), 'track left by horses, animals on the move', etc., developed in French.

placca, placcare. Metal plate, plaque: to plate.

Placca 1812 Bernardoni (= *lamina, piastra*): T-Bell.; 1877 F-A. ('badge of a service or order'); Rig. <Fr. *plaque* (B-Al., M-D., Pr.) 1611 Cotgrave. Verb *placcare* in Tomm. e Bellini, a metalworker's and goldsmith's term, esp. 'to plate with precious metal'. The authors prefer *doppiare*. <Fr. *plaquer* (B-Al., M-D.) 13th cent. <Middle Dutch *placken*. Also in Tomm. e Bell. is *placcato*, 'plated' as above, but more usually a substantive (as in Fr.) = 'gold-plate'. The phon. adapt. of Fr., *placchè*, is earlier (1832, acc. to B-Al.). <Fr. (*métal*) *plaqué* (T-Bell., B-Al.), 1802 both in sense of plated metal and wood veneer.[1] (Cf. *controplaccato* (Migliorini, *Suppl.*) 'plywood', < Fr. *contre-plaqué*.)

plafone. Ceiling of a room.

First attested in Fr. form, *plafond*, 1877 F-A., 1886 Rigutini; *plafon* in 1883 Manfroni; adapt. *plafone* in Panz., 1st edition, 1905 (as Milanese). Fr. word *plafond* (and adaptation); *platfond* 1559 Gardet. It. *plafonare* in Manfroni 'to plaster a ceiling' is no doubt an Italianised version of Fr. *plafonner* (*platfonner* 1690, Furetière).

---

1. Littré notes that *plaqué* is used more than *doublé* for 'rolled gold' (*vide dublè* above).

plancia. Plank, etc.

Panz., 1905, as a military term (shelf in barracks upon which soldiers keep their kit: *vide* Migl., *Suppl.*, *plancia*). The meaning 'plank', 'board' is registered by Panz. under the Fr. form. Certain tech. senses are attested during the course of the 19th cent., notably 'plate', 'engraving for a book' (*vide* B-Al.'s article and dialect forms there cited).

plateau. Geog.: Plateau, tableland.

1895 Garollo (= *altipiano*). Later editions of Panz. have *plateau* 'tray' (VI [1931] onward). Fr. word (both senses) *plateau*; *platel* 12th cent.

polonese. Music, dance: Polonaise.

Milanese *polonesa* 1897; *polonese* 20th cent., acc. to B-Al., who also have *polonese* (adj., archaic) 'Polish' (for *polacco*) in 1839. <Fr. *polonaise* (B-Al, M-D.), 1820 B-Wart.

pompa, pompare. Pump.

Pompa 1804 Alb., *Diz. univ.*; *pompare* 1813 Stratico, *Vocab. di mar.* Both in F-A., Rig., Panz. Alberti gives them as maritime terms. 'Gallicismi ormai dell'uso e registrati' (Panz.). Both appear in Oudin (*pompare* in sense of 'faire une pompe d'eau') and again in Veneroni, but indigenous *tromba*, *trombare* appear to have been the only terms in actual use until the Napoleonic period. I suspect that Veneroni had not enough knowledge of technical usage to query Oudin's entry in this instance. <Fr. *pompe*, 1517, *pomper* 1611 (Pr., Panz., M-*Stor.*, p. 660).

pompiere. Fireman; (pl.) fire-brigade.

1839 *Panlessico* (B-Al.); 1840 Azzocchi *Voc. domest.*; Ugol.; F-A., Rig. <Fr. *pompier* (Panz., B-Al., M-D., Pr.), 1750 *Arrêt du parl. de Grenoble* in this sense. Also *pompiere* 'chi cerca l'effettaccio', Migl., *Suppl.*

pompon. Milit., naut., fashions: Pom-pom (on hat).

In Venet. 1829, Boerio: 'Voce fr. introdotta negli ultimi passati anni tra i militari italiani' (Pr.); *pompone* 1839 B-Al.; *pompò* 1877 F-A. Fr. word (and adapt.), 16th cent.

popeline. Textiles: Poplin.

1895 Garollo; Panzini: *popelin* Panz., 5th edition, 1927. Fr. word *popeline*, 1735, B-Wart. (Panz., B-Al., Pr.) < English *poplin* (1710 *OED*) < Fr. *papeline* 1667 (ultimately from the place-name Poperinghe). *Vide* Battisti, *L.N.*, VII, 1946, 10 and Vidos, *Prestito*, pp. 205-7.

portamonete. Purse.

1871 B-Al.; Petrocchi. Calque of Fr. *porte-monnaie* (B-Al., Pr.) mentioned (under Fr. word) by Arnaldo Fusinato in 1847. *Pormonè* in Milanese (M-*Stor.*, p. 663). A similar calque is *portafortuna* Panz., 2nd edition, 1908 (also in Fr. form) < Fr. *porte-bonheur*, 1876 (Panz., B-Al., Migl., *Suppl.*, Pr.).

porte-enfant. Portable 'carry-cot' for infants.

1905 Panz., 1st edition, 'La voce è stata tradotta con *portinfante* (o *portabimbi*, che non ha avuto fortuna)' (B-Al.). Prati observes (s.v. *garde-enfant*) that 'a differenza di *porte-enfant*, *garde-enfant* pare formato in Italia, forse in Piemonte'; but for Migliorini *porte-enfant* itself is a false Gallicism (*Stor.*, p. 738).

première. Theatr.: First-night, première.

Adapt. *primiera* F-A., 1877; *première* 1895 Garollo, Panzini. Fr. word *première* (*representation*), 19th cent.

prestidigitatore. Conjuror.

1829 B-Al.; also *prestidigitazione*, 'conjuring' 1886 Rig. <Fr. *prestidigitateur*, *prestidigitation* (Boiste, 1829) (Rig., Panz., B-Al., Pr.). 'Sembrano erroneamente a taluni voci più elette di *prestigiatore* e *prestigiazione*, o *giuochi di prestigio*' (Panz.). It. *prestigiatore* is a 17th cent. word (Redi).

prestigio. Prestige, authority, influence.

1871 in sense of *fascino, forza morale, imponenza*, acc. to B-Al.; 1886 Rig.; Panzini. A semantic loan < Fr. *prestige* (Rig., Panz., B-Al.), 16th cent., Yver, which originally like It. *prestigio (-a)* (14th cent.) had the etymological sense of 'spell, magic, conjuring trick'. The semantic development > 'personal authority', 'prestige' occurs in Fr. during the 18th cent. and subsequently passes to It., where it subsists alongside the original signification (*giuoco di prestigio*, etc.). The Eng. semantic loan in this sense dates from 1829; the original borrowing *prestige* = 'conjuring trick', 'imposture' is attested in 1656 (*OED*).

pretensioso. Pretentious.

1840 B-Al. <Fr. *prétentieux* (B-Al., M-D.) 1795.

proprietà, proprio. Cleanliness, tidiness, clean.

Clearly a semantic influence of French in this specific sense, which appears (*proprietà*) in 1877 F-A. (= *nettezza, decenza*), 1886 Rigutini, Panzini ('per *pulizia, decoro, ordine*, è il francese *propreté*, neologismo assai brutto ed anche anfibologico'). Adj. *proprio* 'neat', 'clean', 'tidy' 1871 (B-Al., Rig., Panz.), but the impact of Fr. *propre* had a sporadic effect much earlier. *Proprio* in this sense appears for instance in Goldoni (*Il Ventaglio*, 1763).[1] What we have here is a transfer of meaning motivated by similarity of form, ≠ Fr. *propreté* (abstr. < *propre*), 16th cent. *Proprio* 'clean' is a straightforward semantic loan < Fr. *propre*, originally (12th cent.) 'particular, belonging personally' (cf. 13th cent. It. *propio*, similar sense); the semantic shift to 'arranged befittingly' and from that to 'clean' dates from the 16th cent.).

purè, purea. Culin.: Purée.

Purè 1846 Azzocchi, *Voc. domest.*; 1877 F-A.; Rig., Panz. Fem. *purea* 1883 Manfroni, Panz. 19th cent. sources usually gloss it by *passato*. *Passata* (T-Bell.'s equivalent) was officially put forward as a substitute in 1940 (*vide* discussion of alternatives in Panzini's article, *Diz. mod.* IX). Adapt. of Fr. *purée*, 1314 (all sources agree, except that B-Al. think there may be a Sp. influence in the masc. form, common in southern Italy).

putrella. Engin.: Metal girder.

(Usually an 'I'-section girder.) 1905 Panz.; *potrella* 1910. <Fr. *poutrelle* (Panz., B-Al., Pr.), 1676 Félibien.

quotizzare. To assess (for tax); to subscribe.

Quotizzare 1812 Bernardoni (equivalent to *tassare*); 1877 F-A. (= *sottoscrivere, fissare, ripartire*; example: 'E. e G. furono *quotizzati* per una sessanta di lire per ciascuno . . .'); 1886 Rig.; Panz. (= *sottoscrivere, obbligarsi*). 19th cent. sources and Panzini concur in deriving *quotizzare* from Fr. *cotiser*, 16th cent., 'to tax, assess'. The abstract *quotizzazione*, 1877 F-A., Rig., Panz. is also held to be a Gallicism, < Fr. *cotisation* 16th cent., 'assessment', later 'subscription'. Alberti, 1788, translates Fr. *cotisation* by 'il far la tassa, la quota' and *cotiser* by 'tassare, ordinar la tassa, la quota'.

rabagas. Political turncoat.

'Voce popolare nell '800' (Panz.). Ferd. Martini (Pr.); *rabagà* in Petrocchi. Fictitious proper name *Rabagas*, a demagogue and political opportunist in the play of that name by Victorien Sardou, 1872.

radiare. To cross out, cancel, erase.

1877 F-A. (as officialese, for *cancellare, cassare*); Rig., Panz. ('voce degli uffici e curiale'). <Fr. *radier*, acc. to Rig., Panz. and M-Duro; F-A. derive it from the verb *rayer* rather than the legal Latinism. Fr. *radier* attested 1823 Boiste; Littré still gives it as a neologism

---

1. Act. I, sc. 5; *Commedie Scelte di Carlo Goldoni, Classici italiani* (*U.T.E.T.*) edition, Vol. II, p. 415: 'Un uomo come voi, proprio, civile, galantuomo . . .' The Conte is speaking to Coronato, an innkeeper.

(= 'rayer une inscription hypothécaire; effacer un nom d'une liste'). A semantic loan only, in legal and bureaucratic usage; cf. indigenous *radiare* (Dante) = *raggiare*.

ràpida. Geog.: Rapids, on a river.

1895 Garollo. Panzini has the plural, *ràpide*. <Fr. *rapide* (Panz., B-Al., Pr.), 1611 as an adjective. Cf., however, the autochthonous It. form in place-names, e.g. *Ràpida* (Tuscany) (B-Al.).

razzia. Plundering expedition (originally by Arabs of North Africa).

(Later 'raid by police', 'drive against malefactors', as in Fr.) 1877 F-A.; 1886 Rig. <Fr. *razzia* (F-A., Rig., B-Al., Pr.) 1841, < Arab. *ghaziya* 'raid, incursion'. (Fr. uvular [R] substituted for Arabic *ghain* which it closely resembles). It. *razziare* 'to raid' may be < Fr. *razzier*, 1846 Bescherelle.

reclame. Advertising, advertisement, publicity.

(= *Pubblicità*.) 1873 (B-Al., Pr.); 1877 (the advertisement itself, as inserted in paper, etc.); 1886 Rigutini, as a term imported recently; both give as examples notices of books published. *Reclàm* Petrocchi, Panzini ('voce francese... universalmente accolta'). Fr. word *réclame* (Panz., B-Al., M-D., Pr., etc.), 1842 in this sense; 1762 Acad. as typographical term = 'link-word' from one page to the next, whence 'page-reference to advertisement section of a newspaper' (M-D.). (Also *reclamista* 1908 Panz., prob. < Fr. Alberti only registers *reclamo* (masc., reference to Magalotti) in the legal sense of 'protest, complaint, pursuit for compensation', which also appears in the Fr. > It. section as equivalent to legal Fr. *réclame*.)

redigere, redazione, redattore. Redaction, etc.

(a) 'To draw up an act, compile, compose a literary work' (b) 'Compilation, editing of a journal', etc., also 'editorial staff' (c) 'compiler, journalist, member of editorial staff'. All three 1812, in Bernardoni; (a) and (b) in Parenti, *Catalogo di spropositi* (1839–59), Ugol., F-A., T-Bell. (*redazione* in sense of 'editorial staff'; a typically French use); all three and *redattrice* (fem.) registered as Gallicisms by Panzini. *Redazione* and *redattore* are undoubtedly modelled semantically upon Fr. *rédaction* (1560), *rédacteur* (1762) (19th cent. sources, B-Al.).[1] A French influence in the verb is less certain, though most 19th cent. sources consider it to be at best a Latinism coined in France.

referenza. Reference.

In the sense of (a) 'person who is prepared to give a testimonial on someone's behalf' (b) the testimonial itself. A 19th cent. bureaucratic term, acc. to B-Al. Modelled upon Fr. *référence* in these specific senses (Panz., B-Al., M-D.), 1846 Bescherelle. A Gallicism rather than an Anglicism in view of dating; the first example cited by the *OED* which corresponds closely to that of French appears in Dickens, *Our Mutual Friend*; others towards the end of the century.

regia. State monopoly.

(Esp. referring to tobacco and salt; = *appalto*.) 1831 Lissoni, *Aiuto allo scrivere purgato* (Pr.); Ugol.; F-A. 1877; Panzini (also registers the meaning '*direzione* della messa in scena nei teatri e nel cinema (1932)'. <Fr. *régie* (Purists, Panz., B-Al., M-D., Pr.), 16th cent., Bonivard.

rendiconto, resoconto. Report, relation, account.

Both in Bernardoni, 1812, though B-Al. have *resoconto* as an 18th cent. term. Both are adaptations of Fr. *compte-rendu*, acc. to 19th cent. sources, Panz., B-Al., Pr.

renna, renne (masc.). Zool.: Reindeer.

1835 Tramater (B-Al.); 1850 Rambelli; *renne* and *renno* in T-Bell. <Fr. *renne* (B-Al.,

---

1. D'Ovidio described *redazione* as a 'mezzo francesismo ... spesso richiesto dalla brevità e dalla chiarezza' (*M-Stor.*, p. 734 n. 1).

M-D., Pr.), *reen* 1552 < German *Reen* < ONorse *hreinn*. Alberti gives no direct equivalent to the Fr. word.

rêver, rêverie, rêveur. To day-dream, etc.

'Voci che troviamo frequentemente sia nel Carducci che nel De Sanctis', M-*Stor.*, p. 738. 'Voci... abusivamente usate per *sogno, fantasia, fantasticheria*', Panz., *Diz. mod.* (*rêve* and *rêver*). French words dating from about 1200.

ribotta. Carousal, spree.

'V. volg. toscana, genovese e piemontese' (B-Al.). 1863 Fanfani, *Uso tosc.*, but earlier examples of dialects: Turin, 1814, Genoese, 1851 (Prati). <Fr. *ribote* (B-Al., M-D., Pr.), 1808 d'Hautel (*riboteur* earlier, 1745). It. *ribottare* (1895, Arlia) may be directly from French.

rideau. Curtain.

Ridò 1846 Azzocchi, 1877 F-A. Fr. form at the end of the 19th cent., B-Al.; Panzini. Fr. word *rideau* (1471).

ridotta. Milit.: Redoubt.

1889 Guglielmotto *Voc. mar. e milit.*, acc. to Pr.; 1918 Panzini. <Fr. *redoute* (fem.) 1616, itself a loan from It. *ridotto* with change of gender. (*Vide redoute*, 17th cent. It. > Fr. loans).

riflettore. Reflector.

19th cent., B-Al. as a term of physics; Panzini, as a term of electr. engineering. <Fr. *réflecteur* (Panz., B-Al., M-D.), 1808.

riservista. Milit.: Reservist.

1877 F-A., Panzini. <Fr. *réserviste* (F-A., Panz., B-Al.), 1872 Littré.

ristorante. Restaurant.

1877 F-A. Fr. word *restaurant* also current (1895 Garollo, Panzini). A prestige equivalent to *trattoria* in some degree (*vide* Panzini). Rigutini suggested *ristoratore*, itself condemned as a Gallicism by some authorities when used to mean 'restaurant-keeper' (= Fr. *restaurateur*). *Ristorante* < Fr. *restaurant*, which appeared during the 16th cent. as a quasi-medical term 'fortifying food or drink', a sense which is also documented in Italian (*vide* T-Bell.); first attested in the above sense 1765, when the first restaurant was opened in Paris by Boulanger. Eng. *restaurant* is also a 19th cent. word (1827, *OED*).

ritirata, retrè. Public lavatory.

1859 Carena *Vocab. domest.*; T-Bell.; 1877 F-A., in this sense. The form *retrè* (direct phon. adapt. of French) is registered by Ugolini, 1848. <Fr. *retrait* 1387, *FEW* (Purists, Panz., B-Al., Pr.) a specialisation of the phrase *chambre de retret* 'closet, private room' in Froissart, etc.; cf. also (*chambre de*) *retraite*, 16th cent. The semantic restriction in question dates from the 16th cent.; cf. Montaigne: 'ils (les grands) n'ont pas seulement leur retraict pour retraicte' (Littré) (*FEW*, s.v. *retrahere*, X, 341b, 342a).

rivista. Review.

The senses in question are: (1) 'account or criticism of a literary work' (2) 'periodical consisting of articles of criticism, scientific discussion, etc.' '... *Review* (Eng.) viene calcato in Francia con *revue*, e in italiano se ne trae *rivista*' (Migliorini, *Storia*, p. 662; pre-1860). F-A. (1877) condemn these uses, among others. <Fr. *revue* (Migl., F-A.), 19th cent. in both senses. Both appear in English very much earlier, (1) in 1649, (2) in 1705 (*OED*). In the more recent signification of 'theatrical entertainment purporting to give a review of fashions, events, etc.' both the Italian word (*revue, rivista*; Panz.) and the English (*revue*, 1913) are drawn from French (later 19th cent.).

roccaglie, rocaille. Decorative elements typical of rococo: artificial rockery.

Both 19th cent., acc. to B-Al.; Panzini. 'Voce che si espande da Roma' (B-Al., *roccaglie*). <Fr. *rocaille(s)* (Panz., B-Al., Pr.) 17th cent., Scarron.

rococò, rococcò, roccocò. Rococo.

Rococò and *alla roccoccò* 1870 Fanfani, *Voci e maniere* (Prati); Panzini (= 'out-of-date, old-fashioned'). 19th cent. B-Al.; the corresponding Eng. loan is 1836 (*OED*). Registered by Cherubini (1839) as the name given to a type of carriage then in fashion. <Fr. *rococo* (Panz., B-Al., M-D., Pr.), 1829, Stendhal, a term of artists' slang formed upon *rocaille* (though perhaps also a jocular imitation of *barocco, baroque*).

roncet. Disease of the vine.

(= *aricciamento*). End 19th cent., B-Al. Fr. word *roncet* 1890 (B-Al.) < *ronce* 'bramble'. 'La parola dialettale fr. (Borgogna) fu diffusa nel 1893 da P. Viala' (B-Al.).

rondò. Civ. engin.: Circus or roundabout at the end of an avenue; similar roadway in public gardens.

1843 Cherubini (Pr.); 1864 Rigutini (B-Al.); 1877 F-A. (= *piazzale*). Petrocchi has it as an architectural term (circular part of portico). <Fr. *rondeau* in these senses, acc. to 19th cent. sources, B-Al., Pr.

roulette. Roulette (game of chance).

19th cent. B-Al.; 1895 Garollo; Panzini (also adapt. *ruletta*); *roletta* in Petrocchi. Fr. word, *roulette* (Panz., B-Al., Pr.), not later than 18th cent. in this special signification (the English loan dates from 1745) (*OED*).

rubinetto. Engin., domest.: Tap, faucet.

1835 Tramater; lengthy article describing the *rubinetto* and its applications; plainly felt to be a recent neologism. Alberti translates Fr. *robinet* by *chiave* only. 1877 F-A.; Rigutini has *robinetto*. Both forms in Panz. <Fr. *robinet* (Tram., Purists, Panz., B-Al., M-D., Pr.), 15th cent. Monstrelet; < proper name *Robin* referring to a ram, since the taps were made in the form of a ram's head. One example of *robinetto* earlier in Oudin, translated by *robinet de fontaine*.

rullìo. Naut.: Rolling, of a ship.

1813 Stratico, *Vocab. di mar.* <Fr. *roulis* (T-Bell., B-Al., M-*Stor.*), 1694 in this sense. *Vide rullare*, 17th cent. Fr. > It. loans.

sabotaggio, sabotare. Sabotage: also to damage, thwart.

Late 19th cent. M-*Stor.*, p. 737. 1908, Panz., 2nd edition (also has Fr. form). Adapt. of Fr. *sabotage* (later 19th cent.), *saboter* (13th cent. meaning 'to kick'; the sense 'to do a slovenly job of work' belongs to the 19th cent. [1842, Mozin], whence the above signification) (B-Al., Pr., M-D.).

sabretascia. Milit.: Sabretache.

A leather satchel hanging by straps from the sword-belt. Hussar's uniform. 1st half 19th cent., M-*Stor.*, p. 663. The corresponding Eng. borrowing appears 1812. <Fr. *sabretache*, 1767 < German *Säbeltasche*.

salmì. Culin.: Ragoût of game, salmi.

19th cent. B-Al.; *beccaccia, lepre in salmì* G. Gargiolli (bef. 1876); Petrocchi; Panzini. <Fr. *salmis* (Panz., B-Al., M-D., Pr.); *salmi* 1718 Acad.; abbreviation of 16th cent. *salmigondis*, 'storpiamento del nostro *salami conditi*' according to B-Al., though the earlier It. > Fr. borrowing is doubtful.

salone. Salon, saloon.

1877 F-A. as a Gallicism in the following senses: (a) room where people meet socially ('reception-room' in various contexts) (b) the social gathering itself; example, 'è frequentatore del Salone della Principessa di Papiano' (F-A). (c) 'barber's shop, hairdressing saloon'. To these must be added *salone* in the sense of 'drawing-room' (in an ordinary house) which is somewhat different from F-A.'s (a) above. (Panzini; = *salotto*). None of these meanings appear in Alberti, Tramater and T-Bell. Semantic loans < Fr. *salon* in these significations (F-A., Panz., B-Al., Pr.); originally borrowed < It. *salone* augment, of *sala* (attested 16th cent., in Cellini and continuously thereafter) (see 17th cent. It. > Fr. loans). Meanings (a) and (b), which develop in French during the early 18th cent., are accompanied by that of *salon* 'art gallery' (Voltaire) used initially in connection with exhibitions in the *Salon Carré* of the Louvre (also enters It.; *vide* Panzini) (*FEW*, X, 9–10).

salopette. Overall suit, boiler suit.

19th cent. B-Al. Fr. word *salopette*, 1841. Cf. the synonym *tuta*, also a loan (<Fr. *tout de même*) acc. to Panz., M-D.; coined by the artist Thayant in 1920, entered It. in 1922.

salvaguardare. To safeguard, protect.

= *tutelare, proteggere, custodire, difendere* etc.). 1877 F-A.; Rig.; Panz. <Fr. *sauvegarder* (Purists, Panz., B-Al., M-D., Pr.), 1788, Féraud (*vide salvaguardia*, Fr. > It. 17th cent. loans).

salvataggio. Saving of life at sea, salvage.

1847 Parrilli, *Vocab. militare di marina* (Pr.); T-Bell.; 1877 F-A.; Rig.; Panz. ('*opere, compagnia, stazione, battello di salvataggio . . . sono voci dell'uso marinaresco chè niuno dice altrimenti*'). <Fr. *sauvetage* (19th cent. sources, B-Al., M-D., Pr.), 1796 B-Wart.

sanfasòn (alla-). Adv.: Frankly, carelessly.

'Intendesi specialmente di vesti o di maniera trasandata e sciatta' (Panz.). Fr. form *sans-façons* 1847 Fusinato and Panzini, who also has *alla sanfassò(n)* and *alla sanfassona*; *sanfasòn* in 1877 F-A. Fr. adverbial expression *sans façon*, = 'familièrement, sans cérémonie', mid-17th cent., *FEW* (Panz., B-Al., Pr.), also subst. *sans façon* (masc.) 1865 Littré (*FEW*, III, 360a).

scaglione, scaglionare. Milit.: Echelon (infantry, etc.); to form up in echelon.

Subst. 1835 G. Grassi, *Diz. milit. ital.*; verb in T-Bell. Semantic loan[1] < Fr. *échelon* (B-Al., Pr.), *échelonner* 12th and 15th cent. respectively, but rare until 19th cent.

scaloppa. Culin.: Escalope (de veau).

Scalopa 1895 Garollo; Fr. form *escalope, scaloppa* and adapt. *scaloppina* in Panzini. <Fr. *escalope* (Panz., B-Al., M-D., Pr.) 1864 in the modern (culinary) sense (B-Wart.); mediaeval in sense of 'shell' or 'scale'.

scamottaggio. Sleight of hand; filching.

Later 19th cent. M-*Stor.*, p. 662. Panzini (also has *escamoter* and *escamoteur*). Adapt. of Fr. *escamotage* (Migl., *Suppl.*, B-Al.), 1790; *escamoter* 1560 < Spanish.

sceicco. Sheik (esp. of Bedouins).

1875 Lessona. <Fr. *cheik, scheik* (B-Al., Pr.), 1798 (B-Wart.), < Arabic *šeiχ*. The word occurs sporadically in both It. and Fr. during the Middle Ages; cf. OIt. *scecha* in 1264 referring to a treaty between Pisa and the Emir of Tunis; while Joinville speaks of a 'sarrazin qui avoit à non Scecedin le fil au seic' (Lacurne de Ste.-Palaye, IX, 369a).

sciaccò. Milit.: Shako.

Early 19th cent., M-*Stor.*, p. 664. Ult. < Hungarian *czákó*, but via Fr. military terminology. Eng. *shako* dates from 1815. Version of Fr. *schako, chako*, 1761 (uniform cap of Hungarian hussars), but used widely only in early years of 19th cent.

scialle. Fashions: Shawl.

1808 Pananti; also *sciallo*, 1850 Rambelli, *Vocab. domest.* <Fr. *châle* (B-Al., M-D., Pr.), *chaule* (Anglicising pronunciation) 1770, *chaale* 1772 used sporadically before in relations by travellers in India; e.g. *chal* 1666). Popularised in Fr. owing to influence of English fashions late 18th cent.; may have had a certain currency in Italy before the close of the century.

---

1. It. *scaglione* is attested from Middle Ages (Dante) in the indigenous sense of 'step, stair'; also (equit.) 'canine tooth of a horse' (heraldry) 'chevron'.

sciantiglioni. (pl.). Side-whiskers.

Used esp. in dialects (Piedmont, Milanese, Liguria, Venetia) during 19th cent.; 'non del tutto scomparsa dal linguaggio dei barbieri e parrucchieri' in early 20th cent. (Panzini). Understood to have entered via Milanese *sciantilión* (in Cherubini); Boerio (1829), registering Venet. *santilioni*, describes it as a 'neologismo introdottosi . . . dopo la nostra rivoluzione politica di 1797' and observes that 'le persone colte' call them *favorite* (q.v. above). <Fr. *échantillon* (Panz., B-Al., Pr.) usually explained as a jocular metaphorical extension of the Fr. meaning 'sample, scrap of cloth', etc. (16th cent.).[1]   B-Al. register *échantillon* in 19th cent. It. usage in this particular commercial signification (= *campione, saggio*).

sciantosa. Cabaret singer.

2nd half 19th cent., M-*Stor.* (737). Adapt. *sciantosa* 1918 (Panz., 3rd edition); but the French already in Panz., 1st edition, 1905, defined as 'quella donnetta che si presenta con molta grazia, vesti strane e poca voce a cantar canzonette un po' libere sul palcoscenico dei caffè concerto'. Popularised during the Great War. Fr. word (and adapt.), *chanteuse*.

sciarada. Charade.

B-Al. note that the actual parlour game (prob. invented in France) was imitated in Italy during the 18th cent. The first attestation of the word is that given in Boerio 1829; who observes 'francesismo novissimo fra noi, che nel *Dizionario etimologico scientifico* di Verona (1820) è scritto *Sciarada* come voce italiana'. The derivative *sciaradista* dates from 1837.   <Fr. *charade* (Panz., B-Al., M-D., Pr.), 1770 Sébastien, *Dict. de la littérature*, < Provençal *charrado* 'gossip', 'chin-wag'.

scicche, chic. Elegant, chic.

Scicche end 19th cent. Petrocchi; Fr. form 1895 Garollo. Both in Panzini. '*Chic* è una forma che può essere adoperata da un elegante o da uno che affetta eleganza, mentre *scicche* ha un aspetto plebeo' (M-*Stor.*, p. 738). Fr. adj. and subst. *chic* (Panz., B-Al., M-D., Pr.) 1832, originally artists' slang; of German origin.

scifoniera, chiffonnière. Small chest of drawers, chiffonier.

1877 F-A. ('*cassettoncino, armadino*'). Probably borrowed early in the century; Eng. *chiffonier, cheffonier* dates from 1806. Fr. form in Panzini (= *stipo*); *cifoniera* (Neap.) Panz.; *cifunè(ra)* (Sicil.) B-Al.   < Fr. *chiffonnière* (F-A., Panz., B-Al., Pr.), feminine, in view of the It. feminine form, though this is much rarer in French than the masculine *chiffonnier*: see Littré, who registers *chiffonnière* in Bernardin de Saint-Pierre.

scimpanzè. Zool.: Chimpanzee.

19th cent. B-Al.; *cimpanzè* and *quimpezè* in Lessona. <Fr. *chimpanzé* (B-Al., Pr.), *quimpezé* 1738, La Brosse, from a West African language.

scioppe. Glass of beer.

Sciòp 1883 Manfroni; Fr. graphy in Panzini, who also has the adapt. *scióppe* ('pronuncia centro-meridionale' [B-Al.]). Fr. word (and adapt.) *chope* (Panz., B-Al., Pr.), 1845 Bescherelle, < Low German.

sciovinismo. Chauvinism.

1890 F-A. (Pr.), also Fr. form. Both in Panzini, who makes a slight distinction of meaning between *chauvinisme* itself, 'esaltazione della patria francese' and *sciovinismo*, sometimes applied to Italian situations: 'lo *sciovinismo* . . . vale ad indicare quello spiacente orgoglio cittadino, spesso istintivo, che fa deviare dal retto giudizio'. Fr. word (and adapt.) *chauvinisme* (Panz., B-Al., M-D., Pr.) 1840, Albert Clerc, from *Chauvin*, name of

---

1. A more convincing origin to my mind is that of a visual analogy between sidewhiskers and the 'bare' of a roofing slate (*échantillon* in French), i.e. the square portion of a slate which projects downwards and is visible on a roof or wall from the outside.

patriotic soldier of Napoleonic armies in *La Cocarde tricolore* 1831 (*vide* Migliorini, *Dal nome proprio*, p. 195).

sedicente. So-called, self-styled.

19th cent. B-Al. ('primo Ottocento', M-*Stor.*, p. 662); 19th cent. Purists. Calque of Fr. *soi-disant* (sources agree). Though first attested in the Middle Ages (*c.* 1435, acc. to B-Wart.) and in common use from the sixteenth century onwards (Amyot, etc.), *soi-disant* was a familiar epithet in French Revolutionary propaganda and its equivalent very probably became current in Italian at that period.

segnaletico. Adj., that which identifies.

Esp. *dati segnaletici* 'identification marks, traits', 1901 Manfroni; Panzini (identification marks used by police). *Cartellino segnaletico* 'police identification files' in Darchini, acc. to Prati, who also registered the sense of 'marks by which one identifies race-horses'. <Fr. *signalétique* (B-Al., Pr.) 1836.[1]

segretèr, secrétaire. Writing-desk.

'Cassettone o armadio con vari rispostigli' (B-Al.). F-A. 1877 have *segreterre*. Fr. form *secrétaire* in Garollo 1895 and Panzini. Phon. adapt. of Fr. word (B-Al., Pr.); the semantic shift from 'secretary, repository of secrets' to 'writing desk' occurs in French early 19th cent.

semàforo. Semaphore.

Initially a naut., milit. term (signalling apparatus with movable arms); 20th cent., 'traffic lights' (as in Fr.). *Semaforo* with Fr. accentuation in Tramater, 1838 (also *semaforico* adj.). <Fr. learned Hellenism *sémaphore*, 1812, Mozin (B-Al., Pr.).

semantica. Study of linguistic meaning.

19th cent., acc. to B-Al., Panzini. <Fr. *sémantique* (B-Al., Pr., M-*Stor.*, p. 734), Bréal, 1883.

serra. Greenhouse, hot-house.

1812 Bernardoni (= *stufa*); 1838 Tramater; T-Bell.; F-A., Rig., Panzini. Semantic loan < Fr. *serre* (17th cent.) acc. to the above sources (except Bernardoni) and Prati.

sigaretta. Cigarette.

Masc. *sigaretto* in A. Guadagnoli (1798–1858) (Pr.); *cigaretta* in title of a book printed in Modena 1845 (Pr.); *sigaretta* 2nd half 19th cent. <Fr. *cigarette* (B-Al., Pr.) 1840, *Voleurs et volés* (Dauz.); masc. *cigaret* earlier (1834).

siluetta. Silhouette.

1838 Tramater ('profile portrait', usually cut in black paper and mounted on a white ground). Fr. form in Gherardini (1852–57); *siluette* and *siloetta* in Petrocchi. Panz. has Fr. form and *siluetta*. Generally agreed to be of Fr. provenance. The phrase *à la silhouette* 'something done hastily, sketchily', by analogy with Étienne de Silhouette's brief and unpopular term of office (1759), is attested in French during the 2nd half of the 18th cent. The semantic extension > 'brief portrait, profile portrait' has occurred by the end of the century (*portrait à la silhouette* in Mercier), while the modern signification is approved by the *Académie* in 1835.

sirena. Siren, hooter.

19th cent. B-Al.; originally an instrument for measuring the frequency of vibration

---

1. Certain acceptations of It. *segnalare* are assumed to be semantic loans from French by 19th cent. sources, as opposed to the indigenous connotations; e.g. 'to make famous' (cf. Fr. *signalé*, *segnalé*, 16th cent. It. > Fr. loans) and (with reflexive) 'to cover oneself with glory' (16th cent., V. Borghini, etc.). Bernardoni 1812 observes with disapproval the use of *segnalare* meaning 'to point out, bring to someone's notice'. Similar criticisms are voiced by T-Bell. and F-A., 1877.

of sounds (1875, Lessona), whence 'siren' of a ship, factory, etc. <Fr. *sirène* (Panz., B-Al., Pr.), originally instrument (music, acoustics) as above, invented by Cagniard de la Tour in 1819.

smoking. Dinner jacket.

First attested in Panzini 1905; the earliest example in French is 1890, Rostand, *Musardises*; but the complete English term *smoking-jacket* appears a little earlier (1889 Bourget, *Études et Portraits*). An English word, whose history both in French and Italian is obscure; but the interposition of a French intermediary (affirmed by Prati, envisaged by B-Al.) is scarcely to be doubted in view of the elliptical form and shift of meaning typical of French. Dauzat considers that the new sense—'formal evening wear' as opposed to 'casual home dress'—arose in French: even if this were not so, it is plain that the sense 'dinner-jacket' became established in French, and was transferred thence into Italian. The elliptical form is inadmissible in English.

soarè, soirée. Soirée, elegant evening, social gathering.

Soarè 1881 F-A., 2nd edition, Rigutini; Fr. form in Panzini. Equivalents: *veglia, festino* (F-A.), *veglia, conversazione* (Panz.). Rig. insists that the indigeneous term *serata* is adequate. Fr. word and adapt., *soirée*, 1764 (*FEW*, XI, 517a).

sociologia. Sociology.

1865 Camini (B-Al.); 1875 Lessona. <Fr. learned coinage *sociologie* (Panz., B-Al., Pr.) 1830, Auguste Comte. It. *sociologo* and *sociologico* (Petrocchi) may be modelled upon the corresponding Fr. forms.

sonda. Medic.: Probe, sound.

1853 D'Ayala; Lessona; Rigutini. Verb *sondare (una piaga)* 1877 F-A. <Fr. *sonde* (19th cent. sources, Panz., B-Al., M-D., Pr.), 16th cent. as a surgical term; *sonder*.

sonda. Naut.: Lead-line, sounding-rod.

(= *scandaglio*). 1812 Bernardoni; 1814 Stratico; Tramater, D'Ayala. Unknown to Alberti, who translates the Fr. word by *scandaglio, piombino*; presumably a term of the Napoleonic era. Numerous examples during the 19th cent. of *sonda* and *sondare* used figuratively in a way similar to that of French; as Panzini points out, *scandaglio* is normally used in the purely nautical signification. <Fr. *sonde* (19th cent. sources, Panz., B-Al., Pr.) 12th cent. A clear Fr. influence may be seen in *sondaggio* 'sounding' (esp. figurative), which is, however, a 20th cent. form; *sondeggio* (same meaning) appears already in D'Ayala and F-A. (registered as a Gallicism). <Fr. *sondage* 1769, Morand (B-Al., M-D., Pr.).

sorvegliare. To superintend, watch, watch over.

1812 Bernardoni; 1877 F-A.; Rigutini (claims that the word entered It. through police terminology). Also *sorveglianza* 'supervision, superintendence' (same sources). French verb trans. by '*invigilare, veggiare, aver cura*' in Alberti. <Fr. *surveiller* 1680 (Purists, B-Al., Pr.), *surveillance* 1633 (Purists, Pr.).

soubrette. Soubrette.

1905 Panzini ('servetta nella commedia'); 1930 Della Corte ('attrice giovane dell' operetta'). Fr. word *soubrette* 1640, Faret < Prov. *soubreto* 'qui fait la difficile'.

soufflé. Culin.: Soufflé. (adj. and subst.)

Panz., 1st edition, 1905. Fr. adj. and subst. (*omelette soufflée* 1798, *beignet soufflé* 1835, *sucre soufflé, cuit à soufflé* [Littré]). *Soufflé* as a subst. Boiste, 1829. (*FEW*, XII, 408b).

sovvenire. Souvenir (subst.).

1877 F-A., who reject as a Gallicism the use of *sovvenire* as a substantive meaning *ricordanza, ricordo, memoria* (cf. Panz., remarks upon Manzoni's usage in this respect) and more especially referring to an actual object, i.e. 'gift intended to commemorate a place or happening; ring, keepsake' (= *ricordino* [F-A.], *ricordo*). <Fr. *souvenir* (F-A., Panz., M-D., Pr.).

spahi. North African native levy, *spahi*.

1874 Lessona, Panzini; *spaì* in Petrocchi. Semantic loan < Fr. *spahi* (Panz., B-Al., M-D., Pr.), 1831 in this signification. The form exists much earlier in It. and Fr. alike (It. *spachi* 16th cent., Tolomei; *spahi* 17th cent., Montec.; 1547 in French, in the travels of d'Aramon, French ambassador in Constantinople) but only in the sense of 'Turkish cavalry' (Turk. *sipahi*, < Persian). With the consolidation of French power in North Africa the term was applied to Algerian troops and passed to other European languages in the new acceptation.[1]

spessore. Thickness.

1877 F-A.; 1886 Rig., who observes ironically that a scientist would lose face if he had to use the everyday word *grossezza*. F-A. cite an example of the derived verb *spessare* in a medical report. <Fr. *épaisseur* (Purists, M-*Stor.*).

spionaggio. Espionage.

1886 Rig. 19th cent., B-Al. Panz. <Fr. *espionnage*, 1589, B-Wart.

subire. To undergo, suffer.

1805 Alberti; 1812 Bernadoni; numerous later 19th cent. examples. F-A. cite as current usage *subire una pena*, *subire l'umiliazione*. <Fr. *subir* 1611, Cotgrave (Panz., B-Al., Pr.; 'introdotto ... seguendo l'esempio del fr. *subir*' [M-D.]).

tabagismo. Medic.: Abuse of tobacco; nicotine poisoning.

Panz., 1st edition, 1905. <Fr. *tabagisme* (Panz., B-Al., Pr.), late 19th cent., < *tabagie* 1604 'public smoking-room'.

tableau, tablò. Picture, table, tableau.

Tablò 1846 Azzocchi (B-Al.); Ugolini; 1877 F-A.; Panzini. Various senses, but two predominate in 19th cent. sources: (a) a précis, summing up or brief account, (b) a tableau of people (on the stage, etc.). Panzini mentions in addition the use of *tableau!* as an exclamation: 'si dice in francese *Tableau!* quando si scopre qualcosa di inaspettato, e noi potremmo dire e diciamo *Spettacolo!*' (= 'general consternation', 'collapse of stout party').

table d'hôte. Of restaurant menu, as in English.

1883 Manfroni; Panzini (*vide* articles *table d'hôte* and *tavola rotonda*; possible pejoration of original term). French word used in Italy, as elsewhere (Panz., B-Al., Pr.).

tabù. Taboo.

Tapu, *tabu* 1891 B-Al.; *tabù* 1895 Garollo. A Polynesian word introduced into Europe through English, with a very strong likelihood of a Fr. intermediary between English and Italian. Fr. *tabou* is a well-known Anglicism; occurs first (1785) with Eng. graphy in translation of Cook's voyages; *tabou* 1822. (*L.N.*, I, 161; II, 85.)

tabulatura. Music: Tablature.

1829 Tramater, but an adapted form *tavolatura* in Chambers, 1749. <Fr. *tablature*, 1529 < MLat. (B-Al.).

taburè, tabouret. Stool, footstool.

Tabouret 19th cent. B-Al.; *taburè* 1877 F-A. Fr. form in Panzini. Fr. word *tabouret* (and adapt.), 1552 with this meaning (earlier, 'pin-cushion': mid-15th to early 17th cent.).

---

1. The original Persian form reaches Italian by a third series of contacts in the word *cipai* (19th cent.), 'sepoy' (i.e. Indian levies with British forces in India) from English, or ultimately from Portuguese via English. A French intermediary (*cipaye*) is possible here also. The English use of the word in an Indian context affords a parallel to that of French in Algeria.

tallone. Coupon, counterfoil.

1877 F-A.; *talloncino* 1908 Panzini. <Fr. *talon (de souche)*, acc. to B-Al., M-D., Pr. The architectural and nautical terms may also be influenced by their French equivalents: archit.: 'ogee moulding' 1749, Chambers; naut.: 'sole of rudder', 'after end of keel', Alberti, 1788.

tampone. Stopper, tampon, plug.

1877 F-A. ('cork, stopper'); 1891 Rigutini as a surgical term, 'tampon'; *tamponare* (surgical) 1891 Rigut., Panzini; 'to plug, cork', 1901 Manfroni (also naut. term). A further Gallicism in *tamponare* 'to ram, collide with' (motor vehicles) (M.*Suppl.*). <Fr. *tampon* (B-Al., M-D., Pr.), 1534 < *tapon* 1382. *Tamponare* < Fr. *tamponner* (same sources) 15th cent.; tech. term, railway engineering, 1875. It. *tamponamento* 'collision' < Fr. *tamponnement* (same sources) 1771.

tangheggio. Naut.: Pitching (oscillation fore and aft).

1814 Stratico, who also has the verb *tangare* 'to pitch'. <Fr. *tangage* (change of suffix), *tanguer* (both 1694) < Dutch (B-Al.).

tannino, tanno, tannare. Chem.: Tannin, tannic acid; tan; to tan (leather).

(a) 1828 Omodei (B-Al.) < Fr. *tanin* 1806 (B-Al., M-D., Pr.); (b) (ant.) 1813 Gagliardi (B-Al.) < Fr. *tan*, 13th cent.; (c) 1829 (B-Al.) < Fr. *tanner*, 13th cent. (= *concia, conciare*).

tara. Defect, blemish, vice.

1839 B-Al.; 1st half 19th cent., M-*Stor.*, p. 662. Semantic loan < Fr. *tare*, originally mediaeval borrowing from Arabic via Italian in the commercial senses (see mediaeval loans). 19th cent. lexical purists seldom object to this usage, perhaps because it fulfilled a useful purpose as a technical term in *materia medica* (= *vizio organico o ereditare*; see Panz., who does not register a foreign origin; also *tarato* adj., which exactly corresponds to Fr. *taré, c.* 1500).

tarlatana. Text.: Tarlatan (fine muslin).

(Used esp. for women's evening dress.)   *Tarlatan, tarlatane* 1875 Lessona; Panzini. <Fr. *tarlatane* (Panz., B-Al., M-D., Pr.), *tarnatane* 1723, Savary.

tartina. Slice of bread and butter.

1850 Rambelli, *Vocab. domest.*; Panzini. <Fr. *tartine* (Panz., B-Al., Pr., Migl.) 1642.

tasso. Econ.: Rate of interest, exchange rate.

(= *prezzo, valore, saggio*). 1860, Ugol.; 1877 F-A. 'La misura percentuale dell'interesse e dello sconto . . . in buon italiano, *ragione*' (Panz., s.v. *saggio*). Calque of Fr. *taux*, acc. to Purists, Panz., B-Al., M-*Stor.*

tatuaggio, tatuare. Tattooing, to tattoo.

Tatuaggio 1829 Tramater, 1875 Lessona; *tatueggiare* 1882 (B-Al.); *tatuare* 1891 Petrocchi. <Fr. *tatouage* 1778, *tatouer* 1769 < Polynesian via English (B-Al., Pr.; M-D. derives subst. and verb < English without Fr. intermediary. Panz. is non-committal).

tenuta. Uniform, dress.

Indigenous *tenuta* in the sense of 'possession(s)' is attested continuously from G. Villani onwards. Bernardoni is the first to register the meaning 'appearance', 'bearing' (e.g. 'quell'esercito a una bella tenuta'), which is in turn strongly criticised by F-A. (1877), who add as examples of 'gergo francese' such idioms as 'ha una tenuta molto distinta' for 'ha nobil presenza'. Other purists raise similar objections, which are extended to the meaning 'uniform', 'type of dress', esp. 'evening dress' (*alta tenuta* F-A., Rig.; *gran tenuda* Piacent. already in 1836 [B-Al.]). The military term (1879, B-Al.) must be added to the list of 19th cent. semantic loans from Fr. *tenue* (*grande tenue, petite tenue*).

terrorizzare. To terrorise.

1877 F-A., Rig., i.e. in the wider sense of 'coerce, rule, maintain power by inspiring fear', as F-A's. examples show ('i briganti terrorizzano la Sicilia', etc.). Probably used somewhat earlier; cf. *to terrorize* in English, 1823 (*OED*). <Fr. *terroriser*, 1796, originally referring to the *Terreur* of 1793–94.

timballo. Culin.: Pie, pie-dish.

1839 *Panlessico* (B-Al.); 1850 Rambelli, *Vocab. domest.* <Fr. *timbale* (B-Al., Pr.) in these senses. (*Vide timballo*, 17th cent. Fr. > It. loans).

timbro, timbrare. Rubber stamp; to stamp.

Timbro 1812 Bernardoni (= *bollo, impronta, segno*); 1829 Boerio: 'voce dataci dai Francesi sotto il cessato Governo politico . . . e s'intende quello timbro pubblico degli Uffizii, onde le carte vengono autenticate e validate' (cited Pr.); 1877 F-A. Also *timbro della posta* as an incorrect usage < *timbre-poste*; *timbrare* 1877 F-A. (= *bollare, imprimere il sigillo*). Loans, acc. to F-A., Panz., B-Al., M-D., Pr., from Fr. *timbre*, 18th cent., 'stamp on paper for legal documents and the like'; attested in connection with the postal service (*timbre de la poste*, 1802); *timbrer* (also 1802).

timbro. Acoust., music: Timbre or quality.

1848 Ugolini; F-A. 1877; Rig.; Panzini; all referring in particular to the phrase *timbro di voce*, '. . . metallo, pasta di voce o di suono. Ma pur avendo parole nostre, l'espressione francese . . . è più frequente nell'uso' (Panz.). <Fr. *timbre* (*de la voix*) (B-Al., Pr.) 17th cent., figurative use from *timbre* 'bell'. The corresponding loan in English (*timbre*) appears in 1849 (*OED*).

tiragliere. Milit.: Sharpshooter, skirmisher.

Tiragliör 1879 (Romagna) meaning *bersagliere*, acc. to B-Al.; *tiragliatore* (milit.) 1909 (Pr. B-Al.); Panzini. <Fr. *tirailleur* (B-Al., Pr.), 1808 referring to a corps of riflemen; earlier agent substantive formed on *tirailler*.

tola, tolla. Sheet steel, iron plate.

Tola 1877 F-A. (*lamiera, bandone*); Panz. A Piedmontese word (F-A., B-Al.), spreading to Lombardy, Genoa, Piacenza. *Tolla* is registered by Oudin. <Fr. *tôle* (F-A.; 'probably', B-Al.), 1642 Oudin.

tormenta. Snow-storm, mountain blizzard.

Fr. form *tourmente* (speaking of Apennines) 1830 in Leopardi; *tormenta* 1860 G. Carena; *turmenta* 1814 in Turin. <Fr. *tourmente* 12th cent. (Carena, Panz., B-Al., M-D., Pr.) in the sense of 'mountain storm' only; the naut. term 'sudden storm at sea', 16th cent., Ramusio, Sassetti (also has *tormento*), though ultimately from OFr. *tormente*, entered Italian via the Hispanic languages.

tortiera. Culin.: Pie-dish, baking pan.

Appears in Oudin, whose reference does not, however, appear to be supported by further attestations until the early 19th century. 1829, Tramater (B-Al.). <Fr. *tourtiere*, 16th cent. (Pr.; B-Al. also consider that it may be from Spanish).

totalizzare, totalizzatore. To add up, totalise; totalisator (on race-track).

Totalizzare 1812 Bernardoni, 1877 F-A.; *totalizzatore* (ref. to horse-racing) 1891 Petrocchi, 1895 Garollo, Panzini. <Fr. *totaliser* (B-Al., M-D.) 1829 B-Wart. (prob. earlier), *totalisateur* (Panz., B-Al., Pr.), 1869, Littré.

tourniquet, tornichetto. Surg.: Tourniquet; turnstile.

Surgical term: *tornichetto, tornachetto* 1829 Leone; *tornichetto* 1877 F-A. (who suggest *compressore, guancialetto compressore* instead); Fr. form (in normal use) Panzini. Term of mech. engin., 'turnstile': *tornichetto* 1877 F-A. (who suggest 'contatore'); *tourniquet* 1895 Garollo, Panz. <Fr. *tourniquet* (1575) (Purists, Panz., B-Al., Pr.).

trafiletto. Typogr., journal: Short paragraph inserted between newspaper articles.

1895 Garollo; Panzini (also Fr. word). <Fr. *entrefilet* (Panz., B-Al., M-D., Pr.), 1843 Balzac.

M

trància. Culin., engin.: Slice.

'Slice of bread, meat, ham, etc.', 1905 Panzini. *Trància* 'falcione' 1889 in Ferrara (B-Al.). Panzini (1905) registers *trància* as name of various machine tools used for shearing (esp. metal), shaping or punching. < Fr. *tranche* (Panz., B-Al., M-D., Pr.), 1288.

trattore. Restaurant-keeper.

Mentioned in a letter of A. Cesari (pre-1828) cited by Pr.; 1855, Fanf., *Voc. ling. it.* T-Bell. cite mediaeval examples of which Prati judges one at least to have this signification, though the med. sense of 'broker, trader' could in fact apply to them all. < Fr. *traiteur* (all sources agree), 17th cent., Scarron in this sense; 13th in that of 'broker, factor'.

treno. Railway train.

1874 Lessona (= *convoglio*); probably entered earlier. < Fr. *train* (B-Al., M-D.) which in the sense 'train of wagons or coaches drawn by a locomotive' appears in 1827 and is a semantic loan from English *train* (same sense, 1824) (*vide* Wexler, op. cit., pp. 124–5 and notes). Certain idiomatic 19th cent. uses reflect the French closely, e.g. *treno* for *maniera* (*di vivere*), *essere in treno di . . .* (*être en train de*). (*Vide treno, traino*, 16th cent. Fr. > It. loans.)

trovero, troviero. Lit. hist.: Trouvère.

Trov(i)ero 1891 Petrocchi. < Fr. *trouvère* (B-Al., M-D., Pr.), *trovere, troveor* 12th cent.; revived in 19th cent. under impulse of mediaeval studies. Alberti translates Fr. *trouverre/trouveur* by *trovatore*.

tulle. Text.: Tulle.

Graphies *tull, tullo* 1850 Rambelli; *tulle* 1879 T-Bell., Panzini. Fr. word (and adapt.) *tulle*, 18th cent. < place-name; *point de Tulle* in 17th cent. (*L.N.*, VII, 10).

turbina. Tech.: Water-turbine.

1891 Petrocchi; Panzini. 'Steam-turbine' in 20th cent. < Fr. *turbine* (Panz., B-Al., M-D., Pr.), 17th March 1827 in the correspondence of Ph. de Girard, who claims that the water-turbine was invented by a Frenchman Burdin (Dauz.). The 19th cent. French engineers Fourneyron, Callon and Fontaine undoubtedly played a major part in the development of water-turbines.

turista, turismo. Tourist, tourism.

Torista in F-A., 1877, who refer to the word *touristi* (pl.) on the frontispiece of the *Guida della montagna Pistoiese* by a Prof. A. Tigri (date not stated). Fr. form *touriste* in 19th cent., I. Nievo (B-Al.). *Turista* and *turismo* 1905, Panz., 1st edition. < Fr. *touriste* 1816 Simond (speaking of English), *tourisme* 1841 Guichardet, < Eng. *tourist* 1800 and *tourism* 1811, acc. to F-A., B-Al., Pr. A French intermediary is indicated by early Italian forms, dating, and contemporary references.

turlupinare. To make a fool of, swindle, cheat.

1901 Manfroni; Panzini. < Fr. *turlupiner* (Panz., B-Al., M-D., Pr.), 1615, < proper name *Turlupin* (Migl., *Dal nome proprio*, p. 181).[1]

ultimatum. Polit.: Ultimatum.

1860 Ugolini, 1875 Lessona, Panz.; but adapt. *ultimato* in 1839 (B-Al.).[2] < French *ultimatum* (Panz., B-Al., Pr.), 1798 Acad., taken from diplomatic Latin. *Ultimatum* in Eng. 1731.

umanitario. Humanitarian.

1838 Tommaseo (adj.); Giusti (subst.); 1877 F-A.; Rig. < Fr. *humanitaire*, 1833 M.

---

1. *Turlupini* (pl.) < Fr. *Turlupins*, name of a heretical sect excommunicated in 1372, and *turlupinata* < Fr. *turlupinade* (1653) appear in 1749 Chambers (B-Al.).

2. Earlier (1810) in Foscolo, acc. to Migliorini (*Stor.*, p. 658 n. 2).

Raymond (19th cent. sources, Panz., B-Al., Pr.)., Also *umanitarismo*, 'advocacy of humanitarian ideals' *c.* 1880 (B-Al., Pr.), < Fr. *humanitarisme*, 1838 Balzac. F-A. claim that *umanitario* had by 1877 acquired a slightly ironical connotation because of hypocritical attitudes associated with it.

umanizzare. To humanise.

1838 B-Al. (trans. and reflex.); 1877 F-A. <Fr. *humaniser* (Panz., B-Al., Pr.), 1584 de Barraud.

uniformizzare. To make uniform.

1877 F-A. (who also have *uniformato* 'put into uniform'). <Fr. *uniformiser*, 1725 (B-Al.) (*Vide uniforme*, 18th cent. Fr. > It. loans).

vaccino, -a, vaccinare, vaccinazione. Medic.: Vaccine; to vaccinate, etc.

The relative position of French, English, Italian and medical Latin in this lexical group is not easy to assess. *Vaccino* adj. 'relating to the cow' is a Latinism in both French and English. The point of departure would appear to be Fr. *vaccin* (adj.) in *variole vaccin* (pre-1749) and *vaccine* (subst.) 1749, both meaning 'cowpox' (English had of course the indigenous Germanic word for the disease). When Dr. Jenner speaks of 'the vaccine virus' in 1799 (in a discussion of his discovery) he may either be thinking of the Latinism, the actual Latin word for the disease, or Fr. *vaccine* = 'cowpox' (cf. also 'the vaccine disease' 'vaccine matter', 'vaccine inoculation' (all 1799, *Medical Journal*). The OED is non-committal on this point. Fr. *vaccine* 'action of vaccinating' appears very soon after, 1800, *Décade phil.* (Dauz.), with the verb *vacciner* and *vaccination* in 1801. English *vaccine* as an unqualified substantive, = 'preparation of bacteria with which to "vaccinate" ' appears 1803 in a translation from French (*OED*). The contact between Fr. and It. is less problematical. There is no reason to deny that the It. forms were in turn borrowed from French (B-Al. and Pr. concur). It. *vaccina* = 'vaccine' and *vaccinare*[1] are cited by Gherardini from a text of 1807; the latter and *vaccinazione* are in Bernardoni 1812. As regards masc. *vaccino*, the phrase *virus vaccino* is attested in 1807; *vaccino* subst. in Gherardini (1858).

vagabondaggio. Vagrancy.

1812 Bernardoni. <Fr. *vagabondage*, 1767 (Pr., M-*Stor.*, pp. 660, 662).

vagone. Railway wagon, truck.

1839 A. Bresciani; Parenti; 1840 Cherubini; 1877 F-A., etc. <Fr. *wagon* (B-Al., M-D., Pr.) first attested as *vagon* 1826 (Wexler, p. 117), borrowed from Eng. *wag(g)on*, which gradually replaced the original Fr. term *chariot* during the following decade. *Vagone-letto* < Fr. *wagon-lit*; *vagone-salon* 'Pullman car' < *wagon-salon*.

valanga. Avalanche.

1805 Alberti (B-Al.); 1877 F-A., who discuss it at length and suggest that *valanga* be kept for Alpine regions, *lazza*, *lisciata*, etc., for the Apennines; 1886 Rigutini (as an indispensable term). Used figuratively 1897 (B-Al.) to mean 'mass, overwhelming quantity', etc. Occurs previously (17th cent., Oudin) in the forms *vallanca*, *valanca*. <Fr. *avalanche*, acc. to F-A., B-Al., though the origin of the word and its history in dialects on both Fr. and It. sides of the Alpine watershed is open to debate (*vide* Prati's article and sources cited there).

vapore (masc.). Steamship.

Battello a vapore 1852 Perini (B-Al.); 1877 F-A. (s.v. *pacchebotto*); 1879 (B-Al.). <Fr. *vapeur* (m.), ellipsis of *bateau à vapeur*, calque of Eng. *steam-boat* (1803) (B-Al.).

---

1. It. *vaccinare* ~ Fr. *vacciner* appears at first sight to be a formal criterion of Gallicism rather than Anglicism (opposed to *vaccinate* in Eng.); but the Eng. verb *to vaccine* existed ephemerally alongside *to vaccinate* in the earliest period: cf. 'to have someone vaccined' 1803 in OED.

varietà. Variety show, variety theatre.

Teatro varietà (B-Al., Pr.) in 1893; *varietà* Panzini (also Fr. form). Calque of Fr. *variété* in this sense (Panz., B-Al., Pr.).

versamento. Finance: Payment, deposit of money.

1812 Bernardoni; F-A., 1877, who also condemn *versare* in the sense 'to make a payment'. The indigenous meaning 'supply, provision' (also abstract, = *il versare*) appears in Magalotti, Alberti. Semantic loan < Fr. *versement* (Purists, B-Al., Pr.), 18th cent. as a financial term. *Distinta di versamento* 'credit slip, paying-in slip' is probably a calque of Fr. *bulletin de versement*.

versante. Geog.: Watershed, catchment area.

1839 *Panlessico* (B-Al.); 1875 Lessona; 1877 F-A.; Rig.; Panz. <Fr. *versant* (subst.) (Panz., B-Al., M-D., Pr., etc.), 1823 Boiste.

vetrina. Show-case, shop window.

1841 Lorenzo Molossi (Pr.); Viani; 1st half 19th cent., M-*Stor.*, p. 662. Semantic loan < Fr. *vitrine*, 1836 in sense of 'shop-window'. It. *vetrina* had earlier tech. uses, e.g. 'varnish, glazing' in Baldinucci (1681).

viabilità. Viability.

Referring to state of roads for transport and their efficient upkeep: 1877 F-A., Panzini. <Fr. *viabilité* (F-A., Panz., B-Al.) 1846 Bescherelle. F-A.'s claim that It. *viabilità* (of roads) is borrowed from the Fr. legal and medical term *viabilité* ('ability, fitness to survive, of an infant') is untenable. Two Fr. words are involved, one a Latinism from *via* (*viabilis*), the other a derivative of *vie* < *vita*. Of these the latter also influences Italian in the adapted borrowing *vitabilità*, 1829 Tramater (homoionym of *vitalità*). Cf. also *vitabile* (ibid.), probably < Fr. *viable*, and *vitabilità*, *viabilità* in Migl., *Suppl.* Fr. *viabilité* as a medical term appears 1808, Boiste; *viable* 1546 R. Estienne.

vidimare. To authenticate, approve, visa a document.

1812 Bernardoni, who also has *vidimazione*, 'approval, giving one's visa to a document' and *vidimato* 'approved' (registered as indispensable technical terms); Ugolini; F-A.; T-Bell. 'inutile gallicismo'), etc. <Fr. *vidimer*, 16th cent., d'Aubigné (19th cent. sources, Panz., B-Al., Pr.) < legal Lat. term *vidimus* 'we have seen . . . ' used as a substantive (*donner le vidimus*: parallel idioms with *vidimus* (noun) in Italian to end of 18th cent.).

vignetta. Wood-cut, vignette.

1839 *Panlessico*; Carducci; T-Bell.; 1877 F-A. (also Fr. form). <Fr. *vignette* (Panz., B-Al., *REW* 9350, etc.). *Vignettista* in Migl., *Suppl.* is possibly < Fr. *vignettiste*.

visavì, vis à vis. Adv. or prep.: Opposite, facing.

Vis a vis 1877 F-A., Panzini; *visavì* 20th cent. <Fr. *vis-à-vis*, 14th cent. (Panz., B-Al., M-D., Pr., etc.). Also from French are the senses (a) type of 4-wheeled carriage in which passengers face each other (1840 Cherubini; also adapt. *visavisse*) (b) a double armchair or settee shaped like an S (1877 F-A.).

volante, volano. Mech. engin., auto. engin.: Flywheel; steering wheel.

Some uncertainty attends the relationship of these two semantic loans and the French polysemes from which they are derived. The term of mechanical engineering *volante* (also found as *volano*) 'fly-wheel' (i.e. wheel which regulates and maintains even speed of a revolving mechanism) appears 1836, Foresti (B-Al.); also 1859 Carena (referring to a wheel attached to windlass of a well). <Fr. *volant* (B-Al., M-D., Pr.), which in the 18th cent. referred to a flat plate of metal fixed to the last gear-wheel of a clock's striking mechanism, and which, revolving rapidly, slowed down and evened out the strokes of the bell. Alberti translates Fr. *volant* in this sense by *ventola* (1788). There is no direct semantic connection, therefore, between Fr. *volant* meaning 'flywheel' and meaning 'shuttlecock'. It. *volante* 'steering wheel' of a car, etc., is borrowed from Fr.

in the 20th century, the semantic extension having occurred in French. It. *volante* (fashions) 'flounce' (of a dress), 1877 (B-Al.) is probably a further semantic loan from French.

vol-au-vent. Culin.: Vol-au-vent.

Voluvàn 1876 Gargiolli (B-Al.); Fr. form in Garollo and Panzini. A French compound first attested 1829, Boiste, *vol-au-vent*, for *'vole* (i.e. *je vole*) *au vent'*. Panz. notes that 'in un pranzo ufficiale (1937) la parola *vol-au-vent* fu tradotta nella lista con *ariévole'*.

voltaire. Antimacassar.

Voltèr 1891 Petrocchi. Fr. form *voltaire* in Panzini. Probably a false Gallicism, created in Italian by synecdoche from the style of chair referred to as *fauteuil à la Voltaire*, apparently because it was similar in style to the chair which figures in Houdon's statue of Voltaire (*vide* Migl., *Dal nome proprio*, p. 185).

zeffiro, zephyr. Text.: Light, delicate muslin, esp. for baby clothes.

Panno zèffiro in Petrocchi; *zefir* 1894 Garollo; *zéphyr* in Panzini. Fr. word (and adapt.) *zéphyr*, used figuratively (Panz., B-Al., M-D., Pr.).

zuava. Fashions: Woman's jacket cut like that of a Zouave.

1879 T-Bell. The word *zouave* in its basic sense of 'Algerian soldier', first used in Fr. 1831, enters It. as *zuavo* in the 20th cent.

French Influences on Italian Vocabulary during the Nineteenth Century

Explaining the significance of Gallicisms in nineteenth century Italian is more difficult than it appears to be at first sight. Superficially the lexicologist has everything on his side. There is a wealth of dictionary sources, as we have already seen; the history of the time has been worked over in meticulous detail and, since we are contemplating recent social or linguistic habits and events, introspection or hearsay on the part of contemporaries is a more reliable guide than one can usually afford to admit. To find evidence in abundance makes a refreshing change from the thin, meagre seams of earlier days, even though on occasions it is biased by personal xenophobia or coloured by pedantry. Initially, therefore, one looks forward to a neat, convincing series of interpretations. Only later does one sense where the problems lie and realise how complex the lexico-cultural equation at this period is.

As with Italianisms in sixteenth century French, a great deal of work in this section has already been done. Critical material on vocabulary of the Ottocento is so copious, in fact, that it would be impracticable to refer to individual contributions. Fortunately the need to do so is no longer pressing in view of recent syntheses, and here again I must acknowledge my debt to Professor Devoto's *Profilo*, and to the *Storia della lingua italiana* of Professor Migliorini, who has allotted two very full chapters to the years from 1789 to 1914.[1] The reader will wish to refer directly to these, and to the scholarly sources they cite in connection with each individual aspect of Italian vocabulary at the

1. Esp. *Stor.*, pp. 659–64, 735–9.

time. But a few pointers to guide him through this lexically exuberant century may not come amiss, especially since nineteenth and twentieth century authorities, whatever their standing and whatever the initial reason which leads them to talk about language—social, historical or strictly lexicological—tend to be interested ultimately in Italian as an immanent institution, a national idiom in the process of self-realisation. The result is that Gallicism and everything associated with it comes within the purview of their works only as a marginal phenomenon. For a scholar whose programme is to study the Italian language in its entirety this conception is amply justified. The nineteenth century, as we know well, is dominated by the Risorgimento, the moment in history when political unification of Italy, prepared from a long way back, was finally achieved; and with this impulse to attain political nationhood went a corresponding desire for linguistic unity and the enjoyment of certain ideal benefits thought to accrue from possessing a truly national language. Logically therefore the most productive approach is a centripetal one showing how all events, political, cultural and linguistic converge towards the goal of unification and self-determination. From this standpoint the immediacy of different French influences is seen to vary. Certain military, political and administrative interventions are directly relevant; the cultural impact of France is more or less cogent according to whether it concerns the history of ideas or that of aesthetic innovations, among them literary trends. The role which the French language has to play appears more detached, more episodic. It has a modest walking-on part in the *questione della lingua*, which at this time takes on a special importance because of nationalistic implications. In addition there is its customary function as an indicator through borrowed words of more weighty French influences, which are exemplified with greater or lesser significance according to the different semantic categories.

I shall take this unitary conception as a basic premiss while not feeling obliged to accept all the constructions philologists have placed upon it. The language of a given period is self-limiting, self-defining, and it is always necessary to set borrowings against this primary organic background. But in the nineteenth century an external approach, too, offers special advantages which require to be exploited. We shall find it expedient in this century more than others to view the Italian language from outside, from an uncommitted point of vantage, and see what Gallicisms have to tell about, for instance, Italy's place in the broad context of European life.

Let us begin on this final occasion as previously by an attentive reading of our lists. A two-stage analysis will serve us best this time: a quick glance at the main semantic categories first, before we consider what each separate pattern of content implies and seek out the threads of circumstance that bind them together.

Borrowings may be assorted as follows (see Fig. 1):[1]

1.	Scientific-cum-medical	101 (68+33)
2.	Technological and transport	93 (86+7)
3.	Political and bureaucratic; legal	83 (73+10)
4.	Commercial and financial	84
5.	House and family; foods	71 (34+37)
6.	Amusements and social activities	69 (44+25)
7.	Clothing, fashions and personal adornment	49
8.	Military	41
9.	Naval	29
10.	Intellectual and artistic	35
11.	Exotica	11
12.	Miscellaneous	43
13.	Abstract-general-emotive	104

TOTAL   813

It is interesting to compare these statistics with the eighteenth century (see Fig. 2):

1.	Scientific-cum-medical	27
2.	Technology and transport	16
3.	Political and bureaucratic; legal	28
4.	Commercial and financial	30
5.	House and family; foods	27
6.	Amusements and social activities	11
7.	Clothing, fashion and personal adornments	18
8.	Military	12
9.	Naval	27
10.	Intellectual and artistic	16
11.	Exotica	10
12.	Miscellaneous	7
13.	Abstract-general-emotive	41

TOTAL   270

The size of the nineteenth century list is its most noteworthy characteristic. Comprising 813 words it is the largest in our survey. Each of categories 1 to 6 betokens a major influence; each in itself is numerically comparable to the whole of the corresponding Italian to French corpus. The number of abstract-

1. Technology includes fine crafts. Textiles are classed with Commerce, not Fashion. Numbers cited here are not necessarily congruent with the total of borrowings or number of rubrics appearing in the lists by centuries. Categories overlap; some words are relevant to more than one influence.

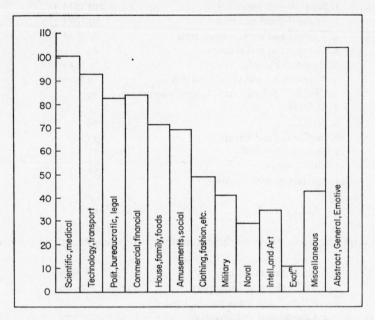

Fig. 1   Summary of Semantic Categories: nineteenth century French to Italian loans

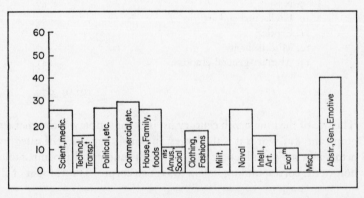

Fig. 2   Summary of Semantic Categories: eighteenth century French to Italian loans

general-emotive terms, though slightly fewer in proportion than in the previous century, is nevertheless still high, as befits a period in which interference movements are of great moment.[1] The nineteenth century inventory is almost exactly three times as long as the eighteenth. Otherwise the similarities rather than the differences are what strike one. Most of the semantic categories have their equivalent in the other period, and the main ones tend to correspond in the same proportion, i.e. in the ratio of one to three, or very nearly so. We might say that the nineteenth century pattern over the greater part of its semantic range is a vastly augmented projection of the eighteenth.[2] One major category, however, escapes from the strict ratio; technological and kindred terms (group No. 2) have expanded far beyond the average, increasing five-fold in the later period. It should not be hard to say why. Terms of warfare on the other hand appear to have become proportionately less abundant, and this too will require an explanation.

During the twenty-five years of the revolutionary–Napoleonic period political issues again come to have a direct bearing on Franco-Italian linguistic contacts, for the first time since the Italian wars in the first half of the sixteenth century.

Culturally and linguistically, as well as politically, the Napoleonic era from 1800 to 1815 and the three years of French domination in the revolutionary or republican period which preceded it shade one into the other to form a continuous, unique historical phenomenon. Yet as far as the impact of France on her southern neighbour is concerned there is a temporary regression in the march of events which forms a break corresponding exactly to our chosen century-by-century division. In early spring 1799 the forces of the Second Coalition moved against northern Italy. By late April Russo-Austrian forces under the Czarist general Suvarov were in Milan. To the reverses suffered by Schérer and Moreau in the north was added that of Macdonald at the crucial battle of Trebbia (17th–19th June). Soon the Parthenopean Republic of Naples followed the Cisalpine into liquidation and nothing remained of France's erstwhile revolutionary states but Genoa, the Republic of Liguria. For practical purposes, therefore, French hegemony is interrupted, to be established once more by Napoleon's reoccupation of the Peninsula in the first campaign season of the new century, hinging on the battle of Marengo (14th June 1800) and confirmed politically by the Peace of

1. A statistical check of all century-lists taken together shows that abstract-general-emotive groups are more numerous *proportionately to the century total* in periods of intimate contact (as well as more numerous in the absolute, of course). Nineteenth century ones account for 11.56 per cent of the total. In residuum periods they fall as low as around 5 per cent.

2. If we amalgamate groups 5, 6, and 7 as equally representative of the overall complex of home and social life, the same proportion of one to three is approximately maintained, i.e. 56 opposed to 189.

Lunéville, 9th February 1801. The point from which our inquiry sets out is therefore clear cut both in time and in matter.

For fifteen years, or one-seventh of the period we now have before us, French influence in Italy was exercised through the Emperor and his representatives of high or low degree, satellite kings, administrators and soldiers. Impressions Italians gained then remained with them and governed their attitude towards the other country long after Napoleon's exile and indeed after his death.[1] The Napoleonic legend revived in France under the Second Empire awoke nostalgic echoes in Italy too.

At the height of his political career Bonaparte enjoyed great personal prestige in Italy. After Marengo as after Campo Formio he was hailed as a liberator, and later exactions or tyrannical *boutades* do not seem to have eradicated wholly this vision of the man of destiny, the harbinger of a new world. His genius for convincingly assuming the personality best suited to the needs of the moment is proverbial; with his background it was no great task to project an image of himself which Italians would recognise and accept as their own. Italian was his first language; on the rare, carefully premeditated occasions when he formally presented himself before the people he scored immeasurable advantages by the simple fact of being able to harangue bystanders in their own tongue. His theatrical self-coronation with the Iron Crown of the Lombards in May 1805 was a calculated gesture, precisely the one needed to secure goodwill for his new Kingdom of Italy before handing over to his viceroy and 'adopted son' Eugène de Beauharnais. With our hindsight and modern experience of political posturing Bonaparte's stagemanship, the plumes and scimitars of his Mamelukes, the togas, laurel crowns and hastily commissioned Roman statues may strike us as faintly ridiculous, but there is scant evidence that Frenchmen and Italians or even subjects of the opposing powers saw them in anything but an awesome, menacing light. Napoleon's influence as an individual is a force we must reckon with.

No doubt we shall never know the truth about the Emperor's innermost feelings towards Italy. In his memoirs he always claimed to have had Italian unification and eventual independence in mind. But events during the imperial period itself show that opportunism largely ruled his actions. His over-riding concern, it would seem, was for the day-to-day advantage which manœuvres in the Peninsula might win for French power, and for himself as the embodiment of that power.[2]

1. In 1830 a wing of the liberals was thinking of Napoleon's nineteen-year-old son, the former *roi de Rome*, as a possible figure-head, while another favoured an appeal to Louis Bonaparte's male descendants.

2. *Vide* Rodolico, op. cit., pp. 569–73, *Idee e sentimenti di Napoleone rispetto all'Italia*. Bonaparte's first unequivocal statement that he desired to see Italy unified appears to have been that made in 1820 on hearing of the rising in Naples: 'Mes chers, mes bons

Lexically, the most immediate commentary on these years of foreign rule is to be found in military vocabulary.

All through the period France had the reputation of being Europe's major military power. In the early 1800s the fact was self-evident. The sheer number of French effectives, quite apart from warlike skills and traditions of infinitely long standing, made preponderance inevitable. At that time the population of France far outstripped any other Western nation. A temporary setback occurred in the Franco-Prussian conflict; yet in the first years of the twentieth century a young nobleman entering upon a military career was still able to see the French army as 'une des plus grandes choses du monde',[1] and most of Europe shared his impression.

Italian elements in the Napoleonic armies were ideally placed to acquire competence in the special vocabulary of warfare which had developed in French and to keep it in mind against the day when a truly national army should be raised. Large numbers were drawn into military service either as volunteers or, more usually, under the edicts of conscription which applied in all French-dominated areas. Thanks to the efforts of its vice-president Count Francesco Melzi d'Eril the refurbished Republic of Italy was able to hand over an army of twenty-three thousand men on the roll to Eugène de Beauharnais, who in his turn worked hard to foster a permanent military caste, aided by his capable war ministers Biragio and Caffarelli. Training closely followed French practice, with the same artillery, cavalry and infantry schools, the same intensive instruction in Bonapartist ideals. In the Regno Italico the army's maximum strength rose to ninety thousand men in 1813: in all one hundred and forty-two thousand men were conscripted from 1805 to 1814.[2] Italian levies served with distinction in other theatres of war, notably in the retreat from Russia.[3]

Recruitment went ahead on similar lines in the Kingdom of Naples, inefficiently at first under Joseph Bonaparte's capricious but relatively mild rule, more briskly later under Murat.[4]

Italiens! Les malheureux sont distribués par groupes, divisés, séparés. . . C'est cet esprit de tribu que je cherchais à détruire, c'est dans cette vue que j'avais réuni une partie de la péninsule à la France, érigé l'autre en royaume. . . . Je me proposais de faire de ces États agglomérés une puissance compacte, indépendante, sur laquelle mon second fils eût régné' (Rodolico, p. 569).

1. Charles de Gaulle, *Mémoires de guerre, L'Appel 1940–42, Livre de Poche* edition, 1954, p. 6. In the nineteenth century, one may add, France also had the notoriety of being the most militaristic of the Western nations.

2. See Owen Connelly, *Napoleon's Satellite Kingdoms*, New York and London, 1965, pp. 50–2.

3. Eugène's Royal Italian guard, for instance, was almost totally destroyed in its successful bid to hold the vital Luzha river crossing (24th Oct. 1812).

4. See Connelly, op. cit., pp. 86–9, 119. Obviously *mobilizzare, mobilizzazione* and

The number of military words introduced was highest in the earliest part of the period, as one would expect. The use of Italian, not French, was compulsory in Eugène's military academies, it is true, but the special vocabulary of warfare at this time was almost entirely French in origin and a whole terminology had to be taken across in thinly veiled adaptations. Once recruits were actually in the field contact with French became direct, not least because Napoleon made it a point of policy always to dilute Italian contingents, like those of other co-belligerents, by dispersing them within a larger corps of French troops from the home country.

Borrowed vocabulary is centred upon the individual soldier, his accoutrements and his duties. Typical items are *buffetteria*, a collective denoting belts, pouches and similar leather equipment, *cartucciera* 'cartridge-belt', *sabretascia*, part of a Hussar's uniform, *sciacco*, *pompon* (*pompò*) and the like; *piantone* 'picket', *appello* and *corvè* (Fr. *corvée*) 'fatigue', usually the more distasteful duties of camp life. A few words are names of newly established corps performing functions which one associates with more modern armies: *genio* ('engineer, sapper'), *pioniere* ('pioneer', occupied chiefly in road and camp construction). But the make-up and tactics of revolutionary–Napoleonic armies were still those of the eighteenth century: large mobile units of infantry supported by echelons of cavalry (*scaglione*), either cantooned in winter quarters (*accantonare*, *accantonamento*) or bivouacked in the field (*bivacco*), strictly limited for reasons of manoeuvrability to only a few kinds of heavy ancillary equipment—cannon (*avantreno*, *colpo di fuoco*), mobile dressing-stations (*ambulanza*) and supply wagons (*furgone*). Other terms relating to field warfare are *piano di guerra* (di *battaglia*), *avamposto*, *piazzare* ('to deploy', when applied to troops).

This conservatism in military matters explains why borrowings were not overwhelming in number, although they were of course very substantial. The basic terminology needed in Italian and other Western languages had already been established along with the techniques referred to.[1]

---

riservista are borrowings which need to be taken in this context: and *demoralizzare*, *demoralizzazione* too, perhaps, though in these loans the politico-revolutionary associations are also strong.

1. It must again be emphasised that our list does not pretend to be exhaustive. Many more borrowings would be revealed if one read through contemporary manuals and reports more vigilantly than I have done. Giuseppe Grassi's *Dizionario militare*, Turin, 1833, and subsequent editions could certainly provide more material, and so could Mariano d'Ayala's *Dizionario delle voci guaste* . . ., Turin, 1853, to say nothing of contemporary French-inspired journals. On the other hand a similar treatment applied to certain late eighteenth century works would doubtless help to redress the balance by increasing the total of known pre-Napoleonic terms—A. D'Antonj's *Architettura militare*, Turin, 1778, for instance.

Fortification was of less account than previously in these campaigns of long-distance flanking movements and battles in open terrain, though one remembers how strategy in northern Italy was based upon possession of the Quadrilateral or group of key fortresses to the south of Lake Garda lying athwart the approaches to Austria. In our list virtually the sole representative of this sub-group is *berma*, a detail of a *glacis* or sloping rampart.[1]

Parola d'ordine and *lasciapassare* are similar in import. Together with *appuntamento*, *semaforo* and *riservista* they represent what we might call the office-work, the rudimentary logistics of these armies on the threshold of the modern world.

The impact of French armies in Italy did not cease with Napoleon's downfall. Expeditionary forces returned to the Peninsula in 1832 and 1849 to maintain the *status quo* with Austria, while as we have already observed, during the crucial period of the struggle for Italian unity forces of Napoleon III and the King of Sardinia undertook joint military action, not always with complete understanding, in accordance with the plans drawn up in July 1858 at the *accords de Plombières* (battles of Magenta, Solferino). The continuity of French military influence is best shown by certain words of barrack-room slang which appear at dates dotted along the road of the century: *berlocca* 'stand-easy' or short rest period during the day's routine; *cicchetto* 'a sharp dressing-down, reprimand' (apparently an extension by antiphrasis from the sense 'nip, tot of liquor'); *musetta* 'kit-bag' (originally 'horse's nose-bag') and *marmittone* 'skiver', i.e. soldier who contrives to avoid fatigues, has himself allotted easy duties, and profits by similar selfish ploys of an underhand sort.[2]

Lastly one word, *mitragliatrice* 'machine-gun' (1875), a calque of Fr. *mitrailleuse* (1870), reminds us that France too had a hand in developing the mechanised weapons which made the grim man-versus-machine warfare of the twentieth century possible.

1. *Ridotta* 'redoubt' in its modern sense appears to have been borrowed much later in the century (1889, Guglielmotti, in our list). *Blindare* and *blindaggio* mainly figure in nautical contexts, but when used in connection with land-warfare they refer to movable protective screens rather than armour upon, say, an emplacement.

2. It is best to consider as *post-Napoleonic* loan-words only those which appear later than Grassi and d'Ayala. Both these authors generally understand that their material dates from the early years of the century, and often say so explicitly. Further, one can trace some borrowings from actual Bonapartist times—in Bernardoni, for instance, or later editions of Alberti—though dialect dictionaries and Restoration sources down to both Grassi and d'Ayala, where they are explained or criticised on exactly the same footing as terms which, according to our present information, are registered first in these authorities. In other words my research into this lexical field convinces me that Grassi and d'Ayala together with most sources up to the mid-century (Botta, Giusti, Cherubini, Tramater, Ugolini, for instance) drew their military documentation directly or indirectly from that earlier period.

And so it comes about that the special vocabulary of war continues to be ready currency between the two languages at the end of our survey, as at the beginning. Its position within the lexicon of special languages, however, becomes progressively weaker from the seventeenth century forward. Even taking other sources of military words into our calculations—Spanish in the sixteenth to seventeenth centuries, German later—does not greatly alter the trend whereby war terms gradually decline in proportion to those of science and industry; it only makes the reversal of emphasis less abrupt. For this reason we might say that for the social lexicologist, despite first appearances, the nineteenth is a century of peace. He stands to gain more useful information from economic historians than from chroniclers of campaigns.[1]

There are others of these historical or political borrowings which are overt, immediately accessible, in the sense that they are taken into Italian as a natural sequel to changes in modes of government. Some are new technical terms directly linked with the foreign regime which was imposed—*prefetto* (1802), a patently Napoleonic Latinism, for instance; *regia*; and in a special connection, *marengo*; also a fair crop of legal-cum-political words: (*corte di*) *cassazione*, (*poteri*) *eccezionali*, *aggiornare*, *vagabondaggio* 'vagrancy' and the wider-ranging abstracts *codificazione* and *legiferare*.[2] A few fall ominously upon the ear: *attruppamento* 'gathering, especially seditious assembly', as in *legge contro gli attruppamenti* 'Riot act'; *terrorizzare*, originally to conduct a purge similar to the *Terreur*, but used in increasingly generalised contexts as the century progressed, and a number of police or security service terms: *sorvegliare*, *sorveglianza* (i.e. police surveillance), *spionaggio*, *segnaletico* as in *dati segnaletici* 'identification marks', *complotto*. These last remind us how much political activity in the first half of the *Ottocento* was carried on by clandestine movements, prominent among them the *Carbonari* we spoke of a little while

1. Overall statistics of military borrowings are as follows: Med.It. > Fr. 26 (out of a century total of 185); Med.Fr. > It. 45 (278); 16th cent. It. > Fr. 51 (462); 16th cent. Fr. > It. 20 (72); 17th cent. It. > Fr. 7 (203); 17th cent. Fr. > It. 29 (100); 18th cent. It. > Fr. 1 (106); 18th cent. Fr. > It. 11 (260); 19th cent. It. > Fr. 1 (81); 19th cent. Fr. > It. 41 (765); total 232 out of grand total of 2512, i.e. 9.24 per cent of all categories. It is interesting to divide the latter into two periods, pre- and post-1600. Before 1600 military loans accounted for 14.24 per cent of all categories; after 1600, only 6.0 per cent.

2. The amended body of statutes styled with the Emperor's approval the *Code Napoléon*, which proved one of the greatest monuments to French hegemony in nineteenth century Europe, took effect in France and direct dependencies during March 1804. It was promulgated in the satellite states after some delay (1st Jan. 1806 in the Kingdom of Italy; during 1805 a six-man commission had translated it into Italian and Latin for use in the Peninsula). Other legalisms in our list are *giurí* (ult. from English), the term of civil law *parcella* 'parcel of land' and ephemeral appelations like *parquet* (*parchè*) for the office of the Procuratore del Re later in the century (q.v., *supra*).

ago, acting by means of conspiracies and attempted *coups d'état* (*colpo di stato*).[1]

A few of the borrowings which go to make up section 3 above are what may most fittingly be called *diplomatic* terms, viz. *attaccato* 'attaché' esp. at an embassy, *ultimatum, paraffare* 'to initial a document prior to its being ratified by the government concerned', *vidimare* 'to approve, give a visa to a document' (especially a passport or safe-conduct), together with *vidimazione*. These are only out-cropping Gallicisms of a very extensive stratum; they draw our attention to the fact that by the nineteenth century France had become the accredited diplomatic language of all Western countries. In discussing *Settecento* borrowings we observed that French, with its newly acquired international standing, was already beginning to take over from Latin in the area of diplomacy, one of its last strongholds. By the early 1800s victory was complete and the status of French remained unchallenged right down to our own time. In the nineteenth century political dominance and the historical accident of French as a European cultural language worked to the same end and made French the supreme international auxiliary.[2]

With political I have included bureaucratic terms, by which I mean close on thirty loans like *autorizzare* 'to authorise' or *personale* 'personnel', especially of a government department, focused on the key term *burocrazia*. Professional administrators and lesser functionaries had acquired unprecedented

1. In 1830 and 1848, most notably, though Italian history up to the 1870s is chequered with plots and counter-plots, many of them associated with supporters of Mazzini and the *Giovine Italia* movement. In northern Italy during 1820 and 1821 the police arrested as conspirators a number of intellectuals whose sufferings in *carcere duro* at Venice and in the Spielberg found a place in heroic literature, thanks to the masterpiece *Le Mie Prigioni* written by one of their number, Silvio Pellico. Among the condemned was young Count Federigo Confalonieri, contributor to the *Conciliatore* (see below), liberal propagandist, economist, reformer and industrial pioneer. After the Restoration, as in the interval between Trebbia and Marengo, many exiles sought refuge in French-speaking countries—Switzerland and Belgium, apart from France itself—and many clandestine activities were directed from there. These expatriates constituted a French-speaking group of considerable importance.

2. In one of the drafts of his uncompleted master work *Della lingua italiana* Manzoni relates a kind of parable to show how the mere fact of being able to communicate is not the same as possessing a language in common. He imagines a conversation between 'tre persone, una ... di Madrid, una di Londra, una di Dresda, ignari ciascheduno delle lingue degli altre due, e aventi ciascheduno un tal quale cognizion del francese' (*vide* Barbara Reynolds, *The Linguistic Writings of Alessandro Manzoni*, Cambridge, 1950, p. 152; also p. 87). Manzoni's choice of French as intermediary is symptomatic of the age, even though it is not his purpose to emphasise this fact, but rather the reverse (he goes on to analyse in a *tour de force* of linguistic perceptivity the shifts, approximations and other devices which each speaker might have to use to make his meaning clear). At the date when this passage was written—ostensibly 1833–36 (*vide* Reynolds, p. 138)—Manzoni had no choice but to cite 'French' as his example or do without his allegory.

influence during the upheavals which marked the *Settecento's* close (*vide funzionario* 1796, eighteenth century list). The position of power which they continued to enjoy in the new century attracted ambitious career-seekers and *funzionarismo* 'excessive demand for employment in public offices' became as in France a recognisable social trend (1877; *vide* word-list. Cf. also *appuntamento* and the use of *piazza* meaning 'situation, job' [*vide piazzare*, note]). A lot remains to be written about what France has contributed to the restricted language of administration and also to officialese in other European tongues. French has long been the most productive source of terms and locutions one has come to regard as typical of, inseparable from, the language of local and central government.

I have just spoken of administrative language and officialese, using a neutral and a derogatory epithet. The layman in any Western country—to venture no farther afield—is aware that there are traits in administrative idiom which place it poles apart from the language of everyday use. A surprising number of them can be detected in the official jargon Italian drew from French early in our period. More interesting still, one can see how these characteristics were acquired by studying the style and semantic incidentals of political jargon at the most important stage in its growth, the late eighteenth and early nineteenth centuries.

Political jargon as we are familiar with it nowadays arose during the last decade before 1800 as a result of intense political proselytism. We have seen how certain central elements of its vocabulary assumed an almost incantatory force—*libertà, patriotto, fraternizzare, rivoluzionario, giacobino, sanculotto*—and observed that this special semantic quality was lost as the political wind shifted. The detached, military, oracular *débit* which revolutionary propagandists affected, first in France, then by a striking transposition of style in Italy too, reappeared in Napoleonic proclamations with certain of its characteristics radically altered. The military resonance and disembodied, authoritative tone still remained, but the vibrant, emotive component tended gradually to be replaced by flat legalising phraseology, often heavily Latinising, in which the self-important suffixes *-izzare, -izzazione, -ismo, -ista* were increasingly used, with their official *cachet* and vague threat of coercion. Examples are *autorizzare* already cited, *collettivizzare, localizzare, nazionalizzare organizzare, terrorizzare, totalizzare, uniformizzare* and their corresponding abstracts *autorizzazione, nazionalizzazione,* etc.[1]

Whatever doubts we may now feel, or the folk of those days may have felt about what their information was worth, Revolutionary propagandists did genuinely strive to inform people. Nineteenth century officialese on the contrary was more concerned to be non-committal, to leave room for man-

1. See observations on these suffixes in Part III, *Formal and non-formal criteria*; also M-*Stor.*, p.643 and ibid., notes 3, 4.

œuvre while still purporting to issue crisp, unequivocal orders which authoritarian government has to give for its very survival. Lexically the upshot was that nineteenth century administrators often found themselves at a fork, obliged to choose between an ambivalent word and one devoid of meaning. Dipping again into our list I find several examples of this kind of bureaucratic jargon: *attivare, mettere in attività* or *realizzare* meaning merely 'to do, carry out'; *paralizzare* in the sense 'stop, suspend' (e.g. payments); *afferente* 'concerning'; as well as a good proportion of the *-izzare/-izzazione* words mentioned.

Gallicism in public offices was a live question all through the last century. Authors of purist dictionaries and other *Antibarbari* were more than usually bitter about these tokens of continuing political dependence on France, as they saw them. There is a nucleus of several hundred barbarisms or alleged barbarisms in governmental, forensic and local government usage which appears in almost all these normative works, a constant, basic vocabulary to which language reformers take exception and which they discuss from decade to decade. A good proportion of these are almost certainly inspired by French. Here is a sample: *assopire* 'to shelve', of a problem; *aderire(a)* 'to join', e.g. a party; *attesa*, as in *in attesa di riposto*, 'in anticipation of...' (loan-creation < Fr. *attente?*); *accommodamento* 'compromise'; *addottare* (of a proposal); *affiliarsi, -azione*; *arretrato* 'late on schedule' (calque of *arriéré*); *carica* 'office, appointment'; *caricare* as equivalent to *segnare, notare, porre* ('caricate questa tabella delle notizie occorrenti e rimandetela' [F-A., 1877]); *centralizzare, -azione*; *compulsare* (*un documento, un archivio*) 'to check, scrutinise'; *datare* ('a datare del venturo mese'); *defezionare* 'to desert'; *demordere* 'to yield, cease to follow up'; *difesa* 'prohibition'; *decesso* 'death' (esp. in vital statistics); *destinatario* 'addressee'; *effrazione* (as in *furto con e.*); *emettere* 'to publish, make known'; *inquietante* 'disturbing' (rumours, e.g.); *insuccesso* 'failure'; *provvisorio* 'provisional'; *regolarizzare; rinvio, -are* 'delay, to reject, remand'; *precisare* 'to specify, make clear' (but often in contexts where nothing is clarified); *segnatario* 'signatory'.[1]

Not every reformer was so intransigent. A critic whose fairness and competence impresses one, G. Bernardoni, published in 1812 a report on official usage for the *Regno Italico*'s Minister of the Interior, Vaccari. A functionary himself, Bernardoni was aware that in the long run officialese is a special language like that of any other profession or technology and therefore indispensable within its context.[2] This is why a good proportion of our borrowings under section 3 do after all give the impression of performing a useful

1. Drawn from Ugolini 1848 and 1855, Fanfani-Arlia 1877 and 1890, Rigutini 1886 and 1891. See reflexions on puristic vocabularies below. The most widely used borrowings are included in our list.

2. *Vide infra*, Part V, p. 712, details of words approved in the *Elenco*.

N

function: *abbonarsi, -amento*; *chilometraggio* meaning 'travelling allowance'; *controllo, -are, -atore*; *constatare, -azione*; *dimissionario*; *demarcare, -azione*; *personale*; *radiare* 'to cross out'; *rendiconto* or *resoconto*; *referenza*; *timbro, timbrare*. *Interpellare* and *interpellanza* 'to ask a question in the House' refer specifically to parliamentary processes and so does *ballotaggio* 'second scrutiny' and of course *parlamentarismo*.[1]

The final link, the cohesive ingredient in this complex of borrowings which I have ranged under the generic heading of *political*, might be called a psychological commonplace—a traditional feeling of one country towards the other. The idea which many Italians had nurtured of France as *fons et origo* of political idealism crystallised into an accepted convention during the initial years of the Revolutionary era. As we saw in the last chapter, France was understood to be the heart-land of enlightened Europe. She had adopted and made her own the doctrines of the new age, which included among their theoretical projects political advancement, human brotherhood in equality and an intentional, willed progress towards a new world order which would be at once just and reasonable. This was for the future: but by accepting her interpretative role France bound herself to ensure that in due course these ideals should be realised. The Revolution added deeds to words and proved the good faith of Frenchmen in this matter, so that even though they may have been seen to fall short of their own ideals on later occasions, the vision of France as the author of a new deal for Europe persisted. It was therefore natural that Italians should seek out France as their ally during the Risorgimento. The balance of power and geographical position demanded it, and this is no doubt the operative reason why the alliance was made; but it is also true to say that the *ethos* of Franco-Italian political relationships favoured it, even at that late date.

Italians like other Europeans were attentive to the systems of political and sociological thought which were conceived in France from time to time during the period we are now contemplating, or which spread from there. This and the previous point explain why so many Gallicisms were borrowed which define or label political doctrines, policies, attitudes, abuses: *autoritarismo* (*autocrate*), *militarismo, collettivismo, collettivizzazione* (*collettivizzare*), *femminismo, umanitarismo, intransigenza, boicottaggio,* (*boicottare*), *assenteismo* (referring originally to English absentee tenure and government in Ireland), *élite, blocco* meaning 'group of political parties', *babuvismo,*[2] *sansimonianismo, com-*

1. The first parliament of the unified Kingdom of Italy met in Turin on 18th Feb. 1861. In the early 20th century *parlamentarismo* became a derogatory term as parliamentary institutions came under an increasing weight of criticism (*vide* word-list).

2. In France Gracchus Babeuf's earlier form of communism ('la terre n'est à personne, les fruits en sont à tout le monde') was proscribed and its supporters made liable to the death penalty by a law of April 1796. The early 19th century was a golden age for social theorists. Other doctrines known in Italy were those of Saint-Simon, Fourier and Leroux

munismo,[1] etc. In like manner actual happenings on the French political scene aroused ready interest in Italy. At the century's end the word *borderò*, which had been borrowed earlier as a common-or-garden civil service term, was heard on everyone's lips as a result of the Dreyfus affair with its famous *bordereau* found in the German embassy waste-paper-basket listing French military secrets apparently handed over to that power.[2] *Comunardo* had its moment in the sun when the ill-fated *Commune* was declared in Paris after government broke down in 1871 as a result of the Franco-Prussian War. *Crumiro* and *crumiraggio* (q.v., word-list) relate to trades union activities ('black-legging') and this was also the situational context of *sabotage/sabotaggio* in the first place. Later in the century *sciovinismo* (*chauvinisme*) was used of excessive Italian nationalism as well as French.

It. *regime* (Fr. *régime*) in its nineteenth century sense of 'form, prevailing system of government' is an appropriate key-word to this lexical grouping (see 18th cent. loans, s.v.), supported by *sociologia* (1865, < Fr. *sociologie* 1830, Auguste Comte).

Of those who disseminated political and social doctrines or acted upon them to the best of their power the great majority were members of the middle classes. The nineteenth century was their age in Italy as it was in France and other Western countries. This holds good for the whole of the period. Only as the twentieth century approached did measures to provide universal education begin to make the mass of people count for something in new cultural trends and therefore in the process of lexical innovation. Oddly enough working people on the land and in cities were in a position to wield greater

(the *socialistes*) and Blanqui, whose extreme left-wing party was active in and immediately after 1848, as well as under the *Commune*.

1. *Comunismo* (< Fr. *communisme*) was first applied to co-operative movements on the land. In and before Marx's time it was only one of several related systems whose influence waxed and waned with the political fashion of the day. Cf. Giusti's slighting description of Giuseppe Montanelli's changing political and moral loyalties: 'Nel '31 il Montanelli fu della Giovine Italia, nel '33 sansimonista, poi socialista e comunista; poi ateo; poi bacchettone, poi giobertiano, poi daccapo Mazziniano' (*Cronaca dei fatti di toscana dal 1845* . . ., *Gr. diz. it.*, III, 448, s.v. *comunista*[2]).

Intellectual or *philosophical* abstracts as we have previously called them fit in admirably here. *Ideologia* < Fr. *idéologie* (1796) sums up the lexically productive qualities we have been analysing. *Altruismo* was coined by Auguste Comte (*altruisme*, 1830), whose philosophy of *positivism* dominated the century until the last decades (*Cours de philosophie positive*, 1830–42). Origins of the word *pessimism* (It. *pessimismo*) go back to the 18th century, though the concept was established by Schopenhauer's philosophy (1788–1860). Associated principally with Romantic literature, it reached Italian as a borrowing from Fr. *pessimisme*. See *ottimismo*, 18th cent. loans. Other terms are *oltramontano, -ismo*, freely used at the Vatican Council of 1869–70 by those who pressed for a definition of Papal infallibility, *dinamismo, egotismo* and *umanitario, -ismo* cited earlier.

2. Also *dreyfusardo, -ista* (M-*Stor.*, 712) and the otherwise undistinguished word *dossier*.

power in the century's opening years, had the organisation existed for them to do so, because the Napoleonic armies needed them for recruits and depended on products of innumerable individual craftsmen for their war material. It did actually happen on rare occasions that the lower orders took a hand in shaping historical events,[1] but such interventions were only episodes. It remains true that the working or peasant classes exerted no political or cultural influence at a level which might affect the fortunes of Gallicism on Italian territory.[2]

French was widely known among the middle and upper classes, as it had been already in the *Settecento*. How many people might have been called bilingual, though, is not at all easy to say. A visitor to Turin in 1831 reported that he 'heard French spoken all round him',[3] and this would have been true even more of the early period in those areas directly occupied by France, if only because many French nationals were there. But taking the mid-century as one's norm, one might say that French was not ordinarily used as a spoken language outside a small minority of the northern aristocracy and upper middle class.[4] The impact of French at all social levels was greatest in the northwest, with its apogee in Piedmont and Savoy, and for that reason its influence diminished when the unified Kingdom of Italy was established and the seat of government shifted first to Florence then to Rome (1871). The same thing happened when, with the reaction against *piemontesismo*, army officers, statesmen and administrators who had played a major role during the *Risorgimento* were gradually replaced by people from the centre and south.

On the other hand a moderately large number of Italians could read French easily, their fluency being proportional to their degree of education and therefore to their competence in other branches of learning, notably in the Classics. We are therefore only concerned at best with the literate population, which in 1861 amounted to approximately one-fifth of all Italian subjects. One would expect a professionally qualified man to know French well, and the same might apply to girls of first the upper classes, then as the century progressed, of the middle and even lower middle, given that they had

1. As when the *lazzaroni* of Naples rose against the Parthenopean Republic in 1799 and returned the Bourbons to power.

2. One small qualification is due here. An interesting Franco-Italian contact on a lower social plane took place through seasonal journeys abroad by itinerant workers from Italy, mainly on the land, but some in building and other trades, particularly before the great period of immigration into the United States began. Presumably they acquired sufficient French to meet the needs of their job. Some may have passed it on to their families. This is another topic on which lexicologists need guidance from social historians.

3. M-*Stor.*, p. 619.

4. In this century as before many well-to-do Italians stayed temporarily in French-speaking countries, often for long periods, and their numbers were swelled by the political refugees we referred to earlier, who were also mainly from the middling levels of society.

attended a good college or perhaps benefited from a French nanny or governess.[1] As in the *Settecento* members of the higher strata of society together with writers and intellectuals often corresponded in French, among them Manzoni.[2]

Thus all through the century, but particularly during the early decades, French fulfilled an indispensable function as an auxiliary to Italian in the sphere of intellectual, scientific and even technological activity.[3] The service French rendered there was in some ways analogous to its position as the language of diplomacy, with the important reservation that its use in technology, say, was more a matter of convenience than necessity and was far from being generally accepted in the way diplomatic French was. On the contrary, there was a steady opposition to French in other areas of usage—or more, in all areas of usage during this period. We shall take this point a little further shortly.

In the nineteenth century works translated into French from other languages continued to be an important source of information for educated Italian readers. Innumerable renderings made the works of German, British, American, Swiss technicians and scientists immediately available to their opposite numbers in Italy. They are usually commendably accurate; often a German or English text gains in precision and readability during the passage through its French *phasis*. Translations of literary texts turn out less satisfactorily. It is notoriously difficult to do justice to a work of literature in translation, and writers of the Romantic and pre-Romantic period, whether hack translators or recognised literary figures, were seldom concerned to render a foreign work with philological accuracy. Usually their aim was the wholly natural one of exploiting the source as material for personal artistic creation. It is an amiable distortion, but distortion none the less, and one which French at that time for reasons that are partly literary and partly stylistic was specially prone to. A good instance of the position of French in this respect appears in the *Conciliatore* of 4th March 1819, where Berchet introduces his forthcoming adaptation of the Sanskrit drama the *Sakuntala*. His version appeared two numbers later. During the course of the article, which is

1. Disparaging remarks by purists about the word *bonne* confirm that it was common by the middle of the century to employ a French-speaking nurse. Savoy provided an ideal source: the region was closely linked culturally to France even before it was ceded to Napoleon III in 1860. See word-list, s.v. *bonne*.

2. Manzoni's *rapport* with French as a young man was typical of his time. In Professor Devoto's words, 'il Manzoni si era affacciato alla tradizione linguistica dal di fuori, dominandone essenzialmente il solo aspetto espressivo attraverso la padronanza del dialetto, e quello tecnico sopranazionale attraverso la conoscenza del francese' (*Profilo*, p. 124).

3. In the early 1800s some Gallophiles went so far as to urge that French should be accepted as the cultural language of Italy, e.g. C. Denina in *Dell'uso della lingua francese*, Berlin, 1803. *Vide* M-*Stor.*, p. 619 and note.

couched in the form of a little play featuring himself and members of the public, Berchet's helpful observation that there are faithful English and German translations available is received coolly: 'E chi non sa d'inglese come fa a legger la Sacontala?' A Latin translation exists, but it has not been printed (the audience expresses disappointment). There is the French translation by M. Bruguière—the laymen's sigh of resignation is almost audible—but, warns Berchet, 'non trovo in essa quelle bellezze che veggo nelle altre due, e che secondo il creder mio non possono provenire che dall'originale'. 'Ad ogni modo,' replies *Uno dei lettori* stoically, 'meglio qualche cosa che niente.' The dialogue rings true. We sense that whether he intended it or no, Berchet in a few introspective lines has characterised an important aesthetic and linguistic relationship very precisely.[1]

The Industrial Revolution came to Italy late for a number of causes among which the repressive political regime after 1815 looms large, together with the economic fact that the chief raw materials needed for industrialisation were in short supply—coal, iron and capital. But most serious of all, the middle classes whose boldness and ingenuity had transformed Britain, France and other Western countries were not fully prepared in the first place to trust themselves with the enterprise of bringing Italy into line with 'the spirit of the century'. During the Napoleonic conflicts middle-class *entrepreneurs* had prospered through the demand for war equipment but had hastened to invest their gains in the traditional security of land.[2] The first half of the nineteenth century is a time of political and economic crusading, when a progressive

1. In its editorial policy, the tone of its contributors, and choice of its articles *Il Conciliatore* is an exemplar of the position adopted by Italian intellectuals with respect to France, other European nations and the world at large during the Restoration. Skimming through a few months' issues we find reviews of Marie-Joseph Chénier's *Henri VIII* and *Philippe II* (relating, that is, to England and Spain) alongside others of Schiller, Grillparzer and Sheridan; a French roving journalist's Petrarchian impressions on visiting Vaucluse; notices on recently published economic, historical and philosophical works, some French—Guingené, *Histoire de l'Italie*, Chaptal, *De l'Industrie française*—but a number of them British—Lauderdale's *Inquiry into the Nature and Origin of Public Wealth* and a medical treatise by T. V. Morgan, *Sketches on the Philosophy of Life* (actually a review of a French translation [1819], not the original English work of 1818). A précis of Benjamin Constant's formal eulogy of the philanthropist Sir Samuel Romilly is another strikingly 'European' article. Most of the *varietà straniere* have a French bias (resettlement of French exiles in the southern U.S.A.) and there are notes on French journals. The impression one goes away with is that France and the French language are valued as *auxiliaries*, as points of reference, but also that they stand as cultural and linguistic *intermediaries*, even at this early date.

2. Traditional since the seventeenth century, that is. Italian sociologists have recognised in this tendency one of the main reasons why commercial prosperity, upon which the Renaissance with all its achievements had been based, fell into decline. Nineteenth century economic propagandists made it their mission to root out this ingrained habit and so free capital for industrial ventures.

section of the *bourgeosie*, mainly from the north of Italy, allied to and in the main guided by a powerful minority of landed aristocracy who shared their hopes for Italy's future, gradually brought a working majority of their class round to their new way of thinking. Their practical programme of action, like their philosophy, was all-embracing and its elements were inter-dependent. Economic and social betterment they felt to be a necessary prelude to concerted political action and hence to natural unity; unity and free associative effort in its turn would foster the industrial power needed for increasing prosperity and progress. Progress, the guiding principle and practical under-pin of the nineteenth century view of life, was understood to imply a perpetual condition of directed, harmonious expansion. As an ideal it too goes back well into the eighteenth century and is attributable in good measure to French thinkers.

Much of this work of propaganda was achieved in monographs by political personalities of the day; men like Gioberti in his *Primato morale e civile degli Italiani* (1843), d'Azeglio in *Ultimi Casi di Romagna* (1846), Cesare Balbo in *Le Speranze d'Italia* (1844) and Mazzini in all of his many-sided repertoire. But for us who are interested in the material effects of the tech-nological age in Italy, in the *things* with which our *words* are associated, the liberal journals of this era are more revealing.[1] The principal ones are *Annali di Statistica* (1824–48), under the aegis of a formidable old revolutionary Gian Domenico Romagnosi, Giacinto Battaglia's *Rivista europea* (1838–48) and the *Politecnico*, founded and controlled by that Admirable Crichton of resurgent Italy, Carlo Cattaneo.[2] Expressing the eclectic, encyclopaedic views of their promoters, these *Annali* and *Riviste* drew their material from many corners of national and international life, rather after the fashion of their short-lived precursor the *Conciliatore* but with greater emphasis on the useful arts and crafts and on applied science, the *cognizioni utili*.[3] A sense of exas-perated dissatisfaction with the present is found in them all, coupled with an exalted, prophetic feeling of optimism for the future.

All these endeavours had their effect upon the lexicon and on Franco-

1. A very full account was given of the journals' economic and technical contribution and their underlying principles a good while ago in K. R. Greenfield, *Economics and Liberalism in the Risorgimento*, Baltimore, 1934. I refer the reader to this work, especially Part II, Ch. 1, *The National Program of the Journals*. All these periodicals deserve to be examined carefully by etymologists. Their popular technical and scientific articles, and above all their *précis* of foreign works in these fields are an excellent source of adapted forms. They go back to the beginnings of modern Italian technology.

2. Carlo Cattaneo, 1801–69, economist, publicist and politician; initiated positivism in Italy, with a social bias influenced especially by the Saint-Simonians. Occupied himself with and had expert knowledge of railways, land reclamation, the fiscal system, agricul-ture, finance, geography, literature, philology and history.

3. Out of fifteen periodicals which by 1830 were being published in Milan seven were devoted to science and technical subjects (Greenfield, op. cit., p. 169). The titles of

Italian borrowings to the extent that France and the other French-speaking regions of Belgium and Switzerland contributed to them by providing information and taking part in mutual trade. The words we have to evaluate under this heading—technological, scientific, commercial, financial categories —are very numerous indeed. Comprising a little over 300 words, or 40 per cent of this century-list, they make up the largest grouping of special vocabularies within the precinct of our study. Most of them date from the later decades.

By spring 1861 the politicians' struggle was as good as over, yet the *operosa borghesia* they had helped to create had barely begun to feel its feet. The first generation of successful industrialists coincided with the Risorgimento's climactic period (Rubattino, Orlando, Cristoforo Crespi and their coevals); those who succeeded them left Italy the industrial country it is today. By 1900 the densely populated northern and western subalpine region was making a contribution to the country's economy very similar, *mutatis mutandis*, to that of Picardy, the Meuse valley or the Ruhr.

Railway terminology is the most characteristic of the engineering vocabularies.

Development of Italy's railway network began slowly because of opposition from the Austrian government who regarded an integrated communications system as politically dangerous. Nationalistic pressure-groups with Cavour as their most successful champion supported new projects for the very same reason. By 1859, twenty years after the first short line from Naples to Portici was opened, Piedmont still accounted for half of the total track mileage. Contacts with France were therefore close; French capital and engineering skill were widely employed.[1] Words borrowed relate to track: *controrotaia, longarina, deragliare, deragliamento*;[2] to rolling stock: *locomotiva, furgone, treno, vagone, tampone, tamponare*; to personnel: *chauffeur, cantoniere*

---

different *Annali* give an idea of their scope: *Annali universali di statistica, economia pubblica, storia, viaggi e commercio*; *A. universali di agricoltura, di economia rurale e domestica*; *A. di fisica, chimica e scienze affini*; *A. di medicina e chirurgia*, etc. The catholic quality of Italian liberalism is seen equally well in the lives of their contributors. Cavour, for example, was a qualified engineer and an energetic company director before he concentrated on the work of statesmanship which assured him his place in history; Massimo d'Azeglio achieved a second fame by his historical novels, which he himself viewed as part of the political struggle (*Ettore Fieramosca*, [1833], *Niccolò de' Lapi* [1841]). Confalonieri found time from his journalism to order a steam engine from Boulton and Watt and build the first steamboat to navigate the river Po.

1. The French engineer E. Biot's work on railway construction *Manuel du constructeur des chemins de fer*, Paris, 1834 was translated into Italian in 1837. Earlier Biot collaborated with the Séguin brothers, engineers to the first French railway company (Lyon–Saint-Etienne, 1826), who were directly in touch with George Stephenson.

2. The last two are very probably from French, though usually cited as Anglicisms (which in any case they ultimately are). English *to derail* does not possess the passive usage 'to *become* derailed' which is normal in French and Italian.

('linesman', whose duty is to look after an allotted section of track); to stations and ancillary buildings: *lampisteria* 'lamp-room' and *garage* 'siding, sheds', etc., a word which acquired this sense in French from its original one of 'canal basin'. The 'block' system of signalling and traffic control were adopted (*blocco, bloccare* in this context). *Raile* 'rail', a crucial, frequently used term which denoted the original invention which made this system of transport possible, was replaced after a time by the native coinages *rotaia* and *binario*. Almost all these forms originated in English but were adopted by Italians from French usage.

Political controversy about railway building was at its height in the later forties, after Count Ilarione di Petitti published his *Delle strade ferrate e del migliore ordinamento di esse* (Capolago, 1845). Cavour intervened with a powerful review article on Pettiti's work in *La Revue Nouvelle*, 1st May 1846 ('Les Chemins de fer en Italie'). It was not the first time he had aired his opinions on the topic.[1] The Piedmontese statesman's policy was clear cut and dynamic. Progress for him came on iron rails, and so did national unification. In 1857 he gave orders to begin work on the Mont Cenis tunnel (more accurately described by the Italian name of *Galleria di Fréjus*) which in 1871 linked France to Italy and gave an unprecedented fillip to industrial expansion. While the work was going forward an interesting temporary mountain railway was constructed over the Mont Cenis pass, with a form of rack and pinion traction known as the Fell system ('il sistema Fell'). *Cremagliere* 'rack' or toothed driving rail and *funicolare* remain to put us in mind of these and similar pioneering experiments.

Appretto, apprettare 'filling', 'finishing' of cloth and *bobina* 'spool' of thread for spinning, also 'spindle', are a meagre harvest for one of the classic manufactures of the Industrial Revolution. Sericulture is not represented in this century list, although silk reeling and weaving was the most lucrative of Italian industries up to the '50s, expanding its production phenomenally to supply and later compete with the silk manufactories of Lyons.[2] Names of textiles taken from French are on the other hand quite plentiful, presumably because of the element of fashion which enters into them. The dozen recorded in our list are only the best-known cloths;[3] by 1900 new names were being

---

1. He contributed an article entitled 'Della strada di ferro da Ciamberi al lago di Bourget e della navigazione a vapore su quel lago e sul Rodano' to the *Annali* in 1840 (Vol. LXIII, pp. 103–7).

2. According to the *Annali* the number of spindles for twisting silk in the Como region alone grew from 2550 in 1830 to 162,000 in 1855 (Greenfield, p. 100). By the later date the textile industry as a whole was securely installed in the region it occupies today, round Gallarate, Busto Arsizio and Monza.

3. *Brillantina* (a glazed cloth with lustrous finish), *calicò, cretonne, crêpe (crespo), grenadina, lamè, madampolam, organdis, peluscio* (originally loaned to French in the 16th century), *percalle, picchè (piqué), popeline, tulle, zeffiro.*

coined for every novelty of weave and texture. French was the main source of them.

Drenaggio and *drenare*, 'to drain' were used from the '50s referring to land reclamation. Several regions of derelict land round Naples were won back and resettled under Ferdinand I and II; a royal decree of 11th May 1855 (coinciding roughly in time with our borrowings) was a pioneering measure of modern legislation on these matters. *Debordare* in its literal sense is a connected term.

Artesian wells—*pozzi artesiani* (1859)— were exploited in France from the Middle Ages in the Artois basin, whence their name, but the attention of hydraulic engineers from other countries was captured by attempts to supply Paris with water by this method (Mulot's drilling at Grenelle, 1833–41; at Passy in 1855–57) and to find water under the Sahara, also in the '50s. Another hydrodynamic term is *turbina* 'water-turbine' for driving machinery, later for generating electricity, a key-word in a branch of engineering where Frenchmen have always been to the fore (*vide* word-entry).

French inventors, too, were responsible for the major techniques of photography, represented by several items in our list: *dagherrotipo, -ia; fotografo, -ia, -are; cliscè (cliché)* 'negative' and *châssis* 'printing-frame'. The last two were also drawn from French as typographical terms, 'stereotype plate' and 'printer's "chase"' respectively, and so form a group with *trafiletto, alinea* and *plancia* in the sense of 'engraving'.

Christofle, pacfong (names of alloys), *lingotto, metallizzare, -azione, lavage* and the pivotal term *ghisa* 'cast-iron' are all connected with metallurgy and preparing metal for manufacture. In my eyes a group of special significance is formed by words relating to the construction of machinery, particularly the heavy steam-driven machinery one associates with the Victorian age and in Italy with names like Ansaldo[1] and Tosi:[2] *putrella* 'girder', *tola* 'sheet-iron', *biella* 'connecting rod', *volante* 'fly-wheel', *ciminiera* 'funnel, smoke-stack', *bullone* 'bolt, screw'—the very atom of mechanical engineering—*montaggio* 'assembly, fitting of machinery', *basculla, carter, châssis* in its usual sense; the names of special trades—*montatore* 'fitter', *fumista* 'stove-setter' and even their working clothes—*blusa, salopette*.

Aviazione, dirigibile 'dirigible balloon, airship' and *paracadute* are forerunners of an array of borrowings in the twentieth century up to and including the

---

1. G. Ansaldo founded the engineering firm which was to bear his name in 1853 at Sampierdarena (Genoa). Though the naval constructional interests were continued and developed (Sestri Levante), a broad range of other engineering activities were included, forming a vast industrial complex by the end of the century.

2. Franco Tosi (b. Milan, 1850; d. Legnano, 1898). Constructional engineer specialising in boiler-making and steam-engine production. Associated particularly with the firm of Cantoni, Krumm & Co. at Legnano, of which he became the owner in 1894.

Great War which may be correlated to France's dominant position in the aircraft industry during its earlier stages. The nineteenth century loans refer to lighter-than-air machines, of course.[1] *Paracadute*, which is attested as early as 1832 and may date from the beginning of the century, referred initially to the large parachute attached to a balloon by which an intrepid balloonist descended to provide the *pièce de résistance* of an aerial display.

Locomobile 'steam traction engine', a modern form of transport needed to handle heavy industrial loads, contrasts singularly with nineteenth century refinements of the ancient craft of carriage-building—the elegant bourgeois *cabriolet, dormeuse* or *faeton*; the *giardiniera* ('waggonette') and *char-à-bancs* (Italianised into *sciarabbà*) mainly used by day-trippers or *escursionisti*; down to plebeian omnibuses (*omnibus* 1835 in Turin; by 1845 a fleet of twenty-five horse-omnibuses was operating in Milan).[2]

I shall include nautical terms under the heading of commercial rather than military vocabulary for the reason that at this time the emphasis rests on mercantile rather than warlike seafaring ventures. Relevant words are: *alaggio* 'towing', *alturiero* (adj.) 'deep sea' (navigation, commerce, etc.), *atelier(e)* used to mean 'shipyard', *amarrare* 'to moor a ship'; parts of a vessel's equipment: *cabestano, pompa, cabina, bidone, cambusa* 'victualling store', *sirena*, (*battello di*) *salvataggio*, 'life-boat'—an obvious link with passenger transport; a number of words still relating to sailing vessels, which until the '80s still carried the bulk of traffic: *droma* 'spare spars', *invergare* 'to set up masts, yards', *gaffa* 'gaff', *olona* 'sailcloth'; *imbarcadero* 'landing-stage', and *passerella* 'gang-way'; *sonda* in the sense of 'sounding-lead' and *sondaggio*; words denoting the movement of a vessel, *tangheggio, tangare* (pitching), *rullio* (rolling). A few words have an exotic cast: *goletta, negriere* (slave-trading ship), *gribana* (kind of wherry used off Picardy and Flanders).

Vapore 'steamship' (also *battello a vapore*) is a highly significant borrowing; it shared its designatory function with *piroscafo*, which appeared at much the same time, and which some etymologists also consider to be a Gallicism.[3]

Though this list of sea-terms is fairly copious we ought not to exaggerate

1. Cf. *aerostato*, 18th cent. Fr. > It. loans.

2. Other technological terms are spread over a number of trades and inventions: *abagiur* (*abat-jour*), *aeraggio -azione, ascensore, avancorpo* (fore-part of an edifice), *plancia* ('plank'), *blocco* (of stone), *plafone, plafonare, parafulmine, béton* ('concrete') and *betoniera* ('concrete-mixer'), all of which have to do with different sections of the building trade; *abrasivo*; *placca, placcare* and *clivaggio* ('cleavage, cutting', of gems), connected with jewellery; *papetteria* (*papeterie*), *cartonaggio, brosciura* (*brochure*), *grattoàr; ceramista* and *grès* 'stoneware' (ceramics); *mortissa* (carpentry); *tanno, tannare; griglia; dentiera; grisou* 'fire-damp'; *tornichetto* 'turnstile'; *cappotta* (*capote*) 'carriage hood' or similar; and *automobile*. There are very few agricultural terms (*serra* 'greenhouse', *roncet*).

3. The learned coinage *pyroscaphe* was applied by the French inventor Jouffroy d'Abbans to an experimental vessel propelled by steam which he tested in 1776; *vide Archivum Romanicum*, VII, p. 87.

the French influence that goes with it. In sea-borne trade and in naval architecture Italy was a prime mover. After a slow start in the early decades of Austrian domination Italian merchant fleets were quickly built up through the personal genius of three enterprising industrialists, Vincenzo Florio,[1] Raffaele Rubattino[2] and Luigi Orlando.[3] In 1881 Florio and Rubattino's successors merged their interests in the *Navigazione Generale Italiana*, and provided Italy with a merchant marine fully able to hold its own with those of Britain, America and France. Maritime trade with France flourished even before Orlando established his line plying between Marseilles and Genoa at the middle of the century, and in the vital years of industrial expansion most of the exchange of machinery and products was carried on by the shipping companies, at least until the Mont Cenis tunnel made land transport a worthwhile proposition commercially. New terminology, however, is not a *direct* function of new trade, as we have seen on many occasions already. One *may* lead to the other; it is the job of social lexicologists to discover what encourages or inhibits borrowing in each interference situation.

The other interesting groups of commercial terms concern the distributive and catering trades, both of which developed phenomenally. Clear-cut distinctions were made between wholesale and retail commerce: *dettagliante*, *vendere in blocco* (also the probable loans *grossiere* 'wholesaler', and *vendere in dettaglio* [*vide* eighteenth century loans, s.v. *dettaglio*]). France appears to have been the first country to concentrate different channels of the retail trade in vast general stores or emporia (*Ménagère* 1846, *Louvre* 1855, *Bon Marché* 1872); their promoters usually styled them 'warehouses' (Fr. *magasin*), laying stress on the size of their establishment and implying that the goods were imported direct, hence sold more cheaply. This shift from the family shop to the supermarket reflected in the semantic development of Fr. *magasin* affected Italy too in due course. The Bocconi brothers' chain of stores *Alle Cento Città d'Italia*, later *La Rinascente*, dates from the end of our period; but *magazzino* was apparently used to mean 'shop' by the '70s.[4] *Bazar* was sometimes used in a

1. Vincenzo Florio, 1799–1868, Sicilian patriot. Built his merchant fleet in the mid-century from proceeds of early successful ventures (tunny fishing and preserving; Marsala wine industry, foundry). His son Ignazio expanded it to over 100 ships by 1880.

2. Raffaele Rubattino, 1809–81, Genoese; furnished the steamships *Lombardo* and *Piemonte* for Garibaldi and the *spedizione dei Mille*. Helped by Cavour to extend his line to transatlantic trade, then via Suez to the Indian Ocean.

3. Luigi Orlando, 1814–96; Sicilian patriot who founded a ship-yard in Genoa adapted for progressive techniques; built the first iron ship in Italy 1845. Managing director of the original Ansaldo company.

4. Cf. F-A., 1877: 'MAGAZZINO—Scambio di Bottega dove si vende roba a minuto, è un forestierismo—Es. *A Roma ci son molti magazzini di vini de' castelli vicini* . . . (other examples). *Magazzino* si dice solo quel luogo dove si tiene molta mercanzia in deposito o in serbo' (but he adds) 'o solo di grandi negozj, dove si vende in grosso, e ci sono merci di ogni genere e in grande abbondanza'.

similar sense, as in French. *Casa di negozio, di commercio* are related borrowings (Fr. *maison* in these collocations) and *vetrina* (Fr. *vitrine*) denoting the sumptuously dressed window of a modern establishment.

My readers who have the pattern of our century lists at their finger-tips will confirm that all contain a modicum of culinary vocabulary, but only one—this one—has a category so large that it requires a full-dress explanation. Up to the eighteenth century names of foods were borrowed adventitiously as fresh dishes and dainties became more widely known. Sometimes an enthusiast like Rabelais went out of his way to acclimatise exotic fare in his own country. It was left to the Brillat-Saverins of the eighteenth century, though, to alter the face of hospitality and make French supremacy in matters of food and drink another universal commonplace like Dutch thrift, English *spleen* or Chinese inscrutability. Eighteenth century France made good cheer a national art; the nineteenth century made it a national industry. Names of new delicacies and cooking techniques poured from French into other languages, including Italian. With the spread of tourism and later, of the holiday industry, the catering trade developed to match it, again largely associated with France and French terminology. Our list has the key terms *hôtel, chef* (*de cuisine*) and *menu* in it, together with *ristorante, trattore, maître d'hotel, table d'hôte, arrangiamento* 'tariff, terms' and no less than thirty-seven foodstuffs and dishes which are really only a fraction of what might be cited.[1] Catering terminology is a vast twilight world where one language diffuses into another and French presides over all.

There has been a surprisingly spirited reaction against culinary Gallicisms during the first half of our own century in all the major Western countries. In Italy opposition was vigorously launched on its way when in 1908 the King ordered that all state banquet menus should be written in Italian (in effect, that they should not be in French, as hitherto). Later, between the world wars, neo-purists made them their special butt, and a foison of proposed substitute terms were invented—*frullato* for *frappé* (drink cooled with crushed ice) and so on. They had a mixed reception. Attempts were made to adapt French words or to reinstate more or less corresponding Italian forms: *frittata* ~ *omeletta, albergo* ~ *hôtel, antipasto* ~ *hors d'œuvre*, which succeeded more easily if the correspondence was total (*menu* ~ *lista, carta*).

How can we account for the feelings stirred up by this rather inconsequential sort of loan, with its frivolous, even potentially comic connotations?

---

1. *Anisetta, babà, bavarese, besciamella, bignè, bordò, bouquet* (of wine), (*vin*)*brulè, charlotte, cognac, consumè, croccante* (crisp almond cake), *cotoletta, crochetta* (*-e*), *entremets, flan, fondant, fonduta* (famous as a Piedmontese delicacy, *fondüa*), *gatò, giambone, giardiniera* and *giuliana* (soups), *hors d'œuvre, macedonia, maddalena, maionese*(*-a*), *margarina, marroni glassati, meringue, mussare* (of wines), *omeletta, purè* (*-ea*), *salmì, scaloppa, soufflé, tartina, trancia, vol-au-vent.*

Perhaps because it implies a slight to Italian cuisine, which many people, and not only in Italy, consider equal in merit to that of any other country; partly because food is strongly symbolic and its terminology comes very close to the private person, but not least because this was a form of written Gallicism flaunted before the ordinary citizen, appearing on the menu of any café or in the window of a *trattoria*. And undoubtedly for many people there is a stigma of pretentiousness upon it, of petty snobbery.

But in the nineteenth century Gallicism in this sphere continued unrestrained, even though experts occasionally fulminated against it. It was felt socially desirable as well as commercially prudent to fall in with this practice. Cookery books and manuals of home etiquette were not content with offering glossaries explaining the names of French dishes, but even advised their readers how to compose menus in the accepted idiom, or in a series of Frenchified solecisms which passed for it.[1]

All in all, in spite of its seeming trivial, this little sector of interference still has a lot to tell us about social motivation and the linguistic limitations of wilfully 'correcting' a form of usage one finds exceptionable for emotive reasons.[2]

1. Giardini's *Dizionario della cucina moderna* is an excellent example. 'Ad ogni piatto di lusso,' the author states complacently in his preface, 'havvi il nome anche in francese per facilitare e servire all'uso, e redigere il "menu" o listino dei piatti che si distribuisce ai conviti.' Very many equivalents are cited, usually like this: 'composta d'albicocche alla minuta = compôte d'abricot à la minute; burro di Mompelliere (sic) = Beurre de Mont Pellier; costolette d'agnello panate = cotelettes d'agneau panée (sic); rognoni di montoni alla moschettiera = Rognons de moutons à la mousquetaire (with a note explaining *rognoni*: "È sotto questo nome che l'arte culinaria se è impadronita delle reni degli animali")'. The whole book is studded with Gallicisms, some conscious, in which case they appear in italics ('mettetevi delle *papillottes* alle extremità del gigot'), but many others are unmarked. Examples are *filetti saltati*, *in garbure*, *crepinette di porco*, *cardons velutée* (sic), *fumet de pernici*, and for good measure some three hundred dishes with *alla* in the title—*alla Perigò*, *alla hochepot*, *alla Soubise*, *alle erbe fine*, *alla moda vecchia*, etc.

2. Other loan-words which could be referred to commerce and business are: *monopolizzare*, *gerenza*, *gerente*, *dattilografo -ia*, *paccottiglia* 'trade goods' for bargaining with natives, *burò* 'servants' registry', *farmacia* 'chemist's shop', *bigiotteria* and *bigiottiere*, *redazione* and *redattore*, *confezione* 'ready-made clothes' and *confezionare*, *località* 'building, messuage', *metraggio*, *articolo* (of goods), *cupone*, and a number of miscellaneous products: *carnè* (*carnet*), *carta velina*, *cartonaggio* 'chocolate-box' and *boîte* (*boatta*) meaning a similar decorated receptacle, *flacone*, *giada*, *gè*, *grès*, *macuba*, *palissandro*. *Reclame* 'publicity, advertising' and *esploatare -azione* are key terms.

Financial and commercial terms are closely connected: as in previous centuries we need make no distinction between the two. Those dating from the 19th century are also a moderately large contingent: *arbitraggio*, *bancarottiere*, *borderò*, *chèque*, *contabile* (see 18th cent., *contabilità*), *corporazione*, *coulisse* (unofficial brokers acting as supplementary to the Stock Exchange), *fondiario* (adj.), (*à*) *forfait* (various idioms), *libero scambio* (also a political issue), *malversare -azione* (also legal), *mercuriale* 'list of market prices', *miliardario*, *montante*, *piazzare* 'to invest, of funds', *quotizzare* both 'to assess' and 'to subscribe', *resoconto* cited

The last of our straight technical vocabularies is that of science and medicine. Scientific vocabulary too has its story to tell; each word may be brought into relation with a discovery, an invention, a trend in scientific inquiry. This is the sector of the modern lexicon where neologisms tend most frequently to be formed on classical roots. In consequence a problem of identification arises, at least from a linguistic standpoint: Latinisms or Hellenisms may be coined, say, by a German, a French or an Italian chemist which are formally homologous and bear no observable marking which reveals their origin. None the less if we are seeking to establish a correlation between vocabulary and cultural history we cannot afford to scout the evidence which scientific coinages are able to provide. Actually we find it not unduly hard in practice to identify the source of a learned technicism because the history of the *signifié* is generally well documented.

Many of the words which concern us are interdependent at the level of content. Those of chemistry may appear in medicine, as when the anaesthetic property of newly discovered substances were made use of in surgery (*vide morfina*). Malaria and swamp-fever (*paludismo*) are linked with land reclamation and new clinical treatments for these diseases, which formerly were endemic over wide tracts of southern Europe; these in their turn were made possible by pharmaceutical research, e.g. the discovery of quinine by two French chemists, Pelletier and Carenton, in 1820. Explorers and colonists incidentally extended the boundaries of geography, anthropology, botany and zoology; as regards the last two we note the important preliminary work of investigation carried out by Ottaviano Targioni-Tozzetti (1755–1829) and Giambattista Casti (1724–1803) in whose works some of the earliest Gallicisms are found (*vide acagiù, caucciù, panzea, caribù, giaguaro*). The reaction against rationalism which accompanied the Romantic movements helped to stimulate speculation about the supernatural and also caused a quickening of interest in occult lore and pseudo-sciences of the human mind, with new editions of Nostradamus, Anton Mesmer's theory of animal magnetism (1733–1815) and Franz Gall's phrenology (*frenologia* 1829 < Fr. *phrénologie*); both had a strong following among influential people in France, where Gall lived from 1807 to his death in 1828. Borrowings in *materia medica* correspond in a satisfactory way to the main contributions which French doctors made in this field: to clinical practice, especially diagnosing pathological conditions—

---

earlier, *tallone* 'counterfoil', *tasso* (as Fr. *taux*), *versamento* 'payment'. *Ammortizzare*, though attested earlier, is effectively a 19th century word (*vide supra*, 18th cent. list.). *Cassa d'ammortizzazione* is definitely so. Sinking funds were set up in Italy on the model of French institutions, in particular the *caisse d'amortissement* created by Mollien in year VIII, based on the British system of Dr. Price and reinstated with a strong financial backing in the budget of April 1816.

introspezione, sonda, sondare;[1] to surgery—*compressa, choc, écraseur, abrupzione, tampone, tamponare, tourniquet*; to microbiological and biochemical research, associated of course with Louis Pasteur and, later in the century, with his *Institut* (*pastorizzare, -azione*); and fourthly, in the field of psychiatric or social medicine—*casa di salute, alienista, alcoolismo, absentismo* (alcoholism brought on by excessive drinking of *absinthe*), *tabagismo, tara, tarato*.[2]

Each of our borrowings under these rubrics could obviously be situated in its historical background with a wealth of factual detail, which unfortunately would go beyond the limits imposed on our survey. But most of them suggest their own interpretation quite clearly, so I am content to add a plain classification of the disciplines under which they fall. It shows how far-reaching French influences in this domain were.

Acoustics:	*fonazione, sirena, timbre.*
Anthropology:	*etnografia, manitù, nomadismo, tabu, tatuaggio, tatuare.*
Archaeology:	*monolito (-e).*
Biology:	*locomotore* (adj.), *organismo.*
Botany:	*acagiù, caucciù, liana, pepiniera.*
Chemistry:	*azoto, grenetina, incoloro, inodoro, morfina, tannino.*
Electronics:	*accumulatore, ampere.*
Entomology:	*calandra* 'weevil'.
Geography:	*accidentato, banchisa, falaise, mammelone, nevato, òasi, plateau, rapida(-e), valanga, versante.*
Geology:	*affiorare, affioramento, faglia, morena.*
Graphology:	*grafologia.*
Linguistics:	*patoà* (*patois*), *semantica.*
Meteorology:	*ciclone.*
Metric System:	*ara, chilometro, litro,* etc.
Mineralogy:	*bauxite, cornalina, dolomia, dolomite.*
Numismatics:	*esergo, marengo.*
Ornithology:	*cormorano, edredone* 'eider', *fregata.*
Physics, Optics:	*riflettore.*
Spiritualism, etc.:	*esteriorizzare, esteriorizzazione, medium; frenologia.*
Zoology:	*caribù, cascialotto, fanoni* 'whalebone', *ghepardo, giaguaro, lamantino, mangusta, moffetta, muflone, pecari, pinguino, piovra, renna, scimpanzè.*

1. Modern clinical practice owes much to the research and example of Napoleon's doctor, J. N. Corvisart, and to the gynaecologist J. C. A. Récamier, also active early in the century. Claude Bernard's part in making medicine an objective, experimental science is well known. The first psychiatric clinic was founded later in the century by another Frenchman, J. M. Charcot.

2. Other medical loans: *atavismo* (links with Darwin and anthropology), *avambraccio, cascè* (*cachet*), *colpo di sole, grippe* (cf. *influenza*, 18th cent. It. > Fr. loans), *crampo, dentiera, endemico, mughetto* (paediatric term), *mutismo* in its strict sense, *pedicure, paralizzare, vaccino, -are, -azione.*

'Ce mode d'influence n'a guère d'exemples dans l'histoire des relations littéraires entre nations civilisées. . . . La présence des Français imprègne, pour ainsi dire, toute la vie des Italiens. Partout, et quoi qu'ils fassent, il leur faut subir la langue des conquérants.'[1] Paul Hazard was speaking of the first period of French domination which ended in 1799, but what he said applied equally well to the second, more permanent occupation which followed it. Such duress could not have failed to provoke a thoroughgoing reaction. The first mutterings of disapproval were heard before the eighteenth century reached its close;[2] by the Napoleonic period the Italian language had found champions with trenchant opinions and a voice to make them known. With the nineteenth century the most fascinating chapter in the long-debated *Questione della Lingua* begins. Philologists have devoted many a page to tracing its different threads—*Trecento* purism, revived with new authority by Padre Antonio Cesari and the Crusca (which Napoleon had reconstituted as an autonomous academy in 1811, by a typically imperious gesture), Vincenzo Monti's classicism, expressed in a *Proposta di alcune aggiunte e correzioni al Vocabolario della Crusca* (1817 to 1824), to which he was the major contributor; both eventually eclipsed by Alessandro Manzoni's momentous contribution, his struggle to discover, synthesise or create a truly natural idiom.[3]

All aspects of the *Questione* at this time provide us with valuable background, but one concerns us directly: the movement of Purism, in so far as it shows itself hostile to Gallicism. Not the positive if somewhat quixotic ideal of Cesari and others who tried to re-establish norms of the fourteenth and sixteenth centuries, but the purism of those who worked systematically in a censorious spirit to weed out barbarisms from the fair field of Italian, above all by waging implacable war against the 'stoltissima smania di sostituire a parole nostre, belle e significative, parole per lo più francesi o infrancescate perchè crediamo di nobilitare con esse e render più magnifici noi e le nostre cose'.[4] Anti-Gallicism in a general way is a plank in every language reformer's platform at this time; even Manzoni, whose linguistic aspirations were above mere political expediency, welcomed during the course of his *Appendice alla Relazione intorno all'unità della lingua e ai mezzi per diffonderla*[5] a

1. Paul Hazard, *La Révolution française et les lettres italiennes*, p. 56.
2. *Vide supra*, 18th cent. Fr. > It. evaluation, p. 419.
3. *Vide* Migliorini, 'La Questione della Lingua', op. cit., pp. 49–67 and bibliography, ibid., p. 75; also M-*Stor.*, pp. 604–18, 684–92 and words cited. The following observations should be read in conjunction with Professor Migliorini's article 'Purismo e neopurismo', still authoritative though written nearly thirty years ago, which forms a chapter of his *Lingua Contemporanea, Biblioteca di Lingua Nostra*, No. 4, 3rd edition, 1943.
4. Rig., 1891, *Prefazione*; refers to a lecture given to the *Circolo filologico fiorentino* on 5th April 1875.
5. Milan, 1869.

O

suggestion made by his critics that a dictionary of Gallicisms should be compiled, so that they might be avoided.[1] At the other end of the scale Cesari roundly condemned *francesismi* but gave little indication of the actual words he wished to see proscribed. The most categorical objections, and the most efficiently documented, come from a group of politically and nationalistically inspired purists active from the forties to the end of the century, who as events later showed were out of the main stream of the *Questione* as represented in its successive stages by Monti, Manzoni, Ascoli and their partisans. These are the people who concern us.

The tradition of these anti-French lexicographers—for their polemic mostly took the form of puristic dictionaries, commented lists of *barbarismi*—goes back to the beginning of the century through the works of A. Lissoni, M. Parenti, B. Puoti, F. Ugolini[2] and others, together with various counterblasts to and apologies for each compilation as it appeared in print. But I regard the later vocabularies—those of the '70s and '80s—as being really typical; above all the successive editions of Pietro Fanfani and Costantino Arlia's *Lessico della corrotta italianità*[3] and Giuseppe Rigutini's *I Neologismi buoni e cattivi più frequenti nell'uso odierno*.[4] These reasoned inventories of solecisms and vulgarisms form a *genre* in their own right. In them the crusading spirit of the day finds an unconventional outlet. 'Lingua e nazione sono la stessa cosa' is their slogan.[5] Fanfani and Arlia speak for all in stating their unshakable conviction that 'la corruzione della lingua ha per consequenza la decadenza del

---

1. Note, however, that Manzoni did not himself follow up this project and obviously gave it low priority.

2. A. Lissoni, *Aiuto allo scrivere purgato*, Milan, 1831; M. Parenti, *Catalogo di spropositi*, Modena, 1839–41, continued by his *Esercitazioni filologiche*, Modena, 1844–58; B. Puoti, *Dizionario de' francesismi e degli altri vocaboli e modi nuovi e guasti*, Naples, 1845, letters A-E (vide L. Rosiello, 'Il 'Dizionario dei francesismi' di Basilio Puoti', *L.N.*, XIX, 1958, pp. 110–18). The most convincing work to stand out against the tide of gallophobia is Prospero Viani's *Dizionario di pretesi francesismi e di pretese voci e forme erronee della lingua italiana*, 2 vols., Florence 1858 and 60, which proves by referring to early texts that many of the censured words were current in the Middle Ages. Some of our lexicographers find his arguments hard to dispose of—like Arlia, who is a Trecentista at heart; but he and others very reasonably point out that many of Viani's *trecentismi* and *cinquecentismi* only reappeared in modern usage through a new, totally unrelated French influence (vide F-A., s.v. *azzardare, abbordare, aggirarsi*, out of many others).

3. Milan, 1877; later editions had the title whetted to *L. dell' infima e corrotta italianità*, Milan, 1881, 1890, 1907; *Giunte* by Arlia (who was responsible for most of the *Lessico*) in 1884, etc.

4. Rome, 1886, 1891 and subsequently.

5. F-A., 1877, *Prefazione*, p. ii. Thirty years earlier Ugolini put the same proposition in more acutely political terms: 'La lingua fu sempre parte principalissima dell'esistenza di una nazione; il perchè fu antico e moderno uso di ogni straniera signoria fare opera per imbastardire e snaturare la lingua di un popolo a meglio soggiogarlo' (op. cit., *Introduzione*, p. vii).

pensiero, e . . . questa è l'avanguardia di una nuova barbarie'.[1] Unexpectedly they make entertaining reading, with their flights of oratory, their passionate outbursts—'tra voci galliche, inglesi, teutoniche e nuove che sboccano tutto-giorno sulle colonne de' giornali, affè di Dio, che la Torre di Babelle diventa un nonnulla!'[2]—and their platonic dialogues between personified words—*Cappa*, for example, a stalwart old peasant, and *Sortù*, obviously a showy, volatile Parisian.[3]

As it happens the Rigutini–Arlia brand of purism was overtaken by both cultural and linguistic events, and the genre fell into abeyance. Unified Italy had no longer cause to be politically thin-skinned; ambitions of the Risorgimento shifted into other channels. Linguistically the problem of combating tyranny from without had taken second place to that of unifying language from within, the controversy accompanying Manzoni's programme for a national tongue. In Devoto's words, 'il problema eterno del bilinguismo si ripropone in termini italiani'.[4] A few new dictionaries were published and older ones revised, but the seam was worked out. When at the beginning of the new century Panzini presented the first draft of his *Dizionario moderno* to his publisher, Ulrico Hoepli, he was told shortly to rewrite it as a plain honest-to-goodness dictionary, 'senza tanti condimenti di osservazioni personali'.[5]

Purists in their generality are among the least qualified to assess a foreign influence aright. Their fault is that they infer that an influence exists from a series of symbols which cannot rightly be interpreted in that light. Most people are not consciously aware what specific activity they are performing when they speak, read a notice or an advertisement or even a book, provided they are genuinely engrossed in the subject. Nor do they as a rule attempt to analyse or take stock of their linguistic possessions at other levels. For 99 per cent of the population language is not something one views detachedly at all, but an essential item of man's make-up like the use of his limbs or his senses. Philologists, on the other hand, used to conceiving of language as a discrete entity and quite rightly recognising in it another form of human behaviour, are apt to project their feelings into language and to postulate

1. F-A., ibid.
2. F-A., s.v. *conforto*. Irony is a powerful resource, too. 'Ecco una bella signora,' observes Rigutini, 'che si è messa in punto per andare a una soirée, o ad una "conversazione danzante". Ella invece di una pettinatura ha una elegante coiffure, al collo le pende un breloque invece di un medaglioncino; la veste à fermata sul petto da una "broche" invece da uno spillone; in dietro in luogo di certo sgonfio o cestino ha il "puff" ' (op. cit., *Avvertimento*).
3. Dialogues, too, between actual people, or purporting to be; for example that between Fanfani and Viani which appears under *aggirarsi* (F-A., 1st edition, pp. 12–13).
4. *Profilo*, p. 129.
5. *Diz. mod.*, 9th edition, p. vi.

similar feelings in others. And from this it is only a step to assume that the attribute a word has for them as trained philologists is an immanent quality detectable by others, and therefore able to be used by others in some symbolic demonstration against the foreign institutions they dislike. This our puristic lexicographers undoubtedly do. They also make some misjudgements in matters of detail—an Anglicism or a Latinism erroneously derived from French; words stigmatised as *brutti francesismi* which Italian in reality gave to others (*bancarotta, carosello, saltimbanco*); figurative usages attacked as Gallicisms which are probably polygenetic extensions in both languages (*sacrificarsi, ristabilirsi*, etc.). But on the whole, making allowances for emotional exaggeration and individual eccentricities, their *corpus* of interference material can be accepted as authentic, providing thus the largest reservoir of information our survey has to draw on. This is certainly the opinion I have reached, and I am strengthened in it by the circumstances I noted earlier when speaking about bureaucratic terms, that each purist collates and methodically revises the work of those who have gone before so that the final body of Gallicisms registered represents the distilled, measured findings of a team of lexicographers rather than any one person. There is also the obvious fact that many of the *barbarismi* are actually recognisable as French words—*armoàr, budoàr, cadò, comifò*—and are often spelt in their French convention—*grisette, chauffeur, bleu foncé*, etc.

So both this repertoire of borrowed vocabulary which the Purists collect and the topical comments they make about it are welcome grist to the lexicologist's mill. And yet it is not immediately clear what construction we can allow ourselves to place upon them. Indeed the more we revolve this problem of explaining our puristic vocabulary the more abstruse it becomes. The *corpus* they present does not include *all* borrowings, nor should we expect it to do. But it is not a cross-section either; on the contrary, it turns out to be strongly biased in certain directions. There is only partial, sporadic coverage of the technical categories we have just been analysing. *Locomotiva, rubinetto* and *bullone* are in, but many more are omitted—*azoto, cabestano, rullío, cormorano, tannare* (I am selecting at random from the foregoing lists). Scientific terms are remarkably few—because they might point to French achievements? Or simply because the purists knew little about science? On the other hand the category we have called *bureaucratic* is well stocked, as we have seen already. There are appreciably more entries, too, drawn from the social, fashionable or domestic sector of vocabulary, the area which we ourselves still have to comment on. But the Purists' real forte is something more narrowly linguistic—semantic borrowings and semantic calque. The more tenuous the Gallicising usage (or so it would seem), the nicer the distinction between what is acceptable Italian and what alien, the more strongly expressed their protests are. For example they find especially objectionable certain metaphorical or otherwise extended uses which are commonplace in French but suspect, or only barely possible in Italian.[1]

The motives they attribute to Francophiles, to the 'servili imitatori del concitato stile francese' also concern us closely. Affectation and snobbery come high on their list, but people apparently also Gallicise through bad habits or through sheer pig-headedness ('spirito di contradizione e di vanagloria' is how Fanfani puts it[2]).

How far were the Purists' fears about a deluge of barbarisms justified? Was Italian vocabulary in danger of being altered radically in its nature by these French influences? What part did the motives they claimed to recognise in their contemporaries' linguistic activities actually play in lexical interference at the time? What do their commentaries add to our interpretation of this most enigmatic century in our survey? The Purists' catalogues are selective; what impression is gained if one supplies the missing semantic categories and looks critically at the whole?

All these are useful queries to have in mind as we turn to the final section of borrowed words, the ones which we have rightly come to regard as occupying a place apart, a place of special relevance in the lexico-cultural confrontation: those referring to human relations and social activities, and as in previous centuries, those belonging to the abstract, general and emotive complex.

Intensity of influence is the topic which dominates the rest of our evaluatory essay.

At this period the steady increase of borrowing from French reaches its extreme limit. I see this as the end of an era. French pressure on vocabulary continued into the twentieth century and certainly before and during the Great War it was as strong, judged statistically, as at any point in the *Ottocento* apart from the years of occupation at the beginning. But all through the second half of the nineteenth century opposition was hardening; and if

1. Examples discussed: *battere* 'to defeat' (= *vincere, superare combattendo*, ideally 'to beat, strike', etc.—though here as in most instances cited it is the abuse of the metaphor that is condemned, its having become accepted as normal practice; *abbordabile* 'approachable, of people'; *abitazione* 'house' instead of the abstract term; *accentuare* 'to lay stress upon, make a point of'; *accesso* in other than medical contexts ('I Francesi, che nelle loro metafore sconfinano, hanno esteso l'accesso a' moti dell'animo, a' sentimenti; e noi come le pecorelle gli abbiam seguiti, dicendo: *Antonio ha spesso degli accessi di generosità*' [F-A., s.v.]); *specialità*, of food; *situazione* 'job'; *scartarsi* meaning *allontanarsi; suscettibile* 'quick to take umbrage' (a late 17th century Gallicism, originally), and very many others, amounting in all to several hundreds.

2. *Vide* F-A., *Prefazione*, p. xv. Rigutini, also, spends a few pages analysing the reasons why words are borrowed, legitimate and otherwise (*Neologismi, Avvertimento*). Among them he detects 'un bisogno esagerato e spesso anche fittizio di voler parole nuove non solo per ogni idea o cosa nuova, ma anche per qualunque più tenue modificazione loro' (ibid.).

Panzini's *Dizionario moderno* from 1905 to 1950 is able to register three thousand actual French words which had a foothold in some register of Italian, this as I see it is due to the rapidly expanding traffic of words in recent times.[1]

With the *Ottocento* influence therefore our 'unit of interference' is rounded off and is seen as a complete pattern. It began and ended in a spell of French domination, with the trend in between completely reversed as a result of the great cultural and artistic impulse of the Renaissance, which as we have seen is mirrored in our sixteenth century borrowings. The sixteenth century Italian to French list is the one to which we naturally turn for a comparison now.

Of the hundred or so items ranged under the abstract-general-emotive rubric several possess distinct polysemic senses which we have already recorded in the technical categories. For example: *pepiniera* (Hortic.) 'seed-bed', and ' "hot-bed" of ideas, training ground' in a sense very conformable to French; *debordare* 'to overflow' and 'to surpass, go beyond the limit'. Many others are abstracts which have a particular, typical application in some special discipline or environment, e.g. *costatare, costatazione* 'to verify, observe' used in philosophy and logic; *sorvegliare* both as a general term and associated with police activity; *effetti*, in current use, but also legal, 'goods and chattels'; *morga*, current for a time in the sense of 'mortuary', and also meaning 'disdain, haughtiness (*altezzosità*)'; *pioniere* military, also 'explorer', then 'discoverer, forerunner' in wider contexts; terms of the metric system—*litro, metro, chilo, chilometro, grammo, ara*, etc., which are scientific yet part of everyday usage; *spessore*, an abstract meaning 'thickness', but used principally in scientific contexts in preference to *grossezza*—and here we can include *incoloro, inodoro* which again are largely scientific though they are helpful words to have for general applications too. There is also the batch of abstracts we have already remarked upon whose effective use was in bureaucratic or similar official phraseology—*subire, attivare, basare* and the rest.

At the core of this lexical category are a number of words which might be regarded as contributing something of value to the lexicon as it stood in those days: *abbrutire -imento, banale -ità, bonomia, chaperon, cliché* (*cliscè*) meaning 'commonplace', *colpo di maestro, colpo di testa, controsenso, effetti* again, valuable because of its collective force; *incosciente, libresco, mal del paese, marrone* (the

---

1. Total numbers borrowed increase as the centuries go by. Italian and French show this trend only imperfectly because in the 17th century there is a period of disengagement, or at any rate one in which relations are less intimate than in the 16th and 18th centuries. The actual figures are: total of words exchanged before 1500, 463; 16th cent., 534; 17th cent., 303; then a continuous rise: 18th cent., 366, 19th cent., 846. But if one brings other languages into the calculation, making a threefold synopsis with the contribution of the Hispanic languages added (strong from 1550 to 1650), this progression comes out very clearly; and even more so if one includes the Teutonic group and its exceptionally large complement of 19th century Anglicisms.

colour), *massacrare*, objected to because of hyperbolical misuse but serviceable in the strict sense, *pretenzioso*, *prestigio* 'prestige', *travedere* 'to catch a glimpse of', *malinteso* 'misunderstanding', *individualizzare*, *umanizzare* and some of the words already listed above (*incoloro*, *macabro*, etc.). Many words of this stamp have become permanent at the appropriate level of usage or made a niche for themselves in certain dialects. There is the usual group of commonly used 'concrete terms' which appears in all centuries where interference effects are strong (those which have a physically identifiable content to which we may say they *refer*): *morga*, *limiere* 'bloodhound', *placca*, *siluetta* and the adjective *bombato* (*bombè*), accompanied by a few names denoting people which again are a part of everyday usage rather than a technical jargon—*bracconiere*, *miliardario*. There are a number of pejoratives: *fumisteria*, *mistificare*, *scamottagio*, *turlupinare*, all concerned with fraud and make-believe; *gargotta* 'low eating-house', *marmittone* meaning political opportunist; *pappiè* 'bumph, screed'; *piovra*, literally 'octopus' but quickly applied to people, 'blood-sucker, harpy'; but none of these are unduly caustic, nor do they probe very deeply into human nature. A hand's-breadth away from them the euphemisms begin, some sufficiently ironical to condemn rather than attenuate: *indelicato* in the sense of 'unscrupulous, unprincipled' (*vide* word-list); *parvenu* as an alternative to *nuovo ricco*; words in the customary taboo categories of death and sickness—*sofferente*, *deperire*—illegality in money matters—*malversare*, *malversazione* 'peculation'—bodily functions—*ritirata*, *retrè*[1] and the less familiar one of 'failure', in which the inhibition appears to be more recent—*insuccesso* (cf. *fiasco* in It. > Fr. list). Sometimes borrowings which at first seem merely to duplicate elements already in the language are found to belong to categories where the sign-function depends upon novel or hyperbolical impact and therefore wastage is great and new equivalents always welcome: *chiarivari* 'din, tumult', *ribotta* 'spree', *cancan* meaning 'shindy, affray', *bisboccia* 'revelry'; also *eccentrico* for *bizzarro*, *strano*. There are a few words belonging to form-classes in which borrowings are rarer, that is, outside the so-called 'autonomous' or 'lexical' categories: the adverbs *all'insaputa*, *alla sanfasòn*, *vis-à-vis* (also a preposition), the conjunction *beninteso* (*che*) and one or two interjections—*maledizione! pardon!*

Taking them all together these central groupings compare quite closely with those of the sixteenth century Italian to French list. They are roughly the same in number; some of the semantic fields correspond—a surprising fact, really, when the cultural environment is so different. But the sixteenth century's abstract-general-emotive words leave one with the feeling that

---

1. *Vespasiana* meaning 'public urinal' is registered in early editions of Panzini with the alternative expression *monumento vespasiano*. It is plainly a version of Fr. *vespasienne*, found in this sense from 1834, *Journ. des Femmes* (Dauz.). Cf. also *water* (*closet*) pronounced [vatẹr], with ellipsis, as in French.

what they gave to the language was more valuable and in all probability more permanent. Here for comparison is a synopsis of the most interesting sixteenth century loans.

affront

attaquer

baste! (interj.)

baster 'suffice'

bizarre

briller

bravache

(se) burler (de)

burlesque

caprice

capricieux

cartel 'challenge'

cavale 'mare'

concert 'meeting'

contraste 'struggle; contrast'

contraster

courtiser

délicatesse

désastre originally astrological term

discoste

disgrace orig. in political contexts

escorne 'snub, rebuff'

faciende 'business, machination'

favori

fougue 'impetuosity'

fougue 'flight'

fracasser

fruste Fine Arts: later general

goffe 'gauche, tactless'

garbe, galbe 'grace, poise'

grotesque Fine Arts; general

intrigue 'snag, involved problem'; later 'plot, intrigue'

jovial orig. astrological term

leste

manquer

médicastre 'quack'

mercadant orig. neutral; pejor. in 17th cent.

mescoler 'mix'

muscadin 'scented pastille'; later 'fop'

numéro

pagnote 'cowardly soldier, scrounger'

pédant 'pedagogue', then 'pedant'

pédantesque

pointille

politesse

poltron

populace 'people'; pejor. later

postiche 'counterfeit, false'

posture

rebuffe 'reprimand'

récolte

réussir

riposte Fencing term and fig. use; both borrowed

risque

robe 'merchandise'

rodomont 'bully'

saltimbanque 'mountebank'

signalé 'famous, of note'

site

soldatesque orig. neutral; later pej.

stenté Fine Arts, then general; 'exaggerated'

strette 'twinge of pain'

supercherie 'excess, insult, cowardly trick'

travestir orig. 'to disguise'

veillaque 'cowardly, vile'

voltiger 'to flit about'

It is not easy, one must admit, to bring both lists within a common perspective. The nineteenth century is lexically a period of transition, of flux;[1] the list before us is a hotch-potch of words appropriate to widely

1. For information about borrowings which were rejected in the twentieth century and on differing degrees of acceptance see Migliorini, 'Purismo e neopurismo', op. cit., esp. pp. 172, 177–8, 181, 196–200.

differing media, registers and even different dialects, often with little or no overlap in use. I have drawn attention to the most significant elements among them, but over and above these there is a fringe of Gallicising usage whose status as evidence for interference is awkward to define.

Nevertheless I believe this fringe of marginal Gallicisms holds the key to the century's loan-word activity, especially the semantic loans I mentioned earlier which make up a large section of it. A semantic loan—a shift in use on the analogy of a foreign related form[1]—is in itself a sign that interference between two languages is operative at the deeper levels of lexis. Different types of semantic loan imply differing degrees of intimacy.[2] To interpret this marginal interference most advantageously, however, we have to begin not by asking *in abstracto* how intense is the contact they indicate, but what the medium or register is in which they first appear, or are mainly found. We can find out a good deal about this from their collocation. It would be worth while preparing a detailed analysis of the habitual collocation of all our borrowings, using those given by the Purists as a starting point, though I find that a series of *sondages* in these authorities is enough to put one on what I think is the right track.

Their pages abound in contexts like *delitto passionale, un sensibile migliora-mento, amare alla folia, in seguito, un grido straziante* (sc. *déchirant*), *un viso patibolare, che superba carozza! sono tanto affarato da non poter venire, l'avvocato arringava con un slancio* (sc. *élan*) *indicibile, vive isolato in campagna, cedere lassa-mente ai moti del timore, un ingegno limitato, la crema della società, la lotta tra il passato e il presente, d'altronde* (*d'ailleurs*).[3] We do not need to analyse many such syntagmas before becoming aware of a threefold pattern which I can best describe by the epithets journalistic, literary, and 'drawing-room' or 'stylish-genteel'.

The form of journalism which has the greatest impact as far as these abstract 'social' groups are concerned is of course the popular press, with special importance attaching to the weekly and monthly reviews, the fashion and other illustrated magazines which were most accessible to francophile

---

1. For detailed observations on semantic loans with definitions see below, Part Four, section 1.

2. A formal criterion which has the same implications is the presence of formal calques and loan-creations, e.g. *campanilismo* ~ *esprit de clocher, sconfessare* ~ *désavouer*. Formal and semantic calques tend to be found in similar conditions, as in our present list.

3. Note that in many instances the significatory *tournure* borrowed is a single complete collocation, or a restricted series of collocations, and not a word in isolation, free to be used in any environment (*messa in marcia, ruda giustizia,* etc.). These form transitional patterns between interference associated with the word as a unit and borrowed idioms which are also very much a feature of the nineteenth century, just as they are of the eighteenth.

middle-class milieux. Many of them were modelled closely on French proto-types: almost all contained articles translated from French and made a special point of reporting the Parisian social events of the day. One can imagine phrases like il *'clou' dell'esposizione* ('high-light' of the exhibition) and *mussare una cosa* (to 'blow up', make much of a situation) coming directly from journalistic sources. If by a sort of 'philological circle' akin to that of Spitzerian stylistics we turn back to the word list for evidence of journalistic activity we find that many borrowings do fit into this background of transfer very well. Sometimes the link can be established beyond doubt, e.g. the words connected with the Dreyfus affair cited earlier or the word *apache* for a member of the Parisian underworld which is known to be a 'silly season' *trouvaille* on the part of French reporters.[1] But there are many other loans which are not immediately connected with the Press's reporting of any particular incident, yet they smell strongly of printer's ink: *dinamitardo*, *petroliere* 'anarchist, bomb-thrower', *giaccheria* (*jacquerie*; used of a popular uprising or demonstration), *linciaggio*, *massacro* and the other over-played figurative words which purists complain about; *dedalo*, *chimerico*, *rinnomata*, (*silenzio*) *glaciale*, (*prove*) *schiacchianti* and the rest; *limiere* 'sleuth', *personalità* 'famous person, V.I.P.', *rabagas* 'political turncoat', *rovescio* 'setback', *razzia* 'raid', for example by the police; also words denoting lurid aspects of *la vie parisienne—bastrè*, *cancan*, *cocotte*, *demi-monde*, *bohème* and their ilk, with some of the theatrical terms and very likely a good proportion of the pejoratives— *ribotta*, etc. The journalistic relationship we are evoking from a contextual standpoint can also be illustrated by appealing directly to content in the technical terms connected with newspaper publishing, that is, by switching from journalese to journalism: *attualità*, *reportaggio*, *reporter*, *intervista*.[2]

Literary *tournures* are less easy to identify, and it is equally hard to trace individual words back to literary influences, though occasionally the im-mediate source in French is known, e.g. *tentacolare*, esp. the phrase *città tentacolari* (Verhaeren, *Les Villes tentaculaires*) or *débâcle*, found in Italian before 1892 but certainly made more widely known by Zola's deeply shocking account of the Franco-Prussian War in *La Débâcle*. Another instance is *piovra* in its literal sense, popularised by Hugo's *Les Travailleurs de la mer*, containing the famous description of the devil-fish which seems to have satisfied some need for a symbol of horror and evil in the European mind at large. Words

1. *Vide* Dauz., *Les Argots*, p. 133.
2. *Giornalismo* itself is probably from French. *Rivista* is understood to be a calque of Fr. *revue* (*vide* word-list). It provides an excellent key-word for all this group, but I prefer to keep it as a token of serious or technical journalism (political, scientific) rather than the popular press. The two kinds of publication are very different in spirit and subject matter and the borrowings associated with each are even more widely dissimilar. This is why I have treated the two quite separately.

which have a literary flavour irrespective of context are *rêveur*, *rêverie* (*vide* M-*Stor.*, p. 738; also p. 736). All through the *Ottocento* Italian writers drew freely on the inspiration which French literature offered. There was a strong, artistically productive bond of sympathy between many authors in the sister countries: Maupassant and D'Annunzio; Pascoli and the Parnassians together with Verlaine; Baudelaire and many of the later Italian poets; Carducci and almost the whole gamut of French writers from Lamartine through Hugo and Sainte-Beuve to Leconte de Lisle. Often these affinities become manifest in their use of language, but much more in composition and style than in vocabulary. There is a palpable link through nomenclature, though, in the names of literary schools—*parnassiani*, *realisti -ismo*, *veristi -ismo* (a loan-creation based on Fr. *réalisme*), *simbolisti -ismo*.

The third undercurrent one detects in the Purists' semantic loans, calques and other complex elements of *lexis* is that of social influences in the narrow sense—up-to-date, fashionable usage. It has a counterpart in vocabulary which is plain for all to see in the words which Fanfani, Rigutini and the others said were borrowed 'per leziosaggine e per grullaggine'. One might call them 'high-life' terms: *bon-ton, bontonista, boudoir* (*budoàr*), *chic, cadò, comifò* (*comme il faut*), *debuttante, distingué, désenchanté, élite, fine fleur, frac, smoking, habitué, lion, lionne, kermesse, sciarada, soirée* (*soarè*), *salone* 'social gathering', *tableau! pardon! magnifico! superbo! perfettamente, alla sanfason.* Many of them coincide with journalese, and rightly so; they had their being almost as much in the pages of gossipy and fashion magazines as in actual *conversazioni* and social coteries. Parisian society was the universal model; one might be tempted to discount many of the words which allude to it as exoticisms, were it not that they could also be used on occasion to refer to Italian social life. Some of them we might aptly style 'boulevard' terms; they include *bistro, scioppe* 'mug of beer', *salone* 'barber's shop' and *frisore* 'hairdresser's', *grisette, midinette, cicca* 'quid of tobacco', *cicchetta* 'dram of liquor', *sigaretta*,[1] as well as *cocotte, bohémien*, and *cancan* mentioned just now. The most intriguing group within this semantic domain is one which has no parallel in previous century lists: words denoting family and communal amusements, usually for the mass of people and usually sponsored commercially. For example, words relating to the circus: *acrobata, equilibrista -ismo*; fairs and sideshows: *illusionista, prestidigitatore, pierrot, montagne russe, marionetta, grand guignol, cartomanzia*; processions: *flambò*; music halls: *varietà, divette, sciantosa, café-chantant, caffè-concerto, soubrette, mimare*;[2] dancing: *tè danzante, serata danzante, festa, veglia, mattinata, trattenimento, cena danzante*; *cotillon, galop*; outdoor games: *canottag-*

---

1. Smoking cigarettes became popular during the Crimean War, in which the Piedmontese fought as allies of France.

2. Words relating to the serious theatre are *debutto* (*début*), *debuttare, foyer, fumoir, première, claque* (*clacche*), *coulisses* ('wings' of a theatre stage).

gio, canottiere, pattinaggio, ciclismo, ciclista; indoor games: *acchito* (at billiards), *china* (term of dice), *domino, écarté, briscola* and the craze of *decalcomania*, all of which are respectable homely pastimes; serious gambling was carried on in the *casino* where *roulette* and *baccarà* were played. Finally, the turf: *pista, totalizzatore*, and the celebrated *turismo, turista* of English parentage. All the others except *panorama* are French in flesh, blood and name, a fact worth recording for reasons we shall see in a moment. I am sure the reader will find as I do that the effect of these sixty words, a remarkably strong muster, is singularly like that of an Impressionist canvas or a verbal painting by Zola or Huysmans. They compose a series of *croquis parisiens*, summing up the gaiety and movement of French cities in the last decades of the century.

Finally the same overtone of social distinction accompanies many of the loan-words denoting personal ornaments and accessories,[1] objects associated with the home and family life[2] and naturally with the vocabulary of fashion, a realm in which France was already *prima inter pares* during the seventeenth and eighteenth centuries, but was now accepted as undisputed and hereditary queen.[3]

What are we to make of the language reformers' claim that these are snobbish and superficial loans? Certainly many of the people who Gallicised most patently were sensitive to social distinctions and atmospheres. They were eager to be in the swim and they took their cue for what was up to date from

1. In our list: *bibelot, bouquet* (of flowers), *broche, breloque (berlocco)* 'pendant', *bretella -e, brillantina* 'hair-cream', *en-tout-cas* (kind of folding umbrella), *fumasigari, lorgnette, lunette* (for *occhiali*), *paciulì* (perfume), *papigliotti* 'hair-curlers', *parapioggia* (= *ombrello*), *portamonete, portafortuna, sovvenire* (= *ricordo*). Cf. also the (men's) hair-styles *favoriti* 'side-whiskers' and *sciantiglioni* 'sideboards'.

2. Cf. in our list: *armoàr, bébé, berceau (bersò), 'arbour', biberon, bidè, boîte à surprise, bonne* (has similar overtones to *miss, fräulein* used for 'governess'), *boudoir (budoàr), charivari* (dust cover for clothes), *cislonga* (Fr. *chaise-longue*), *comò, consolle, croscè, dormeuse* (in sense of 'lounge-chair'), *flacone* '(scent) bottle', *étagère, giardiniera* 'flower-stand', *grattoàr* 'eraser', *lavabo, parquet, porte-enfant, rideau, roccaglie, rubinetto, salone* (drawing-room), *scifoniera* 'chiffonier, side-board', *segretèr* 'writing-desk', *taburè, timballo* and *tortiera*, both pie-dishes, *vis-à-vis* (kind of double settee), *voltaire* 'arm-chair'.

3. *Berta* (pelerine or shawl), *blonda* (lace), *blusa, cappello bombè, bottoniera, cachemir* (also *casmir*), *camicetta, canottiere* 'sports vest' and 'boater' (hat), *carrick* (overcoat), *chemise* (over-coat), *chiffon, corsè, crinolina, dorsay* 'frock-coat', similar to *frac* and also to *finanziera*; *décolleté, foulard (folàr), (maniche) à jambon* 'leg-of-mutton sleeves', *gibus* 'opera hat', *gilè (gilet), giupure, jabot, manichino* (= *indossatrice*), *mentoniera* (trimming of a hat), the key-word *modista*; *négligé, paltò* and *pardessus*, overcoats; *scialle, smoking* 'dinner jacket, tuxedo', *tarlatana, zuava* (sort of bolero). The story of nineteenth century fashions and France is a subject in itself. Among its outstanding personalities was the Empress Eugénie, who launched many of the styles which later caught on throughout Europe (*vide berte* in word-list). She played a central part in the vogue of the *crinoline* which became fashion-able in the 1840s and continued to be worn until about 1860, when it fell out of favour. In 1859 Eugénie appeared at a Tuileries ball wearing a crinoline with 103 hoops.

Parisian society. But it is usually the observer, the outsider, who attributes conceit or arrogance to a speaker, who for his part may indeed be a prey to this sort of feeling, or be aiming to produce the impression that he is; but on the other hand he may be totally unaware of any effect his speech may be having. What we *can* say, at least, is that anyone who wishes to explore his own ideas about what linguistic snobbery means will find more useful material here than at any other stage in Franco-Italian relationships. As for superficiality, a large number of tenuously motivated borrowings usually means close contact, not the opposite. The content of borrowings may be trivial, but the linguistic process they embody is often profound. On many occasions Gallicisms which were replaced by native Italian forms left an indelible mark on the conceptual pattern of the language. *Sfumatura* replaced *nuance*; *ambiente, milieu*; *scapligliatura, bohème*; *sfruttare, exploatare*, etc.; but in the process the native words' habitual context of use was brought into line with that of the French term they replaced.

How well founded is the Purists' charge that borrowing occurred through bad habits and perversity? To accuse a speaker of perversity again implies a value-judgement on the critic's part. If one were required to sum up these marginal areas of borrowing in a single epithet, *compulsive* might be more appropriate than perverse, I think, or better still, *comprehensive*. Words which appear affected or supernumerary may still be borrowed out of a genuine regard for a foreign culture, but casually, as part of a package deal, so to speak, by which foreign influences are imported with all their incidentals and trappings. Our statistics show that once the rate of borrowing has increased beyond a certain volume it tends to rise sharply and reach a level far beyond the average range within which borrowings are normally confined. In the later nineteenth century numbers were raised still further by the agency of mass media, which begin to exert an affect for the first time. From this period onwards cultural currents gradually come to affect a broad stratum of people rather than isolated *élites*. In these circumstances there is a tendency for extraneous material to be fed to the public without discrimination, shuffled into the most convenient acceptable form. One result of this is a spate of uninspired, literal translations, very apt to contain idioms directly transposed and the semantic borrowings we have already dwelt on; another is an efflorescence of journalese. By the end of the nineteenth century the means of delivering information exceeded the cultural stimulus to receive it. This kind of imbalance is peculiarly a twentieth century problem, but its earliest effects are to be seen in the nineteenth in large samples of neologisms such as the one before us now.

For these reasons the metaphor of lexical *exchange* does not suffice to describe Gallicism in the later part of our survey. There is a good deal that is extraneous in the nineteenth century. It is the moment at which *external pressure* upon the receiving language is most intense. France was making an extremely influential, characteristic cultural contribution at this time, and the words relating to it were diffused widely. A remarkably large proportion of the 'social' borrowings as well as those connected with administration, fashion, certain specific technologies and some of the abstracts too are to be found in other European languages—especially English, Spanish and Dutch, but also farther afield (Scandinavia, for example). Not that Italian—to draw out our image a little further—was obliged to *accept* Gallicisms more readily because of this: borrowed neologisms enter a language for a number of reasons which we shall seek to codify in a later chapter, and many of these are quite different in kind from the socio-cultural impulses we have just considered.

Nineteenth century Italians were moved by a deep sense of directivism. Their most cherished aim was to fulfil themselves in terms of national unity, and this they succeeded in doing; but in addition they wished to do so in European terms. They desired like the other nations of western Europe to be modern, to be of their age, an ambition based on the conviction that progress was inevitable, that mankind was in constant movement towards better things, and that it was therefore both practically feasible and morally right to take one's destiny into one's own hands. Italy felt the impact of the western European *ethos*—had indeed taken a large part in creating it through the genius of a Galileo or a Vico—an ethos which we of the mid-twentieth century are at last able to see in all its splendour, with its breathtaking and sometimes terrible dynamism. But for Italy at that time there was a certain leeway to be made up, and she was open as perhaps never before to influences from outside. Far and away the most important source from which these influences emanated was France, and this our word list has shown very fully. But France also served as an intermediary. Culturally and linguistically the smoothest way to Europe was through Paris.

We have a very clear picture of France's dual position as an ultimate and an intermediate source right through the century. We recognised it when we looked through the *Conciliatore's* list of contents. It appeared in every aspect of economic history. Italy's wider affiliations too were well illustrated. Financial support for Italian industrialisation was given by Rothschilds from Paris, but also by financial circles in London, Brussels, Berlin. The Piedmontese collaborated with Frenchmen to establish rail links, sea services; but at the same time the company of Rubattino was constructing its trading stations on the Red Sea with political and material assistance from Britain. We get a good impression of this wider European connection if we look at the ultimate origin of each loan-word. A considerable number entered French originally from a third language, often English, though Spanish, German and Dutch are also represented. There are many Anglicisms in the technical categories[1]

1. Railway terms are an obvious source of Anglicisms.

(sometimes disguised, as [*battello a*] *vapore*, a calque, though French, of *steam-boat*, 1787 in English); one or two are found in political terminology, as in the eighteenth century (*boicottaggio*, *assenteismo*); there are even a few in terms of fashion, social life and entertainment, which as we have seen are strongholds of French influence (esp. men's fashions: *smoking*, *frac*, *carrick*).

The progression from regionalism to national unity, and thence to pan-europeanism with the direct help and intermediary intervention of France, all taking place within the boundaries of the nineteenth century, affords the most dramatic demonstration of lexico-cultural solidarity in our survey. Words, reflecting cultural innovations more accurately when applied to these wider-ranging historical changes, show clearly the trend towards closer co-operation in Europe which will become more intense beyond the point where our survey ends, in the twentieth century, and will move ever closer to the final goal, the logical outcome, that of total integration.

PART THREE

The Formal Aspect

THE FORMAL ASPECT

Preliminaries

On looking over the various loan-word studies written up to the Second World War one is surprised by the amount of space devoted to working out a definition of 'linguistic borrowing' or (as is more usually the case) 'borrowed word'. Even where no normative or puristic bias prompted them to do so scholars were at pains to separate out various classes of loan-word according to what one might call their 'national status'—their relative degree of acceptance into the new language. It was usual to distinguish carefully between *Lehnwörter* and *Fremdwörter*, between 'denizens' and 'aliens', and to give some indication of the transiency or comparative permanence of the term recorded ('casuals', 'nonce-words', etc.).[1] With a shift of interest on the lexicologists' part from the static to the dynamic, from registering precisely a fixed, approved lexicon to investigating on empirical lines the forces which go to mould the ever-changing vocabulary of a language, definitions of this kind were felt to be largely irrelevant.

Paul Barbier first, then a succession of eminent lexicologists including Vittore Pisani, Frazer Mackenzie and the American descriptive linguists who have turned to this branch of linguistic study felt it advantageous practically and more in keeping with scientific fact to define borrowing in more general terms, including under this heading all linguistic phenomena from foreign sources which appear in a given language, however ephemerally. Some scholars interpret 'linguistic phenomena' more liberally than others; Pisani, for instance, speaks of receiving a form of expression from another country.[2] My own preference is for Professor Einar Haugen's broad statement that linguistic borrowing implies the reproduction in one language of linguistic patterns previously found in another.[3]

The type of linguistic entity which may be transferred varies widely. It may consist of phonic patterns including such incidental features as stress. It may concern grammatical features. Borrowing at the lexical level may introduce

1. See the Preface to Vol. I of the *New English Dictionary* (1888), p. xix, and L. Deroy's observations about 'xénismes' and 'pérégrinismes' in *L'Emprunt linguistique*, pp. 223–8.

2. 'Sull'imprestito linguistico', in *Linguistica generale e indoeuropea*, Milan, 1946, p. 55.

3. The actual definition speaks of an '*attempted* reproduction . . . of patterns' (*Language*, XXVI, 1950, p. 212). The qualification is appropriate in view of the subject investigated (minority languages in the U.S.A.).

new forms for word-building, a new word or group of words, or add a new signification, a new habit of use, to indigenous terms; again, it may cause extraneous syntactical patterns to be employed in respect of elements already existing in the language. It may in addition exercise an influence solely upon orthography, independent of any transfer in terms of sounds. Any number of these categories may come into play. There are other ways of describing the different processes by which interference operates. Haugen for instance classifies the same phenomena according to the extent of their morphemic substitution, beginning with *zero morphemic substitution* (LOAN-WORD) where no element of the borrowing language interferes with the form received from without, passing through *partial morphemic substitution* (LOAN-BLEND), as in the case where a suffix in the borrowed word is replaced by a native suffix (e.g. *fonnig, tricksig* in Pennsylvanian German) or where some similar substitution occurs, to reach finally a point of *total morphemic substitution* (LOAN-SHIFT) when the linguistic entity is actualised in a purely indigenous form.[1] Semantic loans are of this type. This classification has the advantage of defining succinctly the status of calques or loan-translations, and of finding a niche for false loanwords (CREATIONS) where a term is felt to be a morphemic importation from an alien source, but has in fact no prototype in the supposed language of origin (cf. the well-known examples *wattman, recordman* in French).[2] Viewing the borrowed material from the standpoint of Saussure in his analysis of the *signe linguistique*[3] one might recognise three main subdivisions, (a) loans which entail the borrowing of the symbol as a whole, (b) those where a new *image acoustique (signifiant)* is linked with a concept already symbolised in the language by some other association, and (c) where a new concept (*signifié*) replaces or is added to the accepted *signifiant*. Situation (c), which in general terms may be called a semantic loan, is considered separately in Part Four below.

Since our purpose is to examine transfer of vocabulary we shall not extend our analysis to formal segments longer than those provided by the lexical unit. The object is to observe what happens to a word from a phonetic standpoint when it passes from one language to the other. As a formal entity a foreign word presents unfamiliar features to the native speaker. His reaction to it will be dictated by the linguistic pattern or patterns at his disposal, both as regards the language as a whole and this term in particular; but the way in which he implements these patterns will vary according to a number of other factors. Important among these is the relationship between his own language and the foreign one. The position of an Italian using a French word in a diplomatic report or of a Frenchman using an Italian musical

1. *Language*, XXVI, 1950, pp. 214-15.
2. See further examples in the discussion of general principles below, pp. 618-20.
3. *Cours de linguistique générale*, 5th edition, pp. 97-100.

term is very different from that of, let us say, a central European striving to master American English. There is no abandoning one language as a whole in favour of another, no continuous, unidirectional development similar to that which arises when an immigrant desires to effect a complete word-importation that will be recognised as authentic by native speakers of the language aspired to.[1] In the case of the Italian or the Frenchman, moreover, a knowledge of the written symbol plays a greater part. To the complicating factor of bilingualism as normally understood must be added a 'third dimension' of bilingualism in respect of the written language only. The educated Romance speaker frequently knows three or more living languages in this way apart from his own.

In the case of borrowing between Italian and French, therefore, where each language is strongly established, the chief *desideratum* is to show how a speaker moulds foreign words according to his own linguistic habits rather than to consider how his own language may be modified by using a foreign idiom: to observe how sounds and forms are realised in the language which accepts them and what changes take place during their transfer.

I shall begin by describing some of the problematical interference situations which are revealed by our material. These examples will lead on to a consideration of the general principles involved. Part III will close with a review of the criteria by means of which French and Italian loan-words may be identified. In this final section I shall compare the value of the phonetic criterion with that of other kinds of evidence available, so raising my sights to anticipate the wider-ranging investigation into semantic and lexical interference as a whole to which the last two parts of my survey are devoted.

Interference Patterns and Problems

I. PALATALISED VOWELS

The palatalised vowels of French, [ö] and [ü], which have no direct equivalent in literary Italian, are rendered either by the graphies *o*, *u*, or (occasionally) *e*. As it happens the number of words containing these sounds which pass from one language to the other is small and the effect of analogy often obscures such evidence as is available. Thus mediaeval It. *fiordaliso* and *produomo* may be affected by *fiore* and OIt. *prode* (mod. *pro*); and even supposing this were not the case, the spelling may be simply a repetition of the OFr. scribal usage, where *o*

---

1. For this reason questions relating to *Sprachmischung* in the sense commonly understood from Windisch onwards are not discussed. The reader is referred to the monographs on immigrant languages cited by Weinreich, op. cit., to Deroy, op. cit., Ch. XIV, *Langues mixtes et langues internationales* and to Weinreich, sections 2.54, *Interference and language shift*; 2.55, *Crystallization of new languages from Contact* and section 3, *The Bilingual Individual* as a whole.

for [ö] (< VLat. [ǫ] tonic free) is found well into the thirteenth century. It. *burro* corresponds to the original OFr. word *burre* ([ü]), not *beurre*. In the French prototypes of OIt. *terzuolo* and sixteenth century *crogiuolo* the suffixes are too unstable for one to trace with certainty a direct transfer of form into Italian.

In French the phonemes /ö/ and /ǫ̈/ are realised as fronted mid-vowels with lip-rounding. Lip-rounding is not a distinctive feature of Italian, though tongue height of course is: and therefore for a monolingual speaker of Italian the phonemes corresponding to French /ö/ and /ǫ̈/ are /e/ and /ɛ/ respectively. These equivalents are in fact registered in our list; cf. the transcription *blè* (pronunciation [blɛ]) for Fr. *bleu* (Meano, etc.) and *scioffè*, *sciaffèr* for *chauffeur*.[1] But most Gallicisms were introduced through written intermediaries, or if by word of mouth, by bilingual individuals who spoke French with differing degrees of precision. Many may have pronounced it absolutely correctly while others only approximated to the desired standard. Approximations and conventional pronunciation may help to explain spellings like *monsù*, *monsiù* for *monsieur* (seventeenth century onwards), *blù*—very usual—and sometimes *blò* instead of Fr. *bleu* (eighteenth century), but generally there is some morphemic equivalent at the back of the user's mind which explains the vowel sound chosen more convincingly. This appears to be the case with eighteenth century *manovra* < Fr. *manœuvre*, which usually has *o* (also *manovrare*),[2] and very probably with nineteenth century *piovra* < Fr. *pieuvre*, as well as the mediaeval examples cited above. The use of [o] is supported by suffixes *-oso* and *-ore* parallel to Fr. *-eux* and *-eur* (cf. *sciaffòr*, s.v. *chauffeur*).[3] As regards orthography the actual French word is, naturally, often used; deliberate Gallicism of this kind is not infrequently found in the luxury trades, e.g. *tailleur* (woman's costume), *coiffeur* (both nineteenth century); cf. also *chanteuse*, *chauffeur*, *viveur*.

No mention has been made so far of the palatal sounds closely similar to those of French which exist in many northern Italian dialects. The palatal [ö] of Genoese is almost certainly responsible for the corresponding sound in Fr. *écueil* (see mediaeval It. > Fr. list), and cases are numerous where the French vowel has passed unaltered into Piedmontese or Milanese, though usually replaced during its further transmission into the literary idiom. To take only

1. Cf. also *floconè*, 20th cent. (Fr. *floconneux*), a heavy woollen stuff. *Vide* B-Al., s.v.

2. *Manuvra*, also 18th cent., is probably dialectal, and so may other /u/ equivalents be. Phonemically a Sicilian dialect would explain this; so would the intervention of a Provençal intermediary between French and Italian.

3. In many cases, as might be expected, adaptation is complete and the corresponding Italian suffix is substituted: *amatore*, *ascensore*; *oltraggioso*, *pretenzioso*, *sciantosa* (*ciantosa*). *Pastorizzare* first appears with the spelling *pasteurizzare* (see the various editions of Panzini). *Capo d'opera* < Fr. *chef d'œuvre* and *franco-tiratore* < *franc-tireur* are obvious calques.

a single example—the French word *dormeuse* (nineteenth century word-list) first appears in Italy in Cherubini's *Vocabolario milanese* and is there transcribed as *dormös*.

There is a similar problem of equivalence in connection with the French phoneme /ü/, but here the question of choice scarcely arises. In most borrowings French [ü] is rendered as *u: brunir* > *brunire, bruit* > *bruito. Bottino* < Fr. *butin* is anomalous, though the explanation may lie in its being at the time of transfer a recent borrowing in French itself from Middle Dutch. There is much vacillation about the rendering of Italian [u] in French loans, where the sound may be rendered phonetically (*boussole, bravoure*) or the influence of spelling may prevail (*brusque, bucentaure, buffe* ('vizor'), *burlesque, buste, capuchon, capucin*, etc.). Orthography exerts the stronger influence in a majority of words, though sometimes only after considerable hesitation (cf. earlier *bourlesque* for *burlesque, arquebouse* along with *arquebuse*). Occasionally dialects intervene here also: *gumène* is probably from Genoese *gumena* (Vidos) rather than Tuscan *gòmena*. The representation of Italian [u] by French *u~ou* is further complicated owing to the fact that French *ou* often serves to render a different sound of Italian, viz., [o̞]. Here the situation is affected by dialectal variations and differences of literary usage arising in Italian and French. As regard the former, the example of Tuscan [u] for [o] countertonic may be cited; a good instance of ambiguity in French is afforded by the situation resulting from the 'learned v. popular' controversy in respect of [o] and [u] during the sixteenth century (examples from our borrowings: [o~u] in *colonel, bocal, escopette*, and the form *fugue* [musical term] < *fuga* alongside *fougue* 'flight', also < *fuga*, but accompanied by the homonym *fougue* 'impetuosity' < *foga*—a different word, though ultimately from the same etymon [Lat. *fŭga*]).

2. l + CONSONANT

Basic situation: [l] before a consonant is preserved in Italian but vocalises [l > ł > u] in French.

Though pre-consonantal [l] is apt to undergo a variety of changes in Italian dialects[1] and vocalisation is found from the Middle Ages onwards even in parts of Tuscany, the literary language itself maintains [l] unchanged. The beginnings of vocalisation in Old French may be traced back to the ninth century, but the main period of change is that of the later twelfth and early thirteenth centuries. Even if one allows for the comparative lateness of this shift in some dialects (e.g. Norman, which has special relevance here) it is unlikely that many Fr. > It. borrowings occurred while French [l] still remained intact in this position, so that It. [l] may have been substituted for Fr.

1. See Rohlfs, I, pp. 401-9.

[u] from the very outset. In the thirteenth century and later the existence of a well-established phonetic equivalent is indisputable. Typical mediaeval examples of relevant loans are *bolgia, oltraggio, oltranza, veltro* and *briffalda*; the latter may be an equivalent suffix, since Fr. *-aut (-aud)* and *-aude* (< Frankish) form a ready parallel to It. *-aldo, -alda* taken from Germanic directly. *Araldo, gialda* and *gialdoniere* are probably similar cases. In *dolzaina* the Middle French scribe's fondness for inserting otiose letters, among them letter *l* (*doulce, herault,* etc.) may have given support to the [l~u] equivalent and helped in some slight measure to sanction its use as late as the end of the sixteenth century (see sixteenth century Fr. > It. loans). Modern examples of [l] for [u] are generally explicable by some precise analogy, e.g. nineteenth century, *salvataggio* < *sauvetage* ≠ *salvare, salvezza*. The first instance of a direct phonetic rendering is *cuccia* < Fr. *couche* (late fifteenth century); cf. also *bodriere, budriere* in Magalotti, etc., < Fr. *baudrier,* and eighteenth century *àuna* < Fr. *aune* (alongside the original loan < Frankish *àlina*).

Care must be taken not to seek an effect of sound-substitution in the cases where the original French lateral has remained unvocalised—in a learned word, perhaps, or an exoticism: e.g. *altruismo* < Fr. *altruisme, alpaca* < Fr. *alpaca, colbac, colbacco* < Fr. *colback.*

Old French nouns with oblique singular in *-el* < Lat. *-ellum* (*bordel, demoisel, ostel*) are borrowed with the corresponding Italian suffix *-ello* during the Middle Ages (*bordello, damigello, ostello*). A far-reaching phonetic and analogical change in French [ɛl(s)] > [ɛau(s)] (twelfth century) > [əo] (by sixteenth century) > [o] (seventeenth century), resulting in the presence of an entirely different stressed vowel, rendered the Italian suffix *-ello* unsuitable as an equivalent; from the seventeenth century onward the graphy *-ò* begins to be used (together with the actual French spelling, on occasions). Examples are: *mantò (manteau), ponsò (ponceau)* in the seventeenth century; *buro (bureau)* (eighteenth century); *bersò (berceau), borderò (bordereau), bordò ([vin de] Bordeaux), cadò (cadeau), gatò (gâteau), rondò (rondeau), tablò (tableau),* nineteenth century.

In French, where the learned group [l]+consonant provided a precedent, Italian [l]+consonant was almost always accepted without alteration.[1] Examples are: Mediaeval: *cavalcade, defalquer, golfe, malvoisie;*[2] sixteenth century: *algousin, altesse, belvédère, balcon, baldaquin, balzan, espalmer, récolte, salcifis, soldat, volte, voltiger;* seventeenth century: *archivolte, catafalque, falquer;* eighteenth century: *alto (contralto), calmande, calque, galvanisme, solfatare,*

1. *Saucisson* (16th cent.) is influenced by *sauce, saucisse; saulcisson* in Rabelais is a graphy only (cf. also *voulste* (= *voute*) in 1508). *Soldars* and *souldars* (du Bellay, d'Aubigné, etc.) are probably alternative spellings of the OFr. word *soudart.*

2. The group [-lf-] in *calfater, calfate* results from the effacement of unstressed [a] in *calafatare, calafato.*

solfège; nineteenth century: *colmate, désinvolture, salterelle, volt*. In an unexpectedly large number of cases—12 of the above—forms with [l] make doublets with earlier native cognate words in which the lateral has been vocalised. Of these some have little interest beyond that afforded by a historical coincidence (*alto~haut; calquer~*OFr. *chaucer*); many, however, exist simultaneously within the same sphere of vocabulary, forming a series of synonyms which raise problems of structural interference on the semantic plane.

3. GROUP s+CONSONANT AND THE PROBLEM OF THE PROSTHETIC 'e'

Basic situation: The groups implicated are [st, sp, sb, sm, sk, sl, sn, sr,] though of these [st] (especially when initial in a word) is the most important numerically. In French groups of s+const. the sibilant voiced, changed to [ð], [χ], or [ç] according to position and was gradually effaced over a considerable period of time which included the eleventh, twelfth and thirteenth centuries, in conformity with the general movement towards a reduction of consonantal groups (produced by the loss of vowels owing to stress modifications) where these did not exercise a distinctive function. Where [s] preceded a voiced consonant or [f] it voiced to [z] and usually passed through the transitional stage [ð] before effacement; before breathed consonants [s] remained, and continued to be pronounced as late as the thirteenth century, usually passing through the transitional stage of a fricative palatal or velar before effacement (*vide* M. K. Pope, §§377, 378). In former times, while the groups were still unreduced, they were inevitably preceded by an 'e' on-glide when initial in Francien (and most other dialects); the same prosthetic 'e' appears whenever an attempt is made to pronounce such a group during the Middle Ages in the normal context of everyday speech. In Old Italian a prosthetic 'i' is fairly frequently attested, and is still found (though more rarely) at the present day in given dialects and in certain syntactical conditions.

Questions of dating, phonetic structure and phonetic equivalents arise here. The group [s] + const. continued to be pronounced in French sufficiently late for some of the earlier Fr. > It. loans to have taken over the [s] of the French consonantal group directly. The number of such borrowings with group in the absolute initial position is small: *spingarda* < *espingole, -ard*, *stanforte* < *estanfort, estainfort* (which may have an abnormal pronunciation in Fr., being itself a loan-word involving initial English [st-] of the place-name *Stamford*) but in other positions the groups are more frequently represented: *bastardo* (*c.* 1300), *destriere* (end of thirteenth century), *mastino* (thirteenth century), *mislea* (late thirteenth century), *mestiere* (13th century), *ostaggio* (fourteenth century), *ostello* (end of thirteenth century), *raspeo* (thirteenth century). From the point of view of signification and context—quite apart from the question of time-lag in dating—almost all these words may have been borrowed earlier, even as early as the twelfth century, when the group [st] (though probably not [sn], [sl], [sp]) would almost certainly be heard still. Later pronounced [st] occurs in Italian where the possibility of a direct phonetic imitation must be ruled out, e.g. seventeenth century *affusto, -are*, seventeenth century *stoffa* and later learned terms coined in French.[1] In some words a direct phonetic transcription of French occurs with the effaced [s] accurately omitted; cf. med. *citerna, valletto* (though here the sibilant in the French etymon was subject to sporadic change—cf. the twelfth century forms *vadlet* [ð] and *vallet* itself, which is the most frequently attested), and in later centuries, *crema* (sixteenth) < *cre(s)me*; *menageria* (seventeenth century) ultimately < OFr. *mesnage*; eighteenth century *crepone* < *crépon* beside *crespone*, which shows the analogical influence of *crespo*, and *meticcio* < *métis* (originally *mestiz* in OFr.), which replaces the sixteenth century Hispanicism with 's', *mestizzo*; nineteenth century, *apprettare* < *apprêter*. A phonetic rendering appears more likely to occur in groups other than [st], i.e. in the cases where a phonetic equivalent is less firmly established.

Conservatism of spelling in French which retains *s* before consonant until the eighteenth century (partly to indicate a lengthened vowel) frequently makes it hard to decide whether the *s* in borrowed words is pronounced or no. As a general rule it must be assumed that the effacement of [s] was more widespread in the Middle Ages than the speech-habits induced by modern pronunciation, with its extensive remodelling, would prompt us to believe. Thus in Villon the line 'frappez a destre et a senestre' rhymes with *maistre* and *estre*, where *s* is silent; the jingle demands that *destre* and *senestre* be pronounced alike; *destre* [dę:trə] suggests the pronunciation [dę:trie(r)] for *destrier*. Was the [s], for instance, omitted from the fifteenth century borrowings *sinistre* < *sinistro*, and *investir* < *investire* (as was the case in *vestir* (mod. *vêtir*)?

It is widely accepted[2] that the group [s]+const. returned to French during the sixteenth century with the reformation of Latin pronunciation on Classical lines and the influence of Italian. If [st] were actually pronounced in all words of Italian origin, however, the dating of the loans would imply that the restoration in general occurred earlier; of the eight cases of medial [s]+ consonant only one (*palescarme*) appears before the fifteenth century; but many others antedate the sixteenth century: *apposter (apposté)*, *embuscade*, *frasque, investir, lustre, poste, sinistre*.

The situation obtaining where [s]+consonant appears in the absolute initial position is somewhat different. Though the pronunciation of these

---

1. There are on the other hand many instances of Fr. > It. loans where the *s* was pronounced in French itself, particularly where the word was ultimately of foreign provenance, e.g. *est* (16th cent.), *brandistocco, scarabotto, filibustiere*, and *lasto*, 18th cent.

2. See M. K. Pope, pp. 152 and 234.

groups was attended with some difficulty (as the prosthetic [e] implies) they nevertheless continued in use during the whole of the mediaeval period. Evidence goes to show that where an initial consonant cluster of this type whatever its source came to be used *in actual speech* before the sixteenth century, it assumed an [e] on-glide. Thus *espatule, especifier, esperme, espère, espirituel, estable* (adj.) correspond to written *spatule, specifier, sperme, sphere, spirituel, stable*. Terms such as *sparadrap, spasme, spongieux* in Mondeville (1314) are early examples of the physician's verbal stock-in-trade; but *spasme*, for instance, appears as *pasme* or *espame* in contexts which suggest day-to-day speech. Other instances without on-glide may be traced to translations from Latin, religious documents or dialects where the initial group is not abnormal, e.g. Anglo-Norman. Loan-words from Italian at this time are treated similarly: *escadre, escadron, escalle, escrime, escueil, esquif, estrade, estradiot, estropier*.

Not until the sixteenth century do Italian words begin to appear without the vocalic glide, and then only rarely in spoken usage, as far as one can tell: cf. the spellings *scandal, scappade, scoffion, scopette, scorne, squirace, stecade, staffette, staphier, stampe* alongside the more usual forms. Examples are frequent in Henri Estienne, who may, however, be suspected of exaggerating the foreignness of his material. Montaigne, one notices, thought fit to replace *stropiat* by *estropié* in his 1585 edition. Among the first writers to use the Italianate graphy is Rabelais, who delights in linguistic curiosities (' . . . mon sbire, mon barigel', also *spadassin* as a person's name). Among the terms which, appearing first in the sixteenth century with the Italian initial group, find permanent places in the language are *spinelle, stalle* (as a religious term), *stance, strapontin, stuc, stylet*. A hint about the situation in spoken French of former days is given by the early history of the word *smalt* ('enamel'), which appears first in official records. One imagines the municipal clerk of the time mouthing the difficult word and writing it out finally as *semalte* (the usual spelling adopted in the sixteenth century). The pronunciation of *stuc* may well have become known in its Italianate form from the actual speech of Italian workers, much as *terrazzo* has become current outside Italy at the present day (pronounced with [ts] in English).

The number of sixteenth century Italianisms in which these groups appear is sufficiently great to imply some influence upon pronunciation as a whole (54 examples of the medial cluster, 31 initial with on-glide). It would perhaps be wiser, nevertheless, to consider the Italian loans as evidence of a change rather than the cause of it. The tendency towards increasing acceptance of this particular sound-pattern is to be explained partly by the influence of borrowings, especially learned borrowings (which far outnumber those from extraneous sources), and partly because of shifts in the underlying phonemic patterns of Middle French and a wholesale reorientation of the language with reference to the norm of the written (i.e. printed) word which characterises the later Renaissance and Modern period.

Among neologisms incorporating these groups Italian loan-words still account for a notable percentage down to the present day. Examples from the seventeenth century onwards are: *cascade, costume, escabelon, espadon, pastel, postiche, rispetto*; *scapin* and *scaramouche* (in which the Italianising pronunciation has a stylistic value), *store, strapasser, svelte*; eighteenth century: *cascatelle, estouffade, lustrine, marasquin, presto, ristourne*; nineteenth century: *casquer, biscotte, fiasco, pipistrelle, vallisnérie, vasque.*

4. GROUPS pl, bl, fl, kl

Basic situation: In literary Italian the lateral normally palatalises via l mouillé to [j], giving [pj, bj, fj, kj]. In French the group remains stable.

Borrowings from French into Italian during the earlier centuries are infrequent; where they occur they present a variety of developments. The outcome which might be expected, viz., a substitution of Fr. consonant +[l] by consonant+[j] is actually attested in a number of cases (*biasimare* < OFr. *blasmer; fiordaliso* < OFr. *fleur de lis; brocchiere* < OFr. *bouclier;* sixteenth century *chiarino* < *clairin, piattaforma* < *plateforme*). It is not unusual, however, to find the group retained; is this to be interpreted as a Latinising or Gallicising graphy, or are the symbols phonetic? It may be assumed that spellings such as *assemblea, assemblare, blasmare, clero* (= *chiaro*) in Gallicising texts of the thirteenth century indicate a French influence of some kind: the evidence afforded by Italian dialects suggests that both orthography and pronunciation are involved. Regional usage in Italy shows a series of developments; [pj], for instance, becomes [tʃ] in Liguria and adjacent localities, [pʃ] near Bergamo and in the Tessino, [kj] (*chiatto* for *piatto*) in Naples and the south. The group is retained unchanged in certain districts bordering on the Rhaeto-Romance area; Rohlfs supposes the phenomenon to have been current over a much more extensive region during the Middle Ages, and infers from this that whatever uncertainty one might have about similar graphies elsewhere, groups of consonant+l in Old Venetian may be taken as representing the actual sound concerned.[1] The fact that [r], the habitual sporadic substitute for [l], may appear in all these groups under different conditions in various dialects is perhaps the best proof of the existence of a pronounced lateral consonant. In the Middle Ages *assembrea* and *assembrare* seem to have been more used than the forms with [l], even in Gallicising texts.

1. Rohlfs, I, p. 310: 'Man wird also annehmen dürfen, dass auch das *pl* altlombardischer und altvenezianischer Texte (z.B. Marco Polo *plano, plu, planto, planura*) die wirkliche Aussprache der damaligen Zeit wiedergegeben hat.' Cf. also his observations upon groups *bl* (p. 297), *kl* (p. 300), *fl* (p. 304).

Loans with consonant+[l] already appear in the literary language during the sixteenth century (*blasone*, *claretto*) and continue to do so with increasing momentum as the modern period is approached. Examples since 1800 are: *aeroplano*, *autoclave*, *blindare*, *blusa*, *clacche*, *cliscè*, *clivaggio*, *declassato*, *dublè*, *flacone*, *placcato*, *plancia*. The group with [j] continues to appear in borrowings, but the cases registered are mainly calques or similar substitutions, e.g. *piano* assuming the sense of 'design, plan' under the influence of Fr. *plan*, *parapioggia* < *parapluie*, *romanzo chiave* < Fr. *roman à clé*. The analogy in *piantone* is less clear, though Migliorini's suggestion of *piantone* 'young plant, seedling' is reasonable.[1]

Except for cases where the [i] forms part of a suffix (as *-ion* in *bastion* < *bastione*, *espion* < *spione*) Mediaeval French has no place for the Italian group cons.+jod.[2] The segments [pj], [bj], [kj] ceased to form part of the sound-system during Gallo-Roman; [fj] is not usual even in Vulgar Latin. Apart from cons.+jod which arises from tonic [ę] (*pied*, *pierre*, *piège*) it is difficult to find an authentic example of the group before the fourteenth century Latinisms of Bersuire and Oresme (e.g. *pieux* 'pious', *expier*), and the application of *sondages* suggests that even in these cases the [i] turns out to be purely vocalic, on account of a following hiatus.[3] It is therefore to be expected that It. *fiorino* and *spianata* would be borrowed as *florin*, *esplanade*, and that *estropier* < *storpiare* (*stroppiare*) would assume vocalic [i]. Occasionally orthography seems to have had an effect, as in *niche* [ʃ] < *nicchia*; unless here, as very probably in the case of *nocher* (It. *nocchiero* < *nauclerius*, *-arius*) the Venetian -tʃ- corresponding to Tuscan -kkj- < -kl- has played a part.

In the sixteenth century there are signs of an Italian graphy, and doubtless pronunciation also, used for local colour; cf. *pianelle*[4] in the Pléiade generally and *fiasque* for *flasque* in Baïf. Other sixteenth century loans are: *babiole*, *estafier*, *floret*, *gonfler*, *implanter*.

It is now quite usual for the Italian groups to be used where the word is clearly felt to be an exoticism—*piano*, *pianissimo*, *fioriture*—and even in cases

1. See *piantone*, 19th cent. Fr. > It. list.

2. Also possibly *rufien*. But It. *ruffiano* (of uncertain origin) may not be a valid example of Latin fl > fj; in any event the influence of Fr. *-ien*, which remains the normal ending of this word up to its remodelling in modern times, is apparent.

3. Scansion provides a convenient check; in earlier times, *lion*, *pier* ('to drink') are disyllabic; *pieté*, *espier*, *champion* trisyllabic; *espieor* (< *espie*, the OFr. forerunner of *espion*), *espierre* tetrasyllabic. *Pioche* (in Froissart) is dialectal, while hiatus occurred in Francien in such words as *piètre*, *pion* (*peestre*, *peon*). Nevertheless an allophonic semi-consonantalisation of [i] must have taken place in certain phonetic contexts even at the height of the OFr. period (cf. development of 1st and 2nd pers. pl. verbal flexions *-ions*, *-iens*, *-iez* in pres. subj., imp. indic., conditional [M. K. Pope, §§ 267, 918–19, etc.]. Reduction of hiatus here appears to date from the later 13th cent.).

4. *Escoffion*, too (another item of dress); but here as in *lampion* the suffix *-ione* is again involved.

where the Italianism would not be generally recognised—as in *fiasco*, provided that the frequency of use during the earlier stages of borrowing was sufficiently high for the word with its unfamiliar consonantal group to enter general usage.

5. STRESS

Apart from the limited displacement of stress which takes place in respect of the *accent d'intensité*, French accentuation is fixed and non-distinctive. Its most common pattern may be regarded as a combination of a word-prosody and a sentence-prosody, the level and evenly divided enunciation of syllables within a word, or of words within a sentence, being modified by a slightly heavier stress upon the final elements of the unit concerned. Italian is more complex; stressed penultimates predominate, but the accent may fall on any other syllable, though the convention remains invariable for each individual word. In Italian, moreover, stress has a phonemic function, as for instance in the pairs *àncora/ancora*, *bàlia/balia*, *nèttare/nettare*, *prìncipi/principi*, *tèndine/tendine*.

The stress of Italian loan-words is remodelled according to the fixed norm of French, often changing the phonetic aspect of the word radically especially when the Italian word is a proparoxyton: *mènsola* > *mensole*; *sèmola* > *semoule*; *pàtina* > *patine*. In Italian, on the other hand, there is ample precedent to permit the importation of French oxytonic stress unchanged. It is noteworthy, however, that French influence has augmented the category of final-stressed substantives far beyond its original (native) complement, above all in the case of words ending in a final stressed vowel. To see the situation in its true perspective we should remember that, if one takes frequency of use into account, a majority of *parole tronche* actually heard in speech are verbal forms (future, etc.), while of oxytonic substantives existing in the language abstracts in *-tà* account for approximately 95 per cent of the total. If the latter are omitted the 'dictionary words' one finds registered which are stressed on the final syllable and which are traceable to native Italian origins form a very modest group indeed (*virtù*, *servitù*, *lunedì*, *testé*, etc.). They are fewer still if one omits items which a strict formal analysis would define as phrases ending in a stressed monosyllable (*finché*, *cioè*, *perciò* and perhaps *lunedí*, *testé*). Indigenous nouns ending in a stressed vowel other than *-ù* (apart, of course, from *-à*) are extremely rare.[1] On the other hand final *-ò*, *-è* and *ì* are well attested in loans from French, the numerical pattern of borrowings being: seventeenth

1. The word *falò*, often cited, was probably in the first place a loan-word from Greek. It is likely too that the well-known poetic term *mercé*—the short form of etymologically regular *mercede*—was also borrowed, this time from Provençal. *Mercé* had a high frequency of use in Old Italian; according to Professor M. F. M. Meiklejohn examples of it are nearly twice as numerous as the other oxytonic abstracts one meets in thirteenth century verse—*beltà*, *amistà*, etc. (M. F. M. Meiklejohn, 'On the Shortening of Certain

century, 10; eighteenth century, 20; after 1800, 80.[1] In other words lexical interference from French has materially altered the proportion of Italian oxytons ending in a vowel (especially a vowel other than [a], since the beginning of the modern period.

Despite the greater flexibility of its stress system Italian also is sometimes impelled to make adjustments to the stress of foreign borrowings, as in the French-inspired learned terms *acròbata*, *aeròdromo*, *autòcrate*, *chilòmetro*, *manòmetro*. The impulse here is in part socio-psychological. Most educated Italians feel instinctively that the proparoxytonic stress is the appropriate one for learned words formed wholly or partly upon Greek bases, in contradistinction to the man in the street, who tends to make them paroxytons. The musical term *òboe* was originally pronounced *oboè* (eighteenth century), i.e. with accentuation directly modelled upon Fr. *hautbois*.

The different stress pattern of a French loan-word is occasionally preserved to prevent homonymy and so assits in maintaining a semantic distinction: in other words a pattern which was non-distinctive in French becomes distinctive in Italian. The word *mantò* (seventeenth century < Fr.) denotes a very different garment from the *manto* or ceremonial mantle used on state occasions. The use of a tonic final vowel in the word *casino* (*casinò*) instead of the more usual paroxytonic stress (under French influence; opposed to *casino* = 'small country villa', also, 'brothel' helped to single out a particular signification (i.e. the one represented by 'casino' in English) and prevent a formal coincidence with the pejorative term.[2,3]

Finally, a French accentuation is sometimes applied to a native Italian term without conferring any advantage of a phonemic nature, e.g. *lillà* for *lilla*; *sigaro* (1882, Rigutini) for *sìgaro*; *mamà* (1789, Pasqualino) and *mammà* (1877,

---

Abstract Nouns in the Duecento', *Italian Studies*, X, 1955, pp. 51–8; details on p. 56). This fact together with other circumstances lead Professor Meiklejohn to suggest that words of the *volontà* ~ *volontade* type were truncated by analogy with *mercé*, and therefore ultimately because of an external (Occitanian) influence (loc. cit., pp. 57–8). My material adds nothing to our knowledge of how Italian *parole tronche* originated, but it does illustrate how the distribution of a particular feature may be notably altered through foreign interference when—as here—the form in question is but thinly attested in the borrowing language.

1. Before 1600 the only example of a borrowed free oxyton in our lists is *tanè* (15th cent.). Words ending in -*è* and -*ò* are most numerous (*caffè*, *canapè*, *burò*, *borderò*, etc.); -*ù* is less frequent (*monsiù*, *bigiù*); -*ì* and -*à* (-*tà*) are infrequent (*colibrì*, *baccarà*, *viabilità*).

2. The Fr. word was itself an earlier loan from Italian in which the stress was remodelled as described above.

3. It would be misleading to include the pair *canapè*/*cànape* (plural of *cànapa*) under this head, since for both grammatical and semantic reasons the correlation would scarcely ever be required (*cànapa* 'hemp' is a generic word little used in the plural, while the *aires sémantiques* are not contiguous).

F-A.) for *mamma*. Here the exotic stress-pattern is—from the formal stand-point—the only Gallicism detectable.

I should add that the whole question of stress-substitution is bound up with that of transmission from one language to another by means of the written word. A literary or scientific term is far more liable to undergo stress-shift. When abnormal stress-patterns are borrowed through the spoken language the changes which ensue are usually more radical. Where stress-shift occurs in a loan-word which we might expect to find borrowed by word of mouth, special care is needed in reconstructing the historical circumstances. Thus Fr. *trafique* < *tràffico* (as opposed to the English loan *traffic*) may be a case of back-formation < *trafiquer*, which also appears in the fifteenth century; or at least the accentuation of the noun may have been affected by that of verbal forms (pres. indic. singular and 3rd plural, for example). But what can we say about a word like Fr. *comite* 'captain, bo's'un' < It. *còmito*? Here, surely, is as good an example of a 'spoken' borrowing as one could hope to find. My own feeling is that there must have been some overriding sense of morphemic equivalence between the two languages totally unconnected with the written aspect of words, since the speakers were often illiterate (as in this instance). This was not consciously applied or even perceived, of course, but was in the nature of a reflex, an instinctive trans-position. To French ears the stress of *còmito*, *unaffected by the other phonetic considerations*, might suggest an equivalent *comte*, or something like it (cf. *comitem* > *conte* 'count' in earlier times). But there might also be an instinctive movement to preserve [i] (which though unstressed was syllabic and distinctly articulated) despite the stress pattern which would tend to efface it by syncope. To do this within the possibilities afforded by French stress would demand that [i] here should become the stressed vowel of an oxytonic, disyllabic word; and though I can conceive that an urge to maintain [i] might take precedence over that for keeping Italian stress intact (which would be less marked, no doubt, in the speech of a polyglot ship's crew hailing from different regions of Italy or even from different parts of the whole Medit-terranean area) I cannot imagine how this could be achieved in practical terms unless the speakers were aware (a) of a general equivalence between the two languages and (b) of certain regular, constant differences: that words spoken *like that* in Italian were spoken *like this* in their own idiom. We shall find this idea of *cognate equivalents* cropping up elsewhere, e.g. in suffixes.

6. NASAL VOWELS

Problems concerning the representation of nasal vowels arise in Italian rather than French, for the reason that the marked effects of nasalisation which characterise the French vowel system find no ready equivalent in Italian. That the nasalisation in upper Italy has not left its mark on French borrowed vocabulary is probably due to the fact that these dialectal traits have exerted little influence upon the orthographical conventions of literary Italian through which the majority of words pass. French usually chooses between oral and nasal vowel in loan-words strictly on the analogy of native terms, i.e. keeping nasalisation in those cases where a nasal consonant blocks the syllable. Thus we find: [a]+nasal;—*bamboche, dilettante* (nasal *a*) as opposed to *camérier, canon* (oral *a*);[1] [e]+nasal;—*crescendo, vendetta* ([ẽ]) as opposed to *chémer, menestre*; [o]+nasal; —*tontine* ([õ]) as opposed to *sonate*.[2] The convergence of [a]+nasal and [e]+nasal to the one sound [ã] in Old French meant that *en* and *an* of Italian words could be pronounced alike,[3] though a distinction was usually maintained in spelling (*credenza > crédence; bastanza > bastance* [both sixteenth century]).

In French to Italian borrowings the corresponding oral vowels are used. Orthography is more important still, pronunciation usually being determined by spelling; cf. the case of Fr. *an* and *en*: *ambulance > ambulanza*, but *accidenté > accidentato, prétentieux > pretensioso*. Morphological considerations sometimes intervene; cf. *corrente* 'country dance' (seventeenth century) < Fr. *courante* (corresponding pres. part.) as opposed to *affluente* (eighteenth century) where the participle coincides exactly with Fr. *affluent*. Adverbial *-mente* is naturally equated to Fr. *-ment*, the corresponding morpheme.

Adapting the French diphthong [ai] from tonic [a]+nasal to Italian presented some difficulty. It appears on rare occasions with the etymological graphy, as in med. *foraino* < OFr. *forain, daino* < OFr. *dain* (*daim*); forms with metathesis suggest that the diphthong was pronounced as such (*danio*; esp. in fifteenth century). Cf. also *dolzaina*, sixteenth century.[4] *Traino, trainare* are inapplicable cases, formed as they are from vowel [a]+palatal (*traginare*). A complication is added by the analogy of the It. suffix *-ano, -ana*, which usually provokes a reduction of *ai* to *a*: hence *ciambellano, chintana. Anziano* < OFr. *anci(i)en* (tonic [a] prec. by palatal) is probably influenced by *anteanus*, the French word's clerkly Latin etymon. In *persienne* (< Lat. *persiana*) > It. *persiana* the analogy extends to the word as a whole, not merely the suffix; i.e. the sense 'Venetian shutter' is a semantic loan.[5] In more recent examples (seventeenth century onwards) the diphthong whether nasal or denasalised is

1. Occasionally an un-etymological graphy *en* is adopted, e.g. *tremplin* (< *trampolino*).

2. The normal Middle French practice of nasalising all vowels before a nasal consonant irrespective of the nature of the syllable presumably affected borrowings as well, i.e. *bonasse* [bõnasə], *canon*[cãno] (see M. K. Pope, op. cit., pp. 172–3 and 176–7).

3. This was the normal practice, and it still applies to some extent at the present day; the pronunciation of Italian *en* as [ẽ] (see above) is comparatively recent (18th cent. onwards).

4. Though here the facts are less clear. The suffix *-ina* soon exerts an analogical influence, giving *dolcina* (cf. also *doussaine > doucine* in French).

5. The same is probably true of *artesiano* (*pozzo artesiano*) < Fr. *artesien*.

Q

shown as *en*, cf. nineteenth century *morena* < *moraine* and the various re-borrowings of *treno*.

A parallel suffix analogy occurs in the earlier stages of French, though more sporadically; cf. the alternative forms *courtisan* ~ *courtisien*, *courtissain*, *partisane* ~ *partisaine*, *pertuisaigne*, *tramontane* ~ *tramontaine*. The normal development, however, is that of *-ano*, *-ana* > *-an*, *-ane* (*portulan*, *soutane*).

Nearer to modern times there arises a tendency for nasals in Italian to be transcribed phonetically, especially where the original French [ã] was spelt *en*. Already in the sixteenth century we have *passamano* < *passement*; later examples are nineteenth century *panzea* and eighteenth century *agreman(i)*, usually found with a flexional ending, but written as *agremà* in nineteenth century purist dictionaries, which also have such graphies as *voluvàn* for *vol-au-vent*. *Randevù* (earlier *rendevosse*, *rendevù*) is found in the 19th century. The substitution here is probably determined by the conventional value given by many Italian speakers to nasal [ã] in a French word, which approximates to the lowered, partially denasalised vowel heard in southern France. Graphies also recognise a denasalisation of [ẽ] in Italian; cf. *grogrè* (< *grosgrain*) contemporary with Goldoni's *andriè* for *andrienne* (where the French word itself has no nasal). Nasal [ẽ] written in the source language as *in* may be similarly rendered (*bastrè* < *bastringue*).

Almost all borrowings of [i]+nasal concern the exchange of suffixes *-in/ -ino*, *-ine/-ina* (*coquin* > *cocchino*, *festino* > *festin*, etc.). Of the many cases involved[1] few show abnormal developments. Orthography exerts an overwhelming influence, maintaining the vowel [i] in the case of It. *-ino* even at the present day, though Fr. ĩ > ẽ occurred in the later Middle Ages. The treatment of the Germanic suffix *-ing* entering Italian by way of French varies according to the date of the original French borrowing. Thus MHG. *virling* > OFr. *ferlin(c)* > It. *ferlino*: but OHG. *-ing* appears as *-enc*, *-ent* in Old French, to which Italian *-ano* normally corresponds (cf. the mediaeval Fr. > It. loans *balzano*, *ciambellano*).

Borrowing of [o]+nasal and [u, ü] (< Lat. ū)+nasal requires little commentary. The former is copiously represented in exchanges of the suffixes *-on* and *-one* (about 60 borrowings in each direction); its phonology offers no divergencies except that in the nineteenth century Italian loan-words borrowed from French forms with *-on* begin to be transcribed more phonetically as *-ò* (e.g. *bombò*, *pompò* for *bonbon*, *pompon*). Borrowings involving [u] or [ü] in nasal environments (the latter pronounced [ũ] in Middle French) are

1. To take only the masculine forms, about 60 It. > Fr., 30 Fr. > It. The feminine suffixes are less numerous throughout, with the exception of Fr. *-ine* > It. *-ina* in the nineteenth century (numerous at that period on account of scientific and technical neologisms).

infrequent (Fr. *tribune, lagune*) : but in any case there is no interference problem here since the comparatively short-lived nasalisation of French high vowels was a redundant feature.

7. THE REPRESENTATION OF FRENCH DIPHTHONGS [ei], [oi], [we], [wa]

The practice of representing French *oi* phonetically (i.e. taking into account the levelling of the diphthong and the formation of a semi-consonantal [u̯]) dates from the early eighteenth century, when words like *hautbois*, *toilette* entered Italian usage. Graphies show that both of the two alternative French pronunciations current then were transferred; the official, literary, socially approved [u̯e] ([we]) and the more plebeian [u̯a] ([wa]). Thus even in the eighteenth century *tueletta* and *toeletta* alternate with *tualetta*, though the graphy corresponding to [u̯e] is more usual—cf. *framboise* written as *flambuese* or *framboè* and *hautbois* as *oboè* (later, with shift of stress, *òboe*). In the nineteenth century on the other hand *oa* predominates; cf. the spellings *armoàr*, *budoàr*, *patoà* (*patuà*), *soarè* registered and generally condemned by Arlia, Rigutini and other contemporary purists. We must also consider here words in which the diphthong [u̯e] or [u̯a] arises from the juxtaposition in French of semi-consonantal [u̯] or the pure vowel [u] and the vowels [e] or [a], e.g. seventeenth century: *moerre* < *moire* (earlier *mouaire*); eighteenth century *piroetta, piruetta* < *pirouette, siluetta* < *silhouette*; nineteenth century *goeletta* < *goëlette*; and more especially in this later period the combination [o], [u]+[a]: *giaguaro* < *jaguar* (with [gu̯]), *tatuaggio* < *tatouage, zuavo* < *zouave*. There was a tendency in the early modern period to interpose a glide consonant in rendering the diphthongs by juxtaposition, e.g. *piroletta* for *piroetta, dovario* < Fr. *douaire, ovatta* < Fr. *ouate* (though the latter is not a very satisfactory example because its ultimate origin is still uncertain). Such cases provide us with additional evidence to support the assumption that there was a perceptible difference in seventeenth century French between [u̯e] which continued VLat. [ę] diphthongised and the diphthong formed by juxtaposition, in which the first element was closer to a true vowel than was the semi-vocalic onset of the diphthong from tonic free [ę].[1,2] Prior to the seventeenth century the diphthong was frequently rendered by [o], as in *contigia* < *cointise, tosone* < *toison* or by [o]+palatal group, as in *cervogia* < *cervoise, gioiello* < *joiel*. Here we must assume that spelling, prompted by etymology, was the chief influence since it would be unrealistic to assign all loans of this kind to the

---

1. I.e. it may well be that in the case of *ouate* and *pirouette* a pronunciation with two distinct vowels was distinctly heard at the time of borrowing.

2. *Tavoletta* for *toilette* is a popular etymology inspired by the early 18th century meaning (see word-entry). Cf. also the alternative form *teletta* ≠ *tela* 'cloth' (the corresponding etymology in Italian).

early thirteenth century or before, when [oi] was still a descending diphthong.[1]

In certain mediaeval Italian words the French diphthong is realised as [e], e.g. *arnese, tornese, torneio, torneiamento* (*torneamento*); cf. also eighteenth century *ardesia*, where the same development occurs.[2] The presence of [e] in such circumstances is probably due not to a single phonetic development but to a combination of several heterogeneous causes. In the first place the It. suffix *-ese* < Lat. *-e(n)sem* is well established from early times and offers a suitable replacement for Fr. *-ois*, particularly where the etymology suggests it, e.g. in *tournois* < *turone(n)sem* appearing in Italian as *tornese*. The direct influence of Latin must not be entirely discounted, especially in a technical word like It. *ardesia* < Fr. *ardoise* (*lapis ardesius* appears in LowLat.). On the other hand LowLat. *torneamentum* (Du C.: text written in France) is more likely to be a version of the vernacular term in view of the already established Latin vocabulary relating to this sport (*hastiludium, nundina*, etc.; see Bezz., p. 122). Latin forms of *arnese* in Italy during the twelfth and thirteenth centuries often reflect the French pronunciation more closely (initial *h* graphy; ending *-esium* suggesting the palatal element of a diphthong). Our problem is to decide what original sound or sounds the Italian vowel *e* or suffix *-ese* represents. The obvious similarity to Provençal *-es* has led etymologists to claim a southern French origin for most words of this type; but the Provençal term is usually considerably antedated by Old French. Further, historical criteria show that at least two of the words—*tournois* (coin) and *tournoiement/tournoi* refer to things first found in northern France. Even with these words a Provençal intermediary is theoretically possible, but it seems hardly likely in the case of *tournois/tornese* especially, which is a banker's term almost certainly acquired by Italian merchants in France itself. If in one example the parallel between It. *-ese* and Prov. *-es* may be discredited, some element of doubt must inevitably attach to the other instances. Supposing therefore that the proximate source is probably Old French, at what stage in the shift [ę > ei > oi > u̯ę] did the loans take place? Could *arnese* and *torneo* have been borrowed in the early twelfth century, before the French diphthong shifted from [ei] to [oi]? Latin forms attested in Italy from 1194 onwards (*harnesium*, etc.) show that this is a reasonable assumption despite the Italian word's late appearance in the vernacular. The Latin attestations in their turn may be subject to 'time-lag', of course. A Latin equivalent to *harnais* appears in France 80 years before it does so in Italy, and was probably even older. There is reason to believe

---

1. The result is similar in the case of [ę] < earlier OFr. [ai] where the influence or spelling may often be seen (e.g. *saio* < *saie*—pron. [seə] in Late Middle French) beside the phonetic spelling (*segnare* < *saigner, attrezzi* < *attraits*). Cf. also 19th cent. *maionese* < *mayonnaise*.

2. OIt. *reame* continues the OFr. form *reame, reemme* (directly < Lat. *regimen*) rather than *roiaume* (*reialme*) in which there is an analogy of *roial* (*reial*).

that the French word had its origin in a Germanic feudal milieu: if Scandinavian, during the tenth century; if Frankish, appreciably earlier.

An additional variable is introduced into the problem by any doubts one may have about the dating of the [ei > oi] change in French, which traditionally is understood to have occurred about 1150 in dialects of the Île de France and neighbouring districts. Norman and Anglo-Norman did not participate in the shift; in these areas [ei] remained undifferentiated or was reduced to a monophthong [ę]. In this circumstance lies the strength of the hypothesis of Norman origin via southern Italy occasionally invoked to explain this class of loans. Thus It. *-ese* in *tornese, arnese*, and *ei* in *tornei, torneiamento* (the latter incidentally bearing a typical OFr. suffix) would correspond directly to Norman dialectal [ei] or would at least continue through analogy a tradition which began when Norman sounds [ei] or [ę] were represented in this way. A similar retention of [ei] undifferentiated is also typical of dialects of the Loire valley during the twelfth century and this may help to accent specifically for the word *tornese*. A further point of evidence is the English word *tourney*, which bears clear marks of its Norman origin.

To sum up: the French *oi* diphthong tends to be shown as *o* in Old Italian (with a tendency towards etymological restoration), but phonetically as *ue* (*oe*) or *ua* (*oa*) in the modern period. There is some evidence that words were borrowed from forms with the corresponding Norman diphthong [ei]. In all cases we have to guard against a possible Provençal intermediary and make allowance for the influence of the indigenous suffix *-ese* which is etymologically equivalent to both OFr. *-ois* and Norman *-eis* as well as to later French *-ais*. The equivalence clearly operates in recent technical terms.[1]

8. CHANGE OF GENDER

The change of gender occurring in French/Italian is closely linked with rendering of borrowed suffixes discussed below. Italian > French loans are usually the ones concerned and a shift from masculine to feminine most frequently results. The most usual situation is that where the masculine suffix of Italian when rendered phonetically in French approximates sufficiently to the feminine form of the recipient language to become accepted as the genuine indicator of a feminine word.

The shift of gender may take place immediately upon borrowing; thus It. masc. *crinolino* (the textile) appears in 1834 as a fem. Fr. word *crinoline*. Similar cases are Fr. fem. *biscotte* (1830) < masc. *biscotto*, and—as far as I can see—fem. *ritournelle* (Molière) < masc. *ritornello*. In other cases equation of gender to form spreads over a longer period; cf. Fr. *ombrelle*, masc. in Montaigne

1. We see this same suffix equivalence applied in the reverse direction in MFr. *pavois* < It. *pavese*.

(1588), which retained that gender down to the later seventeenth century before giving way to the analogical feminine.[1] Sixteenth century It. > Fr. loans include a number of words first attested as masculines and subsequently 'regularised' as feminines; see the word-entries *caprice* and *cartouche*. In some other cases where the feminine triumphed in the long run both genders were used from early examples, e.g. *boussole, escopette* (*chopet*). Fr. *bronze*, 1511 < It. *bronzo* appears immediately as a feminine and keeps this gender through the sixteenth century, reverting to masculine in the seventeenth when the paradigmatic pressure of other masculine names of metals takes effect. The appearance of *ridotta* for *ridotto* is due to the influence of Fr. (*la*) *redoute* during the Great War. Why Fr. *redoute* (itself < It. *ridotto*; *ridotte* in d'Aubigné) should have become fem. is not easily explained, especially when there is some ground for believing that *doute*, which is masc., exerted an analogical influence.[2]

One of the clearest examples of these processes as they apply to French and Italian is that of *stalle*. The desire to preserve final [l] leads to a revision of graphy from the original *stal* (1568, < It. *stallo*) to *stalle* (masc. in Cotgrave), which is interpreted as a fem. in the later seventeenth century. A similar change involving final [l] is *brocatelle* (fem.) < It. *brocatello*, with *brocatel*, *brocadel* (masc.) earlier.[3]

A gender-shift of a slightly different type is shown in *saponetta* (1855, Fanfani) for *saponetto* (Buon. il Giovane). A remark by Alberti (1788) '*Saponetto* ... si prende comunemente per sapone più gentile e odoroso' suggests that this was the name applied to the particular commodity which (as is well known from historical sources) formed an important part of the French perfumery trade. The older Italian form was therefore in all probability altered in gender as a result of direct contact (alternative usage) with Fr. *savonette* (fem.), attested sixteenth century onwards.

Fr. *cigaret* is replaced in the early nineteenth century by the fem. *cigarette*: a

1. I doubt whether the presence of *ombrella* beside *ombrello* in Italian owes anything to a French influence, as some have said, since the fem. form (like the masc.) was actually attested in Italian (*Ciriffo Calvaneo* [Cr.]) long before the word was transferred to French.

2. See entry in 17th cent. It. > Fr. loans, and note.

3. I notice that this type of hypocharacterisation or inadequate morphological marking (in this case, of gender) does not appear to be catered for in the categories proposed by Professor Yakov Malkiel in his authoritative article 'Diachronic Hypercharacterization in Romance', *Arch. Ling.*, IX, 1957, 79–113 and X, 1958, 1–36. It should presumably come under section B ('Deviations involving a change of gender') of his 'Degrees of Deflection from the norm' (loc. cit., vol. IX, p. 88). It could in fact stand as a corollary or converse to sub-section (b) of that rubric, viz., 'shift from a misleadingly determinate to an appropriately determinate form': in our examples what usually occurs is that the misleading form, e.g. Fr. [brokatẹl] < It. *brocatello*, with sounded final consonant suggesting a feminine, is preserved (and actually reinforced by orthography), whereas it is the gender, the function characterised, that is altered to suit.

hint that the corresponding Italian change *sigaretto* > *sigaretta* is linked with the French may be found in the spelling of one of the earliest It. fem. attestations, *cigaretta* (1845).

Feminine *fresque* corresponding to masculine *fresco* in Italian may derive its gender from the word *peinture* or (more probably) may represent an ellipsis of some kind.[1]

Lastly, a reminder that the removal of 'anomalous' characterisation in borrowed words—as elsewhere—may be delayed indefinitely is given by the French word *soffite* < It. *soffitto*, which still remains masculine at the present day.

9. PREFIXES

Since in the Romance languages the prefix has a greater grammatical function and a smaller semantic function than the suffix (in view of its affinity with the preposition and the adverb) and since the grammatical patterns of a language are less amenable to borrowing than the lexical, it follows that total substitution of foreign forms by native morphemes will be more common in prefixes than in suffixes. The truth of this is illustrated very well by the substitutive power of the Italian prefix *a-*, which replaces foreign prefixes in several words. This is not merely a case of paradigmatic analogy occasioned by the frequency of similar forms in Italian; there is as I see it a sense of functional congruity transcending difference of form between one language and another. When in Canto XI, l. 81 of the *Purgatorio* Dante speaks of

> . . . 'quell'arte
> Ch'*alluminar* chiamata è in Parisi',

whatever may be his narrative or stylistic purpose in rejecting the native term *miniare*, the linguistic fact raises no difficulties of interpretation: the poet considers *alluminare* to be a Gallicism, and yet there is no doubt that the actual French term—used in this sense from at least the third quarter of the twelfth century—is not *alluminer* but *enluminer* (Chrétien de Troyes, for instance, refers to '. . . un sautier/Anluminé a letres d'or' [*Yvain*, l. 1415]).[2] We may conclude, therefore, that for Dante the precise equivalent of French *enluminer*, intuitively, was *alluminare*; and by accepting this conclusion we shall more readily understand why Fr. *enrôler* appears as seventeenth century It. *arruolare*, or for that matter (to move outside the realm of Franco-Italian contacts) why Lat. *expectare* and *exsucare* become *aspettare*, *asciugare* in Italian.

I do not intend to imply that the prefix *a-* of Italian was felt consciously to correspond in its grammatical function to that of *en-* in Old French (though the role they play—independently—in each language is roughly the same).

1. See 17th cent. It. > Fr. word-list.
2. See med. Fr. > It. loans, s.v. *allumare*.

The position is a little more complicated than this. Probably the French prefix was functionally inert as far as Italian speakers were concerned, except perhaps that as a syllabic affix it may have prompted them to put *something* there in its place. What I do suggest, however, is that an Italian verb with prefix *a-* was somehow felt to bring out more fully the predicative force of the foreign verb. This explains why Italian *a-* appears in borrowed forms which possessed no prefix in the original; cf. mediaeval *agghindare* < Fr. *guinder*; sixteenth century *accavalciare* < Fr. *chevaucher*; nineteenth century *accantonare* < Fr. *cantonner*.

10. FINAL CONSONANTS AND SUFFIX ANALOGY

The fate of final consonants casts an interesting light upon the way in which transfer of individual phonic elements is conditioned by the analogy of morphemes in the borrowing language which are formally similar. In this position suffixes are the linguistic elements which naturally tend to be implicated.

French contrasts with Italian in its tendency to weaken the endings of lexical units, provoking first the loss of final vowels and subsequently (later mediaeval period onwards) the weakening and effacement of final consonants. The final vowel of a word borrowed from Italian into French is therefore normally omitted, except that an [a] is realised in pronunciation as mute 'e' up to the beginning of the modern period. In consequence the final consonant of a borrowing is in its turn apt to be effaced, a phenomenon readily revealed by fluctuating graphy, e.g. *anqui(l)* ~ *anquin*, *arsenal* ~ *arsenac*, *parapel* ~ *parapet*, *pasquil* ~ *pasquin*, *brigantil* ~ *brigantin*, *cervelas* ~ *cervelat*, *tournesot* ~ *tournesol*, *piedestat* ~ *piedestal*, *caviar* ~ *caviat* ~ *cavial*, *nochier* ~ *nochiel* ~ *nochief*. Such examples, which are more numerous than might be expected, are confined to the late fourteenth–mid-sixteenth centuries, i.e. the period when pronunciation of finals in French was dictated largely by considerations of syntactical phonetics.[1] The general proclivities which they illustrate are clear; but if we wish to make a more detailed interpretation we need to tread warily. The loss of finals could have occurred outside French. Shifts of this sort are frequent in northern Italian dialects: cf. the treatment of final [n], in respect of which the north-west of the Peninsula shows a parallel development to Provençal.[2] This is no doubt the reason why Vidos derives *arsenac* (~ *arsenal*) from Venetian rather than central or Tuscan Italian. Further, alternation of [l] and [r] is endemic in some regions of northern Italy, so that [l] for [r] may be a dialectal trait manifested in finals as in

1. *Vide* Pope, op. cit., §§ 611–24.
2. *Vide* Rohlfs, I, p. 488 ff.

other positions. And several of the 'mistaken terminations' appear in Cotgrave, who is liable to add final consonants in orthography without good reason, especially *t* (e.g. *zanit* for *zani*).

Consonants [t] and [l] are most frequently affected. Because the former was effaced early, *t* was particularly suitable for showing the caducity of finals (i.e. representing zero final consonant). The use of *l* seems less appropriate to us, who are used to giving the letter its normal phonetic value when it appears in final positions in French; but this is a comparatively recent phonetic restoration. *Parapel* may be taken to indicate a pronunciation [parapé] just as *piedestat, caramoussat* for *piedestal, caramoussal* probably represent [pjedestá] ([pjedetá]?) and [karamusá]. *Anquil* < *anchino, brigantil* from *brigantino*, and possibly *pasquil* for *pasquin* < *pasquino* indicate loss of final [n], whether that loss occurred in Italian or French.[1]

Running counter to the movement towards effacement there is an impulse to re-establish finals, more palpable here than in native French words because the usual 'therapeutic' measures combating phonetic deterioration are not the only ones involved. In earlier stages of the interim period (see below, pp. 609-11) there is a tendency to place the exotic term in inverted commas, so to speak, by a play of emphasis and juncture, either to ensure correct reception of an unfamiliar word or to prepare the audience for a shift to the phonemic system of the foreign language. In either case the likelihood of finals surviving is increased. Examples of reinforcement becoming permanently accepted are *leste* < It. *lesto, intrigue* < It. *intrigo, baroque* < It. *barocco, caïque* < *caïcco* (but *caïq, cayc* earlier), med. and sixteenth century *trafique* < *traffico, buste* < *busto* (earlier *bust*, and sporadically *busque*).[2]

The more the termination is phonetically buttressed in this way, the greater the possibility of its being attracted by suffixes, which as established morphemes—crystallised, as it were, by their property of expressing meaning—form powerful nuclei of analogical effect (e.g. *campanille* for *campanil(e)*).

---

1. *Pasquil* is the first example of *pasquin* so far attested, in a letter of Feb. 1536 written by Rabelais to Geoffroy d'Estissac, bishop of Maillezais. Since the letter appears in a handwritten document of the first half of the 17th cent. which claims to be a true copy of the original, it is likely that the -*il* spelling is authentic. A difficulty arises in respect of this borrowing, because the Italian word is occasionally found with the suffix -*illo* as an alternative to the more normal -*ino*, and Rabelais may have taken it direct from the It. form with [l]. No corresponding explanation is available, however, to account for the other words which show alternation between final [n] and final [l]. Was the stressed vowel [i] or [ĩ] ([i] + nasal) for Rabelais? Presumably the latter; certainly not [ẽ], but then [i] + nasal had not lowered generally at that time (except perhaps in Parisian usage, *vide* Pope, §§451-5). *Vide pasquin*, 16th cent. It. > Fr. loans. A hypercorrect orthography is seen in *reversin* for *reversi* 1601 and Cotgr.

2. Cf. in addition the anomalous form *parapete* for *parapet* in Rab., 1546 *Tiers Livre* and 1549 *Sciomachie* (M-Lav., II, 7 and III, 397, 402).

Suffixes

As regards the borrowing of suffixes proper the substitute adopted is largely determined by two factors, (1) the existence or not of a formally parallel suffix in the borrowing idiom (2) the relative strength of the parallel suffixes in the two languages—how well they are attested, how far formally distinctive, how far recognised as operative suffixes; in other words, to what extent they are recommended by statistical, formal and semantic characteristics. Let us for convenience call a suffix which is firmly grounded in this way 'strong'. When suffixes are strong in both languages (e.g. *-in* ~ *-ino*; *-ette* ~ *etta*; *-asque* ~ *-asca*; *-elle* ~ *-ella*) interference during the transfer is slight. Where there is a serious inadequacy in respect of one or more of these three characteristics, the tendency for suffixes to be substituted is great. Thus little-used Fr. *-an*, *-ane* from the stronger Italian suffix *-ano*, *-ana* tends to be replaced by *-ain*, *-aine*.

Suffixes may be lost as a result of phonetic attrition. A case in point is It. *-occo*, which reduces to [ǫ] in French and ceases to be recognised as a separate morpheme (witness the spelling of *tarot* as *tarau* in Rabelais, and *artichaut*) unless reinforced to *-oque* as in *baroque*, above. We have already seen how Italian masculine suffixes are equated to feminines as a result of preserving the finals intact; here again much depends on the strength with which the masculine equivalent of French is established (i.e. the one without final consonant, except in liaison and isolated positions during the later mediaeval and early modern period). For this reason It. *-etto* is readily realised as the strong Fr. suffix *-et* (*floret*, *estivalet*, *ballet*, *stylet*); while in the opposite direction Fr. *-et*, though frequently rendered by direct phonetic substitution in modern times[1] is quite likely to be adapted to *-etto* (e.g. *gilet* as *gilè* or *giletto*, seventeenth century *buffetto* beside nineteenth century *buffè*. There are many nineteenth century examples—*appretto*, *mughetto*, *picchetto*, *rubinetto*, etc. Masculine *-otto* > *-ot* (a moderately strong suffix in French) is often attested (*cavalot*, *estradiot*); there are even cases of false suffixation in favour of this form (*falot* < *falò* and *tarots* < *tarocchi* above).

Interference also occurs between the nominal suffixes and forms of the past participle which resemble them. A vestigial suffix form represented by the ending *-it* results in French from the influence of the Italian past participle in *-ito* (distinguished from the p. part. of Fr. *-ir* verbs not only by orthography but by the actual pronunciation of [t] in certain circumstances at the time when earlier words of this type were borrowed, and also semantically (elimination of the bound morpheme through loss of participial force): *crédit*, *bandit*, *granit*, *favorit* (> *favori* later), *transit*.[2] In such cases as these

1. Cf. *bidè*, *bignè*, *croscè* in 18th and 19th cent. lists.
2. Fr. *candi* (med. loans) possibly reflects a form *candi* in Italian (*zucchero candi*, < Arab. *qandi*) instead of the usual *candito* with attraction of the verbal flexion.

everything depends upon the degree to which the grammatical function remains transparent to the borrower. In Fr. words with *-at* < It. *-ato* the participial force is seldom felt (e.g. *incarnat, cervelat, calfat, soldat*), not so much on account of the impact of native substantives possessing this suffix (*verrat, crachat*), which are quite rare, but simply because lack of transparency resulting from transfer has caused this particular connotation to be effaced. *Renégat* is a separate word from earlier *renié*; sixteenth century *brocat* 'brocade' is so far removed from the p. part. *broccato* that it assumes the suffix *-ard* (*brocart*). To get a just perspective, however, we must recognise that It. > Fr. loans with *-é* do exist (*affidé* < *affidato*), particularly when the predicative force of the word obtrudes itself (*stenté* < *stentato*). The 1585 edition of Montaigne Gallicises *stropiat* to *estropié* (see sixteenth century loans, s.v. *estropiat*).

Italian is more ready to replace the French participle by an indigenous flexion: *-é* > *-ato*. Here again something depends on the implicit verbal force (cf. *affarato* < *affairé, appuntato* < *appointé, debosciato* < *débauché*). Yet recourse to a native equivalent is also common where the predicative implication is more tenuous, e.g. *accidentato* < *accidenté, congiato* < *congé* and, etymologically distinct, but similar in form and principle—eighteenth century *comitato* < *comité*. Cf. also the alternative forms *consumè* ~ *consumato*, *picchè* ~ *piccato, pilè* ~ *pilato*. This conservative tendency which may be taken to represent the fundamental instincts of Italian is overlaid in recent times by a movement towards direct imitation of the foreign sound *-é* and *-ée*, which tend to be realised as a vowel more open than the French: (*vino*) *brulè, dublè, lamè, frappè*, etc. The impulse to substitute an indigenous flexion is even more apparent in borrowings of Fr. *-ée*. Here adaptation, though occasionally total (*portata* < Fr. *portée*) is more frequently of an intermediate kind in which the stressed vowel is retained with It. *-a* added for mute 'e', creating an Italian suffix *-ea*. Examples are numerous, above all in the Middle Ages: *entrea, mislea, giornea, vallea, achinea, contea, trincea*; sporadically, *desinea* for *desinata* < MidFr. *disnée*. Italian *-ea* is still found after French mute 'e' ceased to have phonetic value, e.g. a form *burea* (1709) for *burè* < *bourrée*, *allea* < *allée, panzea* < *pensée*, and the alternative *fricassea* ~ *fricassè, purea* ~ *purè*.

The entire absence of French words terminating in *-ée* from the fem. p. part. Of Italian *-ata*[1] occasions no surprise. We should expect to find a phonetic adaptation or a morphological substitution on the lines of *-ato* > *-at* above. What does raise a problem, and a considerable one, is the fact that the obvious adaptation *-ate* seldom occurs. A suffix with voiced consonant, *-ade*, is almost always used instead. The provenance of *-ade* has given rise to a great deal of discussion, and is still not satisfactorily explained. The word-lists

---

1. *Sigisbée* (18th cent.) < It. *cicisbeo* (onom.) does not of course fall into this category.

indicate that we might be able to make a useful reappraisal by observing more closely its semantic development during the fifteenth and sixteenth centuries.[1]

On the origin of the suffix lexicographers hold conflicting views. Earlier scholars' predilection for an Italian provenance (Hatzfeld and Darmesteter, Marty-Laveaux) has been largely corrected by a later emphasis on Provençal, especially on the part of von Wartburg. The latter idiom was in a favourable position for historical and cultural reasons as well as linguistic ones and a substantial number of words were drawn from this source. Some of the southern French terms can be narrowed down to the Gascon area; this is probably the source of *pistoulade* (Monluc; d'Aubigné, *Les Aventures du Baron de Faeneste*) and ultimately that of *barricade*.[2] Brunot added *harpade* (*Hist.*, II, p. 214), *pomade* ('cidre') (given as Monluc; actually early sixteenth century), *revirade* (Montaigne), *veguade* ('fois, coup') (Rab.) and also *a passades* ('par intermittence'), which he registered in du Bartas, but which goes back to the fifteenth century and is very probably from Italian (see mediaeval loans) (*Hist.*, II, p. 180). Spanish has contributed several terms: *alcade, algarade, armade, capilotade, camarade, à la désespérade, estrade, fanfaronnade, nacarade, panade, parade, peuplade, tornade* and probably *à la soldade, alegrade, verdugade*; Portuguese, *chamade*,[3] the popular etymology *moscovade, pintade* and probably *marmelade, travade*. *Bancade* (space between benches of a galley) may be Catalan or Provençal, while *caronade* (1783, *Encycl. méth.*) is a loan from English *caronade*, a type of cannon made at Carron in Scotland.

The crucial periods for the suffix's development are the fifteenth and sixteenth centuries. In the former it was established as a distinct French morpheme; in the latter it acquired its characteristic meanings. Italian influence entered into both processes—decisively, in my opinion, as regards the second; less obviously but probably also decisively in the first. What we

1. Carl S. R. Collin's monograph *Étude sur le développement de sens du suffixe -ata*, Lund, 1918 (based on earlier articles from 1906) is still useful as a source of examples and of information about forms in the Romance languages, but it no more than touches on the fringe of this problem. The same is true of Luther H. Alexander's thesis *Participal Substantives of the -ata type in the Romance languages*, New York, 1912, which is a very good dictionary of forms but only devotes a page to discussing the *-ade* suffix.

2. Contrary to the opinion of some etymologists the word *gasconnade* is not a Gasconism, any more than *espagnolade* (Cotgrave: 'a Spanish tricke') is a Hispanicism. It is psychologically improbable that it should be, quite apart from other considerations, since ironical terms of this kind are invariably applied to national or social groups other than one's own. Cf. the oft-cited example *filer à l'anglaise* ~ *to take French leave* or the disease syphilis, known (according to the nationality of the speaker) as *le mal de Naples* (1496 in a document from Avignon referring to the expedition of Charles VIII), *napleux* (which apparently goes back to the siege of Naples in 1528) or *il morbo gallico*.

3. Though B-Wart. (like the *D.G.* and Wind) draw it from Italian and allude to the shift Lat. [kl-] > [tʃ-] in certain NIt. dialects.

have to explain is how the influence operated and why it should have been manifested through what appears to be a non-Tuscan form.

Forty-seven of our words in all with the suffix -*ade* were actually borrowed from Italian. The list is: Mediaeval: *ambassade, bastonnade, brigade, cavalcade, embuscade, escalade, esplanade (battre l') estrade, estrappade, gambade, grenade, lançade, (a)passades, salade* (helmet), *salade* (food). Sixteenth century: *arcade, balustrade, bravade, canonnade, carbonnade, cassade, escapade, estafilade, estacade, estocade, façade, fougade, intrade, lancespessade, mascarade, pavesade, pesade, poignelade, pomade, rambade, retirade, saccade, sérénade, taillade.* Seventeenth century: *cascade, écavessade, falcade, incartade, orangeade, pasquinade.*[1] Eighteenth century: *bambochade, estouffade.* Nineteenth century: Nil. It is instructive to compare these figures with those for the suffix as a whole. A list of relevant words up to and including Cotgrave (1611) with Italianisms omitted runs as follows:[2]

abordade	+bouade	carabinade	embrassade
accolade	+bo(u)lade	cargade	enfilade
aiguade	+bourgade	cassonade	escouade
+aiguillade	bourrade	chamade	+esgarrade
aillade	boursoufflade	chopade	espagnolade
+aissade	boussade	choquade	esperonnade
alcade	boutade	cicade	esrafflade
alegrade	+brequenade	clavelade	estoup(p)ade
algarade	brevade	coyonnade	fanfaronnade
alidade	brevetade	condemnade	favade
ambrosiade	brigade	coquillade	feuillade
annonciade	bringade	cornade	+flagerade
armade	bronchade	coutillade	flanquade
+arquebusade	buissonnade	couvade	+flassade
arrosade	cacade	+croisade	fleschade
+aubade	cachebugade	cruciade	fouettade
+ballade	cagade	dorade	fougade
ballottade	calade	dentade	('leap')
barrettade	camerade	debandade	frescade
becquade	cannisade	desesperade	fressurade
benade	capilotade	desgainnade	+fringade

1. In addition *rassade* 'glass beads for commerce with natives' i.e. 'trade goods' (1614, Y. d'Evreux) is very probably connected with It. *raggiare, razzare* 'to shine'. It is, however, possible that the suffix may have been added in French. *Caristade* (beggars' slang: 'hand-out'), which is usually registered as in Vidocq, 1837, though it appears earlier, in 1622, *Caquets de l'Accouchée,* may be a deliberate alteration of dialectal It. *caritade.* There are several other 'possibles'.

2. Forms preceded by + date from before 1500. I have not included words which continue the Greek suffix –άδ–α (nom. άς) as in *monade, ogdoade,* etc., or derivatives which are associated (or seem principally to be associated) with those Hellenisms.

gabionnade	+mezellade	penade	+raillonnade
galopade	mocade	+petar(r)ade	ratepenade
gaulade	+morgade	peuplade	rebuffade
genouillade	mousquetade	pigeonnade	reculade
giroflade	+muscade	pinçade	reposade
glissade	nacarade	pisto(u)lade	revirade
gourmade	niflade	plommade	rodomontade
griffade	onglade	+plonmade	+ruade
grouppade	oblade	poignardade	saluade
+guingade	+oeillade	poinçonnade	sanglade
harpade	orade	poivrade	savorade
harengade	+ostade	pommade	secouade
heurtade	ouillade	('cider')	+sivade
hivernade	+paillade	pommade	+somade
jarretade	palissade	('acrobat's	+sonade
joncade	paloüade	trick')	tenaillade
+journade	panade	pegade	tirade
lentillade	pantalonnade	poussade	vegade
+lievrade	parade	poustaignade	verducade
lignade	(equit., etc.)	promenade	vetade
louade	+pastenade	pugnerade	+vinade
malesuade	+peiregade	+quiade	virade
+margade	pelade	rafflade	Total: 170[1]

Numbers of Provençal and Italian borrowings before 1500 are roughly commensurate—Provençal, 19 plus 3 or 4 possibly from that source; Italian, 14 plus 2 possibles. But there are significant differences between the two groups. A large proportion of the Provençalisms are exotic terms, or hapaxes, or both. Our information about many of them is provided by Godefroy, who in turn brought them to light from a series of fifteenth century legal depositions in which one often found a local (especially southern) term cited, presumably in the interests of accuracy. Thus we learn that *peiregade* (1464) denotes a game of chance; *bolade* is a kind of bludgeon ('leur bailla deux bolades ou massues' 1409: Godef., s.v. *bolade*); *flagerade* is also a cudgel of some sort ('un grant cop d'une flagerade sur le cap' [1476, Godef., s.v.]). More often than not the word has to be defined: 'le suppliant print de l'eaue en ung petit vaisseau appellé en limosin *quiade* (1466, Godef., s.v.); 'margade ou seiche' ('squid'; fifteenth century); 'esgarrade … qui vault autant a dire comme une tres grant plaie' ('scar'; 1411 Godef., *Comp.*, s.v.). *Mezellade*

1. Of the 170 no fewer than 57 are first attested by Cotgrave; most of these have a very limited use and a considerable proportion are hapaxes confined to that author. The total of Italianisms up to 1611 is 42, i.e. almost exactly a fifth of the whole, though as we shall see their importance is greater than this ratio suggests. In the same period between 50 and 60 words are drawn directly from Provençal or very probably so.

(1471) 'space between two furrows' is patently a term of the *langue d'oc*, not the *langue d'oïl*. There are one or two other local measures and items of legal phraseology.[1]

Six terms remain which really did strike root in Middle French usage: *ballade*, thirteenth century in Adam de la Halle; *muscade* 'nutmeg' also thirteenth century, *Antidotaire Nicolas*; *flassade* 'bed-covering, saddle-cover' or similar, Jehan le Bel; *somade* 'load carried by a sumpter-horse', Froissart (the last two abundantly documented in the Middle Ages, though obsolescent by the sixteenth century[2]); *aubade* and *petar(r)ade*, fifteenth century. In the opposite pan of the scales we can throw virtually all the Italianisms. Most of them are still widely used now, as they were in the fifteenth century.

But the most suggestive point of evidence in favour of Italian is this: most of the *-ade* terminations are distinct morphemes in the Italian loans whereas in most of the Provençalisms they are semantically opaque. In neither case are the borrowed derivatives all opaque or all transparent, and these qualities are, naturally, relative; nevertheless forms like *bastonnade*, *escalade*, *cavalcade* are more typical of the loans from Italian, and *muscade*, *pastenade* and *aiguillade* (concrete noun meaning 'goad'), of those from Provençal. This essential difference comes out quite clearly in the thirty-odd words drawn from Provençal during the sixteenth century. In most of them the *-ade* contributes nothing as far as the French user is concerned; even when they possess a significant suffix its connotation is seldom a focal or typical one associated with *-ade* (see below), but usually a direct equivalent of French *-ée* (*abordade*, *dorade*, *giroflade*, *veg(u)ade* = 'time, single occasion'; cf. OFr. *foiiée*, *fiée*).

At what moment did the suffix become productive in French? The answer depends upon our etymological and semantic interpretation of twelve remaining fifteenth century words, among which we may expect the earliest examples of indigenous derivatives to be found: *arquebusade*, *bourgade*, *croisade*, *journade*, *morgade*, *oeillade*, *ostade*, *palissade*, *pen(n)ade*, *raillonnade*, *ruade*,

---

1. *Sivade* 'oats', *brecquenade* 'cereise un poc aigre', *aissade* 'hoe' and *aiguillade* are exotic or peripheral in exactly the same way. *Plonmade* 'balance weight on the handle of an oar' (1382) is a genuine borrowing, but within a highly restricted terminology. *Pastenade* is a special case. The isolated regional form of 1372 (Corbichon) undoubtedly goes back to Prov. *pastenaga*, documented 14th cent. in Ariège meaning 'carrot' and the source of MFr., ModFr. *pastenague* in various sense (*vide FEW*, VII, *pastinaca*, 752–7, esp. 753a). Wartburg, who registers Fr. *pastenade*, *pastinade* 'carrot', then 'parsnip' from the beginning of the 16th cent. (*pastinade domestique* 'panais' in 1501; others 1530, 1536, 1539, etc., ibid., 754a) considers the element *-ade* to be 'apparently an occitanian form' (756a). It could also be an authentic French formation since by that date the suffix had become productive. During the 16th cent. this word is commonly found with alternative suffixes both in French and Provençal which do not show any immediate sign of a shift from the south to the north (*pastinaille* 'parsnip' c. 1543; *pastinaque* 'carrot' 1551).

2. The 15th cent. examples of *flassade* are almost all in actual fact *flassarde*, so the *-ade* termination is sporadic here too.

sonade. Palissade, which appears in Le Fèvre de Saint-Rémy's *Mémoires* referring to the fortifications of Namur is usually held to be a derivative of OFr. *palis* (twelfth century, *Enéas*) 'row of stakes'. I am inclined to think that it could be an Italianism on account of the existence of earlier forms in Italian—*palicciata* in the *Plutarco volgarizzato* and *palizzato* in M. Villani (both 14th cent.) as well as on historical grounds—movement of military terms from the Italian peninsula at this period.[1] The history of *arquebusade* (1478) is bound up with that of *arquebuse* (It. *arcobuso*) which we discussed in the sixteenth century list. It too may well be a direct Italianism. Whatever the origin of *croisade* may be it is almost certainly not indigenous but an external substitute for native French *croisée*, invalidated in this sense through semantic change (influence of Sp. *cruzada*, It. *crociata*? Or a direct formal Provençal counterpart of OFr. *croisée*, specialised in meaning?) *Bourgade* (1418) could be an occitanian form, though an Italianism is not impossible. It. *borgata* is attested as early as the thirteenth century (Ricordano Malispini). Two crucial and most interesting words are *morgade*, 1464 and *ostade*, 1469. In both cases the *-ade* suffix is an approximation in French to a termination in other languages which sounds rather similar. It is therefore clearly a discrete form. The first appears in a text from Brittany: 'Morgade, c'est un poisson, bret. morgadenn' (Godef., s.v.), while the other, a valued weave of woollen cloth, is to all appearances an adaptation of Eng. *worsted*, MEng. *woosted* attested 1293 (*OED*), from the place-name *Worstead* in Lincolnshire. *Ostade* is frequently attested in accounts and inventories during the second half of the century and was indisputably a term in general use. Guillaume Coquillart has *œill-ade* in the sense of 'meaningful or conspiratorial glance' in the phrase *les mots adgencez et œullades, Monol. du Puys*, publ. by E. Picot in *Romania*, XIV, p. 479. Godef. registers *œilades* in the early sixteenth century. I take it to be a native derivative. The absence of an Italian or Provençal equivalent argues for a native origin also in the case of *ruade* (equit.: 'kicking or shying of a horse') in Jean d'Authon, and on a par with *ruade* we can take *penade* or *pennade* ('rearing or bucking of a horse') which continued in vigour right through the following century. I am less sure about the status of *journade* (J. de Wavrin, *Anchiennes Chroniques d'Engleterre*), 'smock or working overall (for men or women)' and *sonade* (O. de la Marche and others in the fifteenth century) 'flourish of trumpets', both of which were in current usage, but there seems no doubt that *raillonnade* (1460) 'crossbow shot' is a French derivative from *raillon* 'quarrel of a crossbow'. I associate it closely with the contemporary Italianisms *lançade* (1460) 'thrust with a lance' and also with *estrappade* (1432) and *bastonnade* (1482) which share with it the implications of 'blow with a weapon' and violence to the person. In *embrassade* (1500) 'act of embracing,

1. Cf. the mid-16th cent. borrowing *estacade*, which denotes a similar military construction.

overt expression of friendship' the suffix is seen to be soundly established and the semantic development launched upon its typical French course.[1]

Investigating the suffix in its mediaeval context thus confirms while ante-dating it somewhat Wind's assertion that 'dès les premières années du XVIe siècle, ce suffixe s'ajoutait . . . à des radicaux français'.[2] French-*ade* had acquired a separate semantic entity, had become a bound morpheme, by the middle of the fifteenth century at the latest. It was firmly established later in the century. Coquillart, Commines and d'Authon, whose works supply examples of several lexical innovations from Italy, are precisely the authors who might be expected to sense the 'separateness' of the Italian form and experiment with similar uses in French.

That it was indeed Italian rather than Provençal which provided the necessary stimulus to create a discrete suffix is vouched for by morphemic considerations, as we have seen. But the actual connotation and the semantic history are more revealing still. Certain meanings typical of Italian were exploited in French, creating eventually a new suffix which has its own special, distinct connotation. The significations concerned are as follows: (1) a meaning-group of which *canonnade* is perhaps the best illustration (though not the prototype) which implies the action of discharging a weapon, some-times once, sometimes repeatedly,[3] together with its effect. There is an accompaniment of technical and argotic overtones (military slang). Examples are *lançade* (1460), *arquebusade* (1478), *canonnade*, *mousequetade*, *escopetade* (the sixteenth century equivalent of 'a whiff of grapeshot'), *pistoulade*, leading to seventeenth century *carabinade*, eighteenth century *fusillade*, *mitraillade*, etc.[4] This group is obviously linked with the allied connotation of rapid, multiple action, especially blows, which begins to be attested during the mediaeval period with the loans *estrappade* (1482) and *bastonnade* (1482), followed by sixteenth century *estafilade*, *saccade*, *écavessade* (1611) and in the same period the French derivatives *sanglade* 'a horse-whipping' (Rab.; < *sangle* 'girth'), *griffade* (1564), *gourmade* (Montlyard, originally a term of horsemanship from *gourme* [mod. *gourmette*] 'curb-chain of a horse's bit'), *gaulade* 'blow with a

---

1. Note the affinities of sound and of sense between *embrassade* and the 14th cent. Italian borrowing *ambassade*. In 1500 verbal humour was going through the most fashionable phase French literature was ever to know; speakers of the time would certainly be sensible of the ironical pun which was available to them.

2. Op. cit., p. 45 n. 4. Brunot gave the date as 16th cent. without further precision (*Hist.*, II, p. 214).

3. The implication '*volley*, from a missile weapon' becomes inherent during the 17th cent.

4. Forms like *frecciata* in the 14th cent. (*Vit. Plut. volg.*; derived from the recent Fr. loan-word *freccia*) show that this suffixal usage was indigenous in Italian during the Middle Ages. It roughly corresponds to that of Fr. *-ée* (*archée*, etc.). *Flechade* in Brantôme is probably inspired by Italian.

R

staff' (d'Aub.) and others.[1] *Souffletade, bousculade*, etc., continue this semantic category later. (2) A more complex notional group implying a concerted undertaking, activity or action of an involved nature: *ambassade* (1361), *camisade* (1552), *cavalcade* (1349), *embuscade* (Alain Chartier), *escalade* (1427) *escapade, retirade* (both Monluc) and in its original sense, *brigade*, 1372 (all loan-words). I associate with these the further signification of 'polished, skilful evolution', e.g. in terms of fencing and equitation: sixteenth century *taillade, estocade, poignelade; parade, pesade, grouppade, reculade* etc. (*vide supra*). All these uses invite irony or pejoration.[2] The step is a short one from 'concerted action' to 'collusion, ruse' (already latent in *camisade, embuscade*[3]); in the second case skill and dexterity easily became sleight of hand, 'pulling the wool over one's eyes' (e.g. *cassade* (1548), a finesse or actual deception at cards). Words for beating, thrashings, are obvious sources of pejoration. A pejorative use has continued to be associated with the suffix (cf. *noyade* 1794), though a more typical connotation is that of an amused irony (*toquade*, Goncourts; *gueulade*, Flaubert, etc.). Out of the various shades of meaning we have just defined—some imported, some developed in French—there arose during the later sixteenth century an overtone of machination coupled with that of pompous, foolish, sly or boastful behaviour, often associated with foreignness (cf. the semantic shift of *bravade* from a neutral or commendatory use to the modern sense, already in Noël du Fail and Grévin). This is seen especially in words derived from personal names: seventeenth century *pasquinade* < It.; but already in the sixteenth century *pantalonnade, rodomontade, fanfaronnade* (prob. < Sp.), *gasconnade*; seventeenth century *turlupinade*, eighteenth century *arlequinade*, nineteenth century *lapalissade* (Goncourts). Here the suffix has profited to some extent from the etymologically distinct form (*i*)*ade* < Gk.-άδ-α (as in *Iliade*) which in the sixteenth century was applied to contemporary epic (*Franciade*) but soon became productive with a mock-epic implication (*Mazarinades, Poissonades*, etc.). To my mind, however, the reverse effect of -*ade* (ironical) on (*i*)*ade* (epic) was even more important.

To return to the formal aspect. The crucial period at which -*ade* becomes active in French coincides with France's re-entry into the northern Italian political and military scene under Louis XI and Charles VIII. In these circumstances the termination with voiced consonant was the natural one to achieve

1. Up to 1611: *bourrade, choquade* (a tautology in that the suffix reiterates the sense of the base), *cornade, dentade, esperronnade, (es)rafflade, fouettade, harpade, jarretade, poignelade*.

2. Cf. the sense of *embrassade*, above; also *barettade* 'exaggerated salutations', in des Periers, Rabelais, du Fail and *fressurades* 'complements of outward courtesie . . . as, the bowing of the knee, or a stooping to touch one anothers knees; trifling, . . . toying, idle gestures', in Cotgrave. Some derivatives are frankly unpleasant in connotation (*coyonnade* [Monluc], *malesuade* [Cotgr.]).

3. Similar traits are inherent in *mascarade*.

acceptance as the typical form likely to be found in Italian words and hence—helped by the analogy of Provençal—the one which was added to the inventory of French suffixes.[1] But to say that *-ade* is a northern Italian form, or a compromise between northern Italian and other languages (Spanish, Provençal, etc.) is not the whole story. It owes its existence as an active suffix principally to Italian; phonetically it has an Italian and a Provençal background: but even more it is a formal entity in its own right. Long before the time when a knowledge of Tuscan Italian came to be a common accomplishment at court under Henri II the new suffix had achieved its status of a *conventional equivalent*. The extent to which this non-Tuscan form—this accepted pseudo-borrowing—became a suffix *à tout faire* is shown initially by the way it ousted early Tuscanisms (cf. the graphies *arcate* ~ *arcade*, *pavesate* ~ *pavesade*, *eustacatte* ~ *estacade* [*vide* sixteenth century list]) and subsequently by its extended application in the several senses outlined above. Semantic developments called the bound morpheme into being: in this instance the linguistic element's phonetic aspect can only be elucidated satisfactorily if we first reconstruct in detail the history of its signification.

The Process of Borrowing: Formal Considerations

It is salutary to return constantly to the axiom that in the ultimate analysis the prime mover in linguistic borrowing—whether formal or semantic—is the individual speaker, the genesis of the transfer occurring at the moment when, upon contact with a foreign spoken or written linguistic element, a given *image acoustique* is formed in the individual's mind. This is the atom, so to speak; but from the atom to the substance and from the substance to the final product many processes intervene. From the actual moment of contact to the beginning of acceptance it is possible to trace the borrowing through a number of different phases and to consider it in the light of many different influences, each having its own characteristics, each intercalated within a broader motivation. We are not obliged to enter the inquiry at the first stage; while it is convenient to do so in analysing contacts between bilingual speakers, the study of interference between Italian and French can be approached more effectively at a level of greater complexity—that of the organised language taken as a whole, i.e. of *langue*.

ACT OF TRANSFER AND INTERIM PERIOD

Although the idiolects of individuals who gallicise or italianise do not concern us greatly, the formal developments in the period immediately preceding

1. Alternative forms with Tuscan [t] are rare before the 16th century, but cf. *cavalcate* for *cavalcade* in André de la Vigne and *cellata* for *salade* (helmet) in 1417.

acceptance into the established language are, on the contrary, of crucial importance.

This preliminary stage is one of fluctuation and experiment, qualified success and temporary rejection, during which the incoming word is subjected to the environment of the recipient language and measured against the template of formal conventions in the new idiom. The extraneous element enters upon what I should like to call the *interim period*. We may catch a glimpse of the vacillation which occurs at this time by arranging the different lexical forms attested in order of dating and comparing earlier examples with the definitive pronunciation. It is usual for the earlier examples of a loan to resemble the foreign etymon more closely, succeeding attestations being more fully integrated into the new linguistic traditions: e.g. *alianza* (1619) becoming *alleanza* in the later seventeenth century; *bambasin* in Marco Polo (< *bambagino* with Venet. -*s*- for -*gi*-) giving way to *bombasin* after the analogy of *bon* had operated; fifteenth century *bocon* (< *boccone*) and sixteenth century *cartoche* replaced by *boucon* and *cartouche* in the sixteenth;[1] *ciamberlano* in G. Villani ousted subsequently by the modern *ciambellano*; sixteenth century *bourlesque* before *burlesque*, *tuorbe* before *téorbe*, *doccia* before *douche*; Fr. *canelature* preceding the adapted form *cannelure*, < *cannellatura*; seventeenth century *soutecouppe* before *soucoupe*, *portoro* before *portor*; and It. *guetri* (< *guêtre*(s)) in 1819 beside *ghette*, which quickly became the permanent form.[2]

The opposite development is less usual, i.e. later attestations closer to the etymon, though it does occur when a word incorrectly received is remodelled later either because it has been heard more precisely or because the influence of orthography has made itself felt: e.g. fifteenth century *camerlin* replaced by *camerlingue*; mediaeval Fr. *rufien* spelt *rufian* later; sixteenth century calque *hautier* giving way to *altier*.

After a lapse of time the stabilising and crystallising influence of usage begins to take effect, perhaps operating (as we have seen) through the prestige of a well-known literary work, or as a result of some chance happening which casts the word before the public in a particular form—its use in a slogan, its presence in some remark made by a widely known individual, or its becoming intimately associated with some specific object or activity which impinges strongly upon the public consciousness. The borrowed material becomes less malleable; the impact of random analogy diminishes and con-

1. There are several examples in the 16th cent. of It. [o] replaced in Fr. after an interval by [u]. The shift in borrowed words forms one aspect of a wider o ~ u alternation typical of this century in which social differentiation and the impact of Classical Latin play dominant roles.

2. Among examples of formal vacillation of this type may be included ephemeral Gallicisms subsequently rejected, e.g. *coregrafia* in Algarotti (Fr. *chorégraphie*), who remarks that the French invented the art in the late 16th cent. (Fr. word received by the Académie in 1740). This was later rejected in favour of the learned *coreografia*.

vention begins to protect the authenticated form from further modification. Stimuli which foster change are damped down to an average, even trend of phonetic and semantic evolution which always remains operative in respect of the linguistic symbol: in short, the borrowing takes its place as an accredited unit of the lexicon.

LACK OF FORMAL AND SEMANTIC TRANSPARENCY. CHANGES ATTRIBUTABLE TO THE ACT OF TRANSFER

During the act of transfer the most important factor governing the reception of a loan-word is its *loss of morphemic and semantic transparency*. The comparative isolation of a borrowed word is a commonplace among lexicologists, and it is undeniable that on many occasions a word's ability to survive is reduced when it is not fully integrated into a formal system or a lexical group.[1] At the moment of contact this inherent instability due to a lack of supporting paradigms is aggravated by a risk of imprecise reception, which is made all the more serious by the fact that the new morphemic group, precisely because it *is* divorced from the patterns of the recipient language, fails to 'trigger off' the mechanism of psychological pre-conditioning which plays a larger part than is generally supposed in the reception of linguistic material.

Many interference phenomena may be explained as a consequence of the formal anarchy prevailing during the earlier stages of transfer. The 'sporadic changes' in general are to be listed under this heading. Traditional categories may conveniently be used in classifying them, if one bears in mind that most examples show traits of more than one category. It is desirable also to distinguish as far as possible between the shifts actually fostered by the temporary relaxation of systemic pressures during the act of borrowing and those which occur in the interim period through purely indigenous impulses.

METATHESIS: Fr. *bribe* > It. *birba* (med.); It. *garbellare* > Fr. *grabeler* (sixteenth century). It. *formaggio* is a direct borrowing of the earlier French form without metathesis (current up to the end of the Middle Ages).

DISSIMILATION AND ASSIMILATION are a little more common: It. *rigattiere* <

---

1. The preservative effect of system is of course a well-known principle applied by scholars in fields other than linguistics. Cf. A. L. Kroeber's observation upon the viability of a cultural practice (*Anthropology*, New York, 1948, p. 402 (cited by Weinreich, op. cit., p. 5): 'If it is thus connected (i.e. "interwoven with other items of culture in a larger pattern") ... it has good expectations of persisting, since large systems tend to endure. But a trait that is only loosely connected and essentially free-floating can be superseded very quickly.' This is not the whole story, though. These implications of system are partly counteracted by the equally notable semantic fact that a striking (even though anomalous) form may provide a more efficient symbol, for the reason that it may make a more forcible phonetic or visual impact.

regrattier (med.); [1] Fr. *riposte* < *risposta* (sixteenth century); dialectal *franella* for *flanella* and *farbalà* for *falbalà*. MFr. *paliscarme* 'ship's boat', alternative graphy *par escalme*, shows a double effect of dissimilation and paronymic attraction which also exists in Italian: *paliscarmo* (Bocc.); Genoese Latin *barga de parascalmo* (1246); Venet. *perischermo* (fourteenth century); Tuscan *palischermo* (sixteenth century); all are ultimately < Gr. πολύσκαλμος 'with many oars'.

APHAERESIS: It. *retaggio* < Fr. *heritage, eritage* (med.). Just as French forms assume a prosthetic 'e', so Italian ones may omit the on-glide of French: fifteenth century *ciarpa*, seventeenth century *sciarpa* < Fr. *écharpe*. There are several instances where a form with aphaeresis exists as well as the unreduced borrowing: *vantaggio, vantaggiare* ~ *avvantaggio, avvantaggiare; razzo* ~ *arazzo* (influence of *di, da*; cf. *da vantaggio* < Fr. *davantage* in Berni [Cr.]); *vanguardia* ~ *avantiguardia* or *avanguardia, chinea* ~ *achinea* (infl. of article). In French: ephemeral *anspessade* for *lancespessade*.

RHOTACISM AND LAMBDACISM: Both developments are only moderately attested in French, the latter usually linked with assimilatory/dissimilatory changes (*contrarier* ~ *contralier, esquarterer* ~ *escarteler, ensorcerer* ~ *ensorceler*) especially in earlier centuries (but cf. *colidor* ~ *corridor* at the present time). Rhotacism was prevalent above all during the sixteenth century, giving rise to forms like *farot* (*falot*), *modère* (*modèle*), *pilure, mérancolie, cristere, porichinelle* (*polichinelle*) and many others so roundly condemned by Henri Estienne in the *Dialogues* (1,199) and the *Apologie pour Hérodote* (I, 314). In Italian rhotacism (which is the more common) often assumes the proportions of a major sound-shift and is particularly widespread in northern dialects (with Genoa as the focal point) where the substitution of [r] for [l] is found not only intervocalically but in pre- and post-consonantal positions. [2]

In view of the presence of both phenomena in either language [3] it is well-nigh impossible to point to any specific shift which occurred during transfer itself. Negative evidence is more readily obtainable, i.e. proof that the actual change occurred in the primary or secondary language. Thus forms such as *assembrea* for *assemblea* in Guittone are native to Italian (and typical of Guittone in particular). Vidos explains thirteenth–fifteenth century *siloc* alongside fifteenth century *siroc* as separate borrowings from Italian before and after rhotacisation; in some similar cases, however, there is a possibility that the Middle Eastern language of the ultimate etymon may account for forms

1. Though the French word itself is of imprecise form; cf. metathesised *regartier*, etc.

2. I omit Sardinian, which does not lie within our scope. For the Italian peninsula proper, see Rohlfs, I, p. 92 (development of [r] before lateral), pp. 364–8 (intervocalic), pp. 402–5 (pre-consonantal), p. 409 (bl ~ br), p. 414 (fl ~ fr), p. 416 (pl ~ pr).

3. Nor are these changes confined to permutations of [l] and [r]; triple alternatives of [l], [n] and [r] are not unknown in the borrowed vocabulary: cf. It. *ceramella, cellamella, cennamella* (*cannamella* by pop. etym.) paralleled by similar forms of the OFr. etymon.

with [l] alongside Italianisms with [r] (e.g. *tolliban* 'turban' (late fifteenth century), *tulban* (mid-sixteenth) < Turkish *tülbend* beside sixteenth century *tourban* ~ *turbant* ~ *turban*). The lambdacisation of *materas* > *matelas* takes place in later mediaeval French, and that of *racchetta* > *lacchetta* in seventeenth century Italian. I consider *coronel* beside the Italianism *colonel* in the sixteenth century to be a native alternative rather than a formal influence of Spanish, as most sources maintain (see word-entry). *Galbe* for *garbe* and *guerrerie* for *galerie* probably bear witness to a French social affectation. Lastly, analogy sometimes determines the phonetic outcome; it is not hard to recognise an effect of the verb *salvare* in *salvietta* for *servietta* (seventeenth century < Fr.) or of *balancer* in nineteenth century Fr. *balancelle* 'little skiff' < *paranzella*.

STRESS: Among the most striking changes which take place during transfer are those induced when indigenous stress patterns are applied to unfamiliar morphemes. Foreign words of which the constituent phonemes can, by and large, be satisfactorily transposed on a one-to-one basis may suffer distortion as a result of a shift in accentuation; the disturbance is all the more profound when the sequence of phonemes which make up a foreign word is accompanied by an incompatible stress pattern and is consequently perceived incorrectly. When a source language has a heavier and more flexible accentuation than a recipient language (as is the case with Italian to French loans) there is a tendency to omit part of the phonic material during the act of borrowing.[1] Provisional changes which result may come to be accepted into the language, giving rise to inefficiently received forms on the lines of mediaeval *camerlin* < It. *camerlingo* (remodelled later); sixteenth century *archipel* < It. *arcipelago* (besides orthographically motivated *archipelague*), *barbe* ('Barbary horse') < *bàrbero*, *bilan* < *bilancio*, *masque* < *màschera*; seventeenth century *argue* < *àrgano*. It will be noted that in most of these loans the Italian originals were *parole sdrucciole*. Proparoxytones are found in early Old French, e.g. *virgene, angele*,[2] but this pattern was discarded well before the end of the Old French period proper. In It. *briscola* < Fr. *brisque*

1. This truncation occurs more readily still when a genuinely monolingual Frenchman pronounces English words. The present writer has noted cases where the second part of a disyllabic English term (i.e. the minor stress) has been entirely omitted in imitative pronunciation (though this may not of course be taken as proof that nothing whatsoever was perceived). Examples of apocope in French borrowings are most frequently to be found in words of Dutch or German origin (especially proparoxytones), i.e. in words which originally bore a very marked tonic stress: cf. *rixdale, risdale* < LowGerm. *riksdaler* or Dutch *rijksdaler*; *choumaque* (beside *choumacre*) < Germ. *Schumaker* or LowGerm. *schomaker*; *varlope, vrelope* ('jack-plane') < Dutch *voorlooper* (see Valkhoff, *Étude sur les mots français d'origine néerlandaise*, p. 219, 89 and 235 resp.). Compare also (in very different linguistic surroundings) the borrowed Pennsylvanian German form [me:maʃi:n] for English *mowing-machine* (P. Schach, 'Hybrid Compounds in Pennsylvanian German', *American Speech*, XXIII, 1948, p. 129).

2. *Vide* Pope, op. cit., paras. 639, 642, 644.

(nineteenth century) the opposite process appears to have occurred, that is, where an Italian, instinctively prompted by his own propensity and that of the people with whom he habitually converses to slur over lightly stressed syllables while strongly emphasising the tonic, mistakenly adds material to a monosyllabic French word.[1]

MORPHOLOGICAL SHIFTS: There are very few examples of changes dealing with the morphological conventions of the language in the sense of flexions or other forms 'propres à conférer un aspect grammatical aux éléments de signification'.[2] We have, however, a clear example of change of conjugation during borrowing in the mediaeval Italian verb *mentovare* for *-ere* (*Novellino*, Dante) < OFr. *mentevoir*.

PARONYMIC ATTRACTION: Up to a certain point[3] effects of paronymic attraction presuppose a loss of semantic transparency in respect of the foreign word or phrase upon which the new form is constructed,[4] and to this extent they may be considered to be promoted by the vagueness of transfer. It is significant that about two-thirds of the examples of popular etymology appearing in the French/Italian lists are ephemeral only, appearing among other alternative forms in the earlier stages of the interim period. *Corporal* for *caporal*, *nouchief* for *nocher*, *tavoletta* for *toeletta* are typical.

BORROWED MATERIAL IN ITS NEW ENVIRONMENT. SHIFTS OF THE
INTERIM PERIOD

Once contact has taken place the linguistic material (which from a formal standpoint is not all equally amenable to adaptation) begins immediately to feel the impact of its formal environment. The situation in its broadest aspect involves a process of compromise between a stimulus on the one hand and a modifying factor on the other. There is a stimulus to import foreign morphemic groups unchanged (since it is the foreign vocable as such which initially presents itself and is recommended for transfer into the receiving language;[5] this is countered by a complex set of modifying influences, a

1. The tendency to supply an off-glide to the pronounced final consonant of the French word would perhaps help to usher in a pseudo-termination.

2. Marouzeau, *Lexique de la terminologie linguistique*, s.v. *morphème*.

3. For limitations of this principle see our further observations on popular etymology below.

4. Conversely lack of semantic transparency may lead to the elimination of a popular etymology motivated in the source language, e.g. the It. military term *casa matta* (lit., 'imitation house', 'false house') becoming Fr. *casemate* (cf. Eng. *casemate*). See also 18th cent. It. *damigiana* and French *dame-jeanne* (Eng. *demi-john*). The same opaqueness may ensue whenever the source word was semantically motivated—not necessarily by paronymic attraction, e.g. *forussi, forussit, fortuscy* (Brantôme) for It. *foruscito*.

5. A potential loan-word is presented in this sense when it is used by a minority of linguistically influential bilinguals, or known to them, and heard by them or seen in

tendency towards disturbance on account of the analogies present in the hearers' mind and subsequently in the mind of all participators in the *langue* concerned.

It may be possible to accept the foreign word without modification, in the sense that the formal elements involved may be allophones of native phonemes (they are in fact often cognate). This is true of the majority of French and Italian vowels, consonants and consonantal groups. The two phonological systems do not differ greatly and were even less divergent in earlier times.[1] The form may on the contrary be totally unacceptable, as with French group [kt] entering Italian, where it is always realised as [tt] (*nottambulo* < *noctambule*, *riflettore* < *réflecteur*) or Italian gemination entering French, where the double consonant is reduced (*canon* < *cannone*, *câpre* < *càppero*, *douche* < *doccia*, etc.).[2]

Our word-lists show no evidence of actual interference at the phonemic level, if by interference we mean the strict sense of a situation where the impact of one language has a permanent effect upon the system of the other. No displacements occur like those one experiences during the formative period of the Romance languages, when the phonemic value of length, accent and quality interacted under what seems mainly to have been the influence of the Germanic languages. Phonological incompatibility on the other hand does occur. There is a minority of formal contacts in which French or Italian phonological conventions have no equivalent in the other language. When this occurs the balance of neither system is disturbed; but it is interesting to see how the receiving language solves the problem of rendering the foreign sounds. We have seen for instance that the French palatal phonemes /ọ̈/ and /ö/ have no phonetically very close equivalent in standard Italian, and that they are commonly equated to Italian /ẹ/ and /ę/, though with many exceptions due to analogy and possibly to other interference effects. Other instances in which incompatibility plays a part have been mentioned in our detailed survey above under *consonant + l*, the *problem of prosthetic 'e'* and

---

writing at fairly frequent intervals. An ideal example is the status of Italian among those who frequented the French court during the 16th century.

1. When for example groups [s] or [l] + consonant were possible in French as in Italian, and affricates were common to both systems. Since both languages normally have recourse to the same graphy we usually lack evidence that any process of adjustment has intervened in these cases, though we know very well from a comparison of the modern idioms that allophonic differences must have existed, and can guess at their nature.

2. Examples in which Italian geminated consonants are implicated run into hundreds. The double consonant of French spelling (*ballotte* < *ballotta*) does not of course reflect the pronunciation. I find no evidence whatever of a causal link between the present French tendency to geminate certain consonants (within narrow limits), especially *l* (*collaborer*, *collègue*, *illégal*) and Italian speech-habits.

stress. It is possible that the group [s] plus consonant was restored in French partly through Italian influence, while the figures given show that French borrowings materially altered the distribution of oxytones in Italian.

As is well known, analogical remodelling in a borrowing language may operate at different levels, either in respect of the individual word, e.g. paronymic attraction and loan-translation (*giustacuore* < *justaucorps*; *terre-plein* < *terrapieno*), elements of word-formation (especially suffixes: Fr. *brocart* for earlier *brocat* < *broccato*) or less extensive sequences like phonic groups or individual sounds, e.g. the total reduction of an unfamiliar termination in It. *blocco* < Fr. *blocus* or of an unusual hiatus in It. *sbranare* < OFr. *esbraoner*. In our material certain patterns of association and analogical disturbance emerge with especial clarity. The trait which characterises them is that they are in large measure conscious substitutions.

It often happens that the historical accident of a common origin in Latin provides cognates which are sufficiently similar in form to provide a basis for substitution and usually not disqualified by being too divergent semantically. Examples are numerous among suffixes: cf. the strong sense of congruence existing between It. *-etto* and Fr. *-et*, *-ella* and *-elle*, *-accio* and *-as(se)*, *-ino* and *-in* and the others we have already dealt with. We are justified in supposing that there exists a force of etymological affinity which encourages substitution between elements of this type, even when the cognates have become appreciably dissimilar formally (as in *-aud* ~ *-aldo* or *-ese* ~ *-ois*). Beyond a certain point this affinity ceases to be recognised and the foreign morpheme falls subject to analogies of a more fortuitous kind (see discussion of Fr. suffix *-el*, *-eau* entering Italian). Occasionally an etymologising equivalent is falsely applied, as when the final consonant of an Italian loan-word received into French suggests a feminine termination instead of the original masculine (see *change of gender* above).

At this freer level of analogy a form of substitution which may be generally termed *false equivalence* makes its appearance; that is, where the imported form calls to mind a morpheme which is etymologically unrelated or ill-matched linguistically in some other way (e.g. Fr. *truchement* (*droguement*), where the influence of Fr. *-ment* has affected earlier *drogman* < It. *dragomanno*; or It. *gridellino*, in which the suffix *-ino* has supplanted the original substantive in the Fr. compound *gris de lin*). The impact of false equivalents is felt at a different linguistic level in paronymic attraction.

Over and above the zones of both etymological and random analogy is a class of substitution dictated largely by psychological motives which we may term a *conventional equivalent*. Here usage, after perhaps a number of tentative adaptations, lights upon one particular equivalent which gains wide acceptance and tends to be pressed into service over a range of situations, its appropriateness in each individual instance ceasing to be called into question.

A case in point is the popularisation of the Fr. suffix *-ade* whose origin we discussed earlier in this chapter, which in the sixteenth century was applied as a substitute for several foreign suffixes of varied origin, among them both northern Italian *-ada* (*-a'a*) and Tuscan *-ata*. The motives behind conventions of this type are largely extra-linguistic, but it is significant that the principle manifested here in the realm of language agrees closely with sociologists' findings about the role of stereotypes in the psychology of social groups. A similar equivalent familiar to English speakers is the termination *-oon* [uːn] for both Fr. *-on* and Sp. *-ón*: *doubloon, maroon, picaroon, saloon*; or again— a close parallel to Fr. *-ade*—the use of *-ado* in English for both masc. and fem. words borrowed from Italian and the Hispanic languages (or which pass for having been borrowed from some similar exotic source): *bravado, bastinado, passado*.

Despite the pressure exerted by etymological parallels and other convenient patterns to which the incoming morphemic group may be equated, in very many instances no single obvious equivalent offers itself; on the contrary there frequently exists a choice of ways in which the French or Italian loan may be rendered. In consequence a borrowing may well appear in many different guises before one form predominates, e.g. the sixteenth century alternatives *sassefrique, sassefique, sassefi, salsifis, sercifi, sercifis* < It. *sassifrica*. The number of forms does not necessarily increase during transfer, though this is the more usual eventuality: the opposite development is occasionally met with, where one form out of many existing in the language of origin is received into the borrowing idiom. Of the numerous Middle French variants *feupe, frepe, ferpe, fripe, felpe* only the latter (one of the least common) is accepted in Italian: *felpa*.

RECEPTION, ASSIMILATION AND EXPLOITATION

Linguistic borrowing is an ambivalent process. It involves on the one hand comprehending and breaking down the material in contact, on the other reconstructing it in conformity with the formal characteristics of the recipient language; a sequence of events which in many ways bears comparison with the procedure of analysis and reconstitution involved in machine translation, to which the terms *catataxis* and *anataxis* are assigned. To describe adequately the total operation of lexical interference, however, not two but three stages must be posited: *reception* (or *comprehension*), *assimilation* and *exploitation*. Negative influences predominate during the first; the verbal material tends to undergo attrition through being imperfectly received (*Aphaeresis*, etc., above). A work of *triage* takes place. The second, *assimilation*, implies the realisation of the borrowed material in terms acceptable to the receiving language along the lines we have just explored. But this is not all.

There is in addition a positive side to the transfer: the contribution of the receiving language. The new idiom not only modifies a borrowed linguistic entity to the extent that necessity demands (integration into the phonemic system, conversion to indigenous flexions and the like); it tends also to exploit or augment the proffered resources. This impulse, which is perfectly in keeping with what we know about the nature of language as a dynamic entity, is discernible in the application of false equivalents and conventional equivalents, but is more plainly manifested in larger formal groupings such as folk-etymology and *calque*. Both of these terms denote a range of phenomena which straddle the boundary between accidental and deliberate change—a fact recognised in the case of *calque* by the subdivisions *loan-translation, loan-rendition* and *loan-creation*. The first (known also by its German title, *Lehnübersetzung*) is generally taken to imply a passive, non-committal exchange of extraneous for native forms, as in Fr. *antichambre* < *anticamera, terre-plein* < *terrapieno, becfigue* < *beccafico, becque-cornu* < *becco-cornuto* or It. *biancomangiare* < *blanc-manger, marciapiede* < *marche-pied, mezzaluna* < *demi-lune* (fortif.), *capo d'opera* < *chef d'œuvre*;[1] but even here the resources of the recipient language are exerted inasmuch as an indigenous equivalent (which may be very distinct formally from the model: cf. *libero muratore* < *franc-maçon*) is deliberately sought; while in some cases an effort of analysis has been applied to a compound which in all probability was no longer motivated in the source language: *sanofieno* < *sainfoin, cervo volante* < *cerf-volant, rayole* (seventeenth century form of *ragiole*) < *raggiola*.

The loan-rendition (*Lehnübertragung*), where the model provides a basis for translation but the resulting word need not correspond in every detail to the original (*patria* : *fatherland*) is less common in French and Italian because of the closer cognate equivalence than it is, say, among the Germanic languages (*skyscraper* : *Wolkenkratzer*, etc.); but we may cite the compounds *cassaforte, rendiconto* (nineteenth century), which both Fanfani and Rigutini equate to Fr. *coffre-fort* and *compte-rendu* respectively, together with *campanilismo* < Fr. *esprit de clocher*. Loan-creations or false loans (*Lehnschöpfungen*) are on the other hand well represented. Here a word is created in the recipient

1. This does not of course exhaust the list, which is very full and would be even more so if segments more extensive than the lexical unit were included, esp. phrases which have an idiomatic unity (e.g. *maestro delle richiesti* (Guicciardini) corresponding to Fr. *maître des requêtes*). To take only military terms: a *sondage* into two pages of Grassi's *Dizionario militare italiano* reveals the following loan-translations corresponding to French terminology: *bastione distaccato, pieno, -regolare, -piatto, -doppio, -a tanaglia, -vuoto, -acuto* (all in Montecuccoli), *batteria da breccia, batteria volante; mezza-luna, luogotenente colonnello, luogotenente generale* (in Redi and Montec. respectively) and a quotation from Scipione Maffei which is a storehouse of such transpositions: '... la singolarità del fortificar del Vauban consiste negli esteriori, cioè nelle controguardie, nelle lunette, nelle mezzelune, nelle tenaglie ...', etc.

language on the pattern of forms which exist generally in the source, but without corresponding to a specific etymon (e.g. the French 'pseudo-English' loans *autostop* and *recordman* (which have also on occasion passed temporarily into Italian). Panzini (*Diz. mod.*, 9th edition, p. 287) cites *porte-enfant* and *garde-enfant* ('child's cradle, of expensive and elegant design') as false Gallicisms: 'Non le trovo in francese. Sono infatti voci di conio franco-subalpino o franco-milanese, che formano mazzo con *Voltaire, Notes*, ecc.' The latter are registered by Panzini elsewhere as false loans (*notes*—a pseudo-French plural meaning notebook, *voltaire* a kind of antimacassar) together with (*vitello*) *thonné* or *vitello tonnato* (i.e. cooked in such a way as to resemble tunny).[1] *Tourniquet* in the sense of 'hairpin bend' on a hill (Prati, Panz.) has no parallel in French, where the normal term is *lacet* or *virage*. If French originals actually existed for It. *crumirismo, crumiraggio* ('blacklegging' during a strike) they must have been of a very transient nature. Both are nevertheless generally felt to be of French origin (< *Kroumir*, name of a tribe involved in clashes during the French occupation of Tunisia).

Not all false loans are accurately described as *loan-creations*. A number of pseudo-forms felt by native speakers to be loan-words are indeed traceable to foreign etyma, but loss of semantic motivation has led to ellipsis and consequent reduction to a single substantive what was initially a transparent phrase. Examples are: mediaeval It. *arazzo* (subst.) from *étoffe d'Arras* (or a similar phrase; cf. *panno d'arasso* in some attestations), eighteenth century It. *rapè* (subst.) < *tabac rapé*. Probably Fr. *faïence* 'porcelain' can be explained in part as an ellipsis of this kind.[2]

There is a sizeable group of terms where the original solecism was committed in French, passing later into Italian, e.g. *smoking* for *smoking-jacket*, *fox* for *fox-terrier* (or *foxhound*) (*vide* Panzini, IX, p. 274), *golf, golfetto* for *golfing-jacket* (Panz., 302), *folding* for *folding camera* (Migl., *Suppl.*, p. 848). The It. and Fr. technical (engineering) term *carter* (subst.; = 'case or housing of a machine') was coined in French from the name of an English inventor, J. H. Carter. I can find no evidence that the word ever existed in English itself.[3]

1. Ibid., s.v. Culinary terms abound in pseudo-forms, as we know. It must be added in the interests of accuracy that Panzini's examples are not always correct; *marbré*, for instance, which he deems a false Gallicism (= 'marbled', of vellum or paper, esp, in bookbinding) is in fact the current Fr. technical term.

2. Ellipsis of a phrase is more usual in technical languages and argots than in the standard. Concerning *faïence*: compare Eng. *delph, delf* ('fine pottery'), initially attested as *Delft ware*, which shows the same combination of ellipsis and false borrowing.

3. N.B. the apparent 'false loan' caused by semantic shift, as when *lorgnette* is used (in English as well as Italian) to mean not the original sense of 'small opera-glass' but that which is signified by *face à main* in French: also the similar effect of derivation from a borrowed word of a kind not consonant with the original language, e.g. late 19th cent. *lorgnettare* 'to ogle, quizz', and the adj. *camionistico* (Migl., *Suppl.*, p. 798) formed on Fr. *camion*.

It is helpful to distinguish two different types of loan creation, (a) those which are accepted, but mistakenly so, as versions of genuine foreign words, an element of verbal snobbery often entering into their use (i.e. false loans), and (b) those which are knowingly created from native elements to match a useful word in the source language (the true loan-creation). The many substitutes proposed in Italian during the '30s of this century in order to rid the language of barbarisms provide excellent examples of loan-creations in the second sense; *autista* in place of *chauffeur*, for instance, or *autorimessa* for *garage*.[1]

As far as folk-etymology is concerned it would be helpful, here also, to maintain a distinction between cases of misunderstanding due to mistaken interpretation (for which paronymic attraction should be used) and those where there is an element of purposeful distortion or exploitation of the model (which may with some justification be called popular or folk-etymology). The distinction is admittedly not always easily drawn. *Nochief* for *nocher* (petty officer of a ship), ephemeral *arcs qui travent* for *architraves* (*arquitraves* in sixteenth century), paronymic attraction due to French in *stanforte* < *estanfort* (< *Stamford*) and even *giustacuore* for *justaucorps* may all be cases of genuine misunderstanding; but since in French and Italian, where utter disparity of form is rare, mistakes of this kind are not so likely to occur as in most interference situations, we may justifiably assume that the majority of paronymic transpositions between these languages are motivated to some extent. The form *burlotto* for *brulotto* adds relevantly to the meaning, as does *tavoletta* for *toeletta*—i.e. *toeletta* (*toilette*) in the original senses of embroidered cloth *spread on a dressing-table*, on which toilet requisites are placed, whence the cloth and requisites as a whole. The outstanding type of folk-etymology found in our lists, however, is the jocular deformation.[2] This is the real motive behind forms such as *salade* (helmet) < *celata* or *sangdedé* (dagger or dirk) < *cinquededa*. It is particularly revealing that a considerable number of the popular etymologies in the sixteenth century list appear in Rabelais, for whom etymological motivation (whether authentic or spurious) is a favourite

1. *Vide* Migliorini, 'Purismo e neopurismo', *Lingua Contemporanea*, pp. 178ff. Cf. also 19th cent. *affarista*, understood by contemporary authorities to be a deliberate rendering of Fr. *faiseur* in the title of Balzac's play *Le Faiseur*.

2. Note how Fanfani deliberately reactivates the constituent elements of the loan-word *agremàn* < Fr. *agréments* (*Lessico dell'infima e corrotta italianità*, article *agremàn*), for purposes of satire and ridicule: 'noi abbiamo gale, guarnamento, ornamento . . . ma ci vuole le agre mani!' Cf. also his humorous remarks about nostalgia and *absentismo* ('chronic alcoholism' < Fr. *absinthisme*) (ibid., s.v. *absentismo*). Some investigation of these *impulsi scherzosi* as they apply to Italian (though not specifically to loans) was carried out by Vittorio Bertoldi in his article 'Esigenze linguistiche del mercato', *Vox Romanica*, V, 1940 (esp. pp. 91–2). Jaberg's article, though older, is still valuable: 'Spiel und Scherz in der Sprache', pp. 67–81 of *Festgabe für Samuel Singer*, 1930.

source of comic effect: cf. especially *brin d'estoc* < *brandistocco, lances pesades* for *lanspessades* < *lancia spezzata, le Besch* for *lebèche (libeccio)*, as well as *sangdedé* above.[1]

DISTURBANCE BY INTERMEDIARY OR ULTIMATE SOURCE

Occasionally the formal realisation of a Franco-Italian borrowing is modified by a dialect through which it was transmitted during its passage from one major language to the other. Dialect interference involves regional usage in Italian rather than French, partly because of the geographical circumstance that the local idioms on the French side of the frontier belong to a third Romance language, Provençal, but mainly because intimate contacts were established at various periods of history between the northern French and the dialect speakers of northern Italy. Up to the sixteenth century most words which entered French were borrowed through direct contact with Italians speaking regional varieties of the language, whether this occurred in Sicily and southern Italy under the Normans and Angevins, with Venetians during the Crusades, with Genoese during Boucicaut's governorship or the inhabitants of Lombardy and states on the Tyrrhenian seaboard during the earlier *Guerres d'Italie*. When in the course of the sixteenth and seventeenth centuries knowledge of Italian came to be a recognised social accomplishment direct verbal contact with Tuscan was possible. On the Italian side, apart from some Norman influence in earlier times, borrowing from central French preponderates. The intermediary role of northern Italian dialects during transfer into Italian itself is much less obvious than that which they assume in shifts from Italian to French since the Italian regionalisms tend to be masked by conversion to Tuscan usage, especially for literary purposes, e.g. It. *fonduta* < Fr. *fondue*, which entered via Piedmontese *fondüa* (Petrocchi). Some idea of the importance of regions such as Piedmont, the Milanese, Venetia and southern Italy in this respect may be gained by noting how many of the first attestations of a French loan in literary Italian are antedated (often by a long period) by examples in Pipino, *Vocabolario piemontese*, (1783), Cherubini, *Vocabolario milanese-italiano* (1839–43), Boerio, *Dizionario del dialetto veneziano* (1829 and 2nd edition 1856), Del Bono, *Dizionario siciliano-italiano-latino* (1751–54). See notes on eighteenth century *barlotta* (via Pied.), *blù* (Sicil.); nineteenth century *carrè* (term in tailoring) (Milan), *comò* (Pied. and Milan), *debutto, -are* (Venet.), *disabigliè* (Venet.), *dormosa, dormeuse* (Milan), *fumista* (Milan) and *pompò, pompon* (Venet.), among many others. As far as

---

1. Travesty with a humorous intention is rife in all military slangs, whatever the language. Three examples for comparison: H.M. Ships *Bellerophon* and *Iphigenia* nicknamed the *Billy Ruffian* and the *Niffy Jane* (Napoleonic Wars); It. *diavoletto!* = 'Boy!' (in Eritrea, etc.), < Arab. *yā walād*; Fr. *ours* = *cheval* during the Great War, < Eng. *horse* (vide Dauzat, *Les Argots*, pp. 80, 105).

Italian to French is concerned numerous dialectal traits have already been discussed: palatalisation of [o] (Genoese) as in *écueil* < [sködd3u] for *scoglio*; NIt. fricatives for affricates and dental fricatives for alveolar fricatives (suffix *-esse*, *-isse* ~ *-iche*, *-asse* ~ *-ache*, *-ise* from northern *-iso* instead of *-igio* as in *artisan, valise*).[1] Other clear examples of dialect intervention are sixteenth century Fr. *grabuge, garbuge* ultimately from It. *garbuglio* (< arch. *bugliare* < Lat. **bulliare*), but with the Genoese/Venetian [d3] < [l]+jod corresponding to l mouillé in Tuscan,[2] and the Venetian forms *sion* (< Lat. *siphonem* with loss of intervocalic const.) and *zani* (< dial. form of caritative Gianni for Giovanni).

The Tuscan sound-shift whereby VLat. [ẹ] and [ę] appear as [i] in initial protonic syllables also affects borrowed words and continues to do so in precisely the same way from the Middle Ages to the present day, as the following examples indicate: *diliverare* (thirteenth century), < Fr. *délivrer*; *mislea* (thirteenth century onwards) < *meslée*; *trinciante* (thirteenth century) < *trenchant*; sixteenth century: *trincea* < *trenchée (tranchée);* seventeenth century: *rimarcare* < *remarquer*; eighteenth century: *ciniglia* < *chenille*, *minuetto* < *menuet, risorsa* < *ressource*; nineteenth century: *dimissione, -ario* < *démission, -aire, ristorante* < *restaurant*, etc. The opposite trend appears in French loans—*récolte* < *ricolta, récamer* < *ricamare*, etc., but not so consistently; cf. *risque* and *riposte*, and a number of words in which the prefix *dis-* is a reflection of Tuscan pronunciation rather than a learned form (e.g. *discoste*).

There is some evidence—slight, but not easily discounted—suggesting that certain isolated anomalies in the recipient language may not be due directly to the source but to characteristics of a third, ultimate source from which the immediate source has borrowed. Anomalous [o] < [ü] in It. *bottino* < *butin* (which was a recent loan in French from Low German at the time when it was transmitted from French to Italian), and the treatment of suffix *-ing* when MHG. *virling* entered Italian from French, as opposed to the same suffix in Gallicisms of Frankish origin, have already been mentioned. To these we may add the case of It. *calesse* (occasionally *calesso*) in Magalotti, Redi, Fagiuoli, etc., < Fr. *calèche*, where [s] for [ʃ] of French is unusual, particularly since an obvious 'etymological equivalent' suffix is available in It. *-eccio*. The French word had itself been recently borrowed (mid-seventeenth century) from German *Kalesche*, probably of Czech or Polish origin. French forms themselves alternate, but between the voiced and unvoiced *chuintante (calèche* ~ *calège, galège)*. Possibly the abnormal reduction

---

1. We can include here an analogous Tuscan/dialectal alternation displayed in verbal forms (*-eggiare* ~ *-isare* [izare], *vide* Rohlfs., III, p. 359): *corseger, ormeger, saccager, spaceger* (and possibly *serpeger, veleger*) as opposed to *galantiser, voltiger*.

2. See Rohlfs, I, p. 461. 16th cent. It. *bagaglio* < Fr. *bagage* may be a hypercorrect formation from what was thought to be Genoese or Venetian dialectism.

of French *blocus* (< Low German *blokhūs*) to *blocco* in Italian may be due to a similar residual effect. There are, naturally, a number of other explanations which might be adduced to account for these anomalies and others like them; nevertheless the assumption still remains a valid one that a small proportion of transmitted borrowings still possessed in the intermediary language some of those 'residual structural irregularities, which might be called systemic fragments rather than co-existent systems' which Haugen concedes to be the only loan phenomena detectable by synchronic analysis in the languages of modern civilisation.[1]

Formal and Non-formal Criteria for the Identification of Borrowings

It has long been accepted that a lexicologist who writes about loan-words should state at some early opportunity in his disquisition the formal criteria by which his alien terms may be identified. One generally assumes as an axiom or fixed point beyond the realm of controversy that evidence got at through historical phonetics is more trustworthy than that which is based on any other constant or codifiable attribute. Most etymologists have accepted that this is true, though some on different occasions have firmly denied it, since the beginning of the century. I should not like to risk passing again over ground already covered; but our brief throughout this programme of investigation has been to contribute to the general pool any information which emerges from our limited, concentrated analysis, whether it confirms, contradicts or simply adds to what is already known, and this is a useful opportunity to bring out a little more clearly the value of other criteria of identification apart from the strictly phonetic one.

The range of formal criteria is very wide. Both the synchronic and diachronic conceptions of linguistic organisation come into play, though in our particular circumstances the former has rather less to offer.

One surmises that a fair proportion of Italianisms and Gallicisms borrowed in the past continued to be pronounced during some stages of their acclimatisation more or less with a foreign articulation and that the words at that time were identifiable because of their anomalous phonic status in the receiving language. This happens with contemporary borrowings and presumably it always did. But to adduce objective evidence of synchronic discrepancy is not easy, for obvious reasons. We may find a word spelt in its foreign convention inserted in a native text; when Montaigne says *ainsi ont les Italiens leurs* doccie (sc. *douches*) or Rousseau speaks of *la* desinvoltura *des Italiens*, or Magalotti intersperses his letters with an *à point nommé* or a *je ne sais quoi*, the words presumably presented themselves to their mind in a foreign phonic guise, and to that of their readers too—in so far as the *image acoustique* of a word

1. 'The Analysis of Linguistic Borrowing', p. 229.

S

is actually shaped up in the mind during the process of reading or comprehending. There are of course many examples in our material of foreign words
interposed like this in a native context, especially during recent periods; in
eighteenth century Italian, for example, where such interventions are
usually made at the whim of the writer (though their spontaneity is only
apparent, since the author is sufficiently disingenuous to set them down in
writing and eventually in print); or again in the nineteenth century, where the
French words used can more fairly be termed elements of *langue*—*habitué*,
bébé, *café-chantant* and so on. Morphological anomalies are easier to detect,
e.g. foreign flexions of number or gender, as when *conoscenti*, *dilettanti* or
bravi!, *brava!* (alongside *bravo!*) appear in certain types of French situational
context, or *élites*, etc., in Italian. However, in all these cases the immediate
criterion from the standpoint of actual research is *orthographic*, not phonetic,
since one has to operate exclusively with printed or manuscript texts.

In practice a diachronic or comparative approach continues to provide the
most efficacious criterion when any period before, let us say, the eighteenth
century is to be covered.

Almost any differences in the sequence of phonological development
between Latin and Italian or French at various moments of history may
help to confirm a foreign loan. Ideally to list them all would mean sum-
marising and comparing the historical phonetics of both languages; in fact a
great deal has already been achieved on these lines by Wind (pp. 36–48) and
Bezzola (pp. 1–11), apart from earlier sources. French linguistic manuals
devote more space to this particular aspect of comparative Romance philology
than their opposite numbers in Italian do and so for the sake of brevity I shall
limit myself to the latter, where the additional indications will be more
useful.[1]

Historical sound-sequences one has to take into consideration most frequently when tracing Gallicisms in Italian are these:

A. SHIFTS INVOLVING PALATALISATION

French k+a > tʃ   : *arciere*, *baccelliere*, *brocciare*, *ciambellano* (very many
                         examples)

k+a > ʃ   : *sciarpa* (as opposed to med. *ciarpa*, *-are*), *sciampagna*

g+a > dʒ   : *bolgia*, *giardino*, *targia*

1. I have observed already how Italian to French loans often coincide formally with
non-popular developments in French; this is why the interest of Romance loan-words is
more immediate for French phonologists than for Italians. Many of the Italian > French
criteria to which Wind and others allude are in effect the converse of those we have
summarised here, e.g. absence of diphthongisation; [k] and [g] before [a] of Latin remaining unpalatalised; unstressed VLat. vowels remaining uneffaced with consequent preser-
vation of consonantal patterns and so on. Apart from the [k] and [g]+[a] criterion, that
of [s] retained before consonant or group is perhaps the one which stands out most in our
lists: see notes on the problem of the prosthetic *e*, above.

pj > tʃ : *accia, accetta, approcciare*
vj, bj > dʒ : *alleggiare, sergente, roggio.*
mbj > ndʒ : *cangiare, frangia*
nd+palatal > ndʒ: *mangiare*
rj > ir : *vairo, dibonaire*
skᵃ > stʃ > ʃ : *maresciallo*
Breaking and
reduction
(e+palatal > i) : *chitare, sire, profitto*

B. LOSS OF UNSTRESSED VLAT. VOWELS
esp. atonic penultimate
Examples: *allumare, fraile, lama, lampa, mastino, mestiere, prenze, sentiero*

C. OTHER VOCALISM
Diphthongisation other than that of [ɛ], [ɔ], e.g. of [a] tonic free > [e]: *cera, clero, ostello,* etc.

D. REDUCTION OF CONSONANTAL GROUPS
largely concurrent with shifts in B.
Examples: medial mn (*dama, reame*), st (*citerna*), lk (*cuccia*) skl (*mislea*), brkᵃ
(*forgiare*) and very many others; see esp. *ceraldo* (ult. < Lat. *character*),
cugino (*consobrinum*), *desinare* (*dis-ieiunare*), *mentovare* (*mente habere*).
initial gu > g (*gaggio*)
final rd > r (*ramparo*)

E. OTHER CONSONANTISM
Lenition and effacement of intervocalics, esp. [t]: *ciaiera* (Lat. *cathedra*), *obbliare*
(*oblitare*), *rollo* (*rotulum*); dental with [r], *foraggio,* etc.

Now although in principle the criterion of etymological comparison has much to recommend it, its practical application to French and Italian reveals certain limitations. Because of the close formal relationship between all the Romance languages a given diachronic sequence of sound-patterns is likely to occur and recur in Italian, French, Provençal and the Hispanic languages under different conditions at different times; the same is true of the various dialects within each language. These circumstances coupled with the direct influence of Classical and Low or Church Latin often introduce so many alternatives that ambiguity makes a comparison impracticable. Wind's synopsis of individual phonetic criteria includes some discussion of these drawbacks as they affect Italian to French loans. French to Italian criteria which depend upon the effects of a more thoroughgoing series of changes in the source language than in the recipient language are less equivocal than those applicable to contact in the opposite direction. Even in identifying French to Italian contacts difficulties arise during the mediaeval period on account of the variety of forms in Old Italian and because of confusion with Provençal where the literary language (the relevant medium during the twelfth and thirteenth centuries) was much closer to French than the spoken dialects were.[1]

Distortion due to analogical effects is still more misleading. The intervocalic [t] in It. *stampita* and *cottardita* corresponds to the normal outcome of Latin [t] between vowels in Tuscany, yet the first is a remodelled verbal ending replacing the cognate Provençal *-ida* in *estampida*, while the second is a borrowing from Fr. *cotte hardie*, where the dental is effaced; the analogy of It. *ardito*, *ardita* has sufficed to restore it. Similar examples may be found at every point in our phonological survey above. One might go so far as to say that analogical interference from established forms in the receiving language is the factor which most effectively directs the formal outcome of Franco-Italian borrowed vocabulary.

The use of suffixes as evidence of foreign provenance deserves special comment. Suffixes are admissible as criteria, but to a lesser extent than is generally supposed. A large number of examples of a certain suffix in borrowed words, for instance, proves nothing of itself; what matters is the relationship between the proportion of actual loan-words possessing the suffix and the total of similar forms in the language as a whole. Suffixes *-iere* and *-aggio* show very well how true this is. Scholars are now agreed, we should note, that both forms may be taken as evidence of French provenance, though this consensus was not reached without hesitation in the case of *-iere*, *iera* < Fr. *-ier*, *-ière*.[2]

The loans appearing in our lists are as follows: (a) *-iere* (*-iero*, *-iera*): mediaeval: *arciere, baccelliere, ber(r)oviere, bordelliere, brocchiere, carriera, cavaliere, celliere, cerviere -o, consigliere, cordigliero, corsiere -o, destriere -o, ferriera, foriere -o, gialdoniere, giardiniere -o, giustiziere, gonfaloniere, laniere, leggiero, levriere -o, messaggiere, mestiere, miniera, origliere, palmiere, paltoniere, pellettiere, paniere, piliere, primiero, rigattiere, riviera* ('river'), *scudiere, sentiero, somiero -e, tagliere, verziere*; sixteenth century: *bottigliere, damiere*;[3] seventeenth century: *bandoliera, bandoliero, barriera, budriere, granatiere, parruchiere*;[4] eighteenth century: *brigadiere, caffettiera, carabiniere, cerniera, chincagliere, crociera, filibusti-*

---

1. *Vide supra*, French to Italian mediaeval loans, Preliminary considerations.

2. The anomalous development of Lat. *-arius* to It. *iere*, and the presence of this suffix beside indigenous Tuscan *-aio*, northern *-er(o)*, certain southern dialects *-aro* attracted the attention of Romance scholars from Diez onwards; cf. Bezzola's summary (*Abbozzo*, p. 3) of the opinions of Caix, Bianchi, Ascoli, Schwan, Körting, Meyer-Lübke, D'Ovidio, Staaff and others, and his reasons for concluding that the origin was French. Rohlfs' recent verdict on the same lines (approved by his reviewers) has pronounced a *nolle prosequi* upon this discussion at present: 'Das Richtige hat schon vor über einem halben Jahrhundert Meyer-Lübke (*Ital. Gramm.*, §486) gesehen, als er für *-iere* französischen Ursprung annahm. In der Tat kann heute kein Zweifel mehr darüber bestehen, dass *-iere* mit franz. *-ier* . . . identisch est, das selbst aus lat. *-arius* hervorgegangen ist' (III, p. 323).

3. And probably *giarrettiera*.

4. Possibly *fuciliere*.

ere, madiere, teiera;[1] nineteenth century: *alturiere, -o, atelier(e), bancarottiere, betoniera, bigiottiere, bomboniera, bottoniera, bracconiere, canottiere -a, cantoniere, cartucc(i)era, ciminiera, cremagliera, dentiera, finanziera, giardiniera, limiere, mentoniera, negriero -e, pepiniera, pioniere, pompiere, première -era, scifoniera, tiragliere, tortiera, trov(i)ero.*[2] (b) *-aggio:* mediaeval: *aggio, (av)vantaggio, baronaggio, boscaggio, carriaggio, damaggio, foraggio, formaggio, gaggio, lignaggio, messaggio, oltraggio, omaggio, ostaggio, ovraggio, passaggio, pedaggio, retaggio, rivaggio, saggio, villaggio;* sixteenth century: *equipaggio* ('crew'), *paesaggio, pottaggio, (bagaglio);* seventeenth century: *appannaggio, equipaggio* 'turn-out'; eighteenth century: *aggiotaggio, bastingaggio, cabotaggio, giardinaggio, libertinaggio, miraggio, tralingaggio;* nineteenth century: *aeraggio, alaggio, apprendissaggio, arbitraggio, ballottaggio, blindaggio, boicottaggio, canottaggio, cartonaggio, chilometraggio, clivaggio, crumiraggio, drenaggio, ingranaggio, lavaggio, linciaggio, metraggio, montaggio, patinaggio, sabotaggio, salvataggio, scamottaggio, spionaggio, tatuaggio, vagabondaggio.*[3]

The number of Italian words ending in *-iere* (*-o, -iera*) registered in a typical compendious dictionary of 40,000 entries intended for use by the general public is 350,[4] so that Gallicisms comprise an absolute maximum of one in 4.2; but since our lists are based on a much more detailed search the true proportion of Gallicisms to native derivatives must be much smaller; probably less than one in ten. For *-aggio* a similar inspection revealed some 50 terms out of the same corpus of entries (both Gallicisms and native formations) as against 58 in our list. Here the situation revealed statistically is totally different: there is little

1. Possibly *formichiere, orologiere.*

2. A number of terms were rejected from the mediaeval list because it was not possible to decide between a French and a Provençal origin. The following may be taken as Provençalisms: *aumoniera, aversiere, ballestriere, bandiera, barattiere, baviera, brughiera, cameriere, candelliere, cervelliera, cimiero, corriere, credenziere, dangiero, forziere, giocoliere, gorgiera, guerriere -o, lauzengiere* (*lozengiere*), *menzognero, palafreniere, passaggiere, preghiera, quartiere, taverniere, visiera.* Ambiguity arises chiefly because in Old Provençal the suffix *-arius* coincided with northern French (*primarius* > *premiers*). Theoretically the feminine of Provençal, being regular at least as far as group [-rj-] was concerned (*primaria* > *premeira* in most dialects and quite frequently in the literary language) should have given a distinctive suffix in Italian; in practice the Italian is *-iera,* modelled upon the masculine or drawn from the common literary form of Provençal. A typical example is It. *riviera* (in the usual sense) of which the southern French origin has never been in doubt.

3. Influence of Provençal *-atge* is less important than that in respect of *-iere.* Though some Prov. > It. loans have this suffix—*boscaggio, visaggio* are probably from *boscatge* and *visatge* —these instances are much fewer in number than their northern French counterparts (21 from OFr. in the Middle Ages).

4. Made up of: *-iere:-* 210; *-iero:-* 30; *-iera:-* 110; a slightly higher proportion of feminines than in earlier centuries. The dictionary in question, chosen at random, was Giuseppe Orlandi, *Dizionario italiano-inglese, inglese-italiano,* Milan, 1951 (intended primarily to be used by Italians).

doubt that the proportion of native creations does not very greatly exceed those of foreign provenance—say two or three times more, if we think in terms of a representative Italian vocabulary of about 120,000 words, rather than the 40,000 our sample dictionary provides. Thus the presence of *-iere* in itself is an extremely unreliable indication of Gallicism whereas that of *-aggio* is a reasonably efficient one. On the same grounds the presence of suffix *-ache* in a French word and *-ea* in Italian is an efficient criterion; though both forms are only sparsely attested in borrowed words native derivations in which they occur are equally restricted (Fr. *-ache* from Norman or Picard dialectisms, plus occasional argotic formations; It. *-ea* from Greek, especially in actual borrowed Hellenisms (-έα or -αιά).[1]

Further information may be gained from arranging borrowed forms statistically, provided that care is exercised to compensate for the wide variation in the total of borrowings from century to century, and the total number in any period is not too small. Adjusted graphs are appended for *-iere* and

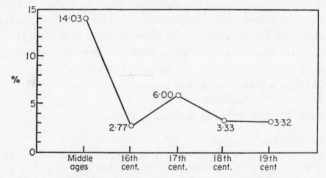

Loan-words in *-iere* expressed as percentage of century totals

-aggio, which are sufficiently numerous to make statistical treatment worth while. It will be seen that although in both cases borrowing was profuse in earlier times the curve for *-iere* shows a consistent diminution as time progresses. This fits in with the usual trend towards dereliction of a symbol resulting from linguistic (mostly semantic) change. On the other hand *-aggio* after a similar diminution recovers markedly from the early eighteenth century onwards. We might account for this reversal in different ways, but the most important fact seems to be that French *-age* was reactivised during the modern period by an extension of the signification 'activity, process of action' (linked with a verb); it was therefore very suitable for creating com-

1. For all this It. *-ea* is seldom put forward as a criterion of Gallicism. Rohlfs (III, p. 289) notes that 'auf franz. *-ée* beruht *contea* und *vallea*, vielleicht auch *scalea*, neap. *corsea . . .*'. The list may be lengthened by ten or so terms; cf. examples in *Final consonants and suffix analogy*, above.

mercial and industrial terms, and many of these in due course became current internationally. The same facts explain the Italian suffix's increased semantic motivation in the modern period as opposed to the Middle Ages, where *-aggio -age* is usually opaque by the twelfth century (*linguaggio, carriaggio, vantaggio, messaggio, ostaggio,* etc.).

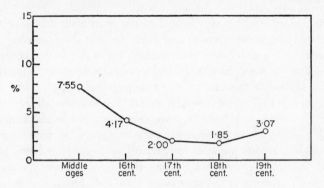

Loan-words in *-aggio* expressed as percentage of century totals

The agent suffix also has an important position in technical vocabularies; but in this function *-iere* was in competition with *-atore* and later *-ista,* both more in keeping with the learned complexion of the restricted languages concerned. Compare the similar clash of *-ier* versus *-eur, -iste* in French.

To serve as a criterion of foreign interference a suffix need not be of extraneous origin. Though the Italian verbal suffix *-izzare,* for instance, is an indigenous learned formation corresponding to *-eggiare* (< Gk. ἰζειν) a substantial proportion of the forms which appear from the seventeenth century are borrowed from French learned derivatives, so that the presence of *-izzare* and its related verbal abstract in *-izzazione* may be taken as putative evidence of a Gallicism. Examples are: pre-seventeenth century: nil; seventeenth century: *brutalizzare, simpatizzare;* eighteenth century: *amortizzare -azione, civilizzare -azione, coalizzare -azione, erborizzare, fraternizzare -azione, generalizzare, naturalizzare, organizzare -azione, realizzare, tranquillizzare;* nineteenth century: *autorizzazione, carbonizzare -azione, collettivizzare -azione, demoralizzare -azione, esteriorizzare -azione, generalizzazione, individualizzare -azione, localizzare, metallizzare -azione, militarizzare -azione, mobilizzare -azione, monopolizzare, nationalizzare -azione, naturalizzazione. paralizzare, pastorizzare -azione, quotizzare -azione, realizzazione, terrorizzare, totalizzare -azione, umanizzare, uniformizzare.*

The suffixes *-aglio, -iglio* (in words which perpetuate the Latin suffixes *-aculum, -iculum*: i.e. anomalous counterparts to Tuscan [-kkj-]) are a doubtful warranty of Gallicism. Apart from ambiguities arising from borrowings traceable to the region where these forms are indigenous (much of Piedmont), cross-currents of analogy set up by suffix *-aglio*, *-eglio*, etc., regularly derived from [l]+jod and the feminine *-aglia* < *-alia*, they admit of no discrimination between French and Provençal etyma. Inspection reveals that in earlier centuries, at least, most words containing this suffix are either definite Provençalisms or not assignable with certainty to either source.[1]

There is other evidence of a formal nature apart from that which may be deduced by comparing etymon and borrowing at the phonological level. That provided by collocation, for instance: the wider formal context often helps to confirm that a given individual word is a newcomer to the language, e.g. *catène* (*cadène*) in the idiom *mat de cathène*, *martel* in *avoir martel de, donner martel à*, *numéro* in *il entend le numéro, robe* in *de bonne roba* (all from sixteenth century It. > Fr. loans). Vidos' *étymologie organique* is a special kind of collocational criterion which has on many occasions proved its use in our list, e.g. in phrases like *cocchin pagliardo* (mediaeval) or *forestiers et bannis* (sixteenth century), where the provenance of one term argues a like provenance for the other.[2] Such evidence is found at every turn in technical vocabularies, e.g. catalogues of products and commercial processes in Savary's *Parfait négociant* or description of armaments and military strategy in Cinuzzi, d'Antonj, Grassi.[3]

Fluctuation during the interim period points to an unfamiliar origin, argotic, dialectal, or—as in our words—exotic. Earliest attestations may indicate the actual source more clearly: e.g. *alianza* (later *alleanza*), where [i] plainly reflects the outcome of stressed [e]+palatal in the Gallo-Romance area.[4] Change of gender and displacement of stress are similar corroborative traits (see above).

Parallel evidence available in other languages may be revealing, e.g. *trafique* (*trafic*) and *ducat* pin-pointed more precisely to their Venetian origin by the parallel first attestation in English which speaks of 'galleys of Traffygo', 1506 (with typical k > g lenition) and Chaucer's simile 'fyne as a ducat in Venyse' (*House of Fame*).[5] The testimony of a word's history in Spanish (now readily accessible in the *Diccionario Crítico Etimológico de la Lengua Castellana*)

1. In our list: *bersaglio, smeriglio* (*imbroglio* is a back-formation either in French or Italian). Others: *artiglio* 'feet of a hawk', *camaglio* 'mail hood', *coniglio* 'rabbit, coney', *miraglio* 'mirror', *orgoglio, sonaglio* 'bell of a hawk', *speglio* 'mirror', *spiraglio* 'ventilation aperture in building', *veglio, vermiglio, ventriglio* 'crop, gizzard of a bird', *volpiglio* 'fox'.

2. 'Nous avons constaté que dans un vocabulaire technique les dénominations des objets appartenant au même groupe d'une part et des objets faisant partie intégrante d'autres objets d'autre part ont la même histoire et la même origine' (B. E. Vidos, 'Etymologie organique', *R. Ling. R.*, XXI, 1957, pp. 93–105. The quotation is from p. 94). Vidos also uses the term *système organique* for a closely related group of words of this type (ibid., p. 95).

3. Cf. the selection of fortification terms cited p. 618, n. 1.

4. *Vide* examples cited in discussion of formal changes in the interim period, above.

5. Mario Praz, *The Italian Element in English*, p. 38.

often confirms or invalidates previous conjectures (*vide* seventeenth century *bigliardo* and *barricata*, among many others).

A certain amount of evidence is afforded by false borrowings. A loan from a third language may have suffered formal distortion during its transmission via Italian or French: cf. the following Anglicisms in Italian whose form betrays their passage through French—fifteenth century *ubino* < *hobby* (Fr. *hobin*); nineteenth century *empirismo* < *empiricism* (Fr. *empirisme*), *utilitarismo* < *utilitarianism* (Fr. *utilitarisme*). Loss of grammatical transparency in *milordo*, *milorde* plainly began in Fr. *milord* ('les milords anglais', etc.).[1] It. *linciaggio* (Lynch law, a lynching) is taken directly from Fr. *lynchage* and only indirectly referable to the English verb derived from the name of John Lynch.

Orthography too opens up many a short cut for the comparative lexicologist. In recent centuries, as we observed earlier, foreign words quite frequently come to be written habitually with the graphy and diacritics they had in their original environment. A further good example of this is to be seen in technical terms of fine art taken into French from the beginning of the eighteenth century—*adagio, piano, presto* and the other musical instructions; *oratorio, soprano, solo, mezzo-tinto* and the like.[2] Often a foreign spelling, or remnants of a foreign spelling, is retained in the earliest attestations but remodelled later according to native practice, e.g. *chi* in a French word reflecting *chi* of Italian (*baldachin*, modern spelling *baldaquin*) or, conversely, French [ʃ] spelt *ch* instead of (*s*)*ci* in Italian; *-ezze* for *-esse* in sixteenth century French, or early examples retaining *s impura* of Italian in the same period; *gu-* before front vowel retained in Italian instead of *ghi-* (*guillotinare* in 1793); *architetture* for *architecture* in Christine de Pisan; *cigaretta* from French instead of *sigaretta* in 1845.

I think the most significant inference one may distil from the foregoing remarks is that purely formal criteria often fail to be precise or conclusive enough. No etymologist since the last century would be prepared to accept without question the bare statement that a certain succession of forms is 'lautlich annehmbar' or 'lautlich nicht möglich', and such affirmations become increasingly suspect as linguistic thought moves ever further from the notion of evolutionary causality behind sound-sequences. In applying etymological principles to practical situations semantic criteria rightly play an important part, and the etymologist must also rely to some extent on circumstances external to language which can furnish him with the proof he needs. The latter are of so heterogeneous a nature that one could not attempt to codify them except in a work exclusively devoted to that purpose; indica-

1. Cf. the examples of false borrowings taken over from French cited above, *General Considerations: Reception, Assimilation and Exploitation*.

2. See evaluation of 19th cent. Fr. > It. loans. Many such words are in general use, or at least are technical terms which are familiar to all speakers: *gala, fiasco, confetti, loto*, etc.

tions of context, for instance, as applied to our material might range from the single fortuitous criterion of fact—say, that MFr. *tramontane, tramontaine* 'North Star' is proved by geographical necessity to be of Italian origin— through various criteria of reference—*baccelliere, conestabile, maresciallo* first used to refer to Frenchmen, *marquis* to Italians; explanatory phrases such as *vino claretto alla Franzese* (*vide claretto,* sixteenth century Fr. > It.)—to historical background of the widest kind, such as France's part in developing and diffusing the concepts of *chevalerie, civilisation, patriotisme.*

Perhaps the most interesting and certainly the most controversial source of external evidence is that provided by the opinions, based on direct personal observation, of writers in the past. My experience while compiling my material was that such impressionistic statements ought to be given serious consideration and certainly should not be rejected out of hand. Typical instances are Pasquier's remarks on the subject of *embuscade*: 'Je ne dirai pas 'imboscade', comme disait le soldat sous le règne de Henri II pour dire qu'il avait esté à la guerre de Parme [i.e. referring to events which took place about ten years before Pasquier began to write his *Recherches de la France*] . . . le mot d'embusche nous est très propre et naturel' or the following reference to circumstances of the mid-fifteenth century in Jean de Bueil, *Le Jouvencel* (1461–66): '. . . Batailles ou eschielles ou escadres, comme on dit en Italie.' Whether animadversions like these are admissible or not becomes an urgent problem in cases where formal criteria are of no value, as in detecting interference confined to the semantic plane. Nineteenth century French to Italian contacts, as we have seen, give rise to many borrowings of this kind: it is also the period most fully documented by personal observation on the part of *littérateurs* and philologists who for divers reasons have the interests of the language at heart. The form in which these opinions are expressed varies from a simple code of diacritics in a dictionary word-entry[1] to long disquisitions upon individual words and idioms accompanied by examples of their use and abuse, the writer's own nostrums and detailed criticism of those offered by his predecessors.[2]

There is of course a great deal in this which would put even the most liberal-minded philologist on his guard. Practical safeguards have to be applied. False information can be weeded out by collating a number of sources, noting anomalies and building up an impression of the reliability of each one. Here too it is helpful to refer to other languages; a wider context may show that purists' objections are unfounded, as when Fanfani and Arlia censure as a French usage the idiom *calcolare*+infinitive to mean 'to intend

1. E.g. Tommaseo and Bellini's symbols for indicating barbarisms and neologisms, or Bernardoni's notation for the purpose of singling out from examples or erroneous usage those which are 'expressive' or indispensable as technical terms.

2. See evaluation of 19th cent. Fr. > It. loans.

(doing something)', or the word *tramvia* as 'del francese tramvoie'. There is a further series of safeguards which is less mechanical. The risk of taking imprecise assertions as genuine facts is in inverse proportion to one's knowledge of the motives, linguistic sensitivity and personal idiosyncrasies of the author. It is easier to believe a man who has practical knowledge of his subject and its terminology, the military strategist Tensini, for instance, when he observes that the rubble from undermined fortifications 'da' Francesi vien chiamata *la breccia'* (= Fr. *brèche;* see sixteenth century Fr. > It. loans). There is all the difference in the world between the acceptability of opinions expressed by a sixteenth century propagandist and the personal impressions of a modern Italian lexicographer. Different puristic approaches—return to the authority of archaic models, purification and codification of language in an era of cultural authoritarianism, aggressiveness towards foreign importations as one facet only of a wider xenophobia—lead to different degrees of distortion; the personality of the author and the form in which he chooses to couch his opinions are equally relevant factors. When satire and invective creep in, scholarly accuracy goes by the board—as is only too often the case with Estienne, and not infrequently with Arlia, whose tirades against 'brutti barbarismi . . . voci francesi, inglesi, spagnuole e di Oga Magoga',[1] above all those 'che vengono dalla riva della torbida Senna' rightly put linguists on their guard.[2]

Against instances of wrong-headedness and ill-interpreted evidence to be found in the testimony of a purist like Arlia must be set the far larger number of occasions when his intuition proves to be at one with the most recent etymological research.

There is something to be said, after all, for considering carefully the impressions gained by the 'man on the spot', even though the practice of doing so runs directly counter to strictly objective scientific method. It is well known that the difference between the premises of descriptive linguistics and those of traditional etymology in their approach to criteria of this kind runs parallel in many respects to that which distinguished the Behaviourist school of psychologists from their predecessors who remained true to Introspective methods. But although behaviourist techniques are widely accepted there is still an appropriate place in all studies which have some bearing upon the human mind for recourse to the direct opinion of speakers and writers, provided that an efficient and objective system of control is applied. It is not justifiable to dismiss such impressions as a vague subjective *Sprachgefühl.* The lexical resources of a literary language are handled and developed

1. *Vide Lessico dell'infima e corrotta italianità,* article *Square.*
2. As also do many of his observations of a more technical character, e.g. 'oggi si ha la smania di mutare in maschile i nomi di genere femminile' . . . F-A., *Lessico,* article *Intimo.*

by men who have an innate linguistic skill and a feeling for the medium of their art. They take part in its creation, and are often at pains to lay down a policy for its future development. It would be unwise to reject without a hearing even the subjective impressions of writers such as du Bellay, Cesarotti, Baretti, Manzoni and D'Annunzio.

PART FOUR

The Semantic Aspect

THE SEMANTIC ASPECT

PRELIMINARIES

The aim of the present part, quite simply, is to make some reasoned statements of fact and principle about our material as a whole in terms of semantic analysis, that is, taking the meaning of individual words as a point of departure rather than their form. It consists of four articles. The first illustrates and discusses an important branch of lexical interference which is not observable in purely phonetic terms, since it is confined to adjustments in the semantic application of words already current in the borrowing language—the group of similar influences generically called *semantic loans*. During the course of the preceding chapter we had occasion to note instances where the formal outcome of borrowed material was determined in some degree by the sense (effects of *calque*, loan-creation, paronymic attraction), so the meaningful element has already played a part in our description of modes of borrowing; semantic loans make up a third category (parallel to the numerous examples of borrowings treated in the formal chapter where meaning was in principle irrelevant) in which transfer entails no phonetic change and the criterion of formal distinction therefore remains inoperative. The other three articles pick out certain major themes of semantic analysis and develop them in the light of our data. The first of these, *Pejoratives and Pejoration*, revises definitions and gives a historical account with reference to Italian and French of what is for us the most outstanding case in which emotive or affective factors are involved in a word's signification. The others, *Change of Meaning*, and *Synonymy and Near-Synonymy*, in turn appreciate borrowed significations from the two cardinal viewpoints of *diachronic* and *synchronic* analysis. In all four essays inferences are drawn both about French and Italian vocabulary and about semantic borrowing, pejoration, semantic change and synonymy as a whole.

SEMANTIC LOANS

A WORKING DEFINITION

The subject of semantic borrowing—a word's acquiring new meanings under the influence of related words in a foreign language—is still a controversial

637

one in spite of the careful attention devoted to it by scholars since the war.[1]
Problems which arise may be attributed for the most part to disagreement
about terminology—a disagreement which often appears to be superficial,
but which in reality conceals important differences in approach. These reflect
in their turn the different interests of those who have explored this field of
linguistic borrowing in the past. One result of this diversity is that terms and
definitions used currently can not be accepted as definitive; there is clearly a
considerable work of analysis and codification to be carried out. This is a
matter for the future: at present we have to employ the terminology as it
stands. Professor Einar Haugen of Harvard, whose research into different
forms of linguistic interference was largely responsible for renewed interest
in this type of loan, and whose authority in these matters is accepted, took an
important step forward when in 1950 he codified semantic borrowing in these
terms: 'Some foreign loans appear in the language only as changes in the
usage of native words. Such changes will be classed as "shifts", which will be
made to include all changes that are not strictly phonological and grammatical. Complete substitution of native morphemes has taken place. When
this occurs in simple stems, two possibilities result according to the degree
of similarity between the new and old meanings of the word. If the new
meaning has nothing in common with the old, it may be described as a
LOAN HOMONYM. This is the situation when AmPort. has substituted its
word *grosseria* "a rude remark" for English *grocery*; the result is that the word
grosseria has two homonymous meanings. In a dictionary they would presumably be listed as two separate words. When there is a certain amount of
semantic overlapping between the new and old meanings, one may speak
of a LOAN SYNONYM, which only adds a new shade of meaning to the native
morpheme.' The American scholar then subdivides loan-synonymy, and
gives as an example (which we may take as typical) the substitution in
American Portuguese of native *livraria* 'book-store, home library' for English
library instead of using the Portuguese word *biblioteca*.[2] It will be noticed that
the definition rests upon a contrast between two opposites, loan-homonymy
and loan-synonymy, a dichotomy which virtually everyone (the present

1. Cf. W. Betz, *Deutsch und Lateinisch. Die Lehnbildungen der althochdeutschen Benedikti-
nerregel*, Bonn, 1949 (esp. introduction); Einar Haugen, 'The Analysis of Linguistic Bor-
rowing', *Language*, No. XXVI (1950), pp. 210–31, esp. section 10, *Loanshifts*; Uriel
Weinreich, *Languages in Contact (Publications of the Linguistic Circle of New York No. 1)*,
New York, 1949, esp. pp. 47–50; H. Kronasser, *Handbuch der Semasiologie*, Heidelberg,
1952, section 14, *Lehnbedeutung*; Einar Haugen, *The Norwegian Language in North
America*, Philadelphia, 1953; Louis Deroy, *L'Emprunt linguistique (Bibliothèque de la
Faculté de Philosophie et de Lettres de l'Université de Liège*, fasc. CXLI) Paris, 1956, pp. 93–
102; U. Weinreich, 'Unilingualism and Multilingualism', in the volume *Linguistique* (ed.
A. Martinet) of *L'Encyclopédie de la Pléiade*, Paris, 1961, esp. section 5.5.

2. 'The Analysis of Linguistic Borrowing', p. 219.

writer included) accepts as fundamental. Professor Haugen has developed his methodology in several respects since then, principally by shifting emphasis on to two terms which did in fact also appear in the original draft, namely *homophones* and *homologues*. A *homophonous* semantic loan occurs 'when the usages have nothing but a phonetic contact, as when American Norwegian *fil* "file" comes to mean "field" ' ('The Impact of English on American Norwegian letter-writing', *Studies in Honor of Albert Morey Sturtevant*, 1952, p. 94). 'In most cases', he continues, 'there is both a semantic and phonetic similarity, as when AmN. *korn* "grain" comes to mean "Indian corn", and then we may call the extension *homologous*' (ibid.).[1] Other scholars have contributed other useful definitions. However, our purpose on this occasion is not to discuss the methods of analysis available[2] but merely to interpret our own information in the most convenient way which presents itself. I shall therefore keep to the original *schema* proposed by Haugen, with two minor changes which the particular circumstances of Franco-Italian contracts warrant: I shall replace as occasion demands the term *loan-synonymy* by *loan-polysemy* which in many situations evokes more accurately the relation between established (indigenous) and borrowed senses; and I shall detach from the comprehensive rubric of loan-synonymy the special case of *semantic calque*, i.e. where translation of form occurs between source and borrowing languages during transfer of meaning (e.g. Fr. *dada* 'hobby-horse' coming to mean 'special occupation or preoccupation' under the influence of English *hobby* or German *Ente* meaning 'lying newspaper report' under the influence of Fr. *canard*). The latter will be classed as a distinct third category of semantic loan.

NUMBERS AND PROPORTIONS

The percentage of semantic loans as a whole is unquestionably higher in Italian than in French. In the former they account for roughly one in nine

---

1. It will help the European lexicologist to find his way around if he notes that *extension* in American terminology means 'semantic loan', and that semantic borrowing is classified as a sub-section of *loan-shifts* which are defined as consisting entirely of native morphemes. The latter category therefore includes *loan-translation* as well, i.e. what is traditionally known as *calque*. Haugen has gone considerably beyond these dichotomies I have cited in refining his terminology. There is no point in pursuing this further here; I refer the reader to the articles cited already, to which we may add his review of Weinreich, *Languages in Contact* (*Language*, Vol. XXX, No. 3, 1954) and of R. P. de Gorog, *The Scandinavian Element in French and Norman* (*Language*, Vol. XXXV, No. 4, 1959).

2. For a critique of some of these see my article 'The Analysis of Semantic Borrowing' in *Essays presented to C. M. Girdlestone*, King's College, Newcastle upon Tyne, 1960, pp. 125-41. In correspondence arising out of this article Professor Haugen kindly passed on to me some of his more recent thoughts on these matters. As I see it, however, his position and those of other American linguists have not altered in principle during recent years, though the definitions framed latterly suit the analysis of immigrant speech rather better than the original, more obviously taxonomic synonymous/homonymous model which we are using here.

T

(11.1 per cent) of the total borrowings, in the latter only about one in sixteen (6.25 per cent). It is naturally hard to obtain anything like precise statistics, and the figures upon which this comparison is based are, we must insist, no more than provisional approximations.[1] The risk of error is very great in past centuries because a prior attestation of a certain form may at any moment reveal that what was initially thought to be an integral loan (i.e. a borrowing in its entirety) was no more than a semantic extension. But if the overall figures of semantic loans are open to question from certain points of view, the relative proportions in French and Italian are much less so since the same constant of error is in force on both sides.[2] The main explanation for this disparity is a formal one which has nothing to do with semantic conditions; viz., homophony is more likely to arise between established Italian words and Gallicisms than in the case of loans in the opposite direction. Consequently the probability that a new meaning will become current without the acquisition of a new form is greater in Italian than in French. We observed certain effects of Italian formal conservation earlier when speaking about adapting Gallicisms to Italian phonetic patterns. The same factors operate here. An Italianism may enter French with little adaptation because the varying degrees of learned borrowing in French provide intermediate patterns, nearer to Latin, which often happen to be closely in accord with those of Italian. French 'popular' forms on the other hand, resulting as they do from a series of more radical phonological developments, frequently possess no close parallel in Italian and are consequently likely to be accepted into the language only after analogical modification (in diachronic terms, a *regressive* modification) has taken place, as a result of which they will very probably become homophonous with already established 'popular' cognates in Italian.[3]

About one-eighth of the total number of semantic loans are cases where the semantic borrowing occurs not in relation to an established native word but to a loan-word taken earlier from the same source language, e.g. mediaeval

1. Some statement other than a simple qualitative appraisal is needed if we are to have any real idea of the position of semantic interference. The figures themselves can if necessary be revised later as more information becomes available.

2. The proportions stated are extrapolated from extensive samples of the word-lists. The lists themselves, as we have already said, err on the side of caution and are apt to understate the number of borrowings which actually took place. In addition they represent the more resistant strata of borrowings, in other words the homonymic rather than the polysemic loans. Polysemic loans are unusually frequent in 19th cent. Italian, and we have cause to believe that their influence was even greater than the 19th cent. list implies. The gap between proportions 1:9, 1:16 could perhaps be slightly reduced, but the essential disparity still remains.

3. An occasional example may be found of a semantic borrowing which arises because an *Italianism* is remodelled by analogy with a popular French word, though cases are extremely rare: e.g. 16th cent. *relief* (term of fine art) < It. *rilievo*, alongside native *relief*, backformation < *relever* (11th cent., *Alexis*; = 'leavings' from the table).

It. *dama* 'lady' < Fr., + sixteenth century *dama* 'counter' or 'man' in the game of draughts, also < Fr.; mediaeval It. *approccio -are* 'approach' < Fr., + sixteenth–seventeenth century *approccio -are* 'to dig approaches (milit. term)' < Fr.; sixteenth century Fr. *cavalier* < It., + seventeenth century Fr. *cavalier* (tech. term of fortification) < It.; seventeenth century It. *canapè* 'sofa' < Fr., + nineteenth century *canapè* (culinary term) < Fr. The situation is not always so precisely determinable. The two senses of It. *mina* borrowed from French ('mine' (for metals) and the ephemeral one of 'mien, appearance') appear in the sixteenth century at much the same time as the Hellenism *mina* (measure of capacity: 'bushel').[1] The position of the eighteenth century loans in respect of the It. word *pensione* ('board, boarding-house', etc.) varies according to whether one considers mediaeval It. *pensione* 'ecclesiastical stipend' to be a direct Latinism or borrowed *via* French. A problem of the same sort arises in the case of *blocco*.

A similar proportion (about one-eighth of the total) are cases in which a given semantic loan is followed at a later period by a second one in respect of the same original word, i.e. another form of dual influence. Examples are OFr. *escarpe* 'criminal' (thieves' slang < dialect form of *escharpe* < *escharpir* 'to shred, tear up') + sixteenth century *escarpe* 'shoe' and also 'escarpment' in fortification, both < It.; mediaeval It. *sortire* 'to draw lots, apportion', etc., + sixteenth century 'to make a sortie' < Fr., + nineteenth century (ephemeral) 'to go out', also < Fr: mediaeval It. *barra* 'barrier', etc., + eighteenth century *barra* 'bar of a river' and 'tiller of a ship', both < Fr.

LOAN HOMONYMY

The most clear-cut grouping which emerges from our material is that in which by the process of borrowing a new linguistic sign is introduced whose form is identical with that of a sign already existing in the language but whose meaning is quite distinct. This should be considered as the typical loan homonym as far as established languages are concerned. A second integral loan—a complete lexical unit—is superimposed, figuratively speaking, upon the indigenous word, with the result that a previously existing form is found related to a new meaning. The essential fact is that we have two separate lexical units or signs distinguished by context in the way homonyms usually are. Examples are the French verb *parer* 'to parry (a blow)', borrowed from Italian in the sixteenth century, beside indigenous *parer* 'to prepare, adorn'; seventeenth century It. *buffetto* adapted from Fr. *buffet* 'sideboard', as opposed to indigenous (onomatopoeic) *buffetto* 'blow, buffet'; eighteenth century *calandra* 'calendar for finishing textiles' and nineteenth century *calandra* 'weevil' (both from French) beside *calandra* 'lark' attested from the thirteenth

---

1. 17th cent. It. *mina* 'mine used by sappers' is on the other hand clearly a semantic loan from French.

century; seventeenth century *barletto* 'carpenter's vice' adapted from Fr. *varlet*, alongside *barletto* (modern *bariletto*) 'small barrel'; sixteenth century *mousse* 'ship's boy' from It. *mozzo* alongside *mousse* in the earlier senses of 'moss' and 'foam'. Usually a broad difference of meaning on the synchronic plane corresponds to a greater divergence historically, i.e. from an etymological standpoint. Often the loan-homonyms are etymologically unrelated in the sense that one or both are drawn from non-Romance languages, e.g. Fr. *civette* 'civet' (animal or perfume) < It. < Arabic, and *civette* 'chive'; Fr. *falot* 'lantern' < It. < Greek, and *fal(l)ot* 'fellow'; or Fr. *flasque* 'powder horn', etc., < It. and *flasque* adj. 'flaccid', also 'cheek of a gun-carriage', both probably < Dutch *vlakke* in different senses. Borrowings cognate within the Romance languages do often enough provide equally striking differences of meaning, witness the nineteenth century Gallicism *accidentato* (of terrain) and *accidentato* 'victim of an accident'; eighteenth century *borgognone* 'iceberg' from French and the geographical name 'Burgundian' (*borgognone* was also an earlier loan from French in the sense of 'helmet', which became a purely historical term in the sixteenth century); eighteenth century *filetto* (culinary term from French) and *filetto* diminutive of *filo*, 'border, bezel' in jewellery, '*fraenum* of the tongue', etc. But in general the principle holds good that between cognates the semantic disparity or ' "leap" of meaning' which characterises the loan-homonym—to use Weinreich's eminently apposite phrase[1]—tends to be less marked.[2]

LOAN SYNONYMY

The remaining loans are those which in some way may be said to show a 'logical, gradual extension of meaning'[3] between the original and borrowed senses; the ones that is which are called loan synonyms in the terminology generally accepted. We have discussed the term's limitations elsewhere, and agreed with Weinreich[4] that the situation which offers the most useful parallel here is not that of synonymy, but of polysemy, i.e. a word's possessing two or more similar senses or (in diachronic terms) retaining its previous senses while acquiring new ones.[5]

1. *Languages in Contact*, p. 49.

2. No doubt the words' common origin explains adequately why the 'gap' of meaning is narrower. We cannot, however, rule out the possibility that some slight measure of etymological awareness exists in lexical contacts similar to that adumbrated in the formal chapter above (p. 616), especially in the Middle Ages, when those at least who were sufficiently educated to write were frequently aware that Old Italian and Old French were closely related; while at the same time Latin—still in current use—provided a common point of reference for all those speaking Romance tongues.

3. *Languages in Contact*, p. 50.

4. *Vide* ibid.; also n. 34.

5. Homonymy and synonymy form a polarity, one opposed to the other, yet they are not the opposite extremes of one single relationship or situation, e.g. similarity of form,

SEMANTIC CALQUE

When semantic borrowing is accompanied by *calque* or translation of the formal element rather than unaltered adoption or simple adaptation, the term *semantic calque* is available for use (example: Fr. *dada* 'hobby' in addition to the sense 'hobby-horse', on the analogy of Eng. *hobby*). Current terminology varies, however, because authorities have different ideas about the category's scope and relative importance. Most do not distinguish between semantic calque and semantic loan in its wider aspects presumably because from a purely semantic standpoint the two are felt to be congruent.[1] In doing so they choose not to take the formal shift peculiar to calque into account. But there is rather more at issue than a simple distinction on grounds of formal disparity inasmuch as semantic calque presupposes a high degree of intention, an effect of deliberate adaptation and therefore a strongly developed feeling for the language on the borrower's part. This awareness of a semantic pattern in a foreign language as well as one's own combined with a perception of the semantic relationship which exists between the two languages and a conscious desire to exploit the parallelism—all of which we sum up by the word 'translation'—is the truly characteristic trait of semantic calque. In contrast,

or similarity of meaning. The contrast between them is a contrast of two factors in each case, i.e. both form *and* meaning. Semantic loans as we have defined them (and as lexicologists accept the term) are loans of meaning as opposed to loans of form (or loans of form and meaning together), a new habit of *usage* brought about by interference between two languages. They should therefore be classified as far as possible in terms of one factor only, meaning; or more precisely in terms of affinity of meaning (see also *Essays presented to C. M. Girdlestone*, pp. 131 and 137).

1. In his well-known article 'Notes sur les Calques linguistiques' (*Festschrift für Vilhelm Thomsen*, Leipzig, 1912) Kristian Sandfeld cut across the traditional division whereby formal (integral) loans are kept separate from semantic loans when he classed together under the title of *calques linguistiques* both formal calque or loan-translation (examples from our lists: *capo d'opera* < *chef d'œuvre, intervista* < *entrevue*) and semantic calque. He thus recognised that a similarity of kind exists between the two and implied by the same token—though he did not state it in so many words—that semantic calque and semantic loans proper are distinct categories. French scholars usually follow Sandfeld's terminology. Others, on the contrary, extend the term calque (or its equivalent in other languages) to mean both loan-translation and semantic borrowing as a whole (Sp. *calco*, for instance). We must observe *en passant* that when semantic calque is *not* considered separately it is inevitably treated as a case of loan-synonymy. This can be misleading. The meanings acquired by a process of semantic calque may well resemble the original (indigenous) significations, but they can also be very different. If we are to suppose (for the sake of argument) that *no* translation of form had taken place, and try to envisage the types of semantic affinity which they would represent if they were ordinary, straightforward semantic loans, we should find that a certain proportion of them would have to be classed as loan-homonyms rather than polysemic loans (see examples in *Studies presented to C. M. Girdlestone*, p. 131).

loan-polysemy ideally implies that the act of borrowing is carried out beneath the aegis of the receiving language only. In loan-polysemy it is not necessary as a matter of principle that the borrower should be aware of both the formal and semantic situation in the source language. He must perceive the formal resemblance between the foreign word and his own; the foreign meaning will of course be different, but it must not be so different that he is unaware of a semantic affinity. In other words the context of use will be sufficiently similar to make a shift from native to foreign use easy (e.g. French-Canadian *introduire* (*quelqu'un*) for 'to introduce (someone)' i.e. in the sense of Fr. *présenter*). But since in French and Italian the formal resemblance of translation equivalents is often very close we cannot always tell whether a semantic loan has in fact been translated, i.e. created knowingly in the receiving language through awareness of the foreign semantic pattern, or only adapted, i.e. simply made to conform to the phonetic conventions of the borrowing language without the intervention of a more fully informed analysis. To put it another way, in our material the semantic loan's formal aspect is not a reliable clue to the degree of awareness or intention which presided over the borrowing of the foreign signification. Furthermore, a word may be partly translated, partly adapted. In Franco-Italian contacts the formal link is in most cases easily recognisable even when an actual translation has taken place, e.g. *jalousie* 'venetian blind' < It. *gelosia* (sixteenth century), *appuntamento* 'stipend' < Fr. *appointement* (nineteenth century); or even in loans where the phonetic divergence is slightly greater: *bilanciare* 'to hesitate, be undecided' < Fr. *balancer* in this sense; *seducente* 'charming, fascinating' < Fr. *séduisant* (both nineteenth century). Other semantic calques are less transparent: *appoggio* 'patronage, support, "push"' < Fr. *appui*; *attaccato* (diplomatic term) < Fr. *attaché*; *carica* 'appointment, post' < Fr. *charge*; *coperto* 'place, "setting" at table', or 'table-cloth' < Fr. *couvert*; *impegnato* in certain senses of Fr. *engagé*; *schiacciante* as in *prove schiaccianti*, 'overwhelming, indisputable' < Fr. *écrasant*; and *straziante* (as in *un grido straziante*) 'piercing, heartrending' < Fr. *déchirant* (all nineteenth century uses). Even so it is difficult to think of a French-Italian calque on quite the same footing as a corresponding English or German one, where the forms are palpably unrelated; compare It. *gusto* '(aesthetic) taste' and Germ. *Geschmack*, both apparently influenced by Fr. *goût*, sense transferred early eighteenth century.[1] In the past lexicologists have tended to ascribe undue importance to semantic calque at the expense of other forms of semantic interference, presumably because it is superficially more striking and therefore more easily detected. Its relatively minor role in closely cognate languages helps us to reduce this aspect of semantic interference to its rightful proportions.

1. The metaphor may ultimately be a Hispanism in French. It was known to Spanish authors of the Golden Age.

LOAN-POLYSEMY

In loan-polysemy an acute problem of identification arises. The difficulty is intrinsic. There is least doubt that a polysemic loan has occurred when the semantic innovation concerned is smallest: yet the more trivial the semantic divergence happens to be, the more likely it is to pass unnoticed. Further, it is an ineluctable fact that whereas homonymy (implying lack of semantic affinity) is an absolute state and consequently can be objectively demonstrated, polysemy (implying resemblance or relation of meaning) is *relative* and *unstable*. It is relative because meanings can be similar to a greater or lesser degree, and unstable because polysemy is a diachronic process rather than static situation; a process whereby uses of a given word diverge, with the result that the content of a linguistic sign is altered, rather than a relationship of meaning which exists at any one moment.

(a) *Relativity. A Scale of Comparison*

However justified in principle Haugen's complaint about 'the lack of any satisfactory method of classifying degrees of semantic similarity' may be[1] it usually proves possible to make an intuitive assessment of semantic affinity sufficiently accurately to separate loan-homonyms from polysemic loans in a majority of cases, even in earlier periods. Some semantic loans fall unavoidably in the no-man's land between the two opposites but these turn out to be very much a minority. One has the impression that since the causes which motivate borrowing in each of the two main categories are of a different kind, semantic loans tend to be either of one sort or the other. Must the assessment be purely an intuitive one? Can a more objective scale be devised? The fact that we are concerned here with cognate languages suggests a way of resolving the difficulty. The semantic 'gap' might be gauged by referring to the developments in meaning which took place in the source or lending language up to the moment of contact, and using them to describe the difference between the original word in the receiving language and its corresponding semantic loan. Most kinds of semantic change are represented, both shifts and transfers. They include:

(i) Changes in semantic extension (in most instances, *restriction*,[2] with specialisation from a general to a technical sense): *affluente* (geog.) 'tributary',

1. 'The Analysis of Linguistic Borrowing', p. 220.
2. It seems to be a rule that the borrowed sense will be a restricted one compared with the indigenous term—a technical word, perhaps, or a specialised sense in common usage. The point is worth noting for further examination, since at first sight there is no apparent reason why a generic or abstract usage should not be borrowed in the way that abstract or generic integral loans often are, and become a semantic loan in respect of the same form existing already in the language in a restricted sense. Similar tendencies are revealed in semantic shifts (see below).

eighteenth century < Fr. *affluent*; *barra* 'bar of a river' as opposed to 'bar' in general, eighteenth century < Fr. *barre*; *grosso* name of a coin and of a kind of cloth, fourteenth and eighteenth century < Fr. *gros; pause* (musical term), sixteenth century < It. *pausa*. Often the change is little more than a shift of application: *amatore* 'amateur' (sport, etc.), nineteenth century; *ombrer* in the special sense of 'to shade a drawing' (fine arts) sixteenth century < It. *ombrare*.

(ii) Ellipsis: *articolo* (of commerce; in a journal), nineteenth century < Fr. *article (de fond,* etc.).

(iii) Place-name, proper noun to substantive: *bavarese* (culin. term) nineteenth century < Fr. *bavaroise*; *persiana* 'type of shutter' eighteenth century < Fr. *persienne*.

(iv) 'Pejoration' and Euphemism: *créature* 'sycophant, yes-man' sixteenth century < It. *creatura*.

(v) Metaphor: It. *domino* 'piece in a game of dominoes', nineteenth century < Fr., a visual metaphor from *domino* 'mask', itself a semantic loan to Italian during the eighteenth century; *liquide* (adj.) 'free from debt, liquid, of assets', sixteenth century < It.; *cavalier* 'cannon mounted upon a mound of earth' (i.e. like a horseman in the saddle), sixteenth century < It. *cavalliere*.[1,2]

These indications suggest that to construct a scale of the kind Haugen would like to see available might not be an impossible undertaking, though admittedly one beset with difficulties. One of these has to do with the problem—well known to etymologists—of parallel semantic development or polygenesis of metaphor. An effect of semantic borrowing is to forestall or by-pass a change of meaning which could equally well have occurred in the receiving language itself, given the right conditions. Might not the new usage result from an indigenous shift which happened to take place in both languages at the same period? How far, for example, are we justified in attributing to foreign influence usages like eighteenth–nineteenth century Italian *abbordabile* 'approachable' (of people), *amabile* and *amabilità* 'kind, kindness, pleasantness', *piccante* 'piquant, pungent' (figuratively), *formalizzarsi* 'to take offence', *sofferente* 'invalid, poorly' or any other of the considerable stock of slightly modified meanings which nineteenth century purists censure as Gallicisms?[3] The final decision rests with the etymologist. One has to 'replace language in its

---

1. The original French word *cavalier* in its usual sense of 'horseman, rider' was itself an Italianism.

2. Only in exceptional circumstances do polysemic loans correspond to metaphorical shift in the source language. In most semantic innovations of this kind the 'leap of meaning' is so great or, in I. A. Richards' terminology, the angle of the metaphor is so wide that a resultant semantic loan is necessarily a loan *homonym* (cf. *barletto* 'carpenter's vice' (above) from *varlet* 'servant, labourer').

3. See 19th cent. Fr. > It. influences.

background',[1] to reconstruct in detail the history of relevant lexical elements in both languages, making use of all criteria which offer reliable information. Often the true pattern of events emerges unequivocally, but when it does not we can at least put forward a reasoned opinion. Thus we can say for instance that the sense 'relating to the present day' in It. *attualmente, attuale*, and that of 'modernity, up-to-date news', etc., in *attualità* were borrowed in succession from their French counterparts during the later seventeenth century, the eighteenth century and the nineteenth century respectively.[2] A similar semantic modification following French usage appears in the Italian word-family *brutale, brutalità, brutalmente* and *brutalizzare*—from the etymological signification of 'pertaining to or resembling brute creation, animal' to that of 'brutish, violent' (i.e. the same sense as ModEng. *brutal, brutality*, etc., which were likewise affected by French).[3] The impulse provided by external example is particularly difficult to specify in words whose application alters as a result of ellipsis, as in the case of It. *uniforme* '(military) uniform' which shifted from the general connotation of the original adjective via the phrase *abito uniforme* but in all probability did so on the analogy of the same shift in French *(habit) uniforme*.[4] On the other hand nineteenth century It. *agghindare* 'to dress up, trim up' (as opposed to the nautical term borrowed during the Middle Ages), which some have held to be a semantic loan, is in my opinion an indigenous development to which transfer of meaning by metaphor and the effect of certain phonetically similar words have both contributed.[5]

(b) *Instability. The Diachronic Aspect*

A natural consequence of the transitional nature of polysemy is that surveys of word-borrowing conducted according to traditional norms are apt to register few polysemic loans. They tend to pass unnoticed unless some unwonted impulse leads contemporary observers to record ephemeral lexical usage in permanent form. The opportunity which nineteenth century Italian purism provides in this respect is without equal in Franco-Italian contacts, although as far as French is concerned a limited amount of information may be gleaned from anti-Italian works of the late sixteenth century, among which Henri Estienne's *Dialogues* occupy a prominent place, as we

1. K. J. Hollyman, *Le Développement du vocabulaire féodal*, p. 2. The phrase 'replacer le langage dans son milieu' sums up the etymological procedure adopted by Dr. Hollyman in that work.

2. See under *attuale*, 18th cent. loans.

3. See under *brutalizzare*, 17th cent. Fr. > It. loans. Cf. in addition the semantic development of It. *libertino* (under *libertinaggio*, 18th cent. Fr. < It. loans).

4. See 18th cent. loans. Cf. also the similar cases of ellipsis under the influence of foreign usage in *locomotiva* and *vaccino* (*vaccina*), 19th cent. Fr. > It. loans.

5. See *agghindare*, med. Fr. > It. loans.

have already seen. We recall how Philausone uses *fatigue* for 'thankless task' (< It. *fatica*) and *stance* for 'residence, stay' (< It. *stanza* in the abstract).

It might be supposed that polysemic loans would be likely to disappear as a result of clashes between related meanings. There are, to be sure, a few grains of evidence to show that similarity of meaning can provoke intolerable ambiguity: witness the clash between the original sense of It. *parrucca*, 'scalp, head of hair' and the meaning of 'wig, perruque' borrowed from French in the seventeenth century; the obsolescence of Fr. *fatigue* 'thankless task' (above), of It. *villa* meaning 'town' on the analogy of Fr. *ville* or of Fr. *caresse* 'beloved' (subst.) used as an appellation by Rémy Belleau (< It. *carezza*). But we must not try to infer more than the evidence allows. There are several reasons why semantic loans fall out of use—reasons which apply equally to loan-words in general and indeed to any elements of vocabulary. Where a lexical usage becomes archaic because of clash or incompatibility, context is at least as important a factor as similarity of meaning: but quite apart from this, incompatibility within the pattern of vocabulary (whether of form or meaning) accounts only partially for the phenomenon of obsolescence; the major factor is the positive one of *utility*, the efficiency of a certain habit of reference as a means of communication, considered according to the requirements of a given cultural situation. We shall inquire later why lexical innovations are received into the language, merely observing for the present that as many loan-homonyms as loan-synonyms figure among the usages which are subsequently rejected; cf. sixteenth century Fr. *amasser* 'to kill' (< It. *amazzare*), *estrade* 'street' (< It. *strada*), *fermer* 'to stop' (< It. *fermare*), *mat* 'mad' (< It. *matto*).

Occasionally, though rarely, it comes about that a clash resulting from similarity of meaning causes the *original* term to be rejected, while the loan-polyseme continues in use.[1] A notable example is that of It. *parrucca* 'wig' cited above. The new meaning was acquired in the later seventeenth century on the analogy of Fr. *perruque* and quickly replaced the primitive sense of 'scalp, head of hair' during the earlier eighteenth century.

OBSERVATIONS AND INFERENCES

I. *Importance of Semantic Borrowing*

The proportion of semantic as opposed to integral loans is high in French and Italian, mainly because of the close formal affinities between the two, but also because extensive semantic interference is typical of periods when contact is extremely intimate. This condition is fulfilled during at least five of the

1. An explanation why the *borrowed sense* seldom supersedes that associated with the *original word* is probably to be found in the circumstance mentioned above, that the borrowed sense tends to be more restricted.

eight centuries under review. It is instructive to make a comparison with words from a non-cognate (sc., non-Romance) source—for instance the corpus of Dutch terms entering French examined by Valkhoff, whose work is all the more useful because he undertakes to label examples of semantic influence in his word-lists. We are surprised to see that he records only two contacts of this kind, that of *accise* (seventeenth century) 'excise duty'[1] and *élingue* (fourteenth century) 'sling' (nautical term).[2] Valkhoff's criterion of what constitutes a semantic loan is more selective than ours[3] but with generous allowances made the proportion of semantic loan in respect of Dutch words accepted by French is extremely unlikely to exceed 2 per cent and probably is more like 1 per cent. The Italian and French average of 8.9 per cent indicates a lexical situation the characteristics of which are radically different. Apart from the formal incompatability of Dutch (which means that a homologous term is unlikely to be present already in the borrowing language) we have to remember that the Dutch loans are ill-matched semantically, in the sense that they often refer to objects or circumstances which could not readily be described by a polysemic extension or figurative transfer of existing French words.

The extent of semantic borrowing plainly varies within wide limits from one linguistic situation to another, but my impression is that the percentages in Dutch > French on one side and French > Italian on the other represent roughly the minimum and maximum proportions in which this mode of intra-lingual interference is likely to occur. Taken as a whole the statistics show that one is fully justified in including semantic borrowings in a list of lexical loans. With languages of culture this should always be done.

2. Effect of Parallel Cultural Development

In about one-third of the examples in our lists there is a double or reiterated semantic influence—either a meaning added to a word already borrowed from the same source-language, or two meanings taken in succession. What is the significance of this? Once again the factor of formal relationship plays a part, but there are others. We cannot fail to observe, for instance, how readily each language accepts extensions of meaning, metaphorical usages

1. M. Valkhoff, *Étude sur les mots fr. d'origine néerlandaise*, pp. 41 and 248.
2. Op. cit., pp. 123 and 264.
3. The semantic influences registered are in our terminology polysemic loans. In particular, they are cases where the difference of sense is slight enough to raise the possibility of a native development. If our definition of loan-homonymy were applied, words like 18th cent. *action* 'share in a company' (< Dutch *aktie*, itself < French and therefore ultimately cognate) and 18th cent. *bosse* 'brush for teazing wool' < Dutch *bos* as opposed to *bosse* 'protuberance' < **bottia* and *bosse* 'keg' < **buttia* [non-cognate homonyms]) would have to rank as semantic borrowings (*vide* Valkhoff, pp. 42 and 67 resp.).

and even idioms from the other; how the semantic innovations of one fall in with the other's needs. There is a solidarity between Italian and French at the semantic level as well as at the formal level. Though superficially less striking, it is intrinsically more worthy of note. The solidarity of form is an automatic result of the languages' common origin. It persists over a long period as an extension or prolongation of a state which existed in former times. The semantic solidarity is different; it perpetuates itself; it is a process of mutual supplementation constantly renewed by one contact after another. The fact that this process may be observed in all periods where contact is close—in the Middle Ages and sixteenth century as well as the nineteenth—may be taken as evidence of a more far-reaching non-linguistic correlation, namely, the intimate relationship of Italian and French culture and its persistence as a stable factor in the cultural history of western Europe.[1]

3. Contribution of Franco-Italian Loans towards Definition and Statements of Principle

To some extent differences of opinion between authorities about terminology, and therefore about the underlying principles by which loans of meaning are to be described and classified, may be attributed to their authors' motives in embarking upon the study of interference between languages. It is a striking fact that most of the work upon semantic loans in the past has been carried out with one of two specific purposes in view. There are some studies which deal with particular cases of interference between ancient languages, above all translations of the Bible and contacts between Greek and Latin epic literature.[2] Others (a more recent approach) describe with the help of information collected from informants in the field the gradual process by which immigrant populations acquire a new idiom. The immigrant languages studied are mostly those of the United States.[3] These are two quite separate lines of attack.[4] And though the field which they cover is admittedly vast,

1. The parallelism I have in mind is not a simple one of significations or meanings in the referential sense corresponding to the same cultural facts and events in each case, i.e. the kind of correlation we have observed on innumerable occasions in our historical section above, but something complementary to this; a more intrinsic relationship which might properly be called stylistic as well as semantic, comparable to the phonemic and grammatical 'convergence phenomena' in western European languages discussed by Professor Hans Vogt in his article 'Language Contacts', in Linguistics Today (Publications of the Linguistic Circle of New York, No. 2), New York, 1954, esp. pp. 253-4.

2. Details and examples in Kronasser, op. cit., p. 143, Deroy, op. cit., pp. 94-7 and generally throughout Sandfeld, op. cit.

3. For details of the works in question, which by now are very numerous and provide a major source of information about linguistic borrowing, the reader is asked to refer to the bibliographies compiled by Weinreich and Deroy, op. cit.

4. Our own stands apart from both of them in many respects. How much they differ may be judged from the following quotation, which reproduces the thinking of American

they are only two headings in a prospectus for a wider scheme of research. Before any further progress in definition and description can be expected we need this still broader perspective which nothing but a supply of new data from widely divergent standpoints can give. The practical advantages of checking contemporary interference phenomena against similar situations in past ages, and of comparing the effects in minority languages with those in two equally established languages of culture apply even more strongly here than they did in respect of the phonetic contacts which we considered earlier. This is true not only of semantic borrowings, but also of influences affecting the pattern of the *lexis* in general.

PEJORATIVES AND PEJORATION

The words which according to various accepted definitions may be called *pejoratives* lay special claim to our attention on both practical and theoretical grounds. To explain their uneven distribution from century to century or between one language and the other seems at first sight to be no more than a practical job of statistical analysis similar to those carried out in the historical and formal chapters above, and yet in reality it is a far more complex undertaking. As in the case of semantic borrowing the inherent problem is one of definition. A number of phenomena are referred to in different quarters by the terms *pejorative* (noun and adjective) and *pejoration* which differ fundamentally in essence. The acceptation of *pejorative* in particular varies widely, meaning in some contexts a word which has undergone *pejoration* or *dégradation sémantique*,[1] in others a word which merely possesses as an absolute characteristic an emotive aura of disapproval or unpleasantness.[2] Marouzeau introduced a third major distinction by adding the idea of relativity: '*péjoratif*: terme propre à présenter une notion sous un jour défavorable; . . . avare est

descriptive linguists in a way we can accept as representative: 'Once a loan has been accepted by other speakers, it is no longer an innovation, and ceases to be a loan, except in a purely historical sense. . . . It is a common weakness of loan-word studies that they include as loans a great deal of material which was already naturalised in the period under discussion' (Haugen, *Language*, Vol. XXXII, No. 4, 1956, p. 762). Within these terms of reference, of course, the present work does not qualify to be called a loan-word study. But we must not think there is something paradoxical in these asymmetrical viewpoints. It is all part of the 'historico-cultural' versus 'linguistic' dichotomy that runs through contemporary linguistics, producing gaps which I for one would dearly like to see bridged.

1. The term favoured by Nyrop (*Grammaire historique de la langue française*, Vol. IV, p. 115f.); sc. a semantic change as a result of which a word appears at a given moment with an unpleasant or derogatory connotation not evidenced in previous periods.

2. Nyrop speaks of a *nuance défavorable*.

péjoratif par rapport à économe'.[1] The problem may be envisaged as a diachronic or a synchronic one according to the point of view adopted. If we choose the first, those factors which provoke a shift from neutral to pejorative connotations will form the focal point of inquiry. Foremost among these, in our case, are the impulses towards pejoration attributable to a word's foreign origin. The synchronic approach, on the other hand, will direct attention towards those aspects of the word's total connotation which are the product of *dégradation sémantique* in the past or which contain the nucleus of pejorative developments to come. Our word-lists, in which pejoratives are well represented (about a hundred and ten words are directly or indirectly relevant, i.e. 4.3 per cent of the total borrowings listed) help to show in what respects the definitions of this phenomenon are imprecise, and what conflicting issues of principle cause this imprecision.

Many of the lexical units to which from time to time the generic term 'pejorative' is loosely applied are straightforward neutral borrowings which happen to mean 'unpleasant' things. Very frequently they denote people (sometimes collectively), their personal qualities or modes of behaviour: Fr. *lazarone, malandrin, mesquin, pastiche, postiche, renégat, rufien, saltimbanque, supercherie, veillaque, volte-face,* etc.; It. *abbrutire, claque, deboscia, furbo, libertinaggio, negriere* ('slave-trader'), *oltranza, oltraggio, sabotaggio,* etc. There is no inherent difference between these and any other borrowed words; unpleasant notions, object, situations, actions require to be described in language just as much as those with favourable or neutral connotations. At the same time it is true to say that these neutral/unfavourable words are always potentially pejorative. All can readily take on an affective or emotive bias in suitable conditions—witness, for instance, the ease with which names of persons in the foregoing sample become terms of abuse.

In very many of our *mots défavorables* the emotive accompaniment is so strong that by itself it accounts for the word's importation and subsequent viability. To such words the label 'pejorative' can very fittingly be applied, though with the reservation that in doing so we are including under a single heading words whose affective connotations differ considerably, and were certainly acquired in widely differing circumstances.

In many instances the process of borrowing which has taken place does not add anything to the word's emotional connotation. A pejorative nuance was acquired in the language of origin and both overtones and referential implications were taken across unchanged, the total symbol being applied to analogous situations in the receiving language. Typical examples are: It. > Fr. mediaeval: *canaille, frasque;* sixteenth century: *bravache, gabatine, pagnote, populace;* seventeenth century: *bec(que) cornu, papalin:* Fr. > It. med.:

---

1. *Lexique de la terminologie linguistique,* II, 1943, p. 161. Examples drawn from our lists are *peuple ~ populace; médecin ~ charlatan, saltimbanque; remède ~ orviétan.*

bordelliere, briffalda, marmaglia, truante, etc. The outstanding century is the nineteenth in Italian, where almost all the pejoratives borrowed were taken ready made from French, often in the French form: *affarismo, affarista, arrivismo, arrivista, coterie, gargotta, parvenu, razzia, ribotta, rococo, sciovinismo*,[1] etc.

On other occasions the act of borrowing fails to play a significant role in the pejorative development for an entirely different reason, namely, because pejoration occurred *after* the word had become established in the receiving language. Much depends, naturally, upon the extent to which the borrowing retains its 'foreign' flavour; and here we are on particularly difficult ground. It is hard to say exactly when the exotic aura fades from a loan-word's connotation. Reliable semantic evidence is not easy to come by. In any case, 'foreignness' in a word is not necessarily the same as awareness of foreign origin. But by considering the lapse of time since earliest attestations of a given word's use in conjunction with contemporary indications as to its meaning (both contextual and lexicographical) one can usually confirm that by a certain period integration has taken place and that the exoticism is no longer generally recognised. When pejoration occurs later the fact that a word is borrowed is of course semantically immaterial; an extraneous idiom supplies the original symbol, but the subsequent development takes place in relation to the borrowing language alone. In principle the influences which provoke a subsequent pejorative shift are the same as those which obtain in respect of vocabulary as a whole. Whenever we are tracing the semantic history of borrowed neologisms the possibility that we may be dealing with a change in which foreign interference has no part should never be overlooked; we should be wary, for instance, of attributing to Italophobia the development of sixteenth century borrowings such as *anticaille, grotesque, pédant, soldatesque, bravade, mercadant*.[2]

We shall not consider at length whether the concept of pejoration as manifested on the diachronic plane is a valid one or not, though the proposition deserves at least a passing mention. Those who have touched upon the

---

1. Used from the outset as a term of disapprobation, of self-criticism, in French itself.
2. It is interesting to check these words against Nyrop's list of semantic categories intrinsically subject to pejoration (*Grammaire historique*, IV, pp. 117–37). *Pédant* is one of the actual examples cited under the rubric *École, enseignement* (p. 125); *soldatesque* obviously belongs to §172, *Soldats* (p. 123) and *mercadant* to §178, *Commerçants* (p. 128). The latter is not an entirely satisfactory example because some slight ironical cast may have been present from the time of borrowing. This is, however, open to dispute. Its use in Habert's translation of Horace, 1549 ('un tas de mercadants qui font. . . ./Pour toujours rapiner') may be dictated by metrical needs, as also may du Bellay's 'nos mercadants d'honneur'. Elsewhere it appears as an exact synonym (presumably neutral) of *marchand*. Noël du Fail uses both words alternatively in the same sentence. On the whole *mercadant* seems to have been diminutive rather than pejorative in the first instance (see examples in Huguet, *Dict. de la langue fr. au XVIᵉ siècle*).

subject of ultimate causes in semantic changes of this kind since Jaberg[1] and Nyrop have never seriously questioned the theoretical assumptions made by the earlier scholars. Yet one must admit that the positivistic, 'pigeon-holing' approach characteristic of both these authorities fails to provide an answer to the problem of what actually happens when a *pejorative Bedeutungsentwicklung* takes place. The very existence of a single term 'pejoration' is regrettable, since it sanctions the concept of an isolated, homogeneous train of events which in many ways does not correspond to reality. There is something to be said for the point of view that pejoration does not exist except as a heuristic construct created to help in classifying certain heterogeneous shifts of meaning.[2] In fact the final reality behind pejoration is not *lexical*[3] but *psycho-sociological*[4] or even *psychological*[5] without qualification. For all this it is fair to say that the psychological problem involved is one which the psychologist cannot expect to tackle successfully without an intimate knowledge of lexicology.

We may therefore doubt whether pejoration can justifiably be presented as a lexical process, or indeed as any single process at all in the sense that process implies a unified, continuous, motivated development. But we can have these scruples, and consequently discount the purely diachronic approach, without necessarily abandoning our search for ultimate causes and having to

1. Karl Jaberg, 'Pejorative Bedeutungsentwicklung im Französischen', *Zeit. für rom. Phil.*, XXV (1901), pp. 561–601; xxvii (1903), 25–7; xxix (1905), 57–71. Other important sources on pejoration and pejoratives are: E. Huguet, *Évolution du sens des mots depuis le XVIe siècle*, Paris, 1934, Ch. IV; E. Gamillscheg, *Französische Bedeutungslehre*, Tübingen, 1951, pp. 94–118; E. Lerch, *Französische Sprache und Wesenart*, Frankfurt a.M., 1933, pp. 49ff.

2. The term *amelioration*, incidentally, is an even more obvious subject for Ockham's razor than its antonym. To describe the meaning-change which occurs when *testa* becomes *tête* as an *ennoblissement* is an extravagant figure of speech and also an unnecessary duplication of categories, since the usual formulae for describing semantic shifts may be applied, e.g. metaphor, metonymy and other transfers, effects of slang, or nonlinguistic shifts—Meillet's *causes historiques*, Ullmann's *changes due to linguistic conservatism* (cf. *Principles of Semantics*, 2nd edition, p. 211 and Collinson, *MLR*, XX, p. 104)—as in *marahskalk > maréchal (de France)* and so on.

3. Nyrop's catalogue of *causes intérieures* (Gr. hist., IV, *Dégradation*, §158), though designed to show a 'dégradation . . . immanente' or 'état latent' of pejoration in certain lexical groups is based essentially upon external (logical) criteria.

4. E.g. the attitude towards social inferiors affecting the semantic development of names used to denote the classes or groups concerned; or (more applicable to the present survey) the effect of a critical attitude towards foreigners. There is a temptation, however, to make too much of the social element, probably owing to the influence of scholars like Meillet and Antoine Thomas; cf. the notorious misunderstanding about *captivus > chétif*, thought by Nyrop to reflect a social abuse—the harsh treatment of captives in the Middle Ages—but later correctly interpreted as an ellipsis of the euphemistic phrase *libidinis captivus* ('slave of one's passions') in the Fathers of the Church (Bloch-Wartburg).

5. Pejoration arising out of euphemism, for instance.

be content with a discrete, rule-of-thumb taxonomy in order to describe this phenomenon. We can usefully consider, for example, what elements of semantic content the pejorative term has which the neutral term has not. Our borrowed words confirm that the seat of pejoration is not to be found in the basic sense, the 'unpleasant' meaning, but in the emotional overtones; or more precisely in the subjective bias which is such a salient feature of this kind of word. We might use this characteristic as a basis for definition, and say that a pejorative term in the strict sense—opposed, that is, to the looser signification of 'any word which has at some time been affected by *dégradation sémantique*'—is one which possesses overtones of feeling corresponding to value judgements and subjective attitudes on the user's part, especially reprehension, aversion, contempt and derision. As far as borrowed vocabulary is concerned the last two almost always dominate, though the first two form a nucleus to the entire emotive complex. To put it another way: the subjective element in borrowings is usually more than a passive feeling of annoyance or dislike; it implies a wilful intervention on the user's part, a deliberately contrived effect which appears on the surface as a play of irony. This ironical colouring is the typical trait of our borrowed pejoratives. Often the irony is hyperbolical; more frequently still it manifests itself in a form of lexical substitution which we may call *false* or *transparent euphemism*, i.e. the use of an apparently euphemistic term or similar verbal proxy which derives its communicative force from the very fact that it allows one to perceive at the expense of a little imagination what it pretends to conceal. Thus *boucon*, literally 'mouthful' or 'pill' is understood (with an ironical smile, so to speak) to mean 'poison'—a grimly humorous interpretation no doubt equally current during the Renaissance among Italians and Frenchmen. These hyperbolical or pseudo-euphemistic pejoratives are well represented in our lists: the phenomenon is obviously something more than an isolated procedure of style. Examples are It. > Fr. *casino* ('brothel', eighteenth century), *faciende*, *favori*, *imbroglio*, *intrigue* and probably *retirade*, *volte-face*, etc. A similar disingenousness may be suspected when a high-sounding name is applied to an unworthy thing, as when the notion behind *arrivismo*, *arrivista*, *affarismo*, *affarista*, *parvenu* is dignified by a technical-sounding term, or the idea of prostitution attenuated (and yet at the same time enhanced and sophisticated) by the terms *cocotte*, *grisette*, *fille (de joie)*, *demi-monde*, all of which were current in Italian during the later nineteenth century.[1] We are not concerned here with euphemism in its strict sense, i.e. the psychological buffer-word, the 'expression atténuée ... d'une notion dont l'expression directe aurait quelque chose de déplaisant' (Marouzeau, *Lexique* ...), or with the *dégradation sémantique* which appears as an end product when a true euphemism has run its course,—that is to say when, as Nyrop puts it, 'l'idée déplaisante

1. Cf. also med. Fr. > It. *bordelliere*, 16th cent. *briffalda*.

U

THE SEMANTIC ASPECT

qu'on a voulu cacher sous une expression neutre et innocente a brutalement
percé le voile et l'a sali' (Vol. IV, p. 133). Ideally the true euphemism fulfilling its purpose efficiently should present no pejorative overtones and
certainly no ironical ones when analysed synchronically. In practice some
slight feeling of aversion is always present; once this has increased to the
point where the euphemism has failed, an element of ridicule frequently
begins to be associated with the word in question. It is of course difficult to
decide where euphemism ends and irony begins. There is a progression from
one to the other, running from actual linguistic taboo on one side through
euphemism proper to ironical or transparent euphemism and eventually to
the deliberate use of substitute words (including foreign words) to give a
satirical, witty, comic or heightened effect. I suspect that many words classed
as typical euphemisms (substitutions made perhaps out of respect for religion,
through fear of committing an impropriety or otherwise offending against
social canons) possessed from the outset an ironical or jocular ingredient. Even
the most obvious *false euphemism* on the other hand may embody some measure of serious substitution (e.g. the superstitious element in thieves' slang).[1]

The *furbesco* has a special relevance here. It is well known that irony and
hyperbole are essential elements in the formation of slangs, especially the
narrowly restricted idiom of thieves' jargon, which owes its exclusiveness
in no small measure to the presence of disingenuous 'euphemisms' of the
boucon/casino type, transparent only to the initiated. These comprise a series
of codes which when broken down reveal a play of irony at the expense of
mutual enemies and of the *pègre* itself; it follows that the 'decoding' can only
be carried out efficiently by people to whom these same attitudes of cynicism
and derision are second nature. Most of the items of thieves' slang in our
lists were originally figurative usages in which false euphemism played a major
part, e.g. Fr. > It. *birba* 'food' > 'trick' (to obtain charity), It. > Fr. *casquer*
'to fall' > ' "to fall for" a trick', *gonze* 'fool' > 'person, chap', *manille*
'bracelet' > 'handcuff', *mariol* 'plaster saint' > 'crafty person', etc.

Most interesting of all are those words in which the pejorative/subjective
nuance is acquired during or soon after transfer on account of some prevalent
attitude towards the lending language and the culture it represents. Numerically they are a minority. The group is small even if one allows for the fact
that pejoratives in general are more likely to be current in impermanent

1. I must make it clear that my conception of 'false euphemism' differs fundamentally
from the *faux euphémisme* described by Nyrop in the *Gram. hist.*, Vol. IV, §428 as 'une
expression euphémique provenant moins d'un souci de correction dans la langue et de
bienséance, que d'une fausse pruderie qui se fait un plaisir de trouver de l'indécence
partout, et qui sous le masque de la pudeur s'acharne contre des inconvenances imaginaires'
(p. 308). My term implies no will to deceive on the user's part, whether through *fausse
pruderie* or otherwise. On the contrary, the whole point is that the verbal 'mask' is
intended to be penetrable.

sectors of language—familiar usage, expressive or emotive speech and the like—and so are comparatively difficult to track down in written records of past ages. In the French to Italian lists there are perhaps a dozen examples of words in which ironical overtones arise or are modified to a notable extent during the act of transfer, e.g. mediaeval *ciarpiere*, 'Jack of all trades', *ceffo*, 'snout, muzzle', *ciurmare*, 'to swindle', *tornese*, 'paltry sum, stiver'; sixteenth century *mangeria*, 'trickery, swindle'; nineteenth century *pappiè*, 'screed, bumph'; cf. also the amusing connotations placed upon importations from French like *bon-ton, bon goût (bontonista, buongustaio), élite, fine fleur, crema della società*, etc.[1] Foreign titles and honorifics are very liable to be affected in this way. There are two good examples in It. *monsiù (monsù)* and Fr. *messer*, the former appearing in the seventeenth century, the latter used slightingly of Italians during the sixteenth century, for the most part. The tendency to exploit pejorative connotations of foreign words for satirical effect is very much a characteristic of French, where Italianisms begin to be used for this purpose in the fifteenth century (see above, discussion of the title *Raguet* in seventeenth century Fr. > It. evaluation, p. 345). The trend persists at much the same strength in proportion to the century totals until the later eighteenth century. A title like *Le poltronisme des choses italiennes* in the 'Bibliothèque de l'Abbaye de Saint-Victor' finds its explanation here, as does the success of Monsieur de la Réussite a century later. The contemporary attitudes towards *créatures, braves* and *favoris* at the Valois court is well known. Similar shades of meaning may be detected in seventeenth century *barbacole, caver, galantiser* and *sacripant*, together with *lazzi* and *opéra* in their original senses ('knavery' and 'undertaking of exaggerated importance' respectively). Eighteenth century *castrat, casino, cicerone* and *sigisbée*, too, are all in their way an adverse comment upon Italian civilisation as seen through French eyes.[2]

What does the historical distribution of our borrowings tell us about the relation of pejoration to national or cultural prestige? Lexicologists generally accept as axiomatic the proposition that pejorative loans are most numerous when the language from which they are taken and therefore the civilisation

1. The reader is referred to the nineteenth century Italian purists mentioned in my evaluation above, who abound in observations about this sort of foreign borrowing. These should be accepted with caution, however, since almost all authorities are prone to exaggerate the pejorative content to help in discrediting a foreign term. Similar impulses lead purists to assert that imported euphemisms reveal a dyed-in-the-wool hypocrisy on the part of foreigners in respect of the particular *denotata* involved (e.g. the French attitude to prostitution as seen through Italian eyes).

2. I have noted on several occasions how the names of foreign coins may be used to mean 'paltry, trivial sum'. A similar thrust at the foreigner is made by euphemistic and jocular names for syphilis and similar diseases which we noted earlier, *mal de Naples, il morbo gallico*, etc. In all these terms irony is a more weighty component than xenophobia.

which that language represents are in eclipse, and correspondingly rare when
the language of origin and the associated cultural pattern enjoy high prestige;
i.e.

> Foreign source in disrepute: pejoratives borrowed are numerous;
> Prestige of foreign source high: pejoratives borrowed are few.

The same antithesis is sometimes expressed in terms of pejoration and 'amelioration' (which as I have already said is understood as the acquisition of more
'noble' connotations, an aura of dignity or reputation); thus:

> Foreign source in disrepute: pejoratives borrowed;
> Prestige of foreign source high: 'amelioratives' borrowed.

All these assumptions are open to question. The defect from which they
suffer is the one we have detected already in accepted ideas about lexicology,
and which will crop up again: they have been arrived at logically, by taking
thought rather than observing actual material. It seems logical to assume that
words denoting lofty concepts, laudable qualities, noble achievements and
positions of high social status, all of which have approbatory implications,
should be drawn from a language associated with a centre of cultural
ferment whose standards are high and whose reputation is great. But in
reality it does not necessarily work out this way. I should not care to maintain that status and pejoration are unrelated; but the conditions under which
one affects the other can not be hit off in a simple formula. It is true that there
are certain occasions on record when few pejoratives are borrowed from a
language whose cultural standing happens at that time to be high. In the
twelfth, thirteenth and fourteenth centuries, when the impact of French on
Italian was great, the proportion of pejorative loans was less than 3.9 per cent
of the total importation (10 out of 262). It is noteworthy, too, that French
titles and honorifics adopted by Italian during the thirteenth and fourteenth
centuries remained free from unpleasant associations: *vide dama, damigella,
gentiluomo, madama* and the terms connected with feudalism: *cavaliere,
scudiere, sire*, etc. The eighteenth century French > Italian contact is even more
striking in this respect; here pejoratives are virtually absent (less than 1 per
cent). This is, however, only one side of the picture. That pejoratives may be
borrowed—even those which express aversion or derision at the expense of a
foreign culture—at a time when the source language enjoys great prestige is
amply illustrated by Italian to French contacts of the sixteenth and seventeenth
centuries, where a high rate of pejorative borrowing coincides with the
apogee of Italianism in France. To this extent, therefore, the evidence of our
loan-word lists appears to be self-contradictory. But the contradiction is only
superficial. In reality the whole argument whereby prestige and pejoration are
related in inverse ratio rests on an unsure footing. It is after all not a paradoxical situation for a society to emulate and even genuinely admire a foreign

culture as a whole while objecting strongly to certain aspects of it. Enmity, criticism and ridicule are commonly directed against cultural *foci* from which nevertheless a powerful influence radiates. Irony, which we have seen to be an important constituent of pejoration, is a weapon of defence rather than offence, apt to be directed against those with whom one feels at a disadvantage. But whether the borrower's attitude is based upon a feeling of inferiority or not is irrelevant; what matters is that disapproval of any kind at least implies positive contact. Prestige and the influences which foster semantic deterioration are not incompatible phenomena. On the contrary, both represent the same element of a dual polarity, the opposite sign being apathy, non-interference.[1]

The pejorative/prestige cycle would seem—though this interpretation is put forward with every caution—to assume a definite pattern only when the influence of a dominant language is waning. At such times the proportion of pejoratives may increase slightly up to the point where the source-language has entered fully upon its period of eclipse, when the total borrowing falls to the datum level and pejoratives are drastically reduced in number. This trend is best illustrated by eighteenth century Italian to French loans. Already well under way by the mid-sixteenth century, borrowing of pejoratives continues for the next hundred and fifty years, increasing gradually at a steady rate. By 1700 the Italian cultural and linguistic preponderance of earlier times is quite at an end, yet the influx goes on as strongly as before (more strongly still when considered in proportion to the century totals) until about the third quarter of the eighteenth century. During the later period the pejoratives attested have an undertone of mockery which must surely be more than coincidental (*babilan*, *sigisbée*, *castrat*, *cicerone*, etc., above). There are fewer from the later eighteenth century onward.[2]

Two other points arising from the statistical evidence are worth making. Firstly, the fifteenth century, though a period when borrowing as a whole is

---

1. A further point which complicates one's interpretation of pejorative tendencies is the layering of society within national boundaries. We are aware that in 18th and 19th century Italy, for example, a strongly francophile section of society provoked reaction from others, so that pejoration may have reflected more the attitude of the opposition, the 'average' layers of society, towards their compatriots' snobbery rather than towards France. Much depends of course upon which sections of society are able most effectively to influence usage at a given moment.

2. Figures for It. > Fr. loans are as follows: 12th–14th cent., 5.3 per cent; 15th cent., 13.2 per cent; 16th cent., 5.9 per cent; 17th cent., 7 per cent; 18th cent., 8.6 per cent; 19th cent., 5.5 per cent of total borrowings. The last figure gives rather a false impression. Most of the words concerned are thieves' slang, which in some respects merits a separate semantic category; their chief source is Vidocq's memoirs, a very specialised document. The corresponding Fr. > It. figures are: 12th–14th cent., 2.8 per cent; 15th cent., 50 per cent; 16th cent., 4.3 per cent; 17th cent., 3.2 per cent; 18th cent., under 1 per cent; 19th cent., 3.5 per cent.

proceeding very slowly, presents an unusually high proportion of pejoratives. This applies to borrowings in both directions, though French to Italian loans at the end of the mediaeval period are few and the proportion perhaps unduly impressive. There are only sixteen words taken into Italian from French at this time; but it can scarcely be a pure accident that half of them are pejoratives. As regards French to Italian twelve out of ninety-one words are pejorative in some acceptation of the term, i.e. 13.2 per cent—again a high proportion. It is conceivable that these figures bear some relation, however indirect, to the mood of irony, farcical raillery and cynicism which undoubtedly characterises the age. I do not suggest that in the borrowing of words like *canaille, estrapade, frasque, ciurmare, furbo* there is a one-way relationship of cause and effect between the prevailing moral atmosphere and the words adopted—that they are its direct product, so to speak. The impulses which motivate lexical borrowing have their own *raison d'être*, exist in their own right, and only partly coincide with the wider influences which make the dominant psychological tone of a historical period what it is—in the fifteenth century, effects of international and civil strife, economic crisis due to plague and famine, moral and intellectual disorientation accompanying the decay of mediaeval social, political and religious traditions. But as has often been observed, and as we have shown with reference to our own material, vocabulary both reflects and codifies the attitudes of the social group who use it; so in the fifteenth century the underlying attitudes of mistrust, pessimism, cynicism and mockery correspond closely to the emotional overtones which we have singled out as the essential attribute of pejoratives. It would be interesting to know if pejoratives other than borrowings were more numerous at this period. I suspect that they probably were, at least as far as French is concerned.

Secondly, the percentages of loans from French into Italian are smaller than those from Italian into French.[1] Here also one's first impulse might be to follow a Vosslerian line of investigation and seek for some fundamental social or psychological difference—some diversity in mental make-up between the two national groups which would explain what appears to be clear disparity on the lexical plane. To do so would be to follow a false trail. There is no need on this occasion to have recourse to evidence other than that which the languages provide. The true explanation is to be found in certain specific traits in Italian, in particular the position of regional idioms *vis-à-vis* the national language and the exceptionally important role played by suffixation. As regards the former: our analysis has indicated that there is a close relationship between pejoration and the dynamic-affective function of language, which in its turn is more clearly manifested in day-to-day conversation with family, workmates and friends, where the speaker discloses

1. The overall percentages are: Fr. > It., 3.3; It. > Fr., 6.3.

his own personality, strikes an attitude, expresses feelings, and expects to provoke an emotive reaction in his audience; the environment, that is, where wit, hyperbole and irony are most naturally and most effectively used. In short, pejoratives stand in a particular relationship to what Professor Devoto terms *la lingua espressiva*,[1] in respect of which Italian regional dialects have in the past fulfilled, and still do fulfil, a more important function in comparison with the central or literary idiom than their French counterparts. The second explanatory factor is more cogent still: the practice of using *suffixes* to add subjective and affective connotations to neutral words is far more highly developed in Italian than in French.[2] In proportion as facilities are developed within a lexical system for symbolising emotive overtones by adding an interchangeable bound morpheme, which may be used to augment or transform the signification of any full word, it will become correspondingly less urgent for the language to acquire autonomous signs with inherent affective connotations, or for emotively neutral words to become specialised in an affective signification. To be strictly accurate, the difference between French and Italian in this respect is one of degree only, because in former times suffixation in French was more of an active force than at present. It may be that French made greater use of ephemeral suffixes than is commonly supposed, though evidence here is hard to obtain since ephemeral suffixation is typically an element in the strategy of speech, an affective resource associated especially with *parole*. There are grounds for believing that in the sixteenth century, importation of many words with Italian suffixes (pejorative and otherwise) caused the suffixes themselves to be accepted on a permanent footing (e.g. *-ache*, *-uche*, *-oche*), or brought about a change of meaning in those already established (*-aille*, *-ade*, *-aque?*, *-esque?*).[3] It is likely that this period saw some modification of the *function* of suffixation in French due to Italian interference; cf. the frequent use of suffixes by the Pléiade and in courtiers' speech under the later Valois, though the forms favoured are usually diminutives and caritatives rather than pejoratives.[4]

CHANGE OF MEANING

Anyone with some knowledge of a foreign tongue is aware how frequently alien terms in a language possess significations appreciably removed from

1. Cf. Devoto's discussion of expressive language in Ch. I of *I Fondamenti della storia linguistica*, esp. pp. 32–5, his theoretical division of language into 4 levels, of which *la lingua espressiva* is one, and his observations upon the position of regional idiom in this scheme.

2. Cf. the shades of meaning implied by *-accio* (*-azzo*), *-acchio*, *-uccio* (*-uzzo*), *-occio* (*-ozzo*) and combinations of these suffixes with diminutives and augmentatives.

3. See discussion of the origin and development of Fr. suffix *-ade*, pp. 602–9 above.

4. An outstanding example among non-pejorative suffixes is provided by Fr. *-on* (diminutive and augmentative).

that which they had in the original linguistic background. The truth of this is perhaps most clearly demonstrated in words which have gained currency abroad while retaining unaltered something of their original form or graphy, or both—the *five-o-clocks*, *high-lifes* and their opposite numbers in every other European language;[1] but it applies no less to those importations which have entirely come to terms with their new phonetic environment and which consequently have ceased to stand out formally or orthographically as exoticisms—by far the majority. All words are subject to semantic evolution, whatever their original provenance may have been. Italian and French loan-words endorse this axiom; we should be surprised if they failed to do so. That the meaning of borrowed words changes, often radically, is therefore well known[2] and so too are the conditions which determine semantic shifts in the lexicon as a whole. What we have much less information about is the extent to which semantic change in borrowed vocabulary is influenced by the fact that it *is* borrowed. It is difficult to tell how precise information of this kind will be, but we now know a great deal about the semantic history of Franco-Italian loans and can expect them to give us at least some sound clues to follow up. There is always the possibility, too, that our diggings may bring to light some useful shards of evidence about the loan-word's adjustment to its new semantic milieu.

The effect of semantic change upon our borrowed vocabulary may be considered from the two viewpoints which have already been of service methodologically in analysing formal borrowing—(a) *shifts resulting from transfer* and (b) *shifts during the interim period*.

Shifts resulting from transfer. It is clear in the first place that the content of most borrowed words changes during the act of transfer into the receiving language, and that, as Miss Aasta Stene puts it, 'as a rule the sphere of reference in the language of adoption is more restricted than in the language of origin; the meaning of a word covers only part of the meaning it had in the original language'.[3] Typical examples from our lists would be Fr. *académie* taken from the sixteenth century Italian specialised sense (as in *Accademia della Crusca*); mediaeval It. *giornea* 'journey' or 'battle' (originally of one day's length), a sense which is current in Old French but is only a part of the meanng of *journée*; or It. *paesaggio*, 'landscape' (in pictorial art), borrowed in the sixteenth century from Fr. *paysage*, which has this sense apart from the wider geographical signification. The nineteenth century Fr. > It. influx is par-

1. These are the semantic counterparts to that category of 'false loans' (*vide* pp. 618–19 above) in which the formal element (phonetic or grammatical) has been distorted in the receiving language, e.g. *dancing* meaning 'dance hall', *smoking* meaning 'dinner-jacket', etc. Cf. in this connection the French false loans in Danish examined by H. Aa. Paludan, *Sproglige Misvisere* (*Studier fra Sprog- og Oldtidsforskning*, 166, Copenhagen, 1934).

2. See in particular the examples discussed by Deroy, op. cit., pp. 261–9.

3. Aasta Stene, *English Loan-words in Modern Norwegian*, p. 34.

ticularly rich in restrictions of this type: cf. *bersò* 'arbour' (in Fr., also 'cradle', etc.); *brosce* (*broche*) 'brooch' (also 'spit' and technical senses in Fr.); *choc* 'shock' medical term (in Fr., 'shock', 'blow' in general); *chiffon* (*cifone*) textile only ('rag', 'scrap' in Fr.); *forfait* as a commercial term (also literary usages, 'crime, transgression', in Fr.); *garage* 'garage' for coaches, cars (abstract term meaning 'storage' in Fr., and a technical term of railways); *lavaggio* 'washing' as a technical process (in French, washing both in technical and general contexts).

Not all these borrowings conform semantically to precisely the same pattern. There are interesting shades of difference. New meanings accepted into the borrowing language are seldom identical in all respects with the corresponding restricted usage in the language of origin—they are not, so to speak, an exact *échantillon* detached from the broader pattern of signification which prevails in the language from which they were borrowed. However technical or otherwise restricted it may be, the particular meaning borrowed was probably accompanied in the source language by a constellation of polysemic uses, while in addition both it and they may have figured habitually in subjective or emotive contexts. Some senses are more independent of their polysemes than others and are therefore more viable in isolation than others, but we may assume that an accompanying pattern of polysemic senses originally exerted an effect upon the signification of practically all the words borrowed. In passing from one language to the other a word is stripped of these semantic associations. To put it in traditional triadic terms, the new *image acoustique* passes across accompanied only by a restricted (referential) meaning. We may summarise this conception diagrammatically thus:

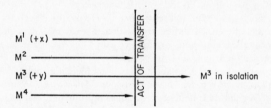

($M^{1,2,3}$ are mutually supporting polysemes: x and y represent emotive and subjective associations.)

One effect of this is that an indigenous speaker of the source language who is acquainted with the borrowing language in addition to his own almost always perceives a semantic difference in the borrowed version of his native word. He has an impression that it is in some way odd or unfamiliar. By shifting the total context of use the very act of transfer, passive though it is, sets in motion the process of semantic change which will thereafter constantly affect the word in its new habitat. We can account for our supposed native speaker's impression of unfamiliarity more precisely: it usually means that an ephemeral or *ad hoc* usage has been raised to the status of an independent, permanent sign, or that a little-used meaning has become generally current, or again, that a figurative usage has been taken as opaque and factual. Many of the words I have cited above illustrate this, but even clearer examples (to draw again from French words used in nineteenth century Italian) are *chef* (i.e. 'head cook' as in English and elsewhere), *clou* 'culminating point, highlight', *élite* 'exclusive social group', *debutto* (*début*) 'entry into society, presentation before the public', *foyer* (of a theatre), *grès* (ceramics) 'stoneware'. Grammatical shifts often heighten the effect of semantic incongruity. The most common case is that in which a past participle loses its verbal element to become crystallised as a simple adjective or even as a noun, e.g. *habitué* (subst.) (nineteenth century Fr. > It.) 'one who frequents (social gatherings, etc.)'; med. Fr. > It. *tanè* 'tan-coloured' (cf. Eng. 'tawny') and *dorè* 'gold-coloured', seventeenth century Fr. > It.

SHIFTS DURING THE INTERIM PERIOD

Once transplanted into the receiving language a borrowed word falls under the influence of its new lexical surroundings and is liable to undergo semantic change. Occasionally this too may involve specialisation of meaning, as when OFr. *mestier* entering OIt. as *mestiere* acquires a special sense of 'funeral obsequies'[1] or sixteenth century Fr. *disgrâce* 'misfortune', *disgrâcié* comes to be used to mean a fall from political office,[2] or sixteenth century Fr. *contraste*, *contraster* 'contention, to struggle, resist' passes to its modern meaning in the

1. Cf. the analogous shift in Fr. *cortège* < It. *corteggio*.
2. Cf. H. Estienne's gloss upon this term, cited by Deroy, op. cit., p. 264. After noting that Italianisms are often used differently in French than in Italian proper, Estienne continues: 'Je vous allegueray pour exemple ce mot *Disgratié*, car je vous confesse que *Disgratié* a vrayment son origine du langage Italien, qui dit *Disgratiato* . . . mais quelques-uns par ignorance l'appliquent à un autre usage que l'Italie n'a appliqué son *Disgratiato*. Car au lieu que *Disgratiato* signifie *Malencontreux*, ou *Malheureux* quelcun qui en passant avet ouy ce mot *Disgratié* de la bouche de quelque emprunteur (qui n'est pas si ignorant), mais n'avet entendu ce qu'il voulet dire, et toutesfois desiret puis apres parer son langage de ce mot nouvellement appris, eut bien grand'haste de dire, *Il est disgratié* non pas pour signifier Il est malencontreux: mais au lieu de dire Il est hors de grace: ou Il n'est plus en grace. Or ne faut-il pas demander s'il fut incontinent suivi des autres courtisans' (*Dial.*, Vol. I, p. 179). It is hard to tell whether the euphemism *disgrâce* 'political eclipse' might have been used in Italian court circles before being taken up by French, though one can say definitely that the typical Italian usage ('misfortune', etc.) continues to be common in early French examples, and that whether French was actually responsible for the special sense or not it is in French that the euphemism achieves general use. Estienne interprets the new signification as a false analysis, a kind of Malapropism (*dis*+*grâce* = *hors de grâce*). I find this unconvincing. The humanist is merely lengthening the list of his opponents' shortcomings by ascribing ignorance to them as well as folly.

seventeenth century by way of the restricted language of art. But for the most part the meaning of a borrowing once it has begun to participate currently in the new language develops according to the contrary process, i.e. from a technical or restricted use to a more general one. Examples like *disgrâce, contraste* are rather infrequent; their minority status is the more striking inasmuch as Italianisms of the sixteenth century taken as a whole stand out as the clearest example of semantic generalisation our survey affords. *Brusque* used initially only of wine, *désastre* term of astrology coming to mean 'disaster', *escroquer* 'to "scrounge", esp. for food' > 'trick, swindle', *intrigue* 'snag, involved problem' > 'plot, machination', *numéro* tech. term in *jeu de blanque* > 'number' in general application, *panache* 'plume' > abstract 'swagger', *postiche* theatrical term > 'false, counterfeit' in general, *posture* term of fine art, 'pose' > general usage and the abstract signification 'attitude', *riposte* fencing term > abstract, *travestir* 'disguise, assume fancy dress' > 'falsify, misrepresent' in general, are semantic developments typical of loan-words of the Renaissance. We have here something rather similar to the transformation which Meillet called a *social change* of meaning, i.e. a technical or restricted term entering everyday usage.[1] Meillet actually describes this change as one which involves a loss of precision. Words entering general use from special languages, he claims, ' . . . ne le font qu'en subissant un changement de sens. La valeur précise et rigoureuse d'un terme tient de l'étroitesse d'un milieu où dominent les mêmes intérêts et où l'on n'a pas besoin de tout exprimer: sorti de ce milieu étroit auquel il doit sa valeur spéciale, *le mot perd immédiatement sa précision et tend à devenir de plus en plus vague*'.[2]

It was to my way of thinking a mistake on Meillet's part to have introduced the notion of imprecision or vagueness of meaning at this stage in his argument; but in any case this particular line of reasoning does not lead in the direction of any very useful conclusions. In reality Meillet's rule-of-thumb analysis tackles the problem at the wrong end. The image we need to have in our mind is not that of abandoning old significatory habits but of creating new ones. In many cases a shift from technical to general usage has indeed come about, but the *use* of words has been broadened as well as their social orbit; and this has been accomplished by a process which essentially is independent of their shift in sociological status. Sometimes there has been a move from concrete to abstract, sometimes from a term denoting a limited individual activity to one denoting that sort of activity in general; but what really counts is that a term with a restricted range of applicability has gained a wider one, and in addition—to describe the event in terms of its most strictly

1. Antoine Meillet, *Linguistique historique et linguistique générale*, 2nd edition, Vol. I, p. 255. The italics are mine.
2. Ibid.

objective component—the frequency of use has risen to a marked degree. Utility in respect of the functions which a linguistic sign has to perform has been enhanced. Words which might well have figured in the language only as ephemeral aliens have acquired such a high semantic value as to seem from our present-day perspective quite indispensable symbols. It is noteworthy, too, how rapidly the shift of meaning followed the word's appearance in the language and how the sense, once adjusted, has remained remarkably stable and entrenched in common usage from the end of the interim period until now. Another group of words which forcefully demonstrates the same process whereby restricted words are channelled into a more useful pattern of signification is that to which I drew attention earlier while commenting historically on French to Italian contacts—the Italian terms of fine art which were received into French during the seventeenth century. Examples are: *attitude* 'pose', *calquer* 'to take a *calque* (of a work of plastic art)', *costume* 'dress, background of a picture', with reference to the necessity to avoid anachronism in these details, *dégrader* 'to shade tones, colours', *élève* 'artist's pupil', *groupe* (of figures in painting, sculpture), *miniature* (of painting only), *morbide*, *morbidesse* (applied to texture and colour values). Corresponding examples may be found in French > Italian loans during the Middle Ages, though there the trend is not seen so plainly.[1]

OBSERVATIONS AND INFERENCES

(a) *Act of Transfer and Interim Period*

Our conclusions in this essay run closely parallel to those reached above in the formal section.[2] A lexical element loses and gains during its transit from one language to another. Existing subjective and affective associations are effaced; the support of context of situation and of congeners in the same semantic field is lost. Here as before we find it valuable to treat as separate entities *transfer* and *interim* period. In the second of these we have to switch our attention to the borrowing language rather than the language of origin. The native lexicon, so to speak, is acting on its own behalf, exploiting the new lexical material. A similar interplay of usage and linguistic requirements will continue to operate as long as the word remains current—which amounts to saying that it will undergo semantic change for an unlimited space of time, subject only in the long run to a proportional wastage of the kind that lexicologists have recently tried to quantify in the glossometric hypothesis. Nevertheless I think there is a valid reason for making a special case of the initial period of a loan-word's existence in a language, the phase in which

1. Pejoratives also provide several good examples of these contingent or 'directed' changes.

2. *Vide supra*, The Process of Borrowing, *Formal Considerations*.

its impact is greatest and its catalysing function in the lexicon most active. During the interim period semantic change occurs more freely, though the speed with which new senses are developed appears to vary from one century to another. The impression I gain from the Franco-Italian material is that when novel and far-reaching cultural transformations are taking place, as at the Renaissance, the tendency to adapt extraneous lexical signs is strongest. Certainly the sixteenth–seventeenth century borrowings in French are our best source for interim changes. On the face of things one might expect the nineteenth century French > Italian influences to produce the same results, but it does not: nineteenth century loans provide many examples of changes during transfer, but very few of interim period adaptation. We have to remember that linguistic changes at all levels, and formal changes as well as semantic ones have been denied free rein in modern times owing to those normative forces which we have seen in action in the later century lists, nor must we forget that the words in these lists were only comparatively recently borrowed. These facts in themselves seem to offer a reasonable explanation why the sixteenth and nineteenth centuries are so different, especially since the closely comparable lexical influence of English upon French during the nineteenth century has had a remarkably similar fortune in the receiving language; and yet I rather think that there may be some more fundamental distinction which might be made, and which might well have to do with what we might call a dynamic or liberal quality in French which makes it more open to lexical neologisms from outside the language.

(b) *Style, Context and Shift of Meaning*

Ultimately the mechanism by which semantic adjustments are achieved is a stylistic one. The borrowed term, divested as we have seen of its habitual semantic accompaniment, enters upon a period of fluidity, of semantic autonomy. Appearing in a host of different contexts, it provides fresh material for figurative expressions and evocative *tournures*. As the number of its actual collocations in use grows, a broadening of semantic range ensues. Gradually certain contexts predominate and become accepted; use defines the signification of the word more precisely. A kind of *restrictive choice* is made which viewed diachronically appears as a shift of meaning. A tradition is established; dictionary definitions and teaching help to stabilise and inculcate it. The influences by which the 'choice' is conditioned are complex. Similar in kind to those which cause a given word to be borrowed, they amount to the same combination of random elements, passive acceptance and active preference or promotion which shape the overall pattern of collective human behaviour in any walk of life. Occasionally the pattern assumes a certain regularity, as in the series of 'fine art' borrowings I have just listed. What we are witnessing here is something like a *Sinnrichtung*, the operation of a *fixierendes Moment* or 'fixative factor', to use Professor Sperber's terminology, that is, a preferred sphere of interest which governs the speaker's choice of expression, more especially in respect of figurative usage.[1] I do not think that it would be fanciful to infer that an innate feeling for the achievements of Italian culture, especially as regards the fine arts, was a feature of some moment in the seventeenth century *honnête homme's* mental make-up; that it was part and parcel of his aesthetic sensibility, his impulse to discriminate and arbitrate, to assay all forms of human creative activity by resorting as it were to the critical equipment of an artist.

There are many reasons why the use of a given linguistic sign may alter. Semanticists have refined upon the topic ever since their discipline was first mooted. The tendency towards a motivated semantic redeployment which I have dwelt on here is only one trait among many which a diachronic semantic analysis might disclose, but it is specially important for our purpose. One thing which this angle of approach brings home to us is that in our sphere of research the receiving language is the principal agent in lexical exchange (which is as much as to say, the activity of bilingual speakers whose linguistic habits are grounded in the receiving language, viewed in relation to the communicative and expressive needs of their social group as a whole, is of primary importance). It might be objected that the shifts which Fr. *travestir, numéro, dégrader, attitude,* etc., have undergone belong to the history of French, and occurred independently of Italian influence; but we have to allow for the fact that repercussions provoked during the period after a new sign is adopted may continue for a great while and that they are all part and parcel of the neological process. It is as a special kind of neologism that a borrowed term may most usefully be envisaged.[2]

SYNONYMY AND NEAR-SYNONYMY

A large proportion of borrowed words in French and Italian as in all other languages refer to new things. When one thinks of a loan-word one usually calls to mind a word whose meaning as well as its form is novel, exotic,

1. H. Sperber, *Einführung in die Bedeutungslehre,* 2nd edition, Leipzig, 1930, esp. pp. 30–2. We need not, like Sperber, speak of a *subconscious* directive; it is enough to suppose that a predisposition, a willing orientation of interest arising from training and prevalent cultural attitudes may have been at work.

2. Other interesting words which change in meaning after being borrowed are: 17th cent. It. *chincaglie (-erie)* 'fancy goods' instead of 'hardware'; med. Fr. *bricole* 'catapult' to the sense of 'strap' and pejorative 'indirect, underhand activity'; also nautical, military and technical terms of stag-hunting, tennis, billiards, angling; *brigade* 'band' to milit. term; *brigand* 'partisan, supporter' to 'highwayman, brigand'; *magasin* 'magazine, warehouse' to 'shop, emporium'; med. Fr. *vogue* 'credit, reputation' to 'fashion'; and 18th cent. Fr. *colis* 'parcel' from *colli* pl. of *collo* 'neck'.

unfamiliar. The symbol as a whole is an entirely new acquisition. This is manifestly true of the vast farrago of purely technical terms which appear in the first and numerically more extensive section of each century's interpretative essay—that is, most of the terms classified in the technical as opposed to the general/abstract/emotive division of our lists. Some are names of products hitherto unknown to speakers of the borrowing languages (*riz, sucre, caucciù, artichaut,* etc.); others are newly introduced commercial processes (*banque, decatissaggio, poste, tontine,* etc.) or inventions (*aerostato, dagherrotipo, ghigliottina*). We remember, too, the multifarious vocabulary of warfare, with its constant innovations in weapons, personnel and tactics; the terminology of nineteenth century science; names of novel amusements or pastimes, and the ever-changing nomenclature of fashion from the *cottardita* to the *crinoline*.

These words account for the major part of our material. But borrowed words are not always unfamiliar in every respect. In discussing semantic loans we have already had an opportunity to observe what an important part is played by formal congruence between established and borrowed items of lexis. What we now have to consider are the effects not of formal but of semantic similarity. Borrowed words which relate wholly or partially to objects, situations or ideas already current, or at least not entirely unknown before and already catered for by an existing lexical sign are more numerous than is generally realised. It is politic to begin by turning a spotlight on these cases of synonymy—for such at first sight they appear to be—because they guide us towards the very heart of the lexical inquiry to which the next chapter is devoted. Synonymy implies a duplication of symbols, one or more alternative words by which to express the same signification—in short, a plethora of lexical resources. If such duplication is possible and certain terms can be freely substituted, what of the supposition that, in some measure (however limited this may be) symbols are semantically interdependent? Plethora, as far as inherent pattern is concerned, is tantamount to anarchy. System depends upon accepted distinctions and gradations; it begins where the indiscriminate ends.

We have said that certain borrowings *appear to be* synonyms. It is a commonplace of traditional semantics, noted by Bréal himself and developed tentatively in his formulation of a *loi de répartition sémantique*, that absolute synonymy hardly ever occurs in practice.[1] It is in fact a useful theoretical starting-point to assume that if the broadest construction is placed upon the word 'signification' so that it includes affective and emotive elements, synonymy in the strict sense does not exist in any single, normal living language. We shall soon find that we need to qualify this formulation quite

1. Cf. Ullmann's remarks upon *semantic differentiation* with reference to Professor A. Carnoy, *La Science du mot, Traité de Sémantique*, Louvain, 1927 (*Principles of Semantics*, pp. 109–114); also E. Nida, *Morphology*, p. 152.

severely, but for the moment a simple statement will serve. On most occasions what we find is not synonymy proper, but homoionymy or near-synonymy. Related words in our own lists frequently differ in respect of their factual or cognitive sense, whether this is a difference of semantic range or overlap, one word including the other within its scope of reference, or whether there is a more or less pronounced divergence in respect of semantic applicability as a whole. *Race* (sixteenth century < It.) and *lignage* both possess the sense of 'breeding, quality'; but while *race* soon came to be applied in the ethnic sense, *lignage* continued to be associated with the statement of an individual's descent. In shape and design a fifteenth century French *médaille* materially resembled a *maille*, yet the former was a work of art and the latter an item of currency or a metal disc with other technical uses. *Récolte* (sixteenth century < It.) implies an enterprise technically more advanced, on a larger scale than *cueillette*. *Alcoolismo* (nineteenth century < Fr.) involves *ubbriachezza*, but it denotes a pathological state where *ubbriachezza* does not. *Ciambellano* and *camerlingo* both refer to important offices: the former is lay, the latter ecclesiastical. In a more homely sphere, while *potaggio* and *minestra* have obvious similarities, we have Panzini's word for it that 'il *potage* (*potaggio*) dei Francesi non risponde se non in parte alla nostra minestra',[1] and that the differences—as he explains with culinary detail—are greater still. Frequently one term of a pair belongs to a restricted *langue de métier*, as in *choc* (medic.) ~ *squasso*; occasionally it appears in an idiom or consecrated phrase, e.g. mediaeval It. *mestiere* (~ *ministero*) in *aver mestiere*, or the use of *crema* (~ *panna*) in phrases which echo French locutions where it implies 'quintessence, most select portion or stratum'.

Frequently one word of an apparently synonymous pair may appropriately be used in emotive or subjective contexts whereas the other may not. Pejorative homonyms like *populace* ~ *peuple*, *ceffo* ~ *capo*, *mercanti* ~ *marchand*, *mercadant* afford good examples. Semantic distinctions associated with differences in subjective overtones were probably more common than we realise at the present day, since the evidence available to us about personal attitudes in the past is necessarily restricted.

Again, the borrowed word may figure only in an idiom drawn from foreign usage, and for this reason may not in reality be a semantic alternative to the native term. A good example is sixteenth century It. > Fr. *gambe* lit., 'leg', in an idiom like *garde la gambe!*, but not used in concurrence with Fr. *jambe* (*vide* sixteenth century It. > Fr. loans, s.v. *ingambe*). The idiom had a valid use in French; the individual word had not.

These and many more examples of homoionymic differentiation between borrowed and native terms which seemed *a priori* to be applicable in precisely the same range of contexts compel us to ask in what circumstances synonymy

1. *Diz. mod.*, s.v. *potage*.

in this sector of vocabulary can occur, or indeed whether it actually does occur at all. The only answer one can give, I think, is that which comes from consulting the word-lists and situating them in their lexical environment. After near-synonyms and pseudo-synonyms have been carefully sifted out we are left with a residue of loan-word versus indigenous lexical pairs where we cannot put forward convincing reasons why at the period when both were current there should have been an appreciable difference of use, or adduce evidence to indicate that there was. In the nature of things we shall never have enough information in some cases to prove conclusively that there was no semantic difference, i.e. that the words were synonymous in the sense we have proposed, and in very many cases it is unlikely that we shall ever be able to prove the contrary, i.e. that the use actually *did* differ. We can, however, state where the areas of apparent synonymy were, and judge whether their existence seriously weakens the basic assumption to which our argument is tending—that signs are essentially diverse within a homogeneous vocabulary.

Examples of words which ought to be scrutinised very closely on these grounds are: *approcciare* ~ *appressarsi, approssimarsi, brocciare* ~ *broccare*, *cangiare* ~ *cambiare, clero* ~ *chiaro, comenzare* ~ *cominciare, frale* ~ *fragile*, *formaggio* ~ *cacio, gorgia* ~ *gola, lampa* ~ *lampada, mangiare* ~ *manicare*, *obbliare* ~ *dimenticare, oreglia* ~ *orecchia, prenze* ~ *principe, primiero* ~ *primo*, *reame* ~ *regno, schifo* ~ *schivo, vairo* ~ *vaio*.[1] Rare, yet easily recognised and exactly determinable, this lexical situation is of a very particular kind and it occupies a niche of its own among interference phenomena. A special name for it would be useful: I suggest symbiosis.[2] A state of symbiosis exists when

1. Most of these pairs are cognates, and so are many of the others I have cited. There is a reason for this. It is easier to detect homoionymy among cognates because the formal similarity gives us a hint that the meanings also may be related. For all this cognate words, even doublets, need not of course be at all similar in meaning. Some are linked fairly closely, like *cavalcade* ~ *chevauchée, espion* ~ *espie, dama* ~ *donna* and the ones just cited. Others turn out to be 'faux amis': *cretino* ~ *cristiano, canaille* ~ *chiennaille, ducat* ~ *duché, tola* ~ *tavola*. Here is a list of other doublets by borrowing: *altesse* ~ *hautesse*, *arciere* ~ *arcadore, attaquer* ~ *attacher, baccelliere* ~ *baccellaro, -aio, balcon* ~ *baucon*, *cadène* ~ *chaîne, cadence* ~ *ch(e)ance, carbonnade* ~ *charbonnée, cavalier* ~ *chevalier, cavalerie* ~ *chevalerie, cavaliere* ~ *cavallaro, -aio, cabriole* ~ *chevreuil, costume* ~ *coutûme, congédier* ~ *congéer, embusquer* ~ *embûcher, esquiver* ~ *eschiver, escrime* ~ *escremie, grotte* ~ *croute*, *maresciallo* ~ *maniscalco, numéro* ~ *nombre, pommade* ~ *pommée, preste* ~ *prêt, réussir* ~ *rissir*, *riposte* ~ *réponse, roccia* ~ *rocca, soldat* ~ *soudé, targue* ~ *targe, se targuer de* ~ *se targer de*.

2. I must point out that the sense in which I use *symbiosis* is quite different from that of Professor von Wartburg's *symbiose* in his celebrated statement about the principles of modern etymology (*Problèmes et Méthodes*, 2nd edition, p. 125). *Symbiose* for von Wartburg mainly corresponds in a general way to what I understand by 'lexical structure', though its full implications are rather wider: 'Nous voyons donc que le regard doit être constamment dirigé vers la symbiose des mots. Les mots ne vivent pas simplement chacun pour soi. La moindre modification, la moindre innovation dans les nuances du sens a aussitôt sa répercussion sur les mots avoisinants', etc.

X

there is in a language at a given time an appreciable body of terms which can be commuted within the same lexical contexts without altering their signification. There are traces of symbiosis in Italian of the eighteenth century, but the only outstanding illustration in our material is afforded by the mediaeval French to Italian influence. The remarks which follow are prompted mainly by the evidence of mediaeval Gallicisms, from which the list of examples cited above were of course chosen.

Symbiosis implies parallelism, concurrence, bilingualism in a state of equilibrium. Though it occurs only during periods when contact is close it does not in itself evince the most intimate or fertile type of interference. Two languages dwell side by side, or more accurately, lexical elements from two distinct sources are concurrent. In the mediaeval period there are other factors which support this interpretation, among them the use of Old French in Italian chronicles and informative works directed towards a popular audience. But by far the most striking evidence of symbiosis as I understand it is provided by the so-called Franco-Venetian language which we had occasion to speak of in an earlier chapter[1]—the composite idiom which, as modern scholarship has shown, arose from the jongleurs' attempts to compose works deliberately in Old French, or at least in a medium which their clients would accept as French.[2] I have already suggested that some ostensible synonyms in mediaeval Italian were probably differentiated by stylistic overtones which fitted them for use in literary and poetic diction. This does not authorise us to assume that the state of symbiosis in Old Italian is simply one in which a literary language is opposed to the language of everyday use, as with Old Provençal and Italian. A literary language is usually the possession of a cultural *élite*. The society which performed and enjoyed Franco-Venetian epics was neither cultured nor select, but the common people, the mass of town-dwellers in northern Italy. In this connection Viscardi makes an interesting contrast between the use by Italians of Old French and Old Provençal: 'Il Gaspary ... riporta l'uso del francese per parte degli Italiani autori di poemi cavallereschi all'idea "che per un determinato genere di poesia bisognasse adoperare di necessità l'idioma straniero" che a quel "genere" appare legato in tutta la tradizione letteraria: "se si volle nell'Alta Italia comporre poesie liriche nel secolo XIII si scrisse in Provenzale; si scrisse in francese quando si vollero narrare le storie venute di Francia". Ma i trovatori d'Italia ebbero del provenzale padronanza piena e l'usarono magistralmente; i troveri, invece, usano un francese sempre, più o meno, inquinato e corrotto: il che significa, in fondo, solo questo: che coloro che, in Italia, composero poemi cavallereschi appartengono a un ambiente meno colto e raffinato di quello cui spettano i poeti italiani che poetarono, in provenzale,

1. *Vide* discussion of mediaeval French to Italian loans, pp. 139-40.
2. A. Viscardi, *Letteratura Franco-Italiana*, pp. 38-49.

d'amore.'[1] Lexical evidence supports this view. The adoption of such a down-to-earth word as *mangiare*, the acceptance from a foreign source of adverbs like *ancora*, *guari*, *troppo*, *volentieri* show that for a considerable period a broad range of the population had a free option to make use either of a foreign term or a native one. Often the native word reasserted itself; in *mangiare* the scale tipped in favour of the foreign word. The fact of lexical parallelism, however, rather than substitution, is what stands out most remarkably in this period.

To return to homoionymy. Needless to say, the semantic difference between homoionyms is seldom one of purely cognitive or purely affective signification. I have deliberately chosen clear-cut examples; on most occasions homoionymic analysis is a much more intricate business. One has to take account of the word's semantic background, particularly in its historical aspect, and also the history of the thing it represents. For example etymologists commonly distinguish *soudart* and *soudoyer* from *soldat* by alluding to their depreciative senses. The Italianism, we are told, was adopted as a neutral term for 'soldier' to offset the pejoration of *soudard* and its formal congeners. What actually happened is a little more complex. During the twelfth to fifteenth centuries there was no true generic word for soldier in the modern sense—if one excepts the sporadic use of *arméz*, a descriptive term, 'armed man'—in the earlier part of the period. The words normally used were specific ones—*chevalier*, *vassal*, *homme* (in the feudal sense), *gens d'armes*, *sergent*, *archer*, etc., i.e. in most cases the actual grades themselves. The *soldat* (*soldato*) is an essentially different phenomenon appearing towards the end of the Middle Ages. He is the soldier who though paid is no longer considered a 'mercenary' in the earlier sense (in effect, a person who has to be bribed to fight, hence 'unreliable soldier, coward') but the normal type of fighting man. We might put it this way: before the later fifteenth century a generic term for 'soldier' in our modern sense was not required, since the notion of professional soldier did not exist divorced from pejorative connotations. Every able-bodied man was a potential soldier whatever his occupation or social standing, within the framework of his feudal obligations. The word *soldat* appeared when the need for it became urgent. There are examples on every hand of cultural changes giving rise to a new situation, so that the new word which seems to be fulfilling the same significatory role as its predecessor is actually referring to a different thing. *Courtoisie* (*cortesia*) of the twelfth-thirteenth centuries is a different concept from *politesse* (*politezza*) in the sixteenth. As a model of manly behaviour the *chevalier* (*cavaliere*) gives way to the *preux d'homme* (*prod'uomo*), while by the sixteenth century this ideal (the man of action) together with that of the *chevalier* as an exponent of *courtoisie* (i.e. ideal of social behaviour) has been superseded by the *cortegiano* (*courtisan*).

1. Viscardi, op. cit., p. 48.

The same developments apply no less to technical vocabularies. Often a series of technical terms which superficially appear to be alternatives refers to a historical sequence of inventions or advances in technique which though applied to the same task are in themselves quite different things; e.g. the words used at different times to denote a ship's compass—*marinette, calamite, cadran (à naviguer, c. de marine), boussole*, of which two at least refer to improvements emanating from Italy (see *calamite, boussole*, mediaeval and sixteenth century It. > Fr. loans resp.).

Consider finally the two words OFr. *marchis* and MFr. *marquis*, the former taken directly from Frankish, the latter borrowed through Italian. Although the duties and status attaching to the rank of marquess changed a little from the tenth to the sixteenth century, in the common grammatical acceptation the two words are synonymous. Yet the one did not duplicate the other; what we have here are not two contemporary synonyms but a historical sequence of terms for what *in abstracto* was pretty much the same denotatum. This pattern of lexical events involves *synonym sequence*, we might say, but not *synonymy in being*.

OBSERVATIONS AND INFERENCES

Lexicologists who examine the relation between a language and the culture which provides its environment and *raison d'être* have in the past attributed too great a significance to synonymy while neglecting the analytical opportunities created by studying near-synonymy or homoionymy. Synonymy is not a pseudo-category, though, at least not for the historical or sociological lexicologist; and therefore despite unresolved controversy about this topic we can accept it as a valid and useful statement that words in an established language are seldom synonymous—or to couch it in Wittgenstein's terminology, the use of two distinct lexical forms is seldom identical.[1]

1. For structural semanticians the position of synonymy in lexis raises problems analogous to those which homonymy presents in morphological description. To the best of my knowledge the most satisfactory answer to them from the descriptive linguist's point of view is that set forth by J. Lyons, *Structural Semantics*, pp. 57–8 and 74–6. Lyons defines synonymy on classical Firthian lines, i.e. by regarding meaning as a 'complex of functions, . . . each function being the use of some language form or element in relation to some context' (*vide* J. R. Firth, 'The Technique of Semantics', *Trans. Philol. Soc.*, 1935, pp. 54, 72). The only objection I would raise concerns Lyons' statement of the limiting case where absolute synonymy occurs, viz., 'that two forms might be synonymous in only one context' (p. 74). I should say rather that the ideal case of synonymy would involve a number of contexts, but that our two hypothetical forms would need to be synonymous in *all* of these. I have said already why a referential schema with its 'prior notion of "meaning" independently defined' remains indispensable for us, even though we may be accepting it largely for its heuristic value; and conversely, why an exclusively contextual conception of meaning is inappropriate *in this particular instance* for the same practical reasons (*vide* methodological considerations above).

Synonymy in the strict sense implies redundancy: and redundancy, as linguists are well aware, has both a passive status and an active function in language. It may be fortuitous, residual, a matter of so much undynamic weight in the linguistic mechanism, or it may be motivated and productive. Linguists recognise its utility in aiding perception at the phonological and morphological levels—to overcome the ill effects of background noise, perhaps, or of too marked idiosyncrasies in the pronunciation of individuals. They are also familiar with the contribution it makes towards learning a language.[1] Benefits accrue from redundancy at the lexical level when a child or a foreigner learns new words by equating a number of alternative (i.e. redundant) contexts. Similar advantages are obtained in a rather different way by a child or foreigner's being able to equate a single word with a range of significatory resources which have the same overall meaning, that is, idioms and periphrases of varying length; or to put it in another way, the existence of synonymy between words and longer lexical segments. To this process true synonymy (between one word and another) contributes nothing. On the other hand homoionymy or near-synonymy does. The broad similarity of contexts in which near-synonyms tend to appear helps in clarifying fine semantic differences between them, the parallax or slight difference of viewpoint, so to speak, making for greater precision.

The one aspect of linguistic activity where synonymy does perform a useful office is the aesthetic one, and more especially, in the technique of style. Synonyms enable an author to control more easily the architecture of his periods, to suit their prosody to their content, and to gain greater profit from rhetorical or other amplificatory devices. See how Montaigne is enabled to build up the effect of the following *expolitio* by having three alternative verbs to hand, a stylistic richness made possible by pressing into service the loan-word *baster*:

Et si un seul suffisoit, pour neant y seroit l'autre sans besoin: et l'ordre des choses ne peut recevoir celà: comme il n'y a pas deux Soleils, par ce qu'un seul suffit; les bestes et les hommes n'ont pas deux testes, par ce qu'ils en ont assez d'une; il n'y a pas deux mondes, par ce qu'il baste d'un.[2]

This turn of style based on synonymic resources is Montaigne's personal gloss upon the undistinguished, factual Latin of Sebond's fifteenth century treatise.[3] The whole translation has a fervour which is absent from its

1. See A. Martinet, *Éléments de linguistique générale*, 2nd edition, Paris, 1961, pp. 185-7; also id., *A Functional View of Language*, Oxford, 1961, pp. 140-1.

2. *Théologie naturelle de Raymond Sebon*, trad. en franç. par Messire Michel, Seigneur de Montaigne, Paris, Guillemot, 1611, p. 18.

3. The original text runs as follows: 'Si ambo essent necessarii, tunc semper unus indigeret altero, et necessario semper deberent esse conjuncti ad invicem ... Si autem unus sufficeret, superfluum esset ponere alterum sine necessitate; et hoc ordo rerum non

original, a subjective pungency which Montaigne gives to his work largely by his stylistic attack, as in this gobbet.[1]

Stylistic considerations apart, however, synonymy contributes little to the economy of vocabulary, and for this reason alone we may hesitate to class it as a permanent feature of lexical structure.

Permanence, too, is an attribute which has to be taken into account. Even if borrowed and indigenous words appear to be synonyms *in esse*, they may give a different impression when regarded as elements of language *in fieri*. Apparent synonymy may do no more than reflect a state of transition towards a new economical pattern of lexical signs. Many of the borrowed equivalents in our lists in actual fact only remained current in the receiving language for a short time.[2]

The cumulative effect of all these small insights into the nature of synonymy as one actually perceives it in a closely knit sample of words is to confirm most of what traditional lexicology has always asserted. One can make out a strong *a priori* claim that in cultural vocabularies like those we are investigating absolute semantic identity between borrowed and native words is not found, provided one allows for the intervention of different dialects, of different social or literary registers, of persistent emotive connotations and the like, and provided one is prepared to concede that lexical economy requires a certain time to work itself out.[3]

permittit, unde non sunt duo soles, quia unus sufficit; neque in animalibus et hominibus duo capita, quia unum sufficit. Ita non sunt duo mundi, quia unus sufficit' (*Raimundi de Sabunde Theologia naturalis seu Liber creaturarum*, Solisbaci, sumtibus (sic) J. E. de Seidel, 1852, p. 13).

1. The concept of stylistic synonymy I have exemplified here must not be confused with the more familiar situation of words which typically possess literary associations, in contradistinction to those which do not. It may of course be that *baster* differed from *suffire* in this way, just as it might in respect of any other semantic qualification, i.e. that there was a difference of register between the two. A distinction of register—literary, say, as opposed to non-literary application—may ultimately explain the case of *symbiosis* cited earlier.

2. Examples: *escaper* and *escamper* for *échapper* and *décamper; discoste* for *lointain or distant; mescoler* and *mescolance* for *mêler and mélange; baster* itself, just cited, also *bastance* for *suffisance;* several of the mediaeval Italian synonyms listed above, and a considerable number of 19th cent. Gallicisms to which native terms correspond.

3. It seems to me that these provisos are no harder to accept than those one customarily writes into a prospectus for structural analysis at other linguistic levels—scope for free variation, 'systemic fragments', 'residual structural irregularities' and so on, as well as the whole assumption of a uniform, precisely delimitable *langue* or less extensive corpus. This raises no problem for me, since I am going to shift emphasis on to the diachronic implications of my material, agreeing with Haugen that 'to identify the results of a historical process like borrowing is not possible by a purely synchronic study' ('The Analysis of Linguistic Borrowing', p. 229).

But synonymic—or better, homoionymic analysis is not so important in itself as in the attitude of mind it generates. This line of research teaches us to look for the reasons why near-synonyms, however similar in use, have nevertheless a different semantic function, and to associate the viability of a borrowed sign with these differences. What is really significant is that one lexical sign has succeeded another, either replacing it or sharing significatory functions with it, with some revision of each sign's range of use, and perhaps consequent semantic repercussions elsewhere. Logically the next step is to ask why this historical sequence of events has taken place, and this in its turn leads one to speculate about the way vocabulary is replenished or supplemented.

It will be my aim in Part Five to explain the function of French and Italian borrowings in this wider neological process.

PART FIVE

Romance Loan-Words and the Neological Process

ROMANCE LOAN-WORDS AND
THE NEOLOGICAL PROCESS

In Part Two above I described borrowed vocabulary in terms of individual lexical units and small clusters of words linked by their common function within a given cultural setting. In Parts Three and Four I turned to a discussion of certain more extensive empirical groupings and broader theoretical issues, firstly from the standpoint of form and secondly from that of content. It now remains to knit together these *minutiae* of information and frame conclusions about our sample of cultural loans—our unit of lexical inter-ference—in all its aspects.

Questions of method and principle will naturally fall to be considered at this stage.

'The vocabulary of a language', observed Professor U. Weinreich, 'more loosely structured than its phonemics and grammar, is beyond question the domain of borrowing *par excellence*.'[1] It is true that most aspects of linguistic contact might justifiably be examined in a chapter which bears the title 'lexical' and the same applies equally to most of the problems which arise. There are several reasons why this should be so, quite apart from the obvious one that words, being more readily borrowed than forms or constructions, provide a more abundant source of information and therefore more readily attract the attention of scholars. For one thing, most interference problems overlap into more than one of the traditional sub-divisions of language, and this is true especially of those which initially or in major part appear to fall within the scope of lexicology alone. I cannot hope to follow all the fresh paths of speculation to which a fund of new research material points the way. My approach will therefore be rigorously selective. Some of the issues have been cleared up already, either explicitly or by implication, in previous chapters. Views have already been expressed on what a loan-word is, how it may be recognised, the sort of cultural and historical information it can provide; traditional methods of loan-word analysis have been criticised. For the rest I shall confine my attention to two questions only, which though simple at first sight give rise to far-reaching theoretical repercussions: firstly, *why are words borrowed?* And secondly, *how can the process of lexical interference best be envisaged and most efficiently described?* In terms of what units, what relationships, what total reality?

1. *Languages in Contact*, p. 56.

RATIONALISATION OF VOCABULARY. A
PRE-REQUISITE TO LEXICAL ANALYSIS

However inspiring it may have been to etymologists of his day (and it was intended to provide inspiration) Gilliéron's famous assertion that *chaque mot a son histoire* has always been a thorn in the flesh of those who seek to formulate general rules about vocabulary.[1] One sees why, in the shadow of this *dictum*, the quest for procedures by which to describe and explain lexical events brought forth more pessimistic remarks than constructive suggestions. Doubts were perhaps most strongly felt by descriptive linguists, most of whom would agree with Professor André Martinet that 'as long as one deals with those meaningful units whose denotative value is imprecise and whose relational value is high, namely grammatical morphemes, the structural parallelism of the two planes (sc. planes of expression and content) can easily be maintained; but the lexicon proper seems far less easily reducible to structural patterning, once certain particularly favourable fields such as kinship terms, numerals and a few others have been dealt with'.[2] Up to the beginning of the present decade linguists (especially American linguists) habitually viewed semantics as a weak point in linguistic studies, partly as a healthy reaction against the mentalism and idealism of earlier schools, and partly as a result of their rigorous standards of operational adequacy.[3] Recent years have seen a radical change. It is now widely accepted that some of the most stubborn problems in linguistic description—those which most urgently need solving—are semantic ones, particularly those which one meets with at the level of lexis. Among others Dr. Noam Chomsky has reserved an

1. Saussure, we note, appears to share Gilliéron's atomistic conception of vocabulary when he comments on the isolative, anecdotal nature of semantic change, which in his opinion 'n'est qu'un accident parmi tous ceux qu'enrégistre l'histoire d'une langue', an accident due to particular causes independent of other changes which might have occurred at the same time (*C.L.G.*, 5th edition, p. 132).

2. A. Martinet, 'Structural Linguistics', in *Anthropology Today*, 1953, pp. 574–86: p. 582. Such misgivings are not of course confined to descriptive linguists. A good example of the attitude which prevails all too frequently among traditional lexicologists is that cited by Deroy (op. cit., p. 22) from the Hellenist Jacques Perret, who speaks of '. . . l'embarras inhérent à la plupart des recherches lexicographiques: l'invraisemblable diversité du matériel rassemblé, la particularité des problèmes posés presque par chaque mot; le lexicographe est vraiment l'homme qui travaille sur de la poussière, sur ce "sable sans chaux" dont Caligula faisait une malédiction.' ('Les Hellénismes du vocabulaire latin', in *L'Information Littéraire* 3 (1951), p. 184).

3. In 1954 it was still possible for members of a symposium on *Language in Culture* held at the University of Chicago to talk disapprovingly of 'mingling language studies with matters of content' and to speak of shelving semantics for a long period, a period which 'may be for a lifetime'. Cf. also Charles C. Fries' observation that 'for many linguistic students the word *meaning* itself has become almost anathema' (*Language*, XXX (1954), p. 58).

important niche for semantics in his project for an inclusive description of language: 'We should like the syntactic framework of the language that is isolated and exhibited by our grammar to support semantic description, and we shall naturally rate more highly a theory of formal structure that leads to grammars that meet this requirement more fully.'[1] Various attempts have already been made to provide generative grammar with a semantic auxiliary, notably by Katz, Fodor and Postal.[2] In addition the longstanding concept of 'semantic structure', which has recently become a focus of attention once more, has been re-examined in the light of transformational procedures by Professor J. Lyons of Edinburgh University.[3] The Katz–Postal hypothesis in its present form does not set us on the road we really wish to travel, even though what the authors term *semantic* elements fairly closely correspond to what we are calling *lexical* items, because the semantic component of their analysis is constituted so as to serve as an ancillary to a grammatical analysis— is exclusively inward-looking, so to speak, and is not concerned with inter-relation at the lexical level.[4] Lyons' semantic analysis too, excellent though it may be as a descriptive (i.e. linguistic) theory, fails to meet our particular requirements because it deals primarily with logico-grammatical structures and is exemplified by words of a principally relational or analytical import. And the same generally speaking is true of the numerous other models of semantic analysis evolved by descriptive linguists from the time of Firth's 'Technique of Semantics' (*Trans. Philol. Soc.*, 1935) onwards,[5] including distributional analysis in its various forms.

What we have to examine and assess are models and metaphors which may help to express the relations between borrowed words and cultural influences as well as linguistic environments, which will allow discussion, so to speak, to move from lexical towards cultural situations as well as in the

1. *Syntactic structures*, s'Gravenhage, 1963, p. 102.

2. J. J. Katz and J. A. Fodor, 'The Structure of a Semantic Theory', *Language*, XXXIX, 1963, pp. 170–210; J. J. Katz and P. M. Postal, *An Integrated Theory of Linguistic Descriptions*, Research Monograph No. 26, M.I.T. Press, Cambridge, Mass., 1964.

3. In *Structural Semantics*; see bibliography. On the subject of semantic structure see also A. G. Greimas' recent work *Sémantique structurale* ('*Langue et langage*'), Paris, 1966, which undertakes to provide an adequate metalanguage for handling all types of semantic inquiry. The author acquits himself remarkably well, though his task is made harder by his extremely comprehensive definition of what the discipline of semantics includes (*vide* esp. p. 5).

4. I.e. the semantic (sc. lexical) elements handled are viewed as a discrete taxonomy, like a dictionary. 'Dictionary' is actually used in this connection on numerous occasions during the course of the *Integrated Theory of Linguistics*; cf. pp. 12ff.

5. E.g. W. Haas, 'On Defining Linguistic Units', *Trans. Philol. Soc.*, 1954, pp. 54–84, esp. 71ff.; id., 'The Theory of Translation', *Philosophy*, XXXVII, 1962, pp. 208–28; and id., 'Semantic Value', *Proceedings of the Ninth International Congress of Linguistics*, Cambridge, Mass., 1965.

opposite direction: in brief, which will bridge the gap between the lexicon and 'the world outside'. For this purpose we need not confine ourselves to an analysis which is strictly linguistic in the descriptivist's acceptation of that term, though we should naturally prefer not to depart too far from the hard core of doctrine upon which linguists are agreed.

I cannot put forward too strongly what I conceive to be the advantage of a survey on the lines followed in this concluding chapter. It is that we have here a precisely delimited *corpus* of borrowings representing a unit of inter-ference between two cultural languages over a long period of time and are contemplating them not only as cultural symbols—a point of view which has often been applied to large ranges of interference vocabulary before—but as lexical or linguistic entities, remembering that, as Marcel Cohen put it, 'le langage, quelles que soient ses relations avec les autres faits humains et sociaux, a ses propres voies d'évolution, et son inertie propre'.[1] The approach is empirical and offers finite conclusions. Others have, of course, investigated conditions in which neologism occurs, as well as the dynamism behind it, and we have already acknowledged a debt to many monographs orientated in this way. The tendency, however, has been to evolve principles and illustrate them with reference to examples chosen from as wide a field as possible, the whole undertaking constituting one phase of a search for semantic universals. All I wish to do is to see what can be deduced from a sample of information which while sufficiently copious for our purposes is restricted when viewed comparatively; sufficiently restricted, that is, to bear intensive examination, yet conventional enough in its make-up to stand as a prototype of neologism in cultural languages as a whole: and to offer this information, well digested and matured, as material for general semantic analysis to be used or rejected by others as they think best.

Any general conceptions which emerge are proffered as having validity within the ambit of this special material. To the extent that borrowed words may be judged a fair sample of the lexicon these findings may prove to have relevance in assessing neologism *tout court*. If so I shall be pleased; but it does not come within the scope of this work to attempt such a wider application.

Linguists have long been aware that relationships of many kinds are seen to bind one word to another when these are viewed from the standpoint of specific, denotational or lexical meaning. Saussure himself assented to the principle of semantic solidarity when in his well-known example of the *constellation de rapports associatifs* surrounding the word *enseignement*[2] he placed likeness of sense (*analogie des signifiés*) on a par with association of form (*communauté des images acoustiques*). The science of etymology has benefited

1. Marcel Cohen, *Linguistique et matérialisme dialectique*, Gap, 1948, p. 11.
2. *C.L.G.*, 5th edition, pp. 174–5.

greatly from an awareness of these affinities. The notion of vocabulary structure in the sense I have just stated has clearly always been a fruitful source of
inspiration to that *doyen* of Romance lexicologists Professor Walther von
Wartburg, both in his capacity of practical lexicographer and of lexical
theorist, as the director of the *Französisches etymologisches Wörterbuch* and as
the author of *Problèmes et méthodes de la linguistique*.[1] There are a number of
different techniques which have been applied to lexical analysis in the past,
and many others are in course of development at the present day. Almost all
have some methodological advantage to offer, while their merits and shortcomings, the soundness or inadequacy of the precepts from which they are
derived all help to refine our ideas about what lexical analysis entails. We
might think of them as the product of a number of basic procedures, something like this:

1. *Use of qualitative indicators* to arrange words, for example, according to
their relative importance as exponents of cultural trends. A stimulating
contribution was made by Matoré's system of *mots-témoins* and *mots-clés*. The
former are 'des éléments particulièrement importants en fonction desquels
la structure lexicologique se hiérarchise et se coordonne';[2] words which
mark a turning-point in a society's development. Examples: *esotérique* 1755,
charlatanisme 1752, interpreted as signs of a reaction against rationalism; *coke*
1770, 'le premier signe de la naissance en France du capitalisme industriel; le

---

1. 'Les mots ne vivent pas simplement chacun pour soi: la moindre modification, la
moindre innovation dans les nuances du sens a aussitôt une répercussion sur les mots
avoisinants. . .' (*Problèmes et méthodes*, 2nd edition, p. 125). We call to mind too his concept of *mots satellites*, affective terms like *vicaire/viguier* in Gilliéron's classical example of
the *gallus/cattus* clash, which 'entourent leurs synonymes du langage normal, non affectif,
tournoyant autour d'eux jusqu'au moment où un hasard heureux permet à l'un d'eux
d'accéder au centre' (*Prob. et méth*, 2nd edition, p. 157); or the point of principle upon
which he criticised Gilliéron's presentation of material in the Atlas Linguistique de la
France: 'L'espace sémantique qui entoure immédiatement un mot central est systéma-
tiquement négligé. Entre les différents mots qui font l'objet des questions se placent la
plupart du temps un grand nombre d'expressions qui leur sont d'une façon on d'une
autre apparentées par leur sens: l'espace sémantique qui sépare les mots du questionnaire
n'est pas vide . . . L'image qu'il (l'Atlas) donne du trésor linguistique ressemble à un
paysage de collines dans une mer de nuages: seuls les sommets émergent; quant aux
dépressions sur lesquelles s'élèvent ces hauteurs et qui forment le lien organique entre
elles, elles restent dissimulées sous le voile opaque des nuages' (*Prob. et méth*., 2nd edition,
p. 159). Cf. Charles Bally's hypothesis of the *champ associatif*, and the insight it affords
into 'areas of semantic overlap' in synonyms; also the same author's survey of inherent
semantic tendencies which forms a part of his comparative study of the characteristic
features of modern French and modern German (*Linguistique générale et linguistique
française*, 3rd edition, Berne, 1950). See in addition Yakov Malkiel, 'Etymology and
word-families', in *Linguistics Today, Publ. Ling. Circle of New York No. 2*, New York,
1954.

2. *La méthode en lexicologie*, p. 65.

jour ou le coke remplace le bois dans la métallurgie, la grande industrie va
naître'.[1] The *mot-clé* is 'un être, un sentiment, une idée, vivants dans la
mesure même où la société reconnaît en eux son idéal'.[2] Examples: *honnête
homme, philosophe, bourgeois*. Belin-Milleron's 'carrefours linguistiques de la
pensée' deserve mention under this heading—words which form a kind of
clearing-house for ideas, e.g. *Loi, Patrie, Union, Peuple, Sacrifice* during the
Revolution.[3]

2. *Attempts to codify the impact of form on meaning*. Lexicologists have always
made allowance in practice for the reciprocal influence of form and meaning,
and have tried on occasion to codify the relationship concerned. P. Guiraud's
essay 'Les champs morphosémantiques' (*Bulletin de la Société de Linguistique de
Paris*, No. 52, 1956, pp. 265-88) is a recent attempt. The author starts in an
interesting way by assuming that if a neologism is not motivated by external
circumstances it must be recommended by its formal associations; but he
fails to exploit the premise fully and goes on to reproduce what are in effect
the well-known and well-proven formulae of Linguistic Geography (particularly as expounded by the late Professor John Orr)—influence of homonymy, paronymic attraction (both accidental and deliberate), contagion,
etc.[4] As yet no new formulation seems likely to usurp the primacy of Gilliéron and Orr's homonymic analysis, though one feels that the last word has
still not been said on this important topic.

3. *Use of statistical methods*, especially word-frequency.[5] Cf. G. U. Yule,
The Statistical Study of Literary Vocabulary, London, 1944; G. K. Zipf,
Selected Studies in the Principles of Relative Frequency in Language, Cambridge,
Mass., 1949; G. Herdan, *Language as Choice and Chance*, Groningen, 1956;
R.-L. Wagner and P. Guiraud, 'La Méthode statistique en lexicologie',
Revue de l'Enseignement Supérieur, 1959, No. 1, pp. 154-9; the various numbers
of the *Bulletin du laboratoire d'analyse lexicographique*, publications du Centre

1. Ibid., p. 67. A danger inherent in the use of *mots-témoins* is that they may turn out
to have been current in the language earlier than at the significant date. This has actually happened in the case of some of Matoré's crucial terms, among them *charlatanisme*
and *magasin* 'emporium'. See W. Krauss, 'Zur Lexicologie der Aufklärung', *Rom.
Forsch. LXVI*, 384-96.

2. Ibid., p. 68.

3. Belin-Milleron, *La Réforme de la connaissance*, Paris, 1942. See P. Guiraud, *La
Sémantique (Que sais-je?* series), p. 98.

4. Cf. also Guiraud's *communication* ' "Écrire comme un chat". Le champ morpho-
sémantique de "chat" ', *Atti del VIII Congresso Internazionale di Studi Romanzi*, pp. 549-
54 (esp. second paragraph) in which the author attempts to distinguish between Gilliéron's approach and his own.

5. For an appreciation of the value of statistical methods see Stephen Ullmann,
Semantics: An Introduction to the Science of Meaning, Oxford, 1962, pp, 253-4. The final
chapter as a whole (entitled *The Structure of the Vocabulary*) is an excellent source of further
information about the approaches I have summarised here.

d'Études du Vocabulaire français de l'Université de Besançon, sous la direct-
ion de B. Quemada, from 1959 onwards; and more recently R. J.
Glickman and G. J. Staalman, *Manual for the Printing of Literary Texts
and Concordances by Computer*, Univ. of Toronto Press, 1966, together with
other information relating to project PRORA (Programs for Research on
Romance Authors) in the University of Toronto, esp. R. J. Glickman, 'An
Integrated Series of Computer Programs for Literary Research', *MLA
Conference 16*, 27th Dec. 1965.

4. *Semantic typology*. A more recent venture, in which Ullmann's article
'Descriptive Semantics and Linguistic Typology', *Word*, Vol. IX, No. 3,
Dec. 1953, pp. 225–40, occupies a key position. A given vocabulary is
described with reference to the proportion of motivated and unmotivated
words, particular and generic terms, devices for conveying emotional overtones, the organisation and distribution of synonymic resources, relative
frequency of polysemy, its characteristic forms, and other similar criteria.

Although lexicologists have always invoked the principle of interrelation
between words or word-groups readily and to good purpose, the conception
of interdependence in the strict sense is exploited far more rarely and less
convincingly, particularly if by 'interdependence' one means the influence
exerted by a total pattern upon its individual components, i.e. a true *Gestalt*
in the original sense of the term as applied first and foremost to psychological
theory. Yet the very nature of the relationship which lexical borrowing
betokens—extraneous unit set against a pattern of established symbols—is
precisely one which suggests a *Gestalt* and which prompts us to look for some
higher entity which can genuinely be said to define the value of the elements
within the system it delimits. How far is the idea of a *Gestalt* applicable at the
lexical level? There are two schools of thought in vogue at present among
lexicologists which have something to offer to those whose research leads
them to think on these lines. They are distinct, even mutually antipathetic;
taken in conjunction they sum up adequately the range of lexical theories we
might expect to be of some use to us. The first attracts the allegiance of those
who see in vocabulary a reflection of a structured conceptual pattern: the
second, of those who feel that words can only be adequately described by
relating them to a wider pattern of phenomena *extraneous* to language. For
the former words stand in a direct (though constantly developing) relationship to a structured 'world of concepts' which forms a closed system analogous
to a phonemic or grammatical system. For the latter words reflect the world
at large, 'the world outside', which may or may not present regularities
that could be termed structures, though whether they do so or not has no
direct bearing upon the method of analysis chosen. The extraneous world,
they say, can be accepted for what it is: scholars other than linguists have
found ways to describe it organically: it provides an ultimate, stable reality

Y

external to language in which to anchor the transient, abstract linguistic fact. The most outstanding example of the former is Professor Jost Trier's theory of the *linguistic field*, which he expounded in its original form in *Der deutsche Wortschatz in Sinnbezirk des Verstandes; die Geschichte eines sprachlichen Feldes*, I, Heidelberg, 1931.[1] The latter point of view is common to onomasiological and *Wörter und Sachen* disciplines in general; but its most interesting application as far as our purposes are concerned is the method of analysis which equates words not to 'the world outside' in its haphazard, individual diversity but to *la réalité sociale*, interpreting the pattern of vocabulary in terms of social structure—or more specifically, in terms of the changing structure of society at different selected periods. The French 'sociological' school of lexicology is the one I chiefly have in mind, coupled with the name of Dr. Georges Matoré and grounded in the principles set forth in his manifesto *La Méthode en lexicologie*.

The gist of Trier's theory has been summed up as follows: 'In the course of his work on intellectual terms in Old and Middle High German, a picture unfolded itself to Trier of a closely knit and articulated lexical sphere where the significance of each unit was determined by its neighbours, with their semantic areas reciprocally limiting one another and dividing up and covering the whole sphere between them. Such an organically articulated section of the general vocabulary is termed a linguistic field (sprachliches Feld); Trier constantly speaks of "linguistic, conceptual, lexical fields", not of "semantic fields" (Bedeutungsfeld) as do the sponsors of rival definitions. Trier's field is therefore an intermediate notion between the individual word and the whole lexical thesaurus of a given synchronous state. In his own carefully phrased definition: "Fields are linguistic realities existing between single words and the whole vocabulary; they are parts of a whole and resemble words in that they combine into some higher units. . . ." This factor of organic and interdependent articulateness . . . explains Trier's contention that there is no gap in the way words cover the whole area of a field, nor in the way fields cover the whole area of vocabulary, i.e. of the universe as reflected by language.'[2]

An important trait of Trier's hypothesis is his distinction between the lexical field and the conceptual field, the first being so to speak imposed upon the latter. A conceptual field is divided into sections by the word mosaic

1. See also: 'Das sprachliche Feld. Eine Auseinandersetzung', *Neue Jahrbücher für Wissenschaft und Jugendbildung*, X (1934), pp. 428–49, in which Trier distinguishes between his own field theory and those of Ipsen, Jolles, Porzig.

2. S. Ullmann, *Principles of Semantics*, p. 157. Ullmann discusses the implications of field theory at some length (*Principles*, pp. 75–6, 152–70). Other detailed *comptes-rendus* accompanied by criticisms are to be found in *Problèmes et méthodes*, 2nd edition, pp. 169–79 and Miss Suzanne Öhman's article 'Theories of the Linguistic Field', *Word* IX (1953), pp. 123–34. See also (among very many other works which bear upon this subject) id., *Wortinhalt und Weldbild; vergleichende und methodologische Studien zur Bedeutungslehre und*

(Wortdecke) of the lexical field. As Miss Öhman puts it: 'A word alone has no meaning but acquires one only through the opposition between it and the neighbouring words in the pattern. For instance in the grading of examination results as *excellent, good, fair, poor, very poor* the word *poor* acquires a meaning only when one knows that the scale of grading consists of five degrees and that *poor* lies in the lower half between *fair* and *very poor*.' But (continues Miss Öhman) 'grading can be expressed by a line; most conceptual fields must, however, be conceived of as two-dimensional. . . . One must try to recognise the boundaries of each single section of the word-mosaic; only then does the content of each single word belonging to a total conceptual field become clear'.[1]

Much has been written against the field theory either attacking it on points of detail or contesting the validity of the approach as a whole. We for our part need only pronounce on those aspects which concern our limited sphere of study. They are three: the notion of 'function' applied to vocabulary; that of a 'mosaic' of lexical fields; that of a *Geistesraum* or 'universe of concepts'.

It has often been conceded—Martinet's observations quoted at the beginning of this chapter are typical of many in the same strain—that there do exist certain groups of words held together by affinity of content which appear to form autonomous units; names of military ranks, numerals, terms of kinship, the nomenclature of colours, or systems of grading like S. Öhman's example, are commonly cited.[2] But these are particular, not to say unique or anomalous situations.[3] In most of these traditional exemplifications

Wortfeldtheorie, Stockholm, 1951 and, more recently, N. C. W. Spence, 'Linguistic Fields, Conceptual Systems and the *Weltbild*', *Trans. Philol. Soc.*, 1961, pp. 87–106. For a sample list of investigations carried out using Trier's methods see Öhman, 'Theories of the Linguistic Field', p. 126, n. 16 and the bibliographical sources mentioned there; also *Problèmes et méthodes*, 2nd edition, pp. 175–6, n. 2.

1. Op. cit., pp. 126–7.

2. *Vide* Ullmann, *Principles* . . . , pp. 154–5 and the works cited there; also Wartburg, *Prob. et méth.*, p. 179.

3. The most interesting of these is the well-known instance of colour-aphasia analysed by Gelb and Goldstein, ('Über Farbenamnesie', *Psychologische Forschungen*, VI, 1925, pp. 127–86; *Journal de Psychologie*, XXX, 1933), in which a patient suffering from amnesia was unable to characterise sections of a spectrum of coloured silks as 'red', 'yellow', 'blue', etc. though he knew that each silk differed in tone from the adjacent one, because he had lost his naming faculty or mental system of reference. But this synchronic problem of analysing *ab initio* a series of phenomena which may be grasped by the senses yet are delimitable in no terms accessible to the senses other than linguistic labels surely cannot lead to general inferences about lexis. If we consider what linguistic activity actually involves we are confronted with an entirely dissimilar train of events. Patterns of designation are learnt by a child through a gradual process of association and re-analysis whose stages are fairly well known, and likewise the classification available to speakers

of field theory the 'conceptual field' concerned is indeed delimited and apportioned by an arrangement of words, but the ultimate articulation of the structure is palpably extra-linguistic, being man-made or directly referable to natural circumstances. A linear sequence of numbers or grades is a mathematical or logical disposition; a military hierarchy is characterised by rules of discipline, degrees of responsibility, scales of pay. The 'pattern' of kinship is of a very special kind we must not expect to find repeated elsewhere: what we are dealing with in this case are the immutable biological affinities of human being, the archetypal pattern, our 'relations' *par excellence*. The same observations about the labelling of natural patterns apply *a fortiori* to G. Ipsen's *Bedeutungsfeld*, especially as put into practice in his earlier works and in those of certain scholars who carried out investigations similar to his and pursued his original line of thinking.[1] 'Field' in this acceptation denotes a group of words which are linked together in that they all belong to one closely knit sector of human activity, usually forming the terminology of a craft or technique, e.g. the special vocabularies of viticulture, sheep-farming, bee-keeping. These culturally and spatially associated terms form a naturally circumscribed communalty within which one can conveniently study, say, changes in technique and the resultant tendencies towards innovation or conservatism in the words used to denote them. There is little reason for calling these congeries *semantic* structures; though they possess a certain internal cohesion it resides in the nature of things and not of words. I doubt whether the term 'structure' could be applied to that sector of human activity which the words as a group denote without doing violence to its accepted meaning. Perhaps what really lays these traditional instances—numerals, ranks, etc.—open to the charge of anomaly is that they fail to exemplify an essential component of the field hypothesis—the concept of a strategic, organic interplay between concepts and the words by which they are denoted or actualised.[2] Just what this delimiting factor, this semantic mechanism

of a language was created in a hand-to-mouth fashion over a period of time—by referring to colours in terms of visible objects (often deliberately, as when the names of dyestuffs are exploited for trade purposes) or by evoking more remote synaesthetic analogies.

1. *Vide* Ipsen's articles 'Der alte Orient und die Indogermanen', (*Streitberg Festschrift*, 1924, pp. 200–37) (original formulation of his 'field of meaning') and 'Der neue Sprachbegriff' (*Zeitschrift für Deutschkunde*, 46 (1932), pp. 1–18) (revised version of hypothesis, catering for formal as well as semantic relationships). A short bibliography of studies similar to Ipsen's is given by Öhman, op. cit., p. 125, n. 8.

2. This assumption is usually made in field theory, though seldom formulated explicitly. It comes out much more clearly in the branch of psycholinguistic studies known as *ethnolinguistics*, which is closely related to field theory in other ways as well. Ethnolinguists, we recall (they are also referred to as anthropological linguists and *Sprachinhaltsforscher*), maintain that 'each language is . . . the shaper of ideas, the program and guide for the individual's mental activity, for his analysis of impressions, for the syn-

which operates between one sign and another on the synchronic plane may be is hard to envisage. There is perhaps a play of conceptual patterns when a child learns its native tongue; at the level of *parole*, too, a speaker no doubt subconsciously chooses between near-synonyms on grounds of semantic range, register, taboo associations and so forth as part of the tactics of speech. It is a more difficult enterprise to say what a semantic system actually implies in practical terms in cases other than those where the *denotata* themselves are arranged in logical or natural structures, though not necessarily an impossible one. Psychologists are constantly discovering more about the way words are associated on a conceptual as well as a formal plane. It may well be that the psycholinguist will succeed in providing field theory with more adequate operational premises to work on by discovering more about these semantic conventions, these 'rules of the language game', to use Wittgenstein's phrase. But for us, at present, this particular trail goes cold here.

The image of a 'mosaic' of fields is the Achilles' heel of Trier's hypothesis. The Munster scholar's opponents have felt unable to accept that concepts or groups of concepts (and hence the lexical units associated with them) are coterminous, even as a methodological construct. In addition most authorities are inclined to discount the scholar's subjective impression which imposes order where in fact there is anarchy—or at best a series of partial, fragmentary regularities. Von Wartburg voices the general opinion: 'Trier ... pose comme postulat que l'image tout entière du monde, telle que l'individu et la communauté linguistique la portent en eux, peut être subdivisée d'une façon continue et organique en partant du haut, c'est à dire de l'ensemble, de manière à constituer des champs de plus en plus petits. Et à l'intérieur de ces champs, les domaines sémantiques des mots qui les constituent s'intégreraient de la même façon pour former une mosaïque sans vide. Il est possible en effet qu'à la hauteur spirituelle où se meut sa recherche, à savoir dans le domaine de l'intellect, on ait la révélation d'une image de ce genre. Mais de vastes spheres de la vie et par là même de la langue ont des limites confuses ou même pas de limite du tout, exception faite pour le savant qui les y introduit pour lui-même ... L'impression d'un champ naît souvent du fait que, dans l'espace sémantique, les écarts sont plus ou moins grands. La disposition générale du vocabulaire d'une seule et même langue est fort différente chez deux individus différents; ceci tient à l'inégalité des expériences de la vie.'[1]

thesis of his mental stock-in-trade' (*Language, Thought and Reality: Selected Writings of Benjamin Lee Whorf*, ed. by J. B. Carroll, New York and London, 1956, p. 212). For a sensitive *critique* of this approach see N. C. W. Spence, 'The Basic Problems of Ethnolinguistics', *Arch. Ling.*, XVI, fasc. 2, 1964, pp. 145–56 (review article of Helmut Gipper's book *Bausteine zur Sprachinhaltsforschung, neuere Sprachbetrachung im Austausch mit Geistes- und Naturwissenschaft*, Dusseldorf, 1963).

1. Wartburg, *Prob. et méth.*, 2nd edition, pp. 178–9.

Trier's 'total vision of the world' which at first sight would appear to offer a solution to our problem of a lexical *Gestalt* rests upon what is frequently held even by field theorists to be an uncertain premise. 'The distinction between conceptual and lexical fields', observes Dr. Öhman diplomatically, 'seems somewhat problematic. . . . Conceptual fields can hardly be defined independently of language, i.e. *a priori*.'[1] One and the same weakness under-lies not only the idea of a 'world of concepts' or totality of conceptual fields considered apart [from vocabulary and that of a conceptual field *per se* considered apart from its exponents, but also the very notion of *concept* divor-ced from the word which denotes or evokes it. What we are faced with here is the familiar philosophical problem of 'naked ideas', which is sufficiently well known to require no amplification. Psychologists, too, have always held conflicting views about the extent to which thought-processes function without recourse to language, though most would be prepared to concede that in a minority of instances which are not always easy to determine human thought moves directly from impulse to conclusion, sometimes by visual imagination, sometimes by an intuition whose actual *modus operandi* escapes direct scrutiny. The 'reasoning' of children who are still unable to speak is an obvious case in point. For their part most linguists who have found it necessary to order their thoughts upon these matters would visualise the totality of concepts or *Geistesraum* in much the same way as Saussure does: 'Psychologiquement, abstraction faite de son expression par les mots, notre pensée n'est qu'une masse amorphe et indistincte. . . . Sans le secours des signes nous serions incapables de distinguer deux idées d'une façon claire et constante. Prise en elle-même, la pensée est comme une nébuleuse où rien n'est nécessairement délimitée.'[2] A similar conviction lies behind Bloom-field's statement that 'we do not possess a workable classification of every-thing in the universe, and apart from language we cannot even envisage any-thing of the sort'.[3,4]

1. Öhman, op. cit., p. 128.
2. *C.L.G.*, 5th edition, p. 155.
3. *Language*, p. 124: see Spang-Hanssen, *Recent Theories of the Language Sign*, p. 125. On the analytical and objectivising power of words see Matoré's short but illuminating note in *La Méthode en Lexicologie*, Ch. III, Part 2, *Le Plan psychologique*, in which he develops Condillac's pronouncement that 'on ne peut parler sans décomposer la pensée en ses divers éléments pour les exprimer tour à tour, et la parole est le seul instrument qui permette cette analyse de la pensée', and also Humboldt's opinion (with which Trier also agreed) that strictly speaking, language is not a means of representing truths already known, but rather a means of discovering truths hitherto unknown. Cf. also Professor G. Devoto's amplification of Saussure's theory about the relation between linguistic expression and content in *I Fondamenti della storia linguistica*, p. 14.
4. A word about the relation between a 'universe of concepts' and conceptual dic-tionaries is timely at this stage. It might be expected that conceptual dictionaries, whose avowed aim is to establish a 'Zwischenwelt geistiger Inhalte, die sich zwischen Ich und

Even when a field theorist is confident that he has identified a field of mutually delimiting concepts the traditional lexicologist may still feel able to interpret this same semantic patterning more convincingly in diachronic rather than synchronic terms. The lexico-conceptual field, the apparently strategic arrangement of *signifiés* and *signifiants* at a given moment of time, might seem to him a sort of optical trick, a projection on the synchronic plane of that is in reality a diachronic process of development and re-adjustment to meet changing needs. The motivated distribution of words within a field may strike him more readily as a residual state resulting from changes which have their epicentre elsewhere, e.g. in impulses towards economy operating on the diachronic plane, in a conditioned choice which governs the process of neologism as a whole.

To sum up: from a theoretical standpoint field theory as a method of describing the structure of content in the 'non-grammatical' areas of lexis is open to many objections, though many of these may be answered when psychologists have progressed further in establishing 'moduli in psychological space', to use Professor G. P. Meredith's expression.[1] The metaphorical leap made by Trier and subsequent theorists in transmuting meanings, which are acquired habits of use, into spatial analogies is disturbingly wide. Neverthe-less the heuristic value of these techniques has been proved to be great, and we can develop certain of their practical advantages in handling the abstract-general-emotive section of our transferred vocabulary. Many of our words

Aussenwelt einschiebt' would furnish information about the way concepts are articulated and might possibly provide evidence from which to judge whether the entire notion of 'conceptual space' has any validity at all. (See the introduction to R. Hallig and W. von Wartburg's *Begriffssystem als Grundlage für die Lexikographie, Versuch eines Ordnungs-schemas*, 2. Aufl., Akad. der Wissenschaften zu Berlin, *Veröffentlichungen des Instituts für romanische Sprachwissenschaft, No. 14*; Berlin, Akademie-Verlag, 1962. But if we ex-plore this possibility we soon come round to the conclusion reached by Professor Ull-mann that 'no major gain for synchronistic semantics can be expected from these schemes (proposals for conceptual dictionaries) since by the very nature of things they are based upon extra-linguistic, *a priori* considerations and do not spontaneously emerge from the lexical material itself. They are primarily designed to meet the needs of the lexicographer, not the semanticist interested in the inner structure of vocabulary' ('Descriptive Semantics', *Word*, IX, No. 3, 1953, pp. 226–7). Concep-tual dictionaries in other words start out from the pattern of the world which experience has inculcated in us (not forgetting *linguistic* experience, which also has its part to play) and produce from it pragmatic schedules for classifying items of vo-cabulary which have certain advantages over the customary alphabetical or ety-mological rubrics. In providing a norm or constant by which to standardise diverse lexical studies they answer an important practical purpose which is not, however, directly connected with our own.

1. Lecture to the University of Durham Philosophical Society, 'The Syntax of Psychological Space', April 1956.

are obvious stuff for this kind of analysis, among them the following drawn from sixteenth century Italian to French loans, all of which fit readily into clear-cut fields: the lexical groups *brave, braverie, bravache, rodomont; bizarre, grotesque, goffe, fruste; affront, escorne, rebuffe, supercherie; caprice, capricieux; politesse, délicatesse, galbe, leste; burle, (se) burler (de), burlesque; poltron, pagnote, veillaque, saltimbanque,* and the isolated words *fougue, disgrâce, jovial, panache, posture, signalé.* Names of ranks are numerous: (Milit.) It. > Fr. *lancespessade, caporal, guidon, colonel;* Fr. > It. *bacelliere, scudiere, cavaliere, gonfaloniere, brigadiere, maresciallo,* etc.; (Naut.) *vie avant, comite, majordome, nostre homme.* There are even a few colour terms: *giallo, roggio, blu, gridellino, lillà, marrone.*[1]

Some of the most successful works on lexical and conceptual fields have been those which contrasted patterns at different historical periods. This comparative approach has something of particular value to offer. It brings home to lexicologists the importance of approaching the problem of neologism as one of vocabulary as a whole in a state of emergence. Further, by hypostatising referential meaning in a *concept* and successfully defending the figure on grounds of practical expediency Trier and his followers have made it admissible for lexicologists to handle abstract lexical signs, when circumstances require it, by methods comparable to those onomasiologists use when dealing with objects and activities in the material world.

A word here about the contribution of glossematists, whose descriptive procedure expressly assumes that the meaningful element of linguistic signs has a structure of its own on the *plane of content* parallel to that of formal entities on the plane of expression, and can be analysed in its own right. As it happens the part of Professor Louis Hjelmslev's programme[2] which envisages an exhaustive description of 'content' in the same terms as 'expression' has not yet been worked out fully. Hjelmslev himself 'predicted with certainty' that a complete analytical theory would be formulated at all linguistic levels using glossematic principles,[3] but subsequent exponents of and apologists for the immanent method hold conflicting views on this score and even

1. How far may these words be said to re-classify the spectrum? *Giallo* may be considered to do so; it was borrowed early, at a time when colour nomenclature was developing away from the somewhat coarse-grained division which seems to have been usual in early Germanic, Celtic and Latin itself. *Roggio,* also mediaeval, is an alternative to *rosso.* 18th cent. *lillà* and *gridellino* (much the same colour) are closely associated with textiles and fashions. *Marrone* (late 19th cent.) reassesses the area of *bruno, rosso,* etc., or rather provides a concomitant synthetic sign for this area; *blu,* first used as a naval term ('Admiral of the Blue') has remained peripheral with respect to the established terminology (*azzurro, turchino,* etc.).

2. Expressed in his *Omkring sprogteoriens grundlaeggelse (Festskrift udgivet af Københavns Universitet; Anledning af Universitets Aarfest November 1943,* Copenhagen 1943; translation by F. J. Whitfield: *Prolegomena to a Theory of Language, Indiana University Publications in Anthropology and Linguistics,* Baltimore, 1953).

3. Op. cit., p. 60–1.

doubt whether this part of the agenda can be carried out in every respect without some modifications. Dr. B. Siertsema for instance suggests that the analysis of content should not go into greater detail than the concepts which correspond to linguistic signs—words, inflections, derivatives (whereas Hjelmslev's '*figurae* of content' or ultimate semantic units are smaller entities, viz., 'non-signs found on analysis as component parts of individual signs')[1] because it will never be possible to find an irreducible element of content.[2] Professor Jens Holt on the other hand sets out to realise the glossematists' aims in every particular through his method of *pleremic* analysis (*pleremics* is a term used by Hjelmslev but not elaborated).[3] He has also undertaken to answer the criticisms of Dr. Siertsema and other scholars.[4] Many objections might be brought against Holt's thesis; but an obvious one[5] is precisely that which was met with in connection with field theories, that we have no way of concretising concepts or 'meanings' other than by using linguistic units. A proposal to subdivide linguistic signs into smaller entities by expressing them in terms of other linguistic signs cannot fail to appear illogical. Nor again is it at all clear what Professor Holt means by 'function' operating between these basic *figurae*.[6]

Professor Matoré's *méthode* is also a classification in terms of a total structure, but not a structure of concepts. It is, he stresses, a 'schématisation du réel'.[7] Rejecting the various field theories evolved by German linguists[8]—too hastily, perhaps, and with undue attention to their more eccentric shortcomings—he replaces them by his own conception of a lexical field with the title of *champ notionnel*. This consists of words linked together not as the name might suggest by their semantic affinities but by the common role they play

1. V. Spang-Hanssen, *Recent Theories of the Linguistic Sign*, p. 132.

2. B. Siertsema: *A Study of Glossematics. A critical survey of its fundamental concepts*, The Hague, 1955. *Vide* esp. pp. 154–70.

3. *Plereme* = unit of meaning (content) visualised as a structural entity: corresponds to *phoneme* on the plane of expression. See Jens Holt, *Rationel semantik (pleremik)*, *Acta Jutlandica*, Vol. 18 (1946), Aarhus-Copenhagen. The pleremes of 'wife' would be *human being, adult, female, married* (example given by Holt in his article 'Pleremics', *Proceedings of the University of Durham Philosophical Society*, Vol. I [1959], Series B [*Arts*], No. 6, pp. 49–53).

4. *Vide* the paper 'Pleremics', above, p. 51.

5. Which Dr. Siertsema herself stresses: 'we can only analyse the content of language by means of its expression . . . ' (op. cit., p. 157).

6. For a telling criticism of glossematic theory as interpreted by Dr. Siertsema see W. Haas, 'Concerning Glossematics', *Arch. Ling.*, VIII (1956), pp. 93–110; also the same author, 'On Defining Linguistic Units', *Trans. Philol. Soc.*, 1954, p. 76, esp. n. 1.

7. *La Méthode en lexicologie*, p. 65 (my italics).

8. 'La linguistique allemande *des champs* se mouvant entre des considérations philosophiques abstraites ("volonté communautaire"—"lutte pour l'ordre", etc.) . . . s'est révélée incapable de déterminer des coupes dans l'histoire du lexique et n'a pu formuler que des explications fragmentaires et discutables' (*Méthode*, p. 64).

in characterising a given state of society: 'Il ne faut pas, en lexicologie, être dupe de la ressemblance ou de la dissemblance externes des éléments. De même que des systèmes d'équations différentielles peuvent présenter des affinités tout en différant par la forme extérieure, un champ lexicologique peut comporter des mots qui à première vue semblent n'avoir rien de commun. C'est la parenté sociologique des éléments qui seul importe. . . .'[1] The author's conviction that the only true structure behind language is a sociological one informs the whole of his *méthode*. 'Un vocabulaire', he affirms, 'forme un tout organique'; but only inasmuch as 'tout se tient dans une société'.[2] The view of language as an autonomous system is rejected: 'Le point de vue idéaliste de la sociologie durkheimienne . . . a entraîné de nombreux savants à minimiser de manière inconsidérée le rôle des conditions matérielles et notamment économiques dans l'évolution du langage . . . et même, comme Saussure, à prétendre que les faits de langue se développement d'une manière particulière à l'intérieur d'un système autonome, indépendant des autres faits sociaux. La lexicologie réprouve absolument une telle conception: elle se refuse à être isolée des études sociologiques.'[3] Patterns of vocabulary are constantly undergoing change because new social patterns are constantly emerging: A chaque époque, à chaque génération se développe, selon un processus que la sociologie cherche à déterminer . . . une nouvelle situation sociale suscitant une nouvelle situation lexicologique.'[4] For these reasons Dr. Matoré is led to evolve a complex *hypothèse de travail* which while remaining largely synchronic in technique will allow for a historical perspective. To this end he proposes to establish a series of *synchronies* or cross-sections of vocabulary at given periods, each separated from the next by a lapse of time roughly corresponding to a generation, and to compare each *synchronie* with those adjacent to it in the historical progression.[5] It is assumed

1. *Méthode*, p. 65. It is instructive to observe how in one of Matoré's typical *champs notionnels*, e.g. that of *Art* and *Technique* about the year 1765 (*Méthode* . . . , p. 102) there are some groups of words which can be said mutually to delimit each other (*Métier-Technique-Art*), but the majority though remotely connected in their implications do not abut semantically upon their neighbours in the diagram (*Dieu-Nature-Art-Beau*; *Artiste-Couleur-Couleur locale*, etc.). This implies no weakness in the lexical sociologists' postulates, but if anything in those of the field theorists. One of Matoré's chief reasons for rejecting the semantic field as a framework for analysis is just the fact that concepts do not for the most part appear to form an articulate pattern in terms of related meaning; whereas words which ask to be considered together, which form a *Zusammenhang* for other reasons are often separated by what von Wartburg has called an 'écart . . . dans l'espace sémantique' (*Problèmes et méthodes*, 2nd edition, p. 178).

2. *Méthode* . . . , p. 89.   3. *Méthode* . . . , p. 93.   4. Ibid.

5. In terms of the distinction proposed by Professor M. A. K. Halliday, Matoré's approach is *historical* (involving the comparison of successive descriptive cross-sections) rather than *evolutionary* (diachronic or historical in the Saussurian sense). See M. A. K. Halliday, 'Systematic description in Grammatical Analysis', pp. 54–60 of *Studies in Linguistic Analysis*, Oxford, 1957, pp. 54–6.

that a regular rhythm of change is detectable from one generation to another and that this recurring reaction against the past is an immanent social reality.[1]

Many of the pronouncements upon points of general principle which Matoré makes as a preamble to his *méthode* throw light upon questions we ourselves have to confront in explaining Franco-Italian loans and are at the time confirmed by our observations. His interpretation of the recip.ocal effect of thought upon language and of cultural development upon vocabulary presents a body of doctrine which the student of language contacts can follow and apply with approval. Borrowings are of course only a small part of the lexicon, a minor source of neologism,[2] but they can be fitted in perfectly well to a sociologically orientated *synchronie* as isolated elements and are often very revealing when placed in such a context. However, the *hypothèse de travail* itself has run the gauntlet of many attacks during the past fifteen years. I have stated my own objections to the *idée de génération* elsewhere;[3] if this article of the hypothesis is rejected, social change has no more privileged a status than that of being an individual aspect of the progression of history, and the *méthode* loses the synchronic basis (comparison of successive synchronies) which distinguished it from other ways of drawing a parallel between words and historical events. Those lexicologists who feel that changes in lexis can be explained adequately by relating neologisms directly to the facts of history will not think the loss of immanent pattern serious. And one has to go along with them a considerable way. I need not repeat here the criticism of the 'lexico-cultural parallel' method which was sketched out earlier in the methodological chapter except to emphasise that despite its shortcomings it has a great deal of practical merit. It forms the staple, so to speak, of any attempt to explain vocabulary in terms of external events.

1. 'Tout se passe comme si, à des dates relativement régulières et pour des raisons complexes . . . une génération privilégiée remettait brutalement en question, en accédant à la vie sociale, les représentations collectives de la génération précédente' (*Méthode*, p. 58).

2. For a picture of lexical resources as a whole see E. Pichon: 'L'enrichissement lexical dans le français d'aujourd'hui', *Le Français Moderne*, III (1935), pp. 209–22, 325–44. Cf. also Cesarotti's *cinque fonti* of lexical replenishment: *il fondo della lingua già ricevuta e approvata* (including derivation and similar procedures), *i dialetti nazionali, la lingua latina, la Grecia, le lingue straniere* (*vide* Cesarotti, *Saggio sulla filosofia delle lingue applicata alla lingua italiana*, 1800, Part III, section XIII. To our knowledge no figures have been published of the relative proportions of each source. A statistical check based on our material indicates that so far as French is concerned total foreign borrowings excluding those from the Classical tongues make up about one-tenth or one-twelfth of the lexicon. Italianisms account for about one in forty to forty-five of the total lexicon. The proportion in everyday speech would be appreciably smaller, especially if word-frequency were to be taken into account (though Franco-Italian loans are far from esoteric).

3. *Trans. Philol. Soc.*, 1964, p. 53–4.

Part Two of the present survey exemplifies and, I should hope, justifies the approach up to the very bound of its practical limitations. But its shortcomings are seen very clearly in a lexicological method like this, where everything hinges on the word's exemplification of social reality and intra-linguistic relationships are rejected most categorically. Further, is it in fact true that word-patterns are immediately referable to states of society? It would seem that lexicologists have accepted too readily the proposition that *tout mot vient à son heure*. Societies evolve; are we to understand that lexical patterns respond instantly to social evolution? This could only occur if social and lexical mechanisms were indissolubly combined within a wider *Gestalt*; now though language may be likened in many ways to an institution like that of society, and though it does happen that attitudes, beliefs, notions of vital importance to social structure are realised in operative form only by the process of lexicalisation, it nevertheless remains true that language transcends any other institution or group of institutions in important respects—that it is different in kind from them in certain essentials. One detects an undue preoccupation too with *words*—perhaps because the author accepts without question a triadic or analytical definition of the linguistic sign—when in fact content may be signified by patterns longer than that of the individual term.

The sociological approach is capable of being applied over very wide areas of vocabulary. Most neologisms, loan-words included, can be related to social innovations if we think of these more precisely as the result of human behaviour—new aspirations, inventions, shifts of moral, aesthetic, spiritual values and so on.[1] A place in the *schema* can for instance be found for adjec-

1. Like the changing moral and spiritual attitudes, the differing emphasis placed upon different qualities which bring about those lexical readjustments investigated by Trier in his classical *wisheit-kunst-list* study. Cf. also in this context Professor K. J. Hollyman's description of the inter-related lexical group *fief-alleu-foedus* in conjunction with other terms of feudal tenure (op. cit., p. 41-5). Hollyman's analysis of feudal terms is one which employs a strictly sociological approach while dispensing with any theoretical apparatus akin to Matoré's synchronic *coupe*—necessarily, since the sample of words handled is, like loan-words, only a fragment of the lexical totality. He does not pretend to analyse language, or even to analyse by means of language, but simply to replace language into its proper background—'replacer le langage dans son milieu' (op. cit., p. 2)—i.e. to consider the effect of social changes upon the speaker and hence upon a certain area of vocabulary. What might in a general way be termed a 'social' approach is traditional among most lexicologists formed by French universities. One associates it especially with the work of R. Léon Wagner and the many whom he has inspired: the reader is referred to the extensive bibliographies of modern lexicology in his *Introduction à la linguistique française* and *Supplément*, Geneva-Lille, 1955; also to his book *Les Vocabulaires français*, Paris, 1967 and works discussed or cited there. A second important focus of lexical research is the Centre d'Études du Vocabulaire français at Besançon, which we have already mentioned, associated with the name of Professor B. Quemada, which publishes the *Datations et documents lexicographiques* and the *Cahiers de lexicologie* (see Bibliography), whose contributors represent a good proportion of the progressive

tives and verbs, whose signification by definition tends to be abstract since they are applied to qualities and activities, for the reason that society at a given moment may commend, condemn or otherwise be interested in these qualities or activities. The same applies to a majority of 'abstract substantives' in the traditional grammarians' sense. Eighteenth century Gallicisms in Italian illustrate this well. One has only to visualise the social situations which motivate the transfer from French of Italian *civilizzazione, concorrenza, cosmopolito, deismo, ottimismo, patriottismo,* or even abstracts associated with apparently timeless entities such as mental or aesthetic qualities—*genio, gusto, sensibilità, spirito* (as a semantic calque of *esprit*). The associations evoked are a fair cross-section of the preoccupations of *illuministi* and *philosophes*: the discussion about natural religion; pan-europeanism contrasted with nationalism; principles of perfectability and of economic *laisser faire* along with many others. So patent is their historical relevance that most of these would qualify to be classed in Matoré's terminology as *mots-témoins* of the *synchronie* to which they belonged.

There is a heterogeneous group of borrowed words, however—quite small, but with an importance far in excess of its numerical strength[1]—which is hard to present as a 'reflet de la société', either 'objectivement, comme des réalités indépendantes de l'individu', or 'subjectivement, en fonction d'êtres vivant dans un milieu concret, dans certaines conditions sociales, économiques, politiques, esthétiques'.[2] Most of them are words like *dettaglio, facoltà, faciliter, manquer, risorsa,* i.e. what may be described as analytical, logical or relational terms. These five examples are substantives and verbs, but the problem is illustrated equally well by others of our abstract-general-emotive contingent. Adverbs are a case in point, in particular those whose value is grammatical or functional rather than cognitive or descriptive, e.g. *troppo, immantinente, attualmente* rather than *volentieri, brutalmente.* All these words (a) show a high degree of abstraction and/or (b) have a high frequency of use (c) are semantically divorced from the historical and cultural circumstances of their

---

lexicologists active at the present day. Sometimes a particular social theory is invoked: cf. Marcel Cohen, *Linguistique et matérialisme dialectique* cited earlier.

What we ourselves are interested in here, however, is the conception of a socio-lexical totality evolved by Matoré, rather than research on the lexicon of limited social or economic groups, technologies and so on. In actual fact Matoré's *méthode* itself has been remarkably little used; those originally most concerned with it have tended to move towards the elaboration of semantic theories, especially semantic universals (*vide* Matoré, *L'Espace humain*, Paris, 1964; Greimas' *Sémantique structurale* cited above, and the various works by K. Baldinger, B. Pottier and E. Coseriu referred to by R. L. Wagner, *Vocab. franç.,* esp. p. 167.

1. Approximately 2 per cent of the total.
2. *Méthode,* p. 92.

borrowing. We might in fact speak of a *problem of non-historical terms* which is endemic in lexico-cultural analysis. There are even some concrete substantives which have to be assigned to this category; these possess characteristics (b) and (c) in common with the abstracts, for example Fr. > It. *bastardo, gorgia, roccia, sentiero, villaggio*. They are non-technical, specific, directly referable terms in everyday use (and whose frequency is therefore appreciably higher than that of terms in restricted languages).

It is appropriate at this stage to note that methods of lexical description which envisage vocabulary as a *Gestalt* or totality are not the only ones affected by the problem of non-historical terms. Lexicologists who set out to interpret borrowings by resorting to the formula 'le mot est importé avec la chose.'[1] i.e. those who apply onomasiological methods to lexical contacts, find themselves even more at a loss when confronted by loans of this character. One must add to avoid misunderstanding that this in no way invalidates a *Wörter und Sachen* approach to borrowed material. It merely imposes a precise limitation upon it. The method is not at all a naïve one; a simple statement that words may be described and construed with reference to the things they denote or, translating this into the sphere of lexical interference, that words and things are borrowed simultaneously is only the factual basis of which the onomasiological method rests, the point from which development starts. How sensitive these procedures can be is shown, for example, by Dr. P. J. Wexler's study on French railway terminology borrowed from English,[2] which among other methodologically useful animadversions reminds us that the circumstances in which a technical neologism is created are no less complicated than those, say, in which a word connoting a mediaeval spiritual concept develops, while the light shed on linguistic principle may be notably brighter.

It nevertheless remains true that the practice of 'checking the pattern of names against the correlated patterns of things named'[3] is most effective when applied to concrete vocabularies, where there are material things or observable processes whose identity and development can be studied objectively.

To return to the *non-historical* terms. A sociological approach is not entirely inapposite even with regard to these. Given sufficiently detailed information one might be able to present a historical account of their transfer which would reveal some individual's influence upon the language or which would show them to have been casually implicated in some cultural movement on a wide front. One might equally well draw attention to their standing as signs of an intense foreign influence (which they undoubtedly are) and

---

1. Cf. Hollyman, op. cit., p. 17 and ibid., n. 9.

2. The section on *Motifs et méthodes* (op. cit., pp. 7–12) is specially relevant for us. Cf. also P. J. Wexler, '*FREIN*: the naming of the vehicle-brake', *Cahiers de Lexicologie*, Vol. 5 (1964), II, pp. 69–83.

3. Yakov Malkiel, 'Etymology and Word-families', *Linguistics Today*, p. 145.

therefore of a special kind of sociological phenonemon. But words such as these invite a more immediate explanation than that which the social structure affords; one which has to do with the status of the linguistic sign rather than its content or extra-linguistic associations.

Since the demands and impulses of social groups mould language more than any other factor or set of factors, the sociological approach to lexicology as a whole and therefore to the sub-section of that discipline dealing with the mechanism of interference has very much to recommend it. It enables one to apply the same closely knit, practically verifiable criteria—the pattern of human behaviour in society—to a broad range of linguistic situations. But unfortunately not to every linguistic situation, nor even to every lexical situation, despite some of its sponsors' claims. Applied to our material it proves less efficacious in respect of exactly those examples of lexical interference which we sense to be most significant linguistically, even though they may be inconsiderable in number, irrelevant historically and uninformative culturally. Though we may not agree with the field theorist that semantic patterning is all-important, the structural aspect undoubtedly has its claims and we must take it into account. Loan-words are lexical components as well as cultural tokens. They demand to be appraised in their own right, according to lexical principles. In this domain as elsewhere lexicologists have both a right and an obligation to proceed pragmatically, adapting the most appropriate existing methods to suit their special needs.

THE CHANGING PATTERN OF VOCABULARY. EXTRINSIC AND INTRINSIC FACTORS

Since current theories about vocabulary as a functional pattern or *Gestalt* and as an immediate reflection of extra-linguistic structures leave something to desire from our point of view we find ourselves obliged to fall back upon an older, less sophisticated approach to provide the overall scheme of classification needed. The time-honoured conception of *lexical defectivity* or *inadequacy* remedied by the creation of neologisms is such a one.[1] Though often invoked in a superficial way this interpretation of lexical change was never developed to its full potential in the past. With the *critique* of the foregoing pages in mind I shall attempt to re-cast it and use it to provide a

1. See Nyrop, op. cit., Vol. IV, pp. 444–51, *Insuffisance des mots*, esp. para. 612ff. Von Wartburg also uses the term *insuffisance*, though in a slightly different context: 'Là où une insuffisance se produit dans un système d'expression linguistique la langue se trouve poussée par cette insuffisance même à effectuer une modification destinée à l'abolir' *Prob. et méth.*, p. 148 (speaking of Gilliéron's part in showing the interdependence of linguistic events). See also Devoto, *Fondamenti . . .* , pp. 16–19, where he discusses the lack of parallelism between *lo strumento linguistico* and *la sostanza espressiva*, noting the contrasting points of view of those who maintain that language is a defective medium of expression and those who insist that it is automatically adequate to its needs.

taxonomy in which to locate organically the differing factors, circumstances, impulses which motivate borrowing in our two cultural languages.

Vocabulary taken as a whole may usefully be defined as a very numerous, largely unrestricted collection of linguistic signs or habits of association familar to and shared by members of a given social group which serves to denote, describe, order or actualise various aspects of 'the world outside'— what the late Professor Firth evocatively called 'the general mush of goings-on'—and used for a number of purposes proper to language.[1]

As an *entrée en matière* consonant with traditional defectivity hypotheses we may imagine that the basic situation prevailing in lexis at any given time is one in which there exists a varying differential between cultural circumstances in the broadest sense and the resources of vocabulary available.

The first refinement which needs to be incorporated into the concept of defectivity is a distinction between *extrinsic* and *intrinsic* causes of insufficiency.

A large proportion of words in our list have to do with innovations which arise from the constant force of change operating in the world at large. Some of these changes—inventions, discoveries, new techniques—are such that one may take cognisance of them objectively by employing the recognised procedures which historians have evolved. This is ideally the domain of word-and-thing analysis, of onomasiological methods, and we have already given a sufficiently full account of many of our borrowings by comparing lexical renewal with material innovations in this way. The lexico-cultural parallel fits into our model best at this point, with all its advantages and its accompanying pitfalls.[2] Sometimes it is not immediately apparent that there has been a shift of content and one has to investigate closely to appreciate that an extrinsic shift has taken place, e.g. *caporal* replacing *dizenier*; *soldat* ~ *sou-*

1. These purposes have often been defined. What we have to remember is that they are extremely diverse. They include, apart from communication or exchange of information in the sense customarily stressed by linguists, (a) communication of feelings, i.e. the inspiration and evocation of feelings in others, (b) intellectual analysis, (c) expression of personality, (d) fulfilment of aesthetic impulses, (e) participation in the ritual of life as a social being and betokening one's 'nearness' to one's fellow-men, i.e. the 'phatic' aspect of language.

2. Errors to which the lexico-cultural parallel is prone are not so immediately apparent as its advantages, but they are no less real. They arise from incomplete documentation, faulty interpretation of the linguistic environment as a whole (failure to account for coincidental interference of other languages, e.g. Latin, etc.) and failure to gauge the social and psychological motives for borrowing correctly (*vide* Hope, *Arch. Ling.*, XIV, fasc. 2, 116–20). Further illustrations of the latter are 17th cent. Fr. *gothique* (< It. early 16th cent. *gotico*), which one might at first sight expect to find examples of in the Middle Ages, but which appears two or three centuries later than its ostensible referent (its true referent is the Renaissance concept of or attitude towards that earlier architectural period); and, similarly, Fr. *baroque* referring to a 16th–17th cent. style of art or architecture (actually crystallised in this sense during the first half of the 19th century.)

doyer, homme d'armes; calamite ~ cadran marin ~ marinette ~ boussole.[1] Often
the operative process is not *innovation* in the strict sense but *reassessment* of
existing concepts or conceptual denotata. As an ideal of manly status the
chevalier (whence It. *cavaliere*) gave way to the *preux d'homme* in the later
Middle Ages (> It. *prod'uomo*), while by the sixteenth century the latter,
together with the *chevalier* as the embodiment of courtly behaviour, the
exponent of courtoisie, had both been superseded by a Renaissance ideal
of Italian origin, that of the *cortegiano* (Fr. *courtisan*). *Politezza*, echoed
in the sixteenth century by French *politesse*, was a different conception of
courtesy from twelfth–thirteenth century *cortesia* derived from France
together with the word which denoted it (Fr. *courtoisie, corteisie*, Prov.
cortesia).

Intrinsic borrowings on the other hand are those whose motivation is to
be sought in the changing pattern of the receiving language. Here too, the
factors are diverse, but they may be exemplified by most *semantic shifts* in the
traditional sense applied to these changes from Bréal onwards. Euphemisms
and other types of *dynamic expression* illustrate the cycle of change which may
provide grounds for intrinsic borrowing very clearly. They are well represented in Franco-Italian loans, as in cultural borrowings from any source,
since the foreign word often affords just the degree of attenuation required.
The notorious 'euphemisms of decency' are there in strength: *gabinetto* < Fr.
cabinet; *ritirata* < *retrait(e)*, *luogo di decenza*, an interesting improvement upon
Fr. *lieux d'aisance* in which the creative resources of paronymic attraction are
exploited; Fr. *toilette* used in Italian as in other languages. That this sort of
psychological infection is not confined to recent times is shown by fourteenth
century It. *zambra* (< Fr. *chambre*) used in the sense of 'cesso' (*vide* mediaeval
Fr. > It. word-list). Other *foci* of semantic taboo are represented; illness and
death: mediaeval It. *mestiere* 'funeral obsequies' < Fr. *mestier* (métier), to which
corresponds *cortège* < It. *corteggio*, nineteenth century It. *sofferente*; crime,
especially murder: fifteenth century *boucon* 'poisoned draught' < It. *boccone*
(It. *acquetta* was used in French too); illegitimacy: mediaeval It. *bastardo* <
OFr. *bastart* (*bâtard*) and so on. There are a number of pornographic terms: It.
bordello < *bordel*, *maccherella* < MFr. *maquerelle*; eighteenth century Fr.
casino, casin 'brothel, gaming-house', nineteenth century It. *cocotte, demi-
monde, casa di tolleranza*, etc. Among more unexpected subjects for euphemism
we have the idea of 'failure', which seems to have developed its taboo associations in the early nineteenth century, witness *fiasco* borrowed by French
(originally for a theatrical 'flop'), while the same word in Italian tended to be
replaced by *insuccesso* (Fr. *insuccès*) in similar contexts. Usury, a practice
repugnant to the mediaeval, produced a copious batch of neologisms includ-

1. Numerous instances are to be found among cases of what we have termed *synonym
sequence* (*vide supra*, Part Four, *Synonymy and Near-Synonymy*).

Z

ing It. *civanza* < Fr. *chevance* 'substance, means' as Franco Sacchetti tells us: 'Hanno battezzato l'usura in diversi nomi, come dono di tempo, merito, interesso, cambio, *civanza*, baroccolo, ritrangolo e molti altri nomi' (Crusca).

Our lists remind us that euphemisms are not the only category of dynamic or *inherently defective* signs. Any term whose semantic function is hyperbolical or depends upon affective impact is prone to rapid obsolescence, e.g. words used to connote acts or events which in various ways over-step the accepted norm, such as acts of violence or fraud: mediaeval Fr. > It. *carnaggio*; nineteenth century *massacrare* (< Fr. *massacre(r)* derived from OFr. *macecle*, *maçacre* 'butcher's shop'—cf. parallel English development of *shambles*); mediaeval Fr. > It. *abusione, birba, furba, ciurmare, oltraggio, sorchietanza*; sixteenth century Fr. > It. *mangeria*; It. > Fr. *supercherie, burle* in the same period.[1]

We may include under intrinsic situations the semantic restriction commonly known as *pejoration*, or rather those manifestations of this complex phenomenon in which one may observe an automatic trend towards obsolescence in respect of the original sign, a movement from neutral or stable signification to dynamic signification similar to that which characterises euphemism.[2] Immanent pejorative shifts are foremost among the circumstances which cause *manquer* and *contraste* (I choose two clear-cut examples) to be borrowed in sixteenth century French.

According to Henri Estienne, writing in 1565, the 'native' and therefore

1. A wealth of near-synonyms indicates that in this sphere there is a recurring need to replace significatory habits whose semantic yield has diminished. A recent M.A. thesis for the University of Manchester indicated that in Middle French prior to 1500 the lexical field comprised more than a hundred items (G. C. Birkett, *The Words for Deceit, Treachery and Promise-Breaking in Middle French*, 1966 [unpublished]). See also J. D. Schleyer, *Der Wortschatz von List und Betrug im Altfranzösischen und Altprovenzalischen, Romanistische Versuche und Vorarbeiten*, 10, Bonn University, 1961. Cf. Panzini's remarks on the 'modernity' and acceptability of It. *mistificare*, borrowed from Fr. *mystifier* (19th cent. list), in preference to older terms. I am inclined to see a similar inherent defectivity in words denoting magnificence, grandiosity and related superlatives, e.g. 18th cent. It. > Fr. *grandiose, grandiosité*, 16th cent. *signalé*, 19th cent. Fr. > It. *pretenzioso*.

2. In my model as I have disposed it here, reassessment of concepts through extrinsic influences which is directly reflected in a new pattern of neutral lexical signs and, on the other hand, lexical shifts which have their origin in a similar lexical adjustment, but are complicated by pejoration, appear on opposite sides of the intrinsic/extrinsic polarity. Both phenomena are grounded in the same continuum of psycho-sociological fact, since both may ultimately be traced back to revised attitudes and shifts of interest within social groups (and so of course in the last resort may most other forms of lexical innovation), but there is a natural, a real distinction to be detected here at the semantic level which justifies our drawing a dividing line at this point. The intrinsic/extrinsic polarity which this distinction helps to authenticate also provides its own inherent justification on grounds of its heuristic value.

'correct' equivalent of the Italianism *manquer* 'to lack' is *défaillir*.[1] *Faillir* and *défaillir*, together with the periphrasis *être en défaut*, were the accepted terms during the Middle Ages for both 'to lack, be short of' and 'to fail'. By the early sixteenth century *défaillir* is clearly attested in the sense 'to fall short, be found wanting' (from an ethical standpoint). Already in the thirteenth century *failli* (p. part. and adj.) had assumed the pejorative implications of 'broken, done for' whence 'unreliable, treacherous, faint-hearted'.[2] In the early sixteenth century *défailli* in turn begins to show the same pattern of dynamic-pejorative change and forms collocations in synonymous pairs with *caduc, lâche, mou, vaincu*. The shift from 'lack' to 'fall short' is a natural polysemic modification one meets with in other languages (cf. Germ. *fehlen*, Eng. *to fail*). It is likely, however, that the use of the verb, on which the main onus of signification rested since *faillir* had come to be affected by the paronymic impact of *falloir*, would not have materially altered had not the idea of 'falling short' become linked during the Reformation with that of religious apostasy and falling from grace. Available as a neutral term and well known to bilingual Valois courtiers in its Italian form, *manquer* quickly came to be employed in contexts where *défaillir* and *faillir* had formerly been usual.[3]

French *contraste* < It. *contrasto* enters usage in the mid-sixteenth century and is soon attested widely in texts. Von Wartburg dates the verb from 1541; the substantive *contraste* was probably in use by the turn of the century, though authorities give the first example as in Montaigne. Its function is that of a neutral term denoting opposition, resistance, then argument, debate, struggle (but typically with an abstract, objective implication).[4] In this capacity it meshes in closely with a number of near-synonyms, some long-established, but remains distinct chiefly in respect of its non-committal semantic status[5] from *débat, contestation, lutte* and others, with which it

1. *Traicté de la Conformité du Langage François avec le Grec*, ed. Léon Feugère, Paris, 1853, preface, p. xxii.

2. Examples in *La Vie de Saint-Édouard le Confesseur, Huon de Bordeaux*, etc. *Vide* Godef., III, 701. The sense 'wretched, woe-begone' is still current at the end of the Middle Ages; cf. Villon's famous *croquis* of himself as 'triste, failly, plus noir que meure' (*Gr. Testament*, v. 179).

3. *Manquer* is attested in 1546: there is evidence that it was widely current soon after the mid-century. It may have entered a little earlier in view of attestations of the substantive *manque*. See word-list.

4. 'Opposition, resistance to an advancing army' in Monluc; esp. *faire contraste à* as equivalent to *tenir tête a q'qu'un*. *Sans contraste* is a frequent collocation, implying 'without resistance' (surrender of a castle) in Pasquier, 'without debate, *nem. con.*' of an election, also in Pasquier; 'without difficulty or learned scruples' in Montaigne ('ceci ne s'en va sans contraste').

5. The phrase *Un doux contraste*, for instance, may be used without semantic contradiction (= 'mild reproof, gentle admonition'; *vide* Hug., *s.v.*).

frequently appears in homoionymous or amplificatory pairs (*débat et contraste, contrastes et altercations* [i.e. discussions as to a certain line of action], etc.[1]). It was accepted in the sixteenth century that the substantive *contention* was the original equivalent of *contraste*;[2] its development from a neutral term meaning 'rivalry, emulation (*Ch. de Roland*), striving, effort towards a certain goal', whence 'struggle, contention' to a pejorative one meaning 'subversive activity, wrangling, dissension of a reprehensible kind' may be traced back into the Middle Ages, but is mainly attributable to the earlier sixteenth century and the influence of contexts which have sedition and heresy as their theme.[3] At this point the way is open for a new, contextually uncommitted term: the Italianism *contraste* is borrowed and for a number of decades performs the main significatory function in this area.

The defectivity of signs available in the 'lexical storehouse', as Jakobson termed it, is endemic, self-perpetuating both extrinsically and intrinsically. The constant march of events and socio-cultural innovations is an obvious cause of potential inadequacy from the former standpoint. So is *décalage* or time-lag in certain of the acceptations we specified in our methodological discussion above.[4] On the intrinsic side we have already cited good examples of inherent defectivity in euphemisms and other dynamic terms, a sector of lexis which needs to be extended considerably beyond what has in the past gone under this rubric, or rather what has been envisaged under some other terms roughly implying what 'dynamic' means for us. The chronic defectivity is also intrinsic because certain of the semantic shifts occur inevitably as a side-effect of impulses whose primary aim was to heighten the effectiveness of language for the tasks it has to perform. Imagery and various forms of figurative expression (including those grouped together as 'figures of speech') all have a linguistic function in common: they are expressive devices which

---

1. The verb *contendre*, for example, as opposed to *contraster*, implies something nearer to 'perverse or misdirected opposition' ('Il luy fut dit . . . que s'il persévéroit à contendre ainsi contre raison et vérité, qu'il viendroit à mauvaise fin' [Calvin, *Lettres*; Hug., 478a]) or 'to impugn', esp. when used transitively ('contendre l'honneur de q'qu'un' [Hug.]). The homoionym *conteste*, on the other hand, is limited in its applicability by certain legal associations which are still more clearly discernible in the verb *contester*.

2. Cf. Pasquier's testimony cited in word-entry.

3. For further details see *Trans. Philol. Soc.*, 1964, pp. 63–4. The field of *contention-contraste-lutte* is of absorbing interest and deserves to be investigated more fully. A lot remains to be discovered about the semantic link with *combat, débat, conteste, dispute* and the corresponding verbs, adverbs and adjectives, but it appears that *contraste* and *conteste* entered use at much the same time and had for some time roughly the same opportunity to become dominant in the basic contexts, together with *débat*, which was of course established very much earlier.

4. In particular the third type of time-lag mentioned there, the interval which elapses while a borrowed word (or other neologism) is making its way into general usage. See Part One, end of 'Presentation of word-lists' section.

stimulate and even oblige an interlocutor to take an active part in the process of communication (or the social ritual of conversation, or any other branch of language's business). They serve to whet the sharp edge of language, keeping its purpose bright.[1] But this refurbishing process, this act of stimulation and rejuvenation has its negative side, as is well known. What was at first idiosyncratic, an individual *trouvaille* may gain wider acceptance and establish a new *signifiant-signifié* association, with the result that the former significatory habit becomes increasingly unfamiliar and falls into abeyance.

A good example of metaphor and shift of significatory patterns is provided by two of our non-historical loans, It. > Fr. *posture* and *attitude* (sixteenth and seventeenth century respectively). Both indicate the taking up of a moral or intellectual position, generally with respect to other people. Lexis commonly actualises these relationships by a series of anthropomorphic metaphors inspired by the stance of a human being, as in English *standing, standpoint, status, footing* and the like. French *posture* meaning 'disposition of mind, attitude' was a metaphor of this kind drawn from Italian and first attested in Montaigne; it was first supplemented, then gradually replaced in a majority of contexts, by a second borrowing from Italian *attitude* which first appears strictly as a term of the fine arts in a letter written by Nicolas Poussin in 1637.[2] Other instances of lexical readjustment following metaphorical shift in our lists are mediaeval Fr. > It. *freccia* (< *flèche*), which was supported in its movement to Italian by the use of the original Italian word *saetta* in the transferred sense of 'lighting', and also the subsequent history of French *contraste* implying 'struggle, contention' which we spoke of a little while ago. The notion of 'contrast' meaning 'juxtaposition of forms, colours, etc., in order to heighten their effect' can be rendered effectively by a metaphorical use of words implying 'to conflict, contend', and Fr. *contraste(r)* came to be applied in this way during the seventeenth century, again within the realm of fine art in the first place. The restriction of *contraste* to technical contacts, followed by its reappearance in general usage meaning 'comparison of any like entities in order to bring out their differences' coincides closely in time with the extension of Fr. *lutter*

1. For further observations upon this phenomenon see Ullmann, *Semantics*, pp. 212–18 and sources cited.

2. See my article in *Trans. Philol. Soc.*, loc. cit., pp. 68–9 and word-entries in Part Two above. In Fr. *posture* (< It. *postura* or *positura*) there is some evidence that a figurative use was beginning to develop in Italian itself at the time of borrowing; in the case of *attitude* (< It. *attitudine*) the transfer of meaning seems to have post-dated borrowing, and to have been carried into general usage because of the prestige enjoyed by the fine arts in the higher, linguistically dominant levels of French society. As in all our examples the basic impulses leading to semantic change are mixed; here we find an effect of pejoration in respect of *posture* working in the same direction as the intrinsic tendency to metaphorical expression.

to abstract contexts. Prior to the seventeenth century *lutter* (OFr., MFr. *loitier, luitier* dating back to the *Chanson de Roland*) essentially meant the sport of wrestling, hand-to-hand combat, and occasional examples of its use meaning mental strife are clearly figurative.[1]

When because of extrinsic changes or ambiguity traceable to an intrinsic source a lexical sign becomes deficient in respect of its original semantic value it might in theory be said that there exists in the new overall semantic pattern a semantic gap, or, to use the metalanguage of descriptive linguistics, a *case vide*. In practice however the concept of a 'hole in the pattern'[2] of significatory resources, whatever interpretation one lays upon it, cannot be applied to lexis to gain the kind of methodological advantage that it affords, say, in phonemic analysis, ultimately because of a difference in nature between the two linguistic levels. Taken literally the idea of a *case vide* in the lexicon is quite misleading. The resources of lexis can never be defective or interrupted in the absolute sense since the very nature of language as an articulated system of signs ensures that it is capable of framing new utterances with which to handle any new situation that might arise. Communication and expression draw upon many expedients. Outside language, gesture, ostention and calling attention to the mute evidence of physical circumstances all play a part. Linguistically they may entail the use of phrases or periphrases of varying complexity. Sixteenth century French purists and their fellows in nineteenth century Italy are, we find, hardly ever at a loss to find some phrase (as opposed to a single word) which renders the sense of a foreign term adequately. Henri Estienne suggests (*un homme*) *sujet à ses fantaisies, qui a ses façons* instead of the Italianism *bizarre*. Fanfani and Arlia supported by other purists of the *Ottocento* put forward (or register as already in use) *cacciatore clandestino, di frodo* for the Gallicism *bracconiere*; *vita sregolata, il viver licenzioso* for *deboscia*; *lampada all'inglese* for *chinchè* (Fr. *quinquet*); *navigazione di spiaggia, litorale* or *di capo in capo* for *cabotaggio*, together with hundreds of similar expressions. All are presented as direct equivalents of single extraneous terms, not merely explanatory glosses of them.

1. Cf. Calvin, *Inst. Chr.* (1560), cited Hug.: 'Il a esté requis qu'il combatist contre les forces de l'enfer, et qu'il luitast comme main à main contre l'horreur de la mort éternelle'; or Montaigne, *Essais*, II, 11: 'Elle (sc. la vertu) demande un chemin aspre et espineux, elle veut avoir . . . des difficultez estrangères à luicter, etc.', where the passage as a whole consists of a series of bold, concrete images applied to an abstract moral situation. The earliest dating cited for Fr. *contraste* in a sense other than that of contest or struggle is usually 1669 in Molière with the technical artistic signification; but contexts may be found much sooner in which the word (especially the verb) is already well advanced towards its later metaphorical sense and may suitably be translated by 'conflict, clash, by dissonant with', e.g. 'contraster aux mœurs publiques' in Montaigne. See also *Trans. Philol. Soc.*, loc. cit., p. 70, n. 1.

2. *Vide* A. Martinet, 'Function, Structure and Sound-Change', *Word* VIII (1952), pp. 19ff.

The lexical defectivity is therefore relative only, not absolute. Diachronically, as a word shifts towards new acceptations, is used in new contexts, a periphrasis may be convenient to avoid misunderstanding; conversely a new situation created by any of the factors we have mentioned can be signified by an utterance framed for that purpose, but may require to be signified with increasing precision as the interim period progresses. Synchronically the question is not whether certain expressive resources exist or do not exist, but whether they are semantically adequate or not.

It is thus possible to envisage what we might call, drawing a metaphor from the realm of natural science, an *ecology* of vocabulary. At a given moment certain *denotata* may be signified comparatively inefficiently at the level of lexical units, though they are able *ex hypothesi* to be handled linguistically. There may exist, so to speak, an 'ecological niche' in which a more efficient term could maintain itself, that is, would commend itself by its utility to speakers of the language and be sanctioned by a sufficient body of the linguistic community to pass into usage. This conception offers several advantages over that of semantic gap or void, or the old theories of lexical inadequacy. It implies a lexical lacuna, but only in the special sense appropriate to our conception of lexical structure and the neological process, that is, one based on the principle of comparative efficiency rather than absolute defectivity; comparative efficiency between various signs or combinations of signs available at a given time, and in the case of loan-words, between indigenous signs or combinations of them and the significatory resources offered by a foreign language.

The ecological model, I suggest, provides us with a serviceable theoretical basis to build on. It is convenient scaffolding for the organised description of many diverse impulses and patterns inside and outside language which account for borrowing in languages of culture. Though simple it is not naïve, but on the contrary is capable of supporting a certain amount of theoretical amplification, though this is not our business at the present moment. One of its ingredients needs, however, to be expanded a little more fully, and that is the conception of *efficiency*. By efficiency I mean the aptness of vocabulary to respond to all the calls human beings make upon it in using language, i.e. to act as a means of self-expression as well as communication, as a tool for logical or intellectual activity, a medium of art, a gesture in social ritual and a label or *signum* for various purposes. Not infrequently it turns out that one of the functions other than factual communication accounts for a term's efficiency. Borrowed usages associated with several of the loan-homonyms and loan-synonyms cited earlier in our chapter on semantic loans were adopted solely because of their social overtones, their up to date or argotic flavour (*amasser* 'to slay', *fermer* 'to stop', *vague* 'beautiful', *caresse* 'darling', etc.). Their semantic efficiency—transient, as it turned out—resided in these marginal implications. Affective and aesthetic overtones may be efficient in a comparable way.

LEXICAL ECONOMY

An impulse towards economy appears to underlie shifts in the composition of vocabulary analogous in some ways to the immanent forces which some scholars recognise as the motive power behind phonological change. This naturally does not mean that we should assent to anything so formulaic as Bally's *univocité*, the principle that every lexical sign tends ideally to have a single *valeur*, and each *valeur* to be represented by one sign, and so on.[1] Nevertheless brevity does play a part in the economical distribution of lexical resources and consequently of borrowings, as purists' alternatives put forward to replace words of foreign origin show very well. To be fully efficacious as an equivalent a native term must be so both formally and semantically; the substitutes offered by purists inevitably fall short in one or other of these ways.[2] Typical entries in a puristic dictionary contain on the one hand single terms or succinct expressions which are formally and etymologically acceptable but semantically divergent, and on the other more or less extensive translation equivalents accurate semantically but cumbersome. Of the latter the vast majority are brief collocations, so that the interplay between the two lexical units *word* versus *collocation or syntagma* is what economy as a factor in lexical interference is chiefly about.[3] I have already cited examples of puristic equivalents some of which show a marked insensitivity to the need for terseness. We find Fanfani and Arlia for instance urging their readers to use *viaggiatore pedestre* for *turista* and *minuto ragguaglia* or *particolareggiata relazione* instead of 'il francese *détail*' (sc. the loan-word *dettaglio*).[4]

Inherently more important, however, is the economy that informs the choice and disposition of linguistic resources including those of lexis in the act of speech or thinking. Although this strategy, as we might call it, is idiosyncratic in the first place, the nature of social habits and their diffusion is such

1. Charles Bally, *Le Langage et la vie*, 3rd edition, Geneva–Lille, 1952, pp. 53–4.

2. Or both; cf. Rigutini's *matrona regolatrice* for *chaperon* (19th cent.).

3. For notes on economy and the borrowing of larger lexical segments in French and Italian (idioms, locutions, etc.) see *Trans. Philol. Soc.*, loc. cit., p. 74.

4. Henri Estienne, whose linguistic sensitivity is a little more profound and his political sentiments somewhat less so than Arlia's, has on the other hand a certain feeling for the economy of his phrases. Cf. his criticism of the Italianism *acconche* (*vide* 16th cent. list): 'Mais c'est grand cas que tous se soyent ainsi accoustumez à emprunter ce mot Italien *Acconcio*, veu qu'en usant du langage qu'ils ont apris de leur mère, ils peuvent exprimer la mesme chose en diverses sortes: tellement qu'ils ont à choisir. Car ils peuvent dire: *Il est bien en point*, ou *il est bien equippé*, ou *il est en bon equippage*, ou *il est bien en ordre*. Encores en pourroit-on trouver d'autres, si on voulait prendre peine de les chercher. Car on ne disoit pas seulemant *il est bien en point*, mais aussi, *il est bien accoustré de tous points*. Toutesfois le plus court, *Il est bien accoustré . . .* ' (*Dial.*, I, 62).

that there is a feed-back of new acceptable uses from individual *parole* through idiolect to language as a possession of the speech-community, i.e. to *langue*. This is common knowledge to psychologists as well as linguists. Use shapes linguistic tools. It would appear that economy at this level sets the significatory capacity of the individual lexical unit against that of the *ad hoc* periphrases—a general principle, again, which scholars have enshrined in their different versions of the *paradigmatic/syntagmatic* duality.[1] But a lot remains to be discovered about the shift from motivation to opacity in the lexical sign, and the relation between one sort of sign and another at the lexical level. A word, an accepted, conventional semantic counter is economical in that at the expense of the effort demanded by 'recall' it can neutralise a given portion of the reiterative material that requires to be handled when closely similar contexts tend to occur repeatedly, i.e. when the attention of society comes to be focused, to dwell insistently, upon particular concepts or contingencies in the world at large. As a result the intellectual faculty is left freer to handle that which has to remain motivated, or which most usefully remains so, i.e. the areas where 'generative' processes rather than pure recall have their optimal function.[2]

An 'ecological space' may be revealed, paradoxical though it may seem, by a profusion of synonyms in a given semantic sphere, indicating (a) a high pressure of usage in that area of signification (b) uncertainty as to whether any of the suggested terms really express the required meaning effectively, especially when an abundance of translation equivalents appears in a bilingual dictionary entry. As late as 1788 Alberti divided the signification of Fr. *tranquilliser* among nine equivalents: *tranquillare* (which has the widest range, and is the term favoured by purists who subsequently attempt to eradicate the Gallicism *tranquillizzare*), *calmare*, *quietare*, *pacificare*, *mitigare*, *acchetare*, *placare*, *sedare*, *attutire*. There is no sign of the foreign loan *tranquillizzare* < *tranquilliser* until the very end of the eighteenth century, but by the early nineteenth it has appeared and quickly become entrenched in usage.

1. A. Martinet, for example, *Éléments de linguistique générale*, Coll. Armand Colin, 2nd edition, 1961, section 6.6.

2. My use of recall and generation is the customary one and is conveniently defined by J. Lyons, *Structural Semantics*, p. 31: 'By "recall" I mean the reproduction of some complex from memory—taking it from "storage"; and by *generation*, the construction of a form by the individual speaker from elements which are themselves taken from "storage".' Recall takes place of course when any linguistic sign is employed, but the distinction between recall and generation as I am using it assumes that the element of recall in the latter is of secondary importance. What counts is that the precise semantic effect needed is in the first instance obtained directly by recall, in the second by the act of disposing certain elements which in themselves do not serve the semantic purpose required. And, to extend the metaphor of 'storage'—the items needed for generation are usually kept close at hand and are easily taken up when needed, whereas to obtain semantic precision by direct recall may require items to be drawn from areas of storage that are unfamiliar and hard to reach.

During the interim period, when a borrowed usage is gaining ground, qualified contemporary observers often give information about its progress, and consequently about the structural pattern into which it fits. Under Fr. *rendez-vous* Alberti tentatively suggests It. *assignazione, appuntamento*, then adds 'On se sert très-souvent du mot François, et l'on dit *Rendez-vous*'. The Italian French entry is equally revealing: '*Voce Francese, e dell'uso*. . . . Questa voce tuttochè alquanto strana è in uso presso varie nazioni, non trovandone altre più proprie ne' respettivi loro linguaggi.'

Bernardoni's *Elenco di alcune parole oggidì frequentemente in uso* . . . is a catalogue of incorrect usage intended chiefly for administrators of his day, that is of the Napoleonic period. But not all the instances of officialese cited met with Bernardoni's unqualified disapproval. He marked with an asterisk a number of words which though not accepted into the standard language are 'very expressive', and with a dagger those which are 'technical terms and consequently indispensable'. Among those which qualify for the asterisk are: *abbonarsi, -amento* 'to subscribe'; *aggiotatore* 'speculator'; *ambulanza*; *destituire, destitutione* 'to sack, strip of one's offices'; *intrapresa* 'undertaking', variously applied; *polizia*; *risultato* (here the author also invokes the support of literary usage); *statistica* 'detailed description of a country in all its parts', *vaccinare -azione*, and *processo verbale* (Fr. *procès verbal*). The 'indispensable technical terms' include *apprendere, -imento, -ensione* 'to confiscate', etc.; *bancarotta* 'bankruptcy' (for *fallimento frodolento*); *dimettere*, 'to sack', *dimissione* 'notice, resignation' (presumably a term more frequently used, as opposed to *destituire*, etc., above; *dimissionario* adj. 'one who resigns, is resigning' on the other hand is relegated to the limbo of unapproved usages); *licitazione* 'auction sale'; *manoforte* 'assistance'; *responsabile, -ilità*; *transigere* 'to compromise'; *vidimare -azione*, 'to authenticate, pass, stamp'. All these are confirmed or probable borrowings from French. Bernardoni himself recognises a Gallicism in most of them. As the *Capo di Divisione nel Ministero dell'Interno* was a man of insight and judgement in linguistic matters, the *Elenco* is a very suitable source from which to gather examples of French terms which satisfied a need in special languages of the revolutionary and Napoleonic periods.

Purists' efforts to find a suitable native word often end by demonstrating how appropriate the foreign word is and so confirm its intrinsic semantic value and its right to be accepted. Henri Estienne is prepared to allow that he is unable to find an equivalent to *supercherie* (< It. *soperchieria*), 'en la place duquel mot tant s'en faut que nous puissions mettre un autre, qu'à grand'peine le pouvons nous expliquer par periphrase'.[1] La Noue admits that the Italianism *leste* has no exact equivalent in French: 'leste . . . mot tiré de l'italien

---

1. *Dialogues*, I, pp. 101-2. Note that Estienne has a sense of the comparable value of words and periphrases.

auquel nous n'avons point de correspondant. Ils disent un soldat *leste*, à qui il ne manque rien en sa personne ni en son equipage'.[1] During the period of politically controlled purism in Italy immediately before the Second World War authorities were often hard pressed to find a simple Italian substantive by which to replace a *barbarismo*. It often happened that the substitute term officially favoured was a compound, e.g. *vigili di fuoco* for *pompieri* (law of 16th June 1938). At one point a ban on the word *bar* (ultimately from English, but via French) was relaxed after official investigation confirmed that no satisfactory native expression was available.[2]

There is in addition a formal aspect to be considered in assessing a loan-word's relative efficiency. Scholars have found out a great deal about a foreign word's phonetic and phonological integration into its new formal environment, largely through detailed field-work among migrant communities, and we ourselves in Part Three above have contributed some observations on Franco-Italian material. Yet once one moves away from objectively controllable phonological and morphological facts one finds that a number of mistaken ideas about formal interference continue to be widely held, especially if they seem to have a certain aphoristic quality, or to appeal to common sense. For example lexicologists habitually assume that words are more easily borrowed between cognate languages, the foreign form fitting more snugly into the native mould. There is a grain of truth in this, as our study has shown. But it is equally true that a word may be recommended by its phonetic eccentricity. Meaning is enhanced when an object or idea which is unusual or exotic is linked with an anomalous, bizarre form, e.g. It. *bastrè* < Fr. *bastringue* and *cancan*, used also in Italian (note that both are names of exotic dances), Fr. *sabayon* < It. *zabaglione* (exotic food), words like *loggia*, *sbire*, *charivaria* and many another. A loan-word's efficiency in this has a lot to do with its exotic aura, to which formal and semantic elements contribute jointly, and also to its aesthetic value. Interaction of form and content is seen very clearly in the history of the word *vendetta*, initially an exoticism, and still partially so, which Merimée Gallicised to *vendette* in his highly successful novel *Colomba* after its introduction into French some thirty years before in the Italian form. Despite his example the adapted form was not accepted, and the word remained current in its more evocative exotic guise. *Mafia* is a similar borrowing.

1. See Estienne, *Dial.*, I, 116.
2. Cf. the *Confederazione nazionale fascista dei commercianti's* report that 'In merito alla tassa sulle insegne in lingua straniera, e precisamente per quella che riguarda la parola *bar*, il ministro delle Finanze ha ammesso che i Comuni abbiano a esentare tale vocabolo dalla tassa sulle insegne in lingua straniera, perchè la parola *bar* non è perfettamente traducibile in italiano, dato che la corrispondente parola *taverna* non designerebbe affatto il tipo d'esercizio che ormai suole indicarsi col vocabolo *bar*' (cited Panz., *Diz. mod.*, s.v. *bar*).

Also fallacious is the theory that borrowed words are 'sterile', 'incapable of producing derivatives' in their new milieu.[1] Our own soundings enable us fully to endorse Wind's assertion that 'bien des mots d'emprunt viennent contredire l'opinion d'après laquelle la plupart des mots tirés des langues étrangères seraient inféconds . . . et tout en prenant racine, ne porteraient pas de rejetons'.[2] It is just conceivable that a bilingual who deliberately preserves the foreign pronunciation for some argotic or snobbish reason might hesitate to commit the barbarism of applying indigenous morphemes to the foreign base, but in normal conditions of linguistic usage, i.e. with monolingual speakers, a foreign word that has entered current parlance is accepted precisely on a par with other lexical items and its later developments are not aberrant.[3]

Paronymic attraction, which plays its part in shaping a loan-word formally, as we have seen, also intervenes in the 'ecological' pattern by virtue of the fact that influences of meaning on form have their counterpart in effects of formal association within lexical fields. There is a formal aspect to most of the lexical substitutions we have cited so far. The history of contendre/contraster/lutter owes something to that of OFr. contrester 'to withstand', documented from the Roland to the sixteenth century (but falling obsolete, we note, during the period before contraster was borrowed),[4] and of the back-formation contrest which dates from the fourteenth century. It is not beyond the bounds of conjecture to suppose that lutter remained restricted to physical activity and that polysemy in the direction of 'mental conflict' was inhibited, to some degree, by the well-known lutter/lutin/nuitin/Neptunus semantic complex.[5] The late Professor John Orr showed how the history of manquer

1. Cf. E. Bonnaffé, Dictionnaire des anglicismes passés dans la langue française, Paris, 1920, p. 22: 'Tandis qu'autour d'un mot français se groupe toute une famille, ceux-là (sc. les mots d'emprunt) sont isolés comme des étrangers' (cited by Wind). Also Bezzola, Abbozzo, p. 12: 'Un secondo indizio (that a word has been borrowed) noi lo troviamo spesso nella vitalità relativamente piccola del prestito; nell' incapacità di crearsi dei nuovi sensi e dei derivati.' Terlingen too seems to countenance the hypothesis (op. cit., p. 40). One contrary example out of many in French and Italian is the 13th century borrowing schifo, which had a more numerous 'progeny' in Italy than in its native country, e.g. schifare (Guittone), schiferià, schifiltà (Bocc.), schifiltoso (B. Davanzati), schifoso (Segneri), etc.

2. Op. cit., p. 22.

3. Sometimes formal efficiency implicates the 'word family' rather than the isolated word, as when a foreign source provides adjectival or agent derivatives to correspond to a native substantive, e.g. the Italianisms cardinalice (<It. cardinalizio) corresponding to cardinal (Latinism), ferroviaire (It. ferroviario) corr. to chemin de fer, aquafortiste (It. acquafortista) corr. to eau-forte, or the Gallicising adjective fondiario (Fr. foncier) corr. to fondo, fondi and probably manifatturiero (Fr. manufacturier), passionale (passionel: usual collocation, crime passionel), raziale (racial), volontario 'strong-willed' (volontaire).

4. Still current later in the 15th century, however, since it was borrowed at this point by English; cf. Caxton, 1498: 'He contrested or gaynstood him in bataylle' (OED).

5. An association between lutter and lutin is still present in Montaigne's mind, i.e. later 16th cent.: 'Aussi disoit-on que ce n'estoit qu'aux lutins de luitter contre les morts.'

(and hence *défaillir*) is linked to that of OFr.–MFr. *mentir* 'to break one's word, to fail someone', through congruence in certain registers at a given point in the verbal paradigm (*manquiez* ∼ *mentiez*),[1] and we have already referred to the *faillir/falloir* dichotomy. One could cite very many such instances. The fortunes of sixteenth century Fr. *réussir* (< It. *riuscire*), for example, are affected by those of its cognate OFr. *rissir*, *reissir*, though the latter had deviated semantically to a series of specialised uses during the Middle Ages.[2]

Despite the influence exerted at different points in the ecological schema by formal association, however, it is wiser all things considered to orientate one's analysis upon exclusively semantic points of reference, calling upon phonological or morphological criteria to support, extenuate or delimit one's deductions as the occasion requires rather than attempt a co-ordinated formal-cum-semantic analysis after the style of morpho-semantic field hypotheses.

LEXICAL ECOLOGY: THE COMPARATIVE ASPECT

In the last resort tactics adopted to impose order upon one's material derive from one or more of three traditional linguistic approaches—descriptive (synchronic), historical (diachronic) and comparative. So far we have exploited only the first two. Our conception as a whole is neological, i.e. historical, but we have profited from synchronic methods by using the evidence of a word's collocations, 'the company a word keeps'[3] to establish its meaning and have put forward a formulation of lexical economy founded on relative efficiency within lexis at a given moment of time. The 'ecological' model possesses in addition a comparative aspect.

Though borrowing is only one kind of neologism out of many it stands apart from other modes of lexical renewal in one particular respect: the symbol to be borrowed already exists and has proved itself to be viable in another lexical environment. There is no question of 'a concept or experience seeking linguistic expression'[4] when we are dealing with loan-words, nor is there any need to posit an 'interlingua of naked ideas from one language to another', as J. R. Firth ironically put it. An insufficiency is revealed and a borrowing promoted as a result of comparing two languages.[5] When

1. 'On Homonymics', *Studies Presented to M. K. Pope*, Manchester, 1939, pp. 260–6.
2. Cf. MFr. *reissue*, *rissue* 'afternoon'; also referring in some dialects to sundry scratch meals taken during the working day (*vide FEW*, III, p. 297).
3. The phrase is Professor Randolph Quirk's.
4. Hollyman, op. cit., p. 19, n. 1 and sources cited there.
5. Thus in its second, comparative, dimension also our ecological model of lexical interference is enabled to avoid what we recognised to be the major pitfall of field theory, viz., the notion of a concept *in vacuo*, in any state, that is, other than crystallised in the form of words.

Cesarotti complains that 'la lingua nostra, al paro delle altre, è povera in proporzione dei bisogni dello spirito, e domanda d'esser arricchita di nuovi termini'[1] he is not thinking of abstract, intellectual concepts *per se* which Italian was unable to express, but—prompted, no doubt, by the multilingual dictionary of a certain K. W. Buttner of Göttingen which he had recently read—drawing upon his knowledge of other languages which by comparison were richly endowed in that lexical area; and we can guess that French was very much in the front of his mind. To take the specific example of our *non-historical* terms: in the source language words like Fr. *ressource*, It. *riuscire*, Fr. *détail* acquired an enhanced value as lexical symbols when they developed in such a way that they attained their modern signification. In accepting the borrowings *risorsa*, *réussir*, *dettaglio* the receiving language turned an extraneous semantic pattern to good account. A lexical inequality between two languages ceased to exist; an inadequacy in one was remedied by adopting an advantageous mode of symbolisation from the other. This way of envisaging lexical neologism, we should note, is in step with sociologists' view of cultural progress as a 'transfusion de civilisation' resulting from an 'inégalité des sociétés'.[2] The study of lexical interference at the level of *langue* necessarily includes a comparative study of two or more sign-systems.

RELATIVE DIFFUSION OF LOAN-WORDS

There are a number of scholarly precedents for comparing the *relative diffusion* rather than the *provenance* of borrowings—comparing the contribution which words from one given source make to a number of other languages. Towards the end of last century a German scholar, F. Rümelin, worked out comparative figures for French loan-words in Dutch and German and reported that of about three hundred 'cultural' loan-words which passed from French into German there were only forty-two which failed to appear in Dutch also; i.e. six-sevenths of the borrowings in German are also in Dutch.[3] French, he surmised, had a certain contribution to make to civilisation which was naturally the same for all Western cultures; hence the remarkably close congruity. Our own lists provide excellent matter for a similar comparison in the diffusion of terms connected with the Italian Renaissance, one of the most

1. *Saggio sulla filosofia delle lingue*, Part III, section VII, p. 89.
2. Marcel Cohen, *Langage et transfusions de civilisation*, Annales sociologiques, 1943, Series E(3). Cf. Hollyman, op. cit., p. 17: 'Au point de vue social, la raison de l'emprunt réside dans le développement inégal des sociétés. La connaissance est une fonction différenciée entre les sociétés. Si l'on nomme *civilisation* les acquêts de la connaissance, alors on peut dire qu'il en résulte des transfusions de civilisation.'
3. F. Rümelin, *Die Berechtigung der Fremdwörter*, Freiburg i B. 1887. See Salverda de Grave, *Quelques Observations sur les mots d'emprunt*, p. 149. Stephen Ullmann's book *Europe's Debt to the English Language*, Royal Hungarian University Press, Budapest, 1940 has a similar aim (study of English words in Dutch, German, French and Italian).

telling contributions to European culture during the whole of our era. A large
number of words relating to the arts, architecture, commerce, warfare and
the like have their formal and semantic equivalents in French, Spanish,
English and other European languages. An excerpt from a trilingual list of
architectural Italianisms, for example, might run like this:

French	Spanish	English
niche	nicho	niche
piédestal	pedestal	pedestal
pilastre	pilastra	pilaster
relief	relieve	relief (relievo)
stuc	estuco	stucco, etc.

or military terms:

French	Spanish	English
bastion	bastión	bastion
bataillon	batallón	battalion
cartouche	cartucho	cartridge
casemate	casamata	casemate
cavalerie	caballería	cavalry, etc.

The parallel is not confined to technical terms but includes a broad range of
semantic categories, e.g. *courtisan* ∼ *cortesano* ∼ *courtesan* < It. *cortegiano*,
or *bravade* ∼ *bravata* ∼ *bravado* < It. *bravata*. Because of linguistic and cultural
differences English stands a little apart from Spanish and French, but between
the Romance languages even ephemeral terms and society jargon have their
parallels, e.g. Fr. *martel* ∼ Sp. *martelo* 'pang of jealousy, whim, caprice', < It.
martello; Fr. *salvatiquesse* ∼ Sp. *salvatiqueza* 'coarseness, boorishness', < It.
salvatichezza.

And yet this equivalence is by no means complete, though it appears to be
at first sight. There is an area of disparity between one language and another
which is easily overlooked for the good reason that negative criteria alone
reveal it, the absence of words rather than their presence. *Motto* 'device,
watchword' and *vista* (earlier *visto*) are current in English from the late sixteenth and mid-seventeenth century onward, but not in French. In the former
scorn < It. *scorno* prospered; in the latter it died out after a brief period of
use. Only the prestige of French enabled an Italianism like *riposte* to reach
England.[1] A number of the temporary Italianisms in sixteenth century
Spanish listed by Terlingen had no parallel north of the Pyrenees, however
ephemeral.[2] The abstract *fougue* obviously fulfilled a need in French, whereas

1. Transfer through intermediary languages introduces a measure of irregularity into
apparently symmetrical lists of technical nomenclature like the ones just cited.

2. Among them are the adjectives *sólito* 'accustomed, wonted', *mesto* 'sorrowful',
pazo 'mad', *esmarrido* 'bewildered, dismayed', *esdrújulo*, *esdrúchulo* 'proparoxytonic'
(referring initially to a verse ending in this kind of foot, < It. *sdrucciolo*), the substantives
trastulo 'toy, pastime' and *raguallo* 'comparison' (op, cit., s.v.).

in English It. *foga* was rendered when necessary by *mettle* (*metal*), *fire*, *spirit* or *heat* as well as a goodly number of more approximate equivalents. *Réussir* and *manquer* which so happily fill a *lacuna* in French have no analogues in Spanish.[1] Quite the contrary with It. *goffo* 'clumsy, boorish' (early sixteenth century, Cellini), which made its greatest impact in the Spanish peninsula, where *gofo* has maintained itself down to the present day and has had several interesting polysemic extensions of use in the past.[2] French *goffe* appeared in Geoffroy Tory's *Champfleury* (1529), defined with a passing reference to Italian usage as 'chose lourde et mal seyant', and was well entrenched as a fashionable catch-word over an extensive period in the later sixteenth and early seventeenth centuries, after which it gradually fell into obsolescence.[3] An example of a 'relational' term appearing only in English is *scope*, which the *OED* and other English authorities derive from It. *scopo*, 'a marke or but to shoot at, a scope, purpose, intent or room' (Florio, 1598), ultimately from Gk. σκοπός. It is attested in the '30s of the century.[4] No corresponding loan appears in French, where the same intellectual situation is handled at that time by using *portée* (dating from the twelfth century) and *étendue* (fifteenth century) or by resorting to extended constructions, e.g. *champ*, *liberté d'action*, *donner carrière à*, or again by periphrases based on *place* meaning 'space, room' available from the fifteenth century forwards.[5] The Spanish words which did duty in like contexts are *alcance* and *lugar*.[6]

Even where corresponding Italianisms are attested in all three languages the frequency of use in each may vary widely.

1. We are concerned in this context only with It. *mancare* in the figurative sense of 'to lack', not the original, etymological one of 'to maim' (cf. Sp. *mancar*) from which the abstract Italian signification developed.

2. Attested late 16th century, for example, as a term of fine art meaning 'dwarfish, stunted figure' in a painting.

3. In English of the same period *goff(e)*, or *guff* is actually found, but vary rarely ('A Goffe, fool, *morio, bardus*', Peter Levins, *Manipulus vocabulorum, A dictionarie of English and Latin Wordes*, 1570 [*OED*]).

4. Meaning 'room for exercise, opportunity or liberty to act', 1534 in an official report of Henry VIII which speaks of giving malefactors 'too great a scope of unreasonable liberty'. The sense 'implication or drift of an assertion' appears two years later in Archbishop Cranmer ('The scope and effect of both my sermons stood in three things' [*OED*, q.v. for further 16th cent. examples in a wide range of uses]). *To have scope, to give scope* (for) are common 16th cent. idioms.

5. In the sixteenth century there were also a number of established Latinisms which appear equally in French, Spanish and English, forming a common denominator of semantic resources, so to speak, which can be disregarded since it was available to all three languages. The most important are *opportunité*, first met with in Old French of the 13th century (Sp. *oportunidad* 1438, *opportunity* late MEng.; all three had developed from the original sense of 'the fact of being timely' to 'favourable moment, latitude for action' by the early 16th cent.) and *capacité*, c. 1350 (*capacidad* 1438, *capacity* 1480).

6. A Sp. *escopo* is actually found in Golden Age Spanish, but was very little used.

As I see it this lack of parallels at certain points in a homogeneous pattern of lexical diffusion, this semantic anisomorphism between different receiving languages, is open to interpretation in two totally different ways. In the first place, one may attribute the discrepancies—and for that matter the pattern of borrowing *in toto*—frankly to chance, to the random outcome of human behaviour and historical accident. We can fine down 'behaviour' in this context without too much difficulty to the apparently random activity of speakers and writers in the way they take up foreign words and incorporate them into speech and literature, and of the public in the way it chooses to pass them on and publicise them; 'historical accident' we may rewrite as the chance success of a particular publication, its author's relative influence for reasons remote from those of his linguistic or literary accomplishment, the fortune of external events which make cultural contact possible, and the like. On the other hand we may seek to explain lack of symmetry in certain areas as a result of differing needs in each borrowing language depending upon the pattern of lexical signs already available in each and their relative efficiency at a given moment. Thus one might experiment with the proposition that the success of It. *garbo* as a loan-word in French and Spanish, for instance, may have been due to a need for some further term expressing formal beauty, grace (Fr. *galbe*, initially *garbe*; Sp. *garbo*) accentuated by the loss in later mediaeval times of numerous items in the lexical field of beauty associated with *courtoisie* and courtly romance, e.g. Fr. *avenant, gent, coint*, etc.; whereas English, which quickly rejected *garb* (in its pristine sense of 'formal beauty') was well furnished with the traditional Germanic vocabulary applicable to this field—*lovely, comely, fair, handsome*, etc., and their derivatives.[1] Of the two standpoints I prefer the second, because it is consistent with the assumption that borrowing is capable of being interpreted rationally and organically: an assumption justifiable on grounds of practical necessity in the first place, since it is impossible even to rough out a working hypothesis if one assumes *a priori* that anarchy prevails, that regularities discernible in our material are fortuitous; but even more because the whole trend of our research indicates that an organic interpretation can be realised. We may therefore take it that the relative diffusion of borrowings, if handled circumspectly,[2] can tell us at

1. For details of attestations in Spanish and English see *Trans. Philol. Soc.*, 1964, pp. 81–2 and notes.

2. It is easy to see what safeguards will be needed to ensure accuracy. Evidence will be most acceptable when one is considering the repercussions of a clear-cut, homogeneous cultural influence between closely or fairly closely related social groups, and when the receiving languages which serve these related social groups are themselves closely related to the lending language—cognate, if possible. More distantly connected languages usually serve more diverse cultures—this is after all one of the reasons for greater linguistic divergence—and therefore the asymmetry attributable to what we might call the practical or historical accidents of transfer (see above) will be greater and harder to

least something and possibly a good deal about semantic anisomorphism in culturally related languages, and hence about the impact of intrinsic semantic patterning upon the adoption of foreign words.

We have already glimpsed in Parts Two and Four aspects of the problem posed by accidental, random or capricious impulses in borrowing. This is a perennial topic, and most of those who study loan-words are impelled to comment upon it, usually under the rubric of utility versus redundancy. Since some have made this distinction a corner-stone in their analysis of motivation it will be appropriate to give it a passing glance, if only to confirm that it is tangential to our own interpretation.

NECESSITY VERSUS LUXURY. A MIRAGE OF INTERFERENCE STUDIES

Lexicologists have grappled with the premise that whereas some foreign importations are borrowed as of right, because they are needed, others appear to be transferred merely as a result of trivial, otiose or even perverse motives and are consequently supernumerary to the language and alien to its natural genius. Terlingen traced a distinction between borrowing *por necesidad* and *por ornamento* back to scholars of the *Siglo de Oro* (Juan de Valdés, *Diálogo de la lengua*, c. 1535),[1] but in its typical form the discussion stems from Tappolet's distinction between the 'necessary' borrowing (*Bedürfnislehnwort*) and the 'luxury' borrowing (*Luxuslehnwort*),[2] or from a modified though still unconvincing version of Tappolet's dichotomy, Jaberg's distinction between the necessary borrowing and the 'handy' or 'convenient' borrowing (*Bequemlichkeitslehnwort*).[3] The latter category was in turn accepted by Bezzola,[4] though the Italian scholar had his own views about the opposition between 'necessity' and 'luxury' as a whole. It is rather disappointing to find Professor Deroy reviving the original antithesis under the guise of *nécessité pratique* and *raisons de cœur*,[5] despite his claim that he does so largely through practical motives—'Cette opposition est commode, même si elle est un peu arbitraire et ne correspond pas toujours aux faits

identify. Using English, for example, in conjunction with our material may best be viewed as an exploratory device—an external indicator which will give us a hint where to look for anisomorphic patterns within the Romance languages themselves.

1. J. H. Terlingen, op. cit., p. 28.

2. Ernst Tappolet, *Die alemannischen Lehnwörter in den Mundarten der französischen Schweiz*, Basle, 1913, pp. 53–8.

3. Karl Jaberg, articles in *Sonntagsblatt des Bund*, 16th and 23rd Dec. 1917.

4. R. R. Bezzola, *Abbozzo . . .*, pp. 14–15. Bezzola's distinction between *prestito per comodità* and *prestito di valore affettivo* (ibid., pp. 16–17) is to my mind the best interpretation of these categories ever achieved.

5. L. Deroy, *L'Emprunt linguistique*: heading of Ch. VI and VII respectively.

avec toute l'exactitude souhaitable.'[1] Some earlier works reflect their authors' reservations more strongly. 'Sa classification [i.e. Tappolet's] qui présente le grand avantage de mettre une étiquette sur deux groupes largement représentés dans tous les relevés de mots d'emprunt', says Wind, 'a peut-être le tort de tracer une délimitation trop stricte. C'est bien dans le domaine de la linguistique qu'il est difficile de dire où finit le besoin et où commence le luxe, "chose si nécessaire"; l'expression d'une nuance nouvelle peut dans certaines circonstances être d'intérêt urgent'.[2] Bezzola goes further by insisting that, 'infatti, di puri "prestiti di lusso" non si potrà ben parlare. Se una lingua accoglie degli elementi eterogenei, *non lo farà mai senza ragione*'.[3] The importance of this last phrase of Bezzola's deserves to be stressed. It actually disposes of the whole question, if one pursues its implications to their logical conclusion. The point at issue is not whether words are adopted from an external source deliberately or casually, legitimately or unwarrantably, with reason, without reason or with greater reason in some cases than others. All borrowing takes place for a reason. Each transferred term bears witness to an impulse, a stimulus which at the time of borrowing was sufficient for transfer to occur. Our text must be the words of Professor L. H. Gray: 'We may regard it as an axiom that each and every word borrowed is taken over for a reason which seems good and sufficient to the borrower.'[4] It follows that on principle we must regard all loans as adequately motivated and therefore 'necessary' loans, even conversational gambits or interjections—*comifò, bon-ton, perfettamente! maledizione! magnifico!*—and non-committal or omnibus words—*realizzare, arrangiare*, etc.[5] Further, since even these *trivia* made a particular, operationally adequate significatory contribution to the lexicon in the context appropriate to each, one may justifiably discuss their viability in *semantic* terms, quite apart from any social, psychological or other impact they may have possessed or represented.

A 'necessity versus luxury' formulation has no place in objective loan-word analysis. It is a relic of the time when the chief intention of linguistic study was normative and research into lexical interference an ancillary to purism.

A further pragmatic distinction which has remained latent in our analysis of the comparative diffusion of Gallicisms and Italianisms (and which is implied also in the 'necessity versus luxury' dichotomy) can now be stated explicitly. It is the contrast between forces which cause new lexical resources to be provided from a point outside a given language, and those which

1. Op. cit., p. 171, n. 2. Cf. the other mutation of the same hypothesis cited by Deroy, ibid., p. 172.
2. Op. cit., p. 10.
3. *Abbozzo* . . . , p. 14. The italics are mine.
4. L. H. Gray, *The Foundations of Language*, 2nd edition, 1950, p. 130.
5. The reader is asked to refer to our observations on 19th cent. French to Italian loans.

stimulate or govern the demand for innovation from within; between the *internal* motivation associated with the borrowing language and *external* pressure deemed to be exerted by the language of origin: or to formulate it still more sparely, between lexical borrowing and lexical lending.

INTERNAL AND EXTERNAL FACTORS. THE
CONCEPT OF PRESTIGE

It is a remarkable fact, and a suggestive one to the lexicologist who is disposed to view his data empirically, that most observations made about *borrowing* in practice show greater regard for the creditor than the debtor. Loan-words are usually contemplated as lexical entities *imposed* in some sense from without. One normally finds this external impulse associated with social history or the history of ideas, in much the same way as we ourselves have done in the appropriate place, and described with reference to cultural influences—that commodious phrase whose help we cannot forgo, but which none the less can often prove a false friend. And so by stages one reaches the final amplification, which consists in adding a value judgement to the concept of external coercion and speaking of the *prestige* of a foreign cultural pattern or of its concomitant language, interpreting borrowing as a whole in terms of cultural superiority or inferiority.[1] One speaks of the prestige of Old French in north Italy during the Middle Ages, exemplified by the mixed Franco-Venetian idiom; the prestige of French during the eighteenth century evinced by its universality. Meillet cited Greek and Norman-French as typical prestige languages *vis-à-vis* Latin and English. To assume that a foreign language may command admiration (or respect, or envy, according to the subjective attitude one adopts) because it is a token of an admired social group or the vehicle of a literature of outstanding repute, and that this may foster lexical importation is a methodically useful premise which is perfectly acceptable so far as it goes. But 'prestige' like 'culture' is a difficult term to use appropriately. Defining it even by implication as a force emanating from a foreign source and exerting pressure upon indigenous social groups means stepping a fair distance down metaphor's road. It would clearly be wrong to dismiss it as one of Stuart Chase's 'semantic blanks', but I should certainly want to call an account of borrowing in terms of prestige alone a superficial one, or more accurately—exploiting again the accepted terminology of descriptive linguistics—a *surface* as opposed to a *deep* mode of interpretation. A more intimate classification may be achieved by shifting the ground of one's inquiry to the opposite side of the external–internal polarity

1. Cf. Terlingen, op. cit., p. 24: 'Una vez alcanzado cierto nivel de cultura, el roce de una comunidad lingüística con *otra de cultura más avanzada*, no dejará de dar origen a una transmisión de elementos de ésta a aquella (et seq.).' The italics are mine.

as we have just defined it and picturing the process of interference as depending not so much on 'influences' as on needs felt and advantages exploited by speakers of the receiving language. It is sounder practice linguistically (and historically too, no doubt) to think of human beings welcoming or accepting new ideals, sources of inspiration or forms of behaviour from outside rather than external cultures bestowing them. Thus a loan-word qualified to be listed under the *external* rubric as a typical item imposed by the force of prestige may be seen from the *internal* standpoint to possess an argotic function, to be a means of affirming one's solidarity with a certain social, artistic or technical group, or to act as a *signum de classe* which serves to maintain, advertise or claim the user's right to a given social status. Further, these semantic advantages may prove to be the operative cause of borrowing, and yet they may remain undetectable from a purely external point of view. Borrowings motivated by commercial and other forms of economic or material interest—what Vittorio Bertoldi called *le esigenze linguistiche del mercato*—also have their internal motivation.[1] Is an alien name applied to a homely product evidence of foreign commercial hegemony? In external terms, possibly so; but it is equally a token of the home producer's shrewdness and linguistic awareness in assessing precisely what the total meaning of the extraneous word is for speakers of his own tongue. The semantic implications of a borrowing, as we have proved so often already, may be very different in the receiving language from those connoted in the source.

Even exoticisms have a decidedly important internal ingredient—terms referring to things, institutions, people associated exclusively with the 'lending' culture—which one might consider to be ideal examples of external loans. Much of the aura which surrounds (or surrounded in the past) words like *doge, condottiere, podestat, dôme* (meaning *duomo*, cathedral), *campanile, lagune, maquis* is in the eye of the foreign beholder.

False loans are obvious evidence of constructive intervention on the receivers' part improving on the material provided externally,[2] and so are borrowings used for their contribution to the resources of the literary medium —for local colour, perhaps, or for their poetic or other stylistic overtones.[3]

When applying the principle of internal and external influences to specific borrowed material workers in the field of lexical interference will find it handy to have available the terms *induced* borrowing (lexical contribution instigated by speakers of the receiving language) and its opposite, borrowing which is *imposed* (proffered by the source language and recommended by the external prestige patterns we have just discussed).

1. *Vox Romanica*, V (1940), pp. 87–105.
2. *Vide supra*, Part Three, pp. 618–19.
3. For examples *vide infra*, pp. 739–40.

A FINAL DICHOTOMY: LINGUISTIC
VERSUS EXTRA-LINGUISTIC

In what has gone before we have succeeded in drawing two major lines of demarcation across our chosen lexical territory. One is represented by a dichotomy or polarity between two attributes we have styled intrinsic and extrinsic, and the other between the attributes internal and external, both applicable to impulses which set the neological process of borrowing in motion and to the factors which govern it. There are other oppositional patterns or progressions which can provide a lead from which to explain the process in certain of its details, but their scope is narrower and their importance not so over-riding as is the case with these two, which are crucial.

It is not an accident that our rationalisation of lexical borrowing fits snugly into this antithetical mould. For one thing, contradictions arise inevitably from different lexicologists' approaches to interference studies, as to vocabulary studies of any sort. These discrepancies we have already pin-pointed and judged according to their merits. Secondly, and more cogently, ambivalence is inherent in the nature of vocabulary, irrespective of the preconceptions with which one approaches it. The point needs to be developed a little more fully.

In reality our interpretational model is dialectic rather than antithetical. The two major distinctions or standpoints we have derived from our borrowings are reconcilable, in that together they compose a final comprehensive opposition which sums up the two-fold nature of the material whose organisation we are trying to reveal. I should like to call this ultimate distinction *linguistic* as opposed to *extra-linguistic* without further ado, even though these terms and the difference they connote are strongly controversial among linguists and likely to remain so. It might be less tendentious to call it *semantic* as opposed to *cultural*, since it is the predominantly semantic interest of lexical interference that makes it worthy matter for the linguist's attention. The final *schema* therefore appears as follows:

PRIMARILY LINGUISTIC	*PRIMARILY EXTRA-LINGUISTIC*
(SEMANTIC)	(CULTURAL)
INTRINSIC	INTERNAL
EXTRINSIC	EXTERNAL

Unfortunately the simplicity of this convenient figure is deceptive. Its articulation is more complex than it seems to be initially. The reader will note that I mark my rubrics *primarily* linguistic or extra-linguistic; the need for this qualification arises from a second point of principle which is also crucially important. As I see it the antithesis between linguistic (semantic) and extra-linguistic (cultural) factors in borrowing cannot rightly be viewed as a continuous progression or vector running from one extreme standpoint to the other. The semantic element of our interpretation is different in kind. It does not complete the total picture of interference stimuli in the sense that it can be added to social, literary, psychological explanations for borrowing, on the same footing as these, to augment and round off their findings; but rather it stands as a parallel interpretation, interlinked with the cultural approach but overlapping and transcending it. I have tried to show, and this indeed has been the main theoretical goal of my exposé, that interpreting lexical interference in semantic terms *alone* is a viable undertaking which can lead to a comprehensive description—remembering always that if there are any weaknesses in the diachronic interpretation based on semantic adequacy which I have presented, these are matched by many areas of ambiguity which still exist in semantic theory as a whole. A description which takes cultural or historical premises as its prime data, on the other hand, can not be applied effectively to each and every category of borrowed word (*vide* our observations earlier about non-historical terms). But although both approaches are applicable to a large portion of borrowed vocabulary as valid alternatives, it is plain that certain words are especially appropriate material for semantic analysis while others are obviously bound up more closely with situations in 'the world outside'. It is equally obvious that any single neologism may be viewed as a token of more than one influence—very likely of several different ones, linguistic as well as extra-linguistic. To this extent an element of choice enters into our description; it is the function of our research procedures outlined in Part One above to indicate what the choice should be in the case of each borrowed word.[1]

We have arrived now at a stage where it should be possible to answer the questions posed earlier in this chapter: Why are words borrowed? How can the process of lexical interference best be envisaged and most efficiently described? In terms of what units, what relationships, what total reality?

Many of the problems raised have already been worked out during the course of our discussion so far: I think it best for brevity's sake and for ease of reference to recapitulate these and present the remaining points in synoptic form. The linguistic/extra-linguistic distinction I have just elaborated will provide a suitable taxonomy for this purpose.

---

1. Thus from the linguistic (semantic) standpoint *euphemism* rightly belongs beneath the *intrinsic* rubric because of its important role as a force which causes changes in the patterns of lexical signs; but it is also legitimate to list it as a psychological factor, i.e. an extra-linguistic element. To my way of thinking the former affiliation is more noteworthy than the latter, but the choice a lexicologist would make for practical purposes would naturally depend upon the aim of his research at the time.

I. A DIACHRONIC MODEL FOR
DESCRIBING AND INTERPRETING
LEXICAL BORROWING IN LANGUAGES OF CULTURE

A. *LINGUISTIC*

THE SEMANTIC APPROACH

Our field of inquiry is the changing pattern of lexical signs available for use in French and Italian, and our purpose, to describe and account for changes in this pattern. All our material may be considered from a semantic viewpoint, as a process whereby the semantic resources of *lexis* remain adequate to their linguistic function. Very often the motives for borrowing are to be sought in a language's need to keep abreast of a constantly changing world with its new inventions, techniques, historical, political, economic or social situations, and interests. In such cases the replacement processes may conveniently be called *extrinsic*. Usually the words concerned are *concomitant loans* in Terlingen's sense; they are well suited to an onomasiological or word-and-thing treatment. There are other borrowings which leave one with the impression that an established semantic pattern is undergoing change, that maintaining the 'ensemble de conventions nécessaires'[1] involves re-allocating, refining or elaborating significatory resources in use at a given time. In this limited but semantically important sector, which we have called *intrinsic*, lexical innovation is closely bound up with the semantic economy of the receiving language —with inherent tendencies to semantic change, the pressure exerted by related signs within a semantic field and the like. This is the sector in which the concept of semantic structure may be invoked.

Replacement is a process of change, not a state: our intrinsic model will therefore be a diachronic one, based on the comparative efficiency of lexical signs available to the receiving language—efficiency which in this instance is maintained or enhanced by exploiting semantic conventions already established in a foreign idiom. A practical method of describing and explaining this process is furnished by the consciously structural application of etymological data which we have called *semantic ecology* (pp. 709ff).

The ecological model also has its comparative aspect (pp. 715ff).

Formal elements also come under the *intrinsic* heading,—that is, in so far as formal factors have a bearing upon the eventual meaning of a borrowed word.[2]

1. Saussure, *C.L.G.*, p. 25.

2. See Part Three, observations on paronymic attraction and analogy, esp. *Borrowed material in its new environment* (pp. 614-17) and *Reception, assimilation and exploitation* (pp. 617-21). The influence of bound morphemes (e.g. suffixes) is also important and deserves to be investigated more intensively, in particular the way in which a bound morpheme may serve as a substitute for a distinct free morpheme or even a periphrasis (consider the semantic work done by the borrowed suffixes It. *-izzare, -izzazione* or Fr. *-ade*).

Further Examples

1. '*Grammatical*' words. Form classes other than substantives, adjectives and most verbs belong to the intrinsic section. The only ones of note are adverbs: *vide supra*, p. 699, also *ancora, guari*, (med. < Fr.), (*à l'*)*improviste* (sixteenth century < It.), (*all'*)*insaputa* (nineteenth century < Fr.); but cf. the conjunction *beninteso(che)* and *vis-à-vis* used as a preposition (both nineteenth century < Fr.).

2. '*Logical*' terms. Among words which plainly serve to heighten the efficiency of vocabulary as a dispensation for communicating and thinking are those which act as logical tools, or in some like manner help to make expression and formulation more articulate. A number of generic and collective terms are foremost among these. There is a pressing need for lexical signs which will enable the speaker to stand back, as it were, and view situations or ideas from a distance. Several of our borrowings mean something like 'equipment', 'gear', i.e. are generic with regard to concrete or technical categories: mediaeval It. *arnese* < Fr. *herneis, harnais* in its general sense, seventeenth century *attrezzi, attiraglio*, nineteenth century *effetti* 'goods and chattels' and ephemeral Fr. *robe* (sixteenth century) < It. *roba*, usually meaning 'merchandise' but also used figuratively, together with corresponding predicates meaning 'to equip' or 'prepare' without reference to a specific trade; mediaeval It. *adesare* and sixteenth century *abbigliare*.[1] What is implied by the lack of these 'synthesising' words or their acquisition in given circumstances has often set linguists and anthropologists arguing. Von Wartburg's pronouncement is one of the most apposite: 'La formation des concepts linguistiques repose précisément sur une abstraction se développant progressivement. Cette abstraction fait halte à un certain point, point qui représente l'optimum de clarté et qui allie à un reste de valeur concrète suffisant pour rendre le concept maniable et saisissable à l'homme moyen, un contenu assez riche pour donner corps audit concept. De même que dans la formation des concepts scientifiques, on constate ici l'application de la loi qui veut que tout accroissement du contenu d'un concept s'accompagne d'un rétrécissement de son extension. On pourrait comparer le point où les deux tendances se font équilibre au foyer d'une lentille. C'est le point de cristallisation des concepts linguistiques, et ce point n'est pas identique dans toutes les langues ni à toutes les époques.'[2] We must add to this that language needs provision for making statements about the same events at differing levels of abstraction, and consequently a series of increasingly generic signs may be instituted, each of which performs a useful function and so fills an 'ecological' niche. In this way Fr. *chiourme* (sixteenth

1. Collective and generic terms are often 'dynamic' in the sense indicated above (pp. 703-4) since they may have euphemistic or hyperbolical uses.

2. *Prob. et méth.*, pp. 180-1.

century < It. *ciurma*) and It. *equipaggio* (nineteenth century < Fr. *équipage*) may be said to occupy an intermediate position between terms for 'sailor' in general and the designations of individual ratings, both of which categories are well catered for in French and Italian (with the help of a number of loans). The generic or 'synthesising' term adds an element which is not provided by any or all of specialised signs it comprehends. Italian *risorsa*, for instance (< Fr. *ressource*), which the nineteenth century lexicographer Arlia rejects as superfluous because at least twenty-seven synonyms exist already in the language[1] includes in its signification something of all these individual attributes, but in addition may be used in well-attested contexts where none of the other terms would be appropriate. What it contributed was therefore a significatory element the Italian lexicon previously lacked, and which French was able to provide.[2] Other logical terms fall into *relational* and *analytic* or *dioristic* categories, e.g. *attitude, manquer, posture, réussir* (to have an outcome), *controsenso, dettaglio*, etc., cited earlier. One or two of them have a qualifying function, e.g. *sedicente* (< *soi-disant*). There is a place here, too, for what Panzini called the 'voce unica e facile',[3] words which the lexicographer like many purists before him attributed to a slovenly disregard for precision. An imprecise or omnibus term has its important part to play in speech because of its vague, provisory nature, as a deliberately non-committal equivalent; or even as a psychological stand-by in case of fatigue or tem-

---

1. *Vide* F-A., 1877, s.v.: 'Oggi com'oggi ad *Ajuto, Assegnamento, Rinfranco*, altrimente non si dice che *Risorsa*. Ci sono anche le voci *Rientro, Rincalzo* nel significato di *Guadagno*, e anche *Ripresa*. E questo per quanto concerne cose materiali attinenti alla vita. Vediamocene ora al morale. Dicono: *Tizio è uomo di grandi risorse*, dove l'idea è quella di saper trarsi d'impaccio, da molestie, ovvero quella di saper architettare mezzi per raggiungere un fine: nel primo il vocabolo è *Ripiego, Spediente*; nel secondo *Partito*'. Ugolini (Arlia goes on to observe) offered the following alternatives: *Mezzo, Spediente, Rimedio, Aiuto, Conforto, Ripiego, Sostentamento, Profitto, Provento, Rendita, Emolumento, Entrata, Ristoro, Presidio, Sussidio, Argomento, Compenso, Rilevamento, Utile, Riparo*.

2. Dr. Paul Schach cited some interesting examples of generic terms borrowed by Pennsylvanian German speakers from English which illustrate exactly the 'ecological' situation to which we are drawing attention ('Hybrid compounds in Pennsylvanian German', *American Speech*, Vol. XXIII (1948), pp. 120-34). Thus the word *fence* was borrowed because 'the German immigrants had a plethora of words designating specific types of fences, but apparently no one word which could be used to refer to any and all kinds of fences' (p. 126). Pennsylvanian farmers had plenty of words denoting the *handle* of different tools, etc.—*Griff, Handgriff, Handhabe, Schaft, Stiel* and so on—but nevertheless found it useful to adopt a generic term *handle* from English (p. 127).

3. *Diz. mod.*, s.v. *complotto*: 'A noi non mancano, secondo i casi, le parole: trama, cospirazione, congiura, intrigo. . . . È il solito caso: l'italiano ha sinonimi di sottile uso, il francese ha *la voce unica e facile*.' The distinction one makes between a true generic and a facile umbrella term is largely subjective, of course. *Risorsa* is usually cited by 19th and 20th cent. purists as the typical omnibus word.

porary aberration.[1] The Italianism *faciliter* from the fifteenth century onward and the Gallicisms *arrangiare, realizzare, salvaguardare, sanzionare, situazione, posizione* in the nineteenth century were often used in contexts of this sort.[2]

This sector of our intrinsic loans provides a modicum of useful material for the neo-Humboldtian 'content analysts' (*vide supra*, p. 690, n. 2).

Names of colours, ranks, numerals and the other hierarchical groups commonly cited as examples of structural patterning automatically qualify as intrinsic borrowings (*vide* examples above, p. 694; add the ordinal number mediaeval It. *prim(i)ero*).

B. *EXTRA-LINGUISTIC*

I. CONCOMITANT LOANS.[3] LEXICO-CULTURAL PARALLEL

Since 'language is a complex inventory of all the ideas, interests and occupations that take up the attention of the community',[4] it follows that neologisms, borrowed neologisms included, are capable of interpretation in the light of innovations and new departures of all kinds within the linguistic community that accepts them. Most loan-words have been interpreted at this primary level in one monograph or other during the past century and the method remains valid, as we have already said, within its limitations.

The area of borrowed vocabulary handled under this section coincides in great measure with that which relates to extrinsic innovations in *lexis*, though the point of view from which we are now approaching it is totally different. There we were thinking of the contributions made to significatory resources; here we are relating words to activities, situations and impulses in the world at large, i.e. to cultural entities.[5]

The following is a list of the semantic categories of concomitant loans which were established empirically during the course of our historical survey in Part Two. They apply to French and Italian, of course, and do not purport to be an ideal taxonomy. A few typical examples of borrowings are added after each section.

1. Cf. Wittgenstein: 'Is it always an advantage to replace an indistinct picture by a sharp one? Isn't the indistinct often exactly what we need?' *Philosophical Investigations*, p. 34.

2. These words, too, often have a dynamic (euphemistic) ingredient. They tend to be of bureaucratic or journalistic origin, as we have seen.

3. I use the term applied by the late Professor Terlingen to this kind of loan-word. It sums up the circumstances of borrowing quite clearly. We need not search farther for an adequate label. *Vide supra*, Part One, p. 22.

4. *Selected Writings of Edward Sapir*, Berkeley, 1949, p. 90.

5. The *concomitant* category is still inward-looking in the sense that one's chief purpose in using it is to seek explanations why words were borrowed, but the outward cultural aspect nevertheless remains dominant. This is also the appropriate point in the model where one may consider what loan-words can tell us about history, either by confirming information provided in advance by historians or, more rarely, by adding to what was previously known.

Agriculture (*giardino, espalier, récolte, sanofieno*)

Amusements and Pastimes; several sub-categories: fencing (*botte, escrime*), tournaments (*torneo, lizza*), dancing (*burè, gavotta, cancan*), gaming (*caver, reversi, lotto*), miscellaneous (*gala, marionetta*), etc.

Architecture (*cornice, fronton, coupole, estradosso*)

Crafts (*médaille, basana*)

Culinary and Food (*vermicelle, consumè, maionese, omeletta*)

Diplomatic and Administrative (*ambassade, burocrazia, autorizzazione*)

Exotic (*doge, lama, bora, carbonaro* [ambivalent category[1]])

Falconry (*girfalco, laniere*)

Fashions and Clothing (*caleçon, pantalon, fisciù, blusa*)

Feudal terms and Chivalry (*scudiere, omaggio, cavaliere*)

Finance and Banking (*banque, solde, libero scambio*)

Home and Social Life; several sub-categories: rooms (*appartement, salon, gabinetto*), furnishing (*origliere, buffetto, armoàr*), activities (*villégiature, debuttante*), etc.

Horsemanship (*balzano, chinea, manège, mézair*)

Hunting (*veltro, corsiere*)

Journalism (*trafiletto, dinamitardo*)

Legal (*assise, lettere patenti, processo verbale*)

Literary (*madrigal, sonnet* [ambivalent category[1]])

Meteorological (*calme, est, bonasse*)

Military (*spingarda, bataillon, bombe, bivacco*)

Music and Opera (*basson, opéra, solfège, ància*)

Nautical (*alleggiare, boussole, nocher, tangheggio*)

Painting and Sculpture (*finiment, gouache, aquarelle, impressionismo*)

Personal adornment, Jewellery (*chignone, agremani, goliè*)

Philosophy (*altruismo, empirismo*)

Political (*riotta, coalizione, patriotto*)

Public life and Ceremony (*livrea, catafalque, cortège*)

Religion (*baldaquin, nonce, cardinalice*)

Scientific; several sub-categories: botany (*mughetto, belladonna*), anthropology (*feticismo, meticcio*), natural history (*avocette, caribù*), geography (*affluente, solfatare*), physics (*galvanisme*), etc., etc.

Technological (*brasque, ghisa, bobina, lavaggio*)

Theatre (*scaramouche, improviser, comparse, caffè-concerto*)

Titles (*dama, marquis, damigella, cugino* [ambivalent category[1]])

Trade and Commerce; several sub-categories: textiles (*sargia, brocard, calicò*), ceramics (*majolique, faïence*), commercial practice (*douane, trafique*), tradesmen (*artisan, pellettiere*), industries (*confezionare*), etc., etc.

Transport (*carrosse, calesse, giardiniera*)

---

1. By ambivalent category I mean one whose loan-words serve as tokens of two radically different cultural influences. For different concepts of 'literary' elements in vocabulary see below, AESTHETIC FACTORS and *Italianism, Gallicism and the Literary Medium*; for further implications of honorifics and lexical *exotica* see below, ibid., *The Métier of Literary Art*.

2. SOCIAL FACTORS

Linguistic communication implies a speaker and a hearer, or a number of each. It is therefore axiomatically a social activity, and consequently there must exist a plane of relationship on which linguistic history may be related to the history of society.

(a) *Impact of Social Groups*

Many of the socio-lexical parallels established in Part Two under the rubrics *Amusements and Pastimes, Home and Social life, Fashion, Court Life and Courtoisie,* and from a rather different angle, *Political, Diplomatic and Administrative* terms qualify to be included in a broadly based *social* conspectus. It is prudent, however, to confine investigation to the kernel situation of social contact, the mutual influence of French and Italian social groups as a whole, returning again to Hollyman's dictum that 'au point de vue social la raison de l'emprunt réside dans le développement inégal des sociétés'.[1] We have seen from our comparison of Gallicisms and Italianisms that only on three occasions did so marked a cultural imbalance occur that speakers of one language were led to emulate the culture, and through it, the language of the other country on a comprehensive scale. The periods are well defined. They are 1150–1350 and 1700–1900 (and beyond) for French to Italian loans, 1450–1700 for Italian to French. Lexical importation at these periods affects a great majority of the linguistically important groups within the nation. Interaction between social groups *within* the respective national grouping is less clear, though as a field of study it promises more, since the social unit in question—'class' of society, *coterie*, profession, etc.—can be defined more precisely than 'nation', which is an ethnic and geographical as well as a social entity, and as far as Italy and France are concerned requires to be redefined from century to century. An intense foreign influence on these less extensive groups may turn out to have little effect on the receiving language as a whole. The sixteenth century Italian influence on French proved to be profound, but only because the exclusive social group for whom Italian was felt to confer social status set norms of behaviour for the rest of France at the operative time. We have seen that the strong current of lexical borrowing associated with the Renaissance persisted throughout the following century and have offered a linguistic explanation why it should be so. A social factor also intervened. Though the aristocratic Valois society of the earlier sixteenth century exercised political, social and therefore linguistic power throughout the nation it had helped bring into being, its supremacy did not remain unchallenged. Vocabulary confirms that from the 1560s onward there was a definite tendency towards intervention on the part of the middle class, who as a rule were unsympathetic

1. *Vide supra*, p. 716.

towards Italy (p. 236). In the seventeenth century, however, those who
inherited the courtly tradition and for whom Italianism still maintained its
rights acquired once more the power to impose themselves culturally, as
politically, making their own linguistic norm the token of political and
cultural hegemony, while at the same time ensuring that any other social
development which might have founded a linguistic tradition of its own
remained quiescent.

The middle-class influence takes over, apparently abruptly, at the point
where Gallicisms begin to dominate the lexical dialogue for the second time,
i.e. in the early eighteenth century. In reality a professional or bourgeois
domination of linguistic events already pervades the French to Italian
importation from 1600 to 1700, i.e. the minor importation of that century.
Most of those who threw themselves so wholeheartedly into the work of
the Crusca (p. 348ff.) were from the professional classes: in this respect as in
others Magalotti and Redi were typical of their time (p. 350). The nineteenth
century reflects a middle-class way of life in virtually all its aspects,
particularly lower middle class, with an emphasis on trade and commercial
occupations; but impulses of a popular or heterogeneous stamp are to be
found from the beginning of the century. Their importance steadily increases
as our survey reaches its term.

(b) *Foreign Language as an Aid to Social Development*

Another strictly sociological situation affecting our borrowings is that where
neologism through recourse to a foreign language is actively canvassed for
its beneficial effect on social (or national) development.

Examples: certain eighteenth century French-Italian loans associated with
the policy of the Verri, Beccaria and the Milan school, together with other
reformers of the period; in a general way, nineteenth century trends in the
questione della lingua, associated with Manzoni and the replacement of Gallicism by a national idiom.

3. SOCIO-PSYCHOLOGICAL FACTORS

There is a sense in which one may regard the basic apparatus of lexical replenishment in the face of extra-linguistic needs as psychological, since from
the cultural or social standpoint the motives which our model is intended to
particularise may be conceived of as incentives or stimuli, of preferences and
conditioned choices experienced by and acting upon people using vocabulary
instrumentally in the course of their daily lives. Further, the linguistic
resources whose mutations we are seeking to account for, exist in their
ultimate reality as a series of traditionally established associative habits, that
is to say, mental habits. Often intimate impulses of the human psyche are seen

to have an immediate effect on the neological process—those which lead to euphemism, for instance, or, to a lesser extent, to pejoration. In this province as elsewhere we can exploit the useful distinction between aspects of our extra-linguistic interpretation which are outward-looking and those which are inward-looking. The outward-looking aspect is the psychological aspect proper, that which engages in speculation about mental phenomena as such. This we may provisionally exclude from our model, remembering, however, that many facets of content and vocabulary studies are at one with psychological research and that psychologists at this very moment are pushing ahead with their own elaboration of semantic structure which logical linguistics may well find hard to fit into its own technical cosmos, and equally hard to ignore. Since the extra-linguistic half of our model is to remain blank at this point, euphemism (for example) will only figure as a linguistic (intrinsic) factor. The 'inward-looking' or lexically relevant aspect is left for our consideration, and this I shall term *socio-psychological*. The place it occupies in our model is of special importance. It is important lexically because lexicologists traditionally put human impulses at the top of their list whenever they attempt to explain why words are borrowed, and whether we concur in accepting this scale of priorities or not, we at least need to be clear about what socio-psychological factors imply before we can pass judgement on them; it is important schematically because in this sector we begin to appreciate how complex the extra-linguistic forces which regulate borrowing really are, while at the same time perceiving new pragmatic groupings which might prove useful for further research. This as I see it is the open-ended sector of our extra-linguistic schema.[1]

3(A). SOCIO-PSYCHOLOGICAL: EXTERNAL

From an external standpoint socio-psychological impulses may be described in terms of *prestige* (*vide supra*, p. 722).

Like the lexico-cultural parallel and social factors, prestige effect is a blanket term, a skeleton key to open all doors; it too may be invoked to contribute to one's account of the vast majority of loans in our lists.

3(B). SOCIO-PSYCHOLOGICAL: INTERNAL

A less superficial, more objective explanation may be achieved by investigating the same socio-psychological impulses exclusively from the standpoint of the receiving language (*vide supra*, the internal/external polarity, pp. 722-3). From

---

1. A corresponding 'growing-point' in the linguistic (semantic) half of our diptych is provided, I suggest, by the *ecological* metaphor. Examples of further research topics in the psycho-linguistic sphere: influence of mass media on neologism from 1850 onwards; effects on language of stereotypes and the persistence of traditional attitudes.

this new vantage the stereotyped explanation provided by the undifferentiated term *prestige* is resolved into a spectrum of somewhat diverse propensities: linguistic snobbery, use of vocabulary as a social *signum*, argotic impulses, even frankly material motives.

(a) *Linguistic Snobbery*

Many of our loans may be understood to reflect impulses of social pretension, affectation, stand-offishness. Certainly they have often been interpreted in this way in the past. Almost any of the words which gall the purists are worth while scrutinising for this sort of overtone. The nineteenth century French to Italian list is the happiest hunting-ground for them (q.v., pp. 563-71), but similar uses were attacked as pretentious in the earlier period of the major French to Italian influence, i.e. the eighteenth century, while in the opposite direction the vogue of Italianism at court in the mid- and later sixteenth century was censured on similar grounds. All such terms may imply that social snobbery was being gratified, but as we have already suggested in our nineteenth century evaluation, it does not follow that they necessarily did so. Here, too, we once more have to cry *distinguo*. For snobbery may be regarded in two different lights: firstly, as an urge to maintain exclusiveness or independence against the pressure of an environment of which one disapproves—French used by courtiers in Czarist Russia is an oft-quoted example[1]—and secondly, as a positive desire to foster cohesion within a social group and proclaim one's allegiance to it by showing one's proficiency in the restricted language associated with the *milieu* in question. We have of course no brief to devise an anatomy of snobbery. This would mean trespassing on the 'outward-looking' psychological territory which we have deliberately skirted round. But it does appear that our material contains no sure evidence of *emprunts par pur snobisme* as Deroy interprets them. Where anything like this occurs it falls into the second category, i.e. is attributable to 'solidarity' or quasi-argotic impulses.

(b) *Signum Factor*

'All in all', observed Sapir, 'it is not too much to say that one of the really important functions of language is to be constantly declaring to society the psychological place held by its members.'[2] I prefer to interpret the upper-class Italianate usage of the sixteenth century in terms of this objective signum potential, despite Estienne's insistence on the subjective, perverse element in his compatriots' jargon. Some of the words he puts in the mouth of Philausone may be trivial in the sense that they were infrequently heard—oddities on

1. Cf. also Deroy, op. cit., p. 182: 'En Allemagne, au temps de la Gallomanie (*die Alamodezeit*) il était de bon ton de farcir sa conversation de mots français dans le but avoué de sich en parlant von der *canaille* zu distinguieren.'
2. *Selected Writings*, p. 18.

the fringe of signum vocabulary proper—or may even have been invented by him for the purpose of caricature, but others turn up in a number of authors, often in semantically neutral contexts. *Acconche, accoster, baster, brave, burler, caprice, capter, cartel, délicatesse* (for *délicateté*), *escorne, goffe, gofferie, martel, passéger, se targuer de* are all words which appear to have gained currency in this register, and the same was probably true of many words which came to be fully accepted into general French usage since that time.[1]

(c) *Argotic Function*

In Franco-Italian loans the *signum function* shades imperceptibly into the argotic function. Social psychologists have still a great deal to discover about the accepted status of different trades and professions in previous ages, and could well gain one or two clues from the fluctuating attitude towards the restricted languages associated with them. Hunting and hawking terms had a widely accepted standing in the Middle Ages, and not only because of their links with the higher orders of society (*vide* pp. 131-2, French to Italian loans). Terms of horsemanship, which have the same kind of reputation, are scattered over all the century lists up to the eighteenth; fencing terms have a similar spread, but with the difference that this restricted terminology is strongly supported in the sixteenth century by a sudden rise to popularity of military terminology, which seems to have strayed beyond its usual social limits far more at that time than in other periods when the general involvement in military matters was at least as great. In the seventeenth and eighteenth centuries society found it acceptable and even a matter of pride to be conversant with specialised skills in the fine arts. Our material shows strikingly how a number of restricted words proper to that field of activity gained a foothold in everyday usage (*vide supra*, pp. 666 and 668).[2] Argot in the strict sense of the word is also clearly represented in Franco-Italian contacts, though from the nature of thieves' slang as a cryptic, formally and semantically disguised medium it is hard in many cases to say whether a word was borrowed

1. For information on socio-psychological factors as observed in the speech of bilingual groups, especially immigrant communities, consult Weinreich, *Languages in Contact*, pp. 83–110, *The Socio-Cultural Setting of Language Contact*. Cf. also his diagram of *stimuli and resistance factors* affecting the speech of bilinguals (in minority groups, that is) ibid., pp. 64–5. It is interesting to compare the 'All interference' and 'Lexical' sections of Professor Weinreich's synopsis with our own model and the matter of this chapter generally, remembering that the objects of research are rather different—gradual transfer of allegiance from minority to majority language, as opposed to replenishment of the resources of the majority language itself; *lingua dell'uso* as opposed to cultural (literary) idiom, etc.

2. Note the following borrowings from earlier periods which extended in semantic application and breadth of usage in precisely the same way: 14th cent. It. *laniere* 'cowardly' and 16th cent. Fr. *briller*, from hawking; 16th cent. Fr. *courbette* from horsemanship and *riposte* from fencing.

BB

or not, or from whence. Thieves' slang appears in our lists at two well-bounded periods: the later fifteenth century, where the movement is largely into Italian (*birba*, *ciurmare*, *maccherella*, etc., with the key-word *furba*[1]), and the nineteenth century, where the movement is largely from Italian (*dabe*, *frangin*, etc., with the key-word *maf(f)ia*[2]).

(d) *Material Motives*

These are immediately detectable in the lexical category of commercial terms I spoke of earlier, where the choice of an appellation is made with an eye to commercial advantage; that is, where V. Bertoldi's 'esigenze linguistiche del mercato' come into play. In his words, 'la denominazione vuole . . . indicare in genere la provenienza esotica della merce per giustificarne il prezzo elevato'.[3] One need not construe this solely as a matter of hard-headed finance, and still less of verbal chicanery. The problem basically is to marry an appropriate, effective name to a material object. A label which has successful associations (including commercial success) will tend to be used in other contexts. In this way names of coins pass between French and Italian, as *luigi*, *ferlino*, *ducat*, *carlin*, *florin*; this is why many seemingly random and opaque appellations of textiles, for example, have a surprisingly long history and may be traced with gradual modifications through the whole of our survey (*moncayar-mohair-moire-moerre*; *gros-grosso-grossograno*, etc.; *saie-saia-saione*; *serge-sargia* and so on). Bertoldi's rubrics *nomi esotici* and *termini pseudo-geografici*[4] have many representatives in our collection: (*panno d'*)*arazzo* from Arras, (*tela di*) *rensa* from Reims, *cretonne*, *cretone* from Creton in Normandy,[5] *stanforte* via French from the English place-name Stamford, *casimiro*, an eighteenth century loan via French from Eng. *kerseymere*, formed on *kersey*, 'coarse say'—yet another transmutation of the French word *saie*. The key-word *stoffa* < Fr. *étoffe* (*estoffe*), a commonplace term in French, was borrowed to denote a luxury product; Alberti in 1788 defines it as 'pezza di drappo di seta o di altra materia più nobile'. Many other categories of trade, technical and professional terms are internally motivated in this way—virtually the whole of culinary terminology borrowed from French, for example—and so for that matter are many other types of concrete substantive. Bertoldi was right when he said that they comprise 'uno dei settori più vitali e più mobili del lessico'.[6] Market terms deserve more attention than has

1. Cf. also *gergo*, 16th cent. Fr. > It. list. *Vide supra*, p. 145-6.
2. *Vide supra*, p. 458.
3. Loc. cit., p. 97.
4. Loc. cit., pp. 100–1.
5. Note the ephemeral adaptation *cretonina*, in which the caritative diminutive suffix reaffirmed and reinforced the approbatory aura with which the base-word itself was imbued.
6. Loc. cit., p. 105.

been given them up to now, and the same applies to technical terms as a whole. These after all make up the greater part of any quota of neologisms, and they are as deeply implicated in the normal processes of linguistic development as any other words.[1]

4. AESTHETIC FACTORS

(a) *Fine Arts in General*

Owing to the nature of the content they express, terms of the fine arts have certain traits which set them apart from terms of trades and crafts in general and entitle them to a separate niche in our taxonomy. Any technical vocabulary viewed as a conceptual field in the sense accepted by Ipsen and others— that is, as an onomasiological family—may be split up into a lexical hierarchy in which different levels of terminology represent different affiliations within the group. Details of the pattern vary, but the words tend to fall into two main sub-families; on one hand, names of created objects or artefacts, the end-product of the craft or technology in question; on the other, names of processes, techniques, elements of organisation by which production or artistic creation are carried on. The label, as we have seen, is an important element of the product.

If for the purpose of comparison one sets terms of the fine arts beside terminologies of the crafts and trades, those of the fine arts appear wanting in some respects, show *lacunae* at certain points which are filled in the other special vocabularies. The difference lies in the first sub-family, and the reason for it is that creations of the arts are not susceptible to naming in the way

1. I should make it clear that by 'material motives' in this acceptation I do not mean the normal impact of material culture as betokened by concomitant loan-words, which is catered for under section 1 above. Nor am I considering the prestige of the *exotic product*, which is again an external factor, but rather the prestige attaching to the word itself, which though no doubt ultimately linked with the wider-ranging prestige of the exotic source is in its individual essence an extrapolation made in the receiving language —a fiction, if you will, created by the borrowers themselves. Readers may care to consider whether they perceive a similar propaganda or 'publicity' distinction between the following pairs of material or market names, drawn from widely different centuries (the borrowed word comes first): 13th cent. *alluminare* 'to illuminate a manuscript', which Dante dubs a Parisian word, as opposed to *miniare*; 19th cent. *dublè, placcato* 'rolled gold', opposed to *similoro*; 19th cent. *hôtel* ~ *albergo*; later 19th cent. *plafon(e), plafond* 'ceiling' ~ *soffitto, soppalco*, etc.; 18th cent. *giruetta* 'weather-vane' ~ *banderuola, mostravento*; 19th cent. *prestidigiatatore, illusionista* 'conjuror' ~ *prestigiatore*; *sciantosa, ciantosa* 'singer, cabaret artist' ~ the native word *cantatrice*; 18th cent. Fr. *cantatrice* 'trained, professional singer' as opposed to *chanteuse*, which in its turn replaced med. and 16th cent. *chanteresse*; 16th cent. *balle* 'ball', esp. in *jeu de paume*, which ousted med. *pelote, esteuf*; 18th cent. *dentista* ~ *cavadenti*; 14th cent. *pellettiere* 'furrier, skinner' ~ *pellicciaio, pellicciere*. One surmises that apart from possible regional differentiation the relationship between *formaggio* and *cacio* may well be accounted for in this way, together with a number of other technical terms in our lists which superficially look like exact synonyms.

those of the trades are. This is not quite so simple as saying that the end-product of a craft is concrete, that of an art essentially abstract. It is partly that the product of art is unique, rather in the same way as the individual human being is unique, and like the human being it may be given a 'personal' name ('The Madonna of the Rocks') but not denoted except as a *genre*. Thus the achievements of the fine arts express themselves in styles rather than things. Gallicism and Italianism in the trades and crafts may be gauged by means of the names relating to the things in question; similar influences in the fine arts—take music, for example—may also be detected, but in terms of values peculiar to the art itself. A musicologist will identify Italianism in an appropriate piece of music, but he will seek it in musical texture, colour, phraseology, instrumentation and similar components proper to that art.

(b) *Literature*

Literary art is different again. It adds a dimension of its own, for the reason that language supplies the medium in which a work of literary art is wrought. Here the categories of *technique* and *achievement or execution* are accompanied by a third one which we might call *material* or *medium*. The latter is perhaps to be preferred in view of the different use we have made of the term *material* in preceding pages. These several distinctions or attributes may be summed up tentatively in a figure, as follows:

Linguistic relevance of a foreign influence

	A PRODUCTION	B PRODUCT OR ACHIEVEMENT	C MEDIUM
CRAFTS AND TECHNOLOGIES	Technique, process, organisation, tools etc.	Artefact (object) or service	—
FINE ARTS	Technique, genres, instruments etc.	A painting, a symphony etc.	—
LITERARY ART	Technique, genres etc.	A poem, a novel etc.	Language

A, B and C represent different aspects of the art or craft.

Column A is lexically relevant, i.e. lexical elements may stand as tokens of non-lexical influences.[1]

Column B is lexically relevant in the case of crafts and technologies but non-linguistic in the arts, with the proviso that execution or achievement in literature may be limited, channeled or inspired by the medium, language.[2]

1. For an interpretation of borrowed musical terms, see 18th cent. It. > Fr. evaluation, pp. 367-72. Observations of the plastic and pictorial arts are spread widely, but see esp. the 17th cent. It. > Fr. evaluation.

2. If other resources of language were the object of our analysis—idiom, syntax or prosody, perhaps—we could not afford to leave this qualification unamplified. But the

Column C is relevant only to literary art; it operates at all levels of language, with lexical elements playing an important part.

(c) *Italianism, Gallicism and the Literary Medium*

In French and Italian the principal influences which left their mark upon the recipient language are as follows. Not in every case does the linguistic influence extend to vocabulary, though when it does evidence of it is documented in our lists.

1. *The contribution of Old French to the traditional literary medium in mediaeval Italian.* Applies especially to the romances and epics, but to some extent the lyric as well, in conjunction with Provençal, which of course exerts the major influence in that genre. See discussion above pp. 138–44, the evidence of the Franco-Venetian mixed idiom, and notes on borrowings in Dante and G. Villani; also the position of the literary register in the situation of symbiosis observable at this period (*vide supra*, ibid., and p. 672).

2. *Sixteenth century influences of Italian on French* (see sixteenth century evaluation, esp. pp. 245–6). Mostly centres upon the Pléiade, with du Bellay as an especially important source,[1] though other authors before and after the mid-century readily include Italianisms in their poetic medium—Gringoire, Marot, etc.

3. *Marinism and the baroque.* Italian impact on French lies mainly in imagery and extended stylistic devices, e.g. periphrasis.

4. *Later seventeenth and eighteenth centuries*: influence of Classical French on Italian. Mostly affects literary themes, *genres* and treatment, but when the literary language is affected what tends to be involved is the stylistic register as a whole (cf. Goldoni's observation that Italian possessed no register suitable for high comedy corresponding to the French of Molière, and his consequent preference for French itself at this level).

5. *An incidental contact, though significant*: Italian preferred by certain *dilettanti* of the eighteenth and early nineteenth centuries as the language of *libretti* and musical lyrics (*vide supra*, eighteenth century It. > Fr. evaluation, pp. 370–1).

6. *Romanticism, and liberalism in the use of vocabulary associated with the movement.* Extending the scope of vocabulary to include archaisms, dialect and restricted languages of many kinds—a typical linguistic resource of the

---

stylistic use of *vocabulary* is only marginally implicated in this more fundamental and infinitely more knotty problem of how far a strictly *linguistic* analysis can elucidate *literary* achievement.

1. Some of the Italianisms reputed to be spurious or trivial borrowings appear in du Bellay and perhaps a second source such as Brantôme, e.g. *caparelle* 'kerchief which covers the bosom', *chambelle* 'cake', *corame*, 'leather', *fantesque* 'serving-maid'. My impression is that the poet used them deliberately, and that for him they possessed distinct *valeurs stylistiques*.

Romantic poet and novelist—has an aspect relevant to interference studies in the use of exotic terms for their stylistic yield (see section 4 below).

(d) The Métier of Literary Art

Relevant words have been cited at several points in our evaluations. Groups 1, 2 and 3 below may be treated as *concomitant loans* (*vide supra*, section B.1.). To recapitulate briefly, they comprise:

1. *Genres*: mediaeval Fr. *nouvelle*, mediaeval It. *lai*, *romanzo* (courtly or Arthurian romance); sixteenth century Fr. *macaronée*, *macaronique*, *sonnet*, *burlesque*, sixteenth century It. *farsa*; seventeenth century Fr. *idylle*.

2. *Literary schools and movements*: sixteenth century Fr. *pétrarchisme*, *-iste*;[1] nineteenth century It. *parnassiano*, *realismo*, *verismo* (loan-creation based on *naturalisme*), *simbolismo*, etc.; eighteenth century It. *purismo*, *-ista*, sixteenth century Fr. *académie*.

3. *Technique of style, versification*: sixteenth century Fr. *stance*, *tercet*; seventeenth century Fr. *improviser*, *lazzi*; eighteenth century Fr. *concetti*.

4. *Local colour and the exotic*. Especially associated with French authors of the earlier nineteenth century, Stendhal in particular. See observations in nineteenth century It. > Fr. evaluation, pp. 453-8. Often a formal element enhances the exotic aura. Mutual influences of form and content explain for example why adaptations of *roulette* in Italian failed to prosper; the word's foreign associations (with Monte-Carlo?) were too intimate a part of its meaning to be cast off by integrating it formally. See remarks on *vendetta*, *bastrè*, etc., above, p. 713.

5. *Humour and satire*. Like a clown's ragged clothes and piebald make-up, the garb of language has power to make its wearer comical or ridiculous. Italian and French were used in this way from early times down to the nineteenth century; Pope Boniface VIII is made to speak an italianised French in Geoffroy de Paris' rhymed chronicle (early fourteenth century), while macaronic Italian is a faithful stand-by of French burlesque: *vide supra*, p. 346, n. 1 and references to Garapon, *La Fantaisie verbale*. For Gallicism in the comic register see observations on the conventional Frenchman in Italy, seventeenth and eighteenth century evaluations, pp. 345 and 421ff. respectively. A foreign word may provide a peg to hang weightier satire on, as when Rabelais in the prologue to his fourth book plays ironically upon the Italian greeting *sanità e guadagno!*[2] Interjections and oaths are a well-known resource

---

1. Cf. also the verb *pétrarchiser*, apparently coined by du Bellay.

2. *Vide* M-Lav., II, 268: 'Les Genevoys . . . s'entresaluant disent, Sanita & guadain, messer. Ils ne se contentent de santé; d'abondant ilz soubhaytent guaing, voire les escuz de Guadaigne' (Tommaso de' Guadagni, adviser to François Ier, passed for having lent a considerable sum at exorbitant interest to the King during his imprisonment after Pavia).

of comedy, from whimsical humour to buffoonery—*granmercè! vie! sango-démi! diavol!* and *coion!* (Frère Jean speaking), *couci-couci* (Scarron), *cazzo!* and *ohimè!* in de Brosses and others, *baste!* used by many an author from du Fail to Mérimée. Honorifics and titles are notoriously two-faced, conferring prestige and dignity on one hand, yet rich in humorous possibilities on the other. *Monsù* is the favourite handle for satire in Italian, *messer* (Messer Gaster, etc.) and *signore* in French.[1]

II. METHOD AND RESEARCH PROCEDURES

Most of what requires to be said about practical procedures needed to prepare material for analysis was sketched out in advance in the methodological section above, Part One. I shall reiterate one or two points worthy of close attention, however, and add the substance of findings from the body of our research.

(a) In preparing word-lists one must have in mind the fundamental distinction between *technical* and *non-technical* (abstract-general-emotive) borrowings. The former in the main respond most readily to word-and-thing analysis, i.e. lexico-cultural interpretation; the latter are promising material for semantic (structural) investigations. Words which may be considered (by using frankly introspective criteria, in the first place) to fulfil a semantic need in the language are of especial importance.

(b) It is necessary to have precise information about a loan-word's history, both formal and semantic, together with a formal and semantic description of it in the original, lending language.

(c) It is necessary also to prepare as complete an account as possible of the loan-word's homoionymic environment, the near-synonyms which encompass each borrowing (abstract-general-emotive terms in particular), bearing in mind the difference between *synonym-sequence* and *synonymy in being* (*vide* Part Four, *Synonymy and Near Synonymy*).

(d) Antecedent and subsequent sign patterns in the same semantic area are as important as the lexical field itself, i.e. both synchronic patterns and diachronic sequences are needed. Our 'ecological' approach makes use of both linguistic axes.

(e) Though we are concerned here with loan-*words*, i.e. with lexical signs and their content, it should be remembered that signification even at this

---

1. Hali's tomfoolery in Molière's *Le Sicilien* is familiar to all, but will bear repeating:
'Signor (avec la permission de la Signore) je vous diray (avec la permission de la Signore) que je viens vous trouver (avec la permission de la Signore) pour vous prier (avec la permission de la Signore) de vouloir bien (avec la permission de la Signore)...
D. Pedre.
Avec la permission de la Signore, passez un peu de ce costé.'
(*Association Guillaume Budé* ed., Paris, 1946, p. 215).

level can draw on more resources than the individual word. Homoionymy
in (c) above must therefore include that between words and longer segments.
Thus in interpreting the borrowing *réussir*, for example, one has to take note
not only of words which fulfilled the same or a similar semantic function,
e.g. *assener*,[1] *chevir*[2] or *achever*, but also of earlier idioms like *traire, mener,
venir à (bon) chef, mener à bien, avoir (bonne) issue*.

(f) The distinction between *moment of transfer* and *interim period* is of
paramount importance (*vide* Part Four, pp. 609-11).

1. As in Chrestien de Troyes, *Yvain*, ll. 1503-4; 'Nes Des, s'il an voloit pener/N'i
porroit, ce cuit, *assener*' (ed. T. B. W. Reid, Manchester University Press). This is an
extension of the etymological sense 'to make (a person) sensible, bring to reason'.

2. As in Gerson, *Moralité du cœur et des cinq sens:* 'Sire' (*Raison* speaking to God)
'aidez au gouvernement (of the six senses);/*Chevir* n'en pourroye aultrement' (*vide
Mélanges Hoepffner*, p. 356).

ABBREVIATIONS
RELATING TO AUTHORS AND WORKS
WITH A LIST OF PRINCIPAL SOURCES

Abbozzo: see *Bezz.*

Acad. (*Dict. de l'Acad.*) – *Dictionnaire de l'Académie française*, Paris (ed. and date as specified); *Complément du dictionnaire de l'Académie française*, Paris, 1847.

Alb. *Diz. univ.* – ALBERTI DI VILLANUOVA, Francesco d': *Dizionario universale critico-etimologico*, Lucca, 1797–1805.

Alberti 1771 – ALBERTI DI VILLANUOVA, Francesco d': *Nuovo dizionario italiano-francese (Nouveau dictionnaire françois-italien, composé sur les dictionnaires de l'Académie de France et de la Crusca*, 2 vols., Paris, Marseille, 1771, 1772; also 2nd ed., 1777.

Alberti 1788 – id., *Troisième édition corrigée et considérablement augmentée*, 2 vols., Nice, 1788.

Anc. poés. fr. – *Anciennes poésies françaises* (XVe–XVIe s.), publiées par A. de Montaiglon, 13 vols., 1855–78.

Anc. th. fr. – VIOLLET-LE-DUC: *Ancien théâtre françois, ou Collection des ouvrages dramatiques les plus remarquables, depuis les mystères jusqu'à Corneille*, 10 vols., Paris, 1854 and subsequently (*Bibl. elzév.*).

Arch. Gl. It. – *Archivio glottologico italiano*, Florence.

Arch. Ling. – *Archivum Linguisticum*, Glasgow.

Arch. Rom. – *Archivum Romanicum, nuova rivista di filologia romanza*, Geneva.

Arlia, *Suppl.* – ARLIA, Costantino: *Giunte al Lessico dell'infima e corrotta italianità raccolte da C.A.*, Milan, 1884.

B-Al. (*DEI*) – BATTISTI, C. and ALESSIO, G.: *Dizionario etimologico italiano*, 5 vols., Florence, 1950–57.

B-Wart. – BLOCH, O. and WARTBURG, W. von: *Dictionnaire étymologique de la langue française*, 4th ed., Paris, 1964. Also 2nd ed., 1950; 3rd ed., 1960.

Barbier, *Misc. lexicog.* – BARBIER, Paul: *Miscellanea lexicographica. Proceedings of the Leeds Philosophical and Literary Society*, 1927 and subsequently.

Baretti – BARETTI, Giuseppe Marc'Antonio: *A Dictionary of the English and Italian Languages (Dizionario delle lingue italiana ed inglese)*, 2 vols., London, 1771. The first edition is London, 1760.

BÉDARIDA, H. and HAZARD, P.: *L'Influence française en Italie au dix-huitième siècle*, Paris, 1934.

BATTISTI-ALESSIO: see B-Al. (*DEI*).

Belon, *Observations* – BELON, P.: *Les Observations de plusieurs singularités et choses admirables*, Paris, 1553.

Bernardoni, *Elenco* – BERNARDONI, Giuseppe: *Elenco di alcune parole, oggidì frequentemente in uso, le quali non sono ne' vocabolarj italiani*, Milan, 1812.

Bertoldi – BERTOLDI, Alfonso: *Epistolario di Vincenzo Monti*, 6 vols., Florence, 1928.

Bertoni, *Elem. germ.* – BERTONI, G.: *L'elemento germanico nella lingua italiana*, Genoa, 1914.

743

Bescherelle – BESCHERELLE, Louis-Nicolas: *Dictionnaire national ou dictionnaire universel de la langue française*, 2 vols., Paris, 1845–46; 7th ed., 2 vols., Paris, 1858; 18th ed., 2 vols., 1882.

Bezz., *Abbozzo* (*Abb.*) – BEZZOLA, Reto R.: *Abbozzo di una storia dei gallicismi italiani nei primi secoli* (*750–1300*). *Saggio storico-linguistico*. Sammlung romanischer Elementar- und Handbücher, 6. Band, Heidelberg, 1925.

BLOCH-WARTBURG: see B-Wart.

Bocc. – Giovanni Boccaccio, 1313–75.

Boerio – BOERIO, Giuseppe: *Dizionario del dialetto veneziano*, Venice, 1829.

Boiste – BOISTE, Pierre-Claude-Victoire: *Dictionnaire universel de la langue française, avec le latin, et Manuel d'Orthographe et de Néologie, etc.*, Paris, 1800; new eds., 1803, 1808, 1819, 1823, 1829 and subsequently.

Boucicaut – *Le Livre des faicts du bon messire Jean le Maingre, dit Mareschal Boucicaut*; beg. 15th cent.

Boulan – BOULAN, H.R.: *Les mots d'origine étrangère en français* (*1650–1700*), thesis of Univ. of Groningen, Amsterdam, 1934.

Boyer 1699 – *The Royal Dictionary . . . French and English, English and French . . . For the use of his Highness the Duke of Gloucester*, 2 vols., London, 1699.

Brun. Lat. – Brunetto Latini, *c.* 1220–*c.* 1294.

Brunot, *Hist.* – BRUNOT, Ferdinand: *Histoire de la langue française*, Vols. I to X, Paris, 1905–43; also BRUNEAU, Ch., Vols. XII and XIII, 1948 and 1953 respectively.

Buon. il Giov. – Michelangelo Buonarroti il Giovane, 1568–1646.

C.L.G. – SAUSSURE, Ferdinand de: *Cours de linguistique générale*, 5th ed., Paris, 1955.

Cambridge It. Dict. – *The Cambridge Italian Dictionary* (ed. Barbara Reynolds), Vol. I: *Italian–English*, Cambridge, 1962.

Canti carnasc. – *Canti carnascialeschi*, 2nd half 15th cent. and 1st half 16th cent.

Carena, *Voc. domest.* – CARENA, Giacinto: *Vocabolario domestico*, Turin, 1846; 2nd ed., 1851; *Vocabolario metodico d'arti e mestieri*, Turin, 1853; a third part published posthumously in 1860. Prati's reference is 4th ed., Naples, 1859.

CESAROTTI, Melchiorre: *Saggio sulla filosofia delle lingue*, ed. R. Spongano, Florence, 1943.

Chambers – CHAMBERS, E.: *Dizionario universale di arti e scienze*, 9 vols. + 7 supplement, Venice, 1748–65.

Cherubini – CHERUBINI, Francesco: *Vocabolario milanese–italiano*, 5 vols., Milan, 1839–43; Vol. V (Supplement) 1856.

Complément du dictionnaire de l'Académie française, Paris, 1847.

CORNEILLE, Thomas: see Th. Corneille.

Corominas (Corom.) – COROMINAS, Joan: *Diccionario crítico etimológico de la lengua castellana*, (Berne, 1954), 4 vols.

Cotgr. – COTGRAVE, Randle: *A Dictionarie of the French and English Tongues*, London, 1611.

Cr. (Crusca) – *Vocabolario degli Accademici della Crusca*, Venice, 1612; 2nd ed., Venice, 1623; 3rd ed., 3 vols., Florence, 1691; 4th ed., 6 vols., Florence, 1729–38; 5th ed., 11 vols., Florence, 1843–1923, as follows: first seven fascicules 1843–52, Vol. I, 1863, Vols. I–X, up to 1910, Vol. XI (to *OZOVO* only), in 1923. Together with a *Glossario*, Florence, 1867 (*A-BUTURO* only).

Crescenzio – CRESCENZIO, Bartolomeo: *Nautica mediterranea*, Rome, 1607.

Cresc. volg. (P. de' Cresc. volg.) – Popular version of Piero de' Crescenzi, *Trattato di agricoltura*, 14th cent.

Crusca: see Cr.

D.G. – HATZFELD, Adolphe and DARMESTETER, Arsène: *Dictionnaire général de la langue française du commencement du XVIIe siècle jusqu'à nos jours . . . avec le concours de M. Antoine Thomas*, 2 vols., Paris, 1890–1900.

Datations 1965 – Datations et documents lexicographiques, Vol. 3, 1re Série, letter C, *Ann. Litt. de l'Univ. de Besançon, Publ. du Centre d'Étude du Vocabulaire français*, 1965.

Dauz. – DAUZAT, A., DUBOIS, J., MITTERAND, H.: *Nouveau dictionnaire étymologique et historique*, Paris, 1964.

Dauz., 1947 – DAUZAT, Albert: *Dictionnaire étymologique de la langue française*, 7th ed., Paris, 1947 (or other editions and revised versions, specified by dates).

Davila – DAVILA, Arrigo Caterino, 1576–1631. Refers to his work *Dell'istoria delle guerre civili di Francia*, publ. 1630.

D'Ayala – D'AYALA, Mariano: *Dizionario delle voci guaste o nuove e più de' francesismi introdotti nelle lingue militari d'Italia*, Turin, 1853.

DEL BONO, Michele: *Dizionario siciliano–italiano–latino*, 3 vols., Palermo, 1751–54.

Delboulle, *Not. lex.* – DELBOULLE, A.: *Notes lexicologiques. Matériaux pour servir à l'histoire du français*, Paris, 1880; also unpublished material deposited at the Sorbonne which has been incorporated in the most recent etymological sources (see *FEW, Beiheft;* B-Wart., *Introd.* XXI).

Delvau – DELVAU, Alfred: *Dictionnaire de la langue verte*, 2nd ed., Paris, 1867.

DEROY, Louis: *L'Emprunt linguistique*, Bibl. de la Fac. de Phil. et Lettres de l'Université de Liège, fasc. XLVI, Paris, 1956.

DEVOTO, Giacomo: *Fondamenti della storia linguistica*, Florence, 1951.

Devoto, *Profilo* – DEVOTO, Giacomo: *Profilo di storia linguistica italiana*, Florence, 1953.

Dicc. lengua castell. – *Diccionario de la lengua Castellana . . . compuesto por la Real Academia española (Diccionario de Autoridades)*, 5 vols., Madrid, 1726–37.

Dict. de l'Acad.: see Acad.

DIONISOTTI, C. and GRAYSON, C.: *Early Italian Texts*, Oxford, 1949.

Dittamondo – Il Dittamondo, by Fazio degli Uberti (1st decade 14th cent.–post 1367), largely composed 1318–60.

Diz. encicl. ital. – *Dizionario enciclopedico italiano dell'Istituto dell'Enciclopedia Treccani*, 12 vols., 1955–61.

Du C., Du Cange – DU CANGE, Charles du Fresne, Seigneur: *Glossarium mediae et infimae latinitatis, conditum a Carolo du Fresne Domino du Cange, ed. nova a L. Favre*, 10 vols., Niort, 1883–87. Incl. Vol. IX, L. Favre, *Glossaire français faisant suite au Gloss. med. et inf. lat.*

Enciclopedia italiana Treccani, 37 vols., Rome, 1929–38.

Encycl. – *Encyclopédie ou dictionnaire raisonné des sciences, des arts et des métiers, par une société de gens de lettres, p.p. Diderot et D'Alembert*, 17 vols., Paris and Neuchâtel, 1751–65.

Encycl. méth. – *Encyclopédie Méthodique ou par ordre des matières*, 4 vols., Paris, 1782–91.

F-A. – FANFANI, Pietro and ARLIA, Costantino: *Lessico della corrotta italianità*, Milan, 1877; 2nd ed., *Lessico dell'infima e corrotta italianità*, Milan, 1881; 3rd ed., Milan, 1890.

F.M. – *Le Français Moderne. Revue de synthèse et de vulgarisation linguistiques*, etc., Paris.

Fanfani, *Voc. dell'uso tosc.* – FANFANI, Pietro: *Vocabolario dell'uso toscano*, Florence, 1863.

Fanfani, *Voc. ling. it.* – FANFANI, Pietro: *Vocabolario della lingua italiana*, Florence, 1855; 2nd ed., 1965.

FANFANI, Pietro and RIGUTINI, Giuseppe: *Vocabolario italiano della lingua parlata*, Florence, 1875.

Félibien, *Entretiens* – FÉLIBIEN, André: *Entretiens sur les vies et sur les Ouvrages des plus excellens Peintres anciens et modernes*, 2nd ed., 2 vols., Paris, 1685–88.

Félibien, *Pr. d'Archit.* – FÉLIBIEN, André: *Des Principes de l'Architecture, de la Sculpture, de la Peinture, et des autres Arts qui en dépendent*, Paris, 1676; 2nd ed., Paris, 1690; 3rd ed., 1697.

FEW – WARTBURG, W. von: *Französisches etymologisches Wörterbuch, eine Darstellung des gallo-romanischen Sprachschatzes*, Bonn and Basle, Vols. I–V, 1922–1950; Basle, Vols. VII–XII, 1955–66, XIV, 1961, XVI–XVII, 1959 and 1966 (other vols. in progress).

Florio – FLORIO, John: *A World of Wordes, Or most copious, and exact Dictionarie in Italian and English, collected by Iohn Florio*, London, 1598.

Fournier, *Hydrographie* – FOURNIER, G.: *Hydrographie contenant la théorie et la pratique de toutes les parties de la navigation* (including a glossary of nautical terms), Paris, 1643.

Franc. Sacch. – Franco Sacchetti, *c.* 1330–*c.* 1400.

Furetière – FURETIÈRE, Antoine: *Dictionnaire universel contenant généralement tous les mots françois tant vieux que modernes, et les termes de toutes les sciences et des arts*, 3 vols., The Hague and Rotterdam, 1690; other eds., 1694 and 1727.

G. Vill. – Giovanni Villani, *c.* 1280–1348.

Gam. (*EWF*) – GAMILLSCHEG, Ernst: *Etymologisches Wörterbuch der französischen Sprache*, Heidelberg, 1928.

Garollo, *Picc. Encicl. Hoepli* – GAROLLO, Gottardo: *Piccola enciclopedia Hoepli*, 2 vols., Milan, 1892–95.

Gay, *Gloss. Arch.* – GAY, Victor: *Glossaire archéologique du moyen-âge et de la renaissance*, 2 vols., Paris, 1887 and 1928.

Gherardini, *Suppl.* – GHERARDINI, Giovanni: *Supplimento a' vocabolarj italiani*, 6 vols., Milan, 1852–57.

Giorgini, *Nov. vocab.* – GIORGINI, G. B. and BROGLIO, E.: *Novo vocabolario della lingua italiana secondo l'uso di Firenze*, 4 vols., Florence, 1870–97.

Godef. (*Comp.*) – GODEFROY, Frédéric Eugène: *Dictionnaire de l'ancienne langue française et de tous ses dialectes du IXe au XVe siècle*, Paris, 1880–1902; also *Complément*, Paris, 1893, 10 vols.

GOHIN, F.: *Les transformations de la langue française pendant la seconde moitié du XVIIIe siècle* (1740–89), thesis of Univ. of Paris, Paris, 1902.

Gr. d'Haut. – D'HAUTERIVE, R. Grandsaignes: *Dictionnaire d'ancien français, moyen-âge et renaissance*, Paris, 1947.

Gr. diz. it. – *Grande Dizionario della lingua italiana*, ed. Salvatore Battaglia, Vols. I–IV A–DUU, Turin, 1961–66 (in progress). Used to Vol. II, 1962.

GRAF, Arturo: *L'Anglomania e l'influsso inglese in Italia nel secolo XVIII*, Turin, 1911.

Grand dict. univ. – LAROUSSE, Pierre: *Grand dictionnaire universel du XIXe siècle*, 17 vols., Paris, 1865–76, incl. two supplements, 1878, 1890.

Grand Larousse encyclopédique, 10 vols., Paris, 1958–64.

Grassi – GRASSI, Giuseppe: *Dizionario militare italiano*, Turin, 1817. The edition generally referred to is the posthumous one published at Naples, 1835.

GUGLIELMOTTI, A.: *Vocabolario marino e militare*, Rome, 1889.

Guittone – Guittone d'Arezzo, *c.* 1230–94.

H. Est., *Dial.* – ESTIENNE, Henri: *Deux dialogues du nouveau langage françois italianizé et autrement deguizé*, ed. Ristelhüber, Paris, 1885.

HATZFELD and DARMESTETER: see *D.G.*

HAZARD, Paul: *La Révolution française et les lettres italiennes*, Paris, 1910.

Hobier – HOBIER: *Construction d'une gallaire*, Paris, 1922.

HOPE, T. E.: 'Loan-words as Cultural and Lexical Symbols', *Arch. Ling.*, XIV, pp. 111–21, and XV (1963), pp. 29–42.

HOPE, T. E.: 'The Process of Neologism Reconsidered with Reference to Lexical Borrowing in Romance', *Trans. Philol. Soc.*, 1964.

Hug. – HUGUET, Edmond: *Dictionnaire de la langue française du seizième siècle*, Vols. I–VI (*SIL–*), Paris, 1925–65 (in progress).

Iacopone – Iacopone da Todi, 1230–1306.

It. Dial. – L'Italia Dialettale. Rivista di dialettologia italiana, Pisa.

JACONO, Antonio: *Dizionario di esotismi*, Florence, 1939.

Jal – JAL, Auguste: *Glossaire nautique; répertoire polyglotte de termes de marine anciens et modernes*, 2 vols., Paris, 1848–50.

KLEMPERER, V.: 'Italienische Elemente im französischen Wortschatz zur Zeit der Renaissance', *Germanisch-Romanische Monatschrift*, VI, 1914, pp. 664–77.

Kohlmann – KOHLMANN, G.: *Die italienischen Lehnworte in der neufranzösischen Schriftsprache seit dem 16. Jahrhundert*, thesis of Univ. of Kiel, Kiel, 1901.

KÖNIG, Karl: *Überseeische Wörter im Französischen (16–18 Jahrh.)*, *Beiheft zur Z.f.r.Ph.*, No. 91, Halle, 1939. Also 'Premières traces en français de quelques mots orientaux', *F.M.*, IX, 1941, pp. 129–44.

L.N. – Lingua Nostra, Florence.

La Curne – LA CURNE DE SAINTE-PALAYE: *Dictionnaire historique de l'ancien langage françois ou glossaire de la langue françoise depuis son origine jusqu'au siècle de Louis XIV*, publ. par L. Favre, 10 vols., Niort, 1875–82.

LANDAIS, Napoléon: *Dictionnaire général et grammatical des dictionnaires français*, 5th ed., 2 vols., Paris, 1840.

LAROUSSE: see *Grand dict. univ.*

Lavisse – LAVISSE, Ernest: *Histoire de France depuis les origines jusqu'à la Révolution. Publié avec la collaboration de MM. Bayet, Bloch, etc.*, 9 vols., Paris, 1900–11.

Leone – LEONE, A., FANTONETTI, G. B. and ODOMEI, A.: *Dizionario dei termini di medicina, etc.*, 2nd ed., Milan, 1828; 3rd ed., Milan, 1834.

Lessona, *Diz. univ.* – LESSONA, Michele and VALLE, Carlo: *Dizionario universale di scienze, lettere ed arti*, 2 vols., Milan, 1874–75.

Littré – LITTRÉ, E.: *Dictionnaire de la langue française*, 4 vols. and supplement, Paris, 1863–72.

Livio volg. – Livio volgarizzato. Popularisation of Livy's *History of Rome* dating from 1st half of 14th cent.

LYONS, John: *Structural Semantics*. (Publications of the Philological Society, No. 20), Oxford, 1963.

M-D. – MIGLIORINI, Bruno and DURO, Aldo: *Prontuario etimologico della lingua italiana*, Turin, 1950.

M-L. (*REW*) – MEYER-LÜBKE, W.: *Romanisches etymologisches Wörterbuch*, 3rd ed., Heidelberg, 1935.

M-L., *Gr. der rom. Spr.* – MEYER-LÜBKE, W.: *Grammatik der romanischen Sprachen*, 4 vols., Leipzig, 1890–1902.

M.L.R. – Modern Language Review, Cambridge, 1906ff.

M-Lav. – MARTY-LAVEAUX, Charles: *Les Œuvres de Maistre François Rabelais. Accompagnées d'un Commentaire . . . et d'un Glossaire*, 6 vols., Paris, 1868–1902.

M-Stor. – MIGLIORINI, Bruno: *Storia della lingua italiana*, 3rd ed., May 1961.

M. Vill. – Matteo Villani, beg. 14th cent.–1363.

Mach. – Niccolò Machiavelli, 1469–1527.

MACKENZIE, Frazer: *Les Relations de l'Angleterre et de la France d'après le vocabulaire*, 2 vols., Paris, 1939.

Manfr. – MANFRONI, Franceso: *Dizionario di voci impure od improprie*, Turin, 1883.

Marco Polo volg. – *Marco Polo volgarizzato*. Version of *Il Milione* by Marco Polo (1254–1324) dating from 1st half 14th cent.

Matoré, *Méthode* – MATORÉ, Georges: *La Méthode en lexicologie (Domaine français)*, Paris, 1953.

MEANO, Cesare: *Commentario dizionario italiano della moda*, Turin, 1936.

Ménage, *Dict. etym.* – MÉNAGE, Gilles: *Dictionnaire étymologique ou Origines de la langue française*, Paris, 1650; id. Paris, 1964.

Ménage, *Origini* – MÉNAGE, Gilles (MENAGIO, Egidio): *Le Origini della lingua italiana compilate dal segnore Egidio Menagio*, Paris, 1669; 2nd ed. with additions, Geneva, 1685.

MEYER, Paul: *De l'expansion de la langue française en Italie pendant le moyen-âge, 12ᵉ–13ᵉ* siècles, Rome, 1904.

Migl., *Dal nome proprio* – MIGLIORINI, Bruno: *Dal nome proprio al nome comune*, Geneva, 1927.

Migl., *Saggi Novecento* – MIGLIORINI, Bruno: *Saggi sulla lingua del Novecento*, 2nd ed., Florence, 1942.

Migl., *Suppl.* – MIGLIORINI, Bruno: Supplement to Panzini, *Dizionario moderno*, 9th ed. (*Appendice al Dizionario Moderno*), bound with 9th ed., Milan, 1950.

MIGLIORINI, Bruno: *Che cos'è un vocabolario?*, 2nd ed., Florence, 1951.

MIGLIORINI, Bruno: *Lingua contemporanea*. 3rd ed., Florence, 1943.

MIGLIORINI, Bruno: *Lingua e cultura*, Rome, 1948.

MIGLIORINI-DURO: see M-D.

MIGLIORINI, *Storia*: see M-*Stor.*

Minsheu – MINSHEU, John: *Mynshaei emendatio vel amendis expurgatio necnon augmentatio sui ductoris in linguas (Guide into the Tongues) sive Etymologici Onomastici sui diversarum linguarum*, London, 1627.

Monaci – MONACI, Ernest: *Crestomazia italiana dei primi secoli;* Città di Castello, 1889; *Nuova edizione per cura di F. Arese*, Roma, Napoli and Città di Castello, 1955.

MONELLI, Paolo: *Barbaro dominio; cinquecento esotismi*, Milan, 1933; 2nd ed., 1943.

Montec. – Raimondo Montecuccoli, 1604–80.

Mozin – MOZIN, abbé: *Dictionnaire complet des Langues Française et Allemande . . . par l'Abbé Mozin . . . et plusieurs autres*, 2 parts, Stuttgart and Tübingen, 1811–12; 2nd ed., 1823–28; 3rd ed., 1842–46.

Nicot – NICOT, J.: *Thresor de la langue francoyse, tant ancienne que moderne*, Paris, 1606.

Not. lex.: see Delboulle.

Novellino – *Il Novellino*. Collection of *novelle* dating from later 13th cent., from 9 MSS and in several versions (see Monaci, 1955, No. 154, p. 478). Prati refers to the *Cento novelle antiche*.

Nyrop, *Gr. Hist.* – NYROP, Kristoffer: *Grammaire historique de la langue française*, 4th ed., 6 vols., Copenhagen, 1935.

NYROP, Kristoffer: *Linguistique et histoire de mœurs. Mélanges posthumes*, trad. par E. Philipot, Paris, 1934.

OED – *A New English Dictionary on Historical Principles*, Oxford, 1888–1933.

Oudin – OUDIN, Antoine: *Recherches italiennes et françoises*, Paris, 1640; *Seconde partie des recherches italiennes et françoises, contenant les mots françois expliquez par l'italien*, Paris, 1642. Also *Dictionnaire italien et françois*, Paris, 1663.

Panlessico – *Panlessico italiano*, 2 vols., Venice, 1839.

Pantero Pantera – PANTERA, Pantero: *L'armata navale*, Rome, 1614.

Panz. – PANZINI, Alfredo: *Dizionario moderno*, Milan, 1905. Re-edited on nine occasions in 1908, 1918, 1923, 1927, 1931, 1935, and (ed. by A. Schiaffini and B. Migliorini), 1942, 1950, 1960. The editions most frequently referred to are I, II (1908) IV (1923) and IX (1950).

Parenti – PARENTI, Marc'Antonio: *Catalogo di spropositi*, Modena, 1839–43, a series of articles continued as *Esercitazioni filologiche*, Modena, 1844–58.

Pèl. Charlem. – *Le Pèlerinage de Charlemagne*. Prob. 1st half 12th cent.

Petrocchi – PETROCCHI, Policarpo: *Novo dizionario universale della lingua italiana*, 2 vols., Milan, 1887–91.

PIANIGIANI, Ottorino: *Vocabolario etimologico della lingua italiana*, Rome and Milan, 1907.

PIPINO, Maurizio: *Vocabolario piemontese*, Turin, 1783.

POPE, Mildred K.: *From Latin to Modern French with Especial Consideration of Anglo-Norman*, Manchester University Press, 1934, reprinted 1952.

Pr. (*V. Et. It.*) – PRATI, Angelico: *Vocabolario etimologico italiano*, Milan, 1951.

Prati, *Voci di gerganti* – PRATI, Angelico: *Voci di gerganti, vagabondi e malviventi studiate nell'origine e nella storia*, Pisa, 1940.

PRAZ, Mario: *The Italian Element in English*. (Essays and Studies by Members of the English Association, No. 15), Oxford, 1929.

PUOTI, Basilio: *Dizionario de' francesismi e degli altri vocaboli e modi nuovi e guasti introdotti nella nostra lingua italiana*, Naples, 1845.

R. Est. – ESTIENNE, Robert: *Dictionnaire françois-latin*, Paris, 1539; id., *corrigé et augmenté*, Paris, 1549.

R. Forsch. – *Romanische Forschungen. Vierteljahrsschrift für romanische Sprachen und Literaturen*, Frankfurt a.M. (initially Erlangen).

R.H.L.F. – *Revue d'histoire littéraire de la France*, Paris.

R. Ling. R. – *Revue de Linguistique Romane*, Lyon and Strasbourg (earlier: Paris).

Rab. – François Rabelais, *c.* 1494–*c.* 1553.

Rambelli – RAMBELLI, Gianfrancesco: *Vocabolario domestico*, Bologna, 1850.

Raynouard – RAYNOUARD, M.: *Lexique roman ou dictionnaire de la langue des troubadours*, 6 vols., Paris, 1844.

REW: see M–L., *REW*.

REYNOLDS, Barbara: *The Linguistic Writings of Alessandro Manzoni. A textual and Chronological Reconstruction*, Cambridge, 1950.

Rezasco – REZASCO, G.: *Dizionario del linguaggio italiano storico ed amministrativo*, Florence, 1881.

Richelet – RICHELET, Pierre: *Dictionnaire françois contenant les mots et les choses, plusieurs nouvelles remarques sur la langue française ... avec les termes les plus connus des arts et des sciences*, Geneva, 1680; id., *dernière édition exactement revuë, corrigée & augmentée*, Geneva, 1963.

Rig., Rigutini – RIGUTINI, Giuseppe: *I neologismi buoni e cattivi più frequenti nell'uso odierno*, Rome, 1886; 2nd ed., Rome, 1891.

Robert – ROBERT, Paul: *Dictionnaire alphabétique et analytique de la langue française*, 5 vols., Paris, 1951–64.

Rodolico – RODOLICO, Niccolò: *Storia degli italiani*, Florence, 1954.

Rohlfs–ROHLFS, Gerhard: *Historische Grammatik der italienischen Sprache*, Berne, 1949–54.

Roland – *La Chanson de Roland*, *c.* 1100.

Rom. Forsch. – *Romanische Forschungen, Organ für romanische Sprachen und Mittellatein*, Erlangen.

Rose – Le Roman de la Rose, by Guillaume de Lorris and Jean de Meun; post-1229.

S.A.T.F. – Société des Anciens Textes Français, Paris.

SACHS, C. and VILLATTE, C.: *Enzyklopädisches französisch-deutsches und deutsch–französisches Wörterbuch*, 2 vols., Berlin, 1874.

Sainéan, L. de Rab. – SAINÉAN, Lazare: *La langue de Rabelais*, 2 vols., Paris, 1922–23.

SALVERDA DE GRAVE, J. J.: *L'Influence de la langue française en Hollande d'après les mots empruntés*, Paris, 1913.

Savary, *Dict. de comm.* – SAVARY DES BRUSLONS, Jacques: *Dictionnaire universel de commerce. Ouvrage Posthume du Sieur Jacques Savary des Bruslons. . . . donné au public par M. Philemon-Louis Savary, son frère*, Paris, 1723.

Savary, *Diz. di comm.* – SAVARY (fratelli): *Dizionario di commercio*, 4 vols. (transl. of the French work), Venice, 1770–71.

Savary, *Parf. négoc.* – SAVARY, Jacques: *Le Parfait Négociant, ou instruction générale pour ce qui regarde le commerce de toute sorte de marchandises*, etc., 2 vols., Paris, 1675; 2nd ed., 2 vols., Paris, 1679.

SAYA, A.: *Contribution de l'Italie à l'enrichissement du lexique français*, Messina, 1905.

Schiaffini, *Momenti* – SCHIAFFINI, Alfredo: *Momenti di storia della lingua italiana*, Bari, 1950; 2nd ed., Rome, 1953.

Sidrac – Le Livre de Sidrac, end 13th cent. Italian version dates from 14th cent. (*Libro di Sidrac*).

Stolonomie – *Stolonomie. Traicté contenant la manière de dresser, fournir, équiper et entretenir en tout temps en bon ordre une armée de mer* (see below, Vidos, Bibliography, p. 642).

Stratico – STRATICO, Simone: *Vocabolario di marina*, 3 vols., Milan, 1813–14.

T-Bell. – TOMMASEO, N. and BELLINI, B.: *Dizionario della lingua italiana*, 8 vols., Turin, 1858–79.

Tav. rit. (Tavola Ritonda) – 'Volgarizzamento del libro de' Cavalieri erranti, detto comunemente La Tavola Ritonda' (Crusca); 14th cent.

Terlingen – TERLINGEN, Juan H.: *Los italianismos en español desde la formación del idioma hasta principios del siglo XVII*, thesis of Utrecht Univ., Amsterdam, 1943.

Tes. volg. (Tes. Brun. Lat. volg.) – Popularisation of Brunetto Latini, *Il Tesoro (Le Trésor)*, attributed to Bono Giamboni (2nd half 13th cent.).

Th. Corneille – CORNEILLE, Thomas: *Le Dictionnaire des arts et des sciences. Par M. C. de l'Academie Française*, 2 vols., Paris, 1694.

Thévet, *Cosmogr.* – THÉVET, André: *La Cosmographie universelle illustrée de diverses figures des choses remarquables vues par l'auteur*, 2 vols., Paris, 1571.

Thierry – THIERRY, Jean: *Dictionnaire françois–latin, par Jehan Thierry*. Paris, 1564; id., *corrigé et augmenté*, Paris, 1572.

Tob.-Lomm. – TOBLER, A. and LOMMATZSCH, E.: Altfranzösisches Wörterbuch, Vols. I–VI (*OZVALE*), Berlin and Wiesbaden, 1926–65 (in progress).

Tr. dóu Felibrige – MISTRAL, Frédéric: *Lou Tresor dóu Felibrige, ou dictionnaire provençal–français embrassant les divers dialectes de la langue d'oc moderne*, 2 vols., Aix-en-Provence, 1878.

Tr. Philol. Soc. – *Transactions* (earlier: *Proceedings) of the Philological Society*, London, 1842–

TRACCONAGLIA, G.: *Contributo allo studio dell'italianismo in Francia, I, Henri Estienne e gli italianismi*, Lodi, 1907.

Tramater – *Vocabolario universale italiano*, comp. a cura della Società Tipografica Tramater e C., 7 vols., Naples, 1829–40.

TREVELYAN, Janet Penrose: *A Short History of the Italian People from the barbarian invasions to the present day*; 4th ed., London, 1959.

Trévoux – *Dictionnaire universel françois et latin*, Trévoux, 1704 (3 vols.); Paris, 1721 (5 vols.); Paris, 1732; Nancy, 1734; Paris, 1743 (6 vols.); Paris, 1752 (7 vols.); Paris, 1771 (8 vols.).

Trist. Ricc. – *Romanzo di Tristano*, end 13th cent. Version based on Codex Riccardiano 2543: see Monaci, 1955, No. 130, p. 387.

Ugol. – UGOLINI, Filippo: *Vocabolario di parole e modi errati*, Urbino, 1848; new eds. Florence, 1855, Naples, 1860.

ULLMANN, Stephen: *Précis de Sémantique française* (Bibliotheca Romanica series prima, *Manuales et Commentationes* IX), Berne, 1952.

Ullmann, *Principles* – ULLMANN, Stephen: *The Principles of Semantics*, Glasgow University Publications, LXXXIV, 2nd ed., Glasgow and Oxford, 1959.

V. Et. It.: see Pr. (Prati).

Valkhoff – VALKHOFF, Marius: *Étude sur les mots français d'origine néerlandaise*, Amersfoort, 1931.

Veneroni – VENERONI, Giovanni: *Dittionario francese ed italiano*, 2 vols., Venice, 1709; other eds., 1724, 1729.

Viani – VIANI, Prospero: *Dizionario di pretesi francesismi e di pretese voci e forme erronee della lingua italiana*, 2 vols., Florence, 1858–60.

Vidos – VIDOS, B. E.: *Storia delle parole marinaresche italiane passate in francese. Contributo storico-linguistico all'espansione della lingua nautica italiana*, Biblioteca dell'Archivum Romanicum, Series II, Vol. 24, Florence, 1939.

VIDOS, B. E.: 'Contributo alla storia delle parole francesi di origine italiana', *Archivum Romanicum*, XV, 1931, pp. 449–79.

VIDOS, B. E.: *La forza di espansione della lingua italiana*, Nijmegen–Utrecht, 1932.

VIDOS, B. E.: 'Le Bilinguisme et le mécanisme de l'emprunt', *R. Ling. R.*, XXIV, 1960, pp. 1–19.

Vidos, *Prestito* – VIDOS, B. E.: *Prestito, espansione e migrazione dei termini technici nelle lingue romanze e non romanze: problemi, metodo e risultati*, Bibl. dell'Archivum Romanicum, Series II, Vol. 31, Florence, 1965. (Incorporates a number of articles by Vidos referred to individually elsewhere.)

VISCARDI, A.: *Letteratura franco-italiana*; Istituto di filologia romanza della r. università de Roma. *Testi e manuali a cura de G. Bertoni*, No. 21, Modena, 1941.

VOSSLER, Karl: *Langue et culture de la France*, trad. A. Juilland, Paris, 1953, pp. 177–81 (Italian borrowings).

Vox Rom. – *Vox Romanica. Annales Helvetici explorandis linguis Romanicis destinati*. Berne, Erlenbach.

Wartburg, *FEW*: see *FEW*.

Wartburg, *Prob. et méth.* – WARTBURG, W. von: *Problèmes et méthodes de la linguistique*, 2nd ed. augmentée et refondue, avec la collaboration de Stephen Ullmann, Paris, 1962.

WARTBURG, W. von: *La Posizione della lingua italiana nel mondo neolatino*, Leipzig, 1936.

WEINREICH, Uriel: *Languages in Contact. Findings and Problems*, New York, 1953.

Wind (W.) – WIND, Bartina H.: *Les Mots italiens introduits en français au XVIe siècle*. Doctorate thesis of the University of Amsterdam, Deventer, 1928.

Zacc. *Raccolta* – ZACCARIA, E.: *Raccolta di voci affatto sconosciute o mal note ai lessicografi ed ai filologi*, Marradi, 1919.

Zeit. f.r. Phil. (Z. f.r. Ph.) – *Zeitschrift für romanische Philologie*, Tübingen.

References to Petrarch's works are drawn from *Rime e Trionfi di Francesco*

Petrarca, Classici Italiani No. 12, a cura di Ferdinando Neri, publ. by U.T.E.T., Turin, 1953.

Further details of Italian literary sources, with editions used by different authorities, may be found in the *Indice degli autori citati* of the *Grande dizionario della lingua italiana* (see Bibliography, *Gr. diz. it.*), and in the *Tavola delle abbreviature degli autori e dei testi* accompanying each edition of the Crusca (Cr.), and also in Vol. VIII of Tommaseo e Bellini (T-Bell.).

INDEX VERBORUM

This index is limited in scope to the 'word-list' sections of Part Two (The Historical Aspect).

Numbers printed in roman relate to words which appear as rubrics to individual word-entries; those in italics, to words which are to be found within the body of the word-entry itself, or in notes.

The more significant variants of form and graphy are included.

A. ITALIANISMS IN FRENCH

B. GALLICISMS IN ITALIAN

DD

kermesse (chermesse) 500

lacchè, 333
lacchetta, 262
ladio, 107
lai, 107
laido, 107
lama 'blade', 107
lama (-à), 399
lamantino, 500
lambrì, lambris, 399
lamè, 500
lampa, 107
lampasso, 399
lampista, 501
lampisteria, 501
lancinante, 399
laniere, 107-8
lasciapassare, 501
lasto, -a, 399
lavabo, 501
lavaggio, 501
leggero, 108
leggiere, 108
legiferare, 501
lengnaggio, 108
lettere patenti, 108
letto di giustizia, 399
leuto, 108
levriere, 108
levriero, 108
liana, -e, 501
libero muratore, 396
libero scambio, 501
libero scambista, 501
libertinaggio, 399
libresco, 501
licantropia, 333-4
licantropo, 333-4
liccia, 108
ligio, 108
lignaggio, 108
lillà, lilla, 399-400
limiere, 501
linciare, linciaggio, 501
lingeria, 334
lingio, 334 n. 1
lingotto, 501
lion, lionne, 501-2
litro, 502

liuto, 108
livrea, 258
lizza, 108-9
locale, 502
località, 502
localizzare, 502
locomobile, 502
locomotiva, 502
locomotore, 502
locomozione, 502
loggia, 109
lògia, 109
(a)lona, 509
longarina, 502
lorgnette, 502-3
lorgnon, 502-3
lucerna, 334
luigi (d'oro), 334
luna di miele, 503
lunette (pl.), 503
lupo cerviere, -o, 109

màcabro, (macabro), 503,
maccherella, 109
macedonia, 503
madama, 97, 109
madampolàm, 503
maddalena, 503
madiere, 400
maestro d'(h)ostello, 503
magazzeno, magasèn, 503
magazzino, 503
maionese, -a, 503
maître d'hôtel, 503
malardo, 109
mal du pays, 503
malebolgia, 85
malinteso, 504
maltalanto, 110
maltalento, 110
malversare, -azione, 504
mam(m)ellone, 504
mancia, 110
mangeria, 258
mangiare, 110
mangusta, 504
manichino, 504
manioca, 400
manitu, manitù, 504
manovra, 400

manovrare, 400
mantò, 334
marabutto, 400
marcia (milit.), 259
marcia (mus.), 259, 401
marciapiede, 400
marciare, 258-9
marengo, 504
marescialla, 259 n. 4
maresciallo, 259
margarina, 504
marionetta, 504
marionette, 504
marmitta, 504
marmittone, 504-5
marna, 401
marrone, 505
marron glacé, 505
marroni glassati, 505
martingala, 259
mascheretto, 401
massacrare, 505
mastino, 110
matinée, 505
mattinata (musicale), 505
mayonnaise, 503
meccia, 260
medesimo, 110
medium (medio), 505
meesmo, 110
melassa, 401
melea, 111
menageria, 334
menestrello, 505
mentoniera, 505
mentovare, 110-11
menu (menù), 505
mercuriale, 505-6
meringa, 506
meslea, 111
messaggiere, 111
messaggiero, 111
messaggio, 111
messere, 121
messidoro, 401
mestiere, 111
metallizzare, -azione, 506
metallurgia, 401
meticcio, 401
metraggio, 506

INDEX RERUM

abstract-general-emotive complex, 144–6, 272, 374, 434–5, 533, 535, 564–6, 669, 699, 741

abstract terms, 66, 237, 319, 353, 374, 435, 451

accords de Plombières, 539

-ache, French suffix, 628

act of transfer, 609, 742
  formal changes attributable to, 611–14
    aphaeresis, 612
    dissimilation and assimilation, 611–12
    metathesis, 611
    morphological shifts, 614
    paronymic attraction, 614
    rhotacism and lambdacism, 612–13
    stress, adaptation of anomalous, 613–14
  semantic changes attributable to, 662–4, 666

-ade, French suffix, 601–9

administrative terms: *see* political

aeronautics, terms of, 552–3

aesthetic factors, 737–41; *see also* fine arts, literary, local colour, musical terms, poetic vocabulary, stylistic considerations

affective or emotive terms, 22, 64–5, 237, 319, 434, 652

-aggio, Italian suffix, 626–9

agricultural terms, 138, 425

Algarotti, F., 416, 417, 418

analytic, dioristic or relational terms, 435, 728

antiquarianism: *see* exoticisms

Arabic influence, 54, 56, 132

archaeology, terms of, 460

architectural influences, 229

architectural terms, 63, 311–12, 373, 423, 434, 460

argotic function, 312, 723, 735

Ariosto, 229, 230, 273

attraction, morphemic: *see* morphemic equivalence

Aubigné, Agrippa d', 150, 239, 247–8

Avignon, papal court in, 64, 65

Baretti, Giuseppe, 417, 634

baroque, influence of, 343–4, 353

Bartas, Guillaume du, 273

Beauharnais, Eugène de, 536, 537, 538

Bellay, Joachim du, 239, 245, 437, 634, 739

Bernini, visit to Paris, 311

Berry, duc de, 63, 65

bilingualism, 438–41, 579

blanket or omnibus terms, 435, 728–9

Boccaccio, 137, 146, 229

Bologna school, influence of, 312, 313

borrowed vocabulary, lexico-cultural evaluation of, Part Two, *passim*, 14–15, 146–7, 237, 441, 697; *see also* semantic grouping

borrowing, process of, formal aspect, 609–11, 617–18
  random or capricious impulses in, 720–2

borrowings, criteria for the identification of, 623–34
  étymologie organique, 630
  evidence of other languages, 630–1
  formal criteria, 23, 623–31
  orthographical criteria, 631
  semantic criteria, 631–2
  testimony of contemporaries, 632–4

botany, terms of, 271, 424

Boucicaut, maréchal de, 56, 57, 621

Brantôme, Pierre de, 150, 241, 247–8, 739

Brosses, Charles de, 312, 355, 372–4, 424, 741

Buonarroti il Giovane, Michelangelo, 348–9

bureaucratic terms, officialese, 435, 542–4, 712; *see also* political, administrative, diplomatic terms

calque, 618

Carbonari, 452, 540–1

777